THIRTEEN WAYS OF LOOKING AT THE NOVEL

Jane Smiley

·

Thirteen Ways of Looking at the Novel

ff

faber and faber

First published in the USA in 2005
by Alfred A. Knopf

First published in Great Britain in 2006
by Faber and Faber Limited
3 Queen Square London WC1N 3AU

Printed in England by Mackays of Chatham Ltd

The right of Jane Smiley to be identified as author of this work has been asserted in accordance with Section 77 of the Copyright, Designs and Patents Act 1988

Grateful acknowledgement is made to Edition Rodopi for permission to reprint an excerpt from the essay "Salman Rushdie's Satanic Verses", by Julian Samuel from US/Them, Transition, Transcription and Identity in Post-Colonial Literary Cultures, edited by Gordon Collier. Reprinted by permission of Editions Rodopi.

A CIP record for this book
is available from the British Library

ISBN 0–571–23110–1

2 4 6 8 10 9 7 5 3 1

We are not told of things that happened to specific people exactly as they happened; but the beginning is when there are good things and bad things, things that happen in this life which one never tires of seeing and hearing about, things which one cannot bear not to tell of and must pass on for all generations. If the storyteller wishes to speak well, then he chooses the good things; and if he wishes to hold the reader's attention he chooses bad things, extraordinarily bad things. Good things and bad things alike, they are the things of this world and no other.

—MURASAKI SHIKIBU, *The Tale of Genji*

CONTENTS

A HUNDRED NOVELS

THIRTEEN WAYS OF LOOKING AT THE NOVEL

1 · INTRODUCTION

The end of September is a great time to have a birthday if you want to be a writer. Jane Austen might be December 16 and Shakespeare April 23 and Charles Dickens February 9, but for a sheer run of greatness, I challenge anyone to match September 23 through September 30—F. Scott Fitzgerald, William Faulkner, T. S. Eliot, Marina Tsvetayeva, William Blake, and Miguel Cervantes. And, I used to add (to myself, of course), *moi*. There is also a gratifying musical backup—George Gershwin on the twenty-sixth, my very own birthday. I never hesitated to bring anyone who cared (or did not care) to know up to date on late September (Ray Charles, Dmitri Shostakovich) and early October (John Lennon) birthdays. It was rather like listing your horse's pedigree or your illustrious ancestors—not exactly a point of pride, but more a reassurance that deep down, the stuff was there, if only astrologically.

But in 2001, the year I turned fifty-two, whether or not the stuff was there astrologically, it did not seem to be there artistically. All those years of guarding my stuff—no drinking, no drugs, personal modesty and charm, good behavior on as many fronts as I could manage, a public life of agreeability and professionalism, and still when I sat down at the computer to write my novel, titled *Good Faith,* my heart sank. I was into the 250s and 260s, there were about 125 pages to go, and I felt like Dante's narrator at the beginning of *The Divine Comedy.* I had wandered into a dark wood. I didn't know the way out. I was afraid.

I tried hard not to be afraid in certain ways. Two weeks before my birthday, terrorists had bombed the World Trade Center in New York. Fear was everywhere—fear of anthrax, fear of nuclear terrorism, fear of flying, fear of the future. I felt that, too, more than I was willing to admit. I tried to remind myself of the illusory nature of the world and my conviction that death is a transition, not an end, to discipline my fears to a certain degree. And my lover and partner was diagnosed at about that time with heart disease and required several procedures. I feared that he might also undergo a sudden transition and I would be bereft of his physical presence, but I also believed that we were eternally joined and that there was no transition that would separate us. This is how we agreed to view his health crisis. Physical fears were all too familiar for me—I had been wrestling with them my whole life, but in the late 1990s, divorce, independence, horses, Jack, and a book called *A Course in Miracles* had relieved most of them.

When I sat down at my computer, though, and read what I had written the day before, I felt something new—a recoiling, a cold surprise. Oh, this again. This insoluble, unjoyous, and unstimulating piece of work. What's the next sentence, even the next word? I didn't know, and if I tried something, I suspected it would just carry me farther down the wrong path, would be a waste of time or worse, prolong an already prolonged piece of fraudulence. I wondered if my case were analogous to that of a professional musician, a concert pianist perhaps, who does not feel every time he sits down to play the perfect joy of playing a piece he has played many times. I had always evoked this idea hopefully for students—however such a musician might begin his concert, surely he would be carried away by his own technique and mastery; after a few bars, the joy contained in the music itself would supply the inspiration that was lacking only moments before. But I didn't know that. Maybe that sort of thing didn't happen at all.

I came up with all sorts of diagnoses for my condition. The state of the zeitgeist was tempting but I refused to be convinced.* I reminded myself that I had lived through lots of zeitgeists over the years, and the geist wasn't all that bad in California. The overwhelming pall of grief and fear and odor and loss reached us more or less abstractly. Unlike New Yorkers, we could turn it off and get back to work, or so it seemed. But perhaps I was sensitive to something other than events— to a collective unconscious reaction to those events that I sensed in the world around me? I felt scattered. Even after I lost my fascination with the images and the events, my mind felt dissipated and shallow. It didn't help that I was annoyed with everything other writers wrote about the tragedy. There was no grappling with its enormity, and everything everyone said sounded wrong as soon as they said it. After

---

*I think now that for me, as for most Americans, the September 11 attacks were simply too huge to comprehend.

this should come only silence, it seemed, and yet I didn't really believe that. I believed that the world was not now changed for the worse— that anyone who had not reckoned upon the world to deliver such a blow, after lo these many years of genocide, mass murder, war, famine, despair, betrayal, death, and chaos, was naive. I believed at the time that if the world was a little changed, then perhaps it was changed for the better. The images had gone global, moving many individuals to look within and find mercy and compassion rather than hatred and anger. Hatred and anger were the oldest old hat, but mercy and compassion were something new. If there was more of those, and there seemed to be, then the turning point had actually been a turning point. Only time would tell. At any rate, surely talking was good, writing was good. Communicating was good, the antidote to the secrecy and silence the terrorists had attempted to foist upon us. Perhaps, I thought, I would stay scattered until the collective unconscious pulled itself together and raised itself up and put fear aside.

But really, events were events. I had known events and written through them, written about them, written in spite of them. I had grown up during the cold war, when obliteration seemed imminent every time the Russians twitched. I had an engagement photo of my parents from a newspaper; the headline of the article on the reverse side was "Russians Develop H-Bomb." Fear of terrorism, I thought, was nothing compared with the raw dread I had felt as a child. The problem with the novel was not outside myself, or even in my link to human consciousness. Perhaps, I thought, it was my own professional history. I had experienced every form of literary creation I had ever heard of—patient construction (*A Thousand Acres*), joyous composition (*Moo, Horse Heaven*), the grip of inspiration that seems to come from elsewhere (*The Greenlanders*), steady accumulation (*Duplicate Keys*), systematic putting together (*Barn Blind*), word-intoxicated buzz (*The Age of Grief*), even disinterested professional dedication (*The All-True Travels and Adventures of Lidie Newton*). I could list my books in my order of favorites, but my order of favorites didn't match anyone else's that I knew of, and so didn't reveal anything about the books' inherent value or even about their ease of composition. I didn't put too much stock in my preferences, or even in my memories of how it had felt to write them.

But I had penned a concise biography of Charles Dickens, and maybe I had learned from Dickens's life an unwanted lesson. I wrote the Dickens book because I loved Dickens, not because I felt a kinship with him, but after writing the book, it seemed to me that there was at least one similarity between us, and that was that Dickens loved to write and wrote with the ease and conviction of breathing. Me, too. When he took up each novel or novella, there might be some hemming and hawing and a few complaints along the way, but his facility of invention was utterly reliable and he was usually his own best audience. In the heat of composition, he declared almost every novel he wrote his best and his favorite, even if his preferences didn't stand. Toward the end of his life, though, his energy began to fail. When he was fifty, planning a new publication, he plunged rapidly into *Great Expectations* and wrote in weekly parts, modifying an earlier plan for the novel and producing a masterpiece largely because his journal needed it. When he began *Our Mutual Friend* a few years later, he was taxed almost beyond his powers. Several numbers were short, he complained of his lack of invention, and he didn't really like the novel much, though a case can be made (I have made it) that it is one of his most perfect. And he died in the middle of his last novel, *The Mystery of Edwin Drood,* having not quite mastered the whodunit form. Even Dickens, I thought, even Dickens faltered in the end, though you might say that he was careful and nurturing of his talents— abstemious and hardworking. He always deflected his fame a bit, wore it lightly. Was the lesson I had learned from Charles Dickens that a novelist's career lasts only a decade or two, can't be sustained much longer even by the greatest novelist (or most prolific great novelist) of all time?

Look at them all—Virginia Woolf, twenty-three or twenty-four years. George Eliot, twenty years. Jane Austen, twenty years, Dickens, twenty-four years, Thomas Hardy, fifty years of writing, but less than half of that novels. James Joyce, D. H. Lawrence, F. Scott Fitzgerald, William Faulkner, Miguel Cervantes. Short short short. I had meant to write my whole life. Surely modern life and modern medicine and modern day care and modern technology and modern publishing would make Henry James the paradigmatic novelist, not Jane Austen. I wondered if novel-writing had its own natural life span and without knowing it, I had outlived the life span of my novel-writing career.

Another thing I learned about Dickens was that after 1862, he began to live a much more active life than he had before. In 1856, he left his wife in a scandalous divorce and took up with a much younger woman. Sometime in the very early 1860s, the younger woman disappeared. Some authorities think that she and her mother moved to

France and that Dickens visited her there, in a small city or town, and that possibly she produced a child. Dickens's work was based in London, his family was near Chatham in Kent, and his beloved was in France. Dickens traveled back and forth incessantly, sometimes spending only a few days in each place. He also embarked on several arduous dramatic reading tours. It may be that such a schedule dissipated his energy or his concentration. I found myself in that, too. Once, when I lived in Ames, Iowa, where errands were easy and day care was exceptional, I had hours on end in which to marinate my day's work. After I moved to California, gave in to my obsession with horses, and became a single mother, to fritter away an hour meant to fritter away most of the day's allotted writing time. Distractions abounded, and they all seemed important. But then, I had always had children, I had always had something else to do during the day—not riding and horse care, but teaching and professorial responsibilities.

If to live is to progress, if you are lucky, from foolishness to wisdom, then to write novels is to broadcast the various stages of your foolishness. This was true of me. I took up each of my novels with unwavering commitment. I did not begin them by thinking I had a good subject for a novel. I began them by thinking that I had discovered important truths about the world that required communication. When I was writing *Duplicate Keys,* for example, a murder mystery, I was convinced of the idea that every novel is really some sort of mystery or whodunit because every novel is a retrospective uncovering of the real story behind the apparent story. I thought I might write mysteries for the rest of my life. When I was writing *The Greenlanders,* it was obvious to me that all novels were historical novels, patiently reconstructing some time period or another, recent or distant. Horse racing, medieval Greenland, farming, dentistry. I would get letters and reviews from all sorts of people who found themselves reading with interest about subjects they had never thought of before. But at the end of each novel, I would more or less throw down that lens along with that subject. My curiosity was always about how the world worked, what the patterns were, and what they meant. I was secular to the core, and I investigated moral issues with the dedication only someone who is literally and entirely agnostic would do—my philosophical stance was one of not knowing any answers and not believing that there were any answers.

While I was writing *Horse Heaven,* though, I embarked on a spiritual discipline that was satisfying and comforting. I came to believe in

God and to accept a defined picture of Reality that took elements of Christianity and combined them with elements of Eastern religions. It was not an institutionalized religion, but it was a defined faith and had a scripture. It was called A Course in Miracles, and it completely changed the way I looked at the world.

The essential premise of A Course in Miracles is that God did not create the world and that the apparent mixture in the world of good and evil is an illusion; God is not responsible for apparent evil. In fact, the world itself and all physical manifestations are illusory, an agreed-upon conceit that is useful for learning what is true and real, but otherwise a form of dreaming—bad dreaming. The essential falsehoods of the world are that beings are separate from one another, that bodies are real and of primary importance, and that the physical preexists the spiritual. A Course in Miracles, like many Eastern religions, maintains that the world, all physical things, all elements of the universe, and all dimensions, including time, are a mental construct, and that the Mind or the Source preexists matter and is connected to itself all the time and in every way. It took me about three years to turn my image of the world upside down and to become comfortable with this new way of thinking. It wasn't hard, though it was disconcerting at the beginning. The payoff, other than my conviction that these ideas were true, was that I grew less fearful, more patient, less greedy, and more accepting. I greeted events more calmly as a rule, and didn't feel that old sense of vertigo that I had once felt much of the time. I got analyzed, or therapized, or counseled. My counselor shared my beliefs. Together we fixed my relationships and my worldview.

But perhaps the result was no more novels? Perhaps the novel is an agnostic sort of form that not only can't say much about God, but also is even uncomfortable with God as a shadowy background figure? I was eager to detach myself from my habit of having expectations, since I had found the disappointment of my expectations crushingly painful over the years, but I wondered if that also made my work less engaged. Was the old truism that I had hated so much really true, that art, or at least novelistic art, is created out of pain and lack? I had resented and resisted that idea for years; art, I thought, is created out of observation and insight. You don't write a novel to salve a wound, but to bear witness. Nevertheless, something another writer once told me niggled in my brain—I had met Peter Taylor toward the end of his life when we were both at the Key West Writers' Festival. I asked him if he had ever had a dry spell, and he said yes, for a few years in his forties and fifties, when he and his wife had a set of especially beloved friends and he was happy.

If I had consulted my mother, she would have said that horses were wrecking my life at last. All through my horse-obsessed adolescence, she had opposed every horse fantasy I had, because women she knew had horse-crazy daughters who were in her opinion going nowhere fast. They were never going to be famous or accomplished, were always going to waste their lives riding. She had foiled me then and thought her victory was permanent—I went to the college where she hoped I would go, I became a novelist as she hoped I would, and I had had unlooked-for, vindicating success. Between 1977 or so and 1993, I had lived what was essentially a domestic life—husband, house, and children, plus university teaching. I hummed along, apparently performing my duties, but really half absent. Always my mind was pondering whatever novel I was writing. Sometimes the preoccupation was like the after-vibrations of a rung bell—words or sentences I had written that day would recur and recur, and I would feel gratified or simply fascinated by them. At other times I would nurture the next day's work or plan larger plot twists or meditate over how to go on. My novels were unceasingly in my mind. Only at night did I exert myself to stop thinking about them, because if I allowed them in, I wouldn't be able to sleep. No doubt I appeared absentminded to my friends and family, but they didn't have anything to compare it to—that's just the way I was.

After 1993, the horses intruded upon and then displaced the novels. My preoccupation went through several stages; fears and second thoughts, worries, anxiety combined with feverish research made up the first stage. I read horse books, horse magazines, got on Internet horse message boards. I cultivated equestrians and trainers and vets. Writing novels was now something I did when I was sitting at my desk, but not when I was cooking dinner or lying in bed. I fiddled around between *Moo* and *Lidie Newton* so much that my husband feared I might never write another book. Then I fell off the horse and broke my leg, so there was nothing really to do other than write *Lidie Newton*. And then came *Horse Heaven,* which was, for me, book heaven. I had successfully combined my two obsessions, and the result was pure joy every day. As far as I was concerned the book had only one flaw, that its composition ended far too soon, and I had to go on to something else. Whatever the lasting virtues of the book are (and I am no judge, especially of that one), it was perfectly suited to me and my sensibility. It was funny and poignant by turns, it had a large cast, it was written in the omniscient third person (which allowed stylistic exuberance), and it had horses in every chapter except one. Some readers have told me they are sorry when it ends, but no reader is nearly as sorry as I was. It was clear after that book that the appetite of the general public for horses horses horses could be satisfied rather easily. I could spend my life learning about horses, but not, perhaps, expressing what I've learned.

But had the literary ruminations the horses had displaced been essential to novel writing? The answer to this depended on one's theory of creativity. I hadn't ever had much of a theory of creativity beyond making a cup of tea or opening a can of Diet Coke and sitting down at the typewriter or computer. The first and last rules were, get on with it. But perhaps that getting on with it that I had taken for granted for so many years was dependent upon those half-attentive ruminations during diaper changes and breadmaking and driving down the road? Or maybe teaching had stimulated me? Week after week for fourteen years I had expounded about writing, given tips, analyzed student stories, come up with suggestions, fielded questions. Both consciously and unconsciously, I had considered difficulties in my own writings and worked out solutions for them from rules I blithely laid down in class. I wasn't doing that anymore, either. Nor was I reading much fiction. Some of my reading time was taken up with horse books, but most of what I had to spare was going to research—the Civil War and Kansas, horse racing, Charles Dickens. In addition to not thinking much anymore about my own novels, I didn't think much anymore about anyone else's novels.

I did construct a new theory of creativity. Its truth seemed borne out by the experience of writing *Horse Heaven.* Rather than planning and working out in advance, as I had done with most of my earlier novels, I willingly entered a zone of randomness. I sat down at the computer every morning, focused on what I had written the day before, and waited for inspiration. If it didn't seem to be precisely what I had expected, I went with it anyway. My pleasure in the process and the product was a revelation. I didn't need to plan! I didn't need to work something out! I could just put myself into the properly receptive state of mind and be given the words, the stories, the adventures! My joke was that my retired racehorse, Mr. T., was dictating from out in the barn; he was my muse—my inspiration, my expert, and my voice from beyond.

A theory of creativity is actually just a metaphor. A pool of ideas, a well of memories, a voice. The word "inspiration" is a metaphor for creativity—a nice one, the ingoing of breath and spirit, breath and spirit both being ubiquitous, available with only the most minimal involuntary exertion, as natural as life itself. Some writers wrestle with their muses, wrest stories from them. Others imagine their brains working, hydraulic pumps or clockworks or computers. A metaphor is a way of capturing a feeling in words, and creating is a feeling. I have sometimes imagined it literally as a feeling of the brain exerting itself as a muscle does. But all metaphors of creativity are both descriptive and prescriptive. A pool of ideas may run dry, a muse may desert, the mechanical brain may cease to work. Mr. T. died. Dickens was exhausted and frightened by his diminishing inventiveness. My own metaphor bothered me. Was I not receptive enough anymore? Worse, was what I was receiving not worth receiving?

Time to face my real fear—that my book wasn't much good. I once heard Michael Chabon say that the idea for *The Amazing Adventures of Kavalier & Clay* came to him suddenly and all at once; all he had to do was write it out. That had been my experience with several novels, and I had confidently stated more than a few times that the execution of a good novel was inherent in the idea from the first. But that was when I was certain all my ideas were good. It may come as a surprise to those who don't care for my work that I'd hardly ever doubted the significance of any idea I'd had, and I'd had very few ideas. I'd written twelve finished works. I'd had fourteen ideas. The two that did not make it into print were a novella about a woman who is married to a jazz musician (I wrote a rough draft, but when I reread it, it didn't seem to have a point), and a novella about a horse-riding Realtor (sixty pages that just kept expanding with no actual story). The structure of all of my completed novels was fairly apparent to me from the beginning, and I had written with an increasing energy and sense of direction as I went through the rough draft. My commitment, but also my sense of what I was doing, never really faltered—inventiveness was for elaborating or vivifying the original conception, not for conception itself. The different forms I used supplied what you might call craft interest. I would try a tragedy, or an epic, or a comedy. The rules for each were different, and so the technician inside me would have something to figure out. The inner citizen would take up social or cultural issues. The inner artist would focus upon more elusive elements of beauty, rightness, truthfulness, newness. Each novel was an experiment in a particular form, sometimes a conscious contrast to the form I had tried last. I suppose I would say that the inventiveness and variety of literature itself produced a strong response in me; each novel was my answer to a particular literary proposition, a particular method of telling a story.

I was not immune to criticism, but I saw many negative reviews as reader dissatisfaction with the parameters of a particular form. For example, comic novels often offend as many people as they please because each reader's capacity for tolerating irreverence is different; what seems tame to one reader seems right to another, what seems corrosive to one reader seems hilarious to another. Novels with a large canvas sometimes fail to provide an intense emotional experience; novels with a narrow focus can seem claustrophobic. Many reviewers and readers loved *Horse Heaven,* but others found it too confusing and were unable to get involved. And then, there were all the happy endings. I love happy endings and consider them a philosophical and aesthetic challenge, but they are disappointing and untrue to some people. Entropy or loss is more satisfying. That seemed to be the lesson of *A Thousand Acres.* Over the years, countless readers have come up to me and declared how much they love *A Thousand Acres.* I've always wanted to say, "Oh, you're kidding." I find that novel interesting, moving, and challenging, but I don't find it lovable, or even very relate-to-able. I sometimes suspected that to love it is to reveal something unfortunate about oneself. But that isn't actually true. What many readers are responding to, I think, are focus and intensity. The novel has an unrelenting quality to it that is inherently involving and comes from the form of tragedy itself. Though I loved *Horse Heaven,* not everyone else did, so I took some of the negative responses to it as permission to write *Good Faith,* a smaller and more single-minded novel that made use of a story I thought was both interesting and important. I wrote up my proposal, sent it in, got my advance, and began.

From the beginning, though, I was disappointed that it wasn't *Horse Heaven.* I made ethical artistic choices and proceeded in good conscience, but I didn't *like* it. And yet, the thing I wanted to do artistically intrigued me, and I felt it had to be done in a certain way to sustain the illusion of the novel. I considered my main character and narrator appealing. In his way, he was not unlike the narrator of Kazuo Ishiguro's novel *The Remains of the Day,* who tells a story on himself that he doesn't quite understand. But the stylistic pyrotechnics of *Horse Heaven* that I had enjoyed as much as anything I had ever written were not appropriate, and I felt diminished inventiveness as well as diminished pleasure. It was like dating someone new who was nice enough but not nearly as exciting as the old boyfriend who had moved to Europe. I stuck with it. I had gotten a third of the advance. My horse was not winning at the track; no other sources of income (such as movie deals) were presenting themselves. I pegged along, inventive enough to keep writing but not inventive enough to surprise myself. At the halfway mark, I stopped and read through what I had written. It was more interesting than I had thought. The energy of that realization pushed me forward another sixty pages. By now, though, I was looking for terminal symptoms. One day I waited for inspiration, got some, went off in a completely new direction, then had second thoughts the next day and tried something new. This was a symptom, indeed, a symptom that I didn't know what in the world I was doing, and it was way too late in the game for that. My heart sank. No, my flesh turned to ice. No, my eyes popped out of my head. No, my stomach churned. No, all I did was close the file on my computer and walk away. But that was very bad.

I decided to read a hundred novels. This book is the fruit of that course.

2 · What Is a Novel?

SIMPLICITY

An inexpensive paperback book from a reputable publisher is a small, rectangular, boxlike object a few inches long, a few inches wide, and an inch or so thick. It is easy to stack and store, easy to buy, keep, give away, or throw away. As an object, it is user-friendly and routine, a mature technological form, hard to improve upon and easy to like. Many people, myself among them, feel better at the mere sight of a book. As I line up my summer reading of thirty-four novels written in the twentieth century, I realize that I have gained so much and such reliable pleasure from so many novels that my sense of physiological well-being (heart rate, oxygenation, brain chemical production) noticeably improves as I look at them. I smile. This row of books elevates my mood.

The often beautiful cover of a book opens like the lid of a box, but it reveals no objects, rather symbols inscribed on paper. This is simple and elegant, too. The leaves of paper pressed together are reserved and efficient as well as cool and dry. They protect each other from damage. They take up little space. Spread open, they offer some information, but they don't offer too much, and they don't force it upon me or anyone else. They invite perusal. Underneath the open leaves, on either side, are hidden ones that have been read or remain to be read. The reader may or may not experience them. The choice is always her own. The book continues to be an object. Only while the reader is reading does it become a novel.

But it turns out that a novel is simple, too. A novel is a (1) *lengthy,* (2) *written,* (3) *prose,* (4) *narrative* with a (5) *protagonist.* Everything that the novel is and does, every effect that the novel has had on, first, Western culture, and subsequently, world culture, grows out of these five small facts that apply to every novel.

The longest novels that stand alone in one volume are just under 1,000 pages—Henry Fielding's *Tom Jones** would be a good example. The shortest run under 100 pages—Joseph Conrad's *Heart of Darkness* would define that end of the continuum. Most novels run 300 to 400 pages, or 100,000 to 175,000 words. If a competent reader can read 30 or 40 pages in an hour—that is, 12,000 to 20,000 words—then most novels take ten hours to read. Length is a bland and reassuring quality, but it is no blander or more reassuring than any of the other qualities. Prose, for example, is usually simpler to read and more casual than poetry. We are accustomed to reading prose, and we talk in a sort of prose. Narrative, too, is a natural form. People tell stories from their earliest years and continue to narrate as long as they can remember and care about sequences of events. Almost always, their stories have themselves or their friends as protagonists. A story requires a protagonist—that is, a human or a humanlike conciousness who acts or is acted upon in the course of the story. Most people with the normal brain development and structure that results in a sense of self live with a protagonist every minute of every day, and that protagonist (*proto*— first, plus *agon*—combatant) is himself or herself. A protagonist is the most natural thing in the world.

Every novel has all of these elements. If any of them is missing, the literary form in question is not a novel. All additional characteristics— characters, plot, themes, setting, style, point of view, tone, historical accuracy, philosophical profundity, revolutionary or revelatory effect, pleasure, enlightenment, transcendence, and truth—grow out of the ironclad relationships among these five elements. A novel is an experience, but the experience takes place within the boundaries of writing, prose, length, narrative, and protagonist.

The most necessary of the five qualities of the novel is writing. The paradox of writing is that it is permanent, and so it may be forgotten. Author and reader agree that images and ideas set down in writing may come and go because they do not have to be stored in memory. Hazy notions and vague pictures that have to do with the writing certainly remain in the memories of both author and reader, as do strong emotional impressions that author and reader alike feel upon reading

---

*For plot synopses of works discussed, readers may consult the section "A Hundred Novels" in the latter half of this book.

certain sections of the novel, but exact wordings can be largely forgotten. The same is not true of poetry. A poem must be remembered word for word or it loses its identity. In fact, poetry is often learned and remembered word for word, as when students memorize Hamlet's famous soliloquy ("Who would these fardels bear?") in spite of the fact that they have only the dimmest idea of what the words mean. The words may have the power of an incantation even in the absence of comprehension. The memory, though, sets limits upon what is to be remembered. The history of epic poetry, for example, shows that poets used set forms, rhythm, rhyme, figures of speech, and already familiar stories as mnemonic devices to aid in both the composition and the transmission of poetry from poet to poet and from poet to audience. Novelists have no need to do so. Particular stylistic tricks or turns of phrase are not necessary as mnemonic aids to the continued existence of the novel, and so the author is free to explore language and ideas that are hard to remember in detail. The novelist can go on and on, adding scenes, ideas, characters, complexities of every sort, knowing that they are safe from the effects of human memory—they will exist forever exactly as printed and will not evolve by passing through the faulty memories of others.

Writing allows the elaboration of prose. Since memorization is unlikely to begin with, it may be made all the more unlikely by the use of a style that is unmemorable. Prose slips by, common as water. Readers have no defense against it other than boredom. But because it is so common and often colorless, the writer can use it in many ways, from the blandest, most objective, reportlike purposes to the most vivid, evocative, lyrical purposes. James Joyce and Virginia Woolf famously exploited metaphorical and lyrical possibilities of English prose that Defoe and Trollope did not. Prose may slow down and quicken, invoke and state, flower into figures of speech, flatten into strings of facts, observations, assertions. It may pile detail upon detail or summarize years of action in a few pages (as in the middle section of *To the Lighthouse*). Prose usually privileges the sentence, using punctuation to define the beginnings, endings, and complications of thoughts, and sentences are easy. They are what we learn and, often, how we learn it. Even though we don't use them in speech as much as we think we do (in fact, people who talk in whole sentences are generally thought of as pedantic or "prosy"), when our thoughts assume formal shape, they organize themselves into sentences. Poetry, in its search for concentration and sharp effect, contracts. In prose, one thought leads to another—it expands. Although thoughtless expansion is a fault to be guarded against, inspired expansion gives us the novels of Proust and Tolstoy, or Laurence Sterne and Halldór Laxness. Prose is both sneaky and powerful, and is naturally narrative, since sequences of events have some inherent organization, and it is naturally expansive, since events can often be broken down into smaller events and extended backward and forward in time.

In *Aspects of the Novel,* E. M. Forster writes of narrative—that is, of "what happened then?"—almost with contempt. Even the lowliest bus driver, Forster says, could show an interest in suspense, in a sequence of events. He almost admits to wishing that novels could be written without narrative, without what he seems to think is the lowest common denominator of art. But they can't be. It is not only that the novel was invented to tell a lengthy and complicated story that could not be told in any other way, it is also that without the spine of narrative logic and suspense, it cannot be sufficiently organized to be understandable to the reader. Even more basically, a sequence of sentences, which is the only form sentences can occur in, must inevitably result in a narrative. The very before-and-after qualities of written sentences imply, mimic, and require the passage of time. There are minimally narrative novels, but the more lyrical and less narrative a novel is, the shorter it is, until it becomes a short story, which may, indeed, dispense almost entirely with narrative and become a series of impressions or linguistic effects or rhetorical flourishes, as happened with American short stories in the 1960s and 1970s. Narratives are as common as prose; they are the way humans have chosen to pack together events and emotions, happenings in the world and how they make us feel. Even the most informal narratives alternate what happens and how it feels (or what it means) to some degree. Even the most formally objective narratives (such as police reports) imply the emotions that rise out of the events, when at the same time they are suspending conclusions as to the meanings of the events.

Because narrative is so natural, efficient, and ubiquitous, it, like prose, can be used in myriad ways. The time sequence can be abused however the writer wishes to abuse it, because the human tendency, at least in the West, to think in sequence is so strong that the reader will keep track of beginning, middle, and end on her own. Nevertheless, the commonest bus driver can and often does take an interest in what happens next, and so because the novel requires narrative for organization, it will also be a more or less popular form. It can never exclude bus drivers completely, and is, therefore, depending on one's political and social views, either perennially compromised or perennially inclusive.

Perhaps the most important thing about narrative is that it introduces the voice of the narrator. In every novel, some voice is telling the story. The narrator may or may not personalize his voice. He may try to let the story seem to tell itself, as Kafka does in "The Metamorphosis"; he may come forward in what seems to be his own voice, and talk about the characters as if he and the reader were observing them together, as William Makepeace Thackeray does in *Vanity Fair,* or Kate Atkinson does in *Behind the Scenes at the Museum.* He may tell his own story in the first person, as Ishmael does in *Moby-Dick.* In every case, the reader must relate somehow to the voice of the narrator. In every case, the story is colored by the idiosyncrasies of the narrative voice, and how those idiosyncrasies strike the reader. Even the blandest, or most charming, or most skillful narrators have their detractors, because this aspect of the novel is irredeemably social, and draws constantly upon the reader's semiconscious likes and dislikes. Some narrators offend, some narrators appeal, but all narrators are present, the author but not the author, the protagonist but not the protagonist, an intermediary that author and reader must deal with.

The most obvious hallmark of novels is length. The novel was invented to be long, because what early novelists wanted to communicate could not be communicated in a shorter or more direct form, and also because length itself is enjoyable. *The Tale of Genji* runs 1,000 pages. Genji lived a long life and had many wives and concubines. His maturation and his greatness could not be depicted in fewer pages. *Don Quixote* is 700 pages long. Quixote's adventures and humiliations need to build upon one another. The paperback edition of *Ulysses* is 783 pages—the intricacies of Leopold Bloom's day out in Dublin require it. Length, too, is simple. It begins as a mere adding on, though adding on may quickly turn into elaborating or digressing or complicating or subordinating and analyzing. For an author, adding on may amount to no more than keeping going, day after day accumulating episodes and stories, getting paid by the word and so writing more words. For a reader, adding on may offer primarily the pleasure of familiarity—the characters or the narrator's voice or the author's way of thinking become something the reader wants to continue to experience. In a novel, length is always a promise, never a threat.

When the protagonist enters, a novel becomes specific, and even peculiar, and loses the generality that the other four elements seem to offer. The protagonist shapes the other four elements to himself. The narrative must be appropriate to him—it must grow out of his circumstances and teach him something. He must interact with the elements of the plot in a believable as well as an interesting way. The narrative and the protagonist are the chicken and the egg, the thesis and the synthesis. Neither precedes the other, nor exists without the other. A generic story line—for example, "a stranger comes to town"—becomes illuminating and interesting only as it becomes characteristic, only as it becomes the sole property of a particular protagonist. Similarly, the protagonist must prove himself worthy of the length of the novel written about him. If he is trite or blandly conceived, if he doesn't grow as the novel gets longer, the reader will lose interest in him. (It is true, though, that the novelist doesn't rely solely on psychological complexity to maintain the reader's interest in the protagonist. He may substitute sociological complexity if his theory of human nature is more realistic than romantic.) The length of a novel can become a problem for the protagonist—the author and the narrator may be tempted to leave him behind (as Cervantes sometimes puts Don Quixote to sleep when the other characters wish to talk about love problems). In some very long novels, the protagonist's role grows nominal as the landscape fills up with fellow characters and their stories take precedence over his. Even so, the protagonist, as he originates the story line and its circumstances, always remains the organizing figure in the novel, and the main plot must resolve his dilemma, however many other dilemmas it also resolves.

The protagonist is the fulcrum of the author's relationship to the narrator, and the prose, or style, of the novel continuously presents the shifting balances among the three. The prose, like the narrative, must be appropriate to the protagonist. It must express something about him that it could not express about any other protagonist and demonstrate his worthiness to be the protagonist. In some sense, the author, the narrator, and the protagonist are always in a state of conflict that is always being reconciled as the narrative moves forward. Henry

James's *The Portrait of a Lady* is a good example of this conflict. The evidence is that James himself is sympathetic to Isabel Archer from the beginning to the end of the novel. He portrays her as especially attractive, having qualities of innocence, beauty, and charm that set her apart from women around her and that appeal to men and women alike. More important, she is potentially courageous—that is, the quality of courage is within her, but she has not had much occasion to exercise it as the novel opens. James the author wants Isabel to demonstrate certain ideas he has about the way the world works in general and about the psychology of women like herself in particular. James the narrator defines and redefines Isabel's qualities by the extensive use of analysis, especially by analogy and extended metaphor. James the narrator deems it his job to talk about Isabel (and everyone else) unceasingly, to characterize everything she does and thinks in relation to some norm of thought and behavior (represented by several of the other characters). This habit of James the narrator does not serve Isabel over the long haul of the novel, in fact eventually works to demean her. Her courage does come into play several times, in her unhappy relationship with Gilbert Osmond, but by that time the fact that James the narrator has always stayed one step ahead of her by so relentlessly characterizing her in a way that she could not characterize herself means that her courage doesn't have the effect of elevating her soul, or showing her growth. What James the author would like to demonstrate about Isabel through an emotional effect upon the reader of pity and terror has been frittered away by the narrator's habits of storytelling.

Examples abound on the other side, too, of the narrator finding just the right narrative method for portraying his, or in this case her, protagonist. Kate Chopin's *The Awakening* is also about a woman in an unsatisfying marriage. It is evident from the beginning of the novel that Edna Pontellier is in for a major change in her situation. Her husband is conventional and irritable, and she knows that she doesn't love him and never has. Chopin's prose, however, does not press upon the two of them. The narrator spends as much time depicting the world of southern Louisiana as she does depicting the changes in Edna—in fact, much of the reader's sense of the changes in Edna grows out of how sensuously Edna begins to see her world. As her world enlarges and becomes more vivid, her ability to confine herself to the bourgeois corner that her husband and children inhabit grows less and less. Chopin the narrator lets her prose flower in sync with the consciousness of Edna, and when Edna makes her choice at the end, the reader understands, sympathizes with, and is moved by it. The test of a well-chosen and well-executed narrative voice is the climax of the novel. We can read *Pride and Prejudice* ten times and still feel conscious pleasure when Darcy and Elizabeth connect. Wanting to know what happens next turns out to have nothing to do with our anticipation, and the relationships developed among the author, the narrator, and the protagonist as demonstrated and developed by the prose turn out to have everything to do with it; as we grow to like Elizabeth and Darcy more and more through Austen's handling of them, we desire their reconciliation more and more.

Paradoxically, given that novels are always referred to as "fiction," the fictive nature of the novel is its most contingent quality. "Fictiveness" arises in part out of length. As a narrative elaborates and prose extends itself, the connection of the protagonist and his story to literal truth becomes more and more tenuous. Lengthy prose is required to be interesting—otherwise the reader won't go on with it—but we can contrast lengthy prose based on fact, such as narrative history, which gains interest through the compilation of authenticated facts, with novels. The historian is required to give up dramatic interest in the pursuit of accuracy, but a novelist must give up accuracy in the pursuit of narrative drive and emotional impact. Even if the novel is based entirely on what the novelist himself has experienced, he will rework the experiences to make them more vivid and evocative, and, indeed, more logical and comprehensible. In reworking them, he will betray, or transcend, the original experience.

Edith Wharton remarked that the job of the novelist is to thoroughly think through each element or aspect of his or her novel. The resulting feeling of completion is essentially fictional. An author may excavate her memory to come up with every aspect of the experience she wants to depict. If she switches for even a sentence or two out of her own point of view and memory into that of another character, she has yielded to the urge to write something more complete than what she knows for certain. And, as Proust would have maintained, the construction of memories themselves, and their arrangement into a logical and understandable order, may make them fictional, but also makes them worth reading about. In other words, lengthy written prose narratives with protagonists are all fictional, but fiction is what results from the other qualities, not what dictates them.

COMPLEXITY

The fact that while the novel seems to be limitless and universally capacious, it is actually much more particular in many ways results from how its five characteristics combine. As an example, let's consider writing and length. Because a novel is a printed book, subject to laws of intellectual property and also subject to commerce, it goes into the world as the author composed it. It retains its purity and constitutes a direct communication from one person to another. A reader who doesn't like what an author has to say may close it, burn it, recommend against it, give it a bad review in a publication, or even censor it, but she doesn't thereby destroy it, as she would if she simply retold the story, leaving out the objectionable parts or adding a little bit of sentiment or clarification here and there. A novel is known to be a book. A redaction of a novel, by Hollywood or Broadway or *Reader's Digest* or a paraphrase or any other means, is known not to be a novel, not to be authentic. A novel can be dropped or outmoded or rediscovered by readers, but it can't be changed into something else, in the way that the stories that were the bases of epic poems or traditional folktales were changed in the telling.

Controversies raised by a novel can become general; a book such as *The Awakening* or D. H. Lawrence's *Lady Chatterley's Lover* can be greeted with outrage, or prominent thinkers can declare that a book such as de Sade's *Justine* should never be put into the hands of young girls. Novels as popular, irreducible, available books promote argument about the issues they explore, and indeed are often meant by their authors to do so. As books, censored or outlawed novels become precious. Restrictions enhance the reader's desire for a private experience—that of reading a banned book—and so promote the very subject they are about, the individual's sensation of coexistence with the group. As a book, a novel enhances its reader's sense of power. Don't like the author? Throw the book away. Think this obscure book is better than that famous one? State your opinion. Disagree with the very respected author? You may, because the book is in your hands, in your power, which makes you the author's equal. But the book itself you cannot destroy.

Imagine the roster of heroes and heroines that novels have carried around the world. David Copperfield stands beside Frankenstein and not far from Scarlett O'Hara and Count Dracula, Anna Karenina, Scrooge, Uncle Tom, Jo March, Becky Sharp, the Count of Monte Cristo, Don Quixote and Sancho Panza, Elizabeth Bennet, Captain Bligh and Captain Ahab. Some have received a boost from the movies, but others have not. The protagonist, made accessible by prose and interesting by narrative and familiar by length, and then dispersed by the written word, has entered the lives and minds of millions and re-created them, at least a bit, in his or her own image. The significance of this combination—writing and ordinary protagonist—has changed the way people relate to literature and, indeed, to themselves. A protagonist is usually interesting not because he is someone special (in fact, it is harder to write about someone special) but because something happens to him. Because the novel has to be long and organized, he has to become interesting as he deals with the thing that happens to him. This typical transformation from an ordinary person to someone worth remembering comes to seem both routine and appealing, encouraging readers to see themselves as potentially interesting and their lives as potential material for novels. Thus are the moral lives of readers encouraged to develop complexity; thus are new characters born out of old ones. When Jean Rhys, who grew up in the Caribbean, read *Jane Eyre,* her direct experience of a world that she felt Charlotte Brontë had not understood caused her to reimagine the monstrous Mrs. Rochester as an abused and abandoned child, used as a commodity by her relatives in their attempt to ally themselves to Rochester's fortune. Rhys's novel, in turn, heralded a reconsideration of many aspects of European colonial exploitation in the Caribbean, which has resulted in astonishing works by such disparate authors as Paule Marshall, Jamaica Kincaid, and Edwidge Danticat.

Other combinations of the novel's five basic characteristics have important implications, too. A long prose narrative offers accessibility through the prose, and entertainment through the narrative. A common complaint about young English girls in the eighteenth century was that they chose to read novels when they should have been reading sermons. When the entertainment of narrative came in the door, it was thought, self-improvement flew out the window. Length adds complexity, enhances enjoyment, and at the same time promotes persuasion. Sometimes a reader disagrees with everything a novelist says but is seduced by some charm or other—intelligence, wit, suspense—to keep reading. By the end of a long novel, the author has had many hours to win the reader over, and the reader may find herself entertaining thoughts and ideas willingly that were once alien or even distasteful to her. In *The Picture of Dorian Gray,* by Oscar Wilde, Dorian pores over a novel given to him by Lord Henry, which does more than anything else to persuade him that he wants to live a life of sensual pleasure at any cost. Readers commonly feel, after reading a long novel about some time or place that they have no actual experience of, that they now "know" that time or place intimately—perhaps more intimately than they "know" their own surroundings. With length, details pile up, the imagination fills in, experience becomes more and more vivid.

Prose, in combination with the relationship between the protagonist and his group, makes a realistic narrative more likely (though there are plenty of novels that are not realistic). Since prose is the style average people use to talk about money, family relationships, work, survival, getting from here to there, trivia, and also the style of jokes and memos, newspapers and letters, it makes writing about common things easier. Prose makes it more likely that the protagonist will be ordinary, more subject to the effects of money, work, survival, and trivia than to the effects of heroism or high destiny. Prose deflates the hero, as poetry and drama inflate him. As it adds up, prose moves on to the next event, and forces the characters and the reader to move on, too, giving novels life and hope, even when the story explicitly being told is dreary and hopeless. Prose implies that events can be organized, understood, endured, and survived. When the curtain falls on a great tragedy, that is the end of those characters and that situation, and often the audience is meant to feel shocked and bereft—worked up to a high pitch of feeling by the climax, and then dropped over the cliff of the denouement. That's what catharsis is all about. In novels, though, prose plus the protagonist plus the group tend to block catharsis, reminding the reader that whatever emotions we suffer, life goes on.

But the most important essential characteristic of the novel that arises out of its structure, out of the combination of narrative and length, is that it is inherently political. It is possible to have a short story, a drama, a novella, or a movie that explores a single consciousness or a single experience. A hundred pages that emphasize a single mind is not at all unusual. But a novel—a story that runs a hundred pages or longer—must for the sake of context and variety include other characters. In many ways, it is easy to see why this is. Focusing on the workings of a single mind gives rise to questions of why that mind works that way, or under what circumstances the mind works in that way, or how that mind is unique (thereby warranting such focus). The reader knows it is highly implausible that a single human mind has no social context, and the author knows this, too, so even as a mere filling in of the blanks, the author begins to depict the group that the protagonist is part of. Inevitably, the subject of any novel comes to be the coexistence of the protagonist and his group. As the group takes shape, so the protagonist takes shape. As the novel lengthens and the group becomes more detailed, so the protagonist's relationship with the group becomes more detailed; and as the details mount up, so does the requirement that the author have a theory of individuals and groups. The narrative, and therefore the logic, of the protagonist's relationship to the group must express some explicit or implicit theory, and inevitably many of these theories are political, because politics is about the division of power in human groups. Even authors who choose not to be political, such as Italo Svevo or Laurence Sterne, end up falling somewhere on the political spectrum, because the very assertion that all of life is personal is political.

Virginia Woolf offers an interesting paradox. In her essay "Mr. Bennett and Mrs. Brown," Woolf maintains that the reality of life is personal—the experience of consciousness—and that such authors as Arnold Bennett and John Galsworthy, who pay explicit attention to social, cultural, and political arrangements, are missing the point. The point, as Woolf suggests in *Orlando,* is the thrilling experience of the present moment. Everything else is a sort of dry dust that falls away, insignificant and distracting. Many of Woolf's most famous works move from character to character, moment to moment, attempting to capture and renew the sense of wonder that exists apart from and inside of social, cultural, and political arrangements. Woolf is, in this sense, apolitical. But in another sense, she is very political, because the logical outcome of her method is a radical democratizing of the novel. No consciousness is privileged. No class, no degree of virtue or talent, no amount of money, no uniqueness of perspective gets to own the depiction of consciousness. A child, such as James in *To the Lighthouse;* a troubled man, such as Septimus in *Mrs. Dalloway;* a not very appealing person, such as Bernard in *The Waves,* can have as important and revealing experiences as any heroine of Dickens, any hero of Trollope. The author's job, according to Woolf, is to preserve exceptional moments, not to award them to exceptional people. Woolf, it is well known, democratized the novel without herself being democratic— she was often snobbish and disdainful, and she liked to hang around people of her own class and intellectual attainments. But her own predilections are of absolutely no importance to her argument. As soon as her argument went into the world, it transformed the world's sense of what is and what is not important, at least as far as subjects of the novel are concerned. Woolf's novels aren't overtly about power, but they show that power, especially the power of true observation, does not have any necessary connection to status or beauty.

And not only is the novel inherently political, it is also inherently liberal—that is, it embraces the rights and obligations of individualism. This is easy to understand as soon as we realize that a lengthy prose narrative must be well organized to be readable. A novel's organization depends upon distinct and readily identifiable characters. They begin by having names and go on to have appearances, characteristics, and histories. Thus, purely for the sake of organization, the novel promotes the idea of individuals' having memorable idiosyncrasies and importance. As a result, it appeals to the reader's sense of her own distinctness and importance. And novel-reading cannot be a collective experience. Just as, without Hamlet to remind the audience that appearances are deceiving, the audience of a drama might believe in the legitimacy of Claudius' rule, so, too, without authorial reminders of the importance of "the people" or "the nation," novel-readers might forget the existence of the collective (as opposed to a group of distinct individuals) entirely. In a society that promotes conformity, novel-reading—one person experiencing both the mind of another person and her own mind experiencing—is a subversive force.

Additionally, the liberal continuum that the novel runs upon is rather narrow. The protagonist has only a few choices in his necessary relationship to the group—he can be subsumed, he can make a comfortable connection, he can make an uncomfortable accommodation, he can refuse to accommodate and remain apart, or he can be destroyed by the group. The author's predilections, theories, and temperament will combine with the logic of the plot to dictate one of the five. But whatever happens to the protagonist, the individuals of the group constitute a countervailing balance—they are all more or less as individuated as he is, and so true conformity, of the sort required under communism or theocracy, is not possible in a novel. Additionally, the most individualistic outcomes are generally depicted tragically—if the individual remains or becomes isolated, his victory is at the very least a Pyrrhic one. It may vindicate his views of the corruption or emptiness or shallowness or brutality of society, but it does not demonstrate that isolation is a happy state. Edith Wharton's *The House of Mirth* is a good example. Lily Bart is a sympathetic and attractive young woman, but she has no means of support. She is best suited to earning her living by marrying someone wealthy whom she doesn't particularly like or respect, but she can't bring herself to do so, even at the cost of her life. In a very muted moral victory, she takes an overdose of a sleeping mixture and dies in a small, dirty room; the class she once belonged to goes on, undamaged and unaware of her fate. In Franz Kafka's *The Trial,* Josef K. is expelled, bit by bit, from the fairly comfortable and conforming life he had been leading. Finally, for no substantial reason, he is killed by the side of the road. His fate is "necessary" but not preferable. Wharton writes as a "realist" and Kafka writes as a "surrealist," but they share a view of what is true about the individual's relation to the group. The fate of Julien Sorel in *The Red and the Black;* the fate of Pechorin in *A Hero of Our Time;* the fate of Anna in *Anna Karenina;* the fates of a multitude of other protagonists are all similar—undone, whether deserving or undeserving, by society.

But it is possible for some protagonists to be integrated into their group, though this happens mostly in English and American novels. Only the darkest Dickens novels disallow some kind of happy marriage at the end, and in my favorite, *Our Mutual Friend,* the two couples (Bella and John, Eugene and Lizzie) and their friends the Boffins and Mortimer Lightwood form a strong and happy circle within the larger, more corrupt London world. In *Uncle Tom's Cabin,* Tom dies, but Cassy and Eliza and their families form a cohesive, happy, and activist group at the end. In *Middlemarch,* Dorothea marries Will Ladislaw, and Mary Garth marries Fred Vincy. In *Ulysses,* of course, Leopold Bloom comes home at night, welcomed into the arms of Molly. Nevertheless, no novel is ever about how everything turned out well for everyone through the achievement of utopia, whether of faith or of politics. The protagonist *must* contrast to those around him to be the protagonist. This means that his fate sets him apart, happy or sad.

The novel is inherently political, but the organizational demands of the novel form mean that it doesn't fit easily into political ideas of class or group blame or virtue. Every important character in a novel is portrayed as having moral complexity. If a character is solely evil, or is solely good, or solely a victim, then he or she is a figure or a symbol of something but not a protagonist, not possessed of agency, which in a novel is the only standard of real importance. A protagonist in a novel, of whatever ethnic background and in whatever time period, cannot be wholly good or wholly bad and still be interesting enough to read about. And novelists have no actors to give nuance to the characters they create—for example, bringing subtle depth or charisma to an Iago. Consequently, readers with an essentially political agenda, looking for models of proper thinking and behavior, are hardly ever going to find them in novels. The novel always promotes complexity as both an organizational principle and a narrative principle. My favorite example of a novel character who cannot be assimilated by any political group is Tom in *Uncle Tom's Cabin*. Tom never acts as a member of his class—a slave, he consistently offends by refusing to yield his conscience. Given the choice to run away when he is sold to a dealer, Tom chooses to go along rather than endanger the economic well-being of the plantation and thereby his family. Given the choice between death or the betrayal of another slave by Legree, Tom chooses death. Given the choice of killing Legree, by Cassy, Tom refuses to imperil his immortal soul by committing murder. In every circumstance, Tom makes his decisions according to his conscience and then hopes for the best, always bolstered by the conviction that this world is ephemeral and one's true reward is in heaven. In the context of the novel, Tom is virtuous, but his virtue is based on an understandable logic. Although he is often the object of others' designs, he sees himself as the agent of his own fate. Outside the context of the novel, his complexity has never been understood. In our day he is seen as craven and accommodating, hardly a man at all, while in Stowe's day his very assertion of agency flew in the face of accepted views of slave, and black, behavior.

When we survey our hundred novels, and all of their hundreds of relatives and neighbors, it seems at first as if they are impossibly diverse, but the five essential qualities of the lengthy written prose narrative with a protagonist have actually limited their variety and the number of things they are capable of communicating, and this is as true of *The Tale of Genji* (1004) as it is of *Atonement* (2001).

3 · Who Is a Novelist?

I had not then read any real novels. I had heard it
said that George Sand was a typical novelist. That had
prepared me in advance to imagine that *François le
Champi* contained something inexpressibly delicious.

—MARCEL PROUST, *Swann's Way*

A novel has an author. The desire to write a novel is the single
required prerequisite for writing a novel. It is the only thing
that overcomes all the handicaps—perfectionism, low self-
esteem, depression, alcoholism, diseases of all kinds, immense riches,
economic hardship, deadly enemies, the resistance of relatives and
friends, laziness, retarded professional development, the regular
responsibilities of adulthood, even imprisonment (Sir Thomas Malory,
for example, wrote the romance/protonovel *Le Morte d'Arthur* while
imprisoned during the Wars of the Roses). While the desire to write a
novel does not guarantee that the resulting novel will be a good one, or,
if it is, that the author will produce a string of good ones, it is the only
way to begin. Most often it grows out of a compulsive habit of reading
as a child. It was said of Sinclair Lewis that he was always doing two
things at once, and one of them was reading a book. Charles Dickens
was an avid reader as a boy; his dearest childhood memories were of
reading *The Tales of the Arabian Nights*. I read in preference to almost
every other activity, though I didn't read anything respectable. I liked
the Bobbsey Twins and Nancy Drew. The Brontës, living in a solitary
Yorkshire parsonage with a very eccentric father, not only read compulsively but also wrote compulsively, and had composed many hundreds of pages by their late teens.

Undoubtedly, we were reading for all the wrong reasons—escape, pleasure, avoidance of responsibilities and human contact. We were reading because it was easy and fun and because we were unsupervised. We were reading to find companions more congenial than those around us. We wanted to fill our heads with nonsense and tune out practical considerations. We were not, most likely, athletic or useful sorts of children. We were reluctant to help around the house or to go outside and play. We did not have very good manners, because in numerous ways to be cited later, reading books is deleterious to good manners. We did not have good sleep habits, because if we had, we would not have read under the bedcovers with a flashlight, or held the book up to the moon that shone through the window, and ruined our eyes. We were reading because we had two lives, an inner life and an outer life, and they were equally important to us and equally vivid. A novelist is someone whose inner experience is as compelling as the details of his or her life, someone who may owe more to another author, never met, than to a close relative seen every day. A novelist has two lives—a reading and writing life, and a lived life. He or she cannnot be understood at all apart from this.

I once asked a woman mathematician whether it was true that math talent went with the Y chromosome, a tendency to allergies, lack of social skills, and left-handedness. She told me that she didn't think so, but that the large population of left-handed male mathematicians with allergies felt most comfortable with their own sort because they had no social skills, so it was a self-selecting profession. Novelists are self-selecting in a similar way. Most children's books and fantasies are about introverted, highly imaginative heroes or heroines who overcome outsider status, either so they can join the group or so they can transcend the group; children who read a lot of books come to identify with those sorts of protagonists and come to be like those sorts of protagonists. Novels for children and young adults are soothing and reaffirm the young reader's sense of worthiness. The child, who may have few friends, gathers around himself or herself an array of characters who are entertaining and forgiving and enlightening.

From our habit of reading, we unconsciously imbibed hundreds of character portrayals, thousands of word usages and sentence structures, thousands of metaphors, similes, and circumlocutions. We saw countless motives analyzed, innumerable behaviors described. We followed plot after plot from exposition to denouement. In assuaging our loneliness or our boredom we also learned what it took to make a novel, though most of us didn't try it at first. We were interested in content, but the intuitive knowledge of form entered along with the content and became part of our mental furniture. A good example of this process, for me, was my love of Sherlock Holmes stories, and, in particular, my frequent rereading of *The Hound of the Baskervilles* when I was eleven and twelve.

Although I was an avid reader, I was not a sophisticated one, and when I took up Holmes, I had only the dimmest idea of most of the things Watson talks about in the novel—I could hardly picture a moor or a mire, I had never seen a convict or been to London. I did not understand what an "avenue of yews" was or know why the Baskerville estate passed from one distant relative to another. I could not imagine the dastardly crime committed by the ancestor Hugo Baskerville that was the source of the family curse. No one I knew spoke with the formality or the diction of Holmes and Watson. I knew the two were friends. I knew Holmes solved mysteries. I had read Agatha Christie and Nancy Drew. I loved dogs. I imagined the hound itself as an extra-large Great Dane, like the one who lived on the property behind us, but black.

I am sure that the first time I read *The Hound of the Baskervilles,* I had no idea what the solution to the mystery was, and I am sure that Conan Doyle was perfectly able to convince me that Holmes was the world's greatest deducer. I am sure that the identity and motive of the killer came as much of a surprise to me as it did to Watson, and to the readers of Conan Doyle's day who made the novel so popular. But I can't remember, because I read the novel many times, until the details of the mystery, and even certain phrases and effects, were completely, though unconsciously, memorized. I read it because of the air of dark fascination that hung over the setting and because of the exciting appearance of the hound itself, with his phosphorescent face and huge size (I was sure I could have made friends with that hound, no matter what they said about him, and I pitied the way they treated him). I reread it because Holmes was never not in control of the situation, and to him, all dangers were exciting and all mysteries were puzzles. I read it because it was reassuring (as *Giants in the Earth,* by Ole Rölvaag, and *The Bridge of San Luis Rey,* by Thornton Wilder, books I was required to read in school, were not); Conan Doyle's worldview was solid, and even innocent. *The Hound of the Baskervilles* was entirely appropriate reading for a twelve-year-old.

What I learned from it was not what I read it for. Each time I reread the novel, knowing the tricks and the deceptions of the plot, I learned how the tricks and the deceptions worked together logically. The novel had two stories—the story as it unfolded on the surface, and the story of what had happened. The two stories had to mesh perfectly for Holmes's recapitulation to be convincing, but the surface story had to successfully hide the real story for the recapitulation to be interesting. Both stories had to bolster Holmes's claim to special intellectual status, as did everything he said, all of his mannerisms, and everything he did. Watson could make claims for Holmes, but Conan Doyle had to depict Holmes in a way that made good on the claims, at least in the eyes of a twelve-year-old. Rereading any novel over and over, for whatever reason, makes it fall into pieces. The veil that suspense and style throw over construction on the first reading or two lifts, and the author's plotting becomes more and more clear. I learned about the logical construction of plot and the clear construction of character. *The Hound of the Baskervilles* was not the best novel I read at that time in my life, but it was the most clearly constructed. As I reread it today, it seems obvious and pedestrian, but I imbibed a good deal from it early in my literary career because it was complicated enough to interest me, but not so complicated as to be utterly seamless and impossible to dissect.

And so, literature itself and novels themselves are one of a nascent novelist's primary inspirations—it may be that they are *the* primary inspiration in most cases, because most children and adolescents have no perspective on their lives, so they don't often have any idea that their lives are unusual or worth writing about. Unhappiness, isolation, even what others would call adventures are just the stuff of every day. Or we can look at it another way and say that literature, the great river of novels, enters into individuals and extends itself into the future through them, because there is no other way for it to do so. A novelist is someone who has volunteered to be a representative of literature and to move it forward a generation. That is all.

The second great inspiration for a novelist is language. Some novelists have a distinctive genius for language, and all forms of language as spoken and written energize and inspire them. Dickens is a good example of a novelist who sought out and delighted in all forms of writing and talk—he walked the streets of London through many nights, talking to people he met and listening to others. He was a great lover of the theater, and not only respectable drama, but also all shows and spectacles. As an actor, he was a noted mimic. He loved jokes,

songs, and rhymes of all sorts. He worked hard editing several magazines, and his letters to his authors show that he paid close attention to
their style. He wrote and rewrote—often he would rewrite his books
between serial publication and volume publication. He was a justly
celebrated letter writer. He was, of course, a great prose stylist, with
many voices and dictions at his command, as inventive with words as
any English writer ever. Clearly his relationship to the English language went beyond love to something more intimate, something more
living, something like breathing. Dickens introduced certain types
of characters into the English novel—characters such as Sam Weller
in *The Pickwick Papers,* whose flow of speech is a flow of self-
representation and a flow of wisdom, too. But what came first, Sam or
his way of talking? If we imagine Dickens in his early twenties, all
ears, preternaturally alert to the myriad voices around him, then characterization becomes the fruit of language rather than vice versa.
Dickens's books are peopled with embodied voices who talk first and
submit to the plot later.

Of course, there are other novelists who have distinctive styles,
clearly styles that owe a great deal to the linguistic universes of their
youth—William Faulkner, Marcel Proust, Franz Kafka, Nikolai
Gogol, Nancy Mitford, Garrison Keillor. All of these novelists have a
claim on our attention because the way in which narratives are wedded to the telling of them is striking and profound. Others, many of
them women (though I think Flaubert fits in here), such as Jane
Austen, Alice Munro, George Eliot, Edith Wharton, and Elizabeth
Bowen, are especially subtle and precise. They don't cause the language to do more, but they cause it to communicate more perfectly and
efficiently. George Eliot, in her use of analogy and extended metaphor,
as well as in her very nuanced deployment of conceptual words that
would seem dry in the hands of another novelist, is especially good at
depicting a whole range of ideas that other authors hardly seem to
have thought about. Whereas Dickens's work is vividly picturesque,
Eliot's is vividly smart. *Middlemarch* is an entire education in the
sources and results of human feeling, and also in how capaciously and
fully it is possible to think about things.

Novelists are not the only artists, of course, who are inspired by language. Obviously all of the literary arts depend upon writers with verbal fluency. The novel has proved exceptionally difficult to analyze
stylistically, though, because of the multiplicity of voices prose may
include. Each time a character speaks, he is likely to speak in a way

that differs from every other character and also from the narrator because distinctiveness is one of the main methods an author has to organize his characters so the reader can keep them straight. The writer with a tin ear is at an organizational disadvantage compared with a writer with a good ear.

To dare to write about many different characters, and to keep them straight without the help of actors, is in some ways a bold endeavor. It imposes several duties upon the author. I have mentioned order, in the sense that the readers don't want to get the characters mixed up, but there is also the progress of the plot. Characters in dialogue are required to more or less move the story along. If they are just sitting around chatting meaninglessly, then the novel comes to be about the meaninglessness the characters are demonstrating. Meaninglessness can be demonstrated only so many times before the reader decides to close the book. The voices of characters are also required to seem authentic. The captain of a whaling ship must talk as a captain of a whaling ship would talk—with characteristic vocal mannerisms and with typical knowledge. Depending upon his role in the novel, though, a character is also required to have something interesting to say that simultaneously deepens the reader's knowledge of him, deepens the reader's knowledge of the other characters, deepens the reader's understanding of the story, and best of all, deepens the reader's knowledge in general. Novelists who don't love language enough to discern these things in the talk and the writing around them have a much more difficult time becoming novelists than novelists who do.

Fortunately, an affinity for language is common. Possibly it runs in families—my relatives were always telling stories, making jokes, coming up with expressions and sayings. They were talkative, and they took pleasure in talk the way musical families take pleasure in music. Talkative families give children a rich linguistic environment in which to develop their own linguistic abilities. But it seems also true that a child's native language can be better or worse at producing novelists, that the richness and variety of the language (the "langue" as opposed to the "parole") asks to flower into lengthy prose. The question of why the novel, when it took hold, took hold first in England, is always an interesting one, similar to the question of why the Icelandic sagas were written in Iceland rather than Norway. Was it only printing and leisure time and the rise of the literate middle class? Are the necessary origins of the novel as an established art form only material ones having to do with commerce and readership? Or is English itself especially well suited to lengthy prose?

I think it is enlightening to look at Daniel Defoe in this context. Defoe was more or less a hack writer who wrote polemics, speeches, manuals, business guides, ghost stories, and advice books, but money doesn't always drive out art. More often they coexist, with art having the last say. Defoe was a London man; he lived by trade at the heart of a world that was just discovering the power of trade, of shipping, of international exploration and exploitation. He knew and wrote about the ways of the worlds—the world of the poor as well as the world of the rich, the world of the up-and-coming as well as the world of the declining and disappearing, the world of the traveler as well as the world of the captured, trapped, isolated, and abandoned. Defoe also grew up reading and listening to the King James Bible, because he came from a strongly religious Protestant household. Anthony Burgess remarks in his introduction to the 1966 Penguin edition of *A Journal of the Plague Year* that "Defoe was equipped by training, as well as by temperament, to turn into the first really modern writer, his mind disposed to independence, liberalism, scientific inquiry, master of five languages (though Latin and Greek not among them), his interests immediate and practical, not classical and remote" (p. 8).

When Defoe turned to writing novels, it was a small step from the books he was already writing (including a travel journal called *A Tour Through the Whole Island of Great Britain*) to the fiction he is remembered for. He published seven novels in five years. In doing so, he incorporated the stories and the languages of seven vigorous English types into the new middle-class form of literature, the novel, a literature about working, getting by, making the best of the free-market economy as it was constituted in the early eighteenth century (no social safety net, as Defoe repeatedly pointed out). The choice between virtue and gain, or between virtue and survival, was Defoe's constant subject. His characters are always weighing the inner life against the outer life, and Defoe's language has a great deal of psychological sophistication rendered in practical, commonsense terms. Most readers first read *Robinson Crusoe* as children, but it is worth going back and reading it as an adult, after reading many other novels. What is immediately striking is that although Crusoe's adventures are still of some interest, it is mental and spiritual growth that are really the heart of the story, and to depict it requires a supple style. A good example of how all of this works together occurs about 70 percent of the way into the novel, at a point where Crusoe is getting to know Friday. Crusoe begins one paragraph, "From hence, I sometimes was led too far to invade the Soverainty of *Providence,* and as it were arraign the Justice of so arbitrary a disposition of things, that should hide that Light from some, and reveal it to others. . . ." The next paragraph begins, "But to return to my New Companion; I was greatly delighted with him, and made it my Business to teach him every Thing, that was proper to make him useful, handy, and helpful; but especially to make him speak. . . ." This paragraph is followed by one that begins, "After I had been two or three Days return'd to my Castle, I thought that in order to bring *Friday* off from his horrid way of feeding, and from the Relish of a Cannibal's Stomach, I ought to let him taste other Flesh; so I took him out with me one Morning to the Woods . . ." (pp. 193–94, Modern Library edition). In about one page of active and lively prose, Defoe takes up his spiritual doubts and what he does with them, the nature of his growing attachment to Friday and his sense of what sort of person Friday seems to be, and how his obligations to Friday's welfare lead him to act, and lead Friday to react. (In the third paragraph, Crusoe shoots a goat. Friday, unfamiliar with firearms, is astonished at the noise and amazed at what happens to the goat.) Defoe's narrative moves quickly and smoothly from what happens to how the characters feel about it, to how Crusoe gives it meaning (or speculates about it—part of the suspense of the novel is that Crusoe is attempting to work out what things mean over the course of his long stay on the island), and, finally, to new things that Crusoe learns as he explores his home. Defoe is as comfortable with words such as "arraign" as he is with words such as "handy." That he calls his hut a "Castle," refers to Friday as "feeding" and to the "Relish of a Cannibal's Stomach" shows he is fully sensitive to the ironic power of English words to communicate several connotations at the same time, that this is a natural part of his style rather than an effect he is striving for at an especially important juncture of the narrative. Most important, for his purposes, Defoe is entirely comfortable moving between the language of action and survival, which is largely made up of words with Anglo-Saxon roots, such as "Flesh," and the language of religious discourse, which is largely made up of Latinate words, such as "Foundation." Defoe was inspired by the adventures of Alexander Selkirk, the original castaway, but his own inner life told him what to do with Robinson Crusoe.

Defoe was conversant with a wealth of English dialects, spoken and written, urban and rural. In addition to being narrated in the first person, his books are full of dialogue; they also quote advertisements and bills and documents. For our purposes, they sample the English language of the early eighteenth century in a prolific and unexcelled manner. And most important, his books were widely read. Thanks to Defoe, by the time of Fielding, Dr. Johnson, and Samuel Richardson, an example had been set of variety and inclusiveness in English narrative prose.

At the other end of the history of the English novel is *White Teeth,* by Zadie Smith. Smith, too, lives at the Defoean/Dickensian nexus of London as a vortex of disparate stories and languages, and she, too, is clearly inspired by English as a robust and colorful river of words and grammar that has an energy of its own that brings characters, incidents, ideas, social classes, and imaginative worlds together whether they will or no, but the tributaries of her river are no longer only the Thames and the Ware, and they no longer empty into the North Sea, as Defoe's did. Her river begins in the Himalayas and the Blue Mountains of Jamaica, in the Snowy Mountains in Australia and the Highlands of Scotland, all the places that English has flowed into and returned from, altered and enriched. Her London is, like Defoe's, not quiet or traditional, but full of overt and covert conflict, and a little dangerous. A major source of discomfort for some of Smith's characters is the difficulty of fixing on an authentic language that communicates the inner life as well as it does the communal life. English itself, though, Smith can't help demonstrating, exalts the variousness of the characters even while it sometimes hinders their attempts to know themselves.

The inspirational effects of language, of course, lead to the inspirational effects of life, and we normally think of a novelist as someone who has something to say—a view of the world or a story to tell that is mostly autobiographical. Traditionally, great novelists live dramatic lives. Snorri Sturluson, the author of *Egilssaga,* was assassinated. Charlotte Brontë, the author of *Jane Eyre* and *Villette,* died during pregnancy, after watching her two novelist sisters and her brother die of tuberculosis. Herman Melville spent years in the South Pacific. Giovanni Boccaccio was a famous man of letters who also performed diplomatic work for various princes. Marguerite de Navarre was a queen and the sister of a king. Ernest Hemingway shot himself.

F. Scott Fitzgerald and Sinclair Lewis were famously and, depending on your view of drunks, tragically or heroically or obnoxiously dissipated. George Eliot lived out of wedlock with a man who was married to another woman. Edith Wharton was immensely rich and socially prominent. Aphra Behn was a successful dramatist in Restoration London, and traveled to South America as a young woman. James Joyce was blind. George Sand was a member of the French aristocracy who claimed both Chopin and de Musset as lovers. William Makepeace Thackeray's wife was schizophrenic and lived in a madhouse. Lady Murasaki was a woman-in-waiting to the empress of Japan. After many bouts of mental illness, Virginia Woolf killed herself. Vladimir Nabokov's father was assassinated by political rivals, and Nabokov went into exile.

Biographies of novelists invariably assert that some part of the novelist's background or childhood led to the writing of novels and even engendered particular novels. But the three sources of inspiration for a novelist coexist in different ways in different novelists. In my opinion, the desire to write a novel and the affinity for language do more to determine the choice of the novel as mode of expression than the drama of particular life events. While on the one side we have Virginia Woolf, Herman Melville, and Cervantes, whose lives were full of drama before they became novelists, on the other side we have John Updike, Harriet Beecher Stowe, and Flaubert, whose lives were not so different from the lives of most other men and women of their day. Their lives show that what happens to any novelist may only be a corollary to the books he writes, not at all a determining cause.

Nonetheless, some novelists are motivated first and foremost by the desire to make something of their lives and experiences, even if the form of the novel doesn't come naturally to them or is unfamiliar to them. Cervantes, for example, who did not begin writing *Don Quixote* until he was almost fifty, had served as a soldier for most of his life, and had been maimed in the hand in battle. For Cervantes, it was not really possible that the form of the novel should inspire him, since there were not really any novels to do so. He is the paradigm of the aspiring novelist who for whatever reason is deprived of a model and a mentor, and has to make it up himself. Cervantes's strangely modern career as a novelist is evident in the differences between the two volumes of his novel, which were published some ten years apart. In volume 1, Quixote, inversely mirroring the career of his creator, perhaps, has his head turned by reading too many romances of chivalry, and at an advanced age, leaves his impoverished estate and his sedentary pursuits to go out into the world to protect the virtuous and preserve the unfortunate. The idea is a clever and productive one, and affords Cervantes any number of episodes and jokes and comic depictions of the real world of late-sixteenth-century Spain as it contrasts with Don Quixote's romantic ideas. But some of Cervantes's material is recycled from other books, and in places he doesn't quite know what to do with his protagonist. The first volume of *Don Quixote* is lively but episodic and disorganized. At the end of it the author, still new to his form, doesn't seem to quite understand what it adds up to.

By the beginning of the second volume, Cervantes had had quite a few more years to contemplate his protagonist, Sancho Panza, and, more important, I think, his life as an author. The second volume is more sophisticated than the first, and is, in fact, a nascent metafiction, which means it is self-referential, that it takes the nature of novel-writing as a subject, and that it integrates all of its levels of illusion smoothly. What Cervantes had not been able to come up with for his first novel—a convincing ending—he comes up with in the second novel, which also has far more emotional weight than the first. The two volumes together constitute the invention of the novel-of-a-man-at-odds-with-his-world—and it is hard to overestimate the influence of *Don Quixote* on the subsequent history of the novel. For our purposes, though, it also shows that an adult may think and feel his way into writing a novel without really knowing what he or she is doing. The novel is a simple, capacious, natural, and accessible form. If the writer is willing to write, if he has a clever idea, if he is dedicated and patient, if he is willing to work out each incident and idea, he might indeed come up with a worthy and unique work of art.

It is not unusual for even ambitious novelists to publish their first books in their thirties or their forties, and most novelists peak in middle age. Those who write their best work earlier have often, like the Brontë sisters, been writing feverishly since childhood or have written extensively in other forms before turning to the novel. The novel integrates several forms of human intelligence—verbal intelligence (for the style), psychological intelligence (for the characters), logical intelligence (for the plot), spatial intelligence (for the symbolic and metaphorical content as well as the setting), and even musical intelligence (for pacing and rhythm). Not only does it take a while to develop and integrate all five forms of intelligence, but also some intelligences develop more slowly than others. Logical intelligence as it applies to numbers seems to develop rather early, but as it applies to sequences of events (plots) whose connections may not be obvious, it seems to develop later. Spatial intelligence as it applies to visualizing shapes develops in infancy, but as it applies to understanding the links between or among disparate categories (metaphors), it develops as a result of broader experience. And because novel-writing integrates several forms of intelligence and because the novel requires lots of incidents richly worked out to sustain its length, novelists benefit from lots of experience—either many experiences or a few experiences experienced in great detail—but once someone has these, there is no reason why he or she cannot learn to write a novel. Thousands have. Writing novels is one of the few arts where native talent is a contingent rather than a necessary requirement. I return to my first point—the only thing an aspiring novelist needs to write a novel is the adamant and unkillable desire to write a novel. Such a desire gets a novel written no matter how mundane or dramatic the novelist's life has been, no matter how fluent or not fluent his various component intelligences are.

And then, of course, the novel-writing itself affects the novelist, because novel-writing is a transformative act. Let's say a novel is *a hypothesis, a dream, a therapeutic act, an ontological construct,* and *an assertion of self.* The first person to experience the effects of each of these is the novelist himself. The easiest to understand, at least in our day, is the novel as therapeutic act. When Dickens was writing *Dombey and Son,* he used the character of Mrs. Pipchin, who owns the infant school where little Paul Dombey is first sent, to depict Mrs. Roylance, who had been the landlady of the boardinghouse where the twelve-year-old Charles lived when he worked at the blacking factory in the Strand while his father and the rest of the family sat in debtors' prison. In earlier works, Dickens had been leery of delving into autobiographical material. His factory period was a terrible crisis in his young life, and he had been much afraid of everyone associated with it—his fellow boys at the factory, the people in the streets, and Mrs. Roylance herself. But the success of Mrs. Pipchin as a character and the success of the novel itself, both critically and commercially, persuaded Dickens to write about his childhood, which he first did in an autobiographical fragment and then in *David Copperfield.* All through the writing of *David Copperfield,* he loved David and the other characters and identified strongly with them. He was especially sorry to see them go when the novel was completed. More important, he was convinced at the end of David's story that his own story could and should turn out differently than it had in real life. He wrote to his friend John Forster that he longed for the companionship of a woman such as David's Agnes rather than that of his own wife, Catherine. Shortly after the publication of *David Copperfield,* he began to entertain ideas of linking up with other women—first his earliest love, who happened to send him a letter, but turned out, upon meeting, to be a disappointment, and later Ellen Ternan, whom he met in a dramatic performance of a play he had written with Wilkie Collins, and who became his friend and mistress for thirteen years. In the absence of trained professional help, Dickens became his own psychoanalyst, exploring his childhood and youth, diagnosing his circumstances and needs (if not his syndromes and character defects), and acting upon his diagnosis. He did not end up preserving himself from all future conflict and unhappiness, but through writing his novel, he did observe himself and then act upon his observations, which is the paradigm of the therapeutic act.

In both novel-writing and psychotherapy, someone constructs a narrative. The author of the narrative uses various devices to achieve distance from the emotions of the situation, to bring it to a climax, and to resolve it. He gives the situation to a character not quite like himself, or he adopts a narrative voice that maintains a cooler, more analytical view of the situation than his own, or he makes a painful situation comic. The author of the narrative hopes to learn something from the exercise. It may be that the patient in therapy gains more insight into his condition because the understanding he comes to is guided by a trained psychotherapist. But it may also be that the novelist has the advantage, because the requirement of the novel that the situation be resolved so the book can end (and make some money) prompts the author to imagine various possible outcomes for the situation, some of which may be different from the historical outcome. The fact that Franz Kafka could not stop laughing when he read "The Metamorphosis" to his friend Max Brod attests to the distance he was able to achieve from his pervasive sense of obligation toward his family and his father—the story provides a solution; for the time being it's hilarious, even if it doesn't resolve the issue in Kafka's life. Novel-writing may not work as therapy, may sink the novelist into a mire of feelings that he or she cannot resolve (it takes as much wisdom to solve a significant problem in a novel as in life), or it may persuade the novelist that some risky course of action is the proper thing to do (divorce, for example), but the attempt to gain perspective is an attempt to not only come to terms with pain, but also to communicate those terms to others and to make something out of nothing.

This is not to suggest that novel-writing makes people happy. The evidence from the biographies of novelists doesn't support such an assumption (though perhaps they were less unhappy than they would have been if they had not written novels). I think that a good rule of thumb is that novel-writing will make happy a person who can tolerate and enjoy an ever-intensifying experience of himself or herself. Novel-writing forces the novelist to turn inward day after day, year after year. No consolations, in the form of praise, fame, money, or importance can compensate for that effort if it is painful. All feelings of unworthiness will be felt over and over again; all self-doubts, all failures of love and self-respect, every sense of inadequacy will be reexperienced. Novelists who produce book after book find a way to deal with these feelings. In the Fitzgerald/Hemingway/Sinclair Lewis generation, novelists drank heavily, for example. Dickens loved his own work; he always thought the book he was working on, and therefore the person he was being at the time, was the best ever. Tolstoy expressed the same sort of self-confidence. Jane Austen's first audience was her loving and appreciative family. Some novelists denigrate the significance or the artistic effort of their work, telling themselves and others that it is just a way of earning a living—Trollope was such a one. Other novelists develop distancing habits of joking about themselves or the painful aspects of their careers, as Henry James did, or Ford Madox Ford. Novelists who are less prolific may simply not have the self-love, or the strength, or the professional motivation to face inward year after year. Even so, it is the willingness to do so at least sometimes that produces good work.*

A novel is a hypothesis. A novelist shares with a scientist the wish to observe. A novelist also shares with a scientist a partial and imperfect knowledge of the phenomenon he wishes to observe. And so both novelist and scientist say "what if?" What if milk that was teeming with bacteria were to be heated to a certain predetermined temperature and allowed to cool? What if some uneducated country people were to set out on a journey by wagon to take the corpse of their mother back to her place of origin? The scientist then does his experiment, which he

---

*Perhaps it is possible to draw a distinction between novelists and poets. Poets also look inward year after year. But novelists, in the company of their characters, are never quite alone, which might preserve many of them from the suicidal impulses that often overtake poets.

may refine over and over until his findings are clear and unequivocal. The novelist begins his novel. The test of *his* experiment is not whether its results can be reproduced, but either plausibility or accountability. His own mind is the first judge. Do Anse Bundren and his children, the characters in William Faulkner's *As I Lay Dying,* fit into a plausible pattern of human behavior? For this test, the novelist is required to have observed enough people to know what is plausible; in many cases he enlists the aid of friends or editors to help him make this judgment. But the plot point or character action may fail the test of plausibility. In this event, can the author account for it in an interesting or believable enough way to persuade the reader to accept it? For this, the novelist often uses his own experience to supply an unusual but right-seeming or appealing explanation. As the funeral journey of the Bundren family proves implausible, for example, and the author subjects them to a catalog of terrors, each member reacts in an arresting and memorable fashion—not plausible, but logical and idiosyncratic—and the reader is induced to accept their journey as a form of truth, even though it is new to her.

There is always tension in a novel between the hypothesis behind it and how it unfolds. The common authorial experience of seeing characters act in unexpected but logical ways, of having them "come alive," is actually a recognition that the original hypothesis was wrong in some ways and requires modification. In the end, the experiment succeeds only if the author is able to bring it to a logical and fitting conclusion. If he can—as Faulkner does when Anse gets new teeth and introduces his new wife to the children—then he has successfully proposed a hypothesis that exists in addition to everyday life and also comments upon it. Ultimately, the novel has to do what the scientific experiment does—it has to withstand the observation and disagreements of other people. The novelist's hypothesis and the novel that grow out of it have to coincide with the worldview of editors, reviewers, book salesmen, and readers sufficiently for them to accept, at least provisionally, the author's hypothesis. If they do, then the novel, like the scientific experiment, adds to the store of human knowledge.

If a novel is a hypothesis, then a novelist is a person with a theory. In fact, a novelist can't begin to fill four hundred pages of prose about how a protagonist coexists with his group if he doesn't have a theory. Every novel must embody a theory of how life works or it could not have a beginning, middle, and, especially, an end. Characters act only plausibly and events only seem to occur in a believable sequence (or at least a logical sequence) if the novelist has made theoretical order out of observed chaos. Whether the novelist's theory is objectively true, or original, or profound, or rational doesn't matter to the novelist. It only matters that he experiences himself as working out and exploiting his theory. Novelists are often portrayed by their natural enemies, biographers, as thoroughly in the grip of unconscious impulses or addictions or social pressures, or other forces that produce the novels, or produce what the novels really are (as opposed to what the novelists themselves thought they were). Novelists may, like other citizens, be subject to forces beyond their control, but in the writing of the novel, these forces do not matter. The novelist experiences himself as much as the agent of his own work as the scientist manipulating his beakers and test tubes or his DNA markers. A novelist's theory, like any other, has a large component of intuition, but he is active and intellectual in making sense of his theory, applying it, and working it out through his plot and characters. If he weren't, then the reader would never get the sense of a palpable intelligence working through the novel, meeting her own, delighting and challenging her own.

The habit of propounding a theory or a series of theories has an effect on the novelist, of course—it may enhance his sense of authority (Henry James called himself "the Master," and Dickens called himself "the Inimitable"), lure him into boorish habits of gratuitous holding forth, or tempt him to manipulate the people around him in accordance with his theories. Even before a novelist becomes respected or wealthy, he fancies himself as a person with an ironclad theory and a solid set of beliefs. The theory itself is the source of his feeling of knowledge and power. Public recognition may ratify the theory (of course, for some novelists, public acceptance is the cardinal sign that a strongly held theory is probably wrong), but public rejection doesn't necessarily abrogate it. The novelist can always decide that the public just isn't ready for his theory.

But, of course, the novel is a particular type of hypothesis—it is *an ontological construct,* it is a theory of being. A novel proposes that the world has a certain mode of existing. It doesn't propose this by asserting it explicitly, but by depicting it implicitly. A novelist may assert that the world is different than it appears to be; in fact, a novelist *must* do so as a result of the operation of point of view, but he or she cannot assert that the world does not exist because words have concrete referents, and to use them is to insert their concreteness into the reader's mind, a type of elephant-in-the-living-room phenomenon. In its very expression, the novel asserts that the world has being. But at the same time, the peculiarities of the novelist's presentation continuously assert that the world's being is artificially constructed. This is obvious with great and original stylists. It is more subtly apparent with stylists such as the Canadian writer Alice Munro, whose diction is refined and almost flat, but marked, in every turn of phrase and chosen detail, by insight and intelligence. Munro's mind does not appear to be stranger than the reader's mind, as Kafka's does, but it does seem to be wiser, and this feature serves to distinguish her from other writers with similar objective styles.

The novelist's ontology is his most effective form of rhetoric. A novel persuades, as any argument does, but it uses assertion, sensation, and emotion as the prime elements of the argument. The first third of the novelist's argument is "This exists—Gregor was turned into a bug." The second is "This is what it feels like—he could see his little legs waving in front of his face." The third part is "This is what the feelings mean—was he an animal that he was so affected by the sound of his sister's violin playing?" The novelist's main rhetorical device is to evoke emotion in the reader through scenes and figurative language. Some novelists stop with this—shared experience of some charged event is all they want to achieve. Others have a stronger theory—they want the reader to feel the feelings and then accept the novelist's interpretation of them. The great nineteenth-century novelists all more or less fall into this camp. Harriet Beecher Stowe is a perfect example of the extremely ideological novelist. Her emotional insights all refer to themes of sin and redemption as depicted through the example of slavery in America. However skillfully she deploys her tools, she is open and even obvious about the conclusions she wants the reader to draw, and many modern readers who don't share her beliefs find her art suspect. But Leo Tolstoy is no less ideological in his intentions; he is simply more subtle. He does not want the reader to act in a certain way, but he does want the reader to believe in a certain way—he wants to change the reader's inner life so that it agrees with Tolstoy's views. He cared very much that his Russian readership should come to see Russian problems as he did. Only then, he felt, would they adopt useful solutions, homegrown Russian solutions that would differ from and be more suitable than imported European solutions.

The necessity of an ontological theory arises not only out of a novel's length, but also out of its abstract nature. Since it has no being except as a reader's mental experience, it must assume that the world exists in order to itself exist. Words assert that the world exists because they have referents, but they can for a certain period of time exist and have power as mere sounds such as incantations, music, or rhythmic beats. Eventually, though, the experiencer of words wants them to mean something. A hundred and fifty thousand words always assert the objective existence of some sort of world, if only an imaginary one.

Novelists are not professional philosophers or scientists. They are amateurs and avid novel readers, so they are perhaps more likely than professionals subject to peer review to develop a whole theory of being. If we look at our roster of novelists, we have to be struck by two facts: one is that most of them started out as nobodies, and the other is that many of them have come to be regarded as prophets and sages. Their job is to develop a theory of how it feels to be alive. Some novelists are more profoundly skillful at this than others. The source of Kafka's appeal, for example, is that certain experiences that others sense vaguely or portray in passing, such as the experience of feeling a compulsion to constantly work at one's given task ("The Burrow"), or the experience of being mysteriously singled out and persecuted by the impersonal state (*The Trial*), or the experience of sudden, unwelcome transformation ("The Metamorphosis"), Kafka depicts purely and intensely, without adding interpretation or context. The being of his protagonists is felt entirely through these imposed necessities, and thereby intensified. The reader is never invited to read larger meanings into these intensely felt states, but it is almost impossible not to. Simply by choice of subject and clarity of exposition, Kafka is able to suggest more about the nature of being than almost any other writer.

The preeminence of the novel as a literary form suggests that the average reader enjoys having the nature of being, especially the nature of being ordinarily human, mirrored back to her. A novelist is the compleat generalist—he depicts as much as he can of what is around him. If he were more of a specialist, he wouldn't be a novelist, he would have a field of study (if he were more a specialist of words, he would be a poet). If he were more a generalist, he wouldn't be a novelist, he would be a roving bore, spouting theories to anyone who couldn't get away fast enough. A novelist is on the cusp between someone who knows everything and someone who knows nothing.

As a novelist writes more and more novels, he refines his characteristic style. A novelist's style is his or her identity, his or her literary self. Like all identities, it is simultaneously developed and revealed, simultaneously conscious and unconscious, simultaneously the result of choice and the result of predisposition, simultaneously a product of education and utterly idiosyncratic. Style is the great conundrum of literature because it is too particular and vast to be analyzed except in a very rudimentary way, and yet it can be instantly apprehended and appreciated. One of the pleasures of reading a novel is the sense that we are experiencing another person's very nature. Literary style is not oral—it is not like being told a story; it is far more mental—it is like being inside the author's mind. And as a great author matures toward his or her perfectly representative work, his or her style comes to express his or her particular quality of mind more and more eloquently.

Let's say for Jane Austen, it might be *Persuasion:*

There was one point which Anne, on returning to her family, would have been more thankful to ascertain even than Mr. Elliot's being in love with Elizabeth, which was, her father's not being in love with Mrs. Clay; and she was very far from easy about it, when she had been at home a few hours. [ch. 16]

For E. M. Forster, it might be *A Passage to India:*

It so happened that Mrs. Moore and Miss Quested had felt nothing acutely for a fortnight. Ever since Professor Godbole had sung his queer little song, they had lived more or less inside cocoons, and the difference between them was that the elder lady accepted her own apathy, while the younger resented hers. [ch. 14]

For Nancy Mitford, it might be *Don't Tell Alfred:*

After this, incidents succeeded each other. A well-known pederast fainted dead away on seeing M'sieur Clement, and was heaved, like Antony to the Monument, into the entresol. [ch. 5]

For Ford Madox Ford, it might be *The Good Soldier:*

The result you have heard. He was completely cured of philandering amongst the lower classes. And that seemed a real blessing to Leonora. It did not revolt her so much to be connected—it is a sort of connection—with people like Mrs. Maidan, instead of with a little kitchenmaid. [ch. 5]

Even in a sentence or two, the reader apprehends not only what the author is thinking of, but also how he or she thinks—with hesitations and qualifications, sharply and straightforwardly, conversationally, contemplatively. Each author's diction is characteristic, and so is his or her sense of rhythm and directness. His or her mental life, at least with regard to that particular subject, is more and more perfectly expressed by the style he or she uses. He is artful; he chooses; he manipulates; he decides; he judges every word and sound pattern and character detail and twist in the action, and yet every one of these things is automatic, given, natural, right. The mind writing is no longer made of parts— the conscious and the subconscious, the voluntary and the involuntary; it is rather one integrated whole, focused and choosing, from all the words in the language, the single perfect one. And the closer the author comes to his (or her) true stylistic self, the more distinct he be- comes from every other writer who has ever written and the more precious he becomes to the reader. The glory of narrative prose is this very thing, freedom of authorial expression, unmediated by actors or poetical conventions or cameras. For me, the only things at all sim- ilar are self-portraits by artists such as Rembrandt, for whom self- consciousness seems to disappear into the fascination of technical mastery. The novelist telling his story, making his artistic choices, is a continual presence to the reader, and this wonderful sense of presence is the effect of his style.

As every novelist has a style, so every novelist has conviction, which is a type of emotion, not an act of reason. It may take draft after draft to achieve a perfectly natural style. It also may take draft after draft to write with sufficient conviction. This conviction can be about anything—a specific theory of human nature, a particular analysis of a single incident, a simple certainty that the writer knows what is true and has to tell it. Some novelists testify to their convictions—Virginia Woolf, for example, felt that the way humans experience life had been overlooked or betrayed by such novelists as Arnold Bennett and John Galsworthy; her manifesto is "Mr. Bennett and Mrs. Brown." Zora Neale Hurston felt that certain overlooked communities and their inhabitants ought to be portrayed from the inside, in their own lan- guage. Mikhail Lermontov wrote only one novel, *A Hero of Our Time,* but he was driven by the desire to represent a certain type of romantic (you might say pre-Nietzschean sort of sexual, brutal, despairingly individualistic) protagonist; he defended his portrayal in an afterword to the second edition of the novel. Numerous American novelists of the twentieth century expressed convictions about the hollowness and shallowness of American life.

The most basic conviction of every novelist from Lady Murasaki on, though, is that things are not as they appear; this conviction can be added to or modified in accordance with the novelist's particular perceptions. Of course, poets and dramatists frequently express the same conviction, but novelists must express it, because narrative point of view inherently delineates the contrast between what one person thinks and what others around him think. Literary artists who are driven by the feeling that appearances are deceiving and that they know what the truth really is are drawn to the novel for this very reason. (By contrast, if we consider the play *Hamlet,* Hamlet frequently asserts that things are not as they seem in Denmark. He is referring to the crimes of Claudius and their subsequent cover-up. His premise is elaborated symbolically through the poetry as well, but one of the reasons he has to assert his opinion so often is that the appearance of the play has a countervailing reality for the audience. If Hamlet were silenced, and Claudius and his court were presented in some other plot, the audience would suspend disbelief in the actions on the stage as willingly as it does for *Macbeth* or *The Merchant of Venice.* Drama relies on the idea that events and characters are as they appear; otherwise they would carry no emotional power.)

Eighteenth-century English novelists frequently wrote about a plucky or bold or lucky protagonist successfully making his way against a tide of privilege, criminality, and circumstances. At the least, such novels required the conviction that these outcast individuals were worthy of attention; they also required the conviction that their eventual triumph was possible and plausible. *The Princess of Clèves,* by Madame de La Fayette, illustrates the conviction that women have complex inner lives worthy of analysis. *The Tale of Genji,* by Murasaki Shikibu, is imbued with the Buddhist ideas current in tenth- and eleventh-century Japan, and expressly imparts them as motives for the characters and as ways of analyzing the meaning of their lives. Sir Walter Scott's *The Tale of Old Mortality* delineates the ways different forms of religious belief create different personality structures, and how these, in turn, shaped Scottish history. Yukio Mishima's novel *The*

Sailor Who Fell from Grace with the Sea is motivated by a different set of convictions about the nature of childhood than is *Little Women.*

Egotistical or self-aggrandizing convictions fuel the novel-writing enterprise as readily as more altruistic ones do. All convictions go back to the novelist's early sense that his inner life is as real and interesting as his circumstances, that his view of things is as valid as the opinions of those around him. His first feeling of conviction might only be that he has to combat external pressure to conform. Writing powerfully embodies and develops the will to survive. The Czech novelist Arnošt Lustig was eighteen and had lived in three concentration camps when he escaped from a train heading to Dachau and joined the Czech resistance. His many novels about the Holocaust assert not only his characters' will to survive, but also his own. The ways in which Rebecca West's economically and socially insecure Edwardian childhood molded her ambition and will are vividly evoked in her wonderful novel *The Fountain Overflows.*

But convictions change. The paradox of a career of novels is that theories are found wanting, specific convictions dissipate, the novelist comes to see things in a different way. Tolstoy's convictions about marriage when he was writing *Anna Karenina* were different from those he held when he was writing *The Kreutzer Sonata.* A novelist can write a string of novels only if he or she is ready to embrace new ideas with as much conviction as he or she embraced earlier ideas. If the conviction simply dissipates or grows stale, the novels do, too. Some novelists have only one real conviction, which they express effectively a few times before the quality of their work declines. Perhaps F. Scott Fitzgerald would be an example of this. In general, the broader a novelist's interests and sympathies, the longer he can pursue his vocation. Great novelists have plenty of convictions. Later novels may contradict earlier ones—when Boccaccio wrote *The Decameron* he dedicated it to the pleasure of women; late in life he wrote another work that was virulently misogynistic. The theories that change motivate the novelist's ability to do the work because the novelist seizes new theories and ideas with the same enthusiasm every time. He may be consistent only in the passion with which he takes up new theories and applies them. Fortunately, the essential conviction that things are not as they appear is one that almost any novelist can harbor for his or her entire life without fear of contradiction.

And every novelist operates with one other essential conviction: almost from the first moment a future novelist begins reading novels, he realizes that all novels are different from one another, and, much more obviously, different from all plays or all poems. This difference provides him with the conviction that he, too, could write a novel, and with the further conviction that as wonderful as many novels are, none of them is just right. In fact, none of them exactly fits his experience or his opinions or his ideas of form, so he comes up with a theory of the novel, at least a rudimentary one, and puts it to the test: he writes a novel. This conviction is the source of the originality that we prize as readers, when we delight in P. G. Wodehouse one day and in Honoré de Balzac the next. As a relatively recent form (and not until more recently a respectable form), the novel allows the nascent novelist's theory an entry. And then, at least sometimes, the form itself changes as a result of the novelist's convictions.

For some years—twenty or thirty at most—the novelist as a living person coexists with the novelist as a literary persona. Inevitably this coexistence is uncomfortable, and some novelists bear it better than others. The requirements and responsibilities of the literary persona and the living person are different. The first truth about a literary persona is that it is equally the possession of the author and the reader; both create it and both respond to it, since it is made by the act of reading and remembering the novels. When readers are disappointed or angered by the living person of the author, it is because they sense a violation of their own creation. Writers who fail to realize that they have spawned another being, different from themselves but connected, are disappointed, too, or angered by the disappointments and demands of readers. In some cases, innate self-esteem and well-learned good manners go a long way to easing the boundary between the public self and the private self: Edith Wharton, for example, who was well schooled by social position to adopt roles that diverged from her personal preferences, showed unexcelled savoir faire throughout her career, all through the First World War, when she did charity work and war work in France, and in her relations with sometimes prickly colleagues, such as Henry James, who was envious of her commercial success. Other novelists, of course, have been legendary boors, which perhaps they would have been anyway.

But the novelist, too, has a relationship with his literary persona that might be somewhat different from his sense of his living self. The literary persona is a much revised and perfected being. It knows how life works and has a fairly complete theory of human behavior. It knows

how to resolve conflicts and bring about appropriate endings. It is eloquent and fluent. It is consistent and logical. It partakes of the wisdom
of all literature that goes before, but has the self-confidence to modify
it slightly. It has good comic timing, if need be, and a marvelous sense
of the appropriate. More than anything else, it is appealing, because a
novel is never coercive and always works by seduction, so the literary
persona, even if difficult and obscure, is a successful seducer. And
when the novelist reads the works of his own literary persona, he must
react to them—he has been conditioned to react to literature by years
of reading, so he reacts. Some novelists always have doubts about the
literary persona—does it say enough, know enough, or is it a pale
shadow of what it might be? Other novelists are fully confident, and
even fully realized, in the literary persona. Their difficulty is that they
don't feel that they can personally live up to the excellences of the literary persona. While the marquis de Sade's literary persona is superhu-
manly energetic and brutal in his exploitation of women, for example,
the marquis himself seems to have occasionally been a nice man—at
any rate, he had a faithful woman friend for his entire life whom he
does not seem to have exploited sexually in any way. Anthony Trollope, Jane Austen, and Ford Madox Ford apparently enjoyed and
learned from their literary personae. When he read *The Good Soldier*
ten years after writing it, Ford was as delighted as if it had been written by someone else; he called it "My auk's egg"—his once-in-a-
lifetime masterpiece, so accomplished that even he didn't understand
how he did it. Trollope and Austen seem to have written in narrative
voices very close to their own natural modes of thinking and talking,
which would mean that they actually were quite like they presented
themselves.

Novelists are fully capable of taking advice from their literary personae, at least some of it bad. I would make the case that F. Scott
Fitzgerald's bittersweetly tragic worldview, expressed in *This Side of
Paradise* and *The Beautiful and Damned,* and then reconfirmed as he
reread and rewrote and was praised for these same novels, dictated the
tragic arc of his short life. Without the self-reinforcing loop of being
seduced by his own literary assertions, he might have lived longer and
produced more various work. When critics greeted *Jude the Obscure*
with scathing rejection, Thomas Hardy shut down his novelist persona completely and went on as a poet, but in a different and more
robust vein than he had written in as a novelist. It is hardly surprising
that a novel that climaxes with a suicide and the murder of five chil-

dren would end a career, whether reviewers liked it or not. In a different way, Choderlos de Laclos moved away from the calculating, libertine literary persona of *Les Liaisons dangereuses,* even though the novel was famous and successful. He spent most of his life as a happily married family man.

Literary personae aren't necessarily required to typify wisdom, reason, goodness, or even intelligence—some authors, such as Dostoevsky, take passion, radical innocence, holiness, or strong, honest emotion as ideals—but literary personae are required to observe coolly and in detail, since it is the details that progress the story and make it worth reading. This means that every literary persona is at least in some measure less subject to certain venal emotions, such as envy, resentment, feelings of martyrdom and victimization, embarrassment and shame, pettiness and irritability, than living authors are. Even when a narrator, in the apparent voice of the author, expresses such feelings, he is objectifying and observing them, holding them and himself up to the reader's scrutiny. The result of this is that every literary persona is more judicious than almost every author. Perhaps this difference is the source of the endless literary joke, depicted with great wit in John Updike's *The Complete Henry Bech,* about how small-minded authors are among themselves. They are no more small-minded, I would bet, than other living persons, but they are always more small-minded than their literary personae. In the Bech stories, Updike very cleverly gets to have it both ways—in so closely observing the shortcomings of his protagonist, Henry Bech, Updike gets to both claim them and distance himself from them. It is his narrative voice that simultaneously depicts Henry's sins (including murders of unsympathetic critics and reviewers) and forgives him for them. Updike succeeds in gaining the reader as an ally—of course, John Updike would never do what Bech does—without so undermining Bech that the reader refuses to read about him.

Literary personae bear the onus of the author's expectations, and not every literary persona performs as hoped. At the most basic level, not every literary persona gets great reviews and earns lots of money. Some literary personae coincide with the public taste quite nicely, others thrill the critics, and a few transform society, but almost none do all three. Some literary personae are quite complex and hard to understand, such as that of James Joyce. Some are saccharine or sentimental, such as that of Louisa May Alcott. Others are full of contradictions—D. H. Lawrence, for example, is by turns aggressive, salacious, lyrical, insightful, dopey, smart, and embittered. It is important to remember that the author has only limited control over this sort of complexity; his three inspirations—literature, language, and life—combine willy-nilly to create his literary persona, and they may combine in ways that do not at all mimic the way he leads his life or appears to his acquaintances. However, the living author must accept the limitations of his literary persona, and some authors do so more gracefully than others. Few are as lucky as George Eliot, who began life as a plain and deferential country girl and yet was able to educate herself in a way that allowed her to develop a literary persona that expressed such intelligence, compassion, wit, and range of emotion that she achieved considerable wealth as well as universal respect and acceptance in spite of her unorthodox liaison with George Henry Lewes.

As the author gets older and publishes more work, his or her literary persona grows larger, stronger, and more out of control. It may begin to dictate to the author, to limit his freedom of subject and style, even to haunt him, in some sense, especially if earlier work bulks larger in the construction of the literary persona than later work. Readers and perhaps scholars come to know more about the author's work than he does—they might have read and reread a book very recently that the author hasn't read in twenty years, and hold him responsible for sentiments that he not only no longer feels, but can hardly remember. As the oeuvre grows larger and readers come to it differently—almost never, for example, reading the books in the sequence in which they were written—the literary persona takes on more and more layers, made up of more and more things that more and more people have said about it, and also of many things that the author himself might have said in passing to an interviewer, on the radio, or on TV. Many of these layers bear only a glancing relationship to the living author, who gradually diminishes in size relative to his literary persona. The literary persona is a verbal construct but it speaks with a human voice, and to those who don't actually know the author, it seems to *be* the author.

The antidote for the discomforts inherent in such a situation is simple but not easy. The author keeps writing; keeps publishing, if possible; and keeps smiling for the audience and the camera. The more intently he or she focuses on the page being written rather than the career that is developing or disintegrating out there somewhere, the better the work and the happier the living person.

Eventually, inevitably, mortality decides the competition between the living author and the literary persona in favor of the literary persona, and year by year the living author recedes out of currency and out of memory. The documents and facts about his life get lost or cease to be understandable, and he, too, becomes only a literary construct, and now the construct belongs entirely to readers, plus maybe a biographer or a few scholars. This construct should never be mistaken for the formerly living person. The fact is that upon death, the living person is folded into his or her literary persona and is, for better or worse, beyond resurrection.

4 · The Origins of the Novel

From our promontory atop Earth's big bookstore, the history of the novel looks, of course, much different from the way it looked to those who made it. Some novelists and their novels dominate the landscape—Charles Dickens and *David Copperfield,* Marcel Proust and *In Search of Lost Time,* Lady Murasaki and *The Tale of Genji.* Others are fallen monuments—Johann Wolfgang von Goethe and *The Sorrows of Young Werther,* for example. Some novelists can be made out with low-powered binoculars—Balzac, Laurence Sterne. Some who once freely populated the landscape seem to have gone completely underground—Madame de Scudéry and her fellow romancers, or Ouida and Edna Ferber, popular writers of the mid-twentieth century, or "the horde of scribbling women" who so tormented Nathaniel Hawthorne. Every novel that now strikes us as original itself originated in a social and artistic network of some sort, because the canon is always being made, remade, and expanded by novelists themselves out of the present stock of available books. Henry Fielding and other eighteenth-century novelists loved *Don Quixote.* Charles Dickens loved Henry Fielding, Tobias Smollett, and Sir Walter Scott, as well as *The Tales of the Arabian Nights.* Dickens was so influential that later writers shaped their writing in imitation of (or in contrast to) his, and imbibed what he learned from his models second-hand (as well as firsthand if they, too, were fond of his favorite authors). Henry James, who was a young man when Dickens was at the end of his career, gave *Our Mutual Friend* a bad review. He disdained what he saw as the formlessness of the older man's masterworks. When James had become "the Master," Virginia Woolf was making up her mind about what constituted the best models—she not only revived interest in Jane Austen and George Eliot by writing about them favorably, she also learned things from them. And any woman writing novels in English today has read Virginia Woolf and, no doubt, taken her essay *A Room of One's Own* much to heart. The tradition of the novel is a living legacy from older authors to younger ones. An author may go out of favor, and even seem to disappear, and then be revived simply by the regard of an influential figure who gets others interested in him or her (a novelist also can kill an ancestor, as Mark Twain killed James Fenimore Cooper). Readers are almost always partisan to some obscure author or another, and so, as long as a book is available in Earth's big bookstore (which I construe as every bookstore and every used-book store and every library in the world), it has a chance of finding a new audience.

It is not what various academic schools consider to be the great tradition that creates the canon, but what novelists themselves read and carry forward when they write. From the point of view of the working novelist, the history of the novel is just this: plenty of models to learn from and enjoy.

Although the novel was invented several times—most notably in 1004 by Murasaki Shikibu in what later became Kyoto, Japan, and once again in the thirteenth century in Iceland, in the form of the Icelandic saga—the modern novel is usually considered to have originated with *Don Quixote*. Like later novels, though, *Don Quixote* grew directly out of earlier works, and I think it is productive to look for beginnings of the modern novel right where we look for the beginnings of the modern period, and that is in Florence during the Black Death of 1347–51. As everyone knows, the great plague of the middle of the fourteenth century devastated and transformed Europe, killing between a third and a half of the population of most areas. According to historians, some regions, especially in Scandinavia and eastern Europe, did not recover their pre-plague numbers until the middle of the nineteenth century. Florence, a bustling commercial center, was hard hit. A city of over a hundred thousand, large by standards of the time, Florence lost between two-thirds and three-quarters of its inhabitants to the pandemic. Florence was the home of Giovanni Boccaccio, born in 1313, author of many works, including *The Decameron,* a cycle of a hundred stories supposedly told by a group of ten young people over the course of ten days in a luxurious retreat from the horrors of Florence (the characters actually stay out of Florence for fourteen days, but religious duties forbade entertainment on Fridays and Saturdays). Boccaccio

called his work a *commedia,* which in the parlance of the time meant
"any play or narrative poem in which the main characters manage to
avert an impending disaster and have a happy ending."*

Boccaccio, thirty-five, was already a noted man of letters with several works to his credit when he set to work upon *The Decameron.* He
was not especially happy in Florence, having been obliged to return
from the elegant and learned court of Naples in 1341 to a town we
might liken to Dallas as opposed to New York City—a town of money,
commerce, and philistinism, where Boccaccio's literary and scholarly
predilections didn't quite fit in. Before the onset of the Black Death,
Florence was already in turmoil—in 1345, two of the great Florentine
banking houses collapsed when Edward III of England reneged on his
loans, throwing the city into a financial panic. Boccaccio had to scout
about for patronage, and he went looking in Ravenna, where Dante, a
particular idol of his, had died in 1321.

In accordance with medieval convention, all of the strands of Boccaccio's work came from literary antecedents. Compilations of tales
were a common form throughout the Middle Ages, and a look at only
one of the books Boccaccio is thought to have been familiar with illustrates the multiple traditions he was heir to. The *Panchatantra,* written in India in Sanskrit before A.D. 500, was probably familiar to
Boccaccio through a Latin translation of about 1270 called *Liber Ka-
lilae et Dimnae,* or the *Directorium humanae vitae.* The Latin version,
by John of Capua, had been translated from Hebrew, which had in
turn been translated in the eighth century from Arabic. Even Boccaccio's depiction of Florence in the grips of the plague, ostensibly a
firsthand report, was probably borrowed from (or influenced by) an
account of an eighth-century Florentine plague from the *Historia Lan-
gobardorum* by Paulus Diaconus ("History of the Lombards" by Paul
the Deacon).

But the importance of *The Decameron* as an antecedent of the novel
is that it owes as much to Boccaccio's observations of the world all
about him, the present life of Florence in 1348, as it does to its literary
sources—he took the old material and worked it in the fire of current
events. Florence in the mid-fourteenth century was a unique and not
quite medieval city, where the merchant and banking classes were

---

*L. Kip Wheeler, "Literary Terms and Definitions, Comedy," http://web.cn.edu/kwheeler/
lit_terms_C.html.

immensely powerful, where citizens experienced what you might call a modern degree of stimulation and change. As a result, *The Decameron* bears many of the hallmarks of the modern novel—moral relativity, everyday concerns, and uneasiness about, on the one hand, money, and on the other hand, God. It has celebrity named characters in several stories and average Joes (and Josefinas) in other stories. It observes contemporary manners and ideas. The frame provided by the overt depiction of the plague while it is happening provides a solemn and even urgent undertone to the humorous antics of the tales and the sensuous details of the setting. Some of these characters may soon be overtaken by the general disaster, portrayed by Boccaccio as a moral horror as well as a mortal one; the tales they tell of mutability, of jokes and tricks and miracles, prepare them for their fates as well as distract them.

The Decameron, not often read today, is conventionally considered a compilation of erotic tales, but it is far richer than convention implies. Even though many of the plots turn on desire, seduction, and adultery, what makes them interesting and diverse is how the protagonists achieve their ends, and the ramifications of their actions among their friends and associates. The theme of desire is the ground color of the carpet, but ingenuity and idiosyncrasy form the pattern. Some of the tales are quite simple. In the ninth story of the fifth day, for example, a young aristocrat spends all his money futilely pursuing a young woman, who marries another. Now broke except for one cherished possession, an excellent hawk, he moves to a small farm in the countryside. Soon the woman's husband dies, and she and their son move to a large estate that happens to be near the small farm of her former suitor. The child yearns to possess the hawk, and then falls ill. When the woman goes to the protagonist to ask for the hawk, he wants to be hospitable, so he kills the hawk, plucks it, and roasts it for her meal.

After they have eaten, she confesses that she has come to ask for the hawk, but alas. Nevertheless, the protagonist has demonstrated that even now he would do anything for his lady love. Soon enough the child dies—"whether from disappointment at not getting the hawk or from the mortal nature of his illness no one knew"—and soon after that, the mother tells her brothers that she would like to marry her poor neighbor. They consent, and all of the protagonist's desires are realized.

Other stories are little more than jokes or tricks. In the fourth tale of the seventh day, for example, a man locks his wife out of the house. She pretends to throw herself down the well, and when he comes running out, she sneaks into the house and locks him out. She then berates him in front of the neighbors, who call in her brothers, who beat the husband. After they are reconciled, he promises not to be jealous, and to let her do as she pleases, as long as she does it discreetly. In another tale, three men embarrass an elderly and unpleasant judge by pulling his pants down in court.

In one very famous tale (fifth day, fourth tale), a girl who wants to entertain her lover persuades her father that she wants to sleep outside on the balcony because it is stuffy indoors, and also she wants to hear the nightingale sing. He agrees with some reluctance, then locks the balcony doors and draws the curtain. She receives her lover, who climbs the vegetation to get to her. They make love so many times ("causing the nightingale to sing at frequent intervals," writes Boccaccio) that they fall into a sound sleep, and when morning comes, the father unlocks the doors and discovers them. He is enraged, and threatens to kill the lover, but is reconciled when the girl and the lover agree to marry on the spot. Boccaccio uses the figure of the nightingale several more times to indicate the joyous lovemaking between the girl and her lover. The tale uses many joke-type conventions—the daughter's attempt to deceive her jealous father, the happy ending, the mother's coolness in contrast to the father's rage, and wordplay. The effect of the story turns not on character but on plot and phrasing. And it is meant to raise a laugh, which it does—in the prologue to the next tale, the narrator reports, "all the ladies laughed so much that it was some time after Filostrato had finished before they had managed to contain their mirth."

The sixth story of the ninth day also has wordplay, and a punch line, but it shades rather more toward a story, since it concerns the unexpected transformation of one of the characters. In this case, a young man who loves a young woman persuades a friend of his to help him sneak into the family home, where there is but a single bedroom with three beds and a cradle. When everyone is asleep, the first young man creeps into the bed of his beloved. Soon afterward, though, the second young man goes out to relieve himself. While he is out, the wife wakes up at a sound in another part of the house and goes out naked to check things out. When the second young man returns, he bumps into the cradle and moves it, and when the wife returns, she is misled by the position of the cradle and gets into bed with the second young man, who, as Boccaccio writes, "gave her a cordial reception, and without a murmur, tacked hard to windward over and over again, much to her satisfaction." The first young man is afraid to fall asleep and be discovered with the daughter, so he gets up to go back to his bed, but, also misled by the position of the cradle, he gets into bed with the father, and thinking he is with his friend, begins to express his delight in the charms of the girl. The father wakes up and threatens to kill the young man. At this point, the mother awakens and realizes she is in the wrong bed. She saves the day by sneaking into the bed of the daughter, then loudly proclaiming that she has been there all night and nothing has happened. The second young man then starts calling out to the first young man to wake up and stop bragging about doing things that he has only dreamed of. The father starts laughing, the first young man goes back to his bed, and the daughter later convinces the mother that nothing at all happened. "And thus the mother, who retained a vivid memory of Adriano's embraces, was left with the conviction that she alone had been awake on the night in question." Her transformation, though slight, is real—she has enjoyed something illicit and used her wit and discretion to make sure that no ill consequences ensue. Boccaccio's telling gives the whole tale a joyful exuberance that relieves it of its potential for sin and conflict. A later telling, as "The Reeve's Tale," in Geoffrey Chaucer's *Canterbury Tales,* exploits the dark side of the material, but Boccaccio's version reveals a great deal about not only his forgiving view of love and sexuality and his comic turn of mind, but also his graceful and efficient literary style. His choreography of what could be a confusing set of actions is clear and humorous, alternating essential details, such as when the cradle was moved and what people said, with homely nonessentials that give the story verisimilitude (the wife goes out of the room to investigate what the cat is doing). Both the women and both the young men are quick of wit, and the father is fooled, but genially so, in the interests of peace rather than exploitation.

Another tale that Chaucer used ("The Clerk's Tale") is Boccaccio's hundredth, the tale of the patient Griselda, whose husband puts her through one trial after another to test her obedience and her devotion. His motive for testing her so severely even over the objections of all his friends and relatives is that he wants to make sure she knows the proper duties of a wife. Hers for enduring is perhaps a tad more convincing—she is well aware of her humble origins, and she has never considered the goods she attained at marriage to be hers. There is some implication in the last lines that it is her lowly birth itself that endows Griselda with the fortitude to endure the faked deaths of her children, her apparent abandonment by her husband, and his evident remarriage to a much younger woman. Griselda's tale of goodness (which represents, as well, the proper Christian response to all of the apparently senseless blows life and fate afford) contrasts with tale number one, the tale of the wickedest man who ever lived, a man so wicked that he lies in his deathbed confession, and yet a man who, subsequent to his death, gains a reputation for sainthood and whose posthumous influence actually, according to the story, works for good. In these tales and others, Boccaccio explores complex themes of virtue, vice, salvation, psychological motivation, and forgiveness.

Boccaccio was well aware that he was doing something new—at the beginning of the fourth day, he intrudes to defend his work—both that it is written in vernacular prose and that it is written to appeal to women, not scholars. He defends it, paradoxically, as factually correct and as a natural thing for him to do, since he likes women—prose, that is, is meant to be pleasing and accessible. Artistically, though, the main thing Boccaccio had to guard against was the possibility that the stories would run together in the reader's mind and grow repetitious or jumbled. He used several organizational principles to avoid this, including thematic introductions, commentary by the storytellers, and juxtaposition of contrasting tales to one another, as well as a wide variety of settings and plots. But he also used what have become typical novelistic techniques—names, descriptions, quirks of behavior, and characteristic dialogue. His use of these things is so natural that it seems automatic to us, but in fact it sets *The Decameron* off from other medieval works, such as *Le Roman de la rose* and *Le Morte d'Arthur,* whose authors have little understanding of individual psychology. In those works, characters' traits are emblems of their identities or roles rather than ways of being. When the emblem is removed, the character is no longer recognizable to the reader. Action exists in and of itself rather than as a result of psychology. By contrast, in every story of *The Decameron,* the plot grows out of the idiosyncratic nature of individual predilections or desires.

The Decameron became a famous masterpiece almost immediately and retained its allure for hundreds of years. One result of *The Decameron*'s relative "philogyny" (compared with conventional views of women in the Middle Ages) was, for our purposes, the placing of women's concerns at the center of the European novel for the next six hundred years.

The Decameron was the direct inspiration for Marguerite de Navarre's *The Heptameron,* the essential transitional work between the medieval story cycle and the modern novel. In many ways, the European novel as we know it today grew directly out of *The Heptameron,* which is even less well known to modern readers than *The Decameron.* Marguerite de Navarre was a queen, the older sister of François I, who became king of France in the early sixteenth century. Both François and Marguerite were exceptionally well educated—Marguerite spoke five or more languages, wrote both prose and poetry, and took an earnest interest in the religious controversies of the time; though a Catholic, she was in favor of Protestant-style reforms. In her early thirties, she was delegated to negotiate the ransom of François from the Spanish, who had captured him in battle. A few years later, she married Henri of Navarre (a small kingdom in the Pyrenees now known as Navarra, and part of Spain). Marguerite had a strong interest in literature, and commissioned a French translation of *The Decameron,* but more importantly, she wrote (or compiled) a set of tales intended to be a *Decameron* for the new age (the 1550s). Who made up the tales, whether Marguerite herself or Marguerite and a set of friends, how far she got (all that remain are seventy-two tales, thus the naming of the compilation *The Heptameron*), and how the concerns of the tales were to be resolved remain unknown to scholars, but Marguerite stated overtly that the premise of the taletelling was that the tales were all true and that they addressed a single question: is it possible for a woman to know true love and to remain virtuous? This question was to become the central question of most of the novels written in France—and, indeed, in the rest of Europe—until at least the early part of the twentieth century.

Marguerite named her ten taletellers with clues to what seem to have been the names of members of her circle, including Henri, who appears as "Hircan." Each tale is followed by a critique, where the tellers do not just react with pleasure, as they do in Boccaccio, but also discuss the characters' actions and the moral implications of each tale. Far more explicitly than in *The Decameron,* in *The Heptameron,* the characters are concerned with the difficulties of salvation—there is no easy pleasure and ready forgiveness in Marguerite's book. Though Marguerite and her friends were Catholics, hers was a world where

religious controversies were of major importance and where preven-
tion of sin was all-important because redemption was felt to be problematic. All of Marguerite's characters, but especially her taletellers,
were obliged to look within themselves.

By contrast to *The Heptameron, The Decameron,* even with all of its
dark shadings, seems positively rollicking. Boccaccio may include
cruel and misogynistic stories, undeserved cuckoldings, and episodes
that modern readers find barbaric, but for the most part he seems to be
in favor of and forgiving of the pleasures of coupling. For the characters of *The Heptameron,* though, life is full of hard lessons and double
binds, even for the wealthy and privileged. The ten taletellers of *The
Decameron* escape the plague in a pastoral paradise; the ten taletellers
of *The Heptameron* are stuck in a primitive monastery in the midst of
inhospitable and unscenic mountains that are filled with wild animals.
The world itself is unforgiving, and human society is no less so. What
is more troubling for the reader is that Marguerite's tales have so little
variety. If *The Decameron* seems to be an inexhaustible treasury of narratives and characters, *The Heptameron* seems more like an obsessive
nightmare, where the same characters stuck in the same dilemmas
return over and over, though with different names and in different
guises, to be investigated again and again for some bit of new insight
that never turns up. This is fertile novelistic territory.

The fortieth story is particularly striking in several ways. It concerns a man and a woman most of the taletellers know, the comte de
Jossebelin and his beautiful sister, to whom the comte is very close.
Although she is of a marriageable age and has many offers, he refuses
to allow her to marry. She falls in love with his favorite gentleman-in-
waiting; they marry, and live happily, though secretly, for several
years. Their relationship is reported to the comte, who surprises them
in bed. The husband escapes through the window, while the wife
pleads her case—she is an adult woman and her husband is just the
man the comte had always said he wished she could marry, and the
two of them are married in the sight of God. They have never done
anything unvirtuous. Nevertheless, the comte has the husband caught
and killed on the spot, and then imprisons his sister in a remote castle,
where she devotes herself to religion. The comte's six sons "all die mis-
erably," and his daughter inherits the estates. The ten critics try to
work out some way of understanding the cruelty of the story. Hircan
makes the case that the comte must put down the ambitions of the
lower-caste servant, no matter what, but the others are more subtle.

Two of the women, including Oisille, an older woman who is the most religious, and often the conscience of the group, draw the typical virtuous lesson—every girl must mold her passions in obedience to her family obligations. Nomerfide, though, who doesn't offer an opinion about every story, suggests that the experience of true love and true pleasure compensates for death, because the one is rare while the other is routine. She says, "The pleasure, too, must have been rare, and all the greater, since it runs counter to the views expressed by all wise men, and has in its favor the fact that a loving heart found satisfaction and that a soul found true repose." Others remark on the injustice of the comte's actions and contrast that to the nature of true love ("though her body was imprisoned, her heart was free and united with God and her husband"). They also point out the political implications of the story—"in order to maintain peace in the state, consideration [in matters of marriage] is given only to the rank of the family, the seniority of the individuals, and the provisions of the law, not to men's love and virtue, in order that the monarchy not be undermined." Often practical sorts of arrangements lead to marital hell, proposes Dagoucin (who is possibly a priest and an abbot), but not always, agree the others, and the married members of the group then congratulate themselves on their luck and skill in gaining marriages that are loving, pleasurable, and virtuous—"So happy were they all that I think the married couples among them did not do quite so much sleeping as the rest—what with talking about their love in the past and demonstrating it in the present. Thus the night passed sweetly until morning broke" (p. 375).

Story thirty is as strange (and Oisille remarks that it is the strangest story she can imagine), but the taletellers agree more readily upon an interpretation. A woman has a teenage son who is making a play for a servant girl. The girl reports this, and the skeptical mother declares that she will sleep in the servant girl's bed to see if she is telling the truth. The son does appear, but the mother is still reluctant to believe that he means to do anything. She remains quiet, and then, once he begins making love to her, thinking she is the servant, "so fragile was her nature that her anger turned to pleasure. . . . Even as the dammed-up torrent flows more impetuously than the freely flowing stream, so it was with this lady, whose pride and honor had lain in the restraints she had imposed on her own body" (p. 318). The woman gets pregnant. She sends the son off to the Italian wars, gives birth, and sends the baby daughter to her brother, where she grows up. In the meantime, the wars end and the son wants to come home, but the mother is now afraid of her own feelings for him, so she tells him that he can't come home until he has married someone he loves. He visits his uncle, unknowingly meets his sister, falls in love with her, and brings her home as his wife. The mother confesses her sins and their consequences to an official, who gets advice from theologians, and everyone agrees that the woman can never tell the children what has happened, but must do penance for the rest of her life. Part of her penance is the sight she has every day of the love between the married couple—"never were a husband and wife so close. For she was his daughter, his sister, his wife. And he was her father, brother, and husband."

The woman's sin, all the taletellers agree, has had its origins in her prideful sense of her own virtue, and anyway, points out one of the women, "nothing should induce a woman to risk sharing a bed with a male relative. . . . It's not safe to set a naked flame near tinder" (p. 322). Interestingly enough, the conversation then turns to the ways in which Franciscan monks employ preaching virtue as a method of seduction, and then Hircan points out that the monks of their monastery have failed to ring the evening bell because they are hiding behind the hedge, listening to the salacious stories.

What Marguerite and her interlocutors are doing in *The Heptameron* is experimenting with realism and psychology, two essential characteristics of the novel. Whether or not the stories they tell are true, in their critiques, they treat them as if they were. They discuss motivation, social context, and states of mind before, during, and after the action. They situate even the most shocking events in a generally accepted moral context, and use both common sense and religious precepts as guides to interpretation. They also relate the stories to their own lives by reacting to them, allowing the stories to spark discussions of their own histories. Since they are friends, they do something else that friends often do, which is to call into question one another's interpretations by reminding one another of past mistakes or proclivities (though this is always done in a good-natured way and the group is never unfriendly). Because half of the group is women, and one of them is the queen (and another may be the queen's mother), the dilemmas and traps that confront women are taken very seriously. The ways in which women are agents of their own salvation and damnation are discussed in the context of the ways in which women are subject to the will of others. That women have erotic desires of their own is also a given. The opinions of the men do not take precedence, and the opinions of Hircan, the king (Henri was eleven years younger than Marguerite), are often politely overlooked, as if their crudity is to be expected.

Taken as a whole, *The Heptameron* is a kind of rough draft for many novels yet to be written; the stories, for the most part simple and plot-based, but dramatic and full of mysteries, are given depth and complexity by means of critical inquiry.

In fact, strange tales have often inspired novels—Stendhal wrote *The Red and the Black* following a newsworthy trial, for example, and Dostoevsky was similarly drawn to the real-life episode that inspired *Crime and Punishment*. Sensational acts arouse moral curiosity. Onlookers become preoccupied with finding a logic for them that allows them to fit into some theory or other of human nature. Furthermore, the religious beliefs of Marguerite and her friends (Catholic, but with reformist leanings) meant that they mistrusted to some degree the conventional system of precepts and moral rituals. Aware of the Reformation and Counter-Reformation that swirled all about them, they were eager to look within and to discuss, to find a basis of right behavior that was logical as well as uncorrupted. There is a strong sense that notions of class, ethics, custom, and morality that had served in the Middle Ages were breaking down in the middle of the sixteenth century to a degree unknown even during the Black Death, and the point of Marguerite's project is to come up with something, even something provisional, that will serve as a guide to the ten taletellers in lieu of what has been lost. This is a common function of the novel.

Both Boccaccio and Marguerite de Navarre were much interested in individuals. In considering human behaviors and misbehaviors, they gave great attention to motives and idiosyncratic circumstances. They sought to understand how points of view differ from individual to individual, and while they accepted the structure of their societies as givens, they thought that both men and women could act for or against the more brutal tendencies of their societies. They saw both men and women as agents of their own salvation or damnation, and they saw the details of such fates as inherently interesting and illuminating. The controversies of the Reformation promoted a believer's sense of his own individuality—he was responsible for avoiding sin and for feeling and demonstrating the presence of God's grace. This gave him (or her) an awareness of the inner life—first of his own, and then of the inner lives of others. Examples of what to do and what not to do abounded, if only one observed closely enough. All of these habits of mind fed naturally into the rise of the novel, which organizes itself around individuals and pays attention to the inner life and its relationship to the outer life. And the novel requires conflict, especially inner conflict. The inner conflict of the worried, conflicted believer predisposed him or her to a novelistic state of mind.

When Cervantes wrote the first volume of *Don Quixote,* he put together the elements of the novel with an inspired simplicity that achieved a wide and enthusiastic audience. Don Quixote, like every good protagonist, entered into Cervantes's abundance of material and shaped it around himself, but, as with *The Heptameron,* the invention of the novel in *Don Quixote* required a great deal of interpretation and conversation among the characters. To many modern readers, this incessant talking gets in the way of the action, but in fact it was necessary to the engendering of the novel as a form. The novel is self-conscious because modern people feel that they are different from past generations. Don Quixote's conversations with his friends almost all revolve around how current adventures and activities relate to received wisdom, often the wisdom of the medieval romances Quixote is fond of. As the conversations progress, the novel's sense of self-assurance solidifies.

   Don Quixote's inseparable and necessary companion is Sancho Panza. When Quixote first ventures away from his home, under the spell of his romantic books and eager for knightly experience, he goes alone, but it is evident to the reader as well as to Cervantes that his solitude does not strike exactly the right note—for one thing, he has to express his thoughts too lengthily and too clearly. They seem less like thoughts than discourses, making Quixote pedantic and inhibiting the flow of the action. For another, he seems both too crazy and too vulnerable. His own naïveté and incompetence, combined with the casual brutality of the world of seventeenth-century Spain, make him too pure a figure of pity to succeed comically. He needs a buffer and ally as well as a sounding board, and Sancho, who is practical in some ways, though quite innocent in others, serves both functions. Sancho, as a peasant who is loyal to Quixote but skeptical of his theories, stands between the idealism of Quixote and the realism all around, enabling both sides of the novel's inherent binary nature to flower more naturally than they could in *The Heptameron.* Quixote is in distinct conflict with his world—it is how he is defined. In this, he differs from the characters in *The Decameron,* especially, and even from the characters of *The Heptameron*. The variety and richness of those two works para-doxically confirm the social realities that many of the characters of the stories transgress. Even such characters as the sister who watches her brother kill her husband and the mother who is impregnated by her son exist entirely within the social network created by the tales, which in turn are embedded in the social network of the taletelling. The world of *The Decameron* is in crisis, and the world of *The Heptameron* is self-contradictory and frightening, but the addition of each tale to the many previous ones reinforces the reality of those worlds.

Not so with Quixote. The question arises with Quixote, as with every strong protagonist: does he shape the world, or does it shape him? This question is present in the mere process of the author shift-ing his attention from Quixote to the world around him and back to Quixote and back to the world around him, realizing each in ever more detail, fitting each more and more to the other in what you might call artistic unity. This is the essential process and power of the novel—to make one cohesive work of art out of many disparate elements, showing the one character in detail while constantly evoking the many that surround him. *Don Quixote* is the first modern novel because the reader's experience of Cervantes's mind working over this relationship is the first modern example of undiluted authorial consciousness as it unfolds page by page. As with many great works, the original stroke of genius by the author was coming up with a good, simple idea (a middle-aged gentleman who has read so many accounts of knightly courage that he decides to try it himself). That things are not as they seem is the root premise of Quixote's view of the world, but also the root premise of Cervantes's story, because even though things aren't as Quixote thinks they are, they also are not as they seem to the other characters. Only author and reader know the truth. Layers of reality and seeming—of point of view—build upon one another.

The history of the novel demonstrates that this simple idea—points of view evoked and juxtaposed—is inexhaustibly fertile. What *The Decameron* and *The Heptameron* show with their multitude of briefer and sometimes jokelike stories is that before the end of the sixteenth century (at least in Europe), ways of understanding and depicting the inner life were not rich enough to sustain much narrative length. But the plays of William Shakespeare, written in the 1590s and early 1600s, show that self-consciousness and introspection were bursting out all over. By means of asides, soliloquys, prologues, and epilogues, the playwright was pushing against the boundaries of the drama to display

and explore the inner life as well as to address the audience unmediated.* The wars, controversies, and religious movements of the sixteenth century required people to look within—life, death, and eternal
salvation were at stake. The result was the characteristic rhythm of the
realistic novel—action, reflection, action, reflection, action, reflection,
for hundreds of pages. It is a hypnotic rhythm.

That Quixote is chaste and celibate is also significant, both as a
departure from earlier depictions of manly men and as an omen of the
future development of the novel. No more rolling in the hay, no more
easy acceptance of human sexuality, including the sexuality of women.
In Quixote, the opinion of Marguerite's Hircan—that if a woman
doesn't yield to his pleasure, he is justified in killing her as a matter of
honor—gets tossed into the dustbin of literary history.

The religious conflicts of the sixteenth century could not help making sexuality an inflammatory subject, especially since, as both *The
Decameron* and *The Heptameron* demonstrate, one of the great accusa-
tions against the Catholic Church was that while professing celibacy
and holiness, its clergy were universally promiscuous—story thirty-
three of *The Heptameron* specifically treats this subject. We may speculate about why Cervantes deprived Quixote of his sexuality, but the
effect on later novelists was to provide a model of male virtue that was
unusual in its own time but more and more usual in later novels.
According to Quixote's friends and the people he meets along the way,
his chastity is one of his stranger peculiarities, but as the reader becomes more acquainted with him and grows fond of him, his chastity
grows less eccentric and more ideal—evidence of his holy foolishness,
as well as of his foolish holiness. *Don Quixote* was, of course, not the
only reason explicit references to sex were dropped from novels, but it
set a precedent—two entire books could be written about the inner life
of a man who falls asleep whenever discussion of sexual and romantic
relationships comes up. An author could make believable a grown
male character who has no sexual desires. In part owing to the huge
popularity of *Don Quixote,* the novel gave up a large and fertile subject
(at least until the twentieth century), and entered into the idea that
because of taboos on sexuality, discussions and depictions of other,
more public sides of human nature constituted discussions of *all* of

---

*For further discussion of this point, please see Stephen Greenblatt, *Will in the World* (New
York: W.W. Norton, 2004).

human nature. The novel, which is simultaneously public and private, published and intimate, has a special capacity to explore the most intimate subjects, but for three centuries it did not routinely explore them, and its avoidance of those subjects made them more and more difficult to discuss.

As suggested above, the two volumes of *Don Quixote* are not the same. The first volume is a more primitive work altogether than the second. Cervantes is less adept at integrating Quixote and Sancho with the characters they meet along the way, and it shares with *The Heptameron* a quality of disparateness. Shortly after the famous incident of the windmills, for example, Quixote and Sancho attack two friars whom they mistake for kidnappers. They are soundly beaten. Far from an inn, they are taken in for the night by some goatherders, who tell them the sad story of Grisóstomo and Marcela—he has died for love of her, and his funeral is about to take place. This story goes on for some twenty-two closely printed pages, and although it is interesting in the context of the preoccupation of the novel as a form with the dilemma of what is to be done with women, it has very little to do with Quixote's adventures. The same is true of the subplot of Cardenio, Dorotea, Don Fernando, and Luscinda, which takes center stage, more or less, for almost a hundred pages (and includes a subsubplot quite similar to story forty-seven in *The Heptameron*). It is not that these stories are not interesting in themselves, it is that their themes don't fit very well with the themes of Quixote and Sancho's quest. And it is not precisely that Cervantes can't control his material, it is that in the first volume he doesn't realize that it requires control. Quixote and Sancho's quest is meant to be both their story and a frame for other stories. Volume one is more like *The Heptameron*. Volume two is more like a modern novel—in it, Cervantes has learned how to make Quixote and Sancho central to his novel by deepening their characters and making their adventures grow out of who they are. By far the most important of these is their run-in with the duke and the duchess, which takes up more than half of the volume. Quixote and Sancho meet the duke and the duchess in a wood, and the two aristocrats immediately realize they have indeed met the famous knight and his squire. They then use their wealth and power to devise an elaborate practical joke by which they entertain themselves with the spectacle of Sancho and Quixote acting in character. They tempt Sancho with power—pretending to put him in charge of his own island—and they test Quixote with the charms and blandishments of women whom they have paid to tempt him. He remains untempted, but the unrelenting joke exhausts him, and when he goes home afterward, he has lost heart. On his deathbed, he admits that he had been mad, but now he is sane, no longer Don Quixote, but once again Alonso Quijano. His friends plead with him to resume his cause, but he confesses, makes his will, and dies.

Don Quixote was instantly popular—so frequently translated that one of Shakespeare's late unfinished plays seems to have been taken from the Cardenio material of volume one.* It was known all over Europe and, no doubt, Madame de La Fayette, who wrote *The Princess of Clèves* some forty years after Cervantes died, was familiar with, at least, a French translation. But her greatest novel seems to have been much influenced by *The Heptameron,* since she set it in the 1550s, in the court of Henri II, who was the son of Marguerite's brother François. Madame de La Fayette prided herself on the precision of her historical knowledge and her familiarity with court life of her own day; she would surely have known all about Marguerite and her tales (although our modern edition is different from the edition she would have had access to). We can see *The Princess of Clèves* as a lengthier and more psychologically detailed answer to Marguerite's original question: can a woman know true love and remain virtuous at the same time? Every word and action of the princess, from the moment she first sees her lover to the end of the novel, models both true love and perfect virtue, an unlikely but dramatic path through the minefield of women's roles and risks in the early modern era.

The plot is a typical French plot—a woman with some status but limited money and influence takes her beautiful daughter to Paris to find her a husband. In spite of the girl's beauty, she is unsuccessful at first, and when the girl does attract the attention of the right sort of man, it is someone she likes but does not love, Monsieur de Clèves. Out of prudence, the mother, who is in ill health, presses the marriage. Shortly after the marriage, the most desirable man in France, the duc de Nemours, falls in love with the girl. Although she avoids him as much as she can, he is irresistibly attentive, and eventually she falls for him. Her passion is deep and sincere, but as a desperate method of

*See Stephen Greenblatt, *Will in the World.*

avoiding any compromise to her virtue, she confesses her passion to
her husband (with whom she has no children, indicating perhaps that
their marriage is sexless). The husband is both grieved by her love and
gratified by her confidence in him and by her virtue. The triangle, now
positively glowing with the frustrated passion of all parties, persists
unstably for a short time, and then the husband dies, leaving the
princess to marry her lover if she wishes. She does not, partly because
she is aware that the knowledge of her passion had contributed to
her husband's fatal illness, but additionally, because she also knows instinctively that should Nemours possess her as his wife, his passion
would be likely to diminish. As long as the two remain unsatisfied,
their love is equal; were she to yield, inequality, and therefore unhappiness on her part, would ensue. This is simultaneously a mere piece of
logic that promotes a virtuous outcome and an astute insight into the
nature of romantic love as opposed to marital love. Is the princess right
or wrong? She trumps her passions with a choice perhaps more plausible to some people than to others—she declares that she owes her
truest love to God, and she is going to solve her emotional dilemma by
sequestering herself, praying, and doing good works.

   The Princess of Clèves was a great success, and sparked intense discussion of the princess's unusual strategy for maintaining her virtue.
Its plausibility was still being argued in the nineteenth century—
possibly every Frenchman in the history of reading, including Stendhal, considered the princess's choices strange, but a glance at the
seventy-two attempted solutions that constitute *The Heptameron* reveals just how hard Marguerite's riddle was. Madame de La Fayette
understood her novelist's job—willing suspension of disbelief can be
achieved without plausibility when the story is interesting enough to
make the reader eager to read on, and reading *The Princess of Clèves*
is intriguing and exciting. Each time the princess does an implausible
thing, it seems like the only appropriate thing to do in the context of
the story, especially, it seems to me, if the reader is a woman. As a
young girl unprotected by family, wealth, or influence, living in a
world of gossip and intrigue, the princess knows that her position is
especially treacherous—it is probable that the duc de Nemours, for all
of his desirability, *cannot* protect her honor, whatever the power of his
affections. By age forty-five, with something like thirty years of court
life behind her, Madame de La Fayette was certainly a realist about
gossip, status, and intrigue.

At the same time, Madame de La Fayette had to come up with a technique that would put her story across, and she did so—moment-by-moment analysis of her protagonist's state of mind and emotions combined with incisive depiction of court life under Henri II (who is openly unfaithful to his queen). And because the princess has to keep secrets as best she can—given the constant circulation of gossip, she can confide in no one—Madame de La Fayette was forced to anatomize her inner life for the reader to an unprecedented degree, without resorting to Quixote-like conversations between the characters. She pretty much invented indirect discourse—the technique by which an author plausibly "overhears" her character's thoughts and expresses them in a way that seems idiosyncratic to her character. The result is a novel that is strangely modern in its psychological astuteness, far more detailed in this way than any of the works we have so far looked at, and one of the acknowledged great novels of French literature. At the same time, it is not idiosyncratic in its voice, like *Don Quixote*. As a narrator, Madame de La Fayette stays out of the way of the story, rarely intruding in her depiction of the characters. Her intelligence and originality come in her deployment of story, character, and theme rather than in her expression of her own personality. *The Princess of Clèves* was published anonymously. Madame de La Fayette wanted the princess's story to stand or fall on its own rather than suffering or benefiting from any association with her life or her reputation. More important, the novel is not about the princess's eccentricity, as *Don Quixote* is about Quixote's eccentricity. What it offers is an alternative plot about the struggle to conform to an ideal in spite of temptation and social pressure. An extravagant style is appropriate to the one; a correct but self-effacing style is appropriate to the other.

The career of Daniel Defoe, who was a child in London when *The Princess of Clèves* was being published, illustrates not only many things about how novelists take up their vocation, but also a great deal about how the novel was invented and then, as it were, franchised. In the first place, since he was a tradesman, importer, and hack writer, Defoe's class loyalties, daily activities, and sensibility were different from those of his predecessors. In addition, by 1700, when Defoe was forty, European religious conflicts had more or less been decided. The assassinations, revolutions, wars, counterrevolutions, inquisitions, tortures, hangings, burnings, murders, mutilations, and terror that marked the seventeenth century had subsided into a more or less territorial configuration of Catholic and Protestant countries that now competed for colonial wealth and trade domination. Capitalism was not as free or as sophisticated as it would be by the time Adam Smith wrote *The Wealth of Nations* (1776), but it had spread around Europe and was the order of the day in vibrant urban regions. Capitalism, of course, depended upon numeracy and literacy. Defoe was a man of the printed word— he was the first of our originators who depended upon the widespread dissemination of books and pamphlets for a living. As a result, he was drawn to sensational subjects, because they were the most likely to sell. At the same time, Defoe's Nonconformist religious training gave him a sense of sympathetic connection with subjects not previously given serious literary treatment—prostitutes, servants, criminals, working men and women, courtesans, adventurers of all stripes. Defoe knew from going to chapel that all humans could look within and inventory their virtues and defects, and were, therefore, suitable protagonists for novels.

Defoe was no less interested in the condition of women than our four previous authors—both *Moll Flanders* and *Roxana* deal frankly with the stark choices many women must make between virtue and survival. For his characters, though, the choices were neither sentimental nor abstract—giving up one's virtue was often the only way for a woman to survive, and one of Defoe's pamphlets was a defense of women's rights. His great technical innovation, though, comparable to Madame de La Fayette's invention of indirect discourse, was narrating in the first person rather than the third person. One of Defoe's hack writing jobs was criminal confessions. Criminals were celebrities in early-eighteenth-century England. In the complete absence of a social safety net, theft, murder, and other forms of violent crime were commonplace, and prostitution, child abandonment, and child-selling were routine, even though the laws against all of these transgressions were strict, punishments were harsh, and recidivism was the order of the day. Sensational crimes were written up and published, and when especially famous criminals came to be hanged (in public, as examples), writers such as Defoe composed their confessions. Defoe also was used to writing in his own voice—he wrote essays and polemics on politics, he wrote a travelogue of a journey around the British Isles, he wrote about a haunting. When, nearing sixty, he came to writing *The Life and Strange Surprising Adventures of Robinson Crusoe,* the first-person point of view was utterly natural to him, but it changed the nature of the novel, plunging it into the subjective realm and shifting the balance between the inner life and the outer life. The narrative still moved between actions and reflection, but now the actions were depicted entirely through the filter of the narrator's mode of reflection. An author need no longer cultivate a particular style that he used to tell many types of stories—varying his tone, perhaps, but retaining his authority. Defoe experimented with different styles—that is, different inner lives—for different narrators. Crusoe approaches everything practically, including his salvation. Moll Flanders is breezier and livelier than Crusoe—although she has been and remains a bit shocked by some of the things that have happened to her, her vitality seems like her natural counterweight to a sense of sinfulness. The narrator of *A Journal of the Plague Year* is more cautious and precise than either of the other two, almost entirely self-effacing and yet quite particular in his depiction of the catastrophic epidemic. Roxana, the protagonist of Defoe's last novel, is the most complex. She is a realist about what she has been required to do over the years to survive, but she is also tormented by her actions—in particular, at the beginning of the novel, when Roxana's husband abandons the family, she starves with the five children for a while, but, realizing that everyone is going to die, she consigns the baby to the parish and perpetrates a ruse upon her husband's sister (who is more prosperous), to plant the older four children in that family. The oldest daughter is subsequently sent away as a servant by the sister-in-law, but the girl returns to haunt, and endanger, Roxana, who more or less colludes, or at least acquiesces, in her death. It is a dark and complex novel, and the female voice is thoroughly convincing. As a gloss on the theories of Thomas Hobbes and their origins in the social conditions of England, it could not be more convincing.

What Defoe was after was not so much sympathy as empathy—not so much "feeling with" a protagonist, but "sensing through" him or her. All of Defoe's protagonists are morally problematic; all have committed sins and crimes, and, more important, all have committed cruelties, but all are also burdened by awareness of not only the sins but also the circumstances that gave rise to them. This moral ambiguity perfectly suits both the novel's focus on the inner life and also the tendency of prose to proliferate, making finer and finer distinctions at greater and greater length. In fact, Defoe's protagonists (with the exception of his first, Crusoe) tend to be so subjective that the world they live in is depicted only in passing. They hardly bother setting a scene or describing a person or a place. Emotions are portrayed and alluded to, but the realest part of the inner life of Defoe's characters is the activity of weighing right and wrong against necessity and desire. And yet Defoe's novels are filled with energy and rarely depressing. There is no ennui in Defoe's characters. They take an active interest in practical matters—Robinson Crusoe, of course, is famous for his enterprise, but *Roxana* provides plenty of interesting information on many topics, ranging from how to foist your children off upon your relatives (which she must do in a particular way because of parish pauper laws), to how to transfer a large sum of money from one country to another, to how to conduct affairs of mutual benefit with married men. Defoe's characters readily comprehend that survival is a full-time job requiring cleverness and application as well as luck. And because Defoe's women characters are on their own, they have an answer to a perennial European question: what is the purpose of women? It turns out that their purpose is work, same as men.

The Adventures of Robinson Crusoe, which was published anonymously in 1719, was a sensation. Within a year of publication, it was translated into several other European languages in, of course, pirated editions. Defoe's later novels (five in three to four years, along with other books) did not cause quite the stir as his first, and he did not receive royalties—each was a one-off. Defoe died in 1731 somewhat mysteriously, away from his family and hiding from creditors. Did immediately subsequent novelists learn from him? On the one hand, *Robinson Crusoe* was the most successful novel of the eighteenth century, and *Moll Flanders* and *Roxana* went through many editions in which they were cleaned up and morally improved; on the other hand, Defoe's subject matter was so sensational and lacking in respectability that if novelists such as Fielding and Richardson learned something from Defoe, perhaps they would not have admitted it. Intention, though, is not the same as effect. Defoe might not have intended to broaden the audience and the subject matter of the novel; he might have intended only to make money. Even so, he often wrote books with a didactic purpose. His first work, a pamphlet of 1689, justified the Glorious Revolution (the accession of William of Orange, a Protestant and a German, to the English throne). He wrote *The Family Instructor,* the two-volume *Complete English Tradesman,* and *The Complete English Gentleman,* as well as his essay on the rights of women. In fact, Defoe was so successful in democratizing the English novel that writers of later generations of the eighteenth century—into the career of Jane Austen—expended considerable effort giving the novel a higher tone.

Even though writers all over Europe (and the world, if we include *The Tale of Genji* as one of our most original and influential novels), invented and reinvented the novel, it took hold as an established form in England about two generations before it took hold in France and elsewhere owing to the economic and social conditions in England that promoted literacy. One of the first newly literate groups, for example, was the large class of ladies' maids who worked from age fourteen or so in wealthy houses all over England, who had a fair amount of leisure time, who lived in close proximity to books and educated employers, and who were themselves required to exhibit a certain amount of refinement, but the growing eighteenth-century audience for the novel was diverse. As a result, each of the great English novelists of the eighteenth century brought something innovative to the new form.

In 1740, a London printer named Samuel Richardson galvanized the literary world with his epistolary novel *Pamela*. *Pamela* began as a model letter in a small instructional book Richardson had written, meant to show the newly literate classes how to write proper letters on various topics and for various purposes. Pamela's letter is that of a servant girl to her parents about her employment on a large estate. Richardson seems to have quickly understood both the thematic and the dramatic possibilities of Pamela's situation, and, seized by inspiration at age fifty, he became a novelist. Pamela, who is in the Dissenting habit of confessing to her parents to seek their advice on how to live a godly and virtuous life, reports the death of her mistress, and shortly thereafter that her young master, Mr. B., seems intent upon seducing and then raping her. According to Pamela, her sole concern is to maintain her virtue and the purity of her soul for reasons of faith. Mr. B. has her abducted, held against her will, drugged, and pinned down while he attempts to outrage her virtue. He then tries a false marriage. Eventually, though, he falls in love with Pamela and decides to marry her in reality, mostly because he is very impressed with her tenacious grasp upon her virtue and with her literary style, which he has read in her letters. At that point, his sister strongly resists the marriage, and Pamela begins writing about larger issues of the true nature of love and marriage.

Upon publication, *Pamela* was a popular success, which meant that readers all over England and even France (the French polymath and encyclopedist Denis Diderot was inspired by *Pamela* to try novel-writing as well) could make up their own minds about Pamela's logic. The great innovation of Richardson's epistolary form was a sense of intimacy and immediacy. Modern readers might find the idea that Pamela could retire to her closet and write at length about her adventures, her feelings, and her ideas even in the midst of being pursued entirely unbelievable, but Richardson's contemporaries were willing to suspend disbelief for the sake of enjoying Pamela's spirited resistance. In some sense, an epistolary novel is like a movie—we seem to be watching it while it is happening, and it therefore gains an extra degree of unpredictability and suspense. Other types of first-person novels are necessarily written after the fact, which means that the narrator has survived, and assimilated his experiences at least to a degree. The epistolary novel can more closely resemble the actual passage of consciousness through time, especially in an epistolary age, when average people are in the habit of regularly reporting on their thoughts and reading the reports of their friends. There is no denying that Pamela and her novel are simultaneously ridiculous and compelling. Richardson's novel also had a strong (and possibly unintended) political dimension.

The basic question Pamela asks is: do I belong to my master, or do I belong to God? Is her virtue hers to dispose of, her master's to take, or theirs to preserve? When the subject turns to love, do property and class issues trump emotional ones? Has Pamela proved herself and her arguments? *Pamela* is openly and directly about power: what are its limits and how are they to be maintained? The very epistolary unfolding of Pamela's dilemma intensifies the importance of these questions—after all, Moll Flanders and Roxana have already lived their lives. Their task as they set down their adventures is to decide whether and how to repent—to decide the meaning of their adventures. The outcome of Pamela's story is not yet decided as she is writing, so part of her task is to come up with strategies for outwitting Mr. B., at first, and then later, reasons for deciding whether his reformation is real. All of these questions, since they are about power, implicitly link the personal and the political; as soon as *Pamela* gained a multitude of readers, the issues became explicitly political, as highly charged issues in popular novels tend to do. If a reader were sympathetic to Pamela's defiance, might he or she be sympathetic to the defiance of other women to the demands of property and class, not to mention to the sexual urges of men?

One of Samuel Richardson's contemporaries who was not impressed was Henry Fielding. Fielding began as a playwright, but English theaters of his day were subject to licensing laws, and as a result of one of Fielding's satiric attacks upon the government, his theater was closed. He turned to writing novels, and his first effort was a pastiche that mocked *Pamela,* titled *Shamela,* that picked up on some of the sillier aspects of Pamela's story. Fielding had enough success with his short novel that he decided to try another approach, so he wrote *Joseph Andrews,* allegedly the story of Pamela's brother, also a servant, who has his own troubles with Lady B., Mr. B.'s lascivious sister.

Fielding's masterpiece, though, owes more to *Don Quixote,* a book Fielding loved. In *Tom Jones,* his eponymous hero, Tom, is exiled from the estate of his foster father, Squire Allworthy, and forced to seek his fortune on the road to London. At the same time, Squire Western, Allworthy's neighbor, decides to force his daughter Sophia to marry Allworthy's nephew (and Tom's enemy) Blifil, to consolidate the two properties. Tom is an attractive young man, and encounters (unlike Quixote) several challenges to his virtue both on the road and among the worldly aristocrats in London. Finally he finds himself in danger of hanging, but just in time, all of Blifil's schemes are unraveled, and Tom (and Sophia) are saved. As a dramatist, it was natural for Fielding to import conventions of the English theater into the novel, and he did, including wit and comedy, an exciting plot that turns on the villainy of Tom's antagonist, and also the standard comic ending—love, reconciliation, and prosperity (which in pre–Industrial Revolution England meant real estate). Fielding's England was a manly, robust, rough place not that different from Cervantes's Spain, except that a pastoral paradise was to be found in England, among the country estates of such responsible and thoughtful members of the gentry as Squire Allworthy. Fielding was by no means progressive, though he was skeptical of religion and leery of forcing young women to marry against their will. Above all, he was humane. He recognized the temptation for people of privilege to abuse their privileges and overlook their obligations; he portrayed members of all classes acting not only foolishly and ridiculously but also coarsely, selfishly, and brutishly. His dearest virtue (the one that in Tom himself balances all his faults and accounts for some of his mistakes) was openheartedness. But the purpose of the plot of *Tom Jones* is never to spread the wealth around—it is always to consolidate (country) property and attach it to right feeling. If a certain amount of fun can be had in the bargain, so much the better. Because Fielding was classically educated, and because he made a strenuous effort to do so, he raised the tone of the novel by calling *Tom Jones* a "mock epic" and including extensive commentary that explicitly linked the story to classical models. Later novelists could read *Tom Jones* (and Fielding's other novels) with both pleasure and self-satisfaction—he was respectable.

In 1759, Laurence Sterne, too, came to novel-writing from another career. He was a clergyman, accustomed to writing sermons, discussing morals and values, and finding general lessons in specific examples of human behavior. But Sterne was an odd duck and not terribly successful in his clerical role. He was also writing at a time when what was called "feeling" but perhaps what we would call "sentimentality" was replacing sharp satire as the fashion. Defoe's *Roxana,* for example, still in print, was extensively rewritten by late eighteenth-century publishers of new editions to mitigate Roxana's seeming indifference toward her children and her less than satisfactory repentence at the end. And whereas Richardson went from Pamela's two-volume rape in 1740 to Clarissa's seven-volume rape in 1748, investigating ever more carefully and fully both Clarissa's point of view and that of Lovelace, her abductor, Sterne's protagonists, Mr. Shandy (the father of Tristram) and Uncle Toby, were hardly interested in sex at all. Uncle Toby, in fact, who comes more and more into prominence as the novel proceeds, is of a singularly modest turn of mind, much more interested in playing an elaborate form of toy soldiers in his garden than paying attention to the widow over the hedge. What Sterne cared about, what constituted his innovation, was human, and especially male, eccentricity. Defoe's characters, Fielding's characters, and the characters in *Pamela* were intended, at least at the beginning, to typify or represent their categories. As the plots of the novels developed, the protagonists individualized themselves, but the dramatic tradition was so strong in England that thinking of human psychology as typology was automatic—in a drama, the actors inhabit the characters and can't help but individualize them, so the author can focus more on the action than on shades of human uniqueness. Sterne, however, as a writer of sermons, did not organize his characters in the same way, and he was not so attached to plotting as an organizational method. He presented his characters as eccentric from the beginning; in fact, the action of *Tristram Shandy* progresses more and more slowly in part because Sterne's (or the narrator's) theory of psychology is based on uniqueness—the unique circumstances of Tristram's conception (his father cries out in annoyance at the moment of ejaculation) and birth (the doctor presses the baby's nose with the forceps, thereby, by symbolic extension, damaging his penis or his libido). Sterne's ideas have their origins in the vagaries of thought and the contingencies of circumstance. If all novels have two sides—the public and the private—the privacy Sterne explores is even more extreme than that of Richardson because it is more idiosyncratic. Unlike Pamela, Clarissa, and Lovelace, Mr. Shandy, Uncle Toby, and the narrator are not attempting to conform at all. In any novel, what is most original is always what is most intimate (though the converse is not true—often intimacies are related in quite conventional ways, importing the public into the private and showing that an author's ideas of intimacy aren't very original). Sterne significantly extended the private, philosophical side of the novel, as, in *A Journal of the Plague Year,* Defoe extended the public, documentary side of the novel. The very fact that few authors have followed these two models subsequently shows how demanding and unusual they are, and how much more readily the novel shapes itself to the fairly equal representation of inner life and outer life, of the individual and the group.

By the time of Sterne's death, the novel was fully invented and, indeed, franchised. It was a popular and exciting literary form. Enterprising dramatists, poets, and intellectuals were frequently moved to try writing a novel or two. More important, novels were regularly published that became all the rage—sometimes because they were so shocking, at other times because they were so funny or moving. Translations were common, so that novels such as *Don Quixote* and *Robinson Crusoe* were available to numerous readers who lived in places and at times entirely remote from Spain in 1610 or London in 1719. Later authors would go on to expand the scope of the novel, to refine its rhetoric, to challenge its readers, to modify how quality in the novel should be defined, but lengthy written prose narratives with protagonists, narratives that regularly alternated between depicting the actions and the inner lives of their characters, narratives that focused on the adventures of individuals and their context within small groups and large groups, narratives that defined reality sometimes as objective and sometimes as subjective, narratives with complex plots and narratives with hardly any plots at all had made their appearance and did not have to be invented again.

5 · The Psychology of the Novel

Whereupon this worthy knight, whose swordplay was doubtless on a par with his storytelling, began to recite his tale, which in itself was indeed excellent. But by repeating the same phrases, and recapitulating sections of the plot, and every so often declaring that he had "made a mess of that bit," and regularly confusing the names of the characters, he ruined it completely. Moreover, his mode of delivery was completely out of keeping with the characters and the incidents he was describing, so that it was painful for Madonna Oretta to listen to him. She began to perspire freely and her heart missed several beats, as though she had fallen ill and was about to give up the ghost.

—GIOVANNI BOCCACCIO, *The Decameron*

The basic substance of imaginative literature (novels, plays, poetry) is not reason but emotion, which is expressed not by the denotations of words, nor the grammar of the sentences, but through the connotations and colorations of the words as employed by the author's style. Once a story has been put into words, people can analyze it, ponder it, hold it in their minds, come to know it, change it willingly, learn from it. But it exists not as words written in books but as images with feelings attached. To read and then reread a work is to reattach remembered images to unremembered words and to experience again (and sometimes even more sharply) the pleasure of the inchoate becoming specific. Both writer and reader experience the same basic pleasure—something in one form in the mind takes another form on the page, something in one form on the page takes another form in the mind. This is the *essential* pleasure of literature, ideas going into and out of words over and over and over, any time the reader opens a book, or the author takes up a pen.

The sheer length and accessibility of the novel, though, changes a reader's experience of this process in specific ways, because the number of words and their connections expand toward the infinite—ideally, in a hundred-thousand-word book, every word could relate to every other word in some unique way, and no conventional forms (as in poetry) or interpreters (actors and directors) are present to limit or guide the reader's intuition. Scholars and critics have despaired of coming up with a method that is various enough for understanding the novel, and their despair is warranted—in a novel such as Rebecca West's *The Fountain Overflows,* where every word seems to relate to and reflect upon every other word, building layers of meaning and feeling that seem to shift continuously, all critical methods are of only modest usefulness. A lively intuition, though, can make it all out to a satisfying degree. Any reader's list of her ten favorite novels exhausts the interpretive capacities of generations of critics, but is readily accessible, over and over, to the reader herself. In fact, the accessibility of the novel renders critical interpretations superfluous to the reader/author interaction. A novel *may* be read on all sorts of levels, as articles and controversies in scholarly journals show, but it can be enjoyably and correctly read just to see what happens next and to enjoy the company of the author, the narrator, and the characters.

Each of the elements of the definition of the novel has an effect on the psychology of reading the novel. For example, narrative voice is social, and so the psychology of the novel is a psychology of relationships, even if the novel is about an isolated loner such as Robinson Crusoe, or Franz Kafka's Josef K. in *The Trial.* Since the mere existence of the narrative voice implies a teller, a listener, and other beings who are being told about and implies, therefore, relationships, every reader comes to every novel with plenty of experience that bears upon the reading of a novel. The qualities of the voice are automatically present—is it warm, friendly, knowledgeable, soothing, charming, intelligent, self-obsessed, droning, bombastic, mechanical, silly, beside the point, suspect? The reader perceives and reacts to these qualities instantly, without thinking. If she likes the voice and feels comfortable with it, she may not actually think at any time, except to process the characters and events of the narrative, but such processing isn't exactly cogitating. A novel that is a comfortable fit with the reader, whose characters and narrative voice the reader is drawn to and enjoys, whose jokes the reader laughs at, and whose insights the reader understands and appreciates, arouses a sense of friendliness. With such a novel—let's say *Persuasion*—the reader's responses feel harmonious and agreeable. She recognizes the crass insensitivity of Anne Elliot's father and sister and the tediousness of Anne's old-maid existence; she understands how the naval officers and their wives offer a welcome breath of exotic practicality to Anne's social life; she follows the subtle changes in Anne's feelings toward Captain Wentworth; she is in sync with the play of Jane Austen's wit. When she retreats from the flow of the narrative into judgment, it is to appreciate scenes or phrases or even to marvel at them. The relationship the reader has with such a novel feels reciprocal though it is not. The reader is supplying both the give and the take that furnish such a reading experience with a feeling of conversational intimacy. Of course, the author is as familiar as the reader with social intercourse; he (or in this case, she) is using the forms and tones of social intercourse to communicate the ideas in her novel because she cannot help doing so. When an author writes, she is communicating with herself; when a reader reads, she is communicating with herself, but when she feels a sense of kinship with a particular novel, she feels that the author is communicating with her.

If the reader doesn't like the voice, though, she starts to think, should I keep reading this, or should I stop? She weighs her boredom or dislike against what she is getting from the novel. With a novel such as *Vanity Fair,* for example, where the tone of the narrative voice is very cynical and where the characters may be hard to like (and the drawings, by Thackeray himself, might be unappealing), she withdraws a bit from the experience of the novel (maybe even while continuing to read) and concocts an argument about whether to go on and for how long. After another ten or twenty pages, perhaps, she puts the book down and walks away. Sometime later, she comes back and sees the book. Then she makes another decision whether to pick the book up and start reading again. This decision is not unlike choosing to call someone who isn't a bosom friend—will the payoff for picking the novel up again outweigh the discomfort already experienced (and already associated with everything about the novel, including the picture on the cover and the color and smoothness of the paper)? If she picks it up again and goes on with it, she reaffirms her commitment, but this can work in two ways. One way, of course, is that she presses ahead to the end of the novel and finishes it, adding to whatever pleasures she ultimately gets from it a sense of accomplishment and relief. The other is that as her commitment deepens, she comes to resent the novel more and more for being so intransigently itself, and this resentment might cause her to throw down the novel in disgust after two hundred or three hundred pages. If she had simply never picked the novel up again after the first few pages, she might never have felt resentment or disgust at all, just a vague sense that the novel didn't have anything to do with her. Every novel, every narrator can't help offering the promise of a relationship.

Of course, a reader may begin by disliking *Vanity Fair* but be won over in the end to liking it very much. The novelist has many pleasures to offer—the unusual pleasure of the exotic, the intellectual pleasure of historical understanding, the humane pleasure of psychological insight into one or more characters, the simple pleasure of entertainment and suspense, the exuberant pleasure of laughter and trickery, the guilty pleasure of gossip, the tempting pleasure of secrecy and intimacy, the confessional pleasure of acknowledged sin and attempted redemption, the polemical pleasure of indignation, the rigorous pleasure of intellectual analysis, the reassuring pleasure of identification with one's nation or people, and the vicarious pleasure of romance. The reader may gradually set aside the discomfort of incompatibility and come to enjoy any or all of these pleasures by the end of the novel, and if the incompatibility stems more from unfamiliarity than anything else, then she has many hundreds of pages to get used to the novelist's way of thinking and of expressing himself.

If the incompatibility comes from a disagreement in opinions, then the reader has hundreds of pages to understand and to learn to agree with the author's arguments. The author can employ different sorts of logic—the logic of cause and effect as expressed in the scenes; the logic of character—whether thoughts and actions hang together and make sense; the logic of theme—whether the author's argument about how the world works makes sense; the logic of structure—whether the parts of the novel work together. There is also a logic of style—how the diction and grammar the author uses at the beginning of the novel prepare the reader for the diction and grammar he uses in later sections (an example of success on this score is Anthony Trollope's *The*

Last Chronicle of Barset, in which the reader is prepared by the way the author discusses the intricacies of a troubled but loving marriage at the beginning of the novel for his analysis of a troubled and loveless marriage at the end).

The reader may recognize that the author has set out to manipulate her in a certain way, to use one or more of his available logics to persuade her of his ontological theory—Thackeray may have intended to show the inexorable decline of honor among Englishmen of breeding and education—but as the materials of his novel coalesce, she recognizes elements that are contradictory, that the author didn't intend, hadn't thought of, and possibly never understood. In *Vanity Fair,* Becky Sharp disappears ignominiously toward the end of the narrative; unlike Lily Bart, in Edith Wharton's *The House of Mirth,* she is not even allowed the dignity of a tragic death. Without her, the energy of the novel dissipates and the novel's only possible hero, the faithful William Dobbin, discovers himself obscurely dissatisfied with his happy ending. Although Thackeray portrays Becky as a selfish arriviste, a pathological liar who is perhaps capable of murder, and an almost certainly unchaste adulteress, she seems to have certain qualities of insight, intelligence, and vitality not allowed any other character. Thackeray seems to like her in spite of himself, as if only conventional propriety is preventing him from awarding her some final triumph. Did Thackeray intend such a combination of vice and energy? Did he even understand Becky's grandeur? Was she a product of his art or an unintended consequence? A reader can find herself beguiled by the confluence of the authorial intentions and lucky accidents of composition as readily as any other pleasure.

Some authors deploy their modes of seduction more gracefully than others, but what they are all trying to achieve in the reader is what length itself demands: willing suspension of disbelief. There are two halves to this equation: "willing" and "suspension of disbelief." It is far more difficult to make the second half work than the first, because no amount of plausibility really overcomes the definition of a novel as fiction.

Usually, what puts a reader into a state of willingness is an interesting assertion, such as "It is a truth universally acknowledged, that a single man in possession of a good fortune, must be in want of a wife" (*Pride and Prejudice*), or "Ours is essentially a tragic age, so we refuse to take it tragically" (*Lady Chatterley's Lover*), or "It was the best of times, it was the worst of times" (*A Tale of Two Cities*). But a character may also do an interesting or appealing thing, such as "Jewel and I come up from the field, following the path in single file" (*As I Lay Dying*), or "Buck Mulligan came from the stairhead, bearing a bowl of lather on which a mirror and a razor lay crossed" (*Ulysses*). At the beginning of "The Metamorphosis," Kafka has Gregor Samsa change into a bug, perhaps one of the most intriguing first premises in literature. However, in teaching this story twenty-two times to undergraduate students, I found that out of every thirty students, one or two were simply unwilling to believe that Gregor could turn into a bug, and for those students, the story offered no charms at all. It was not that the other students believed that a man in Prague in 1915 turned into a bug; it was that they enjoyed the idea and suspended disbelief, and once they imagined Gregor's bugness, they were open to every other idea that Kafka had to offer.

Willing suspension of disbelief is a strange state of mind—reading nonfiction does not require it and neither does reading poetry, since both are based on logical argument. Many intelligent and educated persons resist it entirely or yield to it only for a brief time, in the darkness of a theater, accompanied by other members of an audience—the world is full of people who are rather proud that they don't read novels. Publishers often lament that the audience for novels is narrowing, and especially that it is losing men. A literary education not only enlarges a reader's willingness to suspend disbelief by extending her range of pleasures, it also strengthens her ability to enter the meditative state, and to be receptive to the influence of another human mind, because it is a state of contemplation that is essential to the true appreciation of the novel. While all art forms promote this state of receptivity, with the novel it is uniquely sustained—it is not possible, for example, to contemplate a painting for ten or twelve hours, the amount of time the average reader would need to read a five-hundred-page novel. Few dramatic productions run for more than four hours, and even that length of time is considered daring. How long is Wagner's *Ring* cycle? Fifteen hours is perhaps equivalent to reading Anthony Trollope's *Can You Forgive Her?*, and nowhere in the region of any of the great meganovels such as Proust's *In Search of Lost Time*.

For some readers, of course, eight to ten hours spent reading a novel in a receptive state of mind is the only quiet, contemplative time they can afford, and the opportunity to suspend so much disbelief, to follow a single line of thought, is comforting as well as entertaining and enlightening. When the reader accepts the first line of a book, she agrees to think about the same things, and in the same degree of detail and in the same order, that the writer has chosen to think about. While she is reading the book, she is thinking about them simultaneously with the author. Although in book form the novel precedes her contemplation of it and may historically precede her very existence, as a novel it unfolds in the author's mind and her mind simultaneously. The recognition of this effect of the novel, and of its uniqueness in literature, was the revelation that enabled Marcel Proust to write *In Search of Lost Time*. Proust knew that he could not achieve the sense of reexperiencing important episodes that he sought if he were to write an overt memoir because a memoir has to seem true (both factual and incomplete). He preferred to use the conceit of a memoir but to write a novel, which enabled him to pick and choose aspects of his experience that he found "useful to my theme," as he said, and to elaborate as much as he wished.

Because of the way that the novel unfolds in the mind of the willing reader, she cannot be "wrong" in her response to it—the fact that the novel is created only in her mind while she is reading it gives her sole possession of it. Outside of literature, maybe the closest thing to this is a guided meditation, where the voice of a guru suggests images and ways of thinking that are intended to result in a particular state of mind. Presumably, as he speaks, the guru is meditating on the same images he is speaking of. But few guided meditations go on for twenty-six hours (the length of a full recorded reading of my novel *Horse Heaven*). Rather, the voice of the guru fades away after a while, having induced in the student's mind an absence of voice or image. A novel, too, induces a contemplative state of mind, but rather than emptying it, it fills it with many different thoughts and feelings. Present with the reader in her mind is the individuality of the writer, whose idiosyncratic phrasing, ideas and emotions, fears and desires are guiding her and influencing her and inviting her to react.

However, not every state of willing suspension of disbelief is the same. A novel directs the reader's contemplation of it. Even when a reader likes four different novels equally, and is equally receptive to them, she won't read Robert Musil's *The Man without Qualities* in the same manner that she will read Halldór Laxness's *Independent People,* or even in the same manner that she will read another great modernist novel such as *Ulysses*. A page-turner offers the pleasure of suspense (this is one of the pleasures of the tale), but in an epic, more than moderate suspense might be a fault. In an epic, the unhappy outcome of the novel is shadowed forth early on. Relentless page-turning gets the reader only where she knew she was going in the first place, and it gets her there faster, without sufficient time to ruminate upon the qualities of the epic protagonist that make him or her interesting and worth reading about. Novels with a large component of travel narrative, such as *Moby-Dick,* are meant to meander so that the writer and the reader can gaze at the scenery and appreciate its exotic qualities. One of the problems some modern readers have with Melville is that they don't have the patience to realize that the psychological and plot elements of his stories are intentionally set into a wide landscape that is meant to comment upon and contrast to the narrow intensity of human desires and preoccupations. A novel such as *The Man without Qualities* is an argument about the nature of modern life presented in a highly figurative and epigrammatic style. If the reader doesn't go slowly enough to follow Musil's argument and think about his analogies—if she isn't as precise in her reading as he is in his writing—then the novel will pass her by almost completely. A romantic novel—let's say *Jane Eyre*—offers the reader still another dilemma. Everything in the plot and character depictions pulls her toward the climax that is to unite the protagonists, but for the story to be worth reading, the protagonists and their ups and downs have to be depicted and read about with care; the suspense of a romantic novel can actually get very strong even though author, reader, and convention all foreshadow the outcome and even when, in rereadings, the reader knows the outcome quite well.

Novels have protagonists; protagonists, like narrators, have points of view. Point of view is like perspective in a realistic painting—it changes the size and shape, the nature and identity, of characters, objects, and events in accordance with their proximity to the viewer. Since a reader naturally has a point of view, her own, she readily accepts the simple humanity of point of view in a novel. By contrast, because at first glance nothing differentiates the protagonist in a play or a movie from the other humans around him or her, an audience member needs to be told whom to attend to and empathize with. Point of view in a movie or a play is superimposed by language, camera angles, stardom, voice-over.

The novel, of course, shares point of view with poetry, sharing also the quality of perspective. But the poem—at least the modern poem—usually does not excel at narrating events (and since the rise of the novel, hasn't been asked to do much of it). It excels, rather, at making events stand still for a moment so that some meaning or feeling can be wrested from them by ever more precise and evocative use of language, language that is supposed to cause the reader to stop rather than go. Action, all going and no stopping, is for plays and movies—movies that have nothing else have action. Even plays that have nothing else have talk, which is a type of action. The novel is the only imaginative form that must have both action and point of view, suspense and reflection. In this it seems to mimic the way life feels.

Every novel, then, is a guided meditation on a common thing, common both in the sense of "mundane" and in the sense of "shared"—action and reflection as perceived from a particular point of view. Perhaps this is the reason novelists are generally run-of-the-mill sorts of people, not experts, not possessed of prodigious resources in any specialized realm. Would anyone read a hypothetical novel by Albert Einstein? We can imagine the publisher's blurb: "In this page-turning, soul-wrenching work of genius, *Time and Distance,* the smartest man of the twentieth century tells the story of a fascinating marriage, the passionate ups and downs and the numbing but illuminating details of daily life, alongside the exciting adventures of new ideas *and* the final flight from tyranny!" Or, perhaps, a novel by Donald Trump, "*Brick by Brick,* a strangely lyrical investigation into wealth, corruption, fame, and fashion." And yet every day we read and enjoy *White Teeth,* which was written by a twenty-five-year-old girl; *Rabbit Is Rich,* which was written by the only son of a schoolteacher from a small town in Pennsylvania; *Persuasion,* which was written by the second daughter of a minor landowner in Hampshire, England; *The Adventures of Huckleberry Finn,* by a small-town boy from a small midwestern state; and *Dead Souls,* written and partially destroyed by the son of a moderately wealthy minor official from Ukraine. It is hard to overestimate the importance of this quality of commonness to the nature of the novel; it enables a reader to relax with a novel as with another person, and also to feel as though the novelist might have something to say of relevance to the reader's own common life.

When NASA sent a capsule into space a couple of decades ago, carrying schematic drawings of a man and a woman, a few mathematical formulas, some music, and several other objects, they did not include a copy of *To Kill a Mockingbird*. Every single novel is far too particular to be representative of the whole human race, but the paradox is that while every novel is too particular and even humble to stand as an emblem of humanity, the commonness of the novel is its most humane and human aspect. This is one of the effects of prose (one that Boccaccio pointed out in *The Decameron* when he was trying to justify its existence in 1350). People grow up narrating, expressing their points of view, elaborating and embroidering upon incidents, telling stories over and over. They do so because they want to fix events in their minds and remember them by endowing them with significance and discovering their meaning. It seems clear that many species of animals communicate vocally, but no other species of animal has been discovered to tell untrue stories.

Untrue stories, as Proust realized, are worth telling only insofar as they remain distinct from true stories. It is this distinction that gives them completion. We can see this effect in both lies and gossip. Lies, of course, require some sort of logic for the liar to remember them and avoid being found out. The very process of working out a lie so it is plausible, though, is what makes it complete and implausible. Liars become smooth because they must—they are rhetoricians above all. Gossip, not a set of lies but a set of inferences, works the same way. A round of gossip always begins with a person everyone knows (a character) doing something interesting but uncharacteristic (shoplifting a blouse). The purpose of the gossip is to add events to the story as they become known (she gets caught, she cries, she is discovered to have another blouse in her purse, the police are called, she goes to the station, her dad calls the mayor, she gets off scot-free) and to account for the twists and turns in the story by means of psychology (that narcissistic bitch, remember when she took the lipstick out of my purse and wouldn't admit it even though I found it right in her locker?) and motive (she said if she didn't get that blouse somehow, her cousin would buy it, and she couldn't stand that), and then a broader interpretation of character (you know she always has thought her cousin was prettier than she is, and she hates her for that, but you'd never know it because she's so sweet whenever the cousin is around). Once the story is complete—when all the events are accounted for and the logic of the original mystery and its relationship to the character are understood—it becomes boring and the gossips go on to something else. It doesn't matter whether the story, the motives, and the interpretation of character bear any relationship to reality (Do you remember when she stole that blouse? Well, it turned out the saleslady put it into her bag by mistake as she was leaving the store. She had paid for the other blouse anyway.); the compulsion of gossips is to fill in all of the details until the incident becomes a rounded whole.

Everyone acknowledges that true stories can never be fully known—too many details lack corroboration, too many witnesses disagree about what really happened. Every true story is unsatisfying insofar as it is required to be true. But since the novel is required to be complete (its dispensation from truthfulness), its acknowledged untruthfulness removes it from the world of consequences. The reader suspending disbelief expects a novel to take place in a designated game area (inside a book) under rules that apply only to the game. The rules are agreed upon ahead of time (for example, that it is possible to experience a time and a place very different from one's own). However serious its subject matter, the reader suspends disbelief because a novel is a form of play. Suffering and brutality can begin and unfold without either the author or the reader lifting a finger to stop them. Horrors depicted graphically in a novel are considered to be far less disturbing than the same graphic horrors in a nonfiction account because they are being used in a different way, as part of the logical progress of a game rather than as an unwelcome or irrational intrusion upon life. And unbelievable happy events also can take place in a novel, as a way for the mind to play over and learn from what it might otherwise not have a chance to experience.

The game quality of the novel gives it meaning and form, because all games begin, have a playing time, and end. It also gives the novel at least a rudimentary raison d'être, since games are a recognized form of learning for young mammals. The author sets up the game and is required to signal to the reader early in the narrative what the rules are. He does this in part by adopting a certain diction and tone right away—*As I Lay Dying,* for example, is a game about the lives of people who speak ungrammatically and are likely to do something unconventional; *A Tale of Two Cities* is a game in which two cultures are going to be contrasted, and the contrasts are going to be marked ones; A. S. Byatt's *Possession* is a game in which romantic relationships and styles of literature in two eras separated by 125 years are going to be compared and contrasted. A plot game, such as a murder mystery, signals the beginning of the plot right away with some sort of sinister event. A game about the workings of the mind puts off the beginning of the plot in favor of narrative ruminations about the nature of the world. A game about what seems versus what is, such as Kafka's "The Metamorphosis," begins immediately describing what seems to be happening—Gregor was transformed into a bug, and this is what his little legs waving in the air looked like to him.

To be truly playful, a game requires voluntary participants—if the author does not construct a game that is interesting enough to participate in, the reader is perfectly free to walk away. If she stays to play, then the playful nature of the game frees her to do things she might not be free to do in life—to question, to contemplate, to fantasize, to experience intense emotions, and to feel no guilt about doing so. The participants in a game *may* learn something that they take away from the game, but they *don't have to.* This is part of the freedom of playing the game. The novel game, like the baseball game, is thus an exercise in freedom, agency, and choice. The author may attempt at every turn to imbue the reader with certain sympathies or to get the reader to believe in a certain chain of cause and effect, but the reader is always free to object or disagree, or, indeed, to correct the author's misconceptions, as authors of bad reviews frequently do.

The gamelike nature of the novel is built on the literary convention of the conceit. The conceit is a form of metaphor or pretense—John Donne's poem "A Valediction Forbidding Mourning" is full of conceits such as "Our two souls therefore, which are one, / Though I must go, endure not yet / A breach, but an expansion, / Like gold to aery thinness beat"—in which the poet and the reader collaborate in a logical quest to understand the unique sort of love the poet and his wife share, using metaphors of quiet death, gold leaf, and compasses. The sensuous qualities of the images bolster the logic of the argument. In the same way, Trollope's novel *The Eustace Diamonds* proposes that the reader and the writer contemplate the character of Lizzie Eustace, whom they will agree to be a beautiful but shallow and ruthless young woman, who will begin the game's train of logical events by keeping for herself a string of valuable jewels that by rights belongs to the estate of a family she has married into. They will further agree that Lizzie has all sorts of relatives and associates who are implicated in her designs in some way or another, to see the effect of Lizzie's ambiguous moral choice upon the social world in which she lives. Lizzie's action works in the social body that she is part of like a radioactive isotope— as it moves around, it illuminates, sometimes in surprising ways, the moral life of the community. Trollope's conceit is that these characters and events are real, just as Donne's conceit is that love can be likened to death, gold, and a compass. The conceit of the poem succeeds if it promotes the logic of the poet's argument and if it is vivid enough for the reader to envision it. The conceit of the novel succeeds if the reader enjoys following it out. But both novelist and reader understand that it is all pretense. No diamonds have been stolen, no men have turned into bugs, no radio station broadcasting wholesome pap from downtown Minneapolis was ever started by a pair of brothers named Ray and Roy, no incognito crown prince has ever pulled a sword from an anvil resting on a stone, no fifteen-year-old French girl was ever subjected to year after year of relentless torture and attack and then killed by a lightning strike. But it is lots of fun to think that all of these things have happened, and more.

As with all games, the novel game has many levels of play. The lowest level is, perhaps, simply following the sequence of the story and understanding what happens and why. Higher levels move toward greater and greater complexity and efficiency, just as professional basketball players execute more plays more quickly and more masterfully than high school basketball players do. A novel with a very high level of game quotient has more and more internal and external references, a denser and denser net of connections between words and of intuitive meanings, and the result is a higher level of abstraction. In a novel such as *Ulysses* or any one of a dozen other modern and postmodern novels, no character, no image, no incident stands alone—everything is part of a network of allusions that constantly offers various meanings and reinforces the playful nature of the novel as a form. This high level of play also shapes a novel's claims to verisimilitude, in fact making the question of verisimilitude part of the discussion of that particular novel. Novelists and readers, of course, take greater or lesser pleasure in the game potential of the novel as a form. To some readers, the various and shifting nature of *Ulysses* constitutes its greatest claim to verisimilitude; to others, the lack of an easily recognizable plot (which is always what makes a novel a public object rather than a private one) indicates self-indulgence on the part of the author. And as any game grows more complex, it becomes more abstract and exclusive—in order not to get lost in the subtleties of play, fans have to be highly versed in the rules and the moves of the game and willing to play the game (read the book) over and over to get everything out of it. The novelist has as many drafts as he wants to enhance the intricacies of the novel; likewise, the patient reader has as many rereadings as she wants to work out the intricacies the novelist has introduced. Obviously, the novel as a game gives itself over to all the tendencies of games to consume insiders and deflect outsiders. Highly referential and inaccessible novels with little plot and very complex characters need help to recommend themselves to normal readers, and so, for example, you can buy a twelve-cassette course of lectures on *Ulysses* that promises to get you through the book in a way that makes sense of it—and makes you want to read it. If you buy the lectures ($79), perhaps you will commit yourself to the project instead of wasting the money. The lectures and the book, it is implied, will have been worth the effort once the reader discovers the riches of the author's imagination, and in addition the reader will have gained the prestige of reading something great, famous, and obscure. Only a novel at the highest level of play with little evident suspense requires so much promotion by those who enjoy it. Jane Austen novels, for example, recommend themselves because they work perfectly well at lower levels of play (they seem true, funny, and suspenseful), even though there is more to be discovered as the reader grows more sophisticated. The fact remains, though, that the reader possesses the novel, and so if she finds that the residue of truth or insight remaining after the intricacies of an extremely sophisticated novel game have been worked out isn't really worth the effort, she is entitled to her opinion.

So far we have talked about the psychology of the novel from the reader's point of view, but the novelist has a psychology, too. Once he has decided to write a novel, he goes through all the stages anyone else goes through who is attempting to learn a skill (see chapters 10 and 11).

Just as the novel is read intuitively, it is composed intuitively. Many great authors give themselves over to the process of composition as to madness or vision—that is, they place the reasoning brain in service to the limbic brain, knowing that intuition is a faster, more efficient, but less knowable and controllable method of creation. The length of the novel requires the productive author to do this daily, often for years. An excellent example of this is an account by Charles Dickens's daughter Kate of an occasion from her childhood when she was ill, and spent the day in her father's study. He would sit at his desk writing, then jump up and go to a mirror, where he would make faces and talk quickly in various accents, then run back to his desk and write some more. He was acting out the drama and dialogue he was writing, with no sense, she thought, of where he was or of her presence in the room. Every novelist experiences a variant of this. Some theorists of creativity call it "flow." Robert Musil, in *The Man without Qualities,* characterizes it quite nicely as follows: "this non-plussed feeling refers to something that many people nowadays call intuition, whereas formerly it used to be called inspiration, and they think that they must see something suprapersonal in it; but it is only something nonpersonal, namely the affinity and kinship of the things themselves that meet inside one's head" (p. 129). He is overtly referring to a sense of synchronicity, but what he is describing is the feeling of writing a novel.

"The things themselves" Musil alludes to are figures, words, images, and ideas given potency and importance by feelings such as indignation, pleasure, incongruity, sadness, fear, eagerness, and repulsion, and sensations such as coolness, smoothness, speediness, dullness, heat, abrasiveness, and warmth. All of these "things," which, of course, are not things at all but mental processes, come and go in the mind until something causes their connections to jell, and some set of them links up in a logic that is evident to the writer but as yet unexplored. The jelling catalyst might be any component of the novel. When I conceived *A Thousand Acres,* the ideas about Lear's daughters and about agriculture had been knocking around in my mind for fifteen years or so, but the exact moment they jelled was when I was driving down I-35 in northern Iowa in late March 1988. The landscape was flat and cold, lit by a weak winter sun, and as I stared out the window, the farm fields seemed enormous and isolated. As soon as I said, "This is where I could set that Lear book," the whole thing came into my mind, and the image of that bleak landscape remained throughout the writing of the book as a talisman to return to every time composition faltered. With *Horse Heaven* the situation was different—I conceived the book before I knew anything about the subject. A phrase I heard on the radio, "spit the bit," suggested to me that the language of horse racing must be wonderfully rich. As I began to learn about racing, each phrase or descriptor I then discovered added its own bit of inspiration to my original idea. In one case the catalyst was setting; in the other, the catalyst was language.

Charles Dickens was an avid seeker of names—he read directories and looked for odd names on gravestones. Even though he was almost always writing to a schedule, he was careful to name his characters in ways that seemed to baptize them and begin their journey. Martin

Chuzzlewit's plot didn't truly form around him when his name was "Chuzzlerigg." For Virginia Woolf, the history of Vita Sackville-West's house caused the jelling of all sorts of thoughts about men, women, literary history, writing, nature, and love. For Harriet Beecher Stowe, the death of her own child from an illness sharpened her sense of the meaning of the slave trade, and she constructed her novel of slavery not first and foremost around the subjection of one man to another, but around women losing their children. Fyodor Dostoevsky wrote *The Idiot* when he was on a lengthy journey in Europe—homesickness sharpened his sense of what it would be like to return to Russia as a perfect innocent. Proust felt *Swann's Way* jell when he tasted a madeleine dipped in lime-flower tisane and was reminded of Sunday morning visits to his aunt when he was a child. As Musil suggests, this seems like an involuntary process, but I believe that is because it takes place in the same part of the brain where other things take place that seem involuntary, too, such as predilections, affinities, antipathies, a sense of rightness, and other passions of all sorts.

But it is not all clear sailing for the novelist once he has tasted the madeleine. The reasoning brain often responds to such an experience by saying no, bad job, not good enough, I don't think so, better not, too dangerous, who do you think you are?, and watch out. Practiced and prolific novelists have to be adept at short-circuiting the cautious and reasonable areas of the brain that get in the way of the process while making use of the logical faculties that organize, support, and oversee the composition of the story itself. Every novelist has to withdraw from a state of inspiration at least once in a while to work out the logical steps of plot, character, structure, theme, and style. The sense that an author has thought through the logics in the work is reassuring to the reader, who wants both sensation and perspective, preferably simultaneously. About three-quarters of the way through Halldór Laxness's great epic of Icelandic rural life *Independent People,* for example, little Nonni, possibly Laxness's stand-in, is taken away from the impoverished family steading to America, where he is to learn a trade. The last person he says good-bye to is his grandmother, who bestows upon him her only two possessions—a kerchief and an ear pick—and gives him her only two pieces of advice: "I want to ask you never to be insolent to those who hold a lowly position in the world. And never to ill-treat any animal." Nonni is deeply affected by leaving home; the chapter is full of lyrical descriptions of the sound of the birds, the look of the family home, the sunlight. All of this is in some sense inspiration—the novelist surveying his homeland from the distance of many years. At the end of the chapter, though, the intelligence of the novelist enters twice—once in the voice of Asta Sollilja, Nonni's older sister, who says, "Say thank you to your grandmother, Nonni. She's given you the only thing she has." And then right away in his own voice as narrator, "And he put his hand in hers and thanked her in silence, for he knew no words that could express his gratitude for such a gift; she was giving him the nation's poorest Christmas to cheer him on his way when he went out into the world, and he knew that henceforth she would never celebrate Christmas" (p. 358). The scene, which is enormously poignant already, is made all the more so by Laxness's choice to underscore the humane and loving feelings he considers most important with a small authorial intrusion, which reflects upon not only general human conditions, but also, it is implied, what the adult Nonni learned from his humble origins.

And so every novelist figures out a way to circumvent the judgmental, reasoning brain long enough to get the novel moving, but also, to use it to discern and clarify the meaning of the material. Every so often an author is so inspired that the whole brain works at a pitch of efficiency, discernment, and appropriateness that the author himself cannot understand. A novelist in the midst of inspiration does not feel the egotistical emotions—Aren't I great? Look at me!—but the selfless ones—Aren't I lucky? Isn't this interesting? Isn't this fun? This doesn't mean that the egotistical emotions don't intervene whenever they can, especially in relationship to other novelists. But the reader's exposure to the mind of the novelist is so prolonged that she can always tell by his tone when he is promoting himself in some small-minded way or when he is serving his characters, themes, and plot. All good novels, even those about how selfish the author is, what a jerk he has been, and what this says about all the other selfish jerks in the world, strive to attain the grandeur of inspiration over the pettiness of self-promotion.

If the novel is a therapeutic act, as suggested above, then the very form of the novel suggests a possible positive therapeutic outcome for the author first of all. The Hungarian theorist of the novel György Lukács pointed out that while from the moment the curtain goes up on the stage, a drama accelerates toward the climax, a novel begins from the first page to back away from the climax. The essence of the novel is retarded action rather than precipitate action. There are all sorts of methods for retarding the action of a novel, from digressions and detours, to the introduction of new characters, to plot twists and changes of scene. A compelling style itself retards the action by inviting the reader to linger over the words and sentences. Every time the action of a novel is retarded, choice enters, and so, every time, a character can choose again whether to pursue one course of action or another. One result of this retarded action is that the inevitability of tragedy is lost. If tragedy is the inability, in the end, to make connection, then the retarded action of the novel repeatedly raises the opportunity of making connection, and most characters, even in the most dismal novels, end up making some sort of connection. In Leo Tolstoy's "The Death of Ivan Illych," the reader may think that at last a novelist is going to have the guts to fade to black. Ivan is dying. He has no relationship with anyone. His family life is entirely shallow and commodified. He is isolated by materialism and pride. Nevertheless, at the last moment, on the last page, when he feels that death is like being shoved into a dark sack, he notices that his son is sad at his passing, and the bottom of the dark sack gives way to light. A similar thing happens at the death of Gregor in "The Metamorphosis"—though Kafka was writing out of Jewish tradition (and Yiddish stories are often the darkest at the end), he still has Gregor sense the light of dawn just at his passing. Why is this? Can no novelist be relied upon to tell the unredeemed truth?

In fact, hope exists in the form of narrative itself, because the narrator cannot stop talking. In the end is the word, and as long as the word exists, the possibility of connection exists, no matter how resolutely the author attempts to prove otherwise. Drama can be ended with an action or a curtain, but the novel must say good-bye, which means it lives on after the action is over. It is in the nature of the novel to say, "We are still alive." Furthermore, the requirement of the novel that the narrator be lucid enough to tell the tale puts a boundary on insanity and other forms of mental disconnection. No novel can weasel out of this hopefulness, because the act of observation removes one, at least temporarily, from the state of being overwhelmed or destroyed by circumstances. For real cataclysm you have to have drama or film.

Sometimes the author himself is the first to react to the hope held out by the very nature of his novel. A character, even the protagonist, dies, but the author changes his life, as Tolstoy accepted Russian Orthodox religion at the end of writing *Anna Karenina,* as Dickens left his wife after writing *David Copperfield,* as Kafka laughed aloud while reading "The Metamorphosis" to his friend Max Brod. Does this mean that no character can have a tragic ending? Nineteenth-century novelists such as Eliot, Flaubert, and James were much interested in bringing the grandeur and artistic respectability of tragedy to the novel but, as I shall argue later, it turned out to be more difficult than they thought.

For the novelist even more, perhaps, than for the reader, the novel is a game. He enters into a state of mind that is akin to the states of mind of players of other games, a state of flow or presence that feels playful to him even as he is writing of terrible horrors. The experience of composition, which is inherently joyful and detached, offsets the contemplation of horror. For some authors, the game aspect of novel-writing is the most inspiring, and the author becomes enamored of the tricks, puns, figures of speech, references to other works, abstract patterns, or insights from other endeavors he has used to structure his novel. In *The Awkward Age,* for example, Henry James tried an unusual play-like structure that contrasts with his more straightforwardly narrated novels such as *The Portrait of a Lady* and *The Ambassadors.* The plot is simple: two young women need to be married off, but none of the eligible young men is quite suitable for reasons of either attractiveness or sensibility. The novel is divided into ten discrete parts, taking place as if on a stage among the same group of characters in a limited number of settings. Each section is told from a different point of view, and James suppresses his usual intrusive narrator's voice, telling the story mostly through action and dialogue. What James gets from this game is immediacy and intensity, and, as in a play, the efficient passage of time. He requires the reader to pay attention or get confused. Although James wrote *The Awkward Age* in the 1890s, before movies were invented, the novel anticipates movies such as the Japanese film *Rashomon* because it uses point of view rather like a camera to select features James wants to emphasize in the ongoing narrative in a way that would not be possible with a drama, and thereby reveal more about each character, perhaps, than would be possible with a more conventional narrator. By his own testimony, James was thrilled with his inventiveness in *The Awkward Age,* but it was and still is one of his more obscure novels because the form has an artificial quality that interferes with the reader's sympathetic identification with the characters.

The author, like the reader, is given a social dispensation as part of his participation in the game—what his characters do is not held against him personally. Many authors make careers of depicting brutality, horror, cruelty, vice, and graphic violence; others make careers of depicting vast wealth and social status, perfect marriages, romantic fervor, and happy-ever-after endings. These writers are not required to be realists because they are not professing to play a realist game. Nor are they "writing what they know." No one expects Stephen King to have performed all the mayhem his characters perform, and they would in fact be shocked if he had. A novelist's life is allowed to be different from the games he plays. In fact, for novelists who write with particular skill about evil (Dickens, Bram Stoker, Stephen King), it is required to be different.

The fact that a novel is a book also shapes its psychology in several ways. In the first place, the novel itself, the unfolding narrative, has no independent identity as an object, as other forms of art such as paintings, sculptures, and pieces of music do; nor can it be recited or performed from the stage—even when, as sometimes happens, a novel is commemorated by a full reading, as *Ulysses* was commemorated in Dublin on the hundredth anniversary of Bloomsday, no one expects listeners to sit quietly in a room listening attentively for the entire duration of the reading. If a novel finds no eager readers, it does not even exist. As a result, every novel has to be helped to find readers. A novel does not have the cachet of rarity—a novel from an edition that sells a thousand copies is not intrinsically more valuable than a novel from an edition that sells a million copies. When both editions first go on sale, they sell for the same twenty-five dollars. Because there are no one-of-a-kind novels, rarity and fashionability never combine to drive up the price of a book. In fact, the more fashionable a novel becomes, the more copies of it are printed, and the higher the residual profit for the author and the publisher—a novel is more like a tomato than it is like a diamond necklace. Every novel, no matter how abstract, wants to sell a million copies, and so every novelist has to offer some reason that his novel might appeal to lots and lots of readers.

Like all purveyors of commodities as opposed to luxuries, novelists are usually perfectly willing to advertise (which is another reason the novel fits in with modern life). Jane Austen's novels were not published under her name, but as "written by a lady." This was not as bland then as it seems now—a lady was a specific being, genteel, well-bred, and respectable. In the disagreements of the period about whether young women should be allowed to read novels (rather than sermons), "by a lady" was like a *Good Housekeeping* Seal of Approval—these novels were harmless (but, of course, they were not, because they gave voice to the aims and desires of young girls, as if those aims and desires were worth considering). Advertising for the novel, especially when done by the novelist himself or herself, is just like any other form of advertising—it doesn't hurt, and it can be educational; it may work, and it may not—but third-party endorsements and great word of mouth work better than anything else.

In fact, though some novelists are more uncomfortable with it than others, the psychology of the novel must include some form of authorial self-justification. How else do ordinary citizens of the modern world justify drawing attention to themselves and their ideas for hours and hours on end? At the base of every novel, then, is an argument the author is making about why a novel is worth writing, selling, and reading. Defoe, who always demonstrates the way the novel fits into commercial culture, knew from his work writing criminal confessions that there was already a market for descriptions of crimes combined with acts of repentance. Harriet Beecher Stowe knew that the evils of slavery she was hearing about in Cincinnati from escaped slaves were unknown to many Americans. Louisa May Alcott knew that adolescent girls needed to realize that there were alternatives to the conventional idea of dependency and marriage current in her day. Rohinton Mistry knew that the lives of poor people in Bombay were almost unimaginable to middle- and upper-class citizens in India and elsewhere. Aphra Behn knew that her experience in South America was unique, and that she had seen things that other English men and women would never see. Zora Neale Hurston knew that the inner lives of poor black people were hidden from mainstream culture. When an author has the conviction that his novel is a timely social and historical document, it seems to justify itself and to carry the author along.

To write about the inner life of a slacker, of someone whose claim to existence is only that his capacity for pleasure is vaster and more refined than anyone else's in the history of the world, might be harder to justify, but Marcel Proust manages to do it—not by asserting his importance but by demonstrating his talents. The opening section of *Swann's Way,* before the tasting of the madeleine, is about falling asleep, humankind's most routine and least regarded activity. As M. carries the reader through these ruminations, he demonstrates that the reader can trust him to deal with all the other more usual and more interesting things that civilized people do as well. To write about the inner life of a child-molester is even more unjustifiable, but in *Lolita,* Vladimir Nabokov has a conviction, too—the assertion of absolute artistic freedom by an author; the story justifies itself by means of the beauty and intricacy of the telling. And to tell the story of an ordinary family, as Anne Tyler does in *Dinner at the Homesick Restaurant,* may be the hardest of all to justify. The Tulls have no pretensions to distinction, other than the normal distinctions of ordinary life; they live at a certain address and have experienced certain events, that is all. Tyler is such a retiring and self-effacing writer that she makes no overt claims for her subject—like Proust, she relies on the telling itself to give it a reason. But in the end, the history of the novel is what justifies the story of the Tulls: the tales of all those other ordinary folks have given both writers and readers the conviction that everyday existence is something to be observed and learned from.

6 · Morality and the Novel

All novels, because they move repeatedly between action and reflection, are simultaneously about private experience and public events. For this reason, morality is a perennial gray area in the novel—characters are always doing things in private that challenge the reader's sense of what is appropriate. *The Decameron* and *The Heptameron* took up topics of sexuality and virtue that were natural to their simultaneously public and private "gossip" structure: ten friends sitting around telling compelling stories, and these topics remained perennial concerns of lengthy written prose narratives with protagonists. The ambiguous public/private nature of the novel makes it ideally suited to portray immoral acts, especially sexually explicit ones, and the history of the novel is marked by books that were burned and banned but gained immortality and widespread distribution anyway.

The very fact that the novel exists in that gray area that is both public and private encourages both sides of any controversy over morality. To begin with, the author's sense of privacy while he is writing permits him to take up subjects and compose scenes he might hesitate to address in company. The book's subsequent entrance into the public arena is generally unaccompanied by the person of the author, but happens piecemeal. Gossip about the novel then builds its desirability. After the first copies are distributed, it is virtually impossible for any authorities to stop their spread, and if a controversy enters the public mind, the desirability of the novel grows—it becomes less like a tomato and more like a diamond necklace as threats to limit or stop its distribution seem about to be realized. The supporters of the novel then may act quite disingenuously sincere, and challenge the very idea that the novel has a public life, because it is always experienced in private and the decision to read such a novel is always an individual one. The usual defense of a controversial novel is that if people are offended, they don't have to read the book (and people who are offended often have not read the book, but are acting on rumor). Because of the practical impossibility of stopping the spread of banned novels, every controversy that becomes widespread reinforces the idea that the zone of the novel is a free zone, a play zone, a zone of privacy, and a zone where the individual's relationship to the group is under active contemplation—in other words, immoral novels reinforce the very idea of the novel, usually making a reader (like a protagonist) more determined to make up her own mind because it is both moral and identity-confirming to do so.

One of the first banned novels was the anonymous *Lazarillo de Tormes,* which was published during the reign of the very controlling and conservative Philip II of Spain, who is also notorious for the Spanish Inquisition and the Spanish Armada. Lazarillo is a child narrator, who happens to observe the hypocrisy, brutality, and lechery of the adults in authority around him. Philip's efforts to ban the novel were absolutely unavailing. It went through many editions and spawned the coarse and comic genre of the picaresque, but the story does not follow Lazarillo as he goes upon a journey—in fact, much of the action is domestic. Lazarillo reports that the priest he serves hoards the bread and the nobleman he is later employed by absconds without paying his rent. Lazarillo's main freedom seems to be expressing an independent opinion about people he should pay respect to. *Lazarillo de Tormes* demonstrates what should be evident, and is in part the subject of *The Decameron* and *The Heptameron*—respectable people often have embarrassing secrets. It is not a very subtle or ambitious work—but its importance was enhanced by the fact of banning. Every banned novel makes the world in which it is banned more and more like itself—a place where individuals have inner lives that they protect and points of view that they value; a place where people of like minds connect through reading the novel, even when it is difficult to do so; a place where prohibited types of connections, often sexual ones, are actively pursued as gestures of resistance, where pressure from the outside reinforces the zone of privacy; and where moral rules are seen to be questions of taste, mores, and custom.

Early novels wrestled with these issues over and over, and their authors had to commit themselves to one side or the other. Though Cervantes seems to have been familiar with and influenced by *Lazarillo de Tormes,* and certainly *The Heptameron,* he decided that sexuality and manly virtue could not be reconciled. It is no coincidence that

Quixote and Sancho leave Quixote's estate and pass most of the plot in the out-of-doors, a public world, where they are subject to the observation and opinions of a multitude of other characters. Part of the comedy of the plot is that Quixote has been misled by the romances he loves to read, and at one point his housekeeper and his servants decide to wall up his library so that not only can he not get at it, he is also supposed to wonder whether it ever existed. Books—romances, in fact, about love—are dangerous. Is Cervantes agreeing with this idea or making fun of it? At this point it is impossible to say, but the effect of *Don Quixote* on the subsequent history of the novel was to shift respectability away from depictions of sex, even as a component of love (private drama), and toward depictions of violence (public drama).

Nevertheless, throughout the eighteenth century, issues of sexuality were the ones that powered the rise of the novel, and authors tried various methods to put them over, including anonymity (Defoe); wit (Fielding); endless, and perhaps numbing, detail (Richardson); a cautionary tone (Susanna Rowson in *Charlotte Temple,* the best-selling novel in the United States at the end of the eighteenth century and the beginning of the nineteenth); and sheer brazen excess (de Sade). On the surface, it may be that the subject of romance seemed simple as well as appealing to eighteenth-century authors—what could be easier than to bring the attractive young woman and the manly fellow to the altar after a few exciting adventures? It is the standard plot of a multitude of plays. But in fact, the use of actors and the public nature of the stage circumscribed what the authors could portray (as did, of course, laws against lasciviousness and public nakedness). As soon as a character is alone in her chamber, though, writing a letter, like Pamela, or hiding out, like Roxana, the pressure on propriety intensifies. The character may set out only to report his or her adventures, but because the novel always moves between action and reflection, soon enough he or she is bringing to bear his or her intentions, desires, regrets, fears, self-justifications, and other, more secret thoughts. If the character tries to merely report actions, they quickly become confusing because without feelings, actions don't carry enough emotional weight to remain clear in the reader's mind. But as soon as the character begins to develop a rationale for his or her actions, the narrative moves toward a confession. And what good is a confession if the character has nothing to confess—that is, no moral dilemma, no temptation to be delivered from? Without drama, a novel ceases to be entertaining and therefore loses its reason to exist.

In addition, of course, eighteenth-century novelists, like novelists before and after them, were eager to depict the world they lived in, and in the world they lived in seduction, sexual predation, rape, sexual slavery, marriages of convenience, marriages based solely on property considerations, prostitution, child abandonment, the sale of children into servitude of all kinds, and, of course, disease, suffering, and early death were commonplace. To raise the simple moral issue of whether a girl should be allowed to fall in love with the man of her own choice or be required to marry the man of her parents' choice was to enter into a train of logic that could lead to all sorts of much more complex and difficult moral questions.

One way to deal with these issues was to address their moral content directly, which is what Voltaire does in *Candide* (1759) when he has Dr. Pangloss propose that "everything is for the best in this best of all possible worlds." Candide himself, his beloved Cunegonde, and Dr. Pangloss then set out upon a whirlwind tour of the known world to test this hypothesis. The answer they come up with is considerably different and more brutal than the answer Quixote comes up with. Whereas Quixote is beaten from time to time, and tricked, and disillusioned, Candide finds wars, famines, epidemics, slavery, gratuitous brutality, and destruction of every kind—political, personal, environmental, social. No person and no place (except for El Dorado, far from Europe, entirely surrounded by impassable mountains, and rich beyond compare) is immune from the wholesale Hobbesian conflict of all against all, and no character, even the beautiful Cunegonde, is safe from the effects of the world. Evil is everywhere. *Candide* succeeds as a polemic, but it doesn't succeed as a novel, precisely because Voltaire sets out his program too clearly and hardly bothers with his novelistic duties of character and plot development. Surprisingly, it is the disreputable *Justine,* by the disreputable marquis de Sade, that makes the point Voltaire hoped to make with the impact Voltaire intended.

Justine was published in 1791, during the French Revolution, and the novel's theme, you might say, is the right of every man of rank to do whatever he wants with any woman he can gain access to, preferably by force. The catalog of brutalized and exploited women in *Justine* runs the gamut from legitimately married wives and daughters of great families to nameless girls from the streets and includes examples of every rank and type in between. According to de Sade, being sold into marriage is the least of it. Women are also sold into slavery, thievery, and prostitution; they are turned over by their guardians to tortur-

ers and necrophiliacs if their guardians themselves don't care to torture and rape them. Young girls are routinely betrayed by both women
and men, by those who like them and by those who hate them. The
only true and lasting motives of anyone in de Sade's world are greed
first and lust second (those who are less lusty gain more profit), though
expounding various theories is also a pastime of libertines of every
class. It is the explosion of theory that differentiates de Sade from Marguerite de Navarre's Hircan. For Hircan, the right to exploit women
is a matter of honor—it bolsters the God-given social order. For a
woman to rebel against it is a form of treason, or even blasphemy. In
Justine, the goal is not to reinforce the social order but to maximize the
exploitation of female flesh. If the women rebel or object, so much
the better in terms of excitement, because the more desirable goal for
the sadist is to inflict punishment since, as one of the men Justine meets
early in the novel tells her, regular sex with women is boring and also
damages the monetary value of the woman in question, especially if
she is young and can be sold into marriage for a large sum. What real
men really want is to be buggered by their servants.

When the men and women Justine meets on her journey around
France are not violating her, they are trying to convince her that even if
what they are doing to her is not right according to conventional
morality, then at least it's natural and inevitable. Many of the sexual
scenes are shockingly graphic, but many are politically shocking, too.
At one point Justine is standing in the shade of a tree, and she sees
a large, wealthy, and scenic monastery in the valley below her. She
goes there for refuge and is taken into a torture ring run by powerful
monks and church elders, who not only cruelly exploit and torture succeeding populations of girls and women, but also murder them for
pleasure and dispose of the bodies on the grounds of the monastery.
She and another girl attempt to escape; she succeeds, the other girl
doesn't. Justine's journey shows her the secret life of all of France—
every château, every wood, every house in town, every church, every
seat of secular or religious power hides one or more libertines, who
constitute a vast, informal conspiracy, or, you might say, a vast, corrupt
governing class unfettered by law or morality.

I don't think a modern reader can read *Justine,* even in the context of
other eighteenth-century novels, without wondering if even a portion
of what de Sade portrayed was true, or if it was all a projection on
his part. It seems obvious that de Sade wrote *Justine* for pornographic
reasons—that is, the plot and the protagonist are there to serve the

author's and the reader's shared desire to fetishize sex and cruelty and to use images for lascivious excitement. De Sade himself asserted that Justine was "capable of corrupting the devil" (possibly an example of authorial wishful thinking). Even so, while most eighteenth-century novels that portray rape, intended rape, or rape through false marriage more or less treat the issue as a personal one—a particular man attempting the virtue of a particular woman (only Defoe has a larger view of the structural disadvantages of womanhood), de Sade makes rape part of the apparatus of state control as expressed by individual members of the ruling class (most of whom possess formal authority; they are not renegades or rogues). He is also the only one who asserts that there is no virtue anywhere in the society—no one person who is not lustful, greedy, ready to kill for the slightest advantage. How does the author really feel about this state of affairs? On the one hand, various mouthpieces for his views make the case that nature is red in tooth and claw, so such cruel relations between people are natural and not to be resisted or regretted. On the other hand, he allows Justine to be unconvinced. In the end she wins, insofar as she is able; she never gives up her attachment to autonomy, and she is spared further suffering through sudden death. Justine is a true heroine; she never betrays herself, always tries to understand and survive, never loses her moral compass. Surely she speaks for the author as much as the men do.

Perhaps the political cast of Justine is accidental to the simple requirement of a novel to have a protagonist. If de Sade's purpose is to portray a world of tortures and temptations merely as a pornographic catalog, then Justine makes a good protagonist—in part a tour guide to this world, in part a foil for it—by striving for virtue. She does what protagonists do, for while it cannot be said that she is transformed by her journey, she is revealed as even more resolute than she appeared to be at the beginning. Perhaps de Sade is simply creating a logical scheme upon which he can hang his inhumane fantasies, but he does give Justine an articulate point of view. Though for the purposes of the plot, she must go on in a way that becomes almost purely existential, since she loses everything but her dignity and her identity and never has reason to hope for anything better than more torture, and is never convinced by the evidence of her own senses or by the arguments of the parade of libertines, she knows what she wants, and she continues to want it. However many times she is violated physically, she is never violated psychologically—she is as virtuous as Pamela at the end. And

the reader never betrays Justine, either, by sympathizing with her ex-
ploiters, no matter how eloquent they are in their arguments. When at
the end she opens a window and is struck by lightning, de Sade's ploy
to get himself out of the novel has the effect of an apotheosis—the singularity of Justine's death suits her singular ability to endure and
becomes a type of anointing. *Justine* shows that whatever an author's
motives for depicting horror, the form of the novel itself molds the
depiction. Ostensibly shocking and immoral, *Justine* actually promotes
a certain moral point of view—that integrity and virtue can be retained and recognized in the face of relentless suffering. In addition, to
expose secret corruption is to challenge its existence because of the
nature of the novel as a common and available commodity.

The degree to which we comfortably read novels that were once
banned, proscribed, or denounced is the degree to which we are
trained by the novel to accept the ambiguous public/private nature of
novels as a whole. If the private side of the novel promotes depictions
of sex, then the public side promotes depictions of violence, which we
also read in private. Because all lengthy written prose narratives with
protagonists concern tension or conflict between the protagonist and
the group, the moral implications of social conflict have always been a
subject of the novel. One way of noting how this works is to look at the
Icelandic sagas, which seem to have been invented entirely to explore
this issue. Violence is as tempting to the writer, of course, as sex,
because it raises the stakes of the plot to a high and dramatic level,
which is enhanced further by the facility with which the author can
move between the blows delivered and the thoughts of those delivering them. Scenes of violence in a novel, for example, don't have to be
burdened by exclamations and asides, like sword fights on the stage;
the reader gets the dual suspense of the progress of the fight combined
with the hidden and usually different progress in the intentions and
reactions of the fighters. As with sexual issues, though, the author
always finds himself wrestling with extra moral questions that an apparently simple fight poses.

   A saga begins with a misfit who gets into a conflict with those
around him. He may be a fairly decent or respected man whose conflict is almost accidental, such as Gisli, in *Gislasaga,* or he might be a
naturally aggressive and pugnacious individual, such as Egil, in *Egilssaga,* but he always has some quality that sets him apart to begin with

(women characters may have these qualities also). In the course of the narrative, a combination of personality and circumstances or luck or fate expands the conflict until it becomes an unresolvable feud. At each stage of the rising action, men of importance attempt to resolve the issues by assigning blame and penalties of outlawry or forfeiture of property or money, and, at every stage of the conflict, some example of graphic violence is included in the narrative—heads are hacked off, men are cut in two from neck to crotch, a man continues to fight while holding his intestines together with his shirt, a family is burned alive in their house. In some cases, as with Gisli and Egil, the misfit is simply too strong a personality to accept his punishment. In other cases, as in *Njalssaga,* the two sides continue to inflame the situation by provoking one another in spite of the penalties. As the conflict spreads through the district—or, indeed, the whole country—the violence gets more graphic. The saga ends either when the misfit is killed, as with Gisli, or when the group can no longer tolerate the violence the feud has sparked, as in *Njalssaga.*

The thirteenth and fourteenth centuries in Iceland were marked by violence and lawlessness all over the island. The probable author of *Egilssaga,* Snorri Sturluson, was himself killed by political rivals. The situation became so desperate in the middle of the fourteenth century that the Icelanders gave up their independence and asked the Norwegian king to resume control of the island (control of Iceland from Europe continued then for six hundred years, until after the Second World War, when the Danes, who succeeded the Norwegians, gave Iceland independence). The history of the sagas shows that Icelanders of the thirteenth and fourteenth centuries wrestled constantly with the nature of social unrest, sometimes locating its origin in personalities, sometimes in circumstances, but testifying always to its ubiquity. In every saga, ever-present weapons and volatile personalities combine to injure the group. But the sagas also show that freedom and intransigence have an appeal—the saga authors can't help admiring the strength of such personalities as Egil, who is not attractive in any way, being churlish, beetle-browed, and short-tempered. He represents some essential Icelandic quality of irreducible independence opposed to the effete courtiers of the Norwegian king. Even so, while the sagas were deeply indebted to the epic tradition and existed side by side with Icelandic epic poems, they were closer to novels than epics. The essential purpose of sagas was not to glorify the regrettable necessity of slaughter—gods like Zeus and Krishna do not enter into the action and try to influence or advise the characters—but to measure the social costs of individualism and its corollary, freedom.

After the Icelanders turned over their government to the king of Norway, the saga, one of the greatest forms of literature in the history of civilization, went out of fashion, replaced by tales and poems that are more like folklore than novels. Without the social struggles that marked the saga era, and the dilemmas of freedom that are so like those that Europeans and their descendants have faced in the past three hundred years, the Icelandic form of the lengthy written prose narrative with a protagonist had no reason to exist.

Novelists gradually became more adept at analyzing what has turned out to be one of the novel's most fertile subjects, the morality of personal relationships, which seems, on the surface, to avoid both the pitfalls of sex and the pitfalls of violence. Perhaps the works of Jane Austen are our paradigm. Her six novels are deemed entirely safe for consumption by the most innocent of readers; "evil" hardly enters her world, except in the form of insensitivity or rudeness. Of course, the smooth acceptability of Austen's work turns out to be an illusion— underneath her proper sentiments and her perfectly modulated tone of ironic reserve there is a sharp, irreverent, and even revolutionary spirit. But in her explorations of personal relationships, she showed that it was possible to write serious, astute, and sophisticated "domestic" novels, and these sorts of novels, largely avoiding both sex and violence, became the staple of the nineteenth century.

Even in these novels, though, potential moral issues abound, along with the power to shock the reader, and far more shockingly cruel, in its way, than *Justine* is that staple of middle school, *Wuthering Heights*. No one has ever considered *Wuthering Heights* to be unsuitable for young girls; most women read it for the first time when they are thirteen or fourteen. There are no sex scenes in *Wuthering Heights,* and many readers doubt whether the lovers, Cathy and Heathcliff, ever have sex. She is a young girl when he runs away; there is no suggestion that she has been unchaste. She is a married woman when he returns; there is no suggestion that she betrays her husband. Whether Heathcliff has ever made love to another woman by the time he returns is moot—he is obsessed with Cathy and appears to have thought of nothing else in his time away. No doubt part of the reason girls love *Wuthering Heights* is that it may (only the author knows for sure) portray the most passionate love as asexual and entirely spiritualized, rather like standing on a high promontory and feeling the wind blowing off the moors. At the same time, there are no beatings or shootings in *Wuthering Heights*. The only blood shed is by a ghost in a dream.

Nevertheless, the theme of *Wuthering Heights* is that any betrayal, any cruelty, any indifference to others, including spouses and children, is, if not justifiable, then understandable, in the context of sufficient passion. A woman who returns to *Wuthering Heights* as an adult most likely feels more uncomfortable with Heathcliff, in particular, than she did as a girl. For one thing, and this is not unimportant, Heathcliff is rude by choice. Since charm is one of the qualities that keeps readers reading, Heathcliff's rudeness has to be compensated for, and it never is. For another, Heathcliff is wantonly cruel to young Catherine and Hareton (whom he has betrayed as a father figure by failing to educate him in any way), because he means to avenge himself upon their dead parents through them, moment by moment and day by day. He oppresses, neglects, and abuses them because they are who they are. In other words, his only redeeming quality grows increasingly abstract as the novel progresses, and he doesn't develop any new ones. The Heathcliff of the novel is not played by Laurence Olivier. He is played by your scary Uncle Hugo, who never liked you for a moment.

None of the characters of *Wuthering Heights* is a model of goodness, and all of their crimes are interpersonal ones. The older Cathy is capricious and selfish; her daughter is cross and petty (though kind, in the end, to Hareton). Hindley is a mean drunk, Edgar is long-suffering but weak, and Edgar's sister is spoiled and impetuous. Young Linton is, as Heathcliff truthfully observes, the worst of the bunch, though that amounts only to being whiny, imperious, and irritating. That nearly everyone comes to a bad end is not the satisfaction that it might be, though, because the reader's experience of the general bad nature of the whole crew is prolonged. Do the characters of *Wuthering Heights* perpetrate even a grain of the harm that the characters of *Justine* do? No. Does *Wuthering Heights* seem in the end to be a nastier novel than *Justine* does? Yes. They are similar in that both are unrelieved and both have endings that are happy relative to the rest of the novel. But it is more disheartening to read about Heathcliff's domestic sins than it is to see the crimes of the ruling class exposed, because the exposure of political crimes seems like a step toward ameliorating them, while Heathcliff's cruelties are specifically directed at those he should be nurturing, and only chance intervenes between him and his victims—

exposure only reminds us of how pervasive domestic abuse is. The paradox is that novelists ended up exploring the rich subject of the morality of interpersonal relationships only to discover that while, on the one hand, this subject was safe from the dangers of sex and violence, on the other hand, achieving in such plots the satisfying feeling of redress is difficult if not impossible.

One of the particular vocations of the novel from the beginning has been the portrayal of brutes, criminals, and psychopaths. The first story of *The Decameron* takes as its protagonist the wickedest man in the world, who likes to lie and steal, who is sexually deviant, who even lies when he is giving his last confession. What we know about his crimes, though, is narrated, because every time he speaks, he lies. The reader accepts him as the paradigm of evil because the other characters of the tale report that he is and Boccaccio's cast of listeners accept their judgment. The story works only if his evil nature is a premise rather than subject to discussion or proof. Boccaccio gives this tale a lot of space, but he doesn't develop his evil character's state of mind in any way. The evil characters in *The Heptameron* are presented in a similarly cut-and-dried way, but Marguerite and her fellow critics speculate about the motives of some of the more egregious perpetrators more than Boccaccio's listeners do. Most eighteenth-century novelists were much interested in motives and rationales for evil actions (Henry Fielding, for example, who seems ebullient and earthy in *Tom Jones,* explored darker themes in *Jonathan Wild* and *Amelia*), and eighteenth-century novels are full of immorality and crime (perhaps the lengthiest depiction of the mind of a heartless seducer is Lovelace, in Samuel Richardson's *Clarissa*). Eighteenth-century libertines and murderers want to communicate. Authors couch their characters' self-revelations as confessions, letters, diaries, and testaments (for example, the memoir of James Hogg's "Justified Sinner"). Even in the Romantic period, as with Lermontov's *A Hero of Our Time* and Julien Sorel in *The Red and the Black,* the psychopath readily enters into the world of communication.

All the way up through the beginning of the nineteenth century, evil was viewed by novelists (as well as other writers and thinkers) as a constant of human nature. A typical example of how evil was depicted is to be found in the work of Sir Walter Scott, not much read now but wildly popular in its own day. Scott's novels regularly took up large social issues. In several novels, he concerned himself with the Scottish religious wars of the seventeenth century, which were bitterly contested ideological conflicts with lingering doctrinal, social, and political ramifications. In Scott's novels, villainy (opportunism, rudeness, snobbishness, unkindness, narrow-mindedness, willingness to do violence) occurs randomly, and membership in certain groups does not automatically translate into venality—some clergymen are decent, others are fanatical; some aristocrats are kind, others are brutal; some ideologues are honorable, others are self-serving. Scott subtly shows how, in times of ideological ferment, virtuous acts and evil acts grow out of the shifting combination in every individual of temperament, circumstances, beliefs, and desires. Events and character interact in a classically tragic way—outcomes have a fated quality. The painful effect of dramatic irony is muted by distance from the period of the narrative—Scott is careful to include images of the peaceful graves of his characters that remind the reader that the passions that motivated the conflicts have vanished as thoroughly as the conflicts themselves— and there is no sense that things could have turned out, or could turn out, differently. Even in a novel as passionately dramatic as Scott's *The Bride of Lammermoor,* in which, as a result of being forced to marry against her will, a young girl kills her new husband and then herself goes mad, a sense of peace and resignation result from the traditional idea that the combination of character and circumstances will always result in what we realize in retrospect was inevitable. One of Scott's innovations, artistically, was to take traditional tragic patterns and apply them, not just to kings and princes, but also to a whole society of characters, high and low, male and female, victorious or defeated. Another was to pay close attention, even in the context of the Gothic- seeming plot *The Bride of Lammermoor,* to the intricacies of psychological and sociological cause and effect. Gothic tales such as *The Mysteries of Udolpho,* by Ann Radcliffe, were all the rage in Scott's day, and he puts plenty of uncanny incidents into his novel, which is set in a gloomy castle in the Highlands where superstitions are the norm, but he links his heroine's fate not to these, but to the stress of her difficult position as a pawn in her mother's quest for power, and the effects upon her own sensitive and uncomprehending nature of the conflicting strong personalities around her. Mysterious events, such as the ominous disappearance of a portrait, have an effect, but only heighten the sense of fear and anxiety already created by concrete conflicts and events. Scott's ability to lucidly synthesize threads of cause and effect much inspired Charles Dickens, who read his works avidly as a young man, but Dickens wasn't interested in the past. He was interested in the present.

In the nineteenth century the theory of evil changed, which changed the nature of morality in the novel, and therefore the portrayal of brutes, criminals, and psychopaths. What was really at the heart of the nature of good and evil, novelists realized, was secrecy and, indeed, silence.

It seems that Charles Dickens, the most influential English author of the nineteenth century, was genuinely drawn to criminals and psychopaths. From the time of *Oliver Twist* (written when Dickens was in his midtwenties), all the way until the end of his career, he excelled at depicting nasty brutes: Sikes, who beats his girlfriend to death in a rage (*Oliver Twist*); Quilp, a choleric, garrulous thief and bully (*The Old Curiosity Shop*); Murdstone, a cold and socially respected tyrant (*David Copperfield*); and Carker, the smiling and Iago-like betrayer (*Dombey and Son*). Every Dickens novel has a different variety—sometimes lascivious, sometimes greedy, sometimes power-mad, sometimes vengeful (Madame Defarge), sometimes merely small and mean (Uriah Heep), but always richly, and even gleefully, realized. Dickens was superbly inventive, but never more so than in his exploration of the psychology of evil. What is important, technically, is that, with each new novel, his way of portraying his perpetrators becomes less and less dramatic and more and more internal. Sikes vents his inner rage when he beats Nancy. He is eloquent as well as cruel, and that's all we need to know about him. Ten years later, in *Dombey and Son,* Dickens portrays Carker the Manager, who plans to steal both Dombey's wife and his fortune. The way in which Dickens's prose slips easily into Carker's mind, revealing to the reader his secret thoughts and plans, especially how the world appears and feels to him, is so effortless that it doesn't seem like anything new, but it is. Carker's inner life is known only to him and to the reader, and his schemes excel in seductive psychological plausibility, drawing the reader into their logic as if Carker were the protagonist, not the villain. The growing internalization of the psychology of all of his characters was a feature of Dickens's work as he matured—in *Dombey and Son,* for example, his characters convincingly and movingly coexist inside the novel, physically together but cut off from one another by differing and often mutually exclusive perceptions of the world that are overcome only through enormous effort. Such insights into the nature of human isolation and subjectivity constitute a large part of Dickens's gift to his readers, but the application of this idea and of Dickens's gift for empathy with sociopathic personalities constitutes a philosophy that has had enormous effect on how modern people understand evil as a form of logic, and even of madness that is internally consistent, unrecognized as evil by the perpetrator, and compelling. By the end of his career, Dickens was as good as anyone who has ever lived at clarifying the motivations of those who harm others.

To each novelistic psychopath of the Dickensian sort, his crimes make perfect sense, and as the reader comes to understand the logic, she is tempted to understand the sense, to become, in some way, less horrified at what has been done and more accepting of violent personalities in general. One effect of this technique is that old questions of sin, evil, and transgression of social norms become, with empathy (which is, remember, not "feeling with" but "perceiving with"), new questions of sanity and mental illness. When the novelist makes the reader understand a logic based on horrific premises, is the malefactor distanced from his humanity, or is humanity enlarged to encompass his logical facility? The novel explores this question repeatedly and offers no convincing conclusion.

At the same time, like Scott, Dickens explored cause and effect—what has made Ralph Nickleby, Scrooge, Jasper, and Headstone the way they are? Some of his explanations are more convincing than others. For example, John Jasper, in *The Mystery of Edwin Drood,* smokes opium, which may explain the extreme degree of his calculating isolation; Scrooge not only has had an impoverished childhood, but also went into business with a partner who encouraged his miserly proclivities. In his most insightful portrayal, that of Bradley Headstone, the stalker in *Our Mutual Friend,* Dickens shows how Bradley's shame at his class origins has combined with his temperamental proclivities (envy and self-repression) to engender an uncontrollable murderous paranoia and obsession. Even when Dickens's specific psychological theories don't hold water, the idea of cause and effect, the idea that there can be a theory of evil (and goodness), does. As early as *Oliver Twist,* Dickens is laying out a how-to manual for making criminals—first you deny them porridge and all sense of self-respect, then you give them criminal associates and teach them a few skills, such as picking pockets and engaging in prostitution. It is a very short step from this sort of causal logic to the advocacy of political and social

solutions for what had always been considered individual moral failings, and Dickens readily made it.

But the novel that had the most sensational effect on the moral life
of its times was *Uncle Tom's Cabin,* the best-selling novel of the nineteenth century in the United States, and a big seller in England and in
Europe, too (both Dickens and Tolstoy read it). Stowe began with a
polemical purpose—to promote the abolition of slavery by disseminating stories of life on southern plantations that she heard from escapees
passing through Cincinnati (where she lived) on the Underground
Railroad. She couched her argument in starkly moral terms, invoking
Christian principles and ideals as a matter of course, and depicting
fairly openly for the period both the physical violence and the sexual
license that slavery produced. Stowe, who lost a young child to illness, was especially moved by the plight of mothers and children who
were separated by traffic in slaves and as a result of slave-breeding
establishments—two of her most memorable characters are Cassy,
whose children have been sold away from her, and Topsy, bred in a
slave-breeding establishment and allowed to grow up without any
nurture whatsoever. But the main protagonist and antagonist are Tom
and Simon Legree, who represent good and evil, respectively. What
distinguishes them from characters of melodrama (at least in the novel,
which engendered any number of stage melodramas throughout the
nineteenth century) is Stowe's analysis of, on the one hand, Tom's
choices in the course of his martyrdom, and on the other, Legree's origins, motives, and psychology. Tom makes virtuous choices for logical
and believable reasons. At the beginning, he allows himself to be sold
south because he knows enough to fear that if the plantation he lives
on goes bankrupt, his whole family is in jeopardy. Once in New
Orleans, he continues to hope that his kindly but feckless master will
free him, as he promises. Once on Legree's plantation, Tom knows
that he is so lost in the bayous of southern Louisiana that escape is a
long shot, and though a slave rebellion is conceivable, a positive outcome is not likely. In addition, Tom is a man of faith who truly believes
that this world is passing, and his real home is with his Savior—why
jeopardize his salvation when very little good is likely to come of it?

Legree has no faith but is supremely superstitious. A hard and
greedy northerner originally, he has no personal or spiritual resources,
no friends, and no sense of order or aesthetic pleasure. His only recre-
ation is drinking, but drinking renders him violent and paranoid. At

no point does Stowe cause the reader to feel sympathy for Legree, but she does provide a believable analysis for his absolute lack of fellow feeling not only toward his slaves but also toward everyone else, and she links this analysis to her analysis of slavery in the United States—the southerners may own the slaves, but northern banks provide the money, earn much of the profit, and turn a blind eye to the injustice of the system.

Stowe's ideas were not original, but the sharp delineation of character required by a novel as opposed to a sermon or an essay aided Stowe's moral crusade because she was able to systematically set up and demolish every argument for slavery by inserting into the reader's head vivid, dramatic set pieces that engaged the reader's emotions while undercutting each proslavery rationale. *Uncle Tom's Cabin* brilliantly employs the natural rhetorical tools of the novel form. It eavesdrops on the private conversations of black characters, and lo and behold, they are intelligent, brave, virtuous, funny, charming—in short, they irradicably demonstrate that slaves are human. It promotes freedom by vividly depicting tyranny. It puts characters such as Miss Ophelia (from New England) and Augustine St. Claire (from New Orleans) in situations where they have to discuss their options and make choices, and because they are sympathetic characters, the reader wants them to make sympathetic choices. As Tom travels from his natal plantation in Kentucky down the river to New Orleans and then into the swamps of Louisiana, he is repeatedly discussed, by slave owners and slave dealers and other slaves—his journey toward martyrdom is Stowe's beautifully disguised catalog of arguments for and against slavery. In the early 1850s, when she was writing, catalogs of arguments for and against slavery were rife, but only the novel form, and Stowe's adept handling of it, could change the terms of the discussion and renew the issues in a way that galvanized millions of people and caused President Lincoln to greet her, some years later, with the remark "So this is the little lady who made this big war." Repeatedly, in *Uncle Tom's Cabin,* Stowe asks the reader to consider and decide the larger and smaller emotional and moral questions of slavery. In the many months that the novel ran serially in the *National Era,* Stowe gave her readers steady practice in deciding against slavery, and in understanding causal relationships between the system of slavery and its moral effects.

What nineteenth-century novelists discovered was that the exploration of cause and effect that is natural to the novel mitigates the idea that evil is random, and that the requirement of the novel form that the protagonist be in a continuously depicted relationship with his society has the effect of placing responsibility. As soon as responsibility is apportioned, both author and reader start to feel that evil can be fixed, and fixed by amateurs, since the novel is always an amateur production. The effect of novels by Dickens, Stowe, and their contemporaries (which were, in some sense, the cultural phenomena of their day similar to *Star Wars* or *Sex and the City* in our day) was to make morality a political question—a discussion of good and bad individual actions and their effects, as always, but also of wealth, power, and influence. The novel has certain inherent characteristics—it is naturally democratic; it promotes individuality and freedom; it is intimate and sociable and connective; it elevates inner life over appearance; it is, often in spite of itself, hopeful; and it is naturally popular. These qualities fit into and exemplify the idea of the modern liberal society and in the course of the nineteenth century came to be seen as moral issues (though they can as easily contradict another sort of society's system of morality as uphold it).

The great conflict of the twentieth century concerned whether morality was made up of a set of personal choices having to do with right and wrong behavior, as described by, say, the Ten Commandments, or whether it was made up of a set of political choices having to do with the inequitable distribution and abuse of power and wealth. All sorts of social and economic institutions that had once been considered more or less the natural order of things became moral dilemmas (and zones of ideological conflict)—slavery, marriage and domestic abuse, child labor, the rewards of capital versus the rewards of labor, genocide in war or as an act of conquest, exploitation and destruction of natural resources, the impoverishment of the human spirit as an effect of labyrinthine and secretive bureaucracy. The novel promoted this moral shift. The novel as a form is usually seen to be moral if its readers consider freedom, individuality, democracy, privacy, social connection, tolerance, and hope to be morally good, but it is not considered moral if the highest values of a society are adherence to rules and traditional mores, the maintenance of hierarchical relationships, and absolute ideas of right and wrong. Any society based on the latter will find novels inherently immoral and subversive.

All through the nineteenth century, novelists explored and exposed social abuses, thereby constantly forcing the moral and the political, the personal and the public, to interpenetrate. Dickens and Stowe had plenty of company—Eliot, Dostoevsky, Hawthorne, Tolstoy, Balzac, Zola, and countless others. Machiavelli would have been appalled. But Machiavelli did not have to contend with a citizenry that was entertaining itself on long train journeys with novels—that is, with routine contemplation of political and moral questions about social and economic arrangements.

If reading a novel is an act that underscores the reader's feelings of agency in a way that audience-based forms of art do not have to, and if novel-readers have no other experience of choice, just this one may indeed politicize them. The novel always promotes moral questions as capable of being understood and decided by individuals. This is part and parcel of the novel's natural allegiance to the notion that things are not as they appear. If things are not as they appear, then the individual (author or character or reader) is required to divine how they really are and to understand the contrast between how they appear to others and how they appear to him. But the protagonist, as he comes to understand the difference between reality and appearance, also is required to sacrifice something. Typically, the equation works as follows: If he sacrifices his own sense of truth, then he is dishonored. If he sacrifices love, life, wealth, position, or any other commonly accepted good in favor of his own sense of truth, then he is damaged or destroyed but not dishonored. If he can mesh inner truth and outer truth with only the sacrifice of illusions or foolish expectations, then he is a character in a comic novel. But in any case, the novel is absolutely wedded to point of view and therefore must train its readers to see that things are not as they appear even if, perhaps, they are; it also trains its readers to make the honorable choice—that is, one's own truth over accepted truths.

Nineteenth-century novelists explored all sorts of moral and political ideas, but the one they kept returning to, the one most central to the novel, was the question of female virtue, which is simultaneously the most apparently personal, the most socially and politically explosive, and the most inflammatory. Just as Dickens and Stowe recast issues of stealing, killing, coveting, pride, avarice, sloth, lust, and even gluttony, anger, and envy as social constructs and political questions, so Gustave Flaubert changed the traditional critique of how and why women exist. *Madame Bovary* is an especially good example of how, without even meaning to, a novelist may transform the world simply by observing it. Flaubert, who had none of the reformist ambitions of Dickens and Stowe, famously remarked, *"Madame Bovary, c'est moi."*

On the surface, this makes no sense. Flaubert is careful to describe Emma in a very particular way—a pretty young woman of peasant background who is not well educated, who marries a man she doesn't care for, and then gets involved in several affairs with other men who treat her badly. She finally commits suicide, leaving behind her a very confused husband and an uncomprehending daughter. Flaubert shows that Emma has no real taste or discrimination and is incapable of any sort of higher mental life. She is out of the ordinary in the stubbornness of her aspirations for some sort of relief from French provincial existence, but entirely ordinary in all of her talents and capacities. Flaubert depicts her minutely but mercilessly and coldly—there is no sense, as in, say, *Moll Flanders* or *Vanity Fair,* that the author has respect or grudging fondness for his heroine. Nor do Emma's problems seem to be caused by the society in which she lives—although many of those around her cheat and betray her, the tone of the novel suggests that everyone is doing the best he can do given his circumstances, and that the circumstances of French provincial life are not amenable to change (unlike the public health system in London, for example, or the existence of Negro slavery in the United States).

What Flaubert adds to Emma is his own experience of the sensuousness of things. When Emma and Rodolphe are walking or driving, for example, the movement of the leaves in the trees or the passage of the carriage down the road is ravishing—to Emma and to the author, and therefore to the reader. To motivate Emma's fall, Flaubert infuses her inner life with exceptional richness, with what must have been his own sensitivity to sensation and to feeling. *Madame Bovary* was an instant and lasting success. Flaubert's embrace of Emma's way of experiencing things imparted to the novel a new degree of psychological insight and refinement and complicated the reader's experience of her lack of traditional virtue. This is not on the surface political, especially since "character is fate" for Emma as much as for the hero of any tragic play. Emma's road to her destiny is a train track downhill, and there is no sense that she can get off the train.

But it is evident that there is something wrong with Emma, and pretty soon the reader begins to wonder about cause and effect. Is her persistent inability to fit into and accept her life her own fault or the fault of the provincial existence that the author clearly disdains? And if the problem lies within, is it something inborn, like looks or temperament, or does it have its origins in some life circumstance—motherlessness, perhaps? While Flaubert follows Emma's ups and downs seemingly moment by moment, he makes no suggestions about the reasons for her lack of fit. How she experiences her discomfort and dissatisfaction is how he represents it. He is more observant than she is, but as an artist, he clearly understands that if he were to subject her to some sort of analysis based on superior understanding, her fall would seem less inevitable and less dramatic. She would go back to being a typical young woman with no strength of character, whom the reader could easily judge and dismiss. The immediacy of his depiction, though, only strengthens the reader's tendency to wonder about the causes and effects that Flaubert ignores. As a result of Flaubert's technique and his identification with Emma, the astute reader can't help wondering whether, if the causes and effects of Emma's mental condition were understood more clearly (better than by the author or the narrator, let's say), perhaps an answer (or a cure) would present itself. And this response is a private one. The reader is not influenced by public conventions, such as those of the stage or the opera, to view the character's fate as a form of spectacle, but rather to view it as very akin to her own fate or the fate of a friend (and gossips always believe that they know what's best for the subject of the gossip, if only she would listen to them).

Obviously, the rise of psychoanalysis (Freud was born a year before *Madame Bovary* was published), both as a theory and as a consumer good, grows out of this idea that causes can be traced and effects modified, and that a prolonged effort to do so is possible and even justified for the most average, Emma-like, readerlike person. Whether or not Freud ever read *Madame Bovary,* we can't help but think that Emma would present a tempting case for him, that he would diagnose her as hysterical, and that he would guide her into talking her way into fitting with the life she cannot abide (in our day, we would be tempted to diagnose her, too, maybe as bipolar or depressed, and to treat her with drugs). By giving Emma his own sensibility in such careful detail, Flaubert succeeds not only in writing a great novel but also in authoring the first, but by no means the last, case history. Just as an overtly political novel such as *Uncle Tom's Cabin* sparks a political response— the nation can be changed to fix injustice—a profoundly psychological novel sparks a response based in psychology—a person can be changed to fit her circumstances (especially if they are defined as all human circumstances). A traditionally moral issue, that of lust (and Emma lusts for all sorts of pleasures, not just sexual ones), becomes a medical one.

And just as the social nature of the novel as a form requires injustice to be redressed, it also requires that personal suffering be relieved.

We cannot imagine the characters of *The Decameron* or *The Heptameron,* with all their troubles, saying "What's wrong with me?" Like Roxana or Robinson Crusoe, they might say "How have I sinned and what am I going to do about it?" After centuries of education by novels, though, the average person has come to be routinely introspective, and to substitute therapeutic dilemmas and political questions for moral rules. All of the ways that morality and politics are tangled together in the novel come together in Marcel Proust's *À la recherche du temps perdu (In Search of Lost Time)*. M., the protagonist and narrator of Proust's seven volumes, has one primary rhetorical task—to maintain the reader's willingness to keep reading until he really gets to the essential points of his argument in volume seven, nearly four thousand pages into the novel; he must make himself attractive, or at least fascinating. He does so by characterizing himself in great detail, and these are some of his characteristics: he is tolerant and accepting of differences in lifestyles, opinions, and ways of doing things; he never demeans groups such as servants, homosexuals, or Jews that are routinely demeaned by others; he has good manners and acts in a generally kind way; he is a supporter of Dreyfus, the Jewish officer in the French army who was slandered and wrongfully imprisoned in the 1890s; he is skeptical of those who claim or seek power and influence; he is good at detecting hypocrisy, self-aggrandizement, social cruelty, and subtle rudeness in those around him, and he shows these qualities to be ridiculous and demeaning; he accepts that humans are complex, with both good and bad characteristics, and he also accepts that good and bad characteristics have little or no relation to success and failure. He is, in other words, the ideal liberal protagonist who speaks even of his own passions judiciously and analytically. He is, also, perhaps, unique in the history of the novel in his ability to hold a reader's interest at length. But M. has what most people would consider immoral proclivities with regard to young women of a Lolita age. He likes to exploit such girls and from time to time reports on his exploits. He shares several characteristics with the men in *Justine*—his most dramatic and in many ways significant accomplishment is to keep his young girlfriend, Albertine, imprisoned in his family home, restricting her movements and enforcing what amounts to solitude for some months, until she finally flees. He is as cruel and narcissistic in his

imprisonment of Albertine as Humbert Humbert is in his imprisonment of Lolita, and exhibits far less shame. And yet Humbert, because
he is disdainful and snobbish in his expressions, rather nasty in his
treatment of others, and always unsociable (in comparison with M.'s
ever-flowing sociability), is a model villain, while M. generally gets a
pass on the villainy front because he is adept at arousing in the reader
both sympathy and empathy. A significant feature of his success in
obtaining the reader's forgiveness for his immoral acts is that the
whole subject of his seven-volume novel is cause and effect; throughout the narrative, he continuously traces threads of psychological and
sociological connection. He often considers the question of what might
be wrong with him, and in the end his very ability to consider it so
thoroughly persuades the reader either to accept what is wrong with
him, or decide that whatever is wrong with him is worth the result. It
is a great rhetorical accomplishment.

Inevitably, as prefigured by *Justine,* the novel must amalgamate
politics and sex, and, as with *Justine,* many readers denounce the amal-
gamation on moral grounds when the real offense is political. A case
in point is *Lady Chatterley's Lover.* Though *Lady Chatterley's Lover*
was banned in England and in America because of its explicit scenes
of lovemaking, it has come to seem merely bracing in its frankness
about sexuality, while it still offers a fairly aggressive critique of early
twentieth-century English society. The premise is simple, and similar to the premise of any number of French novels—the wife of a
wealthy and landed gentleman, unsatisfied with her marriage, takes
up with another man, in this case the gamekeeper on the Chatterley
estate. The novel takes place in the wake of the First World War, and,
significantly, both men have served in the war and been changed by
it—Chatterley is paralyzed and confined to a wheelchair, while Mellors, the gamekeeper, has used the opportunity to become more sophisticated in his thinking and less subservient in his manner. Chatterley is
no long-suffering hero who has transcended his bodily injuries and
found a higher purpose. He is a querulous, whiny, dog-in-the-manger
sort who enjoys exerting the power he has, including his power over
his wife, Connie, just for the sake of seeing others acknowledge it.
Lawrence explicitly renders him as the representative of his class and
his nation in terms of both his economic power and his emasculation.
In spite of Chatterley's suffering, Lawrence isn't nice to him at all, and
that remains probably the only shocking element of the novel (though
there is one scene where, over dinner, Mellors and Connie's father dis-

cuss her sexual behavior in a way that seems more than crude, as well as politically incorrect, of course). Lawrence wrote in a traditional realistic style that makes his critique all the more straightforward and his sex scenes all the more confrontational. Part of the reason that *Lady Chatterley's Lover* has ceased to shock, however, is that it doesn't really challenge Connie's subordinate position. For the sake of sexual pleasure, she shifts "owners," from Chatterley to Mellors, but Mellors is gruff and rude and promises Connie only motherhood, not power or even agency. Nevertheless, the banning of *Lady Chatterley's Lover* had the characteristic effect of making the novel desirable and, in this case, eventually bringing the portrayal of sex on the page so much more into the literary mainstream that what once seemed shocking on the page (when the novel was printed in Italy and Lawrence's friend told him that it was a good thing the compositor couldn't read English or he might have refused to set the type) now seems quaint and sentimental.

Twentieth-century novelists were not able to return to the pre-Dickensian idea of evil as randomly distributed, causeless, and incorrigible, but it was not for lack of trying. Many twentieth-century novelists explicitly rejected the nineteenth-century project of social improvement, but the novel itself defied them. The best some novelists were able to do was return to a Jane Austen–like setting of manners and personal relationships, but all plots require conflict; once the nineteenth-century novelists had broadened the representable world and deepened the representable inner life, had applied complexity to both, and come up with ever more refined and intelligent logical connections, the novel's inherent political (and ideological) nature was revealed, and morality and politics in the novel could never be separated again.

7 · The Art of the Novel

For many generations, the novel had no pretensions to art. The novel was not rooted in classical rhetorical and imaginative forms, nor taught in schools and universities. Because novels were read for pleasure rather than "improvement," novelists were from the beginning autodidacts, reading their own, idiosyncratic "courses" of novels, picking and choosing what to emulate and imitate, often writing in secret and pleasing themselves first of all rather than teachers or scholars. Numerous novelists published anonymously or under pseudonyms—Madame de La Fayette, Daniel Defoe, Jane Austen, the Brontës, George Eliot—doing so because they had something to lose by claiming their work, usually respectability. Novelists who published under their own names were often those who were not socially prominent or who, like Samuel Richardson and Henry Fielding, already had literary lives before they began to write novels. Artistically, novelists were do-it-yourselfers, and what they knew about "the novel" they gleaned from their favorite authors. We know from their own testimony that Forster read James, James read Dickens, Dickens read Smollett, Smollett read Cervantes, Cervantes read Marguerite of Navarre, Marguerite read Boccaccio (and, of course, Forster read Cervantes, Dickens read Scott, Scott read Boccaccio, Scott read Cervantes, Fielding read Cervantes, Dickens read Cervantes, Woolf read Austen, Dickens, and James, Stendhal read Marguerite, Balzac read Stendhal, James read Balzac, Turgenev read Stendhal, Stendhal read Madame de La Fayette, Madame de La Fayette read Marguerite de Navarre, Dostoevsky read Turgenev, Tolstoy read Turgenev, Gogol read Turgenev, Turgenev read Lermontov, Lermontov read Scott, Tanizaki read Tolstoy, Dostoevsky, and Lady Murasaki, and so forth). Though some novelists have had classical educations, many, such as Defoe, Dickens, and almost every woman, had a Shakespeare-type education, "small Latin and less Greek." Many novelists' innovative and lively attachment to vernacular speech and up-to-the-minute forms of expression remained uncontaminated by the early drudgery of translating long passages of Latin and Greek. There was nothing "correct" about the novel to begin with (akin to, for example, the classical unities of the drama), and so every author was free to experiment with what might be incorrect but satisfying. When their own compositions became famous and popular, each novelist's techniques entered into both the narrative and the technical lexicon of the novel.

Seminal novelists and others made a technical contribution to the art of writing novels along with a contribution to the treasury of stories, settings, and characters—later novelists testified to their influence. Cervantes showed not only that a long narrative of an innocent man traveling about the countryside had virtually unlimited plot possibilities, but also that a narrative voice talking about such adventures in a chatty way was both agreeable and reassuring. Madame de La Fayette showed not only that all three participants in a love triangle could be equally sympathetic, but also that a narrator could efface herself sufficiently to seem to enter transparently into the thoughts of each of the participants, thereby raising the story above the level of gossipy speculation into the realm of philosophy. When Daniel Defoe wrote in the different voices of Robinson Crusoe, Moll Flanders, H. F., Roxana, and the others, he showed that an author could do two things at one time—observe his protagonist and embody him—giving the reader a rich empathetic experience while maintaining control of the themes that the life of the protagonist represented. When Fielding combined the conventions of stage comedy with the peripatetic adventures of an apparent reprobate, he showed that the juxtaposition of high and low was stimulating as well as broadening. When Lermontov placed his Byronic protagonist in the precisely and lyrically rendered landscape of the Caucasus, he showed how the Russian novel could be made both grand and irreducibly Russian in spite of imported ideas. When Balzac expanded his canvas by having major characters in one novel turn up as minor characters in others, he began to capture the kaleidoscopic variety of France and especially of Paris, but he also showed that while plots are good organizing devices and lenses for viewing particular lives and incidents, they do not need to dictate the roles particular characters, and, by extension, readers, play.

Each specific contribution was not necessarily *invented* by each seminal novelist. Every period was full of inventors and novelists who are now lost in general obscurity but who were nevertheless read by their contemporaries, whose new ideas were noticed and made use of. Technical ideas about the craft of novel-writing are not intellectual property except insofar as they are wedded to particular words written in particular sequences. Rather, techniques are subtle expansions of perception that stimulate a reader's thoughts about his own ideas and perceptions in new ways.* The novel, in fact, *requires* technical innovation, because there is simply no way to make the time pass and the characters exist within a particular setting without being inventive. Even if I set out to rewrite *Don Quixote* incident by incident with the merest detail changed (let's say, the action happens ten years after the action of the real *Don Quixote*), I will be presented with some challenge or other that requires a technical solution—perhaps the reign of one king has given way to that of another and two or three laws governing travel from town to town have changed, or deforestation has altered part of Quixote's landscape. If a handful of details about Quixote's journey are no longer plausible, then those details ramify into other scenes, and pretty soon I have a different novel altogether, as, indeed, Cervantes himself had a different novel altogether in the second volume of *Don Quixote* from the novel he had in the first. Great seminal novelists may or may not be more rawly original than their contemporaries; what they do is manage to wed originality of technique with depth of insight or breadth of knowledge or charm or some other quality that demonstrates the value of that technical innovation and makes it memorable to future novelists.

An author's technique grows out of his temperament, his intentions, and his ideas, but it also grows out of his circumstances. A good example is Laurence Sterne. Sterne was classically educated, at Cambridge University, and he became a clergyman in Yorkshire, but he had no money apart from his living and the fees he sometimes received for giving sermons in York Minster. Like Defoe, he plied his pen for some twenty years in service of partisan politics, at least in part as

---

*Sometimes the reader doesn't know how stimulated she has been. In retrospect, for example, I can see how much my novel *Moo* owes to David Lodge's novel *Small World,* but at the time, I perceived only that I loved Lodge's novel and that it gave me permission to loosely corral many characters into one capacious narrative rather than to focus on the adventures of a single protagonist. While I was reading *Small World,* I was focusing on the jokes and the Arthurian references. While I was writing *Moo,* I was thinking about coordinating the action of the plot to the period of the school year and working out the ecological theme and structure. *Small World* existed in my mind as a template I was semi-aware of (I had read it once) and remembered with fondness.

repayment for clerical preferments he received from powerful friends and relatives in and around York. The first two volumes of *The Life and Opinions of Tristram Shandy,* however, were conceived as explicitly nonpolitical, a reaction to having incurred the wrath of the Church of England in 1759 with a satire on church politics called "A Political Romance."

Sterne was surprised by *Tristram Shandy*'s wild success, but he reveled in it, even in the negative attention (Dr. Johnson was certain its popularity was a passing fad), and was soon a famous man, consorting with David Garrick, meeting the king, and having his portrait painted by Joshua Reynolds. As usual with best sellers, though, it quickly became apparent that the author had to keep writing to maintain the income stream. Sterne was more than willing to do whatever he could to sustain his popularity—one of the first ideas he had was to publish a volume of his own sermons under the name "Parson Yorick," a character in *Tristram Shandy,* implying an autobiographical link between the racy novel (which, of course, frankly discusses all sorts of bodily functions in addition to sex) and his career as a clergyman. Next, he composed two more volumes about Tristram, emphasizing what he considered to be its strongest selling point: eccentricity. Ultimately he published nine volumes in the 1760s, never changing his tone or his method, though gradually shifting his story away from Tristram and his parents toward the mild and mysterious eccentric Uncle Toby. In his embrace of his signature techniques—bawdy jokes, odd ideas and observations, digressions, thought association—in a ten-year effort to sustain sales, Sterne is almost a parody of novelists in general. And he was right. Though he tried another book—a travel narrative about a journey through France and Italy—it was not successful because it did not have that precise combination of subject and sensibility that seemed so original, and turned out to be so lasting, in *Tristram Shandy.*

With repeated employment, a certain technique ceases to be technical and comes to characterize an author's entire oeuvre and to constitute his original vision. Jane Austen claimed that her works were like miniatures painted on ivory—she was ambitious not for breadth, or even depth, but for precision. She not only knew what she wanted to do and could do (given her secluded life), she also knew how she was distinct from other novelists, and she liked to exploit her distinction. Her technique did not seem to limit her ability to grow, though—each successive heroine is different from the others, each new family is set

into a somewhat larger context than earlier families. Austen's miniatures expand and deepen without bursting off the ivory.

Anthony Trollope, more worldly and more ambitious than Austen
but possessed of a similar judicious, ironic style, wrote forty-seven novels by employing a rigorous system of composition that on the surface
does not even look like a technique as much as a lifestyle—when he
was planning *The Way We Live Now,* he scheduled himself to write
some ten thousand words per week and to complete the two-volume,
950-page (in the Oxford edition) novel in thirty-two weeks. He finished in twenty-nine weeks. For most of his writing career (from age
twenty until fifty-two) he worked as a civil servant in the post office—
he wrote his weekly ten thousand words beginning at about five-thirty
every morning. Trollope was no dull boy—he loved fox hunting,
socializing, traveling, eating, and drinking, and made time for a good
measure of each. In addition, Trollope, who, like Sterne, was sensitive
about the hardships of an impoverished childhood, cared a great deal
about "pecuniary emolument," as Jane Austen would have called it. In
Trollope's autobiography (begun when he was about sixty and published after his death) he related as many details about deals he had
made and the relative success or failure of each book as about more
personal aspects of his life or more artful aspects of his career. The
effect of his autobiography was to diminish his posthumous reputation
as a novelist, but the systematic approach he espoused as a way of succeeding professionally worked also as a narrative technique, a way of
exploring in great detail certain aspects of the inner life and of the
many facets of English bourgeois existence that he is famous for
anatomizing.

It is, of course, impossible to encapsulate Trollope's accomplishments in a few paragraphs, but a passage from *The Eustace Diamonds*
might convey something of his technique:

Lady Linlithgow, upon whom Lizzie's beauty could have no
effect of that kind, had nevertheless declared her to be very beautiful. And this loveliness was of a nature that was altogether
pleasing, if once the beholder of it could get over the idea of false-
ness which certainly Lizzie's eye was apt to convey to the beholder. [p. 358]

A few lines later, Trollope turns his attention to Lizzie's lover:

All this had been tendered to Frank—and with it that worldly wealth which was so absolutely necessary to his career. For though Greystock would not have said to any man or woman that nature had intended him to be a spender of much money and a consumer of many good things, he did undoubtedly so think of himself.

Trollope's methodical habits are evident in both these passages. In the midst of love, there is calculation—Lizzie's beauty against her false nature; Frank's desires and ambitions against his instinctive recognition of Lizzie's nature; and, in both cases, external appearance against internal truth. His style works the same way, though to more poignant effect, in *The Last Chronicle of Barset,* where the calculation is about a minor crime: Does the poor, charitable, passionate, but irritable and stiff-necked curate actually pass a bad check? And who of his associates is ready to believe such a thing, and who is unconvinced? Trollope is a genius of measurement—yes, in his autobiography, he counts up the money and totes up his success, but in his novels he weighs and balances and measures the ramifications of countless decisions, impulses, and feelings, recognizing always that in a tightly interconnected culture, the smallest wrong step can have dire consequences, but also that it is possible to think too much and thereby destroy happiness that impulse might have gained. Trollope was a great analyst of marriage as a series of decisions that turn into a relationship and then, as time goes by and the children grow up, into history and architecture; simultaneously, he was the great analyst of politics as it devolves into feelings and their effects on the nation. If we say that Trollope is the ultimate realist, we are recognizing that his work as well as his life recognized more points of view, more endeavors, more sensations, more things to think about and reasons to think about them than almost any other novelist; that the technique he developed for balancing the attractions of these sensations—in sentences, paragraphs, chapters, characters, and entire books—beautifully mimics the way many people construct their identities moment by moment. Since no novel can simply exist, like a painting or a sculpture, but must communicate something intelligible, the ways in which it can be well crafted are numerous, and since the twin challenges of time and space are always present, novelists never lose sight of technical questions, and technical questions are always rhetorical ones as well.

. . .

At the beginning of the twentieth century, though, novelists began making a case not only that novels were art, but also that certain qualities of certain novels were more artistic than others. Whether a novel should be, or could be, art was not, of course, entirely an aesthetic question, given both the novel's history as morally suspect and its wide appeal. The questions were still to some extent framed in terms of technique, but the ideal was no longer just to promote the novel's ability to communicate more and more details about more and more things, but also to have an aesthetic shape or effect that would be intended by the author and felt by the reader as consciously graceful, beautiful, or "right." The foremost proponent of these sorts of ideas was Henry James, both implicitly in the way he wrote his novels and explicitly in what he wrote about them. As a young man, James reviewed both Dickens and Trollope, and not kindly. Of one of Trollope's novels he wrote, "Life is vulgar, but we know not how vulgar it is until we see it set down in his pages" (review of *Can You Forgive Her?*, quoted in *Oxford Reader's Companion to Trollope*). With *Our Mutual Friend* he was not impressed, declaring it "the poorest of Mr. Dickens's works" (quoted in *Oxford Reader's Companion to Dickens*). And even though James seems to have admired George Eliot and attempted to get to know her and her companion George Henry Lewes, he still considered *Middlemarch* "an indifferent whole." We can tell by his subsequent writings, his own novels, and his essays on the nature of the novel as a form that he aspired to produce something simultaneously less vulgar and less formless than the novels of the great Victorians, and that he wished his work to elevate the novel to the status of art.

James's first successful novel was *The Portrait of a Lady,* published in 1881, when James was thirty-eight. His "lady" is Isabel Archer, an American young woman who is brought to Europe by her aunt, to give her a year abroad before she gets married. Isabel is an appealing, independent-minded young woman who isn't ready to yield to the charms, such as they are, of her American suitor. Soon enough, in England, she attracts the attention of two more men—her invalid cousin Ralph and an attractive aristocrat who doesn't seem to attract Isabel. Giving up the protections of engagement and marriage, though, proves more dangerous than Isabel foresees. Her aunt is blind to the possibility that Isabel might be duped, but when Isabel is left a large inheritance, her fate is decided. She falls into the clutches of the elegant but penniless Madame Merle, who introduces her to Gilbert Osmond, an American in Florence with no visible means of support and an expensive habit of connoisseurship. By the end of the novel it is clear to Isabel that she is trapped—her marriage is an evil, loveless sham (Osmond is portrayed as being a vaguely satanic combination of calculation and vengeful selfishness), her child has died, and she has lost access to Osmond's daughter, of whom she is fond. Everything that Isabel has learned about love and marriage growing up in the United States turns out to be wrong—in Europe, marriage is a pure commodity relationship, and it is the fate of girls (including Osmond's daughter) to be bought, sold, and dominated. Their only choices are to accept their fate knowingly or to undergo it without understanding it. That Isabel would suffer disillusionment is only a measure of her former illusions.

In *The Portrait of a Lady,* James does what he had intended to do— he excludes the vulgar by focusing on a few wealthy and well-educated Europeans and Americans, and he uses intense psychological analysis and careful depiction of settings to fill the spots where the vulgar might have been. The plot of James's novel, so similar to myriad earlier plots about what is to be done with women and what they could conceivably do with themselves, unfolds with great deliberateness as Isabel's friends and the narrator contemplate her fate. Isabel herself is something of a cipher—perhaps she is reserved, perhaps she is independent, perhaps she is unusually innocent, but she seems to recede as the novel progresses. Not knowing what she wants, she turns down many things that are offered. When she does choose something (to take a tour), James does not follow her and show the reader how it affects her. When we rejoin her after the tour, we are supposed to understand how she now contrasts to who she had been before the tour, but the contrasts are hazy because Isabel retains her reserve. For compelling dynamism in her character James substitutes analysis of her in his narrative voice. This has the effect of circumscribing her even further. The narrator expresses his admiration of her, but the reader can't help feeling intuitively that she is as trapped by his reportorial voice as she is by the expectations of those around her. Nevertheless, Isabel's fate is affecting, particularly so because she is very young and Osmond is not especially old, either. The trap she seems destined to inhabit is going to last a long time.

James and his friend Edith Wharton were ambitious Americans. They recognized that, as vital and satisfying as the tradition of the

English novel was, English novels were missing something that French novels possessed—psychological refinement and depth. They wanted to get that depth into their own novels, but to avoid the sordid subjects that were the meat and potatoes of the French novel.

James reveals his basic principle, and basic fear, in his introduction to *Roderick Hudson,* in the uniform edition of his novels that was published as the "New York Edition" in 1907. James is explicit about the fact that as soon as he began to write this first novel (in 1874), he began to worry: "I recall again the quite uplifted sense with which my idea, such as it was, permitted me at last to put quite out to sea. . . . Yet it must even then have begun for me, too, the ache of fear, that was to become so familiar, of being unduly tempted and led on by 'developments'" (*The Art of the Novel,* p. 4). He goes on, somewhat later, in a typically elaborate but telling Jamesian simile: "A young embroiderer of the canvas of life [James himself, of course] soon began to work in terror, fairly, of the vast expanse of that surface, of the boundless number of its distinct perforations for the needle, and of the tendency inherent in his many-coloured flowers and figures to cover and consume as many as possible of the little holes" (p. 5). Throughout the introductions of the New York Edition, James recalls how ideas for novels came to him through a single chance remark made to him at a party or a detail relayed to him over dinner. As soon as a particular "seed' struck him, he would make strenuous efforts not to hear any more of the details surrounding the actual incident or character being related because in his own mind, details and connections were already burgeoning. Prominent Victorian authors, of course, specialized in "developments"—as a result, much of the action in their books had to be a bit melodramatic, if only to have definition.

Henry James, though, wanted to write important novels in which the action was less melodramatic—books not about murders and suicides and virtue beset, but about the progress of the inner life, in which the climax might be only a silent recognition by the protagonist that she has made a commitment fatal to her happiness. Readers had to be educated to understand the weight of such subterranean drama, and so in the course of the three decades after *The Portrait of a Lady,* James disciplined the novel in several ways. He rarely wrote in the first person, but almost always in the third-person limited point of view,* and he often located that point of view in one or two characters present in

*The Turn of the Screw is in the first person.

the action of the novel but peripheral to it, as he relates the bad behavior of Maisie's parents in *What Maisie Knew* through Maisie's uncomprehending eyes, or as he relates *The Ambassadors* through the
consciousness of Lambert Strether. The effect of this was to get two for
one—the events unfold, those centrally implicated act out their drama,
and the effects of their drama on those around them are evident, too.
In the case of *The Ambassadors,* the drama has a more significant effect
on Strether, who decides in late middle age not to let life pass him by,
than it does on the lovers he has come to Europe to break up, and
James gets to simultaneously explore the hidden drama of Strether's
inner life and the overt drama of Chad and Madame de Vionnet's
mildly shocking affair. In his introduction to *The Golden Bowl,* James
refers to something he disapproves of—"the mere muffled majesty of
irresponsible 'authorship'" that results from not locating clearly both
the events of the story and the perspective from which it is to be
viewed. Even when the filtering narrative consciousness is all but
indistinguishable from James himself, the discipline of naming and
characterizing the filtering consciousness organizes the way in which
James the author can talk about the plot and the protagonist. The protagonist is also always set into a specific and carefully rendered social
milieu, which becomes part of the story, on the one hand, and defines
how intimate the novel may get, on the other. James often writes about
subjects that in other hands would be considered immoral (in *The
Wings of the Dove,* a couple concocts a plan in which the man will
seduce and marry a wealthy but dying American heiress to get her fortune; in the course of the novel, the focus of the young man's passions
shifts from one girl to the other), but the strict arrangement of the
material and the effect of James's elaborate style in rendering all feelings and passions analyzable and characterizable enables him to raise
their level of respectability, their level of complexity, and their level of
aesthetic satisfaction. James's work gains a great deal of intensity
through the contrast of the inner life of a passionate or idealistic character with the ironclad proprieties of his or her world, and is quite successful at portraying the pain of compromise, self-knowledge, and
endurance.

Significantly, James was also much afraid of having to go too far
afield. He comments on this in the preface to *Daisy Miller* when he
recalls a visit to New York that he made in the 1870s. He found himself stuck "at the very moderate altitude of Twenty-fifth Street . . .
alone . . . with the music-masters and French pastry-cooks, the ladies

and children—immensely present and immensely numerous these, but testifying with a collective voice to the extraordinary absence . . . of a serious male interest." Prohibited (he implies by financial consid- erations) from investigating what was going on on Wall Street, "and New York was, for force and accent, nothing else worth speaking of," James chose a different milieu to explore in his novels, not a milieu of work but one of leisure. Obviously James was not suited by talent or temperament to make a case for expansiveness as a virtue in the novel, so he made the case for form, a form based, as in classical painting, on perspective. Just as in great Renaissance and Baroque paintings the arrangement of the figures depends for effect on where the painter positions the viewer, so what the reader learns about the story James is telling is carefully controlled by the character (or consciousness) assigned by the author to tell the story. Underscoring this effect is the care and detail with which James depicts settings; many James novels read like a series of *tableaux vivants,* where the American characters are dwarfed by their European surroundings, which embody history and tradition as well as art and beauty. Wherever they come from in America, what the characters do is not about who they are and cannot truly be understood apart from the particular buildings, streets, towns, and landscapes in which they find themselves in Europe. When James fails to follow Isabel Archer on her tour, for example, he indicates that who she is and the context of her decisions about her life are not to be understood as a result of what she does, but as the product of the so- cial context in which she finds herself at the time she is making the decision.

James's argument about what was better and what was best (the depiction of moral dilemmas being better and the ever more refined parsing of motive and character being best, with the hand of the author always masterful but hidden) was not directed at the traditional audience of the novel—let's say the Defoe/Dickens audience, who thought the novel was fine and plenty artful; it was directed at the sort of audience who would have the taste to read and the money to buy the elaborate New York Edition of his works, some twenty-three volumes, and, also, to himself as a celebration and perhaps justification of his lifelong devotion (with a short hiatus in the 1890s, when he wrote unsuccessfully for the London stage) to a suspect form.

James was not a popular writer—he often lamented the poor sales of his novels—but he had a powerful effect on novelists who came after him, and on the very idea of what a novel should be, especially in England and the United States. But other novelists had opinions, too, and one of these was Leo Tolstoy, who in 1898 published his own manifesto, "What Is Art?" Tolstoy, like James, seems to be reacting to the nineteenth-century novelistic social project, but his reaction is diametrically opposed to James's. Tolstoy begins his argument not with the novel but with other commonly accepted forms of art—music, ballet, and drama—and describes the ill-paid and difficult labor that goes into producing such art. He focuses especially on the disparities of social class that these (and other forms) promote and confirm—art is an economic product like any other in that those who work the hardest to produce it have the least wherewithal to understand it or to consume it (the workers can't afford the fruits of their labor). The wrinkle in Tolstoy's analysis is that, unlike James, he considers exclusiveness a bad thing; the problem is not in the uneducated taste of one class of potential consumers, but in the perverted taste of the other class of confirmed consumers (and producers). True art, Tolstoy asserts, would appeal to universal human thoughts, desires, and needs, would be simple to understand, would be inclusive rather than exclusive.

Tolstoy was particularly offended by the erotic content of the art he surveyed, and he contends that much of the purpose of art in his day was to inflame the passions of the jaded upper class; he also attacks notions of beauty and pleasure as class-based and empty. He angrily throws Shakespeare, Dante, and even himself into the trash bin. To us, Tolstoy seems to be purveying a belief in the sort of utopianism that ended up producing the nightmares of the twentieth century, but his polemic is a natural extension of the methods of the nineteenth-century novel—should enough material be organized and clearly arranged according to sometimes subtle but ultimately understandable principles of not only cause and effect but sympathy and empathy, then the wholesale transformation of society into something more like a novel—something organized and connected, something if not happier, then smarter—could follow. The proper art could "fix" society, but improper art (and this is the source of Tolstoy's anger—he is surrounded by improper art) can only damage society. His experience of the peasantry on his estate, to begin with, and other "true Russians" not of the upper class has convinced him that erotic passion in particular, but other forms of greed, selfishness, and brutality as well, have their source not in changeless human nature but in social arrangements and contaminating images and ideas—an extension of the ideas of many nineteenth-century novelists, including Dickens and Stowe, but seen through a point of view more religious and less pragmatic than either of theirs.

Novelists after James and Tolstoy were shaped by their influence in several ways. In England, the next generation of novelists reacted strongly against James in a formal sense, constructing the modernist novel in contrast to the "traditional realist novel" (which was really more or less the novels of Henry James and his English contemporaries such as Arnold Bennett, since James had excluded the stranger characteristics of the novel represented by Dickens, Stowe, Melville, and the Brontës from the realm of true art), but they accepted his basic idea that the novel was, or could be, exclusive rather than inclusive, and that a novel without much popular appeal could do things artistically that a novel with popular appeal could not. They accepted his idea that the audience for a quality novel might not be large enough to support the author by means of commerce; this idea is a truism today, but it was new, and even revolutionary, for Virginia Woolf, James Joyce, and many of their contemporaries.

The Bloomsbury group, which consisted of Virginia Woolf, her husband, Leonard; her sister, Vanessa, a painter; and several other essayists and intellectuals, was bohemian in a sense, but it was never low-class; Virginia's (and Leonard's) novel-writing was never considered less artistically innovative or respectable than the painting, criticism, and essay-writing of the others. The men of Bloomsbury were university-educated in the most socially accepted way; two generations earlier, they would have become clergymen. Thanks in part to the fact that Henry James set up and promoted a socially respectable form of the novel, they could now become intellectuals and artists. In addition, Virginia Woolf looked to her friends and relatives for inspiration. She observed and depicted them, as novelists have always done, but James's precepts gave her an added justification—she was creating art, something new and valuable that had never been thought of before and would be true in a way that previous novels had not been true. She was explicit about this in many essays, in particular "Mr. Bennett and Mrs. Brown," which she revised several times. Her complaint against Arnold Bennett and his contemporaries, realist novelists all, was that they lose the sense of "life" and "human nature" by focusing too much on the materials of the set, on the "upholstery of the carriage"—in other words, that in the always restricted linear discipline of unfolding prose, they have devoted too many words to furniture and not enough to capturing sensations, especially momentary ones. She defends some of the techniques and effects of her contemporaries by claiming that awkwardness and discomfort are necessary corollaries to breaking free from old strictures. Of *Ulysses,* she points out, it "seems to me the conscious and calculated indecency of a desperate man who feels that in order to breathe he must break the windows." But Woolf's attack in 1934 on Arnold Bennett was class-based, also. When he died, she encapsulated his life in her diary: "a shop keeper's view of literature; yet with the rudiments, covered over with fat and prosperity and the desire for hideous Empire furniture, of sensibility . . . I remember his determination to write 1000 words daily; and how he trotted off to do it that night."

For Woolf and her contemporaries, James's imprimatur of "art" and the privacy and status of uncommerciality allowed them to explore what the middle class—the great audience of Dickens and many other Victorian novelists—considered to be uninteresting but also immoral topics. Of course, it is every novelist's claim, standard at least from the days of Marguerite de Navarre, that what is "novel" in his or her work is also important to the true understanding of human nature; it worked in the 1920s to allow a new class of writers with a different set of values and interests into the hitherto popular realm of the novel, and it also worked to promote the artificial bifurcation of the novel into more prestigious "critical successes" and less prestigious "popular successes." It worked, in fact, just the same way for novelists from the educated classes as it always had for other excluded groups, expanding the subject matter, the style, the tone, and the audience for the novel as a form.

For the rest of the twentieth century, novelists, readers, and critics continued to argue about what was artful in the novel, but they accepted James's premise that some novels were art, and other, more commercial ones, were not. E. M. Forster, who was a contemporary of Woolf and Joyce, wrote a book called *Aspects of the Novel* that takes up the issue of "What Is Art?" and addresses James specifically on the subject of form. Forster's witty, benign style is especially generous in some ways—*Aspects of the Novel* has held up over the years because it doesn't seem like merely an advertisement for Forster's own work— but his criticism of James is pointed. After a lengthy appreciation of James's own favorite novel, *The Ambassadors,* Forster remarks, "The beauty that suffuses *The Ambassadors* is the reward due to a fine artist for hard work. . . . Success to the full extent of his possibilities has crowned him. The pattern has woven itself with modulation and reservations Anatole France will never attain. Woven itself wonderfully. But at what a sacrifice!" (p. 159). What most readers object to, according to Forster, is not the difficulty of the prose, but the fact that "they cannot grant his premise, which is that most of human life has to disappear before he can do us a novel" (p. 160). What Forster objects to is the subjection of the novel's natural profusion to the rigors of a structure that is evident to the reader's sensibility, to what is required so the reader will stop thinking of a novel as life (which is disorganized and chock-full of uncontrollable developments) and start thinking of it as art, which is conscious of itself at all times. Forster proposes that the novelist in search of artfulness substitute the model of music for the model of painting, and that he attempt to attain a kind of internal pattern analogous to rhythm. He uses *In Search of Lost Time* as his example. When Proust repeats certain ideas and themes in his four-thousand-page novel, they constitute a "lovely waxing and waning" whose effect is "to fill us with surprise and freshness and hope." The huge French novel is not asked to limit itself and fix itself inside a structure, "and yet it hangs together because it is stitched internally" (p. 165). Unfortunately for his argument, Forster does not point out in contrasting *The Ambassadors* with *In Search of Lost Time* that the former is written in James's customary third-person limited point of view, while the latter is written in an absolutely unashamed first-person point of view, which allows Proust the freedom to digress and yet remain within the consistent voice of a single consciousness. Consistency is Proust's default setting (as it is the default setting of every first-person narrator), so "developments" enliven the narrative but never disrupt it. Whether artistic "rhythm" can be achieved in a novel written in the third person is a question Forster's own novel *A Passage to India* sheds light upon (see below). Needless to say, though, from the perspective of Tolstoy's argument, *In Search of Lost Time* only compounds the problems of art as both immoral and exclusive.

Fortunately for us, all four of our theorists of art in the novel put their theories to the test by writing novels as they thought novels should be written. What we have to learn from looking at their works is not that one or the other had a better or worse theory, but that the form of the novel was in many ways too powerful or too intransigent to be subdued by a mere theory. If we consider *A Passage to India** in light

---

*For plot synopses of *A Passage to India* and *Anna Karenina,* readers unfamiliar with those works may consult the section "A Hundred Novels" in the latter part of this book.

of Forster's admiration of Proust, we see that the novel is Proustian in the sense that all relationships depicted in the novel are personal, and all betrayals are personal, too, as in Proust. When the scene of these relationships and betrayals is transposed from France to India, though, and the characters must relate across highly charged boundaries of race and class, Forster's political insights into Anglo India become profound, and the novel almost unbearably poignant. The primary "rhythmical" feature is the enigmatic Professor Godbole, who appears in several of the scenes, sometimes as a friendly figure, who is always kindly and well-disposed, but sometimes as an unfriendly figure, who hampers the plans of the protagonists; in the end, he is neutral, as if divine. Nevertheless, the "rhythm" of *In Search of Lost Time* and of *A Passage to India* is not what makes each novel memorable—it is rather the intelligence and insight of each narrative consciousness. Proust could employ all sorts of subtle patterning devices, but if his remarks were not regularly arresting and his metaphors not original and apt, the novel would just seem gassy and pretentious. If Forster were not truly interested in the inner life of Aziz, were not authentically empathetic with him and the other characters, *A Passage to India* would be just another example of colonial novelizing. Furthermore, Forster accepts, at least implicitly, the nature of the novel as a social document—he doesn't shrink at all from depicting particular customs among particular people at a particular historic juncture—he doesn't find them fleeting or peripheral, he finds them interesting and worth carefully describing. The effect, in 2005, is to give *A Passage to India* currency. By acknowledging its own specificity and depicting, without overt political theories, a plethora of personal relationships—that is, because it beautifully exploits characteristics natural to the novel as a form—*A Passage to India* seems less dated and more insightful than many other novels of its day.

To the Lighthouse, written three years after *A Passage to India,* offers an interesting paradox. Woolf divides the novel into three sections. The first focuses on an apparently routine summer day before the First World War, and details the more or less idle thoughts of a more or less happy family ensconced at their summer retreat by the sea. Woolf's narrative method is to pass from one consciousness to another, simultaneously telling the story of the day and limning the subjective experiences of each of the characters, including the youngest, James, who is six years old. One of the things Woolf demonstrates about "life" and "human nature" is that time does not move steadily and evenly. Rather, some moments take many pages to describe, as, for example, the moment between when Mrs. Ramsay, James's mother, holds a stocking she is knitting up to James's leg to gauge whether it is long enough, and when she decides it is not and takes it away again. The third section focuses on a routine day after the war, when James, his sister, and their father return to the summer retreat. The family is much reduced, in particular by the death of Mrs. Ramsay, but also by the deaths of two of the other children, one in the war and one in childbirth. In this section, the father and the children manage to achieve a goal promised in the first section, a boat trip to the lighthouse, which no longer has the meaning it once did for James (said to be a stand-in for Woolf herself), but can't help accruing new meanings in the context of both James's losses and his maturation. The short middle section, "Time Passes," narrates the losses of the war in terms of the neglect and deterioration of the house while the family is too preoccupied to visit—in this section, the turning of the light and the passage of its beam through the windows of the house ticks away the passage of time both away from the idyllic era of the first section and toward the compromised but fascinating era of the third section. The result is both artful and poignant, but the paradox, with regard to Woolf's theories, is that her method, the method with which she intends to expand the reach of the novel, cannot actually encompass events of dramatic and historical significance. It magnifies the difficulty the novel has with the passage of time. Dramatic action, of course, is always difficult for prose, and no novel can depict two things at once, but some novels can give the illusion of doing so by ordering vivid and various details unforgettably in the mind of the reader so that when the climax, the biggest piece of action, happens, the reader seems to herself to understand it all—good examples of this are the tripartite climax of *A Tale of Two Cities* (where Darnay's escape is contrasted to Miss Pross's fight with Madame Defarge, which in turn gives way to Sydney Carton's execution) and the climax of Toni Morrison's *Beloved* (where Sethe's recollection of the failed escape from the plantation is set into the context of the other incidents the reader has been introduced to that led up to and resulted from it).

Tolstoy's theory seems not to apply at all to *Anna Karenina*—in "What Is Art?" he repudiates the very claims of such characters as Anna, Vronsky, Karenin, and even Levin and Kitty, to any sort of consideration whatsoever. In particular, Anna, Vronsky, and Karenin, whose passions give the reader entry into what would otherwise be a dry and didactic exercise in Levin's learning to do the right thing in spite of himself, exemplify the very cultivation of the erotic he so deplores. We have to imagine Karenin, the cuckolded husband, as prefiguring the man Tolstoy himself became—immune to the charms of his wife, intimidating and forbidding, more interested in rules and forms than affections or other, softer feelings, and resentful of such passions in others. Fortunately, Tolstoy's ability to observe the world around him, to deduce meaning and order from human behavior, and to attach outer expression to inner feeling is a genius he demonstrates that is much more solid and satisfying than his penchant for theories. He is interested in and sympathetic toward Anna in spite of himself; he understands the destructiveness of maleness against femaleness in spite of himself; whatever the moral claims of universal simplicity, he doesn't rely upon it to carry the reader through his novel, and even more fortunately, the novel itself, having been published and distributed, having become the possession of countless readers, defies its author's urge to censor it.

The lesson we learn from our little survey is that even though our authors' theories would seem to exclude one another's claims to artistry, their actual works do not. Any reader (for example, me) can enjoy and value *Anna Karenina, The Portrait of a Lady, The Ambassadors, A Passage to India, To the Lighthouse,* and *Orlando* with no trouble whatsoever. It doesn't even begin to be difficult to read these six novels in sequence, enjoying them all fully, and, indeed, understanding and accepting them. What we realize when we read them is that they are more alike than different, that they all have the same claims as art, and that individual readers are always likely to prefer one or two over the others.

Of course, Virginia Woolf had another literary critical project besides the exploration of consciousness, which was the promotion of women as worthy authors, both in terms of recognizing the value of what women had already produced and of preparing the ground for future works. In this she was, in some sense, more akin to Tolstoy than to James. While not offering as scathing a picture of the privileged class of artists as Tolstoy offers at the beginning of "What Is Art?," she is no less definite about her belief that the traditional exclusion of women from the artistic class is unfair, wrong, and distorting to art itself. As far as Mr. Bennett and Mrs. Brown are concerned, she champions Mrs. Brown as an example of consciousness—"of unlimited capacity and infinite variety"—but also as a woman—"an old lady."

The assertion Woolf makes, that the absence of women from literary history constitutes a glaring omission, seems obvious today, and shines backward over all the literature that has gone before: Did James really get into the mind of Isabel Archer? Did Shakespeare really get into the mind of Ophelia? Woolf doesn't exactly say no, but she casts a doubt, and it is a doubt that affected much of twentieth-century discussion of literature.

Each of our theorists has had an effect on ideas of art and the novel in the past eighty years, exactly the period when the novel as a form has spread all over the world. The effect has been to make novelists and novels self-conscious by requiring serious novelists to have, and to be able to articulate, at least to themselves, a higher or larger goal. Some novelists have actively pursued Tolstoy's social program—the portrayal of those who can't or don't portray themselves, often in pursuit of a higher social goal. In this category I would put Sholokhov (*And Quiet Flows the Don*), Hurston (*Their Eyes Were Watching God*), Steinbeck (*The Grapes of Wrath*), Faulkner (*As I Lay Dying*), and Mistry (*A Fine Balance*). Some novelists have actively viewed themselves as women writing about women, inserting the perspective of women into the mainstream of literary consciousness. My favorite examples in this category are Alice Munro (*Lives of Girls and Women*), Toni Morrison (*Beloved*), Jamaica Kincaid (*Annie John*), Kate Atkinson (*Behind the Scenes at the Museum*), Margaret Atwood, Fay Weldon, Isabel Allende, Amy Tan, and countless others, including me—this is a rich treasury! Many novelists have followed Henry James. The enclosed, cultivated world of secure property and inherited privilege that he wrote about has disappeared, but the idea that elite novelists write for elite readers, who are cultivated and astute enough to appreciate complex wordplay, intricate themes, dense, even abstruse, analysis of ideas, and subject matter that will offend the average reader, has not. Vladimir Nabokov, for example, not only wrote *Lolita,* in which a cultivated older European man abducts a fourteen-year-old girl and takes her over state lines to have sex with her any number of times, he also expressed the urge to write other books he thought might offend American yahoos—the story of a successful interracial marriage that is productive of children and grandchildren and of "the total atheist who lives a happy and useful life and dies in his sleep at the age of 106." Novelists who seem to aim at high art and who disdain, or at least ignore, commercial appeal include Iris Murdoch (*The Sea, the Sea*), Christina Stead (*The Man Who Loved Children*), John Gardner (*Grendel*), Milan

Kundera (*The Unbearable Lightness of Being*), William Gaddis, Julian Barnes, Will Self, Martin Amis, Jonathan Franzen, and, once again, countless others.

The higher goal each novelist aspires to is always portrayed as a form of truth, and his or her art is meant to more clearly express that truth. How the novel is written reveals the basic features of that truth. For example, the heirs of Henry James tend to feel that one of the duties of art is to be unlike life—to be distinct to the point of artificiality and, more important, to express that distinctness in every aspect of the novel. These novelists want readers to be aware at all times that the novel they are reading is a made thing rather than a gratuitous thing and that the author's intentions and choices have shaped what only seems to be resemblance to life. A premium is put not on simplicity or appeals to the universal, but on complexity and intricacy. Few novelists have been unsophisticated enough to declare an allegiance to beauty— the twentieth century was too ironical an age for that—but for beauty they have substituted other sorts of formal integrity that are perhaps more distancing or off-putting than beauty but serve the same purpose of making the novel cohesive and self-referential.

Of course, the great unsurpassable model of self-conscious artfulness in the novel is *Ulysses. Ulysses* is so self-contained and self-referential that there is a whole mini-industry of writers and scholars whose job is to tell prospective readers that *Ulysses* is worth getting through and how to get through it. Whether Joyce's novel is worth getting through is the subject of 343 sometimes lengthy customer reviews on the Amazon.com Web site (as opposed to 270 for *Moby-Dick,* 246 for *War and Peace,* and only 3 for *In Search of Lost Time*). Readers' opinions are deeply divided, from "the GREATEST novel ever published" ("monigan") to "if being smart means liking this, count me out" ("pinnick"). The outline of Joyce's plot is simple, and relies on the same principle Tolstoy used for *Anna Karenina*—two stories are told in parallel, in this case, not two marriages, but two journeys through a single day (June 16, 1904). One Dubliner, middle-aged Leopold Bloom, sets out from home to do some errands, knowing that his wife, Molly, will be entertaining her lover, Blazes Boylan, at their home later in the afternoon and he can do nothing about it. The other Dubliner, Stephen Dedalus, a young teacher whose mother has recently died, teaches his class and receives his pay. His task is to resist, or perhaps give in to, the temptation to spend his money in a profligate manner in the course of the same day. The climax, for the two characters, is when they meet and connect, fatherlike and sonlike, Odysseus-like and Telemachus-like, late in the evening. The climax, for the reader, is in the last section, Molly Bloom's soliloquy, addressed not to her late-returning husband but to herself (or the reader). Like Woolf, Joyce was in part interested in depicting consciousness as it had never been depicted before—as a series of momentary impressions and thoughts, often insignificant—as they are processed by his characters. What each character sees and feels and thinks, how he reacts both to himself and to what is around him, is not consistent. Joyce wants to capture the fragmentary and contingent nature of subjective experience, to show that it is not logical and sequential but often arbitrary, with no apparent antecedent and no apparent consequence, that in fact the appearance of cause and effect in something like a plot is pure illusion—if time as it passes through the characters' consciousnesses were broken down into small enough segments, no causes and effects would present themselves, and so, perhaps, there would be no reason to act. This, Joyce seems to be saying, is how life works and why it simply goes on. Bloom is not happy that his wife is entertaining Blazes Boylan, but there are so many distractions in the course of the day, and so many reasons not to make a fuss, including his whole history with his wife, that in the end the only possible choice is to go home to her and be happy to see her. At the same time, his chance meeting with Stephen does have an effect on Stephen—his warm and positive nature contrasts to the coldness of Stephen's own father and provides just a tiny turning point for him, away from dissipation and toward the exercise of talents he knows he has but is in the habit of slighting.

But Joyce does not stop with precisely depicting the consciousnesses of each of his three characters—he also, and fairly comprehensively, takes up the history of literature, and uses many different styles and forms to depict the otherwise mundane adventures of his protagonists. Some of these, such as his mimicry of tales of ancient Irish heroes, are virtually incomprehensible. Others require considerable patience on the part of the reader (such as the shift into play format for 180 pages in the middle of the novel). Much of this is so taxing to read that one enthusiastic Amazon.com reviewer suggests not trying to understand it at all, but just letting it wash through, uncomprehended but, presumably, stimulating all the same. Most readers seem to agree that the "truth" Joyce is getting at is that even the most routine sort of day is rich with meaning and implication, and that this is a far truer representation of "life" as it is lived than the more logical and consistent characters and plots most novels have to offer. The trouble with this truth is that many readers don't recognize it as true, and aren't motivated to suspend disbelief. The novelist's only recourse, when readers are recalcitrant about participating in this way, is to find them wanting as readers, and many champions of *Ulysses* do find its detractors wanting, but the difficulty is in using what is a naturally appealing and inclusive art form for exclusive purposes. Is *Ulysses* artificial in the most absolute way? Yes. Is its very artificiality a higher representation of the way life really is? Maybe. Joyce uses techniques of erudition, wordplay, self-referentiality, and unpredictability to reinforce an impression in the reader that *Ulysses* is intended to be art.

An example of a novel that has a Tolstoyan purpose to promote some sort of social good is Zora Neale Hurston's *Their Eyes Were Watching God,* the story of Janie and Tea Cake, an older woman and a younger man who fall in love and go off together to work in the Florida Everglades against the advice of Janie's friends, who think Tea Cake is after her for her money. Tea Cake is not respectable, but he is sexy and fun, and Janie knows he loves her. Together, both of them find the companionship they had not found in other marriages or relationships. The climax to the novel, though, is a hurricane in which, while they are escaping, Tea Cake is bitten by a rabid dog. Janie's last act of love toward him is to see him through the horror of his illness and death, before returning to the life she had left for him.

Their Eyes Were Watching God works like most novels with a didactic purpose—it is clearly and dramatically written, the characters are appealing and easy to relate to—in this case, they are earthy, passionate, and well-meaning. At the beginning of the novel, they embark on a learning curve, and what they learn would, it is implied, be beneficial for the reader to learn, also. Like Eugene Wrayburn in *Our Mutual Friend,* who begins the novel as a cynical idler and progresses toward becoming a libertine, but learns to love and consider others after he is nearly killed, characters in Tolstoyan novels mature through sometimes harsh tests that might as easily destroy them as save them. Janie's story is meant to demonstrate several things to her friends and to the reader. For one thing, even though Tea Cake's end is horrifying, Janie has no regrets and knows that she has experienced a type of passion she would not have wanted to miss for the sake of mere security or respectability. For another, she returns to her former community with a larger sense of humanity and fewer of the prejudices she once had and that she sees around her. She also knows that she is both strong and enterprising, and has no need to act out of fear, as she sometimes had as a young woman. The reader is meant to learn the same lessons about Janie as an individual, but also as a representative of her group, rural black people. Hurston, as a trained anthropologist, was perfectly aware of the power of the novel to open a window for the mainstream reader upon an unknown or unconsidered segment of society, and she was self-conscious about doing so in all of her writings. Her social program was not the same as Tolstoy's—she did not want to remake society in a particular mold—but she did want to correct the mis-appprehensions of those who demeaned people like her characters. Janie is worthy of respect in many ways, and when she extends her respect and love to Tea Cake, who appears on the surface to be a type of ne'er-do-well rogue, the reader is asked to do the same thing.

Like the artful novel, the didactic novel has a characteristic mode of failing. If the artistic novel simply fails to communicate, and therefore in some sense to exist, because it is too forbidding and inaccessible, the didactic novel can be off-putting when it is too prescriptive and not sufficiently descriptive. If the author seems to have shaped the material too strictly in accordance with ideological presuppositions about what is good and what isn't good, the Tolstoyan novel strikes the reader as too simplistic to actually stand on its own as art rather than propaganda. Unfortunately for the highly ideological novelist, ideas change—the first things to die in any novel are those precious social theories that the author labored so intently to understand and incorporate into his work. In Sholokhov's *And Quiet Flows the Don,* for example, the author's descriptions of the brutality of pre–World War I Cossack village life still strike us as authentic, but the idealized romantic relationship of the two young Communists who meet late in the novel seems false. The first sections are obviously the fruit of long observation by the author. The later section is more of an idea about how a relationship could work than a picture of how many relationships *do* work.

The entry of long-voiceless groups into the literary world of the novel was extremely productive of good and interesting novels in the twentieth century. A paradigmatic example would be Alice Munro's *Lives of Girls and Women,* which is the artfully told story of how Del, a Canadian girl from a rather eccentric rural Ontario family, finds her literary voice and vocation as she contemplates her various encounters with "the word," on the one hand, and intriguing local women, on the other. What is extraordinary about Del's life is not her particular adventures. While her experiences are idiosyncratic, they are more or less like the ordinary experiences of many girls that go unconsidered, fall by the wayside, and come to be known as "life" once they are part of the past. Del's gift is the ability to note them and to recognize that, ordinary as they are, they form a pattern that she can derive meaning from, both as they change her and as they reveal how "life" works. Munro's wonderful gifts of insight and stylistic precision are always descriptive and yet they imply a sort of prescription—given a chance, ordinary girls can make something of their lives and avoid the nagging sense of frustration that other women (such as Del's mother and, in a different way, her aunt and great-aunts) endure throughout their lives.

What Munro's novel and other novels like it offer above all things is a sense of authenticity. Whether or not Del is Alice Munro, whether or not *Lives of Girls and Women* actually tells the story of her upbringing, the novel offers the reader what seems to be felt and considered experience. The experience may be that of a Canadian woman, or it may be that of an African man, as in Chinua Achebe's *Things Fall Apart,* or it may be that of a man writing about a woman, as in Arnošt Lustig's *Lovely Green Eyes,* or it may be that of a woman writing about a man, as in Francine Prose's *Guided Tours of Hell.* For many women writers, it was Virginia Woolf who gave permission to speak with authority, and twentieth-century literature flourished as a result.

Nevertheless, even so simple and justifiable a concept as authenticity causes problems in the novel. When the burden placed upon the novel is that it should always and invariably reflect the "truth," the novel's capaciousness and appeal to the imagination are thereby limited. When authenticity is prized and imagination becomes suspect, a novelist's right to portray anyone outside of his experience is questioned. It is the novel itself, with its alternation between the inner life and action, between the individual and the group, between cause and effect, that highlights the question of authenticity, but whether a novel is "authentic" can only come in terms of willing suspension of disbelief, which only the individual reader can decide. Novels such as *Anna Karenina* and Jamaica Kincaid's *Annie John* arouse powerful emotions and also make arguments. Disputes about "truth" are a sign that the arguments they make and the emotions they arouse aren't always in agreement. When the literary culture at large tries to impose an answer by insisting that "authenticity" resides in the sex or the ethnic or national origin or biographical experience of the author, it kills the very thing that makes the literary culture vibrant, which is the sense of freedom, vitality, and power the author feels while he is creating his work.

I, too, of course, have a theory of art in the novel that grows out of my temperament and circumstances, as well as my experience of reading novels, my observations of how novels work, and the age in which I live. The first aspect of my theory contradicts James and Forster—I consider it fairly unlikely that a great novel will have either a shape or a rhythm. Each of the literary and nonliterary forms that the novel is related to (see chapter 9, "The Circle of the Novel") offers different challenges and different rewards. The more expansive the author tries to be, to give his argument heft and wide application, the more he tries to stake a claim to greatness, then the more likely the novel will expand outside of the capacity of the reader to maintain a sense of the whole. All of the great, long, many-faceted novels tempt the reader to skim here and there—all of them are more like rivers than pools, with rapids here and shallows there and lovely glades and marshy spots. The sense of wholeness and perspective that James and Forster consider to be the highest form of novelistic art gets lost in the expanding and piecemeal experience of reading such a novel. I would assert that the highest novelistic art is in the intensity of that experience, in the reader having the sensation—as I have when I am reading Nikolai Gogol's *Taras Bulba*—of brilliant phrases, images, insights, observations, sentences, and paragraphs cascading upon me. Or it is in the sharp, painful sense I feel of unrelenting disintegration in *The Man Who Loved Children,* which is as highly dramatic as Euripides' *Medea,* but far longer and more sustained. But these novels do not stay in my mind as wholes. The very sparkle of the words, the impact of each stunning phrase dissipates or confuses a larger perception of formal integrity. The greatness of these novels, as of many others, is that the experience can only be reexperienced, never quite remembered or grasped, and yet the experience is so subjective and dependent upon my own circumstances when I am reading that what I think is greatness one time might miss me completely the next time I try it. It is in attempting to elude this very intermittence that Henry James ended up, according to Forster, sacrificing most of life. The novel is not like a painting, or anything tangible, and so, in my opinion, it can't aspire to the sort of formal integrity that tangible objects aspire to.

My view is that artfulness in the novel lies not in the product, but in the process and in the cultural position of the artist or novelist. The making of art, the writing of a novel requires the artist to exercise free choice in what to depict and how to deploy his materials. Even in societies that don't prize personal and political freedom—let's say in medieval European monasteries, where monks were employed in illuminating manuscripts and what they were supposed to do was prescribed to them, and the techniques they were to employ were taught them—artfulness came in as an expression of individual personality and intention—a particular face or bird or saint might be depicted with a few extra flourishes or with an unusually expressive posture or gesture. It is free choice that is the sine qua non of art. Even when a craftsman (known in the novel-writing business as a "hack") is hired to write a particular story for a particular audience (as, say, series romance novelists are hired to write under pseudonyms), he may bring a certain amount of free choice to the words he employs, the characters he rounds out with idiosyncrasies, or even the themes he touches upon that distinguish his volumes from the others in the series. His motives for introducing his own individuality may not be at all honorable—perhaps he can't help it, or maybe he just does it to give himself a reason to go to work in the morning and stick it to the boss—but it is his sense of agency that is the beginning of art.

Societies have only a few basic categories of work, and four of them are government, religion, daily survival, and nurturing the next generation. Each of these functions requires group effort, and in each it is essential that the individual subordinate himself or herself to the discipline of the group. A fifth category, apparently present in almost every human society, is the making of art (including the telling of stories). In this category, idiosyncrasy is prized, in part because art is perceived as play and is supposed to be, for lack of a better word, fun. It is the flourishes and the bonuses, the bits of any story that go beyond what everybody knows, that make it fun. In every other category—government, religion, survival, and reproduction—freedom may or may not be present. History is full of conformity and enslavement in the name of politics, faith, production of food and shelter, and child-rearing. All of these institutions can exist without freedom, but art cannot. "Art" is what institutionalizes the basic freedom to make idiosyncratic use of materials, and therefore what institutionalizes freedom. And then, when an artist can choose his subject matter and shape it as he pleases, his freedom is thereby enhanced—when Boccaccio chose to write erotic tales in prose in a manner he thought would be flattering to women (and seductive, no doubt), he had to defend his right to do so, but his exercise of freedom enabled those who admired his work to exercise a similar sort of freedom. And it is significant that Marguerite de Navarre chose to exercise her freedom in order to discuss the strictures placed on women. Because she was a queen, she could do so, but only a few centuries later, women who were not queens at all, women who were simple country girls such as George Eliot, exercised the same sort of freedom. Such freedom in all art is the result of point of view, but in the novel, the importance of point of view is enormously magnified by the voice of the narrator, who must tell the lengthy story from a particular point of view because a story can't be told any other way. As a result, the novel is always about freedom, and readers of novels have an instinctive understanding of whether the novelist is exercising his freedom or whether he isn't—that is, whether he means what he is saying or whether he doesn't—because the novel is based in the most primal human materials, emotion and language.

A dilemma that comes up for readers who agree that the novel can do the Tolstoyan thing—promote laudable political goals—is that many novelists use their materials for what some conceive to be bad ends. Since the novel is inherently political, political disagreements abound. Trollope called Dickens "Mr. Popular Sentiment" and thought he was catering to the bad taste of the English middle class. In 1995, when Rohinton Mistry's novel *A Fine Balance* was short-listed for the Booker Prize, essayist Germaine Greer, who was on the judging panel, declared that she hated it because it was "wrong"—his depiction of life in Bombay as astoundingly brutal, and even futile, offended her because her own experience of India had been different. When Salman Rushdie was put under a fatwa for *The Satanic Verses,* not everyone leaped to the defense either of his work or of his freedom to state his point of view—Naguib Mahfouz challenged Rushdie's right to "insult . . . a prophet or anything considered holy." Canadian novelist and filmmaker Julian Samuel considered Rushdie's critique not radical enough. As he stated in *US/THEM: Transition, Transcription and Identity in Post-Colonial Cultures,* as well as in the online journal *India-Star,* where I read it,

It is a kind of refined and erudite compromise constructed for the soft folds of a safe and international literary aristocracy which sees at least one of its aims as the production of a literature heavy, dank and resonant with slickly manipulated surrealism, but with a great deal of it anchored in perfunctory, riskless experimentation.

But the fact is, just as Samuel and Greer are entitled to their points of view, the essential nature of Rushdie's art is that he is entitled to his point of view also. People and groups who are primarily political or primarily religious or primarily commercial often consider art to be a tool for the promulgation of ideas and programs or a way to sell a product—that is, they consider art to be a more excellent form of technique. Any sort of appeal to beauty or goodness or truth as the highest expression of art will result in such an idea and a novel, in fact, can have several goals—truth or sales or goodness or beauty. Its goal may be a standard and not very interesting one, conceived by the artist wearing his hat as citizen or acolyte or consumer. Tolstoy's goal for *Anna Karenina* was to give Russians a lesson in how to be authentically Russian, but art came in by way of Tolstoy's disgust with what he saw around him and his desire to portray it in detail so others could see what he saw; the novel he ended up with is enormously insightful and beautifully written whether Tolstoy's prescriptions convince or not. According to his autobiography, Trollope was writing for money and status, but art came in and created an unsurpassed portrait of the English bourgeoisie that has outlived its creator.

The artistic value of any novel depends on its assertion of freedom within the society in which it is created. All societies—all political programs—value conformity and strive to limit freedom, but simple nonconformity is not the antidote; the antidote begins with the sense in the artist's mind that he is engaged in and focused upon the task at hand— let's say choosing a word that seems right and stimulates him. It expands itself as he develops ideas he feels are uniquely his in a manner that satisfies him. It completes itself in the mind of the reader, who apprehends and appreciates the word and the ideas, or does not, who is free to assimilate the author's vision and equally free to reject it. The primary question is not "What's good?" but "What do I think is good?" Any novel-reader can answer this question, and it is inevitable that one good novel will lead to another, that reading many novels, which all inevitably contrast with one another and have different ways of appealing to a reader, will teach her not only what she likes but also what there is to like, and why. The value of art is not in the qualities belonging to any particular object but in the freedom that all the objects represent, and the freedom that successive individuals and successive ages possess to esteem, demote, or revive any particular object. Art is the only social system that always carries this freedom, so it is of a value that cannot be overestimated, as it coexists with and counteracts all the other systems that promote conformity. As we survey the shelves at Earth's Biggest Bookstore, we see that this is the one quality shared by every artful decision, every detail we find appealing, every element of every novel that lingers in our memories.

8 · The Novel and History

I n the course of this book we have been looking most often at how the novel operates across boundaries of space and time to give the reader a feeling of kinship with a narrator, an author, and characters who are on the surface quite different from her. But it is also true that as we read Boccaccio, Lady Murasaki, and Marguerite de Navarre, we are reminded on every page of how different our world is from theirs, and how different we are from them. In *The Tale of Genji,* for example, women of a certain class are always hidden away from men. A woman showing only the sleeves of her robe from beneath the shade that seals her off from the world constitutes an erotic invitation. She might never reveal her face even to her spouse, who in the course of their marriage might see only her hair falling all the way to her feet and in some sense veiling her. And in the sixth story of the third day of *The Decameron,* as another example, an unscrupulous lover tricks a married woman named Catella into meeting him at a public bath, where, in an unlit room, he pretends to be her husband and makes love to her; she is so heavily veiled that those who might expose his plot and save her don't recognize her. Once Catella realizes that she has been deceived and therefore raped, her rapist prevents her from telling her husband by pointing out that she is thoroughly dishonored and that any confession will result in harm to everyone—the mere fact that he has raped her has ruined her, not him. Boccaccio, who professes to be a friend to women, is sympathetic to Catella's plight, but he can't give her a way of thinking about her betrayal or a way of presenting her case that enables her to go beyond her initial grief and subsequent recognition that her rapist has overcome her and she had better make the best of it. She gives in and agrees to take her rapist as her lover.

By contrast, in Arnošt Lustig's *Lovely Green Eyes,* the protagonist, a teenage Jewish girl named "Skinny," must enter a Nazi brothel to escape from a concentration camp doctor who is doing murderous experiments on camp inmates. Skinny's survival as a prostitute for German soldiers in World War II is depicted as necessary, full of pathos, and even honorable. One narrative method Lustig employs is indirect discourse—he narrates some of the most painful scenes between Skinny and her tormentors from her point of view, using empathy and a clear, specific style to make her consciousness seem normal, though of course terrified, and the behavior of the men seem evil, mad, or inhuman. The result is that rape—what had been portrayed as - naturally human by Murasaki and Boccaccio—seems monstrous in *Lovely Green Eyes*. And it is not only Skinny's honor that survives, but Skinny's sense of herself, her vitality, and her inner life. It never crosses the reader's mind that Skinny should be dismissed as a consciousness because of what is done to her; in fact, her consciousness becomes all the more interesting, all the more potentially representative because Lustig's novel seeks not to judge Skinny, but to reveal how she assimilates her horrifying and identity-killing experiences.

Let's say that the intermediate steps between *The Decameron* and *Lovely Green Eyes* were *The Heptameron* (in which the storytellers discuss and question traditional ideas), *The Princess of Clèves* (in which a woman's dilemma is made sympathetic), *Pamela* (in which a woman develops her theories and strategy without assistance), *The Bride of Lammermoor* (in which a woman's dilemma is connected to the conflicting intentions and desires of her family and community), *The Portrait of a Lady* (in which the consequences of a woman being insufficiently prepared to make her own decisions is explored), *Anna Karenina* (in which the consequences of adultery for a woman are sympathetically detailed), *The Awakening* (in which the existential despair of having made the wrong marital choice is displayed sympathetically), *Lady Chatterley's Lover* (in which a woman is allowed to change her marital choice and supported in her decision by the author), *Love in a Cold Climate* (in which marital choices and mistakes are seen as comic), *Beloved* (in which traditional ideas of female virtues are shown to be race- and class-based), and *Behind the Scenes at the Museum* (in which women's choices, whether capricious or judicious, are seen to have consequences but are not judged).

Several paradoxes emerge when we begin to look at our list of a hundred novels as a map of the way stations between Boccaccio's era and our own. One of these is that our list of novels by itself does not offer a road from one political system (monarchy) to another (democracy). To include these sorts of political changes we would have to include other literary genres, especially the drama. When kings and queens appear in our list of novels (which they rarely do) they are demoted to minor figures with few lines, or they appear in their private capacity. Kings don't fit because the novel is about how persons relate laterally to one another. Essays, philosophical tracts, books on government, perhaps poems, and certainly histories can be about how persons relate hierarchically in the social and political world. Even so, the novel does offer an emotional justification for democracy. Should Sancho Panza, Oroonoko, Moll Flanders, Frankenstein's monster, Queequeg, Tom, Lily Bart, Josef K., Lolita, and Om, in *A Fine Balance,* really have no say in their own fates? Compared with whom? By what standard?

The novel has gotten us from the manners and mores of fourteenth-century Florence to those of twenty-first-century California, though, and done so by very modest means—not by argument, but by proposing simple, understandable choices about common dilemmas. We've already discussed *Pamela* and the way that Pamela's choice to defend her virtue grows more resolute and even radical as the plot thickens. All novels work the same way. If we look at Edith Wharton's *The House of Mirth,* we see that at the beginning of the novel, Lily Bart's sense of belonging to a certain social class outweighs, for her, any sense that she might make some sort of damaging or even fatal mistake. She feels uncomfortable in certain ways—as, for example, when she finds herself at the country house of a friend and realizes that she can't afford to play cards for money anymore. The reader can't help being in sympathy with her first little decisions—to deflect the incipient courtship of a wealthy but unappealing mama's boy, and to do a little secretarial work for the friend. When she makes her next decision, which is to allow a rather floridly unattractive married man to speculate in the stock market with some of her money, it's a larger and perhaps somewhat more dangerous decision, but the reader can still see Lily's point of view, and has the sense that with luck, she will get what she wants, which is to retain both her independence and her lifestyle. Of course, Lily does not get what she wants, and her luck runs out, but the reader is guided by the author to empathize and to sympathize with her rather than to condemn her. What happens to Edna Pontellier, in Kate Chopin's *The Awakening,* is similar. At the beginning of the novel she finds herself in a fairly common situation—she is married to a man who is pompous and disagreeable. She has a new baby and is feeling rather trapped and maybe a little depressed. The weather is stifling. The first choices Edna makes are quite small— maybe the most dangerous of them is simply to learn to swim—but they change her relationship first to herself and then to the world, and lead, step by step, to much more unusual choices that the reader continues to understand. The terms of Pamela's, Lily's, and Edna's choices are always simple—not so much should she do something today or not, but *how* should she do it?

These novels, of course, are at the highly and overtly dramatic end of the spectrum. Controversial in their own day, they have never ceased to be controversial in some way. But even novels that are apparently rather simple stories, such as those of Jane Austen, work by the same method and have the same effect. At the beginning of *Pride and Prejudice,* Elizabeth's choice with regard to Darcy is only between avoiding him politely and avoiding him impolitely. Her sister Jane's choice, when she gets sick and has to stay for a while at the Bingleys', is between being a pleasant guest and being an unpleasant guest. For discriminating girls such as Elizabeth and Jane, these are choices so simple as to be automatic. Nevertheless, the choices they make turn out to contrast sharply with the choices that other characters make— Darcy's choice to allow his demeaning remark about Elizabeth to be overheard, his aunt Lady Catherine's choice to be overbearing, Elizabeth's sister Lydia's choice to indiscreetly run after army officers, and so on throughout the novel. By the end it is evident that Darcy would be an utter fool to attach himself to anyone less intelligent and witty than Elizabeth, but in Austen's era it was far more standard for a man with ten thousand pounds per year to find a woman with a similar fortune than to throw his status away on a girl with nothing, such as Elizabeth. Page by page, choice by choice, Austen's own fine sense of discernment teaches the reader to take a view similar to hers.

Such transformations in the way a character, or a reader, perceives herself and acts as a result of her perceptions were broadcast into society, and therefore into history, by market forces. In the same way that the popularity of the novel encouraged aspiring novelists to try different techniques in their own works, the nature of the novel as entertainment encouraged, or you might say trained, average readers to think in new ways about themselves and their circumstances. By taking up current concerns and portraying and commenting upon them, the novel made them present and important to readers who might not otherwise have had the education or the connections to take a larger view of their lives. In 1604, Cervantes came to writing *Don Quixote,* the first real novel, from an eventful career as a soldier in the Mediterranean wars, a bureaucrat, and, for five years, a slave to the viceroy of Algiers. He could not help but bring a larger perspective to the premise of his plot, which the reader, who was likely to be living a more circumscribed life, would imbibe along with the story. Cervantes is the model; for many if not all novelists, the European discovery of the world that was taking place while they were writing (throughout the sixteenth century, of course, Spain was being transformed by the wealth that poured into the country from the New World; throughout the seventeenth century the New World was being discovered and colonized by Europe; throughout the eighteenth century, the new colonies were assuming identities and intentions of their own) offered compelling things to wonder about as well as interesting stories to tell. In telling their stories, they expanded their readers' horizons.

If I have to pick a single institution that the novel has changed, and whose changes have in turn fundamentally changed the way people live, I would pick marriage. When characters in many eighteenth-century novels contemplate marriage, it is usually as a refuge from other adventures, which may and, indeed, usually do include threats of rape, seduction, and false marriage, fates that for female characters are worse than death. But the refuge is temporary—most marriages in eighteenth-century novels end quickly through the death of one of the spouses. In fact, the brevity of marriage is often the source of danger for the protagonist, who at the beginning of her story finds herself without two parental protectors, or sometimes even one. For Roxana, Moll Flanders, Pamela, Charlotte Temple (the eponymous protagonist in the best-selling American novel of the eighteenth century), Sophia Western, Justine and her sister Juliette, and a host of other girls, achievement of marriage and a secure home life is unlikely at best. Reproductive life, and therefore the fight for survival, begins at about fifteen; old age begins at about forty. Eighteenth-century novelists returned to these dangers over and over, in part because they were dramatic, but in part because they were typical.

As conditions shifted and Europeans began to live longer, though, novels reflected the change—marriage and domestic life became a more interesting and realistic topic for novelists, a shift that gained momentum during the nineteenth century, and eventually produced, not a paean to marriage and its benefits, but an elaborate critique of marital systems in every novel-writing society. The novelists who wrote these novels were themselves often embroiled in marital difficulties; in fact, it is hard to think of a great nineteenth-century novelist who was happily married. The list begins with Jane Austen, who never married, and runs through Gogol, Lermontov, Balzac, the Brontës, Flaubert, and James (none of whom was married while he or she was writing novels, though Charlotte Brontë and Balzac married at the end of their lives), Dickens, Thackeray, Dostoevsky, and Tolstoy (who were unhappily married), and Wilkie Collins, Eliot, Wharton, and Wilde (whose lives were sexually unorthodox). Novelists were not the only critics of marriage, of course—playwrights such as Henrik Ibsen were as avid to show the hollowness of domestic life as their novel-writing contemporaries.

The critique of marriage presented by novelists in each country owed a lot to the conventions of that country, but the underlying difficulty always had to do with how to consider women; a convention of the novel about marriage was that the most desirable candidate as a bride (such as Dora in *David Copperfield* or Emma Bovary) often proved not to be the most congenial companion for thirty or forty years of cohabitation. Authors, like societies, offered several not very satisfactory solutions to this difficulty. One is epitomized by Madame de Rênal in Stendhal's *The Red and the Black*. Madame de Rênal, the mother in the family Julien Sorel works for as a tutor, has opted to seclude herself within the family and to maintain her unworldly innocence even as a mother. She has no friends, never goes out, and divides her time between church and children. But when Julien, who is good-looking, ambitious, and selfish, appears, she has no defense against him—her innocence leads her to believe that the sexual attraction she feels is unprecedented (as it is in her own experience). Another antidote to bad marriage was a form of caveat emptor—in *Jane Eyre,* Rochester's marital problem grows out of the fact that he had been deceived into marrying his wife as part of a financial scam. The family of his wife, Bertha, used certain courtship conventions, especially the convention of preventing the bride and groom from getting acquainted, to hide the bride's defects until after the wedding (and Rochester, of course, hopes to perpetrate a similar crime against Jane). Nineteenth-century novels are filled with couples who marry entirely in accordance with property and family considerations and have to come up with some way to live out their lives of domestic discord— sometimes animosity and avoidance (as in *Jane Eyre,* and in James

Hogg's *The Private Memoirs and Confessions of a Justified Sinner,* where the unhappy couple live in separate wings of the castle), sometimes the submission of one spouse's personality to the selfish demands of the other (as in the marriage of Lucy's parents in *The Bride of Lammermoor,* where the wife is dominant, or as in Lord Steyne's marriage in *Vanity Fair,* where the husband is dominant).

In French novels, where characters may disregard the obligations of marriage entirely, as Emma Bovary does, or may kill the inconvenient spouse, as Thérèse Raquin does, or may claim the right to have any number of mistresses and lovers as long as it is done with some (though not much) discretion, as countless other characters do, the solution is somewhat different from the solution in English novels. In *Anna Karenina,* of course, Tolstoy makes a dedicated attempt to solve the marriage problem—with Anna, Vronsky, and Karenin he analyzes what goes wrong with a fairly typical marriage, where the wife is virtuous but younger and more appealing than the husband, and then, as a proposed solution, he offers Kitty and Levin as his ideal. Tolstoy is careful to show Levin's education as he courts Kitty and prepares to take up his obligations as a family man and landowner. Tolstoy is also careful to portray Kitty as virtuous, well meaning, not very interesting, and fairly easy to dominate, which makes her a likely prospect as an untroublesome wife and mother. At the end of the novel the implication is that they will conform to the ideal, multiply, and prosper. But Tolstoy was in his late forties when he completed *Anna Karenina.* His views on marriage continued to evolve. By 1891, when he was sixty-three, his critique of marriage, in "The Kreutzer Sonata," was far more extreme. Pozdnyshev, whom the narrator meets on a train, has murdered his wife, thinking she was unfaithful to him, and as a result has developed a theory of the depravity of human relations, in particular the marriage arrangements among the Russian and European upper classes, in which virtue is a pretense, debauchery is the norm, and girls are routinely sold to the highest bidder by their mothers and fathers. Pozdnyshev is disgusted by sexuality itself, asserting that husbands and wives should limit relations to a few days or a week after one child is weaned, for the purpose of conceiving another child. Otherwise a couple should live as brother and sister so as not to interfere with the processes of pregnancy and the nursing of the infant. Pozdnyshev (and there is reason to believe his character was expressing Tolstoy's own ideas) is full of energetic and eloquent conviction in his opinions—he seems to be asserting that the murder of his wife was justified, not only as a husband's traditional response to infidelity, but also by the corruption of male/female relations in general.

Nineteenth-century American novelists often avoided the subject of marriage entirely, as Melville does in *Moby-Dick* and Hawthorne does in *The House of the Seven Gables* (and he does not treat it positively in *The Scarlet Letter*). Twain rarely treats of marriage. Stowe is the only major American novelist who analyzes the institution, and though she was happily married and the mother of many children, she, too, is fully able to portray the tormented relationship of Augustine and Marie, Eva's parents in *Uncle Tom's Cabin.* By the time of Henry James and Edith Wharton, even the conventional pleasures of some of Stowe's couples have disappeared. Only Louisa May Alcott offers the idea that women have several choices—Amy marries into wealth, Meg into the traditional female satisfactions of childbearing, and Jo into her joint career with Professor Bhaer of teaching and writing. The saintliest sister, Beth, though, dies because in some sense she is too good for a typical woman's fate.

Nineteenth-century novelists themselves might have said that they were merely reporting on the qualities of what then seemed to be an unassailable institution, the nature of which predated the invention of the novel. Or they might have said that marriage was fixable—if property considerations were deemphasized, if prospective couples had enough education and self-knowledge, if marriage were simply gone about more carefully, then at least some couples would achieve a companionable and sustained happiness. Nevertheless, by enlisting readers in lengthy dramas of incompatibility, novelists subtly promoted the idea that bad marriages were not simply facts of life and fate. If an alternative, such as Dorothea's second marriage, to Will Ladislaw, in *Middlemarch,* could be imagined, then perhaps it should be imagined without the concomitant trauma of her first husband's death. (Well, maybe not—the reader is glad to see Casaubon go, but what about David Copperfield's silly wife, Dora? She seems less expendable because of her youth and innocence.) What we might call the Emma Bovary effect applies—the author constructs a lengthy plot that implies a train of cause and effect but requires the reader to suspend judgment in order to read all the way to the end of the novel. The reader ends up pondering what is wrong with the situation and having ideas of her own, and most assuredly one of these ideas will be that marriage itself could be constituted differently—that a mistake could be recognized as a mistake and the partners could be allowed to start over. This effect is not necessarily intended by the author, who may assume that the institution cannot change; it is more like a market effect—the author's ideas are taken up and modified as they move away from the source. A novelist such as Flaubert, who strives to present without overtly dictating the terms of his presentation—who strives, therefore, to be as ambiguous (and artistic) as possible—is more susceptible to this effect than a more pedestrian novelist, whose narrative voice is always dictating the terms of his story and therefore interfering with the reader's own ideas. Nor does it matter if the author's novel is generally popular, since more exclusive and sharper, less acceptable ideas filter out into the mainstream as they are translated by what you might call middlemen of ideas—other, more popular novelists, journalists, teachers, and sophisticated friends.

But if fixing marriage was, perhaps, the professed intention of all those nineteenth-century novelists, they succeeded not in fixing it, but in exposing it as perhaps unfixable. The very nature of the novel, in which the protagonists have to contrast in their fates with those around them, meant that no author with any self-respect or ambitions for a realistic depiction of the world he lived in could parcel out happy marriages to everyone in his story. Readers, though, who are the protagonists of their own lives and who are invited to identify with the protagonists of the novels they read, do not care to see themselves as secondary characters, stuck with lives that are merely examples of what the author thinks should be avoided. This is how novels always work—they expose general problems and analyze them in terms of cause and effect; to these general problems, novels propose solutions that apply to a few privileged characters; when these solutions are disseminated, readers claim at least the possibility of such solutions for themselves. Sometimes, of course, the solution proposed by the novel is a passive one, such as acceptance of the idea that evil exists or fate exists and nothing can be done about it. We often react to such novels with special admiration or respect, as I react to *The Good Soldier. The Good Soldier* is told entirely in retrospect by a narrator who has no hope of changing the outcome and not much hope of understanding it—his premise is that certain events have taken place right in front of him, but out of obtuseness and complacency, he was never able to see what was going on until it was too late for anyone to be saved. I read this with enjoyment and appreciation for the author's perspicacity, but even as I am understanding what has happened to Ford's narrator, John Dowell, I am vowing to learn from his mistakes—I will never be so unobservant. The very process of accompanying him while he disentangles his experiences reassures me that they can be disentangled. Even a novel that models acceptance works to undermine it. All novels do, and the resulting aggregation of individual readers' responses turns into a social or political movement to legalize divorce, for example.

In *Orlando,* Virginia Woolf identifies the exact moment when the marriage project of the nineteenth-century novel was completed: 10:00 a.m., October 11, 1928. Orlando runs down the stairs, gets into her car, "pressed the self-starter, and was off." Orlando is only vaguely married. She has property and a vocation of her own. In spite of her noble lineage, once she is driving her car, her "virtue" is no longer central to the reader's experience of her—she is just an anonymous human subject to the inconvenience of other anonymous humans. She goes to a department store and buys bed linens. She has a small existential crisis that the store clerk doesn't notice, goes down the elevator, and leaves London via the Old Kent Road. She wrestles with her experience— four hundred years as a man and a woman—but no one cares whether she is married, unmarried, virtuous, not virtuous. She is not possessed of a companion or protected by an escort. She is autonomous and cannot be mistaken for property. She is, in a word, free, and though her freedom is disorienting, especially in the chaos presented by the equal freedom of everyone else she meets, it is exhilarating.

The other great subject of the novel, of course, is "Who am I?," and this question is the source of Orlando's vertigo when she leaves her house in London and goes out into the city. She doesn't find out who she is until she gets back to her estate and, in particular, to the ancient oak tree that sits on the hilltop that overlooks the surrounding countryside. But even though Orlando's answer is idiosyncratic to her history and status, the question she wrestles with is the question that every novelist and every protagonist has always had to address (Defoe, with his unerring sense of the possibilities of the novel, addresses this subject over and over). Every protagonist in every novel answers this question by situating himself somewhere on the continuum between total isolation and total absorption into his group.

But "Who am I?" is another question that has been transformed by hundreds of years of novel-writing and -reading. The first truly average person to enter literary consciousness was Lazarillo de Tormes, a servant and a child. For earlier writers, such as Boccaccio, the story of an ordinary person or an ordinary couple had to have some sort of ribald premise, or had to be connected to the story of a character of higher status. But Lazarillo offers only averageness; he is the earliest precursor to the Tulls in Anne Tyler's *Dinner at the Homesick Restaurant. Dinner at the Homesick Restaurant* never purports to be a revolutionary document of social history, and yet, by contrast to almost every early novel, it certainly is, because it is about ordinary people, and because it dispenses with romance within the first few pages, when Beck Tull leaves the family. Tyler's novel explores the inner lives of Pearl and the children from an entirely practical perspective, never pointing them toward happiness or transcendence through love or family connection, and never elevating their status as a way of justifying the reader's attention to them. They marry and reproduce, but only as a matter of course. We are not to learn anything special about how they do it, only that they do it idiosyncratically. All of the Tulls are ordinary, but their claim on the reader's attention is no less insistent as a result. *Dinner at the Homesick Restaurant* was, of course, both a best seller and a major Hollywood movie. It is evidence that the novel has changed the nature of human consciousness in two ways—it has made readers and audiences more receptive to the ups and downs of everyday concerns, and it has given everyday concerns more ups and downs.

There are intermediate steps between *Lazarillo de Tormes* and *Dinner at the Homesick Restaurant,* too. Let's say they are *Don Quixote* (in which the opinions of a peasant, Sancho, are given as much space as the opinions of his master), *Roxana* (in which practical methods of daily economic survival are detailed), *Humphry Clinker* (in which the points of view of servants are depicted along with those of masters, in the different styles natural to each character), and *Jane Eyre* (in which the impoverished working woman gets to observe and judge everyone around her), *Thérèse Raquin* (in which the inner lives of entirely ordinary and venal characters are anatomized because they are ordinary, not in spite of it), *Main Street* (in which the geographic diversity of the novel is expanded to include characters outside the cultural center), and *Ulysses* (in which the most grand and elegant narrative methods are applied to an ordinary day). After *Ulysses,* we have *The Man Who Loved Children* (in which high drama is made of an ordinary family) and *The Moonflower Vine* (in which the inner lives of characters who not only think of themselves as ordinary, but are proud to be ordinary, are juxtaposed in a manner that reveals how dramatic each character really considers his fate to be). Just as the line of descent from *The Decameron* to *Lovely Green Eyes* has altered the social and psychological nature of women, the line from *Lazarillo* to *Dinner at the Homesick Restaurant* has transformed the identity of average citizens, women and men.

But identity—Who am I?—is a political as well as a personal question, and as the form of the novel spread around the world in the twentieth century, successive generations of novelists answered it in more and more complex and dramatic political terms: at first I am English, but later I am Russian, I am Austro-Hungarian, I am American, I am Irish (but a speaker of English), but later, I am an Italian speaker in Trieste; I am bilingual (standard English/Mississippi English, Russian/English, English/French, Farsi/English), I am Vietnamese and French, I am Korean-Japanese-American, I am Mexican-American—the novel takes as its very premise that identity is point of view and language functioning together, simultaneously.

As each national literature has appropriated the form of the novel, it has taken up different concerns—worries about ill-conceived marriages crossing boundaries of social class, for example, are not as prominent a part of nineteenth-century Russian novels as of nineteenth-century English novels, but exactly who is English and who isn't is not as central a theme in English novels as exactly who is Russian is a theme of Russian novels. The ubiquity of state authority is not as much a concern of American novels as of German ones, but the attractions of outlawry are not as much a feature of German novels as of American ones. The conflicts between romance and marriage are not of such overriding importance in Scandinavian novels as they are in French novels; in Scandinavian novels everyone works, every day, no matter what his or her status, while in English and French novels, members of certain classes have too much time on their hands. But even though national literatures have their common dramatic characteristics, at the same time that a novelist appears to readers to be declaring, for example, "I am Russian," to himself he is saying, "I may be Russian, but . . ." He cannot help distinguishing himself from the Russians around him. A feature of this sense of distinctiveness that the novel cultivates in both readers and writers is that many authors have been quite self-conscious about importing the form of the novel as a way of either revealing their own cultures to the world or of improving their own cultures by making them more cosmopolitan. Naguib Mahfouz, for example, experimented with using traditional Middle Eastern tale-telling forms in *The Harafish,* but wrote his most famous work, *The Cairo Trilogy,* in the realistic mode of some of the European novelists he admired, such as Balzac. Junichiro Tanizaki was influenced by the great nineteenth-century Russian novelists, as is evident in the realistic style and epic scope of *The Makioka Sisters;* he also translated *The Picture of Dorian Gray* into Japanese and wrote a short story on a similar theme, about a woman who is transformed by a mysterious tattoo. Inspired by *The Tale of Genji* after moving from Tokyo to Osaka, though, he wrote a historical novel about the sixteenth century, *The Secret History of the Lord of Musashi.*

Every national literature grows through an accumulation of specific individualities that coexist within the general impression the reader infers from different novels. The readiness of the novel to take up issues of identity has helped spread the form around the world, because readers and writers of novels are always asking, "Who are you? Are you like me? Are you different from me?" Both of these latter questions are to be answered with a yes, which, of course, like all equivocal answers, leads readers and writers to seek more and more evidence. And just as the novel has encouraged readers to think they can contemplate their own marriages and decide whether to do something about them, and has thereby changed the place of marriage in many cultures, it also encourages readers to think they can identify themselves on their own, to explore and know their own natures. It encourages them to think that such an exploration at length—even, say, at the length of Marcel Proust's *In Search of Lost Time*—is a possible as well as a worthy endeavor. Robinson Crusoe's and Roxana's justification for speaking of themselves, that they have sins on their consciences, ceased to be necessary after two hundred years of novels. M.'s four thousand pages of introspection need no preliminary excuse, only the ongoing justification of being intelligent and well-written enough to reward the act of reading. As we look around the world at the beginning of the twenty-first century, we can see that questions of identity dominate political discourse in the same way that questions about marriage (and about whether women are agents or objects) dominate personal discourse.

The novel in the twentieth century contradicted the separate reductionisms of both science and social conformity. That Proust should have considered himself worthy of so many words is in some sense less surprising than that he should have considered so detailed an introspection possible. Science, in the persons of Freud or Heisenberg (whose principle it was that the introduction of the measuring instrument itself changes the nature of the thing to be measured), would have discounted the value of Proust's efforts had he consulted them. But the novelist and his protagonist are never simply part of a statistical sample, small or large. Every word in its expression of the act of choice and in its distinctiveness from every word that other novelists have chosen to depict similar situations resists any attempt to dissolve the novelist, his protagonist, and his ideas into a larger context. At the same time, the tendency of the novel to expand and of all its parts to proliferate tends to emphasize the particular, leaving the general to be implied. Novelists and their protagonists may act according to general patterns as commonly as fruit flies do, but the burgeoning particulars of every novel dazzle the senses, mask the general patterns, and train the reader to pay attention to differences. What scientists and politicians (and religious leaders) promulgated throughout the twentieth century—that most people are more or less alike, that citizens should conform to certain roles, that certain beliefs are essential to a virtuous life or ultimate salvation—the novel itself could not go along with, whatever the professed beliefs of the novelist as citizen. And the novel requires no license or certification, only desire. The novel asserts that an ordinary person, with steady application, can become an expert upon who he himself really is simply by writing it down in his own unique style. At the end of *Zeno's Conscience,* for example, Zeno explicitly rejects psychoanalysis in favor of what he has learned in the course of writing his memoirs about being himself. His quirks are his identity; he doesn't wish to be cured of them.

In the twentieth century, the pressure to conform came from all sides. If the government was a theocracy, as in Azar Nafisi's Iran, for example, then it was a revolutionary act to read *Pride and Prejudice.** If the government is a corporatocracy, as the U.S. government is now, then reading Edward Abbey's novel about a gang of violent saboteurs, *The Monkey Wrench Gang,* is an act of resistance. If the government was a workers' republic, such as China in the 1960s, then reading any Western novel was dangerous. If entrenched power rests upon notions of the inherent inferiority of a single group, as in Hurston's American

*See Azar Nafisi, *Reading Lolita in Tehran* (New York: Random House, 2003) p. 347.

South, then *Their Eyes Were Watching God* is insurrectionary. But for
the novel, the insurrection in all cases does not lie with the idea that a
different ruling group will be substituted for the old one; it lies with
the idea that individuals will be freed from the most onerous imposi-
tions of rule itself and allowed to identify themselves and act on their
own identities. This tension exists between the protagonist and any
group. The protagonist of a novel makes up his own mind about every
norm, situates himself in relationship to every group. The history of
the twentieth century, a century of constant movement and change, of
shifting boundaries of all sorts, including but not limited to racial, ethnic, geographical, moral, political, economic, and religious, placed a
burden upon every thinking person to define and situate himself or
herself, if only to attain what every protagonist desires, a sense of oneself as an actor in the plot, with a defined, logical, and justified moral
position, a sense that the action of the plot has a meaning, and a sense
that the outcome of the plot is understandable. The popularity of the
novel was a response to this burden.

Some twentieth-century novels did challenge the idea of freedom
and personal agency, but the only way the novel can do so is by showing that a point of view is determined by outside forces. Such is the
thrust of Kafka's *The Trial* and other Kafka works. Part of the shock of
reading Kafka after reading other novels is the profound sense his protagonists have of being restricted and trapped, unable to reach a conclusion about who they are and what is meaningful. Sometimes the
trap is literal—in "The Burrow," the burrowing creature is always
occupied in repairing and improving the burrow that protects but also
constricts him. In "The Metamorphosis," the mind of a man is trapped
in the body of a bug. In *The Trial,* Josef K.'s trap may be real and
bureaucratic or it may be self-imposed by obsessive anxieties. In each
case the simplicity of Kafka's use of the tale form reinforces the sense
of restriction—the sequence of events is all. It is arbitrary and may
have no meaning but it is inexorable, and the protagonist's point of
view is there only to register and record it. In some sense, he is too disoriented by events to have an opinion about them and so he can't learn
from them and his feelings about them have an automatic and rather
animal quality. His point of view is reduced to a series of reactions.
Hermann Broch, in *The Sleepwalkers,* is as suspicious as Kafka of freedom, but the problem his characters have is not that they have no freedom, rather that a sense of freedom is pathological and inevitably leads
to cruelty. But Kafka was born in 1883 and Broch in 1886; they were

not twentieth-century men in some sense. Paradoxically, the effect of their work upon the twentieth century was, like that of *The Good Soldier,* to demonstrate that sense *could* be made of senseless events. At the end of the twentieth century, Kafka's and Broch's heirs, novelists who write about the horrors of history, such as Arnošt Lustig (the Holocaust), Chang-rae Lee (Japanese use of torture in World War II), and Kate Atkinson (combat in both world wars), tend to demonstrate faith in logic and meaning in spite of the scenes depicted. These writers are much more likely than Kafka to construct plots in which freedom can be felt, understood, accepted, and controlled as long as the protagonist can ponder his identity and understand the nature of his connection to the group. The underlying assertion of almost every novel is that meaning exists and can be understood because it can be arranged in a sequence that then takes on some sort of logic. As a result, late twentieth-century novelists seem to find meaning in even the most meaningless and brutal circumstances in part because the early twentieth-century modernists had shown them how to do so—Josef K.'s experiences may be meaningless or at least inscrutable, but at the end of *Guided Tours of Hell* and *Three Pigs in Five Days,* Francine Prose's protagonists, who share a third-person limited point of view with Josef K., as well as his sense of smallness, restriction, and self-absorption, do not have to suffer terminal meaninglessness. Their perplexity might be but an intermediate step to future understanding. As long as they don't die, narrative itself holds out the hope that they will figure things out and learn something.

At the beginning of the twenty-first century, issues of identity are combining with mass communications, high-speed travel, and accelerated resource consumption to engender what seems to be a new phase of history, but questions raised in my hundred novels remain intractably current. In the summer of 2003 I happened to go to Scotland at about the time a Scottish newspaper did a survey of the Scottish novels Scotsmen considered great. At the top of the list was James Hogg's *The Private Memoirs and Confessions of a Justified Sinner,* which I had never heard of. Sir Walter Scott, whose statue was on Prince's Street, was not on the list at all. Hogg's book was almost two hundred years old, but it had an uncanny currency in a time when the U.S. president was saying that he had invaded a foreign country because God told him to do so. I learned from the novel that in certain seventeenth-century Scottish evangelical sects, the inner assurance that one had received God's grace was thought to lead to all sorts of destructive actions. I learned that this feature of "antinomianism" has dogged certain branches of Protestantism from the beginning. As I read about Hogg's "memoirist" Robert Wringham and his familiar tempter, I could not stop thinking about George Bush and Dick Cheney. I saw that the deadly seriousness of religious controversy in the United States perhaps owes more to our Scottish heritage than to our English heritage.

A few months later, I read Garrison Keillor's *WLT: A Radio Romance,* about a fictional Minneapolis radio station on which the homely, wholesome programs broadcast are belied by the backbiting, greed, lust, hypocrisy, and shamelessness that are the constants of life at the station. I recognized Keillor's theme—that the media reduce every idea and pleasure to an advertising gimmick and a lie and prosper by doing so. The darkness of Keillor's vision, which was surprising and a little off-putting when the novel first came out in 1992, seemed prescient and all the more current during the election season of 2004, when lies and spin were the order of the day. I found it difficult but compelling to read Rohinton Mistry's *A Fine Balance,* about the 1975 state of emergency in India, when, according to the novel, Prime Minister Indira Gandhi cheated in the elections, threw the opposition in jail, and retroactively changed election laws. Mistry's very clear and eloquent evocation of the lives of his four obscure and representative characters seemed both lively and hopeless in some way—their individual ambitions and desires are so paltry in the face of not only habit, culture, and oppression, but also population pressure, economic realities, and disorganization. I was fascinated and a little bit horrified by Jennifer Egan's 2001 novel *Look at Me,* which not only straightforwardly addresses the nature of identity in a world dominated by big money, big media, good intentions, mind-altering substances, and the Internet, but also peers into the inner life of a believable terrorist hiding in Rockford, Illinois. I thought of *Justine* when I read in *The Guardian* about a French serial killer who said he went hunting for virgins twice a year. And when I read about the banning of religious symbols, especially the head scarf, in French public schools, and about honor killings of Muslim women living in Europe, I thought of *The Heptameron,* which is a catalog of honor dilemmas in which many women are killed.

In the course of 650 years, Boccaccio and his successors have helped to create a certain kind of world. It is a world not unlike the novel, a world that seems to many people transparent and automatic but isn't.

In this world, everyone, male and female, could become, might be, his or her own protagonist—that is, could develop a rich inner life based on the competing demands of conscience and ambition, selfishness and social connection. In this world each person feels a tension between himself or herself and the group, and also wishes to learn how to negotiate that tension. In this world individual existence has the potential for meaning—it can be understood and possibly changed or at least learned from. Cause and effect can be disentangled and observed. Events don't simply follow one another, as coordinate clauses do in a medieval narrative; they shape one another and grow out of one another, as subordinate clauses do in a modern narrative. In this world the ordinary person can step back, observe both the world and himself or herself, make a judgment, and then make a choice. This world is an agglomeration of individuals who relate to others as individuals. It is a world where "point of view" is a well-developed and important concept, the Western liberal ideal, and a paradox: if you look at a novel or a democracy one way, it is the tale of one person; if you look at it another way, it is a tale of a group. Neither the person nor the group ever gains permanent ascendancy; the two coexist. When, during the 2000 U.S. presidential election, Al Gore was asked to name his favorite book, he named *The Red and the Black*. Part of the reason I put it on my list was his recommendation. After I read it, I couldn't really understand what he liked about it—Julien Sorel seemed quite unlike Mr. Gore would want to seem, a cold, ambitious opportunist who uses and betrays women, then gets into trouble with the law and is executed in the end. But at least Gore's choice was a long and serious novel. The man in charge of the Western world had chosen a children's book, *The Very Hungry Caterpillar,* by Eric Carle. Let's not remark that this book is a tale of gluttony; let's just observe that it isn't a novel, that its choice as George W. Bush's favorite book perhaps reflects the fact that he doesn't read, or hasn't read, any serious novels. After a hundred and more novels of all kinds and degrees of seriousness, I was well aware that the habit of reading novels molds the mind in several significant ways, ways that other forms of literature do not. I wish that my president was reading *Pride and Prejudice*. Or *As I Lay Dying*. Or *The Harafish*. Or *A Journal of the Plague Year*.

After more than a hundred novels and two and a half years of history, I saw that the world I thought was established and secure, at least in the West, is more fragile than I thought, because it is newer than I realized. That a woman could be an agent rather than an object or a

possession, that a marriage can be chosen, then rejected, that an identity can be constructed by an ordinary person—these are difficult
ideas, strange to many, and dangerous to some. The tension between
the individual and the group that the novel depicts is often intolerable
to the group, and for some groups, an individual does not have a right
to a point of view. The routine quality of the novel, the way that novels
seem ubiquitous and benign, pleasurable, or fun, or even tedious to
schoolchildren, masks their subversiveness and helps us forget how
they have remade the world. I saw, with some surprise, that my world
is fragile not only because of forces from the East, but also because
of forces from within the West, forces from Texas, forces from Wy-
oming, forces from the evangelical right, forces from the corporate
world, forces from the world of think tanks and political institutes. We
seem to live in a world now where all thoughts are focused on the idea
of prevailing, of imposing one's beliefs on others, and no thoughts, no
thoughts are given to the costs of prevailing, or even what it means.
Have these people never read *Moby-Dick*? Well, no, they haven't.

These are current concerns that perhaps someday will seem
momentary in retrospect, but they remind me that those who don't
read novels are condemned to repeat the oldest mistakes in literature—the mistake of hubris, a Greek mistake, and the mistake of
attributing one's own emotions to God, a Judeo-Christian-Islamic mistake. Pride, arrogance, moral blindness, and narcissism are endemic
among humans, especially humans who occupy positions of power,
either in society or in the family. But when I have read a long novel,
when I have entered systematically into a sensibility that is alien to
mine, the author's or a character's, when I have become interested in
another person because he is interesting, not because he is privileged or
great, there is a possibility that at the end I will be a degree less self-
centered than I was at the beginning, that I will be a degree more able
to see the world as another sees it. And there is the possibility that I will
be able to reason about my own emotions. In the end I will be more
empathetic (I will understand through the logical connection made in
the novel and my experience of the author's sensibility as expressed in
his style) and I will be more sympathetic (I will feel along with the
characters and perhaps the author).

When I've read lots of long novels, I will be trained in thinking
about the world in many sometimes conflicting ways. One of the great
pleasures of the forty-five thousand pages and more that I read in three
years was something outside of the authors' plot making and character

9 · The Circle of the Novel

The modern novel should be largely a work of reference. Most authors spend their time saying what has
been said before—usually said much better. A wealth
of references to existing works would acquaint the
reader instantaneously with the nature of each character, would obviate tiresome explanations and would
effectively preclude mountebanks, upstarts, thimble-
riggers and persons of inferior education from an
understanding of contemporary literature. Conclusion of explanation.

That is all my bum, said Brinsley.

—FLANN O'BRIEN, *At Swim-Two-Birds*

There is, of course, still another way to consider the novel, apart
from who wrote it and why, apart from how it feels to read it.
All novels exist discretely as items in the catalog of novels, and
every one is like and unlike every other one. We can't really understand any one novel without comparing it to others—not necessarily to
decide whether it is great, greater, or greatest, but just to see how in
any particular novel all the potential ingredients are chosen and assembled. In addition, all novels happen to be related to many other forms
of discourse—the "art" of the novel always has to contend with the fact
that the novel is an essentially compromised form. The novel as we
know it grew out of earlier types of literature and can't be understood
except by reference to them. In addition, the impulse to write a novel
grows out of related impulses to communicate and tell stories, and
the novel can't be understood apart from that apparently universal
human urge.

The easiest way, I think, to conceptualize this aspect of the novel is to imagine an analog clock face with the novel in the middle and the forms of discourse it is related to arranged around the circumference. If we then plot some of our novels around the clock, how the catalog of novels arranges itself is easier to understand, and how novels succeed or fail is also easier to understand. Most authors do not, of course, consciously position their novels in relation to all the others, but inevitably, after the novel is out of the author's hands, it takes up its position in the bookcase, in the reader's mental library, and, for the sake of argument, on the face of our clock.

The clock has twelve stations, of course. Each station represents a specific type of discourse. Each type has essential characteristics and offers the reader a particular form of pleasure. If the reader does not gain the sort of pleasure she expects from that type of discourse, she will be disappointed no matter what other pleasures she does gain (if, for example, she is listening to a joke and it isn't funny, it doesn't matter much whether it is informative or eloquent). Much of a reader's willingness to suspend disbelief grows out of whether she and the author agree on what category or categories of discourse a text falls into.

THE CLOCK

12 ROMANCE

EPIC 11

ESSAY **10**

POLEMIC **9**   THE NOVEL

CONFESSION **8**

DIARY/LETTER **7**

6 GOSSIP

1 TRAVEL

2 HISTORY

3 BIOGRAPHY

4 TALE

5 JOKE

The first five forms exist to allow an author and a reader to communicate systematically about specific types of information:

1. **Travel narrative,** simple in a way, offers a series of adventures and descriptions organized around a journey. The travel narrative is always about something exotic or unknown. The travel involved may be literal—to distant places—or it may be figurative—into the mind of another creature—but if the reader gets no sense of being transported out of her own mundane existence, then the travel narrative has not delivered on its promise.

2. **History** relates a series of past events in a way that will enable the reader to make sense of them systematically, and to relate them to her own experience. Essential to history is the idea that time has passed and that the past is different from the present. The reader is asked to reason and understand; her pleasure arises from a sense that perspective has been achieved upon events that previously seemed chaotic or meaningless.

3. **Biography** is the portrayal and analysis of a single person. The reader wants to feel that she has come to know that person well, perhaps better than the person knows himself, and she also wants to contemplate the nature of humanity. It doesn't matter if the subject of the biography is very like the reader or very unlike her; it is enough that the subject and the reader exist simultaneously in the reader's mind.

4. **Tale** may partake of all the previous forms—it can be about a place, a person, or a former time—but it is always fictional and always entertaining. It can therefore include any entertaining element—magic, trickery, deception, dread, implausible plot twists, happy endings, unrealistic circumstances, and nonhuman consciousnesses—but it must induce pleasure or it doesn't qualify as a tale.

5. **Joke** is a mini-tale, but whereas a tale may arouse feelings of awe, fear, or wonder, a joke only has to arouse a laugh.

Three forms depend on and acknowledge privacy and secrecy:

6. **Gossip** is public speculation about private matters. It uses disconnection and secrecy even while using the tools of communication. Gossip is an inherently popular form, like jokes and tales, and it promotes the idea of common sense over erudition. The pleasure

for the reader is that gossip not only reveals secrets, it also interprets and assimilates them.

7. **Diary/letter** is the most intimate form of discourse. In diaries and
letters, private matters are recalled and analyzed. The pleasure
comes from the sense that the diarist or letter writer is as honest as
he can consciously be, and that his revelations are private ones. The
reader feels that the whole of the narrator's mind is open to her,
that she is as intimate with him as he is with himself, but that, as
with the biography, she may come to understand him better than
he understands himself.

8. **Confession** is the diary as a self-conscious form of rhetoric—
intimacy overheard gives way to an intentional persuasion of the
reader that the confessor's interpretation of events has meaning
and weight. The confession is different from the diary/letter in that
the events being discussed are finished and therefore seen as a
whole sequence rather than unfolding while the narrator is writing. For the reader, the pleasure of the confession is its self-
contradiction—intimacy used rhetorically is likely to be combined
with either deception or self-deception.

The next two forms are essentially rhetorical rather than, like
travel, history, and biography, narrative:

9. **Polemic** uses emotion, as narrative does, but presents it as argument, marshaling events, characters, and insights in service to a
rhetorical point. The pleasure, for the reader, is eloquence intensified by feeling and the sense that the writer is pushing the bounds
of propriety.

10. **Essay,** like polemic, uses logic and example to make an argument,
but gets rid of the emotional fervor, adopting instead a reasoned
and objective tone. The pleasure for the reader is always, as in biography and history, in the sense that the arguments are complete,
well reasoned, thoroughly worked out, and demonstrated.

The stations at the top of the clock are the two main narrative pre-
cursors of the novel, always understood to be fiction, but more formal,
significant, and complex than the tale:

11. **Epic.** The goal of this form (at least among Indo-Europeans) was
to solidify a warrior nation's sense of its own identity and the battle

prowess of its warriors. The epic was essentially tragic, since, as Krishna remarks to Arjuna at the beginning of the *Bhagavad Gita,* there is no avoiding either death or killing in this world. The reader's pleasure in the epic comes from a sharpened sense of what makes up a particular national character.

12. **Romance,** of course, is about love, sex, and relationships. The pleasure of romance comes when the reader recognizes and sympathizes with the idea that a particular connection between two characters is interesting, worthy, believable, and involving.

The novel uses all of these forms. Some novels use many of them, others use only a few, but it is impossible to have a novel that uses none of them. If we take some novels and plot them around the clock, we can get insight both into how these novels work and why some of them seem "great."

We can try out our clock by considering a paradigmatic great realist novel, *Middlemarch,* the most novelish of novels. In *Middlemarch* (which uses history, biography, joke, gossip, essay, travel, and romance) Eliot adopts a tone that is too reasonable for polemic and too objective for a tale. She excludes diary/letter and confession by remaining in the third-person point of view. And *Middlemarch* is not an epic—its characters are influenced by history and are characteristic of a certain time and place, but they do not shape and define Englishness. The biographical subjects are Dorothea, Casaubon, Rosamond, Lydgate, Mary, and Fred. Eliot characterizes each in detail—looks, clothing, domicile, family, social class, aspirations, motivations, actions, reflections—and also locates them carefully in their separate contexts, not only that of the town and environs of Middlemarch, but also in what it means to be a man, a woman, and a human being. She uses their habits and choices to develop and reveal their moral natures. At the end she tells what happened to them after the close of the plot, reinforcing the idea that they have whole lives, as biographical subjects do. But she is no less interested in the history of Middlemarch. The novel is set in a specific time and place—the rural Midlands of England, before the parliamentary reform of 1832 and before the full onset of the industrial revolution, some thirty-five years before the composition of the novel. *Middlemarch* is meant to reliably evoke the earlier era and to reflect upon the changes, for better and worse, between the two periods. Eliot is also aware of how the town functions, and she uses the gossip form in a very sophisticated manner to communicate character and plot information to the reader as well as to build up a picture of the town as a network of social relationships.

The organization of the novel sets it up as an analytical argument and therefore essaylike. Although Dorothea is an appealing protagonist, the reader is not allowed to focus upon her. After the first long section ("Miss Brooke"), the novel shifts to the concerns of other characters, who are delineated as carefully as Dorothea has been. She never quite comes to the fore again as she does in the beginning. Even though she is probably Eliot's favorite character, and maybe a representation of the author herself, the novel focuses on Dorothea's relationships and asks the reader to observe the drama of her inner development rather than to become emotionally involved with it. Restraining the reader's sympathies is perhaps Eliot's motive for depicting Will Ladislaw, who comes to town to edit a newspaper and whom Dorothea eventually marries after her first husband, Casaubon, dies, as not quite worthy of Dorothea—he is no Mr. Darcy. Eliot is making an argument about what a moral life is and how to lead one, and she is interested in the mistakes the characters make as representative mistakes rather than as personal catharses. As beautifully drawn as these six characters are, and as many of the other characters are, the pattern and meaning of their choices are what really interest the author.

Romance, of course, can be presented realistically, almost as if it weren't romance, but no character that Eliot really cares about goes unrewarded in *Middlemarch;* the marriages that are made according to Eliot's prescriptions—Mary's with Fred, Dorothea's with Will Ladislaw—get to be happy. Lydgate, of course, receives no reward—neither professional satisfaction nor conjugal happiness—because in spite of his intelligence and good intentions, he is as undeserving as his shallow wife. He not only cannot understand Rosamond, he also is barred by male arrogance from even trying to understand her until it is too late. The reader can't help infer that the author thinks he should have chosen a plainer, more genuine girl, and that if he didn't have the sense to do so, his fate is deserved.

And that is part of the joke, but only part. Pictures of George Eliot (Mary Ann Evans) always show her unsmiling and sober, a moralist to the core, but *Middlemarch* is full of smart, subtle, and very funny ideas and turns of phrase. She is much slyer than those overt satirists Dickens and Thackeray, for example. Although always aware of life's potential for grief and tragedy, she pokes much ironic fun at Mr. Brooke,

Dorothea's uncle, at Mr. Casaubon, at Fred Vincy, and many of the lesser denizens of Middlemarch. Her favorite characters are those, like Mary Garth and Mr. Farebrother, whose views are leavened with irreverence. *Middlemarch* is a serious but not a somber novel. Eliot puts wit and irony to work as antidotes to sentimentality, recognizing that the piquancy of wit makes the hard work of distinguishing between right and wrong much easier. *Middlemarch* shows that Eliot believed that virtue and pleasure, good nature and right thinking are intrinsically connected in a healthy mind.

Middlemarch shows us that a novel that partakes of at least four or five of our categories seems rich and various, and that a debt to either romance or epic is essential, because these are the "long story" forms (though it is not possible to have a novel that is a pure epic, a pure romance, or a pure combination of the two, because the objective tone of travel narratives, histories, biographies, essays, and, in some sense, polemics, becomes the realistic tone of the novel). If we look at another great artifact of the Victorian period, *Vanity Fair* (travel, history, biography, joke, polemic, epic), we can see that two authors can use five of the same "public" categories but come up with an entirely different type of novel if one of them shifts from the objective tone of the essay category to the angry tone of the polemic category. *Vanity Fair* was intended by Thackeray to be a grand portrait of the England he knew, canvassing the rulers and the ruled, men and women, the middle class, the aristocracy, the landed gentry, the colonialists, the military. But because of its satiric, polemical tone, it becomes an antiepic (the English hero dies anonymously at Waterloo), an antiromance (Amelia Sedley, Dobbin's beloved, turns out to be a disappointment in the end), an antitravel narrative (there is nothing exotic in France, much less India), an antihistory (Waterloo and everything subsequent turn out to be much like the present day of the novel), and even an antibiography in some sense, since Amelia and Dobbin are not portrayed as being especially striking individuals, and Becky disappears from the novel as if she had not dominated it from the beginning. The modern reader might not understand what Thackeray is satirizing, since his polemic is not about any recognizable ideology in the way Dickens's is or Stowe's is. Thackeray was explicitly worried about the decline of the gentleman as an English type—a brave, responsible, mature man of good breeding and good manners, honest, dutiful, and courteous. Most of his satire is directed against men who have the power and pedigree to be gentlemen, such as the Crawleys (landed gentry) and Lord

Steyne (wealth, power, and influence). In some sense his views did not disagree with those of Charles Dickens—both felt that the English ruling class was ruling irresponsibly and selfishly. But while Dickens felt that middle-class virtues of domesticity, hard work, feelings of connection to both those at the top and those at the bottom, inventiveness, and wealth creation were a possible solution, Thackeray didn't see a solution. He was thus conservative in his political inclinations— *Vanity Fair* describes loss and deterioration, and stymies notions of change or improvement. Becky, who seems to be Thackeray's protagonist at the beginning of the novel, is enterprising, imaginative, energetic, and accomplished, but her motives are usually of the narrowest and most selfish kind (the one time she takes pity on someone and extends herself to please her is one of the most moving moments in the novel). Dobbin, who seems to be Thackeray's protagonist at the end of the novel, is unselfish, but he is slow and stolid. Becky's friend Amelia is virtuous but unimaginative and silly. No adult has a responsible relationship with any child and is therefore capable of nurturing good values in the next generation. Some of those who have been disappointed nurse their grievances to the grave (such as Mr. Sedley, Amelia's father) or are too foolish to resist further injury (such as Jos Sedley, Amelia's brother). *Vanity Fair* is overtly political, but like all conservative novels, it seems to be satirizing human nature itself rather than human nature as constituted in a particular way by particular social, economic, and cultural arrangements. Unlike *Middlemarch,* it offers no alternative model through the mechanism of a happy ending, a wholly positive character, a charming narrative voice, or an example of spiritual redemption. The absence of such an alternative reinforces the polemical aspect and removes the potential for analysis—cause and effect show only how history has made both society and personal relationships what they are. There is no indication that they could be different, nor could they be redeemed.

Touches of history, biography, essay, and polemic are the marks of the realistic novel, the ways in which the novelist introduces gravity into his story. Each of the realistic novels on our list uses one or the other. But others do, too. *Dracula* (travel, history, biography, tale, gossip, diary/letter, confession, essay, epic, romance) is especially clever in borrowing the objective, fact-piling style of both history and biography to enhance the eerie weight of what is essentially a tale. In fact, of all the novels on the list, *Dracula* is one of the ones that use the most forms. All mysteries and thrillers are really tales. *Dracula* uses the information-gathering form of the case history to imply analysis and an objective tone to make the tale more plausible and more sinisterly a part of the modern world. In addition, Dracula's five pursuers are heroic; Dracula himself represents good and bad aspects of his Transylvanian history. Mina Harker, the romantic heroine, must be and is saved by her husband and his friends, while other female characters are not. Characters travel not only to Transylvania but also to Yorkshire. Several of the characters write privately of their experiences, and many of the interlocking narratives are in the first person, like confessions. Indeed, Mina's husband has to confess to witnessing Mina, in a scene reminiscent of the marquis de Sade, drinking Count Dracula's blood. *Dracula* is considered one of the best and most perennial examples of the horror genre, and surely this is the reason— Stoker makes very intelligent use of many authenticating novelistic forms to bolster his otherwise unbelievable tale and to reward the reader for continuing to read. But unlike Eliot and Thackeray, Stoker isn't out to analyze or prove a social theory, only to make his tale as exciting as possible, so *Dracula* stays slotted in its genre and doesn't break out into the mainstream of the ambitious literary novel.

Another novel that uses many categories, though with more serious overtones, is T. H. White's modern recasting of the Arthurian legends, *The Once and Future King* (travel, history, biography, tale, joke, gossip, polemic, essay, epic, romance). Although White's novel (actually four related novels written over two decades) is advertised as a children's fantasy novel, it is hard to know what children might make of some of White's crueler scenes and more serious themes concerning power, destiny, maternal seductiveness, and neglect, not to mention betrayal and adultery. White not only weds tale (the Arthurian material), history (extensive details from twelfth- and thirteenth-century English life), epic, romance, and joke, he also jumps suddenly and with sharp changes of tone from one to another. Some characters appear as comic figures, such as King Pellinore and Merlyn, others as realistic characters of considerable psychological complexity, such as Arthur, Guenever, Lancelot, Gawaine, and his brothers. Gawaine's mother, Morgause, has the witchlike features of a character in a tale, but the underlying nature of a seductive, neglectful mother in a Freudian novel. She is too complex to be simply evil, but her effect on her children is damaging and haunting; through them she affects the whole kingdom.

In addition, White had a strong interest in all forms of hunting and hawking, as well as in agriculture and natural history; much of the depiction of his English countryside is in objective, almost scientific, detail (fifty years after its publication, it is a catalog of a way of life lost and an ecosystem denuded by population growth and industrialization, one of White's themes). *The Once and Future King* is also a meditation upon conflict and war, upon the psychological links between childhood and adulthood, and upon the interactions of hatred, betrayal, courage, spiritual deprivation, and Fate. It uses every station on the clock except diary/letter and confession (it even explores, through the Lancelot and Guenever material, the pernicious but inevitable effects of gossip). It takes advantage of both the lighter and the darker ironies implicit in the contrast of romance and epic, on the one hand, with the realistic inconveniences of everyday life on the other. As befits a novel written at the nadir of the modern period, though, *The Once and Future King* expresses no faith in innocence or holy foolishness or the worth of good intentions. It shows that varied use of the different forms related to the novel makes a novel richer and more powerful. If a novelist can use them unapologetically and knowingly, giving the reader funny jokes and real information and a worthy romance and a true sense of the broader national concerns he is getting at, the reader will be willing to suspend disbelief and accept what on the surface might seem to be jarring tonal discontinuities.

A tale is something that tellers and listeners agree, for the sake of entertainment, might have happened, but it always contains the possibility of impossibility—this is the charming hook upon which White hangs his novel, and also the reason it became an animated Disney feature, but the greatest example of an author using the tale form on this list is Franz Kafka's *The Trial*. Everything about Josef K.'s experience is mysterious and problematic. Who are the officials? Who sent them? What are the laws they are enforcing? Why do they act as they do? What is the meaning of their existence, or, indeed, of Josef's existence? Where does the action take place—a particular town (Prague, for example), a mythic town, or Josef K.'s mind? Josef's story is told in an objective and realistic way, as if this were not a tale but an example of a realistic novel, but the names and dates that would anchor it in the way that *Middlemarch* is anchored in the 1830s in the English Midlands are missing. *The Trial* also exploits the promise of the tale to be entertaining—it seems until the end to be a joke. Tricks are constantly being played on Josef K., and many of those around him think his situation is funny as well as worrisome. His dilemma is, indeed, intended to rouse a laugh, only not in Josef K., since he is the butt of the joke. The reader is not encouraged to be entirely sympathetic to him—as Josef addresses his dilemma, he sometimes acts unwisely or oddly, and the reader is allowed to think that she might have acted more intelligently or less neurotically in similar circumstances and thereby achieved a different outcome. Nor is Josef an epic hero. He does not typify his nation—we don't even know what his nation is; he never even tries to act courageously; all he wants is to do the proper thing and survive—he is too eager to subordinate himself to be the protagonist of an epic. Only insofar as the reader identifies with his helplessness is he allowed any tragic dimension at all. The important thing to remember about *The Trial* emerges as we look at our clock— without romance, without travel, without polemical anger, without analytical perspective, without even the introspection of a diary or a confession, Josef K. is a hapless modern man, bereft of all the resources the novel has to offer against the meaningless workings of mechanical modernity.*

That *A Tale of Two Cities* (travel, history, tale, joke, polemic, epic, romance) is meant as a tale is evident by the use of the word "tale" in the title rather than, say, "history" or "story." A tale is meant to be entertaining, and Dickens's tale is—it is full of adventure and excite- ment—but a tale also can always be cautionary in a way that a story or a history cannot be because a tale is traditionally used as an exemplum or parable. Dickens intended his fellow Englishmen to understand that they could still be forced to learn the lesson of the French Revolu- tion if the bureaucracy (the Circumlocution Office in *Bleak House*) and the aristocracy (Lord and Lady Dedlock, also in *Bleak House*) did not

---

*In the second volume of *Don Quixote,* Quixote is the object of an elaborate and cruel practical joke that puts him in a situation similar to that of Josef K. Nothing Quixote can think of or do seems to untangle the confusion, and his humiliation has a ready audience in the duke, the duchess, and their retainers. Quixote, though, is an epic hero with a firm set of beliefs in medieval romantic ideals of chastity, generosity, courage, and faith. He attempts to adhere to his ideals throughout his ordeal, and the reader is a witness to both sides of the equation—the elaboration and enjoyment of the ruse by the duke and the duchess and the growing confu- sion, and then, it seems, despair, on the part of Quixote. He has what Josef K. does not have— a worldview to fall back upon—and it has been learned from literature. Even when this worldview does not work as a formula for fruitful action or as a picture of the world Quixote lives in, it does sustain Quixote's sense of who he is. He does not die meaninglessly and alone, as Josef K. does, but in his own bed, in the company of well-wishers. *Don Quixote* partakes of many of the contributory narrative forms—tale, joke, confession, and even essaylike dis- courses on various subjects are folded into a travel narrative, a history, a biography, an epic, and a romance. The two volumes of the novel seem to encompass the world of the late six- teenth and early seventeenth centuries partly because they encompass nine of our twelve nar- rative forms.

mend their methods of governing. All of Dickens's writing during and for many years after the Crimean War (1853–56) partook of the disgust and contempt he felt for the English Parliament, English bureaucracy, and the English class system. In one letter he wrote during that war, he seemed to think that even his eloquence (which he himself considered "inimitable") could not express the depths of incompetence and venality to which the government had sunk. The tale form enabled him to wed polemic and entertainment and excused him from the realistic requirements of detailed, plausible cause and effect (which can give the reader a chance to disagree with the author's arguments and make up her own mind). Dickens was no advocate of revolution; in *A Tale of Two Cities* he sets forth his nonrevolutionary critique of European society. But he does not use analysis. Instead, he weds techniques typical of the tale—the way, for example, that characters such as Madame Defarge, Dr. Manette, and The Vengeance act in a repetitive, dreamlike manner—to the impassioned eloquence characteristic of the polemic.

In the Evrémonde brothers, the father and uncle of Charles Darnay, he gives us a pair of rapists, murderers, and thieves who are callous, cruel, and scheming, but he gives their crimes a folktalelike atmosphere (late at night in the castle, the young girl dies). When Darnay's uncle is murdered, he even turns into a monster, through the association of his death mask with the castle gargoyles. That Madame Defarge, the sister of the raped girl, and her husband should not only hate the brothers but also desire to torture and kill them is the most natural thing in the world, but gradually Madame Defarge, too, becomes a monster. By contrast, we have the tale of Sydney Carton, who begins as a realistic English type of idle young man of good education and bad habits. Through his love for Lucie he is transformed into a saint, and his execution in place of Darnay is explicitly narrated as a reenactment of the Crucifixion.

Polemics must be eloquent, and it is through an eloquence that is almost incantatory that Dickens addresses the challenge of depicting collective emotions and class warfare. Every novel about class conflict or mass movement is at a disadvantage, because a scene that a film, for example, could effectively put on the screen for a few moments—a rioting crowd or an attacking army—the novelist must string out word by word. To handle this challenge, Dickens uses metaphorical language energized by anger. When he introduces the depredations of the aristocracy, he portrays "Monseigneur," who requires numberless servants merely to serve him his chocolate. "Monseigneur" represents, by synecdoche, the corrupt luxury of the ruling class. When, in the next chapter, Monseigneur goes to his country estate, Dickens describes the landscape: "A beautiful landscape, with the corn bright in it, but not abundant. Patches of poor rye where corn should have been, patches of poor peas and beans, patches of most coarse vegetable substitutes for wheat. On inanimate nature, as on the men and women who cultivated it, a prevalent tendency towards an appearance of vegetating unwillingly—a dejected disposition to give up, and wither away" (p. 103). Toward the end, when Lucie is living in Paris, she watches some women dance the carmagnole. Dickens's description conveys his views about the revolutionaries:

> They danced to the popular Revolution song, keeping a ferocious time that was like a gnashing of teeth in unison. Men and women danced together, women danced together, men danced together, as hazard had brought them together. At first, they were a mere storm of coarse red caps and coarse woollen rags; but, as they filled the place, and stopped to dance about Lucie, some ghastly apparition of a dance-figure gone raving mad arose among them. They advanced, retreated, struck at one another's hands, clutched at one another's heads, spun round alone, caught one another and spun round in pairs, until many of them dropped. While those were down, the rest linked hand in hand, and all spun round together: then the ring broke, and in separate rings of two and four they turned and turned until they all stopped at once, began again, struck, clutched, and tore, and then reversed the spin, and all spun round another way. Suddenly they stopped again, paused, struck out the time afresh, formed into lines the width of the public way, and, with their heads low down and their hands high up, swooped screaming off. No fight could have been half so terrible as this dance. It was so emphatically a fallen sport— a something, once innocent, delivered over to all devilry—a healthy pastime changed into a means of angering the blood, bewildering the senses, and steeling the heart. [Book 3, chapter 5]

The requirements of the polemic demand emotional intensity, and emotional intensity can be achieved with highly figurative language. Dickens had an analysis—he got it from Thomas Carlyle's history of the French Revolution. But the success of *A Tale of Two Cities* as a depiction of the nature of revolutions depends on the narrative tools he gained from the use of the tale and the polemic and how he meshed them with his more typical use of joke, romance, epic, travel, and history.

An author with a different, nonpolemical temperament, such as Ivan Turgenev, may write a political novel that has a polemical story but not a polemical effect. Turgenev's *Fathers and Sons* (biography, tale, gossip, essay, romance) takes up political issues that were current in Russia and Europe in the 1850s, while he was writing the novel— scientific objectivity versus Romanticism. He views them through the lens of the generation gap, but the effect of *Fathers and Sons* is not so much to press an agenda as to weigh the advantages and disadvantages of several agendas and then leave the question open.

Turgenev pretends at the beginning that his story is a simple one; indeed, it has the light, self-contained tone of a tale, never the ponderous, exhaustive air of a history. A young man leaves the university and returns to the family estate. He brings with him his best friend. The first young man is an easygoing, good-looking, and rather immature fellow, but much beloved by his father and his uncle. The second is what we might call "a brain." He has been a brilliant student and he holds the newest German theories, but one of his theories is that all allegiances, and even affections, are suspect. No one of the older generation quite knows what to make of this second young man. When he visits his own parents, they are affectionate, but nevertheless he is estranged from them—he seems to be cold by nature. Ultimately he offends his friend's uncle (an aging exponent of European Romanticism), and the uncle challenges him to a duel, which they fight. The uncle is injured, but more than that, embarrassed.

There are also sisters and mothers in the novel. The two young men are intrigued by a beautiful woman, an example of an independent "new" woman, so the novel takes up the concerns of romance, but the beautiful woman proves more than either of them can handle. The brilliant young man falls for her, but his affections are unrequited, because she is not interested in giving up her freedom. The brilliant young man dies. The first young man falls in love with the younger sister of the "new woman," and the last scene of the novel is their marriage feast, which takes place on the estate where the father has also married his mistress, a local girl who had borne him a son. The last scene presents a pastoral vision of integrated family happiness and strong but courteous affections. All of the characters still living at the end are the feckless ones, the ones motivated primarily by attachment to each other, to the estate, and to doing things more or less as they have always been done, and they are happy enough. They miss the stricter and more ideological characters, but only in an abstract way—their comfort isn't much mitigated by the events of the novel, sad as those might be.

Fathers and Sons is more analytical than any of our other political novels. Each advocate of an ideological position is unsympathetic in some way. The brilliant young man seems to have only the coldest of feelings—any sort of connection is anathema to him, even the connection he feels toward the beautiful, self-possessed woman. The Romantic uncle is clearly old, prissy, and outdated. He may represent passion, but it is the passion of resentment rather than desire. In the end, simple family feeling papers over the differences, which are not resolved, either between the characters or in the author's analysis. To a more ideological writer, such as Dostoevsky, who disliked Turgenev, it must have seemed as if Turgenev came to no conclusion at all. But to modern readers, used to the brutal effects of competing ideologies, Turgenev's conclusion may seem to have the charm of perennial verity—even though the problems of the nation cannot be solved, with a little bit of luck, families can live, reproduce, and enjoy one another. *Fathers and Sons* uses the methods of realism, but its talelike qualities rob it of any sort of bombast; it offers entertainment first and enlightenment only if the reader can understand the subtler implications of the characters' thoughts, actions, and relationships. It is a political novel with tact, content to offer observations rather than a program.

Some novels use the private stations of our clock as models, and one of my favorite early ones is *The Expedition of Humphry Clinker,* Tobias Smollett's 1771 epistolary novel (travel, joke, gossip, diary/letter, polemic, confession, romance). Diaries and letters share the quality of immediacy—as the action is unfolding, the narrator writes what is happening without knowing how it is going to turn out. This can seem artificial, which is probably one reason that the epistolary novel has more or less died out—modern readers are likely to suspend disbelief in many volumes of Proustian introspection without needing the added frame of letters or entries with dates and reasons for writing. Even so, *Humphry Clinker* is well worth reading. It relies on the perfectly natural combination of travel narrative and diary/letter. Five characters—a middle-aged man who is ailing; his sister, with whom he does not get along; their nephew, who has just finished university; their niece, who is just finishing her schooling, too; and the sister's maidservant—embark upon a tour of the spas of England. Each has a correspondent back home, so the sights and adventures of the journey are reported variously by the five letter writers, each of whom characterizes himself or herself, gossips about the others, and sees what the others don't see. Like Sterne and Fielding, Smollett had an earthy sense of humor and a full complement of pet peeves. The polemical edge comes in the letters of Matthew Bramble, the squire who is financing the tour for the sake of his health—Matthew doesn't like much of what he sees on his journey. Even so, the conceit of having five disparate letter writers allows the novel to add up analytically to a less grumpy and polemical whole. Uncle Matthew may be right about many things, but the more exuberant voices of the other characters, and the action (three weddings in the end, and a healthy acceptance of the joys of sexuality) contradict his dark view. Humphry himself, a manservant Matthew hires early in the journey, turns out not to be a character as much as a catalyst for Matthew's redemption. *The Expedition of Humphry Clinker* is a rare example of an author using the forms of diary/letter, polemic, joke, and gossip to generate, in effect, travel narrative, analysis, history, and biography (with some good romance thrown in), and it has the charm of novelty.

At first glance, John Updike's stories about Henry Bech, his literary alter ego, seem like a polemical joke—that is, a satire. Bech's motives are always selfish and fearful. He is lusty but has no taste for reciprocal relationships; he uses literary contacts only to advance his own status; his work is precious to him, but only insofar as it once raised his status or lowered it—he doesn't have much attachment to what he has written or the act of writing it because it doesn't express any ideas or feelings he is committed to. He is full of envy, resentment, self-pity, and a sort of craven awareness of his needs that passes for self-knowledge. In his view, no one on the literary scene is any different. The literary world is divided into fools and knaves—silly women who respect him because they don't know any better are marginally less interesting than smart women who have his number but sleep with him anyway. Men in general are mostly uninteresting or vaguely threatening (until the end, when he decides to revenge himself upon reviewers who have failed to appreciate him over the years). Literary accomplishment is a farce—when Bech becomes president of a famous literary organization he had once respected, he sees all the members as eccentric has-beens and disbands the organization in order to sell the expensive real estate it owns.

And yet Updike's Bech stories are much more fun than *Vanity Fair,* no doubt because Updike's own narrative presence offers an alternative to Bech—because we are aware of Updike observing Bech, the stories become a kind of confession. Bech is Updike's alter ego, but so is Updike Bech's alter ego. Bech is sour, but on the evidence of Updike's style in writing about Bech (pointed but good-natured), Updike is not sour. Bech thinks of no one but himself, but Updike's detailed observations and clear, smooth style show that he thinks not only of Bech, but also of all the women and men Bech meets. Bech's life is one humiliation after another (since even success is some form of humiliation), but Updike makes it clear that it is Bech's own perception that is seeing humiliation where it doesn't exist. For Bech, everything is a personal insult. For Updike, the literary world is large and impersonal. Forces that seem directed at Bech are just the natural ebb and flow of age, time, and circumstance. In one early story, Bech goes to a women's college in the Virginia countryside (travel narrative). He can't take the natural fertility of the campus, and he suffers existential vertigo at not being the center of the universe. Updike beautifully renders the flowers, trees, weather, and lawns that torment Bech, in all their normal, impersonal beauty. They do not torment Updike. He feels comfortable with them, and yet he is no less precise in describing Bech's discomfort.

The disjuncture between Updike and Bech is funny (making use of the joke category) and stays funny from the beginning to the end of *The Complete Henry Bech.* As Bech becomes more outrageous, Updike becomes more daring, and this daring is thrilling, an example of authorial virtuosity that the reader can't help finding enlivening. For Updike, the Bech stories are a mock history, a mock biography, and a mock confession—how would he render so well all of Bech's craven feelings and impulses if he had never experienced them? But they are an essay, too, on how the literary life works, and this analytical component comes from the witty separation between author and character. And they are gossip—the reader can't help being aware that what Updike knows about being a Jewish writer he learned from talking to and about Jewish writers. And then, in the end, when it seems almost too late, Bech gets to have a romance—though not, as might have been expected, with a wife or a lover (he is too jaded and selfish for that). He disdains women too habitually to reform, but he has a baby girl at last, and his final appearance (in front of the Nobel committee, of course) is not about self, lust, or prizes, it is about the little

girl speaking and Bech's honest pleasure, after seventy years, in someone other than himself.

Italo Svevo's *Zeno's Conscience* (history, joke, gossip, confession,
essay, epic, romance) shows, like the Bech stories, that confession
requires a light touch. *Zeno's Conscience* is, ostensibly, the psychoanalytic notes of a prominent businesssman from Trieste, which have been
gathered and are being published as an act of revenge by his analyst,
who writes an introduction. The reader quickly forgets this conceit
because Zeno's voice is more charming and more arresting than the
voice of the vengeful psychoanalyst. When, at the end of the novel,
Zeno decides that he does not want to be cured, the reader can only
agree. Nevertheless, the use of psychoanalysis as a conceit sets up
Zeno's confessions as an organized contemplation not only of who he is
and what he has done, but also of his wife and her family, his business,
and the way life works (or worked before the First World War) in Trieste, which is not quite Italian but not quite central European, either.
Zeno does not order his confession chronologically, but in terms of the
importance of his problems. Ironically, his least important problem,
trying to quit smoking, is also his most difficult. His greatest problem
(he says) is that he was cajoled, or maybe tricked, into marrying his
wife, who was exactly the one sister of four he did not want to marry.
But his confessions prove to him that his marriage is satisfying in a lot
of ways, and that if his life had worked out as he originally planned, it
would have been much worse.

Not many of our novels are confessions, because confession is the
hardest form to pull off. Most authors choose to examine the consciences of others, and, given the pleasures of gossip, most readers are
content to collude in this idea. This is the formal bargain of the usual
type of novel—author and reader will stand a bit to the side of the
characters and observe them, inwardly and outwardly, and will agree
to pretend that the characters are not the author and his friends. Successful observation requires detachment, and the reward of successful
observation is new knowledge. Overt confession places a rhetorical
burden on the author not to embarrass himself and a social burden on
the reader not to be aroused to disgust, dislike, or boredom. Both
Updike and Svevo show that the author can preempt the reader's possibly negative reaction to the confession mode by exercising detachment right at the beginning, by showing that the confession is above all
an exercise in analysis and history, forms that require detachment and

an objective tone. Updike, of course, exercises detachment by naming his negativity "Bech." Svevo exercises his detachment by confessing his most trivial but besetting sin first, and only then going on to concerns that have greater moral complexity.

Now, obviously, both of these confessions are conceits. They are not the actual confessions of John Updike and Ettore Schmitz (Svevo's real name), but the conceit is useful for smuggling in real contemplation of real feelings and events. For the novelist's purposes, the form of the confession is as difficult as real confession—he still has to make his confessing character attractive enough to beguile the reader into continuing to read. Zeno persuades us of his sincerity by telling tales upon himself in which his faults are displayed, by lamenting his faults, and by showing his loving relationship with his wife. In the course of his confession—that is, of portraying himself and his relationships—he also constructs a social history of his place (Trieste) and his class (wealthy merchants) in the pre–World War I era.

An added feature of the confession is illustrated by Nicholson Baker's 1992 novel *Vox* (tale, joke, gossip, confession, essay, romance). In this case, confession is combined with tale in a lengthy but self-contained episode of phone sex. There is no framing device—the reader is not told anything and must infer whatever information she can from the conversation. What seems to be going on is that a man from the West Coast and a woman from the East Coast hook up over the phone. They end up talking for several hours and, possibly, revealing a lot about themselves, but always anonymously. The apparent purpose of the call is mutual arousal, and there is some phone sex, but there is also mere conversation, and some of it is boring. It is never clear whether the callers are being honest or deceptive at any stage of the conversation, but nevertheless, two characters, and a novel, are constructed. Reading *Vox* requires a certain amount of patience, but Baker is full of tricks. He asks us to accept the idea that a novel can be interesting even when it is stripped of all the usual novelistic furniture—not only plot and individualized characters, but also the assurance that what we are reading is significant or pivotal in the lives of the characters. Maybe it is, maybe it isn't. The strict frame of the novel, which begins with the beginning of the call and ends when the callers hang up, means that we never know, and this is part of Baker's joke. Since a tale and a confession (and a joke) may always be untrue without contradicting the premises of these forms or forestalling the payoff, the reader is never uncomfortable doubting *Vox*—she can believe it or not. A tale has to be entertaining (which *Vox* is), and a confession has to seem intimate (which *Vox* does). The pleasure is in the acceptance of the conceit, as in a joke, not in the assertion of truth. If the partners to the call were actual potential romantic partners, not separated by so much distance, then the possible lies would give rise to more tension, but no real romance is likely to eventuate, so the two confessors and taletellers are free to elaborate at will.

Some of these same issues come up in *Wuthering Heights,* which in form is a tale nested in a confession nested in gossip, along with elements of travel narrative, history, epic, and romance. At the beginning of the novel, Lockwood, a renter from southern England, shows up to take possession of a neglected property in Yorkshire. He happens to go to his landlord's house to pay his respects (and perhaps to snoop a bit). He runs into some misadventures that result in an injury that confines him to his bed. To entertain him, his housekeeper, Nelly Dean, who has known the family of his landlord all her life, tells him their story, and her own, since she was implicated in the events. The degree to which she has been implicated, in fact, is one of the facets of the novel most disputed by critics, some of whom see her as a Machiavellian figure manipulating all of the other characters for her own purposes.

Unlike Svevo and Updike, Nelly Dean is thoughtless in her confession. She tells it straightforwardly, perhaps not realizing that the form of confession requires addressing the issue of responsibility. A confessing character is not allowed to be merely a witness, nor can she fudge her own motives for taking certain actions or making certain decisions. For Emily Brontë, using Nelly to tell the story poses several insoluble problems that demonstrate the rhetorical difficulties of confession. The primary one of these is that if Nelly spends too much time discussing her own motives, she shifts attention away from the real story—that of the two generations of Lintons and Earnshaws and their interactions with Heathcliff. A confessing character almost can't help being the main character of his or her own story, but Nelly's story is not the most interesting or dramatic, and if she were to spend more time on herself, she would seem self-involved and misguided. In Emily Brontë's time, the modernism of Svevo and Proust, which could be defined as an intense experience and revelation of the self no matter whether the self has much to offer, was still eighty years in the future—the inherent drama of a situation still largely dictated whether the situation was worthy of a novel. Brontë did the best she could with the compromise of Nelly, no doubt deciding that the tale form she chose (with listener, teller, and tale all portrayed in the novel) would work best for the uncanny and violent material she had to work with, and for the complex time scheme of the story, which combines past and present in the first part, and develops further in the second part, when Lockwood returns to give up the house and gather his belongings.

Indeed, Brontë's material was so shocking and violent that even her sister Charlotte declared to her biographer that she didn't understand how Emily came up with it, or what it meant about her sister's nature, though they lived and wrote together for thirty years. Cathy's capriciousness, Heathcliff's vengefulness, their passion for one another, the elemental brutality of the setting—all of these features of the novel required some sort of remoteness from the everyday Victorian world of the 1840s. By making it all gossip, Brontë could get her novel written and published. The public (those few who read the novel, which was not popular in its day) was given permission to think of it all as hearsay, and, more important, to feel its power at a distance and, if need be, dismiss it, which many readers did. Is Nelly implicated in the fates of her charges? I don't think this question can be answered with reference to the text, but, rather, arises from the way the needs of the material and the forms Brontë employed jostle against one another in the final product.

A. S. Byatt's *Possession* (travel, history, biography, joke, gossip, diary/letter, confession, essay, epic, romance) is a good example of how far an author can extend the forms the novel partakes of and still maintain the sense of forward motion. *Possession* consists of two parallel romance narratives that take place 130 years apart. In the 1980s a young scholar discovers a draft of a love letter written to a mysterious woman by a famous male Victorian poet who is thought to have been uxoriously and faithfully married. He then contacts another young scholar, and between them they ascertain the identity of the letter's recipient, an obscure female Victorian poet whose reputation has been resurrected by modern feminist scholarship. In the course of their scholarly investigation the two academics are drawn to one another, and they finally get together in the modern happy ending. But they uncover a passionate and ill-fated love affair between their two poets that resulted in grief, anger, and, of course, lots of poetry—not a happy ending at all (until the last minute).

Possession is, above all, a tour de force. However the reader feels about the characters and the story, she cannot help being astonished

and impressed by Byatt's array of literary skills. She simply creates
two, three, four entire worlds—the world of modern scholarship is the
least of them, a slightly comic depiction of the nature of academic life,
with its rivalries and jealousies and grant-earning necessities. Inside
this frame she sets the lives and works of her two poets—Randolph
Ash and Christabel La Motte. He represents the masculine—he is a
famous and aggressive man of his time, prolific upon all sorts of manly
themes such as Norse mythology and natural history. She represents
the feminine. She is not prolific at all, and her work is in a Celtic, folkloric tradition of spells and lyrics. Byatt uses and composes in all of the
forms her scholars and poets would be familiar with—poetry of many
types, academic prose, letters, diary entries, tales, even gossip (since
some of what the modern characters learn is in the form of speculation). In the course of intertwining her two narratives and bringing
each of them to a satisfactory conclusion (which involves, for the Victorian narrative, revealing everything that happened and what it meant,
and for the modern narrative bringing the two protagonists together
in the end), Byatt has much to say about the methods and goals of
scholarship, about the nature of literature, about the differences between the Victorian period and ours, and about the relationship of the
intellect to love and passion. The way in which Byatt structures her
novel is a beautiful lesson in arrangement as a simple and effective
method of making an argument (the ghost of George Eliot appears
fleetingly at the beginning of the novel—clearly Byatt learned a great
deal from Eliot's careful architecture). As Byatt presents her narrative
portion by portion, she piques the reader's interest in forms that might
otherwise not appeal—each poem or bit of biography serves to solve a
portion of the mystery and forward the plot, and as a result it is dangerous to skip anything. Byatt is not an especially funny writer, but she
subtly recognizes the operation of irony, especially in the modern story,
so she is witty in the same way Eliot is—as a form of intelligent recognition of the differences between ideals (foolish or not) and reality. She
uses just about every station on our novel-clock (not polemic, perhaps,
athough a minor character expresses a good deal of anger in one section) and then some. Part of the display of Byatt's virtuosity is that she
uses the different forms but does not dissolve them together into one
mix, as some other novelists do—she juxtaposes their different literary
styles and intentions, and uses plot suspense to move the reader forward, as Bram Stoker does in *Dracula*. In fact, one of the pleasurable
uses of our novel-clock is to note connections between novels that on

the surface seem unrelated. *Possession* seems far more serious and literary than *Dracula,* but both require the suspense and mystery of the tale
(which is highly plotted) to energize the form (which could otherwise
seem chaotic). If we were to analyze *Anna Karenina* by means of our
clock, we would see that it is a lot like *Middlemarch* in overall tone and
intention, but since Tolstoy did not employ the wit of George Eliot to
add both liveliness and perspective to his long novel, he had to use
something else, and he used the features of the epic. The epic qualities
of *Anna Karenina* redeem the potential sordidness of the adultery story
and also give the novel as a whole scope and importance.

And so, where does greatness lie? The clock suggests some ideas. Four
of our novels are generally considered great: *Middlemarch, The Trial,
Vanity Fair,* and *Wuthering Heights.* Three of them (*The Complete
Henry Bech, Vox,* and *Possession)* are too new to be judged great, but
they are certainly profoundly respected contemporary works. Six of
them (*Dracula, Humphry Clinker, The Once and Future King, Fathers
and Sons, A Tale of Two Cities,* and *Zeno's Conscience)* have adherents,
but each is in some way eccentric or perhaps limited. Maybe the proper
word to describe their effect is not "great" but "striking."

There is no single quality that the "great" novels share other than
the biographical quality—the sense that the reader comes to understand a character completely, better than the character understands
himself or herself. Becky, Josef K., Dorothea, Lydgate, Heathcliff, and
Cathy are all bodied forth as more knowable and logical than it is
humanly possible to be. The only quality that all of the novels are without is the intimate form of the diary/letter, which might be a coincidence, but also, in relationship to the biographical quality, might mean
that greatness in a novel entails perspective upon the protagonist that
the diarist or letter-writer can't achieve even when the diary form is a
conceit. Three of our great novels have a romantic element. Freud
maintained that the two great human endeavors are love and work.
Perhaps a great novel can run for only two hundred pages or less without romance, as *The Trial* does, though, as *Wuthering Heights* (340
pages) makes clear, work is more expendable. In many novels work
exists more as furniture than motivation, though part of the genius
of several of these novels is serious attention to the meaning of a
life work—Lydgate's medical vocation, Becky's struggle for survival
(since by gender she is excluded from a vocation—this is one of the
great themes of the nineteenth-century novel). Josef K. has a job, but it

is not treated like a vocation—his vocation is trying to figure out what is happening, what is imposed upon him. *Vanity Fair* is explicitly epic, and so is *Wuthering Heights* if we consider the Yorkshire moors a separate country from England, as Emily Brontë seems to have. *Wuthering Heights* may be seen as an epic of the moors.

What is perhaps more significant is that only *The Trial* does not use many of the forms. *Middlemarch* uses seven—romance, history, biography, joke, gossip, essay, and travel; thus it offers the payoffs of relationship understanding, historical understanding, biographical understanding, shared laughter (and perspective, through irony), community wisdom (through gossip), objective analysis, and finally a sense that the mundane English Midlands are actually exotic.*

Obviously, though, what we take away from any of these great novels is more than a sense of broad inclusiveness. Each one has a distinct type of greatness. The voice of George Eliot seems uniquely wise and thoughtful; the voice of William Makepeace Thackeray seems uniquely serious, sharp, and worldly; the voice of Emily Brontë seems uniquely passionate. It is tempting to divorce these types of uniqueness from the general quality and breadth that are natural to the novel and that so many novels have. What seems to be happening is that the author's voice and his or her protagonist's potential fit one another and illuminate one another in a unique way. But in fact, capaciousness works for the novelist in several ways. When he includes many components in his novel, he stimulates his own thinking as he tries to get the parts to mesh—dilemmas of narrative as simple as time sequence and cause and effect require the author to think about the complex connections between his parts and to express these complexities in his style, which becomes more probing and more idiosyncratic. A person of natural wit, such as George Eliot, ends up bringing her wit to bear upon more interesting ideas and relationships between and among ideas and thereby expands the power of her wit. The ultimate feeling

---

*Don Quixote uses almost every form but the diary and the polemic in one section or another— even a sense of history is employed when the second volume reflects on the effects of the first and when Quixote comments upon the supposed decline in civilization that has intervened between the time of his knightly heroes and the present time of the novel. So perhaps the straightest path for a novelist seeking greatness is variety and capaciousness: the novel promises to encompass all things as an effect of its almost infinite expandability; when the author piles word upon word, sentence upon sentence, and incident upon incident, he signals this ambition and is also expected to make good on his promise. In eight hundred pages, ambitions are usually realized or not.

we get from each of these great novels, that of knowing the protagonists abundantly, grows naturally out of all the forms around the clock
they are required to inhabit. Sometimes the parts *don't* mesh—Becky
Sharp does not sit comfortably in her novel the way Dorothea Brooke
sits comfortably in hers, because Thackeray's tone is polemical—his
anger is directed both at Becky and at the world she lives in—but the
greatness of Becky is that she is morally suspect and yet strangely
admirable, stronger, more alive, and yet more vulnerable than the conventional characters who have none of the self-knowledge Becky has.
The jostling of Thackeray's polemical tone with the epic, romantic,
geographical, and historical elements of the novel produce Becky. The
greatness of these capacious novels grows out of how the integration of
the parts stretches and stimulates their authors at every level—the
level of style; the level of structure; the level of characterization; and
the level of thought about ideas, feelings, and sensations. Part of the
author's genius was that he (or she) rose to the occasion provided by
the materials of the novel, but another part of his genius was that
he created the occasion by conceiving the materials of the novel to
begin with.

The Trial, though, shows that radical simplicity and focus, resulting
in an intensity of intimacy that is thoroughly original, is another path
to greatness. What Kafka understands better than anyone is the simple
power of narration—a story is constructed one image and one incident
at a time. Once the images and incidents are expressed clearly, they
exist powerfully and in some sense ineradicably in the reader's mind.
If they are sufficiently compelling, the reader cannot help contemplating them. To qualify them in any way, even by relating them to other
ideas, is to muddy them. *The Trial* is an effective answer to E. M. Forster's lament that attention to "What happens next?" inevitably renders a narrative too common or pedestrian to be truly profound.
"What happens next?" can be a far more interesting question than
those Forster preferred—"Who does it happen to?" "What does it feel
or seem like?" "What does it mean?"—but only if, like Kafka, the
author doesn't acknowledge those questions at all. Kafka's form of
greatness is, perhaps, more original and difficult to conceive of than
the other, more capacious form. I think this is because since the novel is
naturally sociable and it encourages readers and authors to think in
sociable ways, Josef K.'s isolation even when he is talking to someone is
exceptional. Whatever is sociable around Josef K. is strange and maybe
untrustworthy (this is true of the main character of "The Burrow" and

"The Metamorphosis" as well as "In the Penal Colony"). Kafka dispenses with the natural sociability of the novel and comes up with an entirely new and compelling vision. But like the other authors of great novels, he also has a genius for conceiving ideas that are both important per se and capable of stimulating his own most characteristic and insightful thinking. Greatness in a novel does not depend upon perfection of the object; perfection of the object is merely an added dimension to the greatness of certain novels. But every great novel offers incomprehensible abundance in some form—even *The Trial,* only a couple of hundred pages long, is abundantly meticulous, abundantly intimate, abundantly strange, and abundantly original.

10 · A Novel of Your Own (I)

Now that you have decided to begin your novel, you may congratulate yourself. You have not been asked or groomed to
write a novel. You have not gone to novel-writing school, nor
taken a standard curriculum of preparatory courses. Chances are, no
one wants you to write your novel—if they say they do, they are just
meaning that you should get it over with or get on with it. The people
you know actually dread reading the novel you are about to write—
they don't want to read about themselves, they don't want to be bored,
and they fear embarrassment for everyone. You are, therefore, free.

As you write the first word, you are embracing the novel's greatest
tradition, that of obscure beginnings. No other art is so simple or so
cheap to engage in as literature. A lifetime's reading may be borrowed
from the library; a pencil and some sheets of paper may be purloined
without much trouble. You can sit at the kitchen table. You can sit on
the stool in the bathroom and put a board across your knees. There is
no outlay for paints or clay. And since you are writing a novel, you
aren't going to need actors or film or a stage. You aren't going to need a
reader for companionship (a difference between you and poets—your
characters can serve as your companions if you want them to). Perhaps
the nicest thing about beginning your novel is that you don't have to
begin anything again for a very long time if you don't care to, because
after you set down the first thought, every time you come back to that
first thought is a rewrite. Of course, the first thought must be followed
by a second one, and so on, but if you abjure fear, it will be—it is in the
nature of thoughts to follow upon one another.

What you are aiming for is willing suspension of disbelief, and the
first person who must suspend disbelief is yourself. Some beginning
novelists have more disbelief to suspend than others, but even if your
burden of disbelief is heavy, the only way to suspend it is to keep

adding sentences to the ones you have already written. Sheer length persuades, at least to some degree, because it builds an object in the mind. In *Within a Budding Grove,* Marcel Proust's installment of *In Search of Lost Time* about his adolescence, there is a short passage concerning the author's first attempts at writing. Inspired by the conversation of a favorite author, whom he meets at the home of his beloved, M. resolves to begin his own career by setting aside in advance whole days in which he will commence ("it was better not to start on an evening when I felt ill-prepared" [p. 210]). It seems like a good plan, except that he doesn't ever commence, instead finding more and more excuses to put off what he has been planning. Within days he becomes so discouraged that he snaps at his grandmother when she inquires after his "work." The irony that you should note is that what will be his work is already evident—one of his modes of procrastinating is to visit the house where he had met his favorite author. Each night when he comes home from socializing, his mind is filled with the conversations he has heard, which inspire imaginary conversations in which he takes all the roles. All he would need do is write a few of these conversations down, and he would find his work creating itself, as, indeed, it did in subsequent years. What I see in this anecdote is not only that the young Proust wasn't ready to begin, but also that one of the strongest features of his talent, his preternatural ability to observe the social world around him, was announcing itself loudly and clearly when he was still very young. So it is with you.

My favorite anecdote about the ease and pleasure of writing a book comes from Ilene Beckerman, who in 1995 published her memoir *Love, Loss, and What I Wore.* Her initial impulse had been to jot down some memories from the early days of her marriage for her children, herself, and her best friend, so she kept paper and pencils at hand, and every time she remembered something, she wrote it out. Sometimes it was a few pages long, sometimes only a page. She did not write about the memories in any particular order, only when they occurred to her. She filed each page with the others in a manila folder, and after a year she pulled out the folder, read over the pages, organized them chonologically, and had them typed. She made five copies—one for herself and each of her three children, and one for her best friend. Some months after she was finished, the phone rang. It was her best friend, who asked her whether she would mind talking to a publisher about publishing her memoir. Though she was totally taken by surprise, she

agreed. Her friend said, "Now, Ilene, be nice." She was nice. The publisher was nice, too, and made such a success of the book that Beckerman went on to write another and to have an enjoyable experience as
an author and celebrity.

One thing to understand about this anecdote is that she wasn't
merely lucky. She believed in what she was writing—she found it valuable, interesting, and worthwhile, if only as a private record, and she
considered herself capable of achieving her goal. Because of the circumstances of her effort, she had no self-doubts. She knew her audience would be pleased with her gift. Because she was ready to write
when she had a memory, but didn't force herself to write when she did
not, her writing didn't seem first and foremost an obligation, and so
she was able to get into the habit without much trouble. Perhaps her
smartest idea was to keep the folder and the paper and pencils at hand.
A book, and especially a novel, must be a habit. Almost all novelists
cultivate more discipline than Ilene Beckerman did, but what this
anecdote reveals is that the absolutely minimal, simplest, easiest way
of writing can accumulate a book as well as the most dedicated, self-
conscious, ascetic way. Some novelists write by obligation, others by
desire. These are questions of temperament. There is no intrinsically
better way, since the only standard of achievement to begin with (and
for quite a long time) is the accumulation of pages. Another thing both
Beckerman and Proust should show you is that writing is writing, not
planning. The sooner you put words on paper, the happier you will be.

As with any discipline, from playing hockey to baking a soufflé to
playing the violin, there are certain requisite skills that a novelist must
be comfortable with, but they are only skills to be learned, not inherent
talents. If you are comfortable punctuating, spelling, and using understandable grammar (which may or may not be standard grammar),
you will enjoy writing more and better believe that you can do it. Language is a tool the limbic system uses to write the novel in the same
way that a hammer is a tool a carpenter uses or a bat is a tool a baseball
player uses. The more automatic your use of the tool is, the less friction
there is between you and the page. Just as throughout your life you
have taken the time to learn to use many tools, so you must take the
time to learn to use the tool of written language. Your eloquence in
speaking is entirely separate from your potential eloquence in writing.
Eventually the two will merge, but to begin with, fluency in the one
has only the remotest relationship with fluency in the other. If you
were not lucky enough to learn the mechanics of prose style in school,

you can learn them as a protonovelist. They are merely rules and habits. Learning how to write conventional sentences is much easier than quitting smoking, learning to ride a horse, or taking up carpentry in middle age.

Every aspect of novel-writing, from knowing the difference between a comma and a semicolon to being able to conceive a multivolume historical saga of French cosmopolitan life, is as likely to be a skill as a talent. No theory of the workings of the brain has revealed a specific novel-writing center in either the right brain or the left brain. For your purposes, this means that there is no definable end to the process of developing your tools—you will not hit a novel-writing glass ceiling in the way that you might hit a piano-playing glass ceiling or a pitching-speed glass ceiling. Let's imagine a novel-writing pyramid of skills. The bottom layer of punctuation, grammar, and spelling is knowledge you will use in every sentence you write. This, the layer that needs to be mastered first, is the most artificial one. There are several reasons for this. One is that because it is artificial, it requires a good deal of practice—repetition resulting in unconscious employment of the necessary tool. Until spelling, grammar, and punctuation work independently of the conscious mind, their operation will interfere with the operation of the other layers. But, more importantly, the most artificial layer is also the one that defines the activity we are engaged upon—the employment of prose to entertain and enlighten, the making of the repository of our art, which is a written book, the drawing of a distinction between this system and other systems of words. It is through the employment of grammar, punctuation, and spelling that we signal ourselves and the reader to prepare for a certain experience.

Above this bottom layer is a layer of diction, which is familiarity with words and expressions. Sensory data and ideas conceived in the mind go in and out of words and are at the same time incarnated and energized by words. We can imagine it to be a variety of quantum and wave theory of light. The words are the quanta, the mental process is the waves. As the writer composes, waves of thought precipitate into quanta of words, which stimulate waves of thought. Each transformation expends energy but also creates it, because though choosing the right words is an effort, the right words are inspiring. Some writers, such as Vladimir Nabokov, have a particular sort of erudition—a wide-ranging and precise knowledge of all the words available to express a certain idea, which comes from a knowledge of many languages and wide reading in many different fields. Other writers, such as Charles Dickens, excel in reproducing the demotic (the language of the people) because they have sharp hearing and good memories. Their own style is remarkably various—influenced and colored by the general human talent for coming up with sharp and colorful phrases, sayings, slang expressions, and shaping intonations. Other writers, such as Zora Neale Hurston, choose to specialize in a particular dialect because it is expressive and also characteristic of the group she wants to portray. All writers, though, begin with some sort of diction and then develop it. Dickens, for example, began with a remarkable ability to mimic the speech of voluble lower-class characters, shady con men, and politicians, among other types. In the course of his career, he developed a diction for talking about the emotional lives of characters such as Paul Dombey, in *Dombey and Son;* Lady Dedlock, in *Bleak House;* Bradley Headstone, in *Our Mutual Friend;* and John Jasper, in *The Mystery of Edwin Drood.* Even Dickens, perhaps the most inherently gifted user of words ever to write an English novel, didn't have all dictions at his command from the beginning. Any diction is good enough for writing some novel, though. The question is, is it good enough (that is, does it have enough words and do you know how the words are properly used) for writing the novel you want to write? If it is not good enough, the best way to improve it is to learn more about the subject of your novel. One of the ways to learn something is to simply pick up the jargon of your subject. And at the beginning, when you are learning words and writing at the same time, it doesn't matter whether you simply regurgitate the words and phrases and ideas you learn; it matters only that you learn them.

Some writers are afraid of research, thinking perhaps it will contaminate their ideas, but the strangest fact about the novel ("novel" means "new or original") is that novelty and originality are automatic. What is difficult is not to write something new but to write something interesting and true. As any piece becomes interesting and true, it becomes original. On the other hand, many original pieces of writing never find readers because they are solipsistic, tedious, tendentious, or self-indulgent. To pursue truth and interest is much more productive than to pursue originality, which will happen in any case. As evidence, I offer my experience teaching beginning undergraduate students. In the course of some fourteen semesters, with at least twenty-five students per semester, I never mixed up students or forgot their names after I had read their first stories. No two stories were ever alike, even if the students had never written before in their lives, even if, no doubt, some of the students were recycling ideas from stories they had read. The student could not help remaking his material in his own image. But not every story was interesting. The ways that the students made the stories interesting invariably made them more original, but they could get more original without getting more interesting. So from the standpoint of enlarging your diction, do not be afraid of any sort of contamination of your linguistic purity by the research you pursue.

The layer above diction is that of story and character, or plot and protagonist. The special appeal of the novel is the alternation of action and reflection—something happens, it is given meaning by either the narrator or the charactors, then something else happens that grows out of the meaning given the first event, which is then given meaning, and so on, until the climax—the largest action, and the denouement, the final meaning. The balance between story and character is unique to every novel, and the balance between action and meaning is different for every author, but every novel has both. Characters confronted by events must make choices, which reveal and develop their characters. Events are shaped by the choices of those involved in them. Events naturally possess energy that manifests itself as suspense, but mere events can jade the reader if they are too meaningless. Beginning novelists are often naturally event types or meaning types. As you accumulate paragraphs and pages, observe what intrigues you more—setting a scene and making something happen, or considering how the event is to be understood or felt. You will fall into one camp or the other. The side that does not come easily to you is the side you should develop by intelligently broadening your reading and learning how other authors negotiate the pitfalls of each. Fiction is not so much about what happens as about how it happens; how it happens is intimately bound up with who does it.

The primary failure of event and therefore of plot is that what happens is not understandable to the reader. This can be a problem of organization—the sequence of events is not understandable or cannot be visualized very clearly because there is too little material or too much. But even when the events are understandable, they may be implausible, not interesting, or not compelling. The solution for such problems is in character and meaning. Henry James was a great advocate of placing the narrative point of view firmly in the mind of one or

two minor characters present at the action of the novel who happened
to be good-quality witnesses. Their predilections would dictate organization, visualization, and emotional involvement in the action and
also would attest to its significance and interest. A risk of James's
method is that all events and their emotional impact would be second-
hand—the danger for the reader is that she might be lost in the intricacies of the story without enough emotional motivation to keep going.
But even a novelist who doesn't adopt as rigid a system for solving
these particular plot problems as James did must use his characters to
organize the plot and give it significance. If we take Wilkie Collins's
The Woman in White as an example of a novel (a mystery) in which the
plot *must* work, Collins's method, of entering the viewpoints of various
characters (all of whom are a bit clichéd), works admirably—each
diary document pictures the somewhat ridiculous action vividly,
implies that there is more here than meets the eye, and hits the special
emotional note that character is there to supply. The variety enlivens
the proceedings, and the reader is carried along perhaps in spite of herself. The same is true of *Dracula*—if we had to see Count Dracula
from a single point of view over and over again, he would lose his
dangerous powers by becoming too familiar to us; but seeing him
intermittently, combined with witnessing each character's speculations
and dreads, gives the count power without overtaxing the author's
inventiveness.

For many authors, the best combination of clear observation and
immediacy is a first-person narrator narrating his or her "unfolding."
A wonderful example of this technique is Jamaica Kincaid's *Annie
John,* a short novel about the inner life of an adolescent girl on the
Caribbean island of Antigua. Kincaid's style, which is very controlled
but rich, works to finesse the two most serious pitfalls of first-person
narration—the temptation of digressiveness and the temptation of
self-dramatization. The proper balance between action and self-
revelation is hard to find. If the world of the novel gets too complex to
efficiently portray, the first-person narrator can lose himself in the mix
and comes off as paler and less interesting than the other characters,
but if the narrator seems interested in himself to the exclusion of all the
other characters that seem potentially interesting to the reader, he can
seem solipsistic and dull. But views on this vary, and an author can
make a case for anything—the contemporary novelist William T.
Vollmann's argument for writing only in the first person, including in
theoretical and nonfiction works, is that to write in the first person is to

acknowledge that all ideas and opinions are subjective and to take responsibility for them.

Nevertheless, all narrative voices are equally conceits, and as long as you understand that the alternating rhythm of action and reflection, plot and character must feed one another, you can choose any manner of going back and forth that is comfortable to you, the author, and suitable to the subject.

One layer higher on the pyramid, requiring more thought and adding a more sophisticated dimension to your work, are the complementary concepts of setting and theme—or, you might say, the specific and the general. When Captain Ahab sets out on the *Pequod* in search of a particular white whale, he is not the same person as the unnamed captain of the *Bachelor,* a "glad ship of good luck" the *Pequod* meets on the Japanese cruising ground. Melville shows by name and description that first and foremost we are to consider a particular man whose ship is also particular in all its features. The March sisters, in *Little Women,* do not live in California. *As I Lay Dying* does not take place in Paris. *Persuasion* takes place in Bath and *Tristram Shandy* takes place in Yorkshire. Prince Myshkin is not from Trieste and Zeno never visits St. Petersburg. Arnošt Lustig's *Lovely Green Eyes* is not about Mississippi. The Bride of Lammermoor lives in a particular Scottish landscape because the loyalties of her mother, father, and lover are dictated in large part by territorial conflicts that are also religious conflicts, and her fate is partly determined by local superstitions. The originating impulse for many novels is an author's belief that a particular locality is interesting and worthy of entrance into cultural commerce—that Dickens's London is worth looking at, but so is Egdon Heath (Thomas Hardy) or Cairo (Naguib Mahfouz). The paradox is that not only is each of these places equally in the world, each of these places equally *is* the world. The nature of the novel itself asserts this, by contrast to almost all the rest of conventional human wisdom, which states that there are "centers" and "peripheries." In the Earth's Big Bookstore, all novels, no matter where they are set, fall silent and disappear when the covers are closed. When the covers of one of them are opened, the world of that book becomes the center of the world, and the rest of the world and the rest of the books revolve around it. The particular becomes general, and the relationship between setting (which includes all of the characters' circumstances) and theme (which are conclusions to be drawn about the characters' humanity) becomes manifest.

As with character and action, setting and theme feed one another. If your themes are too general, then investigate your setting more closely, and anchor your characters more deeply within their circumstances. If your story seems too trivial, then ask yourself about the connections between these circumstances and the larger human condition. This implies that both setting and theme are equally prone to problems, but this is not true—readers are so likely, either by instinct or training, to extrapolate from the particular to the general, that while they always need help visualizing and understanding specifics, they rarely need help connecting them to a larger concept of humanity. As with action, organization is the key—the real danger with particulars is that they will get confusing and hard to follow, like forest undergrowth that hides the path, or that they will proliferate in a way that suggests that the author is communicating primarily with himself—details piled upon details that are only partially depicted tax the reader's patience. In some ways this presents itself as a feature of style—is the author capable of density and lucidity at the same time? For me, Musil's *The Man without Qualities* rewards patience and attention with special depth and clarity, but many readers find the narrative dry and hard to follow. Likewise, the world is full of readers for whom every detail of *Ulysses* is worth keeping track of, but there are other readers who find this a thankless and tiresome task. Style, though, is the evidence of how the author's mind works. How he selects, arranges, and presents his particulars is the closest we get to who he is. As you write your story, you will inevitably reveal yourself.

Every novel has themes. Most serious authors devote considerable thought to their themes, and, indeed, for many authors, the desire to explore or express certain ideas is the originating impulse for writing a novel. For some authors, the desire to write and the interest in charac-ter come first, and the product is some short stories; after a while, understanding the implications of a larger picture—a longer time frame or a larger group of characters—is inspiring, and a novel is begun. This may happen at about the time the writer is thirty, a good age for integrating what you have learned in childhood and youth. If we look at our list of authors, we can see that those who were writing in their twenties, whether successful or unsuccessful, often recon-ceived their work at about age thirty. Dickens was hugely popular and successful with *The Pickwick Papers, Oliver Twist,* and other episodic novels of his twenties, but when he began *Martin Chuzzlewit* at thirty, he took up his first overarching theme, that of selfishness, to give unity to both his writing and his social theories. Zola, who also wrote and published in his twenties, began his cycle of novels, *Les Rougon-Macquart,* when he was thirty. Henry Fielding's satirical ambitions got him censored for theatrical pieces he staged when he was thirty, so he turned to the novel, publishing *Joseph Andrews* when he was thirty-five. Herman Melville wrote several popular romances in his twenties; he was thirty-two when he published *Moby-Dick.* Henry James wrote *Roderick Hudson,* his first novel, when he was thirty-two. Thirty-two hardly seems young; it is more or less the age when the first stage of maturity is complete, when a marriage is contracted, and when children are born. It seems a culminating age to many people (though from the perspective of twenty-five years on, it seems to have been more like a commencement). At any rate, for an author in his thirties, theories and themes abound, and often, as for Fyodor Dostoevsky, who was arrested, nearly executed, and sent to a Siberian work camp when he was thirty, they consolidate or contradict ideas the author imbibed in his late teens and twenties. It is the sense of whole things coming together, of the flowering of reason and understanding, and of the connections between particulars that had hitherto seemed discrete that give rise to a novel. We may see in this the joy of an author voluntarily revealing himself or herself.

For every novelist, and therefore for you, wherever the larger ideas come from, they must seem at the time you employ them to be illuminating and bringing together intensely perceived particulars, expediting a work that could only be about these characters who are performing just these actions.

At the apex of the pyramid is the element most general and yet most difficult to attain: complexity. Life itself is complex, and every subset of life (marriage, any professional enterprise, reproduction, owning and maintaining a home, any recreational activity) is equally complex. The brain is complex. Any individual activity contains as much complexity as the brain contemplating it is capable of. Complexity is like infinity—within the infinite set of numbers is an infinite subset of real numbers and another of whole numbers. Infinity makes all sets and subsets the same size, even though that is impossible. Thus it is with life and all its parts, including the novel.

More complexity is more fun as well as more true. One thing novelists habitually do is return to the same themes over and over. Since the energy of the novel and of the novelist's career is supplied by the limbic system of the brain, no doubt the conventional view is true, that the novelist can't help revisiting and worrying patterns of meaning and emotion that are important to his sense of who he is, or to his very notions of survival. Even so, when he returns to them each time, he brings new ideas and skills to them and attempts to illuminate them again to make better sense of them.

Any aspect of a novel may be made more complex, but not every aspect. *Ulysses,* for example, is probably the most complex novel in the English language, but the underlying story is not complex at all—two men set out on a particular day to do several fairly routine things. Toward the end of the day, they meet, connect, and then go home, possibly somewhat transformed by the events of the day and their meeting. *Ulysses*'s complexity of psychology and style is imposed upon this simple structure as a theory about the true nature of literature and of life—even the most routine day is a culmination of all that has gone before it; even the most modern novel contains within itself all of the literature the author knows. By contrast, Wilkie Collins's *The Woman in White* has a highly complex plot and structure (different narrators tell different parts as the story unfolds) but a simple and clear style and a conventional theory of psychology (though the sociology of the characters is more interesting). It is an easier read than *Ulysses* but not so highly esteemed by critics. Emotional complexity is a feature of the modern novel, achieved through the general post-Flaubert recognition that characters often harbor conflicting and contradictory feelings about themselves and their situations.

Emotional complexity is easy to communicate—it can be exhaustively explored in a realistic manner, as Robert Musil explores the emotional lives of the main characters of *The Man without Qualities,* using a deliberate style rich in metaphor and figurative language that likens the mysterious emotional lives of the characters to known objects and ideas, as in the following passage, which efficiently details three types of relationships in the first sentence—Ulrich's perception of Diotima's relationship to him, Diotima's imitation of her husband, and her husband's care in his professional relationships—and then pinpoints the nature of Ulrich's ambivalence about Diotima in the next two sentences.

> In his first minutes of withdrawal, Diotima treated him with the bland courtesy—carefully and pointedly overdone—that she had copied from her husband, who made use of it in dealing with young aristocrats who happened to be his subordinates but

who might someday be his ministers. . . . When he was once
more holding her mild, weightless hand in his, they looked into
each other's eyes. Ulrich had the definite impression that they
were destined to be a great nuisance to each other through love.
[pp. 107–8]

Or emotional complexity can be allusively explored through the radical simplification of story and style, as Kafka explores the emotional
life of Josef K. by depicting it and relying on the inherently referential
nature of language to supply ambiguity and larger significance. Emotional complexity is the sine qua non of the serious literary novel.
Often linked to emotional complexity is moral complexity, which
explores the relationship between feeling on the one hand and good
and evil on the other, but moral complexity alone can energize a
novel—Yukio Mishima's novel *The Sailor Who Fell from Grace with the
Sea,* about some boys who murder the stepfather of one of their number, has few attractive characters and a very cool tone, but the author
successfully engages the reader in the dilemmas of his characters'
moral lives and the larger exploration of what the existence of these
characters at this time in history means about Japanese culture and
morality.

You may choose sociological complexity, as Stendhal, Dickens,
Proust, Garrison Keillor, and Rohinton Mistry do, but there is a price
to pay. When characters act out their assigned social roles, even idiosyncratic ones are often condemned as "flat." Simultaneous sociological, moral, emotional, and psychological (not to mention geographical)
complexity is hard to organize and is also hard to represent, because
the reader, required to contemplate many forms of complexity, ceases
to see any of them clearly.

Added to these complexities of subject are complexities of form.
Since the novel engages both the author's and the reader's pleasure in
games, some authors like what you might call tricks—puns, allusions,
jokes, hidden meanings, parallels, and contrasts in composition and
structure. A novel that has to be annotated for the reader to understand enough of the references to enjoy it, or that knowingly uses
obscurity, tempts the reader to dispense with the literary joke. There
may be a payoff for being in on the joke—extra pleasure at its intricacies—but it is tricky to pull off. An author such as Nabokov, though,
can't help asserting ideas about the relationship of seriousness to

games, about the apparent absurdity or triviality of conventions normally taken to be important, affecting, or serious. Complexities of form, however subtle, draw the reader's attention to the form and put the subject in the background. For every reader, the "truthful" balance between the transparency of form and the importance of the subject is different. Some readers more willingly suspend disbelief if your form is complex, and some are more willing if your form is simple. Keep remembering that you can please some of the readers some of the time, and some of the readers most of the time, but sometimes you will please only yourself, and you can never please all of the readers all of the time.

One lesson to be drawn from our pyramid is that there is no proper way to write a novel because there is no way to perfectly balance all the categories in the pyramid. The novel is a linear form because prose happens sequentially, but the parts of the novel, as analyzed in the pyramid, are spatial. No novel can be written perfectly because perfect spatial balance cannot be achieved word by word. At the same time, though, writing a novel is easy because there is nothing simpler than adding word to word, sentence to sentence, paragraph to paragraph, and then going back and reading and writing it over again. To do it, the author simply has to remember that it can't be done, that the ideal edifice that exists in his mind may not be, cannot be, and will never be communicated, *but something will.* That something is the novel you don't know you can write until you get it written.

Since the key to resolving the irresolvable difficulties of the novel for the reader is willing suspension of disbelief, the something about every novel that induces the reader to forgive, accept, or, indeed, to not even notice its flaws is often apparent in a critical remark or blurb about that novel. If we take the example of Milan Kundera's *The Unbearable Lightness of Being,* we read on the back cover that Elizabeth Hardwick considers the novel to be "a work of the boldest mastery, originality, and richness." In other words, she has been induced to believe in the author's technical skill, the freshness of his ideas, and the number of elements he is able to manipulate simultaneously. Her willingness comes from her view that the way in which Kundera weds the narrative elements of the novel to the thematic ones makes the best use of both—the story is compelling and the underlying argument is, also. The melding of theme and narrative induces her as a reader to overlook compromises the author must, by definition, make in composing the novel. Another critic, Jim Miller, is quoted on the cover of the paperback saying, "Kundera has raised the novel of ideas to a new level of dreamlike lyricism and emotional intensity." In this quote, Miller is pointing to the wedding of style—"lyrical" is another word for poetic—and characterization. Essentially he is saying that most novels of ideas are dry and abstract, but Kundera has avoided this trap by conceiving his characters sympathetically and using the evocative effects of a poetrylike prose to separate his subject in tone from raw, realistic, or naturalistic novels. Each of these readers' remarks points to how reading *The Unbearable Lightness of Being* was in contrast to the expectations they brought to reading it, or to other novels of the category it belongs to that have been unable to finesse the compromises inherent in the subject matter. A reader for whom Kundera's novel does not work would recognize the same qualities in the prose and the same alternation of ideas and narrative, but might find the prose too self-conscious and not pictorial enough and the ideas uninteresting or outdated.

You may feel that *The Unbearable Lightness of Being* is a novel that abruptly suffered a fate that all novels suffer sooner or later—the historical circumstances that gave rise to the ideas suddenly vanished, so the novel became, perhaps prematurely, a historical document, no longer current as a depiction of eternal human circumstances. Does the novel lose its artistic qualities of truth, beauty, and freedom thereby? Maybe; maybe not. But all novel-readers react in part to the place of a novel in its historical moment, and they will react the same way to your novel eventually. Words such as "bold" and "original" are time-limited in their power to recommend. However, the fact that your novel will one day seem old-fashioned doesn't mean that it won't eventually seem immortal.

The key for you, the author, is also energy. The word "inspiration" is, of course, rooted in the Latin words meaning to breathe in and is closely related to aspire, expire, transpire, and spirit. At the same time that you breathe life into your work, you are breathing in the stimulus that enables you to do so. It's as easy as that!

Well, maybe not. But every author attests to the two states of writing—inspiration and waiting for inspiration. You may wait for inspiration while writing; you may, and probably will have to, write toward inspiration, possibly with a sense of tedious boredom and heavy toil, but the good news is that inspiration is only tangentially related to product; writers we readers despise were as inspired at their work as writers we adore.

My definition of "inspiration" is "a condition of being stimulated by contemplation of the material to a degree sufficient to overcome your natural disinclination to create." Contemplation of the material creates forward energy—one word, line, thought, image, idea, sentence, or paragraph elicits another. The barriers to the writing of the next word, line, thought, image, idea, sentence, or paragraph come to seem technical when you are inspired—the idea is pressing to get out; you merely have to find the latch that allows the gate to open. The latch might be a new word or a new phrase, but it is the smallest thing imaginable. Something outside of the normal realm of reason is happening, once thought to be a gift of the gods or muses, later thought to be a rumbling of the "subconscious" or "id" (the Latin word for "it").

My theory is that inspiration is emotional memories lingering in the limbic system becoming suddenly activated and asking the frontal lobe to organize and thereby understand them. Robert Musil maintains that it is "nonpersonal" (see above, p. 97) because reason isn't aware of the connections, but I think it is personal—all the emotional memories in the limbic system belong to the individual, they are just not processed by intellection, the area of the brain that gives us our sense of our own identity. Freud maintained that the id was the source of energy; if the id is in the limbic brain, then, indeed, it is a source of energy, in the form of adrenaline, because the limbic brain in mammals governs our earliest feelings of attachment, safety, well-being, aggression, and fear. When a set of circumstances we witness or hear about lights up the limbic system, it is really alerting us to potential threats and urging the frontal lobe to check it out. I like to think that an author feels what Freud called sublimation when he takes that adrenaline and deploys it into a story that is a logical, prolonged, enlightening, and entertaining communication to other humans. Inspiration, or this adrenalized feeling, is often uncomfortable. It also may move the writer to action, since its original purpose is to engage the "fight or flight," "protect or attack" mechanisms in mammals. Maybe this is one reason that some good novelists are bad citizens.

But this is my theory, one I concocted after reading a book called *A General Theory of Love.** Like every theory, my theory is simply a

---

*See Thomas Lewis, M.D., Fari Amini, M.D., and Richard Lannon, M.D., *A General Theory of Love* (New York: Random House, 2000).

metaphor for a mysterious process, and every metaphor either promotes the process or hinders it. The way in which you think of the
energy that motivates you to pick up your pen and add to your writing
will shape your relationship with your writing and your ability to pursue it. Another metaphor I like, that of the river of literary history
looping through each individual writer and being altered by him (or
her), relieves me of worry about originality, because by the terms of
that metaphor, originality is automatic, and so is flow, energy, influence, and some sort of larger purpose. A metaphor for inspiration that
I don't like is one I heard once at a writers' conference: "toiling at the
coal face with a tiny pickax, trying to fill my bucket." An even worse
one, for my purposes, is "Dionysian ecstasy"—too many drunks out
and about for a good realistic novel.

At the end of the inspired thought or paragraph, of course, the
energy subsides with a conscious feeling of exhaustion. Each stimulus
carries the author forward only so far (though each element of the
novel has an inherent half-life and some are longer than others—good
character inspiration lasts longer than good word-choice inspiration).
There is an actual physical feeling of "can't go on," and this requires
the author to develop inspiration-friendly habits. One of mine is to
take a shower. I often find that water pouring over my head stimulates
further thought and further energy, and sends me right back to my
writing. When I was still a student, I found that some authors inspired me—Virginia Woolf, Halldór Laxness, John Steinbeck. Others,
though I was fond of their works, did not—Jane Austen, George Eliot.
I came to think that Austen's and Eliot's works had a too perfectly reasonable surface to seem accessible in any way. Woolf, especially in *To
the Lighthouse,* was no less finished, but the subject of that novel was
the construction of consciousness itself, and how to make art. It made
me want to sit down at a desk and make some, though I had no idea
what to make.

And so, here is your novel, growing day by day. It is about some people
who may be based on friends or relations of yours. It is set in a specific
spot on the globe, and several things happen in sequence, even though
you may not be telling them in the sequence that they happen. You
alternate telling the things that happen with telling what the people
feel about them, and you keep everyone organized by making them
different from one another—their names are not similar, they look
more or less different, and they have distinguishing quirks that also

(two for one!) display the facets of your theme. Much of what you write seems great when you first think of it, and even when you put it down in writing, but when you go back to it a day or so later, it doesn't have the richness or clarity you thought it had. Pressing ahead with it is an intermittent business—the feelings it arouses in you are conflicting, and no feeling lasts very long. Perhaps the idea of sticking with this day after day for many months or years is downright gruesome (though perhaps you fly to your desk every day with a laugh on your lips and a song in your heart). The trick is to make your material so fascinating that you cannot stay away from it, so intriguing that you ignore negative feelings and second thoughts, so rich with interest that the concepts of "good" and "bad" hardly occur to you. Because your goal is a complete rough draft of a novel, and every rough draft, by being complete, is perfect.

For this reason, I advise against rewriting, except for grammar and clarity, until you have the whole arc of the novel complete. The desire to get each scene "just right" works against productivity because it allows you to get in the habit of ruminating upon your self-doubts. In the Victorian period, when novels were published serially in monthly or weekly installments, authors got in the habit of letting forty or fifty pages, thousands of words, go out into the world before the novel was finished or even, in some cases, fully worked out. Publishing serially, for the sake of an income, served as a spur to invention—the luxury of writer's block was out of the question. Dickens told his friend John Forster about going into a shop to buy paper, and overhearing a customer ask for the next installment of the book he was working on. He knew that he hadn't even begun to write it. He reported being stimulated rather than intimidated by the incident. Other authors, such as George Eliot, found publishing serially more difficult than Dickens, but as a group they rose to the challenge and produced an unprecedented body of great literature. You can follow their model by setting aside the tendency to second-guess yourself. Each day, you sit down to your work, reread what you wrote the day before, correct the spelling and untangle thoughts you no longer understand. If there is a sequence of actions that is unclear, fix it as best you can and then go on. Do not worry about finding newer, righter words. Do not worry about fixing major problems of setting or character or theme. Do not make things more complex. Use rereading and fiddling with details to orient yourself in your text and get on with it.

Of course, many novelists will disagree with me—there are novelists who polish every scene and sentence before they can move forward, but to do so is a habit, not a necessity. One problem with beginning as a writer of short stories, which most novelists do, is that in short stories, perfection is a valid goal, and it is fairly easy, psychologically, to go on perfecting a short story for several months without losing sight of the whole piece. The same with poems. But when the whole of the work is a hundred thousand words rather than two thousand words, you simply have to get those words down on paper or you don't have anything to think about or work with. A novel comes alive, even to its author, as it precipitates onto the page. If you prevent it from going forward by polishing each bit, it is much harder for it to take on its own being. And the more of it there is, the easier it is for you not to feel commitment to any particular bit. Tolstoy threw out two thousand pages when he was writing *War and Peace*—he was so willing to go on with it that as he moved his draft toward realization he had a luxurious abundance of material to choose from.

When you begin your novel, you know enough about your material to begin it, but not enough to finish it. As you write, you learn about what you are writing. It may be as simple as coming to a spot where you don't know a proper word or a correct fact. In this case you do a bit of research. By the time you've found the word or the fact, you've also serendipitously learned a couple of other things that are interesting as well. Nothing in the history of novel-writing requires you to generate every word from your deepest and most private being as with, maybe, poetry. Everything, in fact, that carries you out into the world, teaches you to observe, and rewards your observation with some worthy nugget is good. Novel-writing is not pure. Remember, you will be original no matter what. But there may be something else you need to learn, something more in the realm of wisdom than of information. Whatever it is is already present in the words you are writing, though perhaps not fully formed as a concept or a thought. In this case you might make a mental note that there is something missing at this spot and reassure yourself that what is missing constitutes a hole of a certain shape. When you come back to this spot at the end of the rough draft, the shape of the hole will describe fairly exactly the object to be fitted into it. In fact, to write through to the end of the rough draft, in spite of time constraints, second thoughts, self-doubts, and judgments of all kinds, is an act of faith that is invariably rewarded—the rough draft of a novel is the absolute paradigm of something that comes from nothing. Some thoughts and impressions, a few inchoate feelings, some resentments perhaps, or some passions and joys, lots of memories, and several wishes. None of these things has to come to anything; it is, in fact, highly likely, statistically speaking, that over the broad spectrum of humanity, most of such inner fragments will indeed come to nothing, but if you keep at it, yours will coalesce into something quite substantial—the rough draft of a novel.

What if you lose interest in your material? Boredom is only a symptom, and boredom with the material that at first inspired you to write a novel can mean any number of things, but it never means that your material is inherently uninteresting. Even so, the special bonus of novel-writing is that you can stop doing it any time you want to. If you remember at all times that no one ever asked you to write that novel, you will at least be preserved from feeling victimized by your work.

The first thing that boredom can mean is that you don't know enough about your material, and that your action, setting, and characters have subsided into just going through the motions. Ignorance is a self-generating state of mind; one of its characteristics is that it doesn't recognize itself as ignorance. The remedy is to find out more—read more, travel to the spot where your novel is set and spend a few days there, ask questions, look for original documents, engage your senses to gain more knowledge of what you are writing about. If you are bored with your subject, it is fatal to try to think your way out of it.

Another possible reason for boredom is that you are confused about how things take place in your book, so you can't see your way forward to the next step. In this case, remember that the action, whether slight or complex, is the organizational spine of the book. The plot is a piece of logic (so are the characters, though not the same sort of logic). Logic draws conclusions from premises. If you don't know your premises, you will draw illogical conclusions from them, get confused, and then get bored. This boredom feels different from the other sort of boredom—less dull, more avoidant. If you are staying away from your desk because it just seems like too much to handle, then perhaps it's time to make yourself figure out (by rereading, not rewriting) what is going on. This is a good time to make an outline, to assign roles, to draw a picture or a graphic. When I wrote my first novel, *Barn Blind,* I kept a pencil sketch above the stove in my kitchen. All it had on it were six lines, each labeled with the name of one of the characters. Each line traced a different pattern as it crossed the paper—straight, zigzag, sine wave. Somehow the daily contemplation of this graphic enabled me to keep track of the progress of the characters through to the end. Any aid to organization is all to the good. Writing a novel isn't a test—you can cheat any way you want to except copying word for word from another text and claiming it as your own.

Sometimes a feeling of boredom is really a feeling of fear. As the rough draft takes shape, it isn't turning out the way you thought it would. Of course it isn't very "good." Perhaps you are protected against that particular self-doubt by some luck of temperament or discipline. But good or not, it also isn't telling the story you thought it was going to—it is diverging from your presuppositions about it, and you don't know what the results will be in terms of the plot, the fates of the characters, or even the ideas you thought you were going to express. As a result you don't know where you are going, or maybe you suspect that where you are going is a place you don't want to be. There are several ways of approaching this sort of fear/boredom. The primary one is to have faith even in this, that you will recognize your baby and love it no matter what it looks like. The second one is to recognize that this child will never leave the house unless you send it away. Once you get to the end of the rough draft, you can go back and reshape, rewrite, remake it as many times as you want to. It is, after all, only the rough draft, and in rough drafts, all is forgiven. What is happening is that your intuition is conflicting with your reason, and perhaps even taking over from it in the composing of your novel. That is its job. The rough draft is where the intuition asserts its strength and threatens to get out of control, where it shows what it knows that can't be known but only interpreted by intellection. Since from long experience you know that your intuition can get you into trouble in all sorts of ways, it is perfectly understandable that you would feel anxious now, but just keep going. Sometime far in the future, when your novel finds readers, it is your intuition that will speak to them most profoundly. The saving grace of the novel as an artistic process is that it takes a long time to produce. You cannot write a novel on impulse. Writing a novel cannot be a form of acting out or flying off the handle. The very process itself submits impulses to reason and makes something thought-out of them.

For some writers, boredom is a sign that their ability to execute their own work is less sophisticated than their taste in the work of others, and it is, indeed, very disconcerting to find that what you put on the page is something you would disdain if you were asked to review it. If your faculty for passing judgments is highly developed and has been lucrative in terms of both status and money, boredom can be a cover for shame. The critical faculty does not, in any of its stages of development, promote creative freedom. Criticism is about identifying mistakes and proscribing them. If you are adept at criticism and the language of criticism is second nature to you, your lovely first draft will appear to be full of mistakes even while it is accumulating, and you will have plenty of opprobrious terms to apply to it that will enhance your feelings of shame and cause your rough draft to fail in the only way that it can fail—by not arriving at the end of the story. The only remedy for this problem is in the degree to which you are stimulated by the material to ignore your own critical habits and discourse. If your material arouses true passion in you, you might get there. If you treat your novel as a product of your desire for status—as an object of embarrassment or defiance—you are less likely to get there, in just the same way that you are unlikely to raise a happy, well-adjusted child if you are constantly finding him wanting or constantly using his abilities to promote yourself. Avid readers who become novelists are always a little ahead of themselves in terms of taste, but only a little ahead. Admiration for the work of other novelists should remind you of the goal, but not make the goal seem unattainable, should open up your desire to write, not shut it down. Writing novels is an essentially amateur activity. Professional readers and literary types have to be able to dispense with their professional side in order to engage in the amateurism required in the rough draft of a first novel.

Ignorance, confusion, fear, and shame are the enemies of your novel. Desire and pleasure are its friends—the desire to communicate and the pleasure of contemplation. Fortunately, you don't have to permanently resolve the balance of these urges in your life to begin a novel; you only have to cope with them. The task of writing itself is helpful, because writing is an exercise in observation, and it is more or less easy to extrapolate from one form of observation—let's say observing your friends and relatives acting like asses—to observing yourself acting like an ass.

Almost every novelist, no matter how great, begins by portraying his friends and associates thinly veiled in his work. This is a very good idea, because the novel is a demanding interpersonal medium, and it is much harder to demonize or sanctify a character than it is to demonize or sanctify a relative. As soon as you put words in your dastardly brother's mouth, you begin, at least in a rudimentary way, if only for the sake of the plot and future critical acclaim, to see things from his point of view, because if you did not, the character based on him would not be able to speak convincingly. This is one of the differences between the novel and melodrama—the characters in a melodrama speak in clichés because they don't have any thoughts of their own, while the characters in a novel may do or say evil things, but they always have a logical point of view. The effort of understanding the logical point of view of characters you are writing about because you aren't ready to fully imagine hypothetical characters, as you will in later novels, gives you practice in detachment, which helps you detach yourself from ignorance, confusion, fear, and shame, which in turn helps your rough draft progress.

There is a difference between discipline and ritual, even though they sometimes seem similar. Discipline is a form of training, a way of developing good habits or breaking bad ones. Having a set time to write each day and writing for a set period, or writing a certain number of words each day, or taking a class and doing the assignments, or joining a writing group and regularly sharing your work, or engaging in a reading program with specific goals, or being mentored in a systematic way, or even mentoring someone else, are all ways of bringing discipline to your novel-writing, and discipline is essential because of the length of the novel and your need to sustain and cultivate inspiration. And to a certain degree, rituals may encourage rather than deter, if the ritual is a type of formalized preparation for the day's work that distinguishes the time you spend writing from the time you spend doing other things. Some writers maintain a separate writing location—a room at the other end of the house or even an office across town. Others leave town altogether and go to writers' retreats such as Yaddo or the MacDowell Colony. But the danger with rituals is that they can as easily prevent you from getting on with your work as enable you. Any time you begin to think that conditions have to be just right for you to sit down to your novel, chances are you are avoiding it rather than engaging with it, and you need to go back to the section on boredom and think about what the real problem is. Obviously, temperamental and even physical factors can enter into the whole issue—some people are more sensitive to noise than others, for example, and get distracted from anything they are doing by noises that less sensitive people can't even hear. Others don't want to be intruded upon by the phone or visits, while there are writers who welcome interaction, even when they are hard at work (I am one of these, and God knows what I get out of it—perhaps mere social stimulation). If you are sitting at your desk, unable to get down to work because the oven needs cleaning, then ask yourself what oven cleaning would offer your novel. Sometimes idle physical labor promotes inspiration, as when Arthur Miller was building his work cabin and suddenly felt *Death of a Salesman* enter his head as a whole concept. Other times, though, oven cleaning is a way of making yourself seem productive and worthy while avoiding engagement with your work.

Another thing you may wish to do and find helpful is to take on a teacher. The temptation to seek out an adviser and show him or her your work and get advice about it is sometimes overwhelming, even as a mere antidote to loneliness, not to mention self-doubt. But you want your teacher to reinforce your productive side, not your critical side, and not every teacher can do so. For one thing, it is not the responsibility of any writing teacher to be the gatekeeper of literature, but some teachers set themselves up to discourage their students rather than encourage them. Novel-writing is such an idiosyncratic and lengthy endeavor that no teacher can tell you whether you will "make it," or whether you have "talent." You should not be seeking answers to that sort of question, but neither should your teacher be offering them. Your teacher's job is to focus your attention on possible solutions to technical problems, including punctuation and grammar, including larger issues of structure, including plausibility of character motivations, etc. Ideally, he or she will be widely read and capable of enjoying many sorts of novels, will understand his or her craft, and will have the vocabulary to communicate his or her knowledge in a way you can understand. Ideally you will never know whether your teacher actually likes your work, because it is not the business of your teacher to like or dislike your work, but to analyze it, communicate the analysis to you, and enable you to learn from his or her wider experience. I do not think it is a good idea to show your novel to a teacher when the rough draft is only partly written. If the teacher praises what you've written, you may feel encouraged, but what if you get to the end and discover that the very parts he or she praised have to be cut? If the teacher doesn't care for what you are writing, there is another obstacle to the completion of the rough draft. By and large, I think that writing courses and programs offer benefits both as social situations where writing is prized and as places to learn how to write your novel without having to reinvent the novel form, but be wary of your teacher, and try to make use of him or her without taking his or her predilections too personally.

At the same time, it is far better to show your work to a teacher, if you must, than to friends or relatives. You simply will not believe anything that friends or relatives say, whether it is praise or doubt, and then you will ruminate upon it, seek out hidden meanings, and give it weight in your own mind. At the same time, your friends and relatives will use their special relationships with you to infer things about you or themselves that will make both of you uncomfortable. No one no one no one is as interested in your work as you are, not even your perfect beloved. Keep it to yourself until it is ready for display, and if you feel the need for praise and encouragement, give yourself some.

The fact is, at the beginning of your career, you can have too many rituals—and seeking praise from another can be a kind of ritual—but you can't have too much discipline. The more wholeheartedly you throw yourself into as many forms of discipline as you have time for, then the more time you will spend with your work; the more familiar you become with the process for getting it down, the less ignorance, confusion, fear, and shame you will feel about it. If your friends and relatives tell you to stop whining, listen to them, because they are right—nobody asked you to write that novel in the first place. As with all aspects of the novel, you are indeed free to go about writing yours in any way you please, but at least be willing to admit that some ways promote productivity and others don't.

The ultimate fact about novel-writing is that you can never control whether your writing efforts will be successful, but you can control whether they will be enjoyable or satisfying. I once knew a promising first novelist for whom everything seemed more than propitious. A good editor at a good publishing house bought her novel for a substantial sum. The editing and design went well, the book was appealing when it came out, and it had two or three admiring blurbs on the back from respected older writers, but unfortunately the *New York Times* went on strike two weeks before the novel's publication, and no *New York Times* meant minimal critical buzz. The book disappeared out of sheer bad luck, and I've never heard of that novelist again. Her best bet for reviving that book would have been to write another, and her best bet for writing another would have been to enjoy herself the first time, so that her publication fate, while a blow, would not have been a blow fatal to her vocation. My first novel, *Barn Blind,* had a similar adventure that now seems funny—six weeks before publication, my editor was fired. The new editor called me and told me how happy she was to be godmothering the publication, but unfortunately she would be doing it from an island in the South Seas, where she planned to be for the month of publication, overseeing another, more successful author in whom the publishing house had a large investment. A week before publication, I got a letter telling me that all of the editorial workers at the publishing house were going on strike, and asking me not to contact the office in any way during the strike. At just the same time, the much-beloved and very successful subsidiary-rights director took another job and left the company, leaving the selling of my little novel into paperback in the hands of an inexperienced (and on strike) subordinate. The key to my survival as a novelist was not only my general cluelessness as to the meaning of these events, it was also that I had enjoyed writing *Barn Blind* no matter what the critics said or what happened to it in the big world, and I was well into writing my next novel by the time *Barn Blind* was published. I laugh at *Barn Blind*'s misadventures now, but I laughed at them then, too. The great thing, as Henry James would say, is to do that rough draft, recognizing it as your first experience of "the incomparable luxury of the artist."

11 · A Novel of Your Own (II)

I wasn't writing poetry and prose so that the reader
would think me a nice person, but in order that my
sets of words should convey ideas of truth and wonder, as indeed they did to myself as I was writing them.

—MURIEL SPARK, *Loitering with Intent*

Now that you have felt the profound pleasure of completing
your rough draft, it is time to recognize that there is no technical solution to the problems of the novel. You can't pick the
ideal point of view, the right protagonist, the ideal plot, or the perfect
setting; you can only pick ones that offer some benefits and some
deficits. And the ones you have picked and committed yourself to are
constrained by qualities you've given them while not knowing what
you are doing. This is their glory as well as their vulnerability.

When you embark upon the second draft and further drafts after
that, your job is to bring knowledge, taste, judgment, and strategy to
all the aspects you are capable of considering, to think through both
what you intend and the effect you want it to have, to know what
needs work and what does not, and to know when you may bring your
efforts to an end, either because you have made the most of the material, or because you have exhausted your ability to improve it. This, of
course, is a tall order, but you can go about it systematically, assured
that your knowledge of other novels will combine with your responses
to this rough draft as you work through it to suggest not only what is
missing but also how to go about adding it.

After you read your rough draft over, you will be tempted to judge it rather than to analyze it, but your task is above all an analytical one. It is not for you to decide whether, for example, it is "publishable." How could you know? Many novels you have read and enjoyed might not be publishable in today's publishing world. Whether your novel is publishable is, for you, an imponderable, so my advice is to avoid the occasion of sin and try to put this question out of your mind. You have made your commitment; now make the most of it. You will also try to decide whether it is good. Let me answer that for you—it is, but it can be better, and your job in rewriting is to make it better. "Better" is not a global trait, but a group of specific qualities you can work toward one by one, knowing that they work ecologically—as you make one better, it might get out of balance with the others, but it also might make the others better. Every novel is a system. Sometimes the system looks out of balance, sometimes the system looks in balance but rather shallow, sometimes a small change balances the whole system and everything gets better and deeper.

Your first step is to decide what you have written, because, as I mentioned in "The Circle of the Novel," every form contains a promise, and every reader expects the inherent promise of the form to be delivered. *Middlemarch* partakes of many forms, but it is primarily a biography/history. It promises psychological insights and a larger historical pattern, and because of Eliot's exceptional intelligence and remarkably judicious style, it delivers on both promises. *The Good Soldier,* with its intimate tone and objective-sounding title, promises biography but also gossip and even scandal. Ford's psychological insights into the characters, possibly exceeded only by the shocking twists in the plot, deliver to a degree that seems, while you are reading the novel, astounding, but because of the novel's complexity, something about it slips away in retrospect—even Ford himself had forgotten how good it was when he looked at it again after ten years. Toni Morrison's *Beloved* combines history and tale. The tale aspect is used to lure the reader into the story, which promises mystery and entertainment, but it also serves to make the narrative more authentic, as if it were a piece of oral black folklore passing outside of the usual suspect literary forms directly from the protagonist's generation to the reader. The historical aspect of *Beloved* promises not to paper over what really happened to former slaves before and after the Civil War, to at last tell the truth without placating white sensibilities. The two forms fuse perfectly, each one bolstering the other but also leaving the reader free to take the novel personally or not. By contrast, *Uncle Tom's Cabin* uses similar material, but shapes it in accordance with the forms of epic and polemic—simultaneously defining the nation as corrupt, and challenging the reader to do something about it, a very inflammatory combination. Even an enormous novel such as *Ulysses* relies on only a few forms more than on others. In *Ulysses* Joyce obviously had to deliver on the form of the epic—these are the Irish today, June 16, 1904, and every detail about them encapsulates all Irishness that has gone before. What he wedded it to was an essay in literary criticism. If the reader can't understand or respond to Joyce's comments upon and interpretations of literary forms and styles, then chances are she will not get much out of *Ulysses*.

And so, look back at the twelve stations on the novel-clock. Is your novel primarily about travel? Then the reader will look for an experience of the exotic. Is it a history? Then the reader will demand some sort of historical understanding or pattern. Is it a biography? Then the reader will expect to get a thorough understanding of your biographical subject. If it is a tale, then entertainment is required and probably a sense of mysterious doings. If you are aiming for a comic novel, then the joke is your model, and will fail if the reader doesn't laugh. If your novel takes much of its inspiration from gossip—that is, the social conversation of people talking about one another—then your reader will expect both intimacy and something shocking or illicit. If your novel presents itself as a diary or letter, you are promising suspense as well as intimacy. If your novel is a confession, then your narrator is by definition unreliable and your narrative suspect, but cannot be dry or distancing—every word your narrator uses is evidence of his state of mind. If your novel is polemical, then it must be vivid, opinionated, and full of righteousness—there is no reason to adopt a polemical stance, no matter what your ideas, if you can't deliver on outrage. If your novel is analytical, then the reader expects evidence, logic, insight, illumination. If you have chosen to write an epic, then you are obliged to characterize your protagonist and his group (usually his nationality) as different from other groups in particular ways, as having a group identity. And, of course, if your novel is a romance, you have to succeed in persuading your reader that the love match you are proposing is worthwhile, or at least interesting. Normally, every novel is an amalgam of more than a single type, with two predominating. When you have decided what types your rough draft is making most use of, you have to bear in mind what you need to deliver to repay the reader's expectations. You can't deliver less than that, but you can deliver more; or, if you must counter the reader's expectations, you can deliver some sort of recompense in exchange for disappointing her. For example, *Orlando* presents itself as a biography, but it quickly becomes clear that Woolf is not delivering a realistic assessment of Orlando in her life and times, but something more eccentric. Woolf uses fanciful set pieces, authorial remarks, and a gossipy tone about literary history to encourage the reader to keep reading even as Orlando's story becomes more and more unusual. The result is a fairly successful experiment (though not as profound or as polished as some of Woolf's other novels). As you assess your rough draft, keep firmly in mind your primary forms so that you understand what the reader is going to feel she has been promised above all. If, for example, you have promised a romance, but instead of an appealing love story you deliver one joke after another, perhaps you should rethink your intentions.

After you decide what form you are using, it is time to get your action organized. For this you must understand how and why a plot works. Not every novel is organized into a plot, but most are.

A plot has four simple parts: exposition, rising action, climax, and denouement. Each of these parts has a job with regard to the action, the characters, and the themes, but its overall purpose is to organize the material to carry the reader along with at least a certain amount of suspense, giving her the feeling that her familiarity with and knowledge of the material is growing as she reads. The suspense can come in any form. We usually think of suspense in connection with the action: the car is heading over the cliff—will it stop in time? For most sophisticated readers, though, such suspense is pretty old hat, and other types are more interesting. One common one is the suspense of finding out what really happened—not what the real outcome of a particular dramatic event was, but what its real cause was. This sort of suspense often leads to a looping or circular structure. In *Beloved,* for example, the question arises fairly quickly—can Sethe and Paul D, both former slaves on a particular Kentucky plantation, find love and consolation with each other? Whether they can depends on their common history and how each interprets it; the current events of the novel; their separate histories and how each interprets them; and something else, which Morrison keeps hidden for most of the novel. This incident, which turns out to be the escape itself, when planning went awry and torture and death ensued, is something the reader almost forgets about in the excitement of all the other events, but Morrison is very careful to place it at the climactic point of the novel to underline the way in which both Sethe and Paul D have defined themselves with regard to it. It is not until the meaning of all the other events has been organized in relation to the escape that Sethe and Beloved can work out their conflict and Sethe's teenage daughter Denver can break away from the haunted house, initiating the denouement. *Beloved* is a novel with plenty of dramatic action, but the climax is one of theme—the meaning and psychological effects of a particular event rather than the event itself. The climax works not to lift the reader to the highest pitch of excitement but to lift her to the highest pitch of understanding.

You, the novelist, can choose what sort of climax you want because you don't have to provide spectacle, as movies and plays do. As soon as spectacle is present, it is required by the plot to get bigger, and this is the tyranny of plot that many writers can't bear. But you have to provide something that looks like a climax, and you have to get it going about 85 to 90 percent of the way into your novel. So the first thing you are going to do is turn to whatever page comes 90 percent of the way into your rough draft and decide if that's what you want your climax to be, because whatever your climactic scene is, that is also the point of the logical rhetorical argument you are making with your lengthy written prose narrative that contains a protagonist.

Chances are, when you turn to your ninetieth, or nine-hundredth page, it isn't exactly right—perhaps it is unclear, or not very dramatic, or stylistically muddy and confused, or dull. A climax is big, but yours is small. For the time being, you can note down what you observe about your climax—not what is good and bad about it, but what its qualities are. Is it narrative or dramatic? Does it deal with events, images, or ideas? Is it long or short, richly depicted or too quick? A climax should have weight, should say to the reader, "I am important, pay attention to me." Is your climax about the point you thought you were going to be making in your novel? Does it include the characters you think are most important, and does it reveal the most important things about them you want the reader to know? Indeed, do you yourself know what those are? If you were asked to tell everything you learn about your novel from that one page of the climax, what would those things be? List them. That one page of the climax of your novel can tell you a lot about both what you have done and what you want to do, if you let it. Reading it, and a couple of pages around it, is your first diagnostic.

Now, with your climax in mind, go back to the beginning and read through your exposition. The exposition is exactly what it says it is—the place in your novel where you show who the protagonist is, who the antagonist is, and what their conflict seems to be (of course, the nature of their conflict can change as the reader learns more about it). The protagonist is always a consciousness (usually human, but sometimes not, as in *The Lord of the Rings* or any one of thousands of fantasy novels), but the antagonist might not be. Something, however, is in the protagonist's way and blocking his intention or desire. Without something of this sort, there is no plot. A good example of a novel without a standard antagonist is David Lodge's *How Far Can You Go?*, which follows the lives of eight traditionally raised Catholics from about age eighteen to about age forty-five. Each of the eight gets almost equal time at the center of attention, and each is a more or less well-meaning modern urban citizen, trying to live according to both conscience and desire. Their antagonist is the Catholic doctrines of their childhood as each has internalized them. Sometimes the church itself seems to block their desires or spoil their lives, but Lodge never forgets that the church is an impersonal institution variously (and sometimes hilariously) interpreted to its members by individuals who are themselves in conflict about what is true and what is right. Lodge's exposition runs exactly a chapter, 10 percent of the pages of the novel. It is a textbook exposition—gathering all the characters in one place, at Mass, in the presence of their antagonist, naming each, describing what each is thinking, laying out the terms of the conflict each one feels, distinguishing each one carefully from the others so the reader can keep them straight. It has all the qualities of a good exposition—it is clear, it is seductive (in this case, funny, intelligent, unorthodox, and ruefully irreverent in tone), and it is specific. At the end of chapter 1 of *How Far Can You Go?*, the author has set out all of the terms of his side of the bargain. If the reader likes them, she can read on. If not, the chapter is over, and she can close the book and stop quite conveniently right there. Lodge is a popular and successful novelist because he is adept at offering the first sample of his wares. The promise of his style and clarity is that he will be trustworthy and intelligent, that he will keep things witty, and that there will be ideas to think about.

Another, more traditional way of going about your exposition is to start your characters moving and talking as if you were entering their lives suddenly, right in the middle of things, and to hope that what they are doing is interesting enough or appealing enough or shocking enough to induce the reader to read on. In this case, drama is intended to take hold before the reader is given a chance to know what it all means. A good example of this sort of exposition is the beginning of Francine Prose's *Three Pigs in Five Days*—"Every time she turned on the T.V., someone was killing a pig." We find out quickly that an American girl named Nina has traveled to Paris on a writing assignment for a magazine whose publisher is her lover. She is disoriented, staying in a seedy hotel he has booked for her. In the course of an evening and a morning, Prose develops Nina's sense of unease—she is suspicious of the whole setup, but she doesn't know exactly why her planned vacation in Paris is turning out to be more sinister than she had expected. At exactly the 10 percent mark, Nina realizes that the proprietress of the hotel is one of her lover's former mistresses. In this sort of exposition, the author reveals dramatically what Lodge, in his novel, reveals by mixing comment with snapshots of characteristic behavior, but the same economy prevails—you, as the author, have about 10 percent of your novel to show the reader "who," "what," "where," and "when." "How" is for the rising action.

Now read the first 10 percent of your rough draft. You don't have to be as precise as Lodge or Prose, but you do have to decide whether your exposition, such as it is, is inextricably connected to your climax—if the story you promise to tell is the same as the story you tell, and if it is not, why not. You have several tasks. Fortunately, most of them are second nature to you from your reading of other novels. What is your protagonist's name? What are the names of his allies and friends? What are the names of his antagonist and that being's allies and friends? (Some of these corollary characters can come in later, along with neutral parties who may take sides or may function as a chorus to the action.) Where is everyone? When is the action taking place? How is time going to be organized? Straight, continuous chronology? Chronological, but in forward jumps? Some sort of looping structure? Backward? What is the protagonist's biggest problem? What does the protagonist want? What stands in his way? (What really stands in his way might be different from what he thinks stands in his way.) What is the protagonist's characteristic way of doing things—that is, how does his nature make him worth writing about, and if nothing does, then what is your justification for writing about him? (Is he an example of something? Has something happened to him that is worth exploring in spite of his ordinariness?) What is your approach—are you going to stay out of the way and let him more or less reveal himself through action, or are you going to intrude, comment, manipulate, and narrate? You have only a certain number of pages to get the reader used to you as a writer. The more you pack into those pages, the more likely the reader will trust you and be willing to go on to the rising action.

Don't hesitate to take out every novel on your shelves, good or bad, and look at their expositions. If they are books you like, then those authors have succeeded in their expositions and so are worthy of your study.

The rising action is the meat of the novel. We may or may not really remember the other parts, but we do remember the rising action—fabulous scenes, passages of dialogue or narrative, unexpected twists of the plot, authorial insights that pleased or astounded us not only because they were good in themselves, but because they also led to something (the climax) that also turned out to be satisfying. When we cherish a particular novel it is because the author excelled at developing his story and making it as immediate to us as our own experience, because his voice became familiar and even precious to us while we were reading, because we entered into some sort of agreement with him (though perhaps sometimes a troubled agreement) about how the world works. You may have difficulties with your climax and you may have problems with your exposition, but these are as nothing to the dilemmas of the rising action.

What is really going on in the rising action is that something that seems implausible at the time of the exposition—the climax—is being prepared for. It is in the rising action that the novel becomes more and more different from life. Life is full of expositions (people beginning to do something) and full of climaxes (dramatic events), but it is less full of rising action because the rising action is essentially a consciousness of cause and effect and an arrangement of events so they appear to lead to one another in a logical manner. If we return to *The House of Mirth* we can see the challenge. When we meet Lily, through the eyes of Selden, she is an especially attractive young woman—"Miss Bart was a figure to arrest even the suburban traveller rushing to his last train" (p. 4). At the 90 percent mark, Lily begins an interview with her last suitor, a wealthy man named Rosedale whom she finds especially unappealing. She has just lost her millinery job and is in desperate circumstances. Wharton's job, in the rising action, is to make us believe both in Lily's special qualities and in the idea that she can fall so low as to entertain Rosedale in any way. The climax of Rosedale is the climax of Lily's humiliation but also of her special form of integrity. If the climax doesn't work, then Wharton hasn't proved her argument about Lily and the world she lives in.

To take another and perhaps more complex example, let's try *Tom Jones,* by Henry Fielding, which runs to some 950 pages. Fielding's exposition is leisurely, perhaps too leisurely for some modern readers, but exactly at the 10 percent mark, Tom's tutors, Thwackum and Square, who represent religion and science, respectively, and who are always at odds, engage in a debate that turns out to have as its catalyst a fight between Tom and Blifil, Tom's antagonist. This fight begins the train of conflicts that result in Tom's exile from the Allworthy paradise. Tom is still much beloved of Allworthy, and perhaps to Allworthy, at this point, it would be unimaginable that he could ever turn the boy out, but he does, through the machinations of Thwackum and Square. Ninety-five pages before the end of the novel, Tom is about to be hanged, Allworthy is ready for that to happen, and Sophia is openly defying her aunt's instructions to accept Blifil's proposal of marriage.

Even *The Life and Opinions of Tristram Shandy* conforms in some degree to this model, though Sterne wrote the book in volumes, adding more each year to sustain the novel's success. At the 10 percent mark, Sterne shifts the story to Tristram's Uncle Toby, where the story more or less remains. At the 90 percent mark, Uncle Toby, the shyest and most modest of men, declares himself in love with a neighboring widow, surely the most implausible of all the implausible events detailed in the novel.

Why this pattern seems ubiquitous in the novel is worth discussing, but for now, you have plenty of pages to fill to get your apparently normal, or average, or regular, or sympathetic protagonist to the point where he is going to do something that he would never have planned in a million years. This is the very point of your novel.

As you may have noticed in your own reading, most readers are perfectly willing to suspend disbelief and follow the protagonist to any implausible climax if the situation is interesting enough, but your reader's willing suspension of disbelief cannot be taxed too heavily, or you and she will part company. The primary thing you must do is encourage your reader to think about your situation in such detail that she can't help but keep thinking about it. This is what compelling, picturesque, and vivid details are for. Each detail is an insertion into your reader's inner life—a splinter, a thumbtack, a grain of sand, a drop of oil that spreads upon the waters, a bud that blossoms into a silken, fragrant lily, an elephant in the living room.

At the same time, these details must add up logically because every plot, every novel, makes some assertion about causality.

Now it is time to read through your rough draft from the end of the exposition to the beginning of the climax. I suggest that you read through it without stopping, only pausing to make some small mark where something strikes you as out of place, as missing something, as digressive, as boring, as unclear or confusing. Read your draft in a fairly short time—the point of this reading is to try to comprehend the draft as a whole, and to understand the whole arc of the action. You are not to dwell either on the fabulous bits or the terrible bits, and you are not to fix anything, no matter how strong the temptation. At the end of your reading, make as many notes as quickly as possible about what you think of your novel—nothing systematic, just a form of talking to yourself to fix your impressions. I don't think you should record negative feelings you have, though it's perfectly fine to congratulate yourself on the wonders you have engendered. With luck, after these few forms of reconnaissance, you have a sense of your novel as a whole, and it has spoken to you, to your tastes and knowledge as a reader more than as a writer, about what it needs. Your goal at this stage is to have a sense of the draft as a whole, because once you start through it again, rewriting, fixing, adding, subtracting, and sorting through the confusing bits, what you have already written will exert a seductive pull that you want to both acknowledge (that's its job, after all) and resist. Your future reader will be more successfully beguiled if you are more detached and less passive now.

With luck you will come up with a good way to organize the work you need to do. When I was writing *Duplicate Keys,* which was a whodunit, I made a set of cards, one for each scene. On each card I listed the characters who appeared, what they were supposed to do, what they should be doing that they were not doing, and who was supposed to know what at this point. Since a mystery can work only through the careful revealing of information, it was essential that I have a firm understanding of what had and had not been revealed. My cards worked well for *Duplicate Keys,* but when I set about rewriting my next novella, *Good Will,* the card idea wasn't applicable at all. When I wrote *Moo,* I set up a visual chart, with the chapter numbers running across the top and the character names running down the side. Each time a character appeared in a chapter, I put a dot in the square where chapter and character intersected. I could see at a glance which characters were getting lost; when I finished the rough draft, I aimed to have a fairly evenly populated field that represented the novel. When I began the rewrite, I saw that many of the characters had story lines of their own, and that each thread had to be logical and sequential, even though the many threads were woven together into a larger plot. I began the rewrite by dividing the manuscript into the individual story lines, arranging them from largest to smallest, and reading through each as a whole. I then fixed each story line and braided them back together. After that, I went through the whole thing again, working on continuity and transitions.

You have plenty of ingenuity. If you are receptive to your rough draft but detached from it, you will come up with some sort of method that will make your novel palpable to you and spur your inspiration with a sense of progress. Thinking about your novel and grasping it as a whole without going through it over and over will prevent you from making mistakes and falling into difficulties that arise simply from habit.

Now it is time to start through it. You should *want* to go through it. Fear, shame, confusion, and ignorance can deter you as you do your rewrite, just as they may have in the rough draft; the antidotes are the same. This time, though, the momentum is on your side. What you have already written is pushing you forward. What you need to accomplish is smaller than what you have already achieved. For inspiration, keep reading novels. As you aim for perfection, don't forget that there is no perfect novel, that because every novel is built out of specifics, every novel offers some pleasures but does not offer some others, and while you can try to achieve as many pleasures as possible, some cancel out others. For example, it is very hard to achieve both *broad* and *deep*. The prime example of *deep* is, of course, *Madame Bovary*. At the time of its publication, no previous author had ever gone so deeply into the psychology of a single character, especially a female character with all sorts of female weaknesses. *Madame Bovary* was a revelation to its readers and changed the history of the novel, in part because it showed that the reader could make a connection even to an unsympathetic character, even to a woman who was not virtuous. Once Flaubert showed the way, many subsequent novelists used his method to extend the embrace of the novel to many protagonists who might have seemed unlikely in earlier times.

The novels of Henry James also serve as examples of *deep*. When

E. M. Forster says of James in *Aspects of the Novel,* "Most of human life has to disappear before he can do us a novel" (p. 160), he attributes this to James's desire to make of every novel an artistic whole, and certainly this was one of James's preoccupations, but he also wanted to explore particular human feelings and impulses patiently and exhaustively, with intense and careful focus. When we enjoy *The Portrait of a Lady* or *The Ambassadors,* we are according James the privilege of saying a lot about a fairly small thing. James takes very seriously the idea that the unexamined life is not worth living. I may feel as strongly that the unlived life is not worth examining, but when I am reading Henry James, I am learning how to examine in greater detail, with more refinement of sensibility. A modern example of *deep* would be Jamaica Kincaid's *Annie John,* which is short but so evocatively written that we feel we have visited an island, and a consciousness, in the Caribbean in a way not otherwise possible than through this novel. Annie's problem is her vexed feelings for her mother, out of which grow all of her other feelings about Antigua, her father, herself, and the world. If the novel were *broader,* her feelings would be put into context and lose intensity. In the cases of Annie and Emma Bovary, the important thing is not what their feelings mean, but what they are, and whether the reader empathizes with them.

Novelists of the nineteenth century tried over and over to get both *broad* and *deep.* That is one reason their novels ran eight hundred to nine hundred pages. Some nearly succeeded—*Middlemarch* nearly succeeds because after the first section about Dorothea, we retain a strong sense of kinship with her. The scenes of her marriage with Casaubon are affecting as well as brilliantly insightful. But in her effort to depict a whole place at an important time (the town of Middlemarch just before the parliamentary Reform Bill of 1832), Eliot is forced to drop Dorothea and apply her intensity of focus to other characters, like Lydgate and Rosamond Vincy and Fred Vincy and Mary Garth. The result is that although we end up wishing them well, they do fall into an authorial pattern, which is abstract and therefore distancing. Many readers would say that *Ulysses* achieves both *broad* and *deep,* and truly, Joyce enters the mind of Leopold Bloom as thoroughly as maybe it is possible to do, but the idleness of Bloom's concerns in the course of his day and the fact that he doesn't in the end act upon anything he learns, but instead goes to bed with his wife to all intents and purposes unchanged (he will, after all, get up the next morning and have a similar day, except that it won't be recorded for posterity), rob the novel of emotional impact for many readers. In the end, novelists who want both *broad* and *deep* are constrained by the form of the novel—prose elaborating and elaborating—to go on into multiple volumes, as Proust did. And as length increases, readers get intimidated and works become the property of specialists rather than of the reading public as a whole. Even Tolstoy had to make a choice in *Anna Karenina*—he had to limit himself to two couples, Anna and Vronsky and Levin and Kitty. To explore only four consciousnesses (along with a little exploration of Karenin), he allowed himself almost a thousand pages.

You may prefer *broad*. If so, you have plenty of company. Many comic novels, such as David Lodge's *Small World* and my own *Moo,* are broad. So is Naguib Mahfouz's *The Harafish.* But your critics are going to complain that your characters are stereotyped, thinly realized, or not very engaging. Some readers are happy to give up depth for pattern and breadth, for the sparkle of the author's vision, wit, and intelligence; others will tar you with the Dickensian brush—your works are not quite refined enough to be truly great, your psychological insights aren't very astute, you deal in types rather than real people, and finally they don't *care* as much about your characters as they do about the deep ones. But *broad* necessarily makes a pattern and so is intellectual and abstract. *Deep* necessarily hides the author's theories about psychological causes and effects beneath an illusion of unfolding humanity, and so is more emotionally appealing but perhaps not very interesting. Your job is to understand which you want to emphasize and to make the best of the possibilities of that alternative.

Over the centuries, more authors have probably placed their bets on the realistic novel than on any other type. After all, one of the reasons the novel exists is to explore the dilemmas of the author and his contemporaries: Marguerite de Navarre was interested in the love problems that her circle knew firsthand or at one remove; Miguel de Cervantes confronted his knight and squire with typical travelers' adventures at inns and along roadsides in a recognizable Spain. Henry Fielding was careful to set *Tom Jones* during a particular month of a particular military campaign—he used an almanac to be sure he even got the phases of the moon right. Realism is naturally interesting because most people can relate to realistic characters and problems, and realism is natural to the novel because of the mundane—let's say, prosaic—nature of prose. But realism, too, makes compromises. It goes in and out of fashion, and when it is out of fashion it is usually because readers feel that "realism" doesn't quite reproduce the surreal quality of life as they experience it. Realism is no less subjective than fabulism or surrealism, but realists and their readers agree that there is a generally accepted form that reality takes; that it can be depicted, read about, and agreed upon; and that its boundaries are fairly clear and separate it recognizably from unrealities such as insanity, fantasy, wishful thinking, heightened states of consciousness, and dreams. Realism can seem pedestrian and unoriginal, appealing only to readers without any sense of adventure. Realism is dogged by the need for plausibility and accountability. The problem is that plausible events are often not very much fun, while implausible events have to be depicted in detail and accounted for, and these requirements may take more time in the telling than the event is worth. Most literary best sellers are examples of realism, because realism has the widest audience, but most realistic novels get disdained by sophisticated critics as "middlebrow"—not innovative enough to be of interest to the most sophisticated readers. Some critics feel that the possibilities of realism have been fully explored, at least in America and Europe, in the dominant literary cultures. They might wonder if it is really necessary to redo *Madame Bovary.* The realistic novel, though, accepts the importance of the novel as a social document and the need for successive generations to depict the world as it appears to them. The realistic novel expresses the idea that normal life is intrinsically interesting, and that if the novelist is sufficiently insightful and observant, new wine can be poured into old bottles. And anyway, it's nice to have a large readership and maybe get your book made into a movie.

If you are writing a comic novel, chances are it will have limited appeal no matter how funny it is, unless you are writing comforting nonsatirical books like those of P. G. Wodehouse. Every comic effort has a narrower potential audience than every realistic effort, because individual readers differ in their acceptance of the irreverence and disrespect inherent in the comic sensibility. What is scathing and off-putting to some is just right to others. What is mirthful and light to some is flat to others. If writing comic novels weren't wonderfully enjoyable, I doubt that anyone would make the effort, because the rewards are few—no prizes, no respect, and not many sales, only the satisfaction (considerable though it is) of a joke well told. Fortunately, if you are writing a comic novel, it is because you have a certain verbal gift, you can't be stopped anyway, and you understand already that phrase-turning is its own reward.

A comic novel has two aspects, and they are strongly distinguished by the author's political sensibility. Both aspects have to be funny, which is a stylistic requirement. Every witticism is like a small bubble that pops in the text, brightening it and giving it a small push forward, but every witticism sets up the need for another, and most readers want the text to be popping with regularity. Beyond this, though, is the conservative/liberal issue. A traditional comic play, which is the paradigm of comedy, promises several marriages at the end of the fifth act, and these marriages represent social integration and the resolution of conflict. The liberal comic novel offers the same sort of social resolution—it is a funny novel with a comic plot structure, where conflicts are resolved and antagonistic feelings are shown to be illusory. Thus the liberal comic novel at bottom expresses a worldview that is a bit at odds with other types of novels. If, in the realistic novel, the protagonist normally sacrifices something for the sake of knowledge—he ends up not happier, but smarter—in the liberal comic novel he ends up happier *and* smarter. This movement contradicts what many serious readers consider the norm, so if you are writing a liberal comic novel, you have to understand the possibilities of your material in a way that makes happier and smarter plausible rather than implausible. One of my favorite examples of a liberal comic novel is Nancy Mitford's *Love in a Cold Climate,* in which a young girl insists on marrying a confirmed bachelor who is also one of her mother's old lovers, the heir to the enormous family estate turns out to be a penniless young gay man living by his wits in Paris, and all the characters are rejuvenated and redeemed by a large infusion of French style.

The conservative comic novel, which doesn't propose that happiness is a possible outcome, has its own difficulties, because a dark worldview combined with lots of jokes almost inevitably carries a tone of contempt and can be quite distancing for the reader, who enjoys the jokes for a while but can be offended by what she perceives as cruelty. The conservative comic novelist, or satirist, almost inevitably adopts a superior tone that challenges the reader's "naïveté." The jokes have to be especially good and the satire especially smart to sustain the reader's commitment (the novels of Kingsley Amis such as *Lucky Jim* and *The Old Devils* qualify as conservative comic novels).

And while you, the author, are exerting yourself to achieve the impossible, since comic novels are perhaps the most difficult form, you must understand that your effort itself is not appreciated. What could be more honorable and worthy than trying to raise a laugh? And yet, readers and reviewers seem to react with special venom to comic or satiric novels they don't like. I am not sure why this is, but as a result, it's a good thing that writing a comic novel is its own reward.

Experimental fiction can take any form, but essentially it is more or less nonrealistic—you are playing with the narrator/character/novelist relationship and in the process dispensing with the realist illusion that the reader is watching the characters go about their business as if they were fellow citizens, only with special access to their inner lives. You undoubtedly wrote an experimental rough draft because you are smart and inventive and not content to do again what has been done before. You are very aware that a novel is "novel," so you want your novel to live up to the promise of the form. Congratulations. But the special burden of the experimental novel is that you have to continue to be smart, and then get smarter. An intriguing concept will carry you a long way, but not all the way. You have to exploit your material from beginning to end—like jokes, inventiveness begets the need for more inventiveness. At the same time, your inventiveness, I am sorry to say, must have a point that the reader finds enlightening. The promise of any theme-oriented novel, especially one that flouts convention, is that you have a reason and purpose in flouting convention, and that if the reader wades into the unfamiliar stream that is your novel, she will get something out of it besides an unpleasant experience. As with comic fiction, some readers have a smaller capacity to tolerate the unknown, and your audience may turn out to be limited, but if you were interested in writing a standard realistic novel, that's what you would be doing. Remember above all that readers outside of graduate school really do not care what is good for them. It may be that reading your novel (or Henry Miller's novels) will set them straight forever, but they do not care about that in the slightest. Even you, as smart as you are, have no powers over the reader except the usual seductive ones. Experimental novelists are in some ways the most frustrated, because they are visionary. Every experimental novel is a dose of medicine in the form of unpalatable truths or a radical shift in perspective. If you are an experimental novelist, you are probably some sort of malcontent anyway, and your experience writing, selling, and publishing your novel could sour, or further sour, your relationship to society. As a result of all these considerations, your task in rewriting your rough draft is never to compromise, because no reward will compensate you for the feeling that you gave in to weakness, whatever its source. It is easier to do it your way, to polish the jewel until it is just how you want it, and maybe never find a publisher or a readership, than it is to take advice you disdain and end up with a product you cannot in good conscience claim as your own.

Attempt to do your first rewrite as you did your rough draft, as continuously as possible and without consulting anyone. Inevitably you possess the several intelligences that go into writing a novel in varying degrees, and these differences will manifest themselves as you work. If your sharper intelligences are psychological and verbal, you will round out your characters and improve your style, but perhaps your logical/structural intelligence is a bit lacking, so you will not understand how to make the larger structure work—possibly you won't even notice that the balance is off. An interesting novel with structural weaknesses is George Eliot's *The Mill on the Floss,* a book Eliot felt to be autobiographical, even though she gave Maggie Tulliver a quite different life and death from her own. *The Mill on the Floss* is meant to have a plot, with a dramatic climax in which Maggie is lured away by her cousin's fiancé, returns in disgrace, and then dies trying to save her estranged brother in a flood. Really, though, the climax, as dramatic as it is, seems tacked onto the interesting and complex portrait of the drama of Maggie's search for some way to use her intelligence, her passions, and her idealism. The novel purports to be about the conflict, much of it covert, between Maggie and her disapproving older brother, but Eliot never successfully portrays Tom's appeal. Maggie ends up seeming too good for him in a way the author doesn't understand. The structure of the novel gives nearly equal weight to all the parts of Maggie's life—childhood, family, her father's ruin, her relationship with Tom, the love plot. Only Maggie's intensity endures throughout, so a story meant to build dramatically by the accretion of incident ends up seeming arbitrary. A real climax has to seem to solve the problem the exposition poses. The climax of *The Mill on the Floss* merely ends the problem of Maggie's inability to fit into the world and the family into which she was born.

Maybe, like Henry James, you have a genius for structure, even though your style is flat and unevocative. Into that category I would put *Dracula.* Bram Stoker succeeds in achieving his uncanny effects because the mystery they represent contrasts with the pedestrian voices of his narrators, who never pretend to be anything other than average late Victorian folks with some special knowledge, but conventional attitudes, toward love and morality.

The key to the first rewrite is to fix it all the best you can, working through it until you are fairly satisfied not only with the effort you've made but also with the product you've come up with. You might say it is not perfect, but you are reasonably satisfied with it. This means that you and it have more or less parted ways—it more or less stands on its own, setting out its terms and fulfilling them without tempting you to justify it or make excuses for it or, indeed, to sit with a reader and anxiously oversee her reading of it!

As you come to the end of the first rewrite you will have to deal with the denouement, which you have been avoiding. The problem of the denouement is that you have to seem to the reader to know what you have been doing, but not to be imposing any final thoughts about the meaning of the novel, or having last-minute ideas. You also have to get your narrative voice and your characters gracefully off the stage, and you have to stay within the tone you have set up. You cannot betray impatience, even though you are probably relieved to be approaching the end of a lengthy task. The key to a good denouement is not thought, though, but intuition. If you solve all the problems of your novel in successive drafts, if you become throughly familiar with your novel so everything about it, but especially some feeling it gives you, is present in your mind, your limbic brain will provide you with the denouement. You may be dissatisfied with the denouement until the very end because it is literally beyond your understanding but know it is right anyway. The most famous denouement in English literature are the last words of Molly Bloom at the end of *Ulysses,* "and yes I said yes I will Yes." It is famous because it is both appropriate and full of pleasure and hope. It sums up all the ironies of Leopold Bloom's marriage, but also all the good will in Bloom himself.

Now you are ready to show your novel to someone.

Ideally, your first reader will have an editorial sensibility, which may be defined as being interested in the novel as a form, knowledgeable, somewhat detached from you and your life, and without a strong investment of his or her own in what a novel should be (that is, that it should be like something your reader would write). As noted above, relatives, friends, and other novelists do not make the best first readers because they inevitably feel conflicts of interest. However, editorial sensibilities are not as available as they might be, and you may have to show it to someone who is less than ideal. If so, an educated novel-reader would be your best choice, possibly a novelist who teaches creative writing in a summer program.

When you have your conversation about the novel you have written, once again (because this is very difficult) try to direct it toward analysis rather than judgment. Inevitably and unfortunately, the conversation will open with some summary judgment of the novel. You must let this opening go by and pay attention to the subsequent analysis, even if your reader asserts that your novel is a literary abomination typical of your sort of crude and unredeemed sensibility. "Yes, but," is your response—Yes, but what about the exposition? Did you understand who was who and what the problem was? Yes, but what about the rising action? Did it move too abruptly? Was there anything missing in the logic of the sequence of events? Was it repetitive or overlong? Did you understand the themes, and did they become more complex and interesting as you read? Yes, but was the climax both expected and unexpected, surprisingly right after you thought about it? Yes, but did the felicities of style make you want to read on? You should be committed enough by this time to what you have done that the fires of judgment raging all around you cannot deter you from questioning the dragon. This means that your material still fascinates you, draws you to it, enables you to pick out helpful nuggets from whatever else your reader says and ignore the rest.

If your reader is good at his editorial job, he may be able to suggest improvements. If you know your weaknesses—psychology, structure, style, understanding what the larger themes are—you will be better able to listen to these suggestions and learn from them. You don't want to slavishly do what he says—you want to be able to consider a suggestion in the light of not only what you already know about the book, but also of your intentions. I, for example, might have made a strong case to George Eliot for cutting the first two-thirds of *The Mill on the Floss* by 25 percent, leaving a more shapely novel, but she might have decided that in the end, the plot wasn't as important as the texture of rural English life that she wanted to achieve by including those parts I wanted to cut. My cuts, she might have decided, would make a shapelier but less innovative novel, and at her level of experience, she wasn't yet ready, as she would be a few years later, to conceive of a structure that would fully exploit the potential of her material. Or, I might have told her, Maggie's adventure with her cousin's fiancé is too pale and timid to truly warrant her subsequent disgrace. Then she and I might have had a spirited discussion about female virtue in the provinces in the 1830s, about gossip, respectability, and appearances versus reality. Once again the solution to the problem would depend on Eliot's own judgment about what is plausible, what was allowable in the novel of her day, and what she feels comfortable with as a single, self-supporting, female author. In your discussion with your reader, you have the last word, but the more educated and less defensive you are about your novel, the more likely you are to come up with a solution to its problems. Solutions come from the free operation of invention. If, in the face of judgment and analysis, you can retain your ability to play with your material—and, indeed, your playful mood—you are more likely to be able to invent your way to a higher form of your novel.

All the time you are working on your rewrite, be careful to correct spelling errors, grammatical errors, errors of diction, typos, errors of fact, and other small mistakes. To do so bolsters your sense of progress and your sense of professionalism. To fail to do so makes your manuscript look worse than it is and interferes with your ability to contemplate it.

How do you know if you are finished? The first step here is to know yourself. Are you a dissatisfied perfectionist who tends to overdo everything? Or are you a careless sort who loses interest after the first rush of energy? Novels are long projects, and are more difficult to write if you go about it unsystematically. The reader wants both the finished surface and the energy simultaneously, all through the book. Your rewriting should promote both.

One danger of doing too many drafts, especially if you are rearranging events and sequences of action or materially changing characters, is that you can get very confused about what happens when and what you have put in, taken out, and added to. There is no solution to this problem, because the more times you read the drafts through, the more information about the drafts you have to keep straight. If you are getting confused about what is happening, stop, take a long break, give the novel to your astute, editorial-type reader, and ask her explicitly to keep track of the action or the characters or the other things that confuse you. There are two types of confusion. In the first type, you don't know what is going on because you haven't figured it out yet. In the second type, you don't know what is going on because all the things you've written have become disordered in your mind. For this reason, three good drafts, done thoughtfully and thoroughly, are better than ten drafts without a plan. Your novel doesn't have to be perfect to find a publisher; it only has to be promising and engaging. An editor will inevitably have suggestions, and if you feel that you have perfected the novel before the editor buys it, you will be less open to what are probably good suggestions. The job of the editor is to help you—to be able to diagnose both what the novel needs and how to get you to supply it—and one thing a good editor will really help you do is keep track of events, action, and characters.

In the preceding paragraph, I am assuming, of course, that you tend to the perfectionist side. If you are a slob, though, pay no attention to the previous remarks. If your manuscript has coffee stains, crossings out, grease spots, spelling errors, sentences that run off the bottom of the page and around to the back, typos, and if it shows evidence of having been dropped into the bathwater, keep rewriting it until it is neat, sequential, polished, and, as far as you are concerned, perfect. Your standards are low. Try to exceed them.

The feeling you are looking for as you decide whether you are finished is exhaustion. I do not mean literal physical fatigue as much as the sense that you have used up your inventiveness, your intelligence, and your ideas with regard to this story and these characters. While you are still interested in them, you have thought every thought you are capable of about them. Chances are your novel is *not* perfect, and someone else will have a good idea of how it can be improved or at least be done differently the first time he reads it, but you have come to the end of your relationship with it. Print it out; go to a bookstore and buy a book about publishing, which is a whole subject in itself.*

---

*Some incidents that take place at the 90 percent mark:

Orlando: pp. 280–81—Orlando gets the poem she has been working on for hundreds of years published.

Justine: pp. 260–61—Justine is recaptured by her old tormentor, Dubois.

Three Pigs in Five Days: pp. 153–54—Nina in the conciergerie (holding pen for the guillotine during the French Revolution) is betrayed by her lover.

To Kill a Mockingbird: p. 250—The beginning of the Halloween pageant that ends in the children's being terrorized on the way home.

The Idiot: p. 584—Myshkin has his climactic epilectic attack at the big party.

Lady Chatterley's Lover: p. 324—Mellors writes his manifesto to Connie, who is pregnant by him and expecting in the spring.

Madame Bovary: p. 230—Emma poisons herself.

12 · *Good Faith*: A Case History

> I read the article while forcing myself to imagine
> that it had been written by someone else. Then all
> my images, all my reflexions, all my epithets taken
> in themselves, unvarnished by the failure which
> they represented in relation to my aims, charmed
> me by their brilliance, their unexpectedness, their
> profundity.
>
> —MARCEL PROUST, *The Fugitive*

When I closed the file of my rough draft of *Good Faith,* I was on what became page 286 in the published novel. The immediate reason I lost heart was that I had impulsively introduced a heart attack into the narrative (the protagonist's fundamentalist father) and then realized that the death of the father would complicate the protagonist's emotional life and add many pages to a novel that was supposed to begin accelerating toward the climax. Page 286 was about 70 percent of the way into the novel.

For those who haven't read *Good Faith,* its premise is fairly easy to summarize. Joe, about forty, is a small-town real-estate agent in a scenic region; he is newly divorced but generally happy and not filled with high aspirations. At the beginning of the novel, two things happen, apparently independently of one another—a stranger (Marcus) comes to town full of big plans; and an old friend of Joe's (Felicity), the daughter of his partner and married, entices him into having a clandestine affair. It is 1982, the beginning of the Reagan era, when mores are beginning to loosen in the more conservative regions of the United States, and though he is cautious by nature and suspicious of both Marcus and Felicity, Joe allows himself to be seduced by both of them, with consequences that are, to say the least, surprising to him, if not, with the perspective of twenty years, equally surprising to the reader.

The "seed" of *Good Faith* was an anecdote related to me by a friend about his own experiences as a real-estate agent in the 1980s. Since I had written two books about the eighties already (*A Thousand Acres* and *Moo*), I was always interested in how other tales of the eighties fit in with my theories about that regrettable period of American history, and my friend's anecdote fit in perfectly. The anecdote was self-contained and seemed as though it would be easy to expand into a good novel.* Not long before I closed my file, I had, at the 62 percent mark (page 255 in this novel, or equivalent to the beginning of the fourth act in a five-act play), consolidated and reoriented the narrative, in a scene where Marcus assumes greater control over the partnership and Joe closes his own real-estate office, losing his independence and taking a decisive step toward becoming completely vulnerable to Marcus. I did not do this knowingly, but I wasn't surprised later that I had done it—almost every novel gathers itself at the 62 percent mark, changes strategy, and freshens. In *To Kill a Mockingbird,* Bob Ewell lies on the stand about seeing Tom and his daughter having sex. In *The Trial,* Josef K. meets Titorelli the painter; the "process" Josef K. is undergoing expands into new realms of confusion. In *Justine,* Justine arrives at a large château and meets the count, who, while he is violating her, explains to her exactly how sex and marriage work among the French aristocracy. In *Madame Bovary,* Emma begins to give up her attempts at domestic conformity and then goes to see her first opera, *Lucia di Lammermoor,* which quickens her romantic yearnings. In adding a heart attack on page 278, I was adding drama to keep myself entertained, but I also changed the pacing of the novel without getting closer to the point. I cut out the heart attack (no more than a page or two), but this made me feel as though I had lost the thread of the novel entirely and was bored, to boot.

*A few more particulars of *Good Faith*: the novel takes place over the course of about two years and involves the attempt, by Joe and his associates, to develop a dream property, the pristine and luxurious estate of a wealthy local couple who want to divest themselves and move to another property they own in Florida. The cast of characters includes several from the local savings and loan who are attempting to forward financial schemes of their own. In addition to Joe, Marcus, and Felicity, the main characters are Felicity's parents, Gordon and Betty, whose background is a bit mysterious; Joe's parents, who are very strict fundamentalists; two enterprising gay guys who like to buy property and fix it up; and Marcus's sister, who colludes with Marcus, but also warns Joe about him.

I diagnosed my boredom as fear, but I wasn't sure what I was afraid of. Most of the parts of my plot were already in place and I understood them. I knew enough to go on and was fairly clear how I should go on. As I noted in the introduction, I felt considerable underlying fear as a result of the World Trade Center attacks and their aftermath; performance fears rested on top of that, in particular the fear that if the plot wasn't building enough to quicken my pulse, then most likely it wasn't building enough to quicken anyone else's pulse. This is what the boredom felt like. I recoiled at what Henry James would have called "the developments," the very proliferation of dialogue, narration, characters doing this and that, scenes piling upon scenes. Not only did I recoil at what I still had to produce, I also recoiled at what I had already produced. The whole thing presented itself to me as a dusty, sunburned road, and I was trudging down it. As it petered out in the few days after I added and removed the heart attack, I wrote a few things I liked, including a bit of dialogue where Joe runs into a gay couple at the hardware store. These two guys were always witty, so I enjoyed their wit all over again. But it was as if their wit used up my own, and when I read the scene the next day, it did not stimulate any more thoughts.

By contrast, at the 70 percent mark in *Horse Heaven,* I so loved my small sets of characters that I relished each visit with them—each group (say Rosalind, Al, and Limitless, or Deirdre, Tiffany, and Audrey) was a refreshing change from the other groups. Though I dreaded the moment when I would finish *Horse Heaven,* I enjoyed getting there. That novel presented itself to me not as a dusty road but as a collection of bright stages I was privileged to visit. At the 70 percent point in *A Thousand Acres,* which I had not enjoyed writing but which I had found intellectually stimulating, the conflicts among the characters were intensifying, and Ginny's disagreements with her husband, in particular, were emerging into the open. The novel seemed to me to be building steam. I felt myself moving with the characters toward something horrible but alluring and exciting—a nasty, adrenaline-fueled revelation that couldn't be avoided.

In *Good Faith,* I was required by the nature of the plot to be careful and calculating so that the reader, like Joe, would be seduced and beguiled. This was a feature of a betrayal plot that I hadn't reckoned with when I began the novel. All plots are about what happens, and then what happens after that, and so on; usually as events approach the climax, the things that happen next pile on one another more and more energetically. But this plot was about a scheme, and just as Marcus had to think through his scheme ever more carefully, so I had to think through the various aspects of the scheme ever more carefully—it could not lose plausibility, it could not be too exposed, Joe could not appear too foolish, Marcus could not appear to be too insincere, decoy elements had to be supplied that would eventually fit in with the main plot but seem gratuitously lifelike. I had to resist the energy of the plot if it made me careless and yet sustain it for the sake of the reader. And there was no relief, no jumping to other characters and plots, as I had done in *Horse Heaven.*

Perhaps the lesson here was that plotting is hard work—harder than style (which is at least in part natural), harder than character-drawing (which is more or less complete early on, because once the characters are standing up and talking, they operate largely on their own internal logic). Another lesson may be that plotting is a bit airless by nature—the more involved the plot, the more mechanical it is, and the more careful the novelist must be to hide the mechanics. And yet I love to read cleverly plotted novels. They have the extra pleasure of contrivance—if we look at a beautifully made box or listen to a Mozart piano sonata masterfully played, we love to say, "How do they do that?" When I read a P. G. Wodehouse novel, I also say, "How did he do that?"

When I was teaching writing, I would sometimes come across gaps in student stories or spots where the student had stopped writing altogether. When I asked the students why, they would say that they had fallen asleep, or had had to go to work. Almost invariably, outside circumstances had intervened to prevent the completion of the story. But no. When the other students and I read those stories, we quickly saw that whatever the writers themselves thought, it was apparent to us that the story had failed just at that point—if it had not, the writer would have gone on with it in spite of outside circumstances. And so *Good Faith,* too, in spite of the World Trade Center attacks, had failed just at that point, in the late summer of 1983, when Joe had nothing to do but work on the project and no place to go but the office.

When I resumed writing the novel in the second half of October 2001 (after writing the introduction to this book and reading *The Tale of Genji*), the first thing I did was bring on my most energetic character, Marcus Burns. Although I don't like Marcus and am not like Marcus, and in some ways revile Marcus, "Marcus Burns, *c'est moi,*" as Flaubert would say. In *Good Faith,* it is Marcus's desire that initiates the action of the story. He is the one with the appetite and the intention. So I began chapter 21. Joe and Marcus are driving out to the expensive farm they plan to develop. Joe is bored and disgruntled ("the scenery looked tired and uninteresting, the dusty end of summer"—there was my attitude, right there). Marcus doesn't say much at first, but then he begins persuading Joe to do yet another thing that Joe hasn't thought of—find a woman and get married. Marcus, of course, has a plan and a theory. He has picked a particular woman as a suitable mate for Joe—someone good-looking, cosmopolitan, and short; although he is married to a tall woman himself, he has a theory that favors shortness in the wives of powerful men.

In some sense, I was required simply to pass the time for about eighty pages. My job was to accelerate and intensify the rising action without seeming to be going anywhere—the climax had to surprise Joe to work. Any interaction he had with Marcus had two goals—to entangle him inextricably in Marcus's scheme and to lull the reader's suspicions of Marcus. (The reader had to be suspicious of Marcus—without the reader's suspicions, there would be no suspense, but unless the reader's suspicions were lulled, the climax would come on too fast and seem obvious.) For me, the payoff for focusing on Marcus was one I liked. If there is any sort of character I enjoy writing about, it is one who is full of bull, who talks compulsively, and who has plenty of theories that are partially correct but are always manipulative. Jess, in *A Thousand Acres;* Gift, in *Moo;* Leo the compulsive bettor in *Horse Heaven;* and the satanic veterinarian Curtis Doheny, also in *Horse Heaven.* Since I, too, am a compulsive theorizer, I often give these characters some of my own theories. It energizes the characters and energizes me, too, and it prevents me from letting such characters, who have no integrity, get too far outside my sympathies.

And so *Good Faith* resumed, and I almost made my deadline. I had intended to be finished with the rough draft on December 31. I was finished on January 17. I sent it to my editor with some anxiety, because I didn't expect her to like it.

When she did like it, I saw some things about the novel as a form that I had always known about but never experienced, and the first was that it had its own energy and forward motion. The sense of this as it came back to me from my editor's reading was especially strong with *Good Faith* because I felt detached from it. When I sent the first draft of *Horse Heaven* in, my attitude had been much different. I loved the novel so much that I assumed everyone who read it would feel the same. I loved it the way you love a horse or a child—I delighted in it. When the publisher did not respond with a similar love, I hardly noticed because my delight was so intense. That the publisher repeatedly referred to the first draft of *Horse Heaven* as "the material" rather than "the draft" or "the novel" seemed funny to me rather than ominous, partly because I loved "the material" so much that I knew I could rummage around in it and extract from its richness any sort of novel. With *Good Faith,* I was surprised but gratified—I had set up the machine and my editor's response indicated that it ran pretty well, if not perfectly. Since she liked it better than I did, it was my task in the second draft to make it more to my taste. I figured that when we both came to like it, it would be satisfactory and publishable, but the experience of composing the rough draft had been so taxing that I never expected to cherish it.

When I received the manuscript back from my editor and read it myself, I once again liked it better than I had thought I would. Marcus wasn't my friend, but he had a way about him as a character of organizing the action and the themes. Felicity and the gay couple kept both Joe and me in a good mood. Felicity's sense of freedom and the gay couple's sense of irony contrasted refreshingly with Joe's plodding quality. Of course, Joe has to be a plodder, just as David Copperfield has to be a plodder—narrating a novel in the first person is a thankless and arduous task. The most annoying thing, of course, is the constant employment of the word "I." "I did this," "I thought that," "then I did this," "then he said to me"—it is a repetitive and debilitating form of discourse, tied tightly to the action (because digressiveness is usually even more tedious).

There were two things about the rough draft that were quite wrong, though. One was Joe's garrulousness. Joe did tend to babble on, but not in the same way Marcus did. As a person who bullshits for a living, Marcus can indeed numb the listener with theories and ideas; in fact that is his trump card, psychologically. His strategy is to divine in his listeners just what will make them happy, and then weave theories about it without seeming to be actually offering anything. He lulls their doubts partly by seeming to know what he is talking about but also partly by putting them into a half sleep. Perhaps instinctively, Marcus knows that the prey might run if the adrenaline begins to pump. But Joe's garrulousness that annoyed me in the rough draft came from something other than strategy—it came from ignorance, both his and mine. He had a habit of continuing to talk even after he stopped having anything to say, like a bad date. I had the tools I needed to fix this problem once I recognized it—in the first place, I knew much more at the end of the rough draft about every aspect of the novel, so I was no longer as ignorant as I had been when I was composing the rough draft. Where Joe kept talking, knowing vaguely that there was more to say but not knowing what it was, was where I had known as the author that there was more to a particular moment than I could think of at the time. Now I could fill in those blanks. Also, I could just cut him off. I noticed that he had a habit of letting his remarks dribble to a close. As I read through the rough draft, every time I felt myself getting irritated with him, I cut that part—I unsaid it, exactly the way you cannot do on a bad date! By the time I had been through the second draft with these two things in mind, I liked Joe much better and felt that his good qualities were no longer lost in the verbal underbrush.

The last two chapters were a bigger problem and actually required a good deal of thought. The rule of thumb, of course, is that when the climax doesn't work, the problem is in the exposition, but I didn't feel that the rule of thumb fit in this case. Something else was preventing the climax from working, but for quite a long time I couldn't figure out what it was. I finally realized, though, that a book about a scam and a betrayal has two climaxes—the climax of the action, when big things are happening and the narrator doesn't know what they mean, and the climax of the interpretation, when the narrator extracts the real meaning of not only the climax but also of the whole train of events. The problem with my last two chapters was that these two climaxes were mixed together, so the interpretation stole the suspense from the action. As eager as I was to get to the end, I had to continue to be patient in detailing the action, and I had to treat what would normally be the denouement as action—Joe's thought process as he works through what has happened to him needed to be well organized and to progress through time in the same way as any other type of action.

The prose I had already written led me astray and hid the real problems and their solutions from me. I would read along and read along, and on the surface it all looked okay to me. I was falling in the most common way for my own fluency—I was reading as a reader when I should have been reading as a writer. The only way to overcome this problem was to do something that felt drastic as a way of making a break from the dream of the existing text, and that was to rip apart the last two chapters and rewrite them almost completely. The understanding of the problem came after the ripping apart because the ripping apart was the only way I could remove myself from a state of receptivity.

Every form of the novel contains some basic implausibility. The confessional novel, which is retrospective and in the first person, is implausible in the way the narrator has to appear not to know what he surely must know so the plot can unfold in a suspenseful and orderly fashion. Any intrusion of subsequent knowledge into the unfolding plot either confuses the issues or shifts the reader's attention to other questions.* My intention was to put what happened to Joe in the foreground because Joe had been betrayed, and when someone feels betrayed, he or she is likely to go over the sequence of events carefully and even obsessively to work out how or where a relationship went wrong. My real interest was in the emotional experience of betrayal—that was where the drama lay and how the themes gained weight. The author, of course, has to address whatever questions he chooses in a consistent, logical, and orderly manner. He can't unknowingly shift the terms of the discussion in the middle of the narrative or both the themes and the plot will go awry. When I began to bring order to the last chapters—when I began to be patient and not hurry to the end—then the climax sorted itself out. The author feels pulled toward the end, as the reader does, but the author must resist the pull in order to put in all the information the reader needs to understand the ending, and through that the themes of the novel. When I wrote the second draft of the last two chapters of *Good Faith,* I knew the section needed more work, but felt it was no longer a blight upon the whole enterprise.

Another necessary aid to revision was a map of Joe's geographical region, with all the houses and towns and roads and neighborhoods depicted. I went through the rough draft and wrote down every geographical fact, made a list, and drew a map. I fixed inconsistencies and bits of confusion, not because I expected a reader to be able to orient Joe in his world but because I expected myself to. When I was in seventh grade, I remember, my mother gave me *The Annotated Sherlock*

---

*The author can choose to address any questions he wishes, and "what happened" might not be the first choice of many confessional authors—for example, in *Lolita* we know from the beginning that Humbert Humbert is in jail; the story is thereby shifted from "what happened?" to "how did he get here and how are we to account for his attitude and tone?"

Holmes, by William S. Baring-Gould. I thought it would be an author-itatively expanded edition of the detective's adventures, full of pictures and notes that would intensify my pleasure in Holmes's adventures, but Baring-Gould spent a fair amount of space pointing out inconsis-tencies in the stories, and the inconsistencies made me uncomfortable because they challenged my willing suspension of disbelief, just as, when I was six years old and comparing *The Bobbsey Twins* to *The Bobbsey Twins at School,* I was quite disturbed by the fact that in the first volume Nan and Bert were eight and Freddie and Flossie were four, while in the later volume, Nan and Bert were twelve and Freddie and Flossie were six. I didn't want readers of *Good Faith* to worry about such things.*

What I noticed and liked about the rough draft of *Good Faith* was something I had not expected—it went down easy. I attributed this in part to Joe's voice, which was casual and undemanding. I had noticed this in other first-person narratives I had written, and it is the signal virtue of writing in the first person—the conceit of the human voice telling a story is readily accepted by the reader. It is comfortable and familiar and sociable, especially if the voice makes no pretensions to being special, but just seems to be telling the story because something interesting or dramatic happened that needs to be told. Defoe's novels are perfect examples of this—each of his protagonists asserts from the beginning that he or she is just an average person who did something or saw something that ought to be recorded, so the voice is friendly and so the reader reciprocates that friendliness. I had intended Joe to be friendly for narrative reasons—he is a real-estate agent, after all, and of course he has to be at least relatively friendly in order to be betrayed. His natural style is colloquial American English, which is a friendly style. He is more or less a self-effacing guy. Somehow all of this added up, for me as a reader, to a smooth passage of the narrative, a smooth passage of time, really, where events and seasons melt into one another rather undramatically (by contrast to *A Thousand Acres,* which is based on a drama).

It was this way that *Good Faith* had of slipping down easily that remained my inspiration and talisman as I worked through the sec-ond, third, and fourth drafts. It seemed to be the most essential quality of the novel and it seemed to be pretty much there, already present. My

---

*This is not to say that my novels are as perfectly consistent as I would like them to be. At a reading, someone once pointed out that in *Horse Heaven* I have eight horses running in a race, and I say that they have sixty-four legs. Apologies to all!

job was to elaborate on this quality, to make it slip down more and more easily with each rewriting—to perform, in fact, what Marcus was doing to Joe, a seduction. This meant that the sense of Joe's innocence, and the sense of everyone's innocence, even Marcus's, had to remain with the reader almost to the end. As political and cultural events followed one another through 2002 and 2003, this quiet appearance of innocence I felt was part of the novel and essential to it meant that it came to represent my own feelings about the themes of the novel less and less. Jane Smiley the citizen was growing increasingly alarmed and angry while Jane Smiley the author of *Good Faith* was simply pointing out and suggesting a few political ideas and thoughts. In particular, I felt that the deregulation fashion of the eighties was exceptionally wrongheaded and had done all sorts of harm to all sorts of sectors of American life—the environment, consumer protection, the media, and now the financial and business sectors. As a citizen I was humming with ill-suppressed indignation and Cassandra-like predictions of future economic and social collapse, but *Good Faith* could not be wrenched from the tone Joe gave it. His betrayal plot required that he not know what was going on and not foresee what could happen, and the first-person narrative required that I not interfere with his telling the story. In one sense it was good that the novel went down easy; in another sense I couldn't stand how easy the novel went down because the polemicist in me wanted to make sure the reader saw what I saw and understood it as I understood it. However, it was not in me to burst out of my narrative form—either I didn't yet have the conviction or I didn't have the imagination. The novel remained as it had been conceived in 2000, before current events began to accelerate. I could not reconceive it or break up its narrative integrity. I am sure it would have been different if it had been conceived a year, or even six months, later. The only solution to its failures as a polemic was to conceive another novel.*

I finished the final draft and turned it in in August 2002. It felt unfinished and unrealized to me all the way to the end of the process. I worried at the last chapter over and over, mostly sorting out the sequence of events, breaking them down, and organizing them for clarity, but I

---

*I see *Good Faith* as confession and history, with some romance, some essay, a good deal of gossip, a few jokes, some local travel, and even a touch of epic smuggled ironically in, but no letters, no polemic, no tales, and no biography, since Marcus's fate is unknown—ambitious, according to "The Circle of the Novel," but fairly self-effacing because of Joe.

also felt there was some emotional capstone missing. It was small—less a capstone than a tiny bean balancing on the top of a pile of other beans—but essential. I knew that if I left it out, I would know that the novel was unfinished, unintegrated somehow, but that maybe a reader would not know. Maybe the thing I wanted was almost too much, and the novel really didn't need it. Maybe it was a matter of taste. At any rate, I read the novel over one more time, and I did end up adding one last thing, the second-to-last phrase, which is, "for once I recognized something my parents had talked about all my life, and that was the operation of grace in the material world." I added this with an intense sense of satisfaction. It brought several things together—Joe and his parents, Joe's secular view of life and his parents' faith-based view of life, the legal and religious connotations of the novel's title, and the two halves of Felicity (the female protagonist)—her exuberance and her physical grace. At the same time, the word "grace" set up unfortunate verbal and thematic echoes with the name of one of the characters, Marcus's sister Grace. Her name had to be changed, and I thought about this for about a day, trying out typical Catholic names of Grace's generation. I read over some of her lines, and they didn't work with a two-syllable name. I also felt I had to use a name with a long "a" sound, which left few names—not Amy, not Elaine, not any one I could think of other than Jane, my own name.

Naming Grace "Jane" seemed daring in a minor way, simply because of the coincidence with my name, but then I remembered that Jane Austen had named Jane Bennet after herself, and I figured if she could do it, I could, too. I used my "find and replace" utility to change the name (what a fabulous tool that is for a novelist!) and sent the finished manuscript in.

The novel now entered the publication process. Most authors do not have much say over the packaging of the novel because the publishing house considers packaging—how the novel looks but also how it is presented to the public—its domain. I think it is fruitful to think of novels as passing through levels of decreasing privacy—first a notion hardly even realized by the novelist, then a draft understandable mostly by the novelist, then subsequent drafts, each of which has a more public aspect than the last one, then one or more edited drafts, aiming more and more specifically for public existence. The last of these is the copyedited draft, in which an expert in grammar, spelling, and other details of language and continuity makes the novel more or less standard (let's say she ties its shoelaces and buttons its buttons properly). This last draft is then printed and furnished with packaging meant to demonstrate a few things about it and to put the prospective reader into a mood. This mood may be different from the mood of the writer. For example, my mood when I wrote *Good Faith* was green, humid, and breezy—I always had a background sense of the landscape Joe was driving through on his way from open house to open house. When I contemplate the book in retrospect, I mostly picture weather—it is a sensuous book for me and for Joe; never can he separate what happened and what was said from what sort of day it was when that event took place. The mood of the novel package in hardcover, though, is washed-out red, white, and blue, because the publisher chose to highlight the themes of the novel to sell it as important as well as readable. The cover of the novel looks like outmoded advertising of the sort we used to see in the fifties, when a company, by advertising its integrity, made that very integrity seem suspect. The design is witty and smart, and, indeed, when the book designer came up with it, everyone liked it. When publication date rolled around and I received a box of twelve copies, I found opening the box a pleasure. The books looked pink, welcoming, almost benign. Their matte finish was cool and asked, somehow more than the glossy finish of *Horse Heaven,* to be picked up and held in the hand, a dry book against a dry palm. The title page, too, was designed to carry a double message—it looked vaguely like both a stock certificate and a carnival advertisement.

If I sound cynical here, I don't mean to. Since every novel is various and rich with incidents, characters, and themes, its package has to be simplified somehow and made representative. The reader has to be reminded that reading is a pleasure of some sort—perhaps sensual and happy and funny, or perhaps austere and difficult, but I can't imagine that a row of texts differentiated merely by titles and authors would induce large-scale purchases. Once, maybe they did, but we are used to both facets of the object now—the feel and look of the book and the promise of the novel within. My book was to be matte, bright, graphic; the novel within was to be smart and sly, with perhaps a few hidden attractions (good-natured but detailed sex scenes). It took a few commercial risks—there was no telling, for example, if anyone cared about real-estate agents or real estate, no matter how much money was at stake, or if anyone cared about the 1980s. My name on the front was meant to work as a recommendation; compliments gleaned from the publication of previous novels, listed on the back, were to bolster that recommendation, tastefully reminding the reader of my claims to her attention. My job and the publisher's job were related but distinct. The publisher's job was to get the reader to buy; my job was to get the reader to begin reading and keep reading.

When the preliminary reviews came in, about six weeks before publication date, they were full of praise. The novel continued to please others more than it pleased me, which convinced me more than ever that while it owed its existence to my effort and will, it did not owe its nature to my wishes or choices. It was a multifaceted sociable object, a consciousness that people could relate to that was separate from my consciousness, that was human but not *a* human. All books are like this, but if the novelist especially likes a book or feels a kinship to it, his attachments blind him to the independence of the novel and make him feel that his views about the novel are more primary or more important than other readers' views. In fact, they are only different. When I published a novel that I was satisfied with but did not like, I saw that no novel can help communicating many things to every reader, and that the novelist's ideas about what is being communicated are as valid as any reader's ideas, but no more so.

Of course, the premise of every review is that the reviewer is reading and commenting upon his subjective experience of the novel, and that what he may or may not read in the novel has only a relative connection to everything actually in the novel. Packaging goes only so far with a reviewer, partly because reviewers are sent bound galleys, which usually have no pictures (though this, too, is changing). The publisher can offer flap copy and quotes, but doesn't count on putting the reviewer in a receptive mood by sending him something pretty.

Reviewers, of course, are required to exercise their freedom to vote, which is essential and 100 percent good, but good reviews and bad reviews do have different psychological sources. Bad and ungenerous reviews are necessarily more subjective than positive and generous reviews, because as with any other manifestation of ill will, the bad reviewer is indulging in an egotistical display of some state of mind that is supposed to enhance the reviewer's status at the expense of the subject of the review (and I say this having written bad reviews myself). The bad reviewer is required to be eloquent in order to be readable. Eloquence at a novelist's expense can be quite a pleasure for a reader— when Martin Amis's 2003 novel *Yellow Dog* was published, the reviewer for the *New York Times Book Review,* Walter Kirn, wrote a bad review for the ages—so full of good lines that it was a joy from beginning to end. Its negativity, you might say, was large rather than small. While Kirn suggested that Amis was repeating both ideas and techniques, he did acknowledge Amis's seriousness and importance—or rather, he rolled up an intelligent and well-versed appreciation of Amis's work into a display of his own talents that was good-natured rather than peevish, but nevertheless killed *Yellow Dog*. At the time I felt it would almost be worth it to have inspired such a smart review. But maybe not. At any rate, good reviews are all alike (in that they generally agree on the virtues of the book being reviewed), but every bad review is like the mind of the reviewer; it demonstrates the anatomy of his pique. Even so, often in a bad review there is a nugget of something to be learned about the novel one has written and about the nature of the novel as a form. Since every novel is a compromise and most ambitious novels stake their claims to greatness on qualities of idiosyncrasy and excess rather than perfection, reviewers' responses are necessarily going to be strongly rooted in their tastes, which can dictate their response to any feature of a novel—style, psychological insights, plot, themes, aesthetic theories, even setting. And for the author, bad reviews are really no more disquieting than good ones; both equally remove the novel from the novelist's own experience of having written, read, rewritten, and reread the novel and substitute for that experience another person's experience. Bad reviews may be discouraging or annoying, but the trouble with good reviews is that they can replace an experience that may have been quite satisfying with wishes for additional things such as status or money or fame.

What did I learn from the reviews of *Good Faith*?

Of course, it is always nice to be inoculated from the bad-review experience by a few good reviews, and the Sunday reviews before pub date were all good—Paul Gray in the *New York Times*, Donald E. Westlake in the *Washington Post*, and a few others—so by the time Michiko Kakutani's bad review came out on pub date in the daily *Times* I was mostly prepared. Her particular beef was with Marcus Burns: "never even momentarily believable as a persuasive con man," "an obvious phony." Her opinion was not in the majority of those I had read by this time—Westlake, Gray, Ron Charles in the *Christian Science Monitor*, and Richard Lacayo, in *Time*, had been willing to suspend disbelief in Marcus and had even found him intriguing and well portrayed, but it was definitely true that Marcus was the key. A reader who could not find Marcus in any way appealing would never accept his influence over Joe. Kakutani wasn't buying my con man. I thought it was interesting, though, that those who accepted Marcus were men, and Kakutani was a woman. In the novel, Marcus targets men more easily than he does women—his special technique with Joe is to challenge his masculinity in various subtle and not so subtle ways. Of course, an astute woman reader can see that he is not what he purports to be, but then she would not be vulnerable to his methods anyway. When I read Kakutani's review, I knew there was no technical way I could have done anything differently that would have avoided her criticism. The very conception of Marcus was right for me and wrong for her.

But Kakutani's objection raised a more systemic question. Are con men so common in American fiction that the author is forced down a particular kind of plot chute whenever a stranger comes to town? And for the sake of originality, does this proscribe a whole category of stories? This question constitutes a narrative dilemma the author must solve for the novel to succeed. My solution was that there are two sides to every betrayal—the betrayer has a technique, and there is some inherent interest and energy to that technique, as I discovered when I found myself relying on Marcus to get me through the novel in the teeth of Joe's passivity. But I had chosen Joe as my protagonist because I was drawn more to the dilemma of the betrayed. I thought (or felt, since how an author approaches the material is mostly instinctive) that if the attention of the reader were shifted away from the betrayer's technique, then the betrayal would become an investigation of the character development of the betrayed—first how he is fooled and then how he recovers and who he is afterward. The betrayal itself becomes just a certain type of misfortune; misfortune is a broad field and one everlastingly plowed by the novel. The importance of my last chapter, which took me so long to complete, was that it was the heart of the book—Joe's betrayal had to be sudden and upsetting, his reaction clear and believable, his acceptance of "grace" at the end a relief—as deserved as the betrayal and therefore satisfying. Without realizing it when I conceived the novel, I had embarked upon a project that was far more circumscribed by literary convention than my previous novels, and whether or not I was familiar with my antecedents, which I was not, I felt hemmed in while I was writing—there was a narrow path of originality I could make my way down, but it was surrounded by whole regions where potential clichés abounded.

Let's look at the question in another way. Con men are common in

American fiction because they are common in American life—money for nothing, the big score, overnight success—this is the American Dream, no matter how much parents, teachers, bosses, and politicians blather on about the rewards of hard work. So here was the reason why *Good Faith* was conceived from the beginning as a realistic novel—realism is about recurring themes, about how something that happens in one spot in one year is different from a similar thing that happens in another spot in another year. The American novel can't stop talking about con men until American life is no longer about material success.

Other reviewers, including Dan Cryer in *Newsday,* who had liked *Horse Heaven,* and A. J. Sherman (a Brit—more about that later) in the *Baltimore Sun,* found both Joe and the novel too bland. Cryer wrote, "He's easily squeezed but still resilient, too squishy-soft to be of much interest." Sherman wrote, "Greed may be blind, but it is unbelievable when portrayed as quite this dumb." No willing suspension of disbelief there. For these men, Joe's personal qualities didn't arouse respect—a danger that a first-person novel always courts. To cite some examples of the same effect from my list of the hundred novels I read, I didn't care to be in the company of Briony, in Ian McEwan's *Atonement,* or in the company of Charles, in Iris Murdoch's *The Sea, the Sea,* but I quite appreciated M., Robinson Crusoe, and Alice Munro's Del, in *Lives of Girls and Women.* That a narrator's sensibility will not be congenial for many readers is something the novelist simply must accept—a first-person narrator in particular must have integrity and not seem to be trying to please everyone. To read a novel is to have a personal relationship; the resentment in some bad reviews comes simply from having to keep reading about someone the reviewer would prefer not to know.

In general, I learned from the good reviews that as much as I wanted to write a polemic, no one wanted that from me, and I learned from the bad reviews that some people, when confronted by a carefully wrought and subtle satire, prefer something less cautious and more polemical. I also learned that novels not about the World Trade Center attacks were perfectly welcome. A year and a half after 9/11, and a month after the Iraq invasion, there was room in readers' minds for other thoughts and even other temporary loyalties, since the suspense the good reviewers felt and attested to was purely about Joe's well-being, not at all about the fate of the world, or of civilization, or of America as we know it. I would make the case that Joe and his associates did do damage to their world that is still visible today, both in the landscape and in the morality of our public life, but that was a case I was obliged to make outside of the novel, in interviews; in the novel, given the constrictions of the *Good Faith* time scheme and of Joe's voice, it could be implied but not stated. Good reviewers were alive to the implication, but happy that I didn't press it too hard; they commended me for my light touch. Bad reviewers thought the novel was too sunny, Joe's and Marcus's crimes too lightly punished.

Of course, several of the good reviews contained doses of castor oil. Ron Charles of the *Christian Science Monitor* took time to denigrate each of my last three novels by name, calling them "white elephants." Laura Miller in *Salon* bothered to allude to my infamous article in *Harper's Magazine,* in which I said that I found *The Adventures of Huckleberry Finn* boring and *Uncle Tom's Cabin* better than critics would have you believe. Readers of this book will know that with novels, personal preference is always allowed, but *de gustibus non est disputandum* didn't prevent Ms. Miller from administering a belated spanking (and I still find *Huck Finn* boring, which is why I didn't include it in this book).

I encountered *Good Faith* itself again when I went on tour to promote it. My enjoyment of the *Horse Heaven* tour had been renewed every time I opened the book and began to read—and that was how I read it each night, in each bookstore. I picked up the novel as if it were a Bible, opened it in the destined spot, and read that chapter. I enjoyed every single one. I never got tired of the novel, and when I gave my last reading from it, I was filled with regret. Truly, no eager fan loved it more than I did. But I found reading *Good Faith* difficult. No passage seemed to be the right length—there were pretty good insights and paragraphs, a page or two that seemed dramatic and promising as a way of showing the novel off, but twenty steady minutes, self-contained and available, I couldn't find. I tried several bits—when Joe accompanies Marcus and Linda to the closing of their home-buying deal, but it was too long; when Joe and Gordon visit a county supervisor who is a pig farmer, but I got tired of it; when Joe and Marcus visit the golf course of a secret club, but they seemed juvenile to me. Other selections were too short. My editor's favorite selection, Joe and Felicity's hotel scene, was too erotic for me to read in public. The problem in presenting a novel with a plot, I soon realized, was that you must explain what is going on, but if you explain even a bit too much, you take away the charm of the actual execution of the plot, and the reader is less rather than more likely to want to go on with it. I settled on one or two of Joe's conversations with Marcus—examples of seduction, and therefore sly, with plenty of dialogue and forward energy. Even so, I was glad when the tour was over. I was reduced to advertising the novel myself, from the podium, as a late-night novel, one a reader keeps reading without realizing that the time is passing, hardly realizing that anything is happening. That is a valid form of novel, too, and one I could promote without embarrassment, but it seemed like an apology for a less than dramatic reading.

My book tour was a quiet one; no gala events at racetracks and not much media coverage. I had toured in 1998, 2000, 2001, 2002, and now, again, in 2003. Even though I was getting very good reviews, Jane Smiley having a new book out wasn't newsworthy. Every so often I had a whiff of the old nightmare—a *This Is Spinal Tap* sort of tour where the audiences get more and more indifferent and the venues smaller while the artists themselves vapor on about their sources of inspiration. But I did have a small revelation during the tour, and that was that a book tour is also about bookstores, not only about media. When the publisher sends the author to read at various bookstores around the country, essential business contacts are made and reaffirmed. Fame is one thing, but sales are another, and the two things don't always overlap. On your fifth book tour in six years, you might get sent to the small, independent bookshop in the suburbs, while someone else, who wrote a famous book ten years ago but hasn't had anything out since, appears the same night at the nationally known book emporium in the middle of the city. Sometimes I felt that this was a humbling experience, but at other times I felt that it was an experience appropriate to the private side of the novel—a low-profile exchange between the individual writer and the individual reader, taking place in small rooms; an occasion for pleasure but not for celebration. The book tour was long, and, I was told, successful. *Good Faith* appeared on best-seller lists here and there. It would be successful, said a man who works at my publishing company who had predicted in 1991 that *A Thousand Acres* would win the Pulitzer, but it wouldn't win the Pulitzer. Right again.

In August I went on the British book tour. British newspapers were making more of *Good Faith* than American papers had done, partly because American coverage had been complimentary and partly because *Horse Heaven,* being about horses, had made a splash in England

and Ireland, and had been nominated for the Orange Prize, which is a prestigious literary prize for a novel in English by a woman. When *Horse Heaven* was on the short list, there was one English woman, one Canadian, one Australian, one New Zealander, and me. That was a compliment. I believe the bookies had me as second favorite (though the Australian Kate Grenville, in her maiden race, was the one who won, shutting out me and Margaret Atwood, the older stakes-winning mares). Writers from the *Guardian* and the *Times* came all the way to California to interview me, which was flattering.

Book reviewing in England is and always has been somewhat differently arranged than in the United States. Most often, in the United States, writers review one another's books and there is some sense of generosity born of shared time in the novel-writing trenches. It is more common in England for a novel to be reviewed by what you might call professional book assessors. The difference is that novelists can't really help being positive about the form of the novel, and therefore supporting a book at least in a general way, but people whose job is to read dozens of new books in a year and to compare them are required by the task itself to be more neutral, somewhat like an admissions committee at a prestigious university. And that, some would say, is a far too benign view of English book reviewing, which can be quite vicious, rather like English politics. It is perfectly acceptable, and even desirable, in England for a reviewer to show off his talent for eloquent invective at the expense of an author—desirable because it's fun for all, and if a novel is entertainingly killed, that's one less author who will be pulling his chair up to a crowded table. Before *Horse Heaven* there was *The All-True Travels and Adventures of Lidie Newton,* which was entertainingly killed in the *Times* Literary Supplement by, it is true, American Joyce Carol Oates, but killed in the British tradition, without apology, rather than in the American tradition of rueful fellow-feeling.

The British reviews, which I considered only moderately good compared with the most favorable American ones, seemed to more than satisfy the English publisher Faber & Faber, which I took as a sign of bad things that could have happened but didn't. To me, the most interesting one was by Elaine Showalter, an American academic, who not only did not like *Good Faith,* but didn't even use much of her piece to discuss it, instead giving me a glowing review of my Dickens biography, which had appeared to otherwise mixed reviews the year before. She didn't like Joe's narrative voice and the way *Good Faith* made no use of the novel's "polyphonic" possibilities. And, as a matter of taste, I agreed with her—polyphony is more interesting to the sophisticated reader.

In the end, *Good Faith* turned out to be a success, though it didn't single-handedly revive the American economy in 2003, end the Iraq War, or halt the slide of American democracy into the black hole of deregulation. It lingered briefly on a few best-seller lists and found its way onto end-of-the-year "best books" lists in Washington, D.C., Chicago, San Francisco, and Los Angeles. It was named by the *New York Times* as a notable book, and not, as far as I know, considered for any major awards. It had a therapeutic effect, though—the person who told me the original story behind *Good Faith,* the story I thought would be easy to write and was not, the story I thought was unique and was not—found himself more at ease after the writing, editing, publication, and reception of the book. In part this was because he had a chance to observe the story from a more detached perspective than his own—my perspective. In part it was because events in the novel got confused with events in his mind and lost their vividness. In part it was because the novel was funny and his experience came to seem funny through it.

When I think of all my novels, I imagine them spatially, grouped around me on a dark plain. Their covers are only dimly visible, but I know which is which. *Horse Heaven* is large, the closest to me, within arm's length. *A Thousand Acres* is the farthest away—I can hardly see it, and because I rarely think about it, it is hard for me to remember. *Moo* is a little behind *Horse Heaven,* and a shaft of sunlight hits it from one side, making it bright and inviting. *The Greenlanders* is off in the distance, too, but since it is larger and denser, it seems closer. *Good Faith* sits by itself, still floating an inch or two above the plain, not quite landed yet—its bright cover and happy publication keep it suspended for the time being. It is still the one that happened to surprise me, so I owe it some loyalty. It has been fertile, too—spawning this book and, through this book, my next novel, which is just beginning to appear in the distance. The new book looks spherical and self-contained, but jammed with things, like a spaceship made of Venetian glass, shining, intricate, and full of colors, not like any novel ever looked to me before.

13 · Reading a Hundred Novels

The omniscience of novelists has its limits.

—DAVID LODGE, *How Far Can You Go?*

y first idea was to read 275 novels, but I am a slow reader. It took me almost a month to read *Anna Karenina* and almost another month to read *Moby-Dick,* and I decided that anyway, there was not much more to be learned about the nature of the novel from 275 novels than there was from 100 novels (and after all, what with novels I read on the side for fun and for work, the final tally for three years of novel-reading would be closer to 130 than 100). My list is not and was never intended to be a "Hundred Greatest," only a list of individual novels that would illuminate the whole concept of the novel—and almost any list of a hundred serious novels would illuminate that concept. I knew I would be reading books I had read before, books I had always meant to read, and books I had not ever wanted to read but knew were important. I knew I would be omitting lots of books and authors that other readers would consider vital to any understanding of the novel—Hemingway, Philip Roth, Joyce Carol Oates, for example—but not only did I have to start somewhere (with *The Tale of Genji*) and go somewhere (to lots of different countries), I also had to stop somewhere.

There were obvious candidates, especially from the early years, such as *Don Quixote* and *Robinson Crusoe,* but others fell onto the list by chance—I hadn't intended to read any Walter Scott, but Lermontov recommended him (in *A Hero of Our Time*), and once I had read that one (*The Tale of Old Mortality*), I thought I had better try another (*The Bride of Lammermoor*). I hadn't ever heard of *The Female Quixote,* but

Dr. Johnson promoted it when it first came out and he was right—it was lively and inventive. I did intend to read *The Good Soldier Schweik,* but there was controversy about translations. I read one short Dickens (*A Tale of Two Cities*) because I had written about all the others in an earlier book. Sometimes I chose a novel I hadn't read, such as *The Idiot,* because I had read others by the same author and wanted to try something new. I tried to "read" Chinua Achebe's *Things Fall Apart* by listening to CDs in the car, but got distracted. One reason I didn't conceive the list as being any sort of "best of" list was that to understand the nature of the novel, sometimes the reader has to read novels that don't work for her and think about why they don't work—representative lists, unlike "my favorite" lists, have to include uncongenial works (and the reader will see that there are works I found uncongenial in the following bibliography). Most of the time, even if I did find a novel not to my liking once I got into it, I kept reading and included it on my list because something about it was instructive, but not always—I found the style of *The Grapes of Wrath,* for example, too cloying, and I stopped reading. As my list shaped up, it became arbitrary, and that came to seem like a necessary feature of any reading list that takes three years to complete, but not a fault in a list of novels, because random variety is part of the nature of the novel.

When I began to read in the fall of 2001, the novels I read started to work as an antidote to history immediately. In the first week of October I took up *The Tale of Genji,* which, at a thousand years old, was as far from the modern world as it is possible for a novel to be. I read more than a thousand pages in eight days, usually in the evening, closed into my bedroom, with the shades down. I got oriented to Heian Japan by the second chapter, when Genji and his friends sit around one day and discuss women—is it better to marry a beauty but then run the risk that she will cease to please or be seduced by someone else, or is it better to marry a plain, intelligent woman who keeps the establishment orderly and enhances the power of the family? The terms of the discussion were a little different from a modern discussion, but I recognized these young men. After that initial sense of familiarity, I entered into what seemed to me a miraculously soothing experience. For one thing, Genji and Lady Murasaki have a highly developed aesthetic sense. The novel marks the passing of the seasons and the passing of Genji's life with a series of set pieces describing flowers, trees, gardens, and landscapes that do just what they are intended to do—remind the reader of the ephemerality of life and the beauty of art and nature simultaneously. Most of the time the characters communicate by means of poems that are quoted in the text— these poems, too, repeatedly reiterate the theme that every moment is timeless while every life lasts only a moment. In the aftermath of the World Trade Center attacks, there was no better thing to be reminded of.

But at the same time that *The Tale of Genji* was familiar in many ways, it was also irreducibly alien. The women characters in the novel were secluded—they never showed their faces to male characters who did not officially possess them, and the men frequently came into possession by means of abduction and rape. As I was devouring the thousand pages, I was always peripherally aware that an entire millennium had intervened between its author and me, that although I seemed to be imagining Heian Japan well enough, undoubtedly I was wrong— my notion of Heian Japan, though continuous and satisfying and aided by drawings in the text, was utterly unlike what Lady Murasaki knew. Even more amazing was the fact that for all the text promoted the idea of ephemerality, the novel had existed through periods and in places that Lady Murasaki herself could not have imagined. Here I was, on my bed in a room in California, in North America, surrounded by objects such as English pictures of horses from the nineteenth century and Persian rugs and Amish quilts and French doors, eating some chocolate, reading in a language that had not existed when Lady Murasaki wrote her novel. I imagined my being and life as so alien to Lady Murasaki's that I began to feel a bit of vertigo—layers of familiarity and unfamiliarity, of transitoriness and permanence, of there and here, spinning out of the rectangular, boxlike paperback volume of the novel (something she also might not have been able to imagine) and enveloping me. During the hours I was reading *The Tale of Genji,* the attacks on the World Trade Center seemed to diminish in size. History is full of crimes and massacres. Millions have lived and died, and yet the despair of the Lady of the Evening Faces, who worries that she is not pleasing, continues to exist and continues to be affecting.

It was a simple act to go from there to the Icelandic sagas—they came next, chonologically. But they were not nearly so reassuring. If Genji's tale spoke from a long way off about the eternal ephemerality of life, *Egilssaga* and *Laxdoela* spoke from a long way off about the permanence of war, the urge to fight and its costs. We were fighting the Taliban in Afghanistan by that time; Egil was fighting the Norwegian king; the people of Laxardal were drawing up sides and bringing more and more partisans into their conflicts. Gudrun, the protagonist of *Laxdoela,* seemed to sum it all up at the end of the story when she was asked what she thought of all the fighting she had instigated over a piece of clothing. She said, "I caused the death of the one I loved the most." The one you love the most doesn't have to be a man, as it is with Gudrun. It could simply be a place or a way of life. The Icelandic sagas, though I had always loved their intransigence and their irony, did not make me happy in the fall of 2001. The lessons of the sagas, eloquently evoked, had gone unlearned and here we were again, with different motives and bigger weapons but with the same sense of injury and vengefulness and the same old wrong feeling that violence could put an end to something when most of the time it only spawns more violence.

At the height of the anthrax scare, when people were dying and post offices were being closed and there was much discussion in the news of biological warfare, I picked up Giovanni Boccaccio's *The Decameron,* which, of course, takes place during the Black Death—once again, pure chronological coincidence. The opening chapter was riveting. Florence was in the grip of an epidemic that possibly modern Americans cannot begin to imagine. Death, dread, disease, social breakdown everywhere and every day for months. The anthrax scare transfixed and paralyzed the United States in some ways. We had constant speculations and instructions about other biological agents— plague itself, but also smallpox and botulism as well as anthrax. One could only look at oneself, one's loved ones, one's situation, and wonder. But here were the characters of *The Decameron,* seven women and three men and their servants, making up their minds to go out into the countryside, to take a break from the devastation, and to entertain themselves with stories. They go away for two weeks. Given the death rate, when they come back, four to seven of them will die, but they do find repose and they do entertain themselves, and most important for readers, with their tales and their discussion, they reconstitute what it means to be human and civilized even while civilization is disintegrating around them. And they do it with good humor rather than grief. Many of the stories are jokes; many of them are intended to evoke laughter and pleasure. Is *The Decameron* mere escapist fun? In the midst of the anthrax scare, I didn't think so. I thought that it was a reminder of human resilience—not merely that humans survive, but that as they survive, they can't help re-creating complex culture, which includes aesthetic, moral, political, sexual, and sensual ideas. According to Boccaccio, disaster destroys, but it doesn't have to brutalize. The bonds of conversation and social connection are enough to save civilization even in the face of the Black Death. The World Trade Center got smaller again; at least, it got smaller than the Black Death. In a larger sense, that my immediate concerns and fears could be reflected back to me by books and authors so remote from 2001 was a steady comfort all through that autumn—Boccaccio's effort at detachment aided my own.

I had never read or even heard of *The Heptameron,* my next book. I chose it only because it was written in imitation of *The Decameron.* While I was reading *The Heptameron,* the women of Afghanistan were in the news, having been newly liberated, at least in part, from their burkas and their general condition of house arrest. *The Heptameron,* in French, written by a queen, closer to our time by 550 years than *The Tale of Genji,* is about the imprisonment of women—French women, Spanish women, Italian women, Christian women. The women in *The Heptameron* may not wear burkas, but they are closer in their clothing to the Afghan women than they are to me in my jeans and short-sleeved shirts. They wear long, elaborate gowns with long sleeves, and head coverings and sometimes veils. They are possessed by their male relatives and husbands in exactly the same ways Afghan women are possessed. They can be killed instantly for bad behavior, and this is defined as behavior that transgresses male possession. If there is any book that must remind twenty-first-century American and European women that Afghan women are us, then *The Heptameron* is it. It reminds us that what is at stake is not fashion but survival, the very right to think and act and feel autonomously rather than in accordance with the interests and presuppositions of the men around us. The author of *The Heptameron,* Marguerite de Navarre, was interested mostly in freedom of conscience, a topic current in her day because of the Reformation and the Counter-Reformation, but it is clear from her book that freedom of conscience for women can lead anywhere—if your eternal soul is your own responsibility, and cannot be saved through reliance upon a corrupt church, then it is a short and slippery slope from there to all sorts of freedom, first of belief and thought, then of feeling, then of action. I had to think, though, with the Afghan women right there on the front page of the newspaper, and Iranian women and other Middle Eastern women in the news, is the dire road back from freedom and autonomy really blocked? If I am too old to suffer much in some brave new fundamentalist world from the yearning of men to possess and control women, what about my daughters? My granddaughters? Our government was fighting the Taliban, but were they really doing it for the women? Or was that strange but frequently noted effect of enmity going to eventuate where two enemies who seem utterly distinct at the beginning come to look more and more like one another by the end? I certainly didn't want the United States to look at all like Afghanistan, but Marguerite de Navarre seemed to be saying that the shackles and iron maidens of our own past weren't as outdated as I had thought.

It wasn't until I got to the two volumes of *Don Quixote,* some four months after I began, that the books resumed their identities as mere novels, entertaining and enlightening but not prophetic. It was a relief, actually, to read along in that familiar state of interest flowing and ebbing, of laughing at a particular scene, or considering it rather dispassionately, or wolfing it down. I like the uneven way novels control one's awareness. For a moment or two there is nothing but the action or the setting of the story. In the next moment, the words themselves stand out, some felicity of phrasing bouncing off the page as words, as a sentence, simultaneously obscuring and revealing the action and characters, and then in the next moment the novel subsides into a book, not quite compelling enough to stand out against the chocolate beside the bed or a dog's bark outside the room. I like the languor of laying the book down, glancing around the room, and picking the book up, the quiet sounds of one's hands against the paper, of one's own breath and the rustling of one's clothes. And then the characters emerge again.

When I was a young woman, fond of *To the Lighthouse* and *The Waves,* reading Virginia Woolf's diaries, it discomfited me to realize that I was probably just the sort of person Woolf would find vulgar and uninteresting, but as I read through the books on my list, I was happy to enjoy and appreciate novels such as *The Fountain Overflows* and *Love in a Cold Climate* by women (Rebecca West and Nancy Mitford) who would certainly intimidate and disdain the real me in real life, and other novels, such as *Justine* and *A Hero of Our Time,* by men (the Marquis de Sade and Mikhail Lermontov) I would avoid at all costs. Novelists are no better than anyone else (and maybe worse) at achieving intimacy in their personal relations, but the novel crosses boundaries of appearance, manner, and habit more easily than people do, so that was another pleasure of my list—getting to know authors in spite of themselves.

I found that every novel accompanied me through the day. While I was doing errands or cooking or riding a horse, certain features of what I had been reading would remain with me. With *Moby-Dick,* for example, there was a constant sense of the flat openness of the mid-ocean, the rolling steel blue of the sea against the enameled blue of the sky, and within that picture a sense of whiteness—the whiteness of the moon or the sun or human flesh or the whale. When I was reading *The Fountain Overflows,* I went around for a few days with the sense of a golden edge to things, perhaps a synesthetic impression through color of the richness of West's evocation of an Edwardian childhood. An author's style and tone would enter my mind and lodge there, molding me (sometimes reluctantly) to his or her story, and sometimes prepare me for another novel (if, for example, I finished one book in the morning and intended to start another in the evening). To go from *Tom Jones* directly to *Tristram Shandy* was shocking somehow and yet fascinating. The contrast gave me a fleetingly sharper sense of each. Sometimes I could not go from one to another—for example, from *A Tale of Two Cities* to *Madame Bovary.* Somehow these authors seem to exclude one another from my consciousness. Sometimes the transfer was a positive pleasure—I didn't know how little I was enjoying *Ulysses* until I felt myself gladly embrace Hermann Broch's *The Sleepwalkers,* generally considered a difficult and off-putting novel.

I tried to read chronologically, but early on, a review assignment intervened—I agreed to review a biography of Sinclair Lewis, so I thought I had better reread *Main Street,* his most famous book. I was impressed. Not only did Lewis capture the particular feel of life in the Midwest as I knew it several generations after he knew it, he also was sympathetic and generous toward his protagonist, Carol, in spite of her transgressions against female norms. He let her out of the age-old "virtue" trap—not every male novelist was willing to do that. I was soon back in the eighteenth century, but I saw the connections now among Lewis, Defoe, and Marguerite de Navarre. A few weeks later, on a trip and out of books, I leaped forward again and read Edith Wharton's *The House of Mirth.* I began to see a pattern. I grew more and more amazed at how long the woman question persisted in the European novel. As late as Henry James's *The Awkward Age,* the routine sale of women into marriage was a standard plot element of many, if not most, novels. And when the women weren't sold into marriage, they had to wrestle, often unsuccessfully, with what to do with themselves.

If every book inevitably throws up a protagonist and an antagonist, then the hundred-volume book of my reading list did also. I would have expected the protagonist to be one of my favorite authors— George Eliot or Charles Dickens or Jane Austen. And I didn't expect to have an antagonist, but to be impartially in favor of all authors, my brothers and sisters. But the protagonist who kept jumping out at me was Daniel Defoe. I liked everything about him, from his long and productive life to his straightforward depiction of the lives of his characters. I liked his habit of giving advice and yet forgiving his characters' trespasses. He seemed to me to be a person upon whom, truly, nothing was lost. And who should turn out to be the antagonist but Henry James? I didn't like his prissy, domineering manner. I didn't like the way he called himself "the Master." I didn't like how he thought some rich people constituted the whole world. Defoe, of course, was not like that. I read more Defoe. I liked him better. I read more James. I liked him worse (until he got himself tangled up in the prefaces of the standard edition of his novels, and he was so smart and yet so unable to be straightforward that I came to like him after all).

I had other antagonists. Leo Tolstoy was one. I resisted the power of *Anna Karenina,* and especially the importance of Levin's spiritual quest, for almost the entire novel, but in the end I was won over, not by Tolstoy's ideas, but by his skills as a storyteller and psychologist. Nathaniel Hawthorne was another. *The House of the Seven Gables,* which I had liked once and even named my daughter out of, now seemed more than silly and shallow—it seemed to epitomize the strange paralysis of antebellum America's view of itself, prideful and dishonest at the same time. It took me a long time to make a truce with William Makepeace Thackeray. I didn't care for his sour tone. But I had been reading Balzac, and when it occurred to me that Becky was a French character who strayed into an English novel, I could see how difficult it was for everyone, and I fell in love.

My preferences on the list do what preferences always do—they make an outline of who I am, depict me as a reader and as a person. But, I think, they are transitory preferences, as preferences in novels almost always are.

·   ·   ·

Of necessity, because of the way I researched and wrote this book, these hundred entries are more spontaneous, less thought through, and form less of an argument than the other twelve chapters of *Thirteen Ways of Looking at the Novel.* After I read each book, usually on the same day, but sometimes after a day or two, I wrote a mini-essay about that book. Often, thoughts that I had while reading that book were incorporated into the body of *Thirteen Ways,* then subsequently rewritten and integrated with other ideas. *Thirteen Ways* evolved intentionally, but the list of novels I was reading merely extended itself, evolving in some ways but not systematically. To me, it is a journal of my reading. To a reader, I suggest that it be used like an old trunk full of fabric samples or a box of costume jewelry—it is not to be read through from beginning to end in search of a cohesive argument, but to be rummaged about in, in search of something interesting or striking. One entry might lead to another and another, but it doesn't have to.

I should also state that many times I was moved by a particular novel to read more about that author, or to somehow extend my pleasure in the book. If I read a book in a scholarly edition—published by Oxford University Press, say—I would read the introduction, the translator's preface, and the notes. Sometimes I would read more about an author or a period in *Wikipedia,* an online encyclopedia. For novelists such as Sir Walter Scott, who have been the subject of much scholarship, I would consult Web pages devoted to that author for short biographies or lists of works. But each novel inspired me with different sorts of appetites for more information—when I read *Robinson Crusoe,* I wanted to know more about Defoe and his work, so I read his other novels and glanced through his biography; when I read *Dinner at the Homesick Restaurant,* I wanted to know how other readers felt about the novel, so I looked for online reviews. Some novels had inspired other works—after *Jane Eyre,* I read *Wide Sargasso Sea.* After *The Bride of Lammermoor,* I listened to *Lucia di Lammermoor,* by Donizetti. After *A Passage to India,* I watched the movie made of the novel. I did not, however, consult any theorists of the novel who were not themselves prominent and successful novelists, even though there is an entire academic industry based on theorizing about the novel. I knew there would be no efficient way to sort through the theories, but mostly, I preferred to glean my ideas about the novel from the books themselves. My justification for this, as the reader should know by this time, is that novels were invented to be accessible. Specialized knowledge about the novel is something the reader may engage in for added pleasure, but doesn't need to engage in merely to understand what she has read.

In fact, the authors and books on this list constitute a treasure available to all. I came away from reading them with a deep sense of abundant pleasure and no inclination to declare which are the "greatest" or the "best." My purpose will be served if a reader is moved to try a novel she has never heard of before, or one she never thought she would like, if she is moved to reread a novel she loves in a new way, or try again with a novel she has not been able to get through. Of course, I imagine book clubs thumbing though my list and deciding to try something obscure, such as *The Female Quixote* (well, maybe not, but how about Muriel Spark's *Loitering with Intent,* or T. H. White's *The Once and Future King,* or Junichiro Tanizaki's *The Makioka Sisters,* any of which I would recommend to anyone?).

One thing I learned from my course in reading is how rich the tradition of the novel is—how even with uncongenial novels, the struggle to get through is worth it, and with congenial ones, the joy of meeting up with the author's mind is so intense that it hardly seems possible that it must be private, that it can't be communicated, or even expressed. When a novel has two hundred thousand words, then it is possible for the reader to experience two hundred thousand delights, and to turn back to the first page of the book and experience them all over again, perhaps more intensely. Such joy demands to be shared, but really, in the end, all the reader can say is, "Read this. I bet you'll like it."

Another thing I learned is that novels, even those from apparently distant times and places, remain current and enlightening, and also comforting. Many times, I looked up from the page I was reading and thought, "This is right! If only someone from the *New York Times* were reading this, everything that seems so worrisome right now would come clear!" My hundred novels were not outdated at all, but testified, over and over, to the perennial nature of regular human thought—not only are there problems and conflicts that persist in not being solved, there are also the insight and common sense people have brought to bear on those problems. It was not only that misery loves company, but also that Jane Austen *is* a good guide to personal integrity; Anthony Trollope *does* know how marriage works; Honoré de Balzac *is* indispensable when Jacques Chirac refers to the relationship between France and England as *un amour violent.* It's worth remembering *The Makioka Sisters* when the newspaper reports a typhoon in Japan. It's worth knowing that serious thoughts are being thought, and also that serious fun is being made of fools everywhere. It's also worth knowing, in dangerous times, that dangers have come and gone and we still have these books.

Note: Many of these novels come in several editions, and there can be differences even in editions of novels originally written in English. Translations, of course, can be widely different from one another, and the question of which translation is best is impossible to answer—all have their virtues and their defects. Like all interpretations, specific translations go in and out of fashion. Some novelists who are supposed to be difficult to translate appear on this list—Gogol and Stendhal, for example—and the translations of *The Tale of Genji* are so different that several guides exist to help the reader collate them. Nevertheless, I have forged ahead as an average reader does—reading what comes to hand and getting what I can from it. In my experience, the prose speaks for itself—it may not exactly capture the flavor that the author instilled in the original, but if the reader finds it moving and beautiful or striking, she is still getting plenty out of it. In fact, once a novel leaves an author's mind, it becomes the possession of the reader in any case. We can't hope to perceive his subject, or his words, as he did. A translation is separated from his mind by one or two more removes than, say, the original published version of the book, but prose is always more or less accessible.

In every case in this list, I refer to the edition I happened to read, but this list should in no way be construed as an advertisement for any specific edition.

A Hundred Novels

1 · Murasaki Shikibu · The Tale of Genji

TRANS. EDWARD G. SEIDENSTICKER

(1004; REPR., NEW YORK: ALFRED A. KNOPF, 2000), 1,090 PP.

The Tale of Genji has two parts. Genji, the hero of part one, of some 41 chapters and 734 pages, is husband of the mother of Kaoru, the hero of part two, and the grandfather of Niou, Kaoru's friend and nemesis. Each part is self-contained, and each part, in form, is a different sort of novel. Genji's story is about the whole arc of one man's life—his mistakes and his virtues, his experience and what he learns from it, over some forty-eight or fifty years. Kaoru's story begins when he is a young adult and follows out the ramifications of a single relationship, covering some seven or eight years. It seems to be unfinished.

The author, a woman of the eleventh-century Heian court of Japan, also wrote a diary (or may have—the novel is so famous in Japan that it is possible the diary is an early fraud), but there is otherwise not much information about her except what can be inferred from the text. She does seem to have written all but a few chapters of the novel, and she does seem to have served at the emperor's court at the very beginning of the eleventh century.

The structure of Genji's story is simple but inspired. Early in the novel, Genji and his friends, who are all well-born young men of the court, are sitting around comparing notes about women. They discuss women they've known and heard of, trying to decide the relative advantages of women who are great beauties, or of women who are good conversationalists or housekeepers. Are all relationships with women doomed to failure? Are all women doomed to be found tedious in some way? The young men finally give up the discussion, but Genji, who is of an amorous turn of mind, sets out, more or less unconsciously, to test their hypotheses. A secondary main character, who contrasts with him and whose life intertwines with his, is his best friend, To no Chujo.

The modern American reader understands from the beginning that social arrangements in the tenth-century Japanese court are considerably different from ours. Well-born women live in seclusion, surrounded by other women and removed from the gaze of all men except their husbands. A husband customarily has more than one wife; each has a separate room in his palace. All of his children are legitimate. Their claims to status depend in part on the power and influence of their mothers' families and in part on their own good looks and accomplishments. *The Tale of Genji* is about domestic rivalries and intrigues. Whatever might have been happening politically and militarily in tenth-century Japan is entirely absent from the novel, though the male characters often have titles such as "minister" or "general." Much of the novel is taken up with descriptions of clothing, interiors, gardens, and the ritual progress of the seasons. The characters communicate most often by letters and poems, which are reproduced in the text, and which have traditional forms and symbols.

Genji (called "the shining Genji" when he dies) is the astonishingly good-looking son of an emperor and a woman of little power. He is superior in every way, but his superiority doesn't extend to what Westerners would consider moral probity. In particular, he is often guilty of rape and seduction. His most profound relationship is with Murasaki,* whom he takes into his house when she is ten years old, promising to be a father to her. He later seduces and rapes her, then installs her as his favorite wife. When she dies toward the end of the Genji section of the novel, he goes into despair himself and dies soon after. They do not have any children of their own, but she raises several of his children by other women.

The Tale of Genji proceeds at a dreamlike, deliberate pace, rather like a long scroll depicting a journey. The author is adept at description and dialogue, and at reporting the inner workings of the minds of the main characters. The novel is always indescribably exotic, because of what the characters do and the world they live in, but it seems familiar because the details of their relationships—jealousy, frustration, desire, gossip, anxiety, rivalry, intimacy, good fellowship—are utterly

---

*The relationship between Murasaki Shikibu the author and Murasaki the character is not known to modern scholars, but possibly the author was given, or took, the name "Murasaki" to connect her to the starring female character.

understandable. There is nothing even remotely primitive about *The Tale of Genji*. If anything, the level of luxury and convenience depicted, as well as the complexity of daily life, with all its errands and responsibilities and conflicting demands, seem almost modern.

Kaoru's story is structurally more sophisticated, full of dramatic irony of which Kaoru himself doesn't understand the meaning. Born in unhappy circumstances, Kaoru is, to all appearances, an exceptionally sober and unamorous young man. He is very good-looking, like Genji, but of a more serious turn of mind. Kaoru's most interesting quality is his natural fragrance, which is repeatedly compared to the most beautiful and rare sort of perfume. Kaoru seeks enlightenment, and hears of an old prince who has left the world and become a scholar in a villa in a small mountain village. The old prince has two daughters, and Kaoru agrees to watch out for them. He falls in love with the elder daughter, and promotes the affair of the younger daughter with his friend Niou, who is already married to the eldest daughter of the emperor. Kaoru's beloved cannot bring herself to live in the world, and dies shortly after the death of her father. The second daughter marries Niou, but he treats her badly, and Kaoru falls in love with her. A third daughter is found, the daughter of the old prince and a former lady's maid, and she is so like the first daughter that Kaoru falls for her. But Niou finds out that this beautiful secret is being kept from him, and he imposes himself upon her. Kaoru then hides her, but Niou finds her and rapes her. She falls in love with him, realizes she has gotten herself into an insoluble dilemma, and throws herself into the river. The plot twists and twists, and one feature of Kaoru's story that is a development over Genji's story is the social setting—serving women and collateral characters promote and retard the aims of the main characters, and also comment on everything at length in highly characteristic voices. Kaoru's story, some three hundred pages, has a very sophisticated structure indeed, as if the author invented the picaresque eighteenth-century novel (like *Tom Jones*) first, and then the social novel (like *Pride and Prejudice*) a few years later. One thing that changes is the balance of action and dialogue relative to description and narration. Genji's stately progress gives way to Kaoru's dramatic torments; descriptions of nature and ritual give way to a cascade of action that the narrative can hardly keep organized.

The Tale of Genji demonstrates that psychological analysis is one of the inherent features of all lengthy written prose narratives with protagonists: a character acts and the narrator offers a theory of why he acted as he did. Characters in *The Tale of Genji,* like characters in later novels, are sometimes mentally or physically ill. The narrative details the ways in which monks and healers come and perform exorcisms, and evil spirits who are possessing them leave them, often identifying themselves and their motives for possession. These incidents are reported so matter-of-factly that they seem utterly plausible, rather like the medical theories Balzac suggested in the nineteenth century. It is the form of the novel itself, which contrasts distinctive individuals with their social surroundings, that demands some sort of psychological theory. The conventions of the epic, the romance, and the history, which base characterizations on traditional types, aren't complex enough to give rise to the same sorts of ideas.

The Buddhist world of tenth-century Japan is always at the forefront of the narrative. Monks and nuns are characters (Kaoru's mother becomes a nun at a very young age, after Kashiwagi, Kaoru's real father, rapes and impregnates her). Poetic pleas and responses always refer to traditional images of the fleeting nature of love and life, which are also commonplace in the conversation of the characters with one another. In the fifty to sixty years covered by the novel, the fleeting and illusory nature of the world is invoked again and again—children are said to be too beautiful for this world, death strikes suddenly, blossoms fall, seasons pass. Eleven hundred pages seem long but are actually short. It takes something like a week to read about sixty years. Life is short, but a book is shorter. And yet, it has been a thousand years since Genji's tale was set to paper. Long or short? Or simply haunting?

2 · Snorri Sturluson · Egilssaga

TRANS. BERNARD SCUDDER, IN *THE SAGAS OF ICELANDERS,* ED. ROBERT KELLOGG

(1220-40; REPR., NEW YORK: PENGUIN, 2000), PP. 3-184.

Egilssaga, the only saga for which we have a likely author, is written as the biography of a single outstanding man, like *The Tale of Genji.* Like all sagas, Egil's story begins with his progenitors and ends with his descendants, but the saga is exceptionally unified in its focus on Egil and its development of his character and position in relation to his social world.

Egil's world slightly predates Gudrun's—it is the Viking world of ninth-century Norway, during the reign of Harold the Fairhaired, who temporarily unified Norway under his own hegemony between about 880 and 900. Egil's grandfather, Kveldulf ("Nightwolf"), is Harold's contemporary, and Egil is the contemporary of Harold's son Erik Blood-Ax. Whereas the action of many of the sagas focuses upon or is confined to Iceland, the action of *Egilssaga* takes place all over the Viking world—from far northern Norway (Finnamark) to Denmark, Scotland, England, Ireland, and Iceland. The saga is full of Viking raids (which in later sagas have evolved into trading expeditions or explorations after new lands such as Greenland and Vinland). Egil is both a preeminent fighter and a great poet, and the portrait of him develops not by analysis by the narrator, but by means of close scrutiny of all of his actions from age three to his death eighty years later. *Egilssaga* is exemplary in its use of the materials and techniques that were in some sense left over from the age of the epic and that had become less grand and heroic as they entered the age of history and memory.

Kveldulf, his son Skallagrim ("Bald Grim"), and his family have a practical problem: King Harald has vowed to bring all the kings and chieftains of the various districts of Norway under his power, and he is using both war and politics to do so. Those chieftains he cannot buy, he builds alliances against, and tries to frighten off. If he cannot frighten them off, he does battle with them, or attacks them and kills them one by one. Kveldulf sails for Iceland. There is no sense that he is cowardly in doing so, but resentment and a sense of enmity remain. The king gains and keeps his status by fighting. There is no holy or anointed element to the respect the conquered show him; he just happens to be the biggest dog on the block.

Egil commits his first killing as a boy, during a game. The victim is an older playmate who throws him contemptuously to the ground. Egil buries an ax in his skull. Throughout his boyhood, Egil is portrayed as hard to manage; he even threatens to kill his father, Skallagrim. He grows up to be a head taller than most men, bald, and ugly. He is as famous for his ability to write poems as he is for his prowess in fighting, and he is a continuous irritant to Harald's sons. He rarely causes trouble in Iceland, but he relentlessly pursues issues of legitimacy and honor that he considers important even when the odds seem to be against him (eight against one, eleven against one). From time to time his friends attempt to reconcile him with Harald's sons, but in the end, Egil's own pride prevents any but the barest accommodation.

Egil's poems, quoted at length throughout the saga, provide for self-awareness (though since they are composed of highly ritualized figures of speech, the modern reader might find them less than revealing). Several incidents late in his life—the death of his favorite son, an incident with his daughter—also make him one of the most psychologically complex saga heroes. He is not exactly a fighting machine, à la the Terminator (though he is said to have that kind of power), nor is he stupid or unobservant (he is contrasted to other characters who are simply brutes), nor is he without gentler feelings (he loves his wife and family as well as several friends). The author seems to be putting together a complex portrait of a historical figure who is exceptionally manly in the most basic sense—he cannot be taken advantage of even by kings. His pride is not a tragic flaw—he does not suffer a tragic end, but dies in his bed, a very old man, subject to the same indignities as all old men (once, when he pushes himself up to the fire, one of his serving women reprimands him and tells him to get back to bed and stay out of the way).

Egil Skallagrimsson was a historical figure and an ancestor of Snorri Sturluson's. There is no way of knowing how accurate Snorri was in depicting Egil's adventures, but by focusing on him and making each incident of his life logical, Snorri manages to avoid some of the problems that writers of other sagas run into, in particular the sense that a character's actions are against his own interests, that plausibility is being sacrificed to plots, and that what is going on is really not understandable. The reader may not agree with Egil's every action and opinion, but Egil himself is vivid and believable.

Egilssaga demonstrates one of the most effective novelistic techniques—that of simply telling the action and the dialogue in detail without commenting much upon them. As the story accumulates interesting detail (and it does have to be interesting), the reader's unwillingness to suspend disbelief is overcome by the simple effect of imagining what is going on. Then the reader begins supplying cause and effect and meaning as a way of knitting together actions that at first may have seemed random or unbelievable. The anomalous takes shape and becomes simply unusual and therefore worthy of note. Snorri never intrudes, and yet his knowledge, confidence, and absolutely clean and beautifully paced manner of telling the story indi-

cate an author with a great deal of experience—and, indeed, Snorri
was a powerful Icelander of the mid-thirteenth century who also compiled and edited a collection of myths and legends known as *Snorri's
Edda*.

3 · The Saga of the People of Laxardal

TRANS., KENEVA KUNZ, IN *THE SAGAS OF ICELANDERS*, ED. ROBERT KELLOGG

(1250–70; REPR., NEW YORK: PENGUIN, 2000), PP. 271–421.

The prose narrative, novel-like tradition of the Icelandic saga flowered
in medieval Iceland between the first half of the thirteenth century and
the middle of the fourteenth century. Several writers of Icelandic literature are known—Ari Thorgilsson, who wrote the history of Iceland
at the beginning of the twelfth century, and Snorri Sturluson, who
compiled the legends and myths of the prose *Edda* in the middle of the
thirteenth century. Some believe that *The Saga of the People of Laxardal*
was written by a woman.

The action of the saga takes place at the end of the tenth century, at
about the time Scandinavia was converting from worship of Norse
gods to Christianity. After a preliminary explanation of why the original settlers left Norway and how they settled the valley of the Lax
(Salmon) River, the story focuses on two families—that of Hoskuld, a
prominent farmer with several sons, and that of Gudrun, the most
beautiful woman ever to be born in Iceland. As a young woman,
Gudrun has four dreams that predict the fate of her four marriages.
Hoskuld has several sons, of whom two, Kjartan and Bolli, are the
most beautiful and promising. Gudrun is a strong-minded woman—
she gets rid of husband number one in favor of husband number two,
but husband number two is drowned. She then falls in love with Kjartan, and when he decides to go to Norway to seek his fortune, she asks
to go along, but he refuses to take her. While he is gone, Bolli asks to
marry her, telling her that Kjartan has lost interest in her in favor of
the Norwegian king's daughter. When Kjartan returns, wealthy and
more handsome than ever, Bolli and Gudrun are already married.
Jealousy, envy, spite, conflict, and killings ensue. The feud spreads
around the valley, with betrayal and trickery the order of the day, until

at last all family representatives are satisfied with their compensation and Gudrun devotes herself to religion. One of the most famous exchanges in all of Icelandic literature happens at the very end, when Gudrun's son asks her which of her husbands she preferred. She says, "Him I treated worst was the one I loved the best." She means Kjartan, whom she had goaded her husband Bolli to kill.

The writers of the Icelandic sagas were a good deal more cryptic than Murasaki Shikibu. They specialized in the economically rendered but telling detail, and the reader has to be alert to pick up the undercurrents of the story. The contemporary audiences of the sagas were interested not only in what happened, but also who was who and who their thirteenth-century descendants were—the sagas worked as genealogy and geography, not only as stories. And all the saga writers were aware of what the other saga writers were writing about—the sagas had many characters in common and many formal effects in common. For example, it often happens in a saga that a character wants to do something that others think is unwise. When he proposes this course of action, the standard reply is, "You will do as you wish in any case." There is also a customary use of understatement—toward the end of the present saga, men surround the sheep-tending hut of one of the characters. When he injures one of them with a spear thrust through a window, the other members of the ambush remark "that there must be men inside."

The Icelandic sagas were written about an armed society full of hot-headed citizens with strong propensities toward violence. The characters often make choices we might find difficult to understand. At the beginning of the Laxardal saga, one man cheats another out of his half of a catch of fish. A few days later, the cheated man comes up behind him and cuts off his head. He is in turn pursued by the first man's relatives. In spite of her third dream, which predicts the death of her third husband through killing, Gudrun goads and belittles him and promotes conflict. In part, the strangeness of the Icelandic sagas comes from their focus—most were written in a time of widespread fighting about the temptation and curse of widespread fighting (in fact, the society the sagas depict was probably more peaceful than the sagas make it seem). The sagas relate a sequence of events without delving into the psychology of the participants—characters rarely reveal their motivation, except by an ironic sentence or two. The sagas, therefore, add up to a theory of human behavior, but neither the characters nor the narrators discourse about that theory. The theory is simple and brutal—people do what they are fated to do, actions are quite often foolish, only the wisest manage to avoid disaster, and the best attitude is one of stoic irony.

The result is an ambience of impending doom and mischance, and the absence of free will and a sense of spiritual redemption. The characters are enslaved by their impetuosity and pride, benumbed by the repeated destruction of relationships. When they foresee evil outcomes, their expressions of regret are muted and rueful. Not for the Norse men and women those floods of tears that Murasaki Shikibu's characters indulge in. For these Norse, life is so fleeting that they don't even have the luxury to reflect upon how fleeting it is.

For the modern reader, though, the Norse characters share with the Japanese characters unfamiliar moral standards. Gudrun is frequently called the greatest heroine of the sagas, but she does not have the moral characteristics of appealing modern heroines. She is powerful, greedy, angry, envious, treacherous, and unloving, but she is never judged for these qualities. Her beauty and the grandness of her story are what elevate her to greatness. Like Genji, she can commit what we would call "sins" or "crimes" because she exists outside of subsequent Christian moral precepts and outside of the ordinary—that is her claim to being a worthy protagonist.

4 · Giovanni Boccaccio · The Decameron

TRANS. G. H. MCWILLIAM (1352; REPR., NEW YORK: PENGUIN, 1995), 909 PP.

The Decameron is a compendium of tales and stories compiled, translated, composed, and arranged by Florentine man of letters Giovanni Boccaccio during the time of the Black Death (1347–49). Ten young people of means—seven women and three men, and each with one servant—elect to leave Florence, the scene of much illness, death, and social chaos, and go into the countryside for fourteen days. There they find and make use of three beautiful and abundant locations (think of them as perfect resort compounds) to rest and recuperate their spirits before returning to the city. They decide to pass the time singing, dancing, feasting, enjoying nature, and telling stories with various themes, many of them comic or satiric, a few of them macabre or gruesome, several tragic. Some are only a page or two long, some are as simple as jokes, and some are long and complex, exploring social, philosophical, and spiritual themes.

It is hard to convey the richness of Boccaccio's accomplishment, which is surely one of the great prose masterpieces of all time. Boccaccio makes full use of the possibilities of his form. He begins with a graphic and detailed picture of life in Florence during the Black Death. It is not only that the population has been decimated, it is also that the people have been brought to a state of coarse numbness and brutality in their relations with one another, leaving their loved ones to die alone and be buried alone, while they are rioting and carousing, giving up all forms of decorum and prudence.

Boccaccio was a great lover of Dante and *The Divine Comedy,* and later in his life became a friend of the poet Petrarch. Boccaccio was a convivial, influential, and well-connected man in Florence, and *The Decameron* was famous from the beginning of its circulation among the literate classes. One thing that is especially interesting about it is Boccaccio's evident awareness of himself as a target of criticism in the literary rather than the social or political sense. At the beginning of the fourth day, he breaks the frame and addresses some of the criticisms— that some of the stories aren't accurately translated, but also that their subject matter (often of a sexual or erotic nature) is inappropriate or unworthy of literary art. He defends himself from the first charge by challenging his critics to produce originals different from his, and from the second two charges by noting that sexual desire is as natural as hunger. To deny sexual desire, "one has to have exceptional powers, which often turn out to have been used, not only in vain, but to the serious harm of those who employ them."

The tragic and gruesome stories notwithstanding, *The Decameron* is essentially a comic work, and Boccaccio's choice to write it in prose enhances its comic qualities. Most of the stories are about connections successfully achieved, often through guile, but often, also, through love and fidelity. Although several of the stories, especially the last, have a misogynistic cast, the desirability of male-female relations is never in question. Women and men are not perfect, but they are better off in one another's arms having "delight and joy of one another, causing the nightingale to sing at frequent intervals" (p. 396) than not. The ten young people form a perfect comic society, surrounded by beauty and abundance that they can fully appreciate (Boccaccio includes a scene in which the women go away and find a small valley where they swim naked in a clear lake to cool themselves); they have differing opinions but no conflict. They treat one another with courtesy and respect, but for the fourteen days of the taletelling, they do not couple up—their relations remain ones of friendship; the balance among all the participants is maintained.

Though many of the tales are based on traditional material, Boccaccio locates quite a few of them in the Florence of his day, or in other parts of Italy that his readers were familiar with. He uses well-known names—sometimes, he uses a famous family name, such as Cavalcanti, but introduces a fictional member. Like Lady Murasaki and the Icelandic saga writers, Boccaccio is interested in the particularities of his time and place—he is well aware, for example, of the power of the Florentine mercantile class and of the vagaries of the bourgeois life. Many of his characters gain sudden wealth and then lose it through moneylending or trade. He also depicts the increasing fluidity of social and economic class as well as some of the problems of what we would call the professions—doctors and scholars. In other words, while Boccaccio's structure and material are medieval in many ways, the sense of change and possibility, the irreverence toward traditional figures of authority (especially the church), and the individuality of the scores and scores of characters he creates are modern and "prosaic." Prose is for exploring what is unique about situations and characters—we might say that prose is "Aristotelian." Poetry is for exploring what incidents and persons typify—it is "Platonic." Like many prose writers, Boccaccio adopts a rather self-effacing narrative voice—his statement, above, that he does not have the power to defy nature, extends beyond the realm of sexuality and desire to the realm of art and philosophy. The accumulation of telling detail—that is, of psychological truth—is what he is after.

If narrative is about how something happens, and its meaning grows out of specific, and often very tiny, turns of events, then it cannot help but explore the differences between individuals, because events impose choices on the characters, and choices reveal intentions and predispositions that are always made on an individual basis. Quite often the choices contradict conventional rules or standards, and then the narrator and the character must defend or illustrate the rationale for a particular choice. While *The Decameron* does not have the structure of a novel, in that it is not about a single set of characters who are engaged in working out a single plot, it does have the piling on of character and incident that is typical of a novel and that seems to reveal (like *The Tale of Genji*) life as it is being lived around the author. In fact, the verisimilitude of *The Decameron* is so marked that scholars have been at pains to point out that Boccaccio's portrait of the plague in Florence is *not* taken from the author's experience, but from a depiction of the plague in Florence of the ninth century that Boccaccio had read.

As in many great novels, the treasury of detail in *The Decameron* defies analysis, or even sufficient appreciation. The reader (and it *is* a reader—*The Decameron* is too long to be recited, too detailed to be filmed except in an abbreviated form, too various to be dramatized, too huge to be painted) can only appreciate each brilliant turn of phrase or each exquisite irony or each perfect set piece and then move on to the next, allowing them, afterward, to coexist imperfectly but delightfully in the memory, until her enjoyment is renewed with another reading.

5 · Lazarillo de Tormes

TRANS. STANLEY APPELBAUM (1554; REPR., NEW YORK: DOVER, 2001), 103 PP.

While *The Heptameron* (see below) marked, perhaps, the end of something (a medieval way of looking at things, from the point of view of the master class), *Lazarillo de Tormes* perhaps marked the beginning of something—the modern way of looking at things, from the point of view of an average, or less than average, citizen who was interested not in romance or chivalric prowess, but survival. Not quite a novel, more like a story or a fragment, *Lazarillo de Tormes* was an unsuppressible Spanish narrative of the sixteenth century. Published in 1554, it was enormously popular, and continued to be so for the next couple of centuries, however energetically the authorities tried to ban it. It was widely read and imitated, the first, or perhaps the proto, picaresque novel, about the adventures of a lower-class and in many ways disreputable young man, often a petty criminal (though Lazarillo himself is simply impoverished).

The author gives Lázaro (who narrates in his own voice) three or four adventures in finding himself a master and a livelihood, and then seems to lose interest and marries him off to a woman who may or may not be cuckolding him. Lázaro's voice is charming, and the details he relates of the tricks played upon him and others are interesting enough, but the novella seems primitive in comparison with some of

the other works discussed on our list. In addition to being of considerable literary-critical and historical interest, though, *Lazarillo de Tormes*
shows plenty of the characteristics intrinsic to prose narrative—it is a
lively social document concerned with daily life as the author is living
it. Apart from Lázaro, the characters he meets are types, but they are in
no way ideals—a blind man who mistreats him and whom he tricks, a
friar who hoards all his bread, and an impoverished nobleman who
absconds without paying his rent, leaving Lázaro to fend for himself.
Lázaro, though a child and a servant, is perfectly willing to express his
opinion of these characters, and his opinion is not respectful. Though
short almost to the point of being fragmentary, *Lazarillo de Tormes* was
subversive in giving a voice to the hitherto voiceless, and demonstrates
that the novel is indeed a naturally democratic form—promising not
"every man a king" but rather "every man a protagonist."

6 · Marguerite de Navarre · The Heptameron

TRANS. PAUL A. CHILTON (1557-58; REPR., NEW YORK: PENGUIN, 1984), 543 PP.

The Heptameron was compiled (or composed) in conscious imitation of
The Decameron at the court, and probably under the direct supervision
of Marguerite, the queen of Navarre and the sister of François I, king
of France. It was published after Marguerite's death, so it is impossible
to say with certainty that she wrote it, but she did write poetry and did
sponsor much literary activity at court, including the work of Rabelais.
Marguerite died in 1549, at age fifty-seven. A version of *The Heptameron* was published in 1557, and an edition giving credit to Marguerite the following year.

The construction of the story cycle is similar to that of *The Decameron*—a group of men and women are confined to an out-of-the-
way spot and decide to tell ten stories every day until a hundred have
been told, but the frame, and the mood, of the later French work is
decidedly different from that of the earlier Italian work. Whereas Boccaccio's young people leave plague-ridden Florence in search of a
happy land where they can refresh themselves, and Boccaccio devotes
considerable effort to describing the paradises they find, the storytellers of *The Heptameron,* who are older and married or widowed,
come together by chance in the wilds of the Pyrenees after several

frightening misadventures in which the husband of one of the ladies, Longarine, is killed. They take refuge in a monastery while a bridge is being built that will permit their departure. Little space is given to describing the setting, but more space is given to the group commentary at the end of each story. Additionally, they adopt the rule that the stories are to be true rather than from books. It seems that most if not all of the stories were taken from the lives of actual contemporaries of the tellers, who are also largely identifiable—Parlamente seems to be Marguerite herself, and Hircan seems to be Henri of Navarre. The others seem to be noble friends or relatives of theirs. Thus, though many of the stories are artfully told, they occupy a middle ground between gossip and fiction, and they are used by the group for a prolonged discussion of love, faith, virtue, and the true natures of men and women. The argument is unresolved because the manuscript breaks off at the beginning of the eighth day.

The Heptameron has neither the charm nor the comic exuberance of *The Decameron,* but it has a dark, obsessive, compelling quality of its own that carries the reader through many stories that seem in some ways to be about the same thing—how to work out the inequities between men and women, and, if they can't be worked out, how to justify them by appealing to Scripture or natural law. If a hallmark of the tales in *The Decameron* is the lively coupling of all sorts of lovers in spite of all sorts of obstacles, and whose pleasures are approved of by the author, a hallmark of *The Heptameron* is quite the opposite—love and sex are dangerous but unavoidable, and the consequences of passion are almost always dishonor, illness, or death. Hircan is the spokesman for the extreme male position—if a man falls in love with a woman, his love is demonstrated only by his determination to bed her by any means; if seduction doesn't work, then rape is not only justified, but also required. If she resists, then for the sake of his honor he may kill her (at the same time, since Parlamente is his wife and she is present, Hircan often protests that these are abstract rules that apply to others and not to him, since he is entirely satisfied in his marriage). The women use their stories to demonstrate how love and virtue can coexist in certain women, but the terms of women's lives are so circumscribed that the group never agrees about what love is for a woman. They all agree, however, that women's lives are dangerous, especially those of beautiful women, and that there is no real protection if a woman attracts the notice of a passionate lover. In one story, a young man enlists the aid of a serving girl to carry letters to the well-born woman he loves. The father of his beloved (a duke) discovers the activities of the serving woman and threatens her. She pleads with the duchess to send her off to a convent to avoid the duke's wrath, and she does so, but the duke persuades his wife that he doesn't mean to harm the girl. She promises the girl safety on her life and honor, so the girl comes back, whereupon the duke has her imprisoned and hanged, even though the duchess begs him not to. Though this story shocks most of the listeners, the duke has his defenders, who assert that he has the right to treat his servants as he pleases. In this regard, it is important to remember that *The Heptameron* was the work of the actual ruling class—a king, his queen, and their friends. Part of its rhetorical purpose is to maintain status quo power relationships in French society. Although the storytellers lament sometimes that life is the way it is, none of them suggests that it be arranged differently.

The only recourse—and a problematic one it is—is faith and the direct experience of God's love. Several of the storytellers relate stories that they consider show true devotion to religion and virtue, and much of the framing material is taken up with the religious observances of the ten men and women. The leader of the group, an older, very devout woman named Oiselle, conducts lessons from Scripture at the start of every day. The subtext of *The Heptameron* is the Reformation and Counter-Reformation, which unsettled sixteenth-century Europe with anticlerical and evangelical ideas. But while everyone in the group seems to agree with these new ideas in principle, many of them doubt whether they can work in reality, given the importance of position and appearance. The seventy-two stories repeatedly demonstrate that no happiness can be found in the world the characters inhabit— no theory or technique or belief or degree of caution, no amount of power, and no social institution, whether marriage or law, offers protection from the passions of relatives and associates, most of which begin with love and attraction but end with hatred and resentment. The final effect of *The Heptameron* is very dark, and much in contrast to *The Decameron*.

In the face of the Black Death, Boccaccio is able to construct an opposing picture of beauty, virtue, friendship, and forgiveness, where fear and tragedy are more than counterbalanced by honest pleasure and real connection. Two hundred years later, under less obviously trying conditions, Marguerite and her friends depict a cruel and senseless world where treachery is standard and people's lives and reputations are always at stake. Does this reflect the changes brought about by religious ferment? The impasse that feudal notions of power and class had come to? Other cultural and economic uncertainties? Whatever the source, the sense of a culture in conflict is marked. And neither is there any countervailing sense of peace and beauty in the natural landscape—the storytellers are lost in the wilds; at most, they can refresh themselves in a meadow of grass that is hardly described. The impression that *The Decameron* leaves of being an inexhaustible treasure of life's variety gives way to the sense in *The Heptameron* of returning over and over to the same few dilemmas without hope of resolving them. And yet, *The Heptameron* seems a sincere and in some ways innocent work in which the storytellers survey their world as straightforwardly as they can, themselves unaware of the overall effect of their efforts. Out of its contradictions grow some of the most interesting and fertile questions in all of subsequent European prose literature.

7 · Miguel de Cervantes · Don Quijote

VOL. 1., TRANS. BURTON RAFFEL (1605; REPR., NEW YORK: W. W. NORTON, 1999), 335 PP.

The first volume of *Don Quixote* was published in 1605, about fifty years after *The Heptameron, Gargantua and Pantagruel* (1532–64), and *Lazarillo de Tormes*. It is a truism of modern criticism that *Don Quixote* is the first modern novel, but the first volume seems to me more of a piece with the works of the mid-sixteenth century than is generally acknowledged. The premise of *Don Quixote* is that a certain genteelly impoverished gentleman, deluded by reading too many cheap chivalric romances, takes up sword, shield, and cardboard helmet and leaves home on his aged steed, Rocinante, to live as a knight-errant. He employs a squire, Sancho Panza, and devotes himself to a local maiden (to whom he has never spoken), naming her Dulcinea. He then gets into a series of misadventures with mule drivers, goatherds, innkeepers, tragic lovers, clerics, policemen, and other passersby, always asserting against the evidence of his (and everyone else's) senses that his realistic world of Spain under the reign of Philip III is actually a storybook world of queens and castles and knights and enchantments.

Cervantes uses Don Quixote's delusions in several ways, and some of the best parts of the novel are his conversations with Sancho Panza, in which Sancho attempts to disabuse Quixote of his illusions and Quixote attempts to convince Sancho of their superior reality. Nevertheless, more often than not, Don Quixote earns injuries as well as ridicule in his "chivalric" endeavors. He is unhorsed and beaten up more than once, and several times gets into battles that his companions see as sources of entertainment. In the end, he more or less wins Sancho to his side—not because Sancho believes in Quixote's romantic world, but because Sancho loves his master and chooses to defend him against the doubts of others. When the two finally return to their village, and Sancho encounters his wife, he quells her doubts (partly with a subtle threat of marital force after they get home) and makes the same promises to her that Don Quixote has made to him (and that have come to nothing).

The story of Don Quixote and Sancho Panza's travels also serves as a frame for several other stories, told them by travelers they meet upon the road, and these stories bear a striking resemblance to stories in *The Decameron* and *The Heptameron. Don Quixote,* volume 1, is not a modern novel in the sense that it describes a distinct and significant transformation in the mental state of its hero. He goes out deluded and he returns home deluded; what is perhaps different is the reader's interest in and sympathy with him. Cervantes is careful to balance Quixote's comic, pathetic, and noble qualities and (rather like the two earlier works) to provide frequent commentary on his protagonist through the dialogue of the other characters.

Four of the interpolated tales—Marcela's Tale; the Tale of Cardenio, Don Fernando, and Dorotea; the Tale of Anselmo, Lothario, and Camila; and the Tale of the Veiled Woman—deal with many of the same themes and some of the same plot ideas as tales in Marguerite de Navarre's collection. As in *The Heptameron,* all are concerned with how a beautiful woman is supposed to negotiate her rights and obligations in a world of rapists and seducers. Marcela sets the tone when she declares that the death of her lover, Grisóstomo, whom she had never encouraged, is his own fault, and that she is not to be blamed for heartlessness or lack of mercy, since she had openly declared her financial and emotional independence from the world of men, and her beauty, which has lured him to her, is not her fault but God's gift. Soon after Marcela, Don Quixote and Sancho meet Cardenio, another disheartened lover (and fellow madman), who has been betrayed, as far as he knows, by his betrothed, Luscinda, and his best friend, Don Fernando. Not long after Cardenio tells his story, Don Quixote and Sancho meet a woman disguised as a man (when she takes off her cap, her blond hair falls to the ground), who tells the story of her betrayal. She turns out to be the seduced and abandoned betrothed of Don Fernando, Dorotea, and not long after that, the group of friends encounters Don Fernando himself and the grief-stricken Luscinda, who has only just been prevented from killing herself. Luscinda and Cardenio are reunited, Don Fernando repents and is reunited with Dorotea, and the whole group then hears the story of Anselmo, who is married to Camila, but who persuades his best friend, Lothario, to put her love and virtue to the test (somewhat similar to the last tale of *The Decameron,* in which Gualtieri puts his wife, Griselda, to several cruel tests to make her prove the truth of her marital vows, and very much an elaboration of Tale 47 in *The Heptameron,* in which friends from childhood are sundered by the husband's mortal certainty that his new wife and old friend have become lovers). The Tale of the Veiled Woman, in which the daughter of a wealthy Moor, Hadji Murad, engineers her own abduction so she can go to Spain and become a Christian, is also reminiscent of the pan-Mediterranean feel of several of Boccaccio's tales in which Christians and Muslims travel between Europe and the Islamic world because of war, piracy, or trade.

Cervantes's frame doesn't serve him quite as well in introducing these tales, so he puts Don Quixote to sleep and lets the other characters take over for a while—neither Quixote nor Sancho have much to offer in analyzing these love themes, since Sancho is a peasant and Quixote apparently has never had relations with a woman. The tales themselves show that issues raised in the French stories are no more resolved fifty years later in the Spanish ones, though times have changed since Boccaccio—there is a moment in the story of Anselmo and Lothario where the reader can imagine Boccaccio ending the tale with a laugh, right when both Anselmo and Lothario are enjoying Camila. Boccaccio would consider cuckolding a just punishment for Anselmo's compulsive failure of trust and an attentive lover a just reward for Camila's initial resistance. And when, in the earlier tale, Don Fernando comes to his senses and accepts Dorotea as his wife, the reader can almost hear the commentary Marguerite's friends might have supplied for and against Don Fernando's rights and obligations as a lusty nobleman, for and against Dorotea's course of action after the loss of her virtue, for and against Luscinda's failure to complete the suicide she had vowed, for and against Cardenio's failure to revenge himself upon his friend. In particular, the psychology of Don Fernando's redemption would have been far more believable to Marguerite's panel of critics than to us. He does not undergo a character shift, but is merely recalled by the group to the rules and obligations of his social class (after which he can serve as the benefactor of several other characters who need pecuniary assistance, including Don Quixote, who refuses to pay his bill at the inn because no knights in books are ever required to pay bills).

It is hard to say what is notably "modern" in the first volume of *Don Quixote,* unless it is Cervantes's own literary views, which pit the destructive lies of the popular chivalric romances against the more enlightening works of serious contemporary authors that he champions in a discussion between two priests who accompany Quixote back to his home village. But Cervantes's premise, the idea of a man trying to live a knight-errant's life in the Spain of Cervantes's day, is a simple and brilliant comic idea that reveals how different Cervantes himself considered his time to be from the medieval period. In addition, *Don Quixote* is a good example of the best way to write a novel—Cervantes takes a rather simple premise and follows it through its train of logic. Many brilliant works illustrate the value of intelligently pursuing a simple concept—for example, Franz Kafka's "The Metamorphosis" (man turns into a bug), Charles Dickens's *A Christmas Carol* (man is visited by dreams of his past, present, and future). Some concepts are so easily grasped and yet so pregnant with possibilities that they almost unfold themselves, giving the writer a visible structure within which he is free to explore ideas, character, themes, and even styles, as Cervantes does with his interpolated tales.

Miguel de Cervantes · Don Quijote

VOL 2., TRANS. BURTON RAFFEL (1615; REPR., NEW YORK: W. W. NORTON, 1999), 396 PP.

Cervantes published the second volume of *Don Quixote* in 1615, ten years after the first, and it is important to understand that it is a sequel, not a part of the original conception. For novelists, a novel is an experience as well as a product, and part of the experience is the postpublication fate of the novel as well as the novelist's further thoughts and feelings about the characters and the situation. After publication, the world speaks back to the novelist about what had once been his private thoughts, and in Cervantes's case, he was clearly inspired in several ways by *Don Quixote*'s reception. Modern critics seem especially to appreciate the brilliance of Cervantes's "metafiction"—his incorporation of Quixote's response to volume 1, allegedly written about him by Sidi Hamid Benengeli, into his further adventures, as well as his response to the false volume 2, written by a literary pirate and published in the interim. These layers upon layers of embedded fictionalizing prefigure Italo Calvino or Robert Coover. When Milan Kundera says that "*Don Quixote* is the novel all future novels answer to," perhaps it is this, in part, that he is referring to. And it does seem very postmodern (very post–E. M. Forster, let's say) for the novel to be so simultaneously self-referential and playful. Once again, though, I think Cervantes's accomplishment is more on the order of conceiving a simple and brilliant premise—that the reader of books has become the hero of a book—and following it out. To call *Don Quixote* the first modern novel misrepresents how it appeared to the author himself, which was as a book among books, part of a flourishing and much-discussed literary culture that Cervantes had opinions about, not as a precursor to books that Cervantes would never see. When an author seems to predict the future in an uncanny way, it is not because he looks forward to us as we look backward to him, but because he intuits the structure of some or many aspects of the world he is living in, and is adept at extrapolating from it.

The second volume of *Don Quixote* begins about a month after the first ends, when Quixote, recovered from his wounds, decides to embark upon a third tour of knight-errantry, and persuades Sancho, somewhat against his better judgment, to go with him. Cervantes introduces several significant new characters, the most important being Samson Carrasco, a local villager who is a graduate of the University of Salamanca, an educated young man. It is he who tells Quixote about the knight's new fame, but he also, more secretively, decides to cure Quixote of his madness. How to think of Don Quixote's madness and therefore how to treat him is the consistent theme of the novel, and supplies a firmer and more sophisticated story line than the adventures of the first volume.

Don Quixote and Sancho get farther from home than in the first volume, and their adventures have a metaphysical flavor. At one point Quixote sends Sancho to report his lovesickness to Dulcinea. Sancho goes to her village but can't find her, so when he returns, he lies, and says he did see her. Later, when the two of them go to her village to find her, Sancho, covering for the fact that he doesn't know what she looks like (and Don Quixote doesn't know, either), identifies her as one of three peasant girls they encounter as they near the village. Don Quixote is disappointed and upset at the girl's coarseness. He decides she's been enchanted, and for the duration of the novel eagerly seeks the means of her disenchantment. The longest section of the second volume concerns Don Quixote's tormenting at the hands of a duke and duchess he and Sancho encounter hunting in a woodland. The noble pair are familiar with the first volume of Don Quixote's story, and after they realize who he is, they contrive to make him and Sancho the butts of a series of elaborate theatrical jokes. At the end of the episode of the duke and duchess, both Quixote and Sancho have changed. Sancho is no longer interested in the perquisites of governing, but is eager to get back to his village and his family; Don Quixote has lost a measure of his energy. Not long afterward, he is unhorsed by another knight and forced to acknowledge the beauty of that knight's lady, which he finds fatally disheartening.

Quixote does return home, and with another plan, but he soon falls ill, and just as he regains his sanity long enough to repudiate knighthood and his books of chivalry once and for all, he makes his will and dies.

In the first volume, Quixote's adventures are pure expressions of his delusions—he mistakes windmills for giants and an inn for a castle, for example. Those he meets have simple reactions to his delusional actions—they defend themselves against him with greater or lesser vigor. The narrator relates and the reader witnesses his adventures. The interpenetration of points of view is far more complex in the second volume. In the first place, Sancho and Quixote are made self-conscious by the knowledge that not one but two books have been written about them, one false and one true, so they become alert not only to what they are doing but also to whether those they meet have heard of them. Frequently those they meet have heard of them, which adds another layer of consciousness to the narrative. Some of those they meet—not only the duke and duchess—want to manipulate them so they can further witness the revelation of their characters (which, in both cases, are drawn from literary sources—Don Quixote makes constant reference to his books about knights, and Sancho is constantly spouting proverbs, that is, constantly setting his actions and thoughts into a traditional, commonsense frame of reference). The adventures of the second volume are more numerous and less broad, and most of them take place among a better class of people than the mule drivers and innkeepers of the first volume. As a result, there is a greater emphasis on interpretation and a smaller emphasis on action. The second volume is vastly more literary than the first.

In addition, Cervantes is more sophisticated in the manner in which he interpolates his tales. He is still interested, for example, in seduction, in the position of girls and women in contemporary Spain, and in the Moors, but instead of putting Don Quixote to sleep so tales can be told, he incorporates them into Don Quixote's adventures or into the tricks played upon him—he knows his protagonist better and is more able to depict his reactions. And his protagonist is more complex. Don Quixote and Sancho have a great deal of discussion in volume two. This cannot help but enrich both the reader's and the author's sense of what Don Quixote and Sancho are like, and equip the author with greater and greater insight into his characters—one of the miracles of the novel is the way characters are developed and revealed at the same time. That is the illusion of roundness—that a sequence of words/ images is pointing out what is already present in a character, when in fact those things seemingly being pointed out are really ideas that, possibly, the author has never thought of before. If Cervantes's first volume is a sometimes awkward step away from *The Heptameron* and *Lazarillo de Tormes* toward the second volume, the second volume is a more assured step away from the first toward the modern novel, wherein every episode fills in the psychology of the characters until the reader comes to feel what Forster talks about in *Aspects of the Novel,* that she knows these beings far better and more intimately than she knows any real person.

Don Quixote and Sancho are beloved characters because they are not perfect. It is never to be decided whether Quixote is wise or mad, whether Sancho is intelligent or foolish. Their looks and talents and states of mind are secondary to their moral qualities—they are kind, upright, chaste, and affectionate toward one another. They have moods and intentions and desires. In the second volume, they achieve depth of character in both the literary sense—complexity—and in the common usage of the term—integrity. They are tested by events, they are tested by people they meet, they are tested by one another. A more integrated, less episodic plot would involve Quixote and Sancho in a world quite removed from the reader's. As it is, we come to feel close to

them, in part because we are the only witnesses to everything that happens to them.

8 · Madame de La Fayette · The Princess of Clèves
TRANS. WALTER J. COBB, ED. NANCY K. MILLER
(1678; REPR., NEW YORK: NEW AMERICAN LIBRARY, MERIDIAN, 1989), 162 PP.

The ten storytellers and critics of *The Heptameron* propose themselves
a riddle that after seventy stories they cannot answer. It is stated by
Parlamente (probably Marguerite herself) as follows: "Just suppose
that I were able to name a lady who had been truly in love, who had
been desired, pursued and wooed, and yet had remained an honest
woman, victorious over her body, victorious over her love and victorious over her would be lover. Would you admit that such a thing were
possible?" (p. 120). She then tells the story of Amador and Florida
(Story 10), in which a faithful young man eventually attempts the rape
of the woman he loves out of sheer force of desire; she resists and maintains her virtue, denying him all future access to her, but not ceasing to
love him.

Her nine listeners do not all accept her interpretation. Hircan insists
that since Florida only screams, she isn't really resisting, while Oisille
takes the attempted rape as evidence that Amador's love is false. All
seventy stories more or less unsatisfactorily work over the same dilemma—can true love be honorable and still be satisfied? A hundred
and twenty years later, Madame de La Fayette takes up the same riddle
in her most famous novel and answers it more successfully, by drawing
a more intricate and insightful psychological portrait of a husband
and wife, Monsieur de Clèves, Madame de Clèves, and her lover, the
duc de Nemours. Madame de La Fayette sets her novel in the court of
Henri II, son of François I and nephew of Marguerite, and she also
makes allusion to Marguerite's work, as a book of tales. Florida's tale
becomes the tale of *The Princess of Clèves*. It is the first entirely successful use of the novel form.

Madame de La Fayette did several things with her material that
previous novelists had not done. First, she deployed her characters in
order of their importance and interest, and she stuck to her deployment. She devotes most of her text to Madame de Clèves (who is about

eighteen years old during the novel—the whole novel concerns the emotional lives of teenage girls and their somewhat older mates), who has the most unusual dilemma. She concentrates second upon Monsieur de Clèves, who has the second most unusual dilemma, and third upon the duc de Nemours, whose dilemma is straightforward. Around these three are ranged their relatives and patrons, who serve to promote and complicate the action and to witness and comment upon it. Their relatives and patrons are the king of France, his mistress, the queen of France, the dauphin, and the queen dauphine, Mary of Scots (Madame de La Fayette was a countess herself, so this is a ruling-class production like *The Heptameron*). Once she has arranged her characters according to how interesting they are, she maintains her focus upon them, not letting herself get distracted by other interesting material—as Cervantes did, for example.

Most important, she always maintains at the forefront of the narrative the questions of how the characters are experiencing their feelings and why they feel and act as they do. Consciously or unconsciously, Madame de La Fayette discovered that all actions and feelings are representable, even ones that seem unbelievable, if the novelist shows their progress step by step and makes the short connections between each step plausible. In other words, she was able to incorporate uniqueness into the context of the conventional and to do it smoothly and naturally—this is an essential function of the novel as a form. In short, *The Princess of Clèves* works because the author is especially good at organizing, focusing, and thinking through her material—and all of these efforts work together to propel the plot.

The Princess of Clèves beautifully illustrates the relationship between novels and gossip. The novel's setting, the French court, is a dangerously gossipy place. Power, love, influence, politics, status, war, peace, and national alliances all depend upon intrigue and shifting loyalties. Everyone at the court is alert to the body language of everyone else, and ready to infer carefully hidden feelings and then broadcast their surmises. Intimate information is a form of capital to be used in the continuous exchange of power and influence, and women play as resolutely as men. The stakes are high, as is illustrated by the death of King Henri—within hours of his death, former favorites are out, new ones have gained offices and influence, and the entire balance of power has shifted. As the ten storytellers of *The Heptameron* well knew, there is little room for innocence or virtue, and yet sin is a risky game. Madame de Clèves's greatest act of courage is to go among the courtiers seething with passions she can't afford to disclose in any way, and her only relief is the opportunity to leave the court in the normal course of her duties without drawing attention to herself. But the novel illustrates its debt to gossip in a couple of other ways, too. For one thing, the author interpolates several cautionary or illustrative tales, as Cervantes does, but she interpolates them with brilliant grace as gossip. They not only fit, constituting significant interaction between the characters, they also develop the themes and the plot without derailing the action. In particular, though, Madame de La Fayette's focus on her heroine's state of mind and her deft investigation of it reveal a sensibility for whom human motivation is of natural and compelling interest, both in general and in particular. Only an accomplished and astute (and compassionate) gossip could have entered into her characters as fully as she does.

Madame de La Fayette was proud of her depiction of life as it had been lived 120 years before her time. She was proud that she got her facts and her history straight while seamlessly introducing her fictional couple, and no one has seriously questioned that she did so. Nevertheless, a comparison of *The Princess of Clèves* and *The Heptameron* shows that something changed in those 120 years that enabled the author to see both her characters and her form in a more modern way. Marguerite and her friends cannot quite make sense of the true stories they tell—they don't quite understand what love and virtue are, and even though they go over the same material time and again, they cannot make the two fit. There are no happy endings. Rapes, deaths, imprisonments, and other cruelties abound, and explicit religious practice does little to console the characters or brighten their depiction of the world around them. What Madame de Clèves dares to do both times she is in a crisis (when she confesses to her husband that she loves someone else, and when she confesses to the duc de Nemours that she loves him but cannot marry him) is to be honest and, against her better judgment and that of everyone she knows, to trust the men who say they love her. In other words, she expresses true love and faith—and her inner life—in a way that contradicts notions of love and faith that are conventions of the period (passion, ardor, physical attraction). The two men are astounded at how much more they love her even though she has not given them what they want, but she has given them something far more rare (as they know instinctively) and asked them to give her something equally rare—the right to her own feelings. While the characters of *The Princess of Clèves* do not deem themselves happy at the end of the novel, each of them achieves peace—the Princess through the active pursuit of higher thoughts, Nemours through the passage of time, and Monsieur de Clèves through learning the truth about his wife's virtue. The reader, though, has a very happy ending when the princess anatomizes the idea of courtly love and lays it to rest forever.

The modern reader looks for a novel that is irresistibly involving. Though perhaps not the novel's greatest virtue, this is its greatest appeal, a bonus that detaches, calms, and relaxes the reader's mind, no matter how agitating the subject matter—thus the paradox that very disturbing material can be "loved" by millions of readers. The early works we have read so far, while worthy and sometimes great, have not been consistently involving. What Madame de La Fayette succeeded in doing was to take traditional material and use the natural tools of the novel to make something new of it. She had an inherently interesting story; she ably depicted both the individual characters and their social milieu; she organized her material so it progresses relentlessly but not predictably; she thought through her themes, researched her setting, had compassion for her characters. Best of all, though, she successfully negotiated the most important aspect of the novel form—the manner in which an individual character distinguishes herself or himself from his world while acknowledging the pressure to conform. As a result, *The Princess of Clèves* is not only worthy, or even great, it is a page-turner, and a modern novel, too.

9 · Aphra Behn · *Oroonoko* and "The Fair Jilt"

ED. PAUL SALZMAN (1688; REPR., NEW YORK: OXFORD UNIVERSITY PRESS, 1994), 45 PP.

The novel, of course, owes equally to the romance and the history, and *Don Quixote,* especially the second volume, can be seen as the history of a man who took romances too much to heart. Many early novels, to distinguish themselves from romances and to stake their claim to truthfulness, present themselves as histories (and in several languages, notably French and Icelandic, the words for "history" and "story" are the same [*histoire* and *saga,* respectively]). Aphra Behn, the first woman to make a successful career as a writer in England (1640–89), placed her short novel *Oroonoko* squarely in the category of a history by attesting that she herself had known Prince Oroonoko during her stay in Surinam, and that he had related the facts of his earlier life to her himself. Various commentators over the years have used her assertions against her (there is more evidence supporting them than contradicting them) either to claim that she lied or to deny her skills as a literary artist, but claiming to be merely reporting a true story is a standard novelist's assertion, usually employed to bolster the moral and ethical claims of novels in general and for certain novels in particular. Behn had a specific polemical purpose in telling her story, which was to expose the slave trade between Africa and the New World. She could only make a splash by asserting the truthfulness of her account (many of the same issues were to come up 170 years later, with *Uncle Tom's Cabin*). She was well aware that her material was controversial, and it remains so, even though her novel is short, obscure, and entirely the province of academic specialists.

The history of Oroonoko is rather simple. The prince of a populous and prosperous but warlike tribe in West Africa, he falls in love with a beautiful maiden of the same tribe, Imoinda, who also is desired by his grandfather, the king, who designates her as his partner, though he is impotent. For customary reasons, Imoinda cannot thereafter become the wife of Oroonoko, but they don't forget each other, and during a ceremonial dance, she stumbles into his arms, arousing the suspicions of the grandfather, who later that evening discovers the two having a tryst. Imoinda is sold into slavery. Not long after, Oroonoko, too, ends up on a slave ship heading for the New World, as a result of the treachery of the English captain of the ship (who had invited Oroonoko onto the ship as his guest, then put him in chains). Oroonoko ends up at Aphra Behn's plantation in Surinam, where he meets up with Imoinda. Behn takes an active interest in his story and his fate. He and Imoinda are married and she becomes pregnant. They now want to buy their way out of slavery before their child is born a slave, and the English slave owners agree to allow this, but repeatedly betray their word and refuse to free the two. Oroonoko (renamed Caesar) leads a slave revolt. Thinking that he will surely die, he kills Imoinda (with her full cooperation) and then is captured. The uprising is put down; he is tortured, killed, and dismembered, stoic to the last.

In fact, *Oroonoko* owes quite a bit to the romance. Behn clearly imagines conditions in Africa, which she has never seen, to be somewhat like conditions at an elaborate European court, where power, convention, taboo, and intrigue dictate the tragic outcome of romantic personal attachments, and the most worthwhile characters are the best looking and the highest born. Imoinda and Oroonoko conform to standard European ideas of male and female virtue—she is beautiful, loving, and submissive, and he is doughty, handsome, and virtuous. Conditions in Surinam Behn depicts with a greater sense of authenticity, and she spends some of her short narrative describing the Indian population as well as the landscape, flora, and fauna. She also alludes to the cession of Surinam to the Dutch—Oroonoko's story takes place entirely within a recognizable historical context—but Oroonoko remains a romantic hero—his uniqueness is too great and his fate too dramatic for the reader to feel that she comes to know or understand him. Behn does not use dialogue—every scene is narrated—and so Oroonoko's and Imoinda's voices are absent from the narrative (as are the voices of the English slave traders and slave owners). Behn was a dramatist and her other narratives make use of dialogue, but her technique wasn't sophisticated enough (and perhaps her polemical purpose was too great) to risk allowing Oroonoko to speak for himself (though she testifies that he speaks several languages as a result of exposure to Europeans in Africa). Undeniably, though, the tale she tells is a horrifying one; the reader doesn't have to feel a thing for Oroonoko and Imoinda as individuals to recoil at their fate. What happens to them gains power insofar as it is shown to be representative of the way slaves are treated by their English masters in Surinam (and elsewhere, of course). The treacheries and brutalities of the English have a believable idiosyncratic cast that makes the reader nod and believe.

"The Fair Jilt" is a more traditional tale, and is in fact reminiscent of some of the darker tales of *The Decameron*. Miranda, a wealthy young woman who has lost her parents, is beautiful but secretly promiscuous. Her first victim is a young man who has gone into the Franciscan order because his brother has stolen his beloved and married her. Miranda throws herself at him, then accuses him of rape when he rejects her advances. He is put in prison. She then falls for Tarquin, who may or may not be the wealthy pretender to the throne of the Roman Empire. He truly loves her, in spite of her evil nature, and they collude to rob her younger sister of her half of the family fortune by twice attempting to kill her so the money will revert to Miranda. Tarquin is tried and set to be beheaded, but the executioner misses his aim, and

Tarquin is saved, only to demonstrate when he revives that he still loves Miranda, evil though she may be. Through various legal maneuvers they are preserved from execution (though now impoverished) and they learn their lesson, going off to live peacefully together until they die of old age. Miranda's first victim is redeemed and released triumphantly from prison as well. Behn doesn't fully explore the moral implications of this outcome or Miranda's transformation. Like Boccaccio, Behn accepts the existence of evil people. She is less interested in their moral improvement than she is in their adventures and their effect on those around them. She is not a psychological novelist as her near-contemporary Madame de La Fayette is, because Behn is more interested in actions than in reasons, or even in plausibility. That people act and how these actions affect others are as far as she goes. But Behn's work is worth reading not only for historical interest but also because she had an eye for what you might call the wonders of life. She was drawn to strong drama and didn't shrink from depicting violence and treachery, nor from expressing "feminine" feelings and thoughts about it. Her work is unusually bold and sometimes startlingly frank.

10 · Daniel Defoe · Robinson Crusoe

(1719; REPR., NEW YORK: RANDOM HOUSE, MODERN LIBRARY, 2001), 282 PP.

Daniel Defoe was the son of Nonconformists, a merchant, and an active writer and pamphleteer—possibly the most prolific English writer ever. His father was a tallow chandler and his mother was from a family with some connections to the gentry. He lived a very active life—he was briefly the captive of pirates, he went bankrupt several times, he served in the army of William of Orange, he was pilloried and repeatedly arrested for subversive pamphleteering, and he saw his work become both famous and notorious. He started writing novels at fifty-nine, and after his major novels, he published *The Complete English Tradesman, An Essay on the History and Reality of Apparitions, A New Family Instructor,* and *The Complete English Gentleman,* among other titles. In other words, Defoe was a certain type of active, hardheaded English Protestant businessman, and his novels consistently reflect his interest in survival, money, trade, and enterprise in general. His protagonists must make their way in the world, often against very difficult world. It is hard to dislike and impossible to dismiss, yet 286 years later, after intervening centuries of genocide, exploitation, and war, it can't help making us uneasy.

Daniel Defoe · Roxana

(1724; REPR., NEW YORK: OXFORD UNIVERSITY PRESS, 1996), 330 PP.

If novel-writing (and romance-writing) in France was a diversion of the aristocracy, Defoe made English novel-writing an activity of the entrepreneurial middle class, which was largely made up of Nonconformists, whose religious beliefs encouraged continual investigations of conscience. It was fine for, and even required of, Nonconformists that they work hard, live simply, and grow rich, but only in good conscience, and all of Defoe's major novels show the uneasy relationship between doing well and doing good. It is certainly no coincidence, given the preoccupation of European novelists with the condition of women's lives, that through Roxana, Defoe analyzes the relationship of womanhood to money and sex.

The first time Roxana makes an illicit liaison, she has the best possible excuse—her husband has left her and her five starving children. In desperation, she foists her children upon the husband's wealthier relatives (the husband's sister would rather the parish take care of them, but Defoe is explicit about the hardships of the eighteenth-century welfare state). Soon afterward, Roxana's wealthy landlord begins to court her, and manages to win her by means of tact, kindness, and, of course, the goading spur of her degree of want. She is probably in her mid- to late twenties at this point, and very beautiful and desirable. Her lover, a jeweler, takes her to France, where they live in luxury for a time, until he is murdered by robbers while delivering some jewels to a princely client. The client pays a condolence visit to Roxana and falls in love with her. She is attracted by his kindness, generosity, and princely rank, and becomes his mistress for several years. He has other mistresses, but she begins to believe that she is the favorite. All along, she is having both babies and second thoughts, but she is also accumulating money, living frugally, and adding to her principal. It is this lack of sentimentality and this focus on the ways and means of prospering that supply the novel's essential charm and originality. If every novel is about *how* characters live and act—that is, the manner in which they do things reveals who they are—then *Roxana* is about how a representative beautiful woman does what most of the people in the world have to do every day of their lives—how she makes a living, how she manipulates the opportunities and accidents that life and the social system present her, how she employs intelligence, stratagem, and all other available means (looks and charm among them) to make her fortune as a courtesan, but also about what both her methods and her results mean to her, how it feels to be a woman in such circumstances. In this, Roxana is different from almost every female protagonist before her, because her survival is something she makes for herself out of mundane materials such as "bills" (the forerunner of the bank draft), interest-bearing notes, presents, china, household furnishings, and other things bought new and sold at a profit. Throughout the novel, she balances independence and feeling—after experiencing the effects of marital property laws in her first, disastrous marriage, she resists marriage for a long time in spite of her consciousness of sin.

Eventually, though, her conscience catches up with her. Back in London, she at first continues her successes, but then, as she gets older, now possessed of some means, she decides to live even more discreetly than she had been doing, with the help of her longtime maidservant and confidante, Amy. She moves to an obscure end of town, into the house of a Quaker lady. Many years have passed since Roxana gave up her children, and her oldest daughter now reappears, threatening to expose Roxana, but also, in some way, threatening to get close to her. The daughter is done away with by the maid (there is some ambiguity here about Roxana's role in the murder), and subsequently both Roxana and the maid lose everything, though this part of the story is not detailed. The novel turns out to be Roxana's confession.

Modern readers have admired the darkness of *Roxana* and its psychological, sociological, and economic astuteness, but it is by no means easy to understand exactly what Defoe is getting at. On the one hand, Roxana commits sins she regrets, but her downfall is not depicted in any detail, and her pleasure in her growing knowledge of the world and its ways is depicted with substantial satisfaction. Until the arrival of her grown daughter upon the scene, it does not appear that she will suffer—she is as prudent in her personal choices as she has been in her investments. Her daughter poses a dilemma that the ruthless maidservant solves for her—Roxana is passive rather than active in the murder. I think the best interpretation of the novel is that the part of it that would interest an author of, say, 1900—the dreadful psychological and phantasmagorical possibilities of the daughter's pursuit of her mother and the mother's guilty conscience—was not what interested the author of *Robinson Crusoe, Moll Flanders,* and *The Complete English Tradesman.* While he may have known he had a great idea, the novel itself hadn't progressed far enough for him to be able to exploit it. But nor had the theory and practice of women leading independent lives and having independent thoughts. In some sense, Roxana and Amy are good examples of characters getting out of the author's control and leading him into themes he is not prepared to fully explore. Defoe was once pilloried for his political writings. In *Roxana,* he is still taking risks.

11 · Samuel Richardson · Pamela; or, Virtue Rewarded
(1740; REPR., NEW YORK: PENGUIN, 1985), 538 PP.

Pamela illustrates several important features of the novel as a form as well as several turning points in the history of the English novel. Published in 1740, it was a sensation, went into several editions, and was rewritten for the stage in the way novels are sold to Hollywood today. Richardson, who had been a printer and stationer since 1720, published it under his own name, and writers all over London realized that they could earn money as novelists. Richardson not only followed *Pamela* with *Clarissa,* which was also a great success, and several other works, he also continued to revise and perfect *Pamela* until his death in 1761 at age seventy-three. The accepted modern edition is taken from the 1810 edition published by his daughters, including all of the emendations and corrections Richardson made in his lifetime.

Novels always reveal the traces of their original conception, and *Pamela* is a particularly good example of this. Richardson began to write a handbook of model letters in 1739, and a sequence he wrote for this book, letters from a servant girl to her father, grew into the plot we have—a fifteen-year-old waiting maid whose employer dies. She is then pursued and preyed upon by the son, who is a wealthy and powerful member of the landed gentry. She energetically preserves her virtue even to the last extremity—after he abducts her, imprisons her, and attempts to bribe her. He attacks her in her bed while his co-conspirator, a housekeeper he has employed, holds her hands. Pamela falls into a fit, Mr. B. feels remorse, and the rest of the novel is about his reformation. He eventually marries her, and then manages to reconcile his sister and neighbors to the marriage. Depicting models was clearly on Richardson's mind, and in the end he produced not model letters but model characters engaged in model behavior— Richardson wrote for money but he also wrote to educate, and in so doing helped elevate the form of the novel to respectable status in English literature in spite of the risqué nature of the subjects he chose (*Clarissa,* much longer, explores abduction and rape in even greater detail).

It is hard to like Pamela, because she is so obviously a Goody Two-shoes, but the reader simply cannot help getting used to her, and in the end all but the most obdurate are likely to come around, at least to accepting the principle that she deserves to get the guy, the money, and the estates, if not the adulation of everyone she meets. The reason the reader is won over is that she keeps reading, and the more she reads, the more familiar she becomes with the ins and outs of Pamela's reasoning, and in spite of all Pamela's self-praise, her reasoning is astute and complex and the reader can hardly get ahead of her. In addition, her dilemma is a significant one—Mr. B.'s attempts upon her virtue are wholehearted and unrelenting, and they are vividly portrayed. After an interval the reader may find tedious, during which he reforms himself, and Pamela's discourse is reduced to various forms of gratitude for his goodness and condescension, Mr. B.'s sister comes upon the scene and stages what is surely one of the most violent tantrums ever to grace classic literature. And then it turns out that the spoiled, willful manners of the upper classes are part of Richardson's subject matter, and the novel becomes a rather subversive piece of work. The desperation of Pamela's situation and the detail with which it is told work upon the reader's love of suspense, drawing the reader onward in spite of distaste for the tone or the characters, but then the experience itself of reading overcomes that distaste. Richardson's greatest risk—putting the novel in Pamela's voice—becomes the source of its success, because we end up feeling intimate with her in a way that third-person narration would not allow.

Richardson, like Defoe, was born into the artisan class, and he had the same respect as Defoe for hard work, enterprising spirit, self-worth grounded in religious belief, and independent thought. Like Defoe, he was not classically educated, and he had an outsider's view of the gentry. In the last quarter of the novel, when Mr. B. explains why he had never wanted to get married, Richardson shows a good understanding of developmental psychology, marital relations, and class consciousness. The way marriage is supposed to be—the wife obedient, the husband responsible, duties shared, and respect evident on both sides—is contrasted with the way marriage usually is: "the yawning husband, and the vapourish wife, are truly insupportable to one another; but separate, have freer spirits, and can be tolerable company" (p. 464). Richardson also believed in economic self-improvement— doing good and doing well. Like Defoe, he had a taste for psychology that grew out of the requirement that Nonconformists search their souls, and lives, for evidence of God's grace—right thinking and right acting would be rewarded by prosperity as well as ease of conscience. This is not the only way for an author to develop psychological understanding, but it does cause him to ruminate upon trains of cause and effect—how actions and psychology work together through time to create a character's fate (and build a plot). It is not that character is destiny, but that choices are destiny. Both Pamela and Roxana reflect constantly upon the consequences of wrong and right choices, in this world and in the hereafter. They do not consider Fate, for example, and so instead of illustrating, let's say, the workings of a tragic flaw, they model how to get through the day or the week. There is no tragic flaw—each choice that comes up offers the renewed chance of either salvation or damnation. This religion of the middle class, the self-made protagonist, stands in strong contrast to the pattern of aristocratic literature (notably the epic) that preceded it, in which the hero is the dupe of circumstances, and his only choice is the manner in which he meets his fate.

Novels grow, as *Pamela* so clearly illustrates. Richardson rewrote the novel so many times because his plot opened important and interesting themes that he continued to think about, and his thoughts (and perhaps criticisms from friends and fans) reminded him of bits of the story that could be made more plausible or smoother or funnier or clearer. This is a common event in novel-writing, though in our day and age, editors and publishers try to make sure that the novel finishes growing before it is printed. Perhaps it was not part of the author's original intention, for example, to discuss the proper education of gentlemen, and in fact for the first two-thirds of the novel, Mr. B. is an unsympathetic stick figure. It becomes clear, though, that for the sake of plausibility, he has to justify his decision to marry Pamela, and in so doing, he becomes more like her—willing to go on at length about his actions and motivations. Ostensibly he reveals himself, but in fact he is developing new facets of character as Richardson has to account for what he does.

Pamela, in spite of the tradition of abduction and rape in European literature, is implausible. What is the most implausible thing changes as the plot develops. Is it more implausible that Pamela would save herself? More implausible that Mr. B. would be so unrelenting? More implausible that he would want to marry her? More implausible that she would come to love him? More implausible that she would accept his love child from an earlier liaison? Every turn of the plot is implausible, but the detailed narration of *how* each event takes place lays to rest the issue of implausibility. The reader wants to find out what happens, so the reader accepts and goes on. Richardson reasons, persuades, almost numbs the reader, but the evidence of *Pamela*'s classic status shows that he does gain the reader's willing suspension of disbelief.

12 · Henry Fielding · The History of Tom Jones, a Foundling

ED. FREDSON BOWERS (1749; REPR., NEW YORK:

RANDOM HOUSE, MODERN LIBRARY, 1994), 982 PP.

Henry Fielding had been a playwright, but his theater was closed in 1737 by an act of Parliament in retaliation for his satirical attacks on the government of Prime Minister Robert Walpole. It was *Pamela* that inspired Fielding to try fiction. He thought Richardson's novel was so ridiculous that he lampooned it in *Shamela,* then expanded his parody in *Joseph Andrews,* which purported to be the history of Pamela's virtuous brother and Lady Booby, the sister of Mr. B. After the death of his beloved wife, Charlotte, though, Fielding decided to try his hand at something larger and more original with a central character, Sophia Western, inspired by Charlotte. His friend and patron, Ralph Allen, served as the inspiration for the virtuous Squire Allworthy.

Although Fielding was a famous and esteemed writer, *Tom Jones* exhibits complexity and generosity of character portrayal that is unprecedented in his other work, and it justly became a great English classic. We think of it as epitomizing the bawdy, bright energy of eighteenth-century England, contrasting strongly with the darker and more repressed passions of the Victorian period, and while *Tom Jones* is certainly exuberant, it, too, has its shadows and its subversive elements.

Two babies are born to the family of Squire Allworthy. One of these, Tom, is a foundling, apparently the abandoned child of a local girl, Jenny Jones, and the schoolmaster, Mr. Partridge. The other is the son of Mr. Allworthy's sister, Bridget, and her opportunist ne'er-do-well husband, Captain Blifil. Tom grows up good-natured and handsome, but impetuous and lusty. Blifil is far more careful, and it is made apparent to the reader, though not to Mr. Allworthy, that Blifil is a cold, opportunistic hypocrite, just like his father. As the boys near manhood, Tom falls for Sophia Western, the daughter of the neighboring landowner, and she for him, but their relations are complicated by his illegitimacy and by his prior attachment to Molly Seagrim, the daughter of Allworthy's gamekeeper. Tom is hated by Blifil and also by the tutors Allworthy has hired for the boys, Square (the philosopher) and Thwackum (the prelate), who agree on nothing else. Sophia's father, Squire Western, becomes convinced that Sophia is in love with Blifil, and sets his heart on the two of them marrying, which would allow him to join his estate with Allworthy's. When Sophia reveals that she hates Blifil, he confines her to her room and swears he will force the marriage. She escapes and flees to London. In the meantime, Blifil, Square, and Thwackum have engineered Tom's disinheritance, and Tom, too, is on the road.

Fielding is possibly the most intrusive (or second most, after Laurence Sterne) narrator in the history of the English novel. At the beginning of each book and frequently in the course of the rest of the novel, he breaks off the action to comment on artistic or philosophical or political questions, and many readers find this at least a little annoying. But much of Fielding's greatness lies in the qualities he displays in these sections, and to love *Tom Jones,* a reader has to accept and love the voice of the author/narrator (Fielding doesn't differentiate between the two). Tom himself is rather a shadowy character—a good, handsome protagonist and not much else; his dialogue is much more conventional and flowery than that of his author. His appeal is bolstered by Fielding's partisanship and affection, and by his open warmth in comparison to Blifil's sneakiness, but he has few endearing idiosyncrasies. Other characters—Squire Western, his sister, and even Sophia herself—are more vividly drawn, but Tom and Fielding partake of each other in the reader's mind, and I think it is fair to consider Fielding an older and more worldly version of the hero without imputing too much autobiography to the novel.

Tom's journey is what Sterne would have called "Cervantick." In the course of his adventures, he gets into farcical imbroglios at inns, meets various characters who tell him enlightening tales, and becomes temporarily entangled with the army, which happens to have been called up to pursue the ongoing eighteenth-century skirmishes between the Jacobite Catholics and the Hanoverian Protestants (the Battle of Culloden, in which the forces of the Stuart pretender were defeated at Inverness by the duke of Cumberland, a son of George II, took place in April 1746). Fielding is so careful to place the action of the novel in contemporary times that it is likely he used an almanac to make sure he was accurate about the phases of the moon during the action of the novel.

Sophia's journey is the more compelling because it raises the more interesting questions. The reader knows absolutely that Sophia cannot and must not be forced to marry Blifil, because not only does she hate him, the author despises him as well. Nevertheless, her course of action is a moral minefield, because she has to assert herself, but cannot appear to be unfeminine or unvirtuous. The novel is peopled with women who are unable to achieve the proper balance—Miss Western, Sophia's aunt, is portrayed as a good-hearted and strong-willed but laughable spinster whose ignorance is dressed up in military analogies that she gets from her preferred reading of political and military subjects. Lady Bellaston, who seduces Tom when he gets to London, is a hardened courtesan. Sophia's cousin, Mrs. Fitzpatrick, has made the mistake of marrying unhappily and against the wishes of her family, and is destined to end up like Lady Bellaston, if she is lucky. Jenny Jones (Mrs. Waters, whom Tom meets on the road) is kind-hearted and intelligent, but also of low repute, since she lives with men she is not married to. There are only two possible choices for Sophia—to live with her father as a spinster and tend to his needs, or to marry the man she loves, with her father's consent. For most of the novel, both of these choices are impossible. Once Sophia is discovered in London, too, Lady Bellaston and Miss Western collude to force her to marry Lord Fellamar, who attempts to rape her upon the advice of Lady Bellaston—if he does rape her, she will have to marry him, should he be willing to marry his own whore, which he is.

Sophia's own notions of love are considered naive and even dangerous by all of the female characters because, though Fielding does not
say so, should they become universal, they would subvert the property
arrangements that English marriage is founded upon. As with most
other English novels, the only comic solution is the merger of love and
money. Of course, Fielding solves the puzzle—his robust, ironic style
foreshadows that he will.

Much of the plot of *Tom Jones* is designed to solve the riddle of
Sophia's affections and to make Tom worthy of her hand, both as a
man and as a property-holder, but Sophia must save herself without
losing her feminine nature, and she does so by being the immovable
object rather than the irresistable force—her cousin, Mrs. Fitzpatrick,
demonstrates the dangers of acting on her own wishes as opposed to
simply resisting the untoward wishes of others. Nightingale, whom
Tom meets in London, is Mrs. Fitzpatrick's male counterpart—a
young man who seduces a poor young woman and then must be cajoled into marrying her by Tom in the teeth of the resistance of his relatives, and even of his own resistence; he can't imagine what he is
going to do to earn a living if his father disinherits him. Ultimately his
father is persuaded not to disinherit him.

The Fielding question—how can the young people be married off
according to their affections?—turns out to have a rather revolutionary answer: the property-owning parental class must go along with the
inclinations of their offspring, even if the result is mixing of classes and
dilution of assets. The real aristocracy is of the heart and the mind—
much the same conclusion Richardson comes to in *Pamela*. Such is the
gist of *Tom Jones,* the story. As a social document, though, *The History
of Tom Jones, a Foundling,* details the contingent nature of this solution
compared with the vast inequities and immoralities surrounding the
exceptional and blessed central characters. Fielding's narrative tone is
generous, comic, and evenhanded, but his depiction implicitly suggests
that the main difficulties do not reside in human nature but in social
arrangements. Charles Dickens, a more explicitly revolutionary novelist, loved this eighteenth-century predecessor, and no doubt partly for
this reason—Fielding was alive to the idea that social circumstances
could be changed, though he wasn't prepared to suggest wholesale
solutions.

13 · Charlotte Lennox · The Female Quixote

(1752; REPR., NEW YORK: OXFORD UNIVERSITY PRESS, 1998), 383 PP.

The Female Quixote is not about a woman who sets out on a series of adventures with her faithful companion, but about a young girl of aristocratic English parentage who grows up on a secluded estate reading romances, and who takes all her ideas of romance and valor from them. When she comes into contact with mid-eighteenth-century society, her misapprehensions and predilections are startling and disturbing to those she meets, and inconvenient, and even dangerous, to herself, but she persists in them until she is disabused through a lengthy discussion with a learned doctor (possibly modeled on Samuel Johnson).

The Female Quixote, not nearly as famous as *Tom Jones* or *Pamela,* and not, indeed, part of the eighteenth-century canon, except to specialists, is both entertaining and instructive as a work and as a historical document. Charlotte Lennox was a contemporary of Johnson and Samuel Richardson's, who collaborated to help her both write and publish this novel before she was, according to Richardson, yet twenty-four years old. At that point she was already married, widely traveled, and the author of another novel, *The Life of Harriot Stuart.* She went on to write several more novels, but none as popular as *The Female Quixote.*

Like the Cervantes original, the Lennox novel is intended to be comic—to portray the ludicrous effects of an improper education upon a susceptible mind, and like Don Quixote, Arabella, Lennox's protagonist, is entirely estimable apart from her fixation on stories of passion, romance, and war (not the same stories as Quixote enjoyed, but French romances ostensibly set in ancient times though written in the seventeenth century by de Scudéry and La Calprenède).

As with *Don Quixote,* as the story grows, its comic aspects darken and soften, the natural result of prolonged acquaintance with the protagonist. The author's effort to sustain the ridiculous aspects of Arabella's psyche while not losing the reader's sympathy inevitably presents some challenges, but Lennox approaches them cleverly. The first of these is that Arabella, like Quixote, is rude, disputatious, and occasionally aggressive. The novel is a social form—the reader relates to characters as she would to acquaintances—and one of the paradoxes of the novel is that social faults can be more off-putting to readers than moral faults, at least at first. But as in life, the reader takes her cue from others around the protagonist, and in this case, the fact that the sensible Mr. Glanville, Arabella's cousin, finds her appealing and genuine (though he is frequently, and most plausibly, irritated and upset by her ideas) excuses her enough for the reader to go on with her. In addition, Lennox contrasts Arabella with her much more typical cousin, Charlotte, who is more realistic, but also small-minded and shallow. Also, Lennox never allows Arabella to seem entirely in the wrong. Sometimes she comes up with a reasonable rationale for her actions; at other times it is she who is most harmed by her actions, and at still other times we see that at least her actions stem from honorable and generous motives. Her variety keeps her interesting (though I have to admit that the balance isn't perfectly maintained, and Arabella gets tedious from time to time). Lennox is also careful to locate the comedy in the characters around her—a very sophisticated choice for so youthful an artist. Arabella voices absurdities, but the reader doesn't laugh until her relatives and friends react to them. This device is frequently used in movies, when, for example, one character does something and another does a double take, thereby opening up the distance between the action and its meaning that comic perspective requires.

The perennial problem of a novel in which a character is deluded is how to believably undelude him or her, and what comes after that. This is a problem natural to the novel, since the novel is always about whether and how particular individuals fit into their social milieu. Cervantes offers one solution to this problem: Don Quixote is defeated and then falls ill. He wakes up sane but then dies, having no reason to live anymore. Arabella, too, suffers physically (she nearly drowns), but upon recovery, she has a long discussion with the Samuel Johnson–like figure, who appeals to her intelligence with reasoned arguments. She repudiates her former reading, marries Glanville, and lives happily ever after, because, really, all along, her motives were of the best. Some readers accept this ending and some don't, but appealing to her reason makes sense partly because she is always using logical arguments, though based on false authorities and strange premises, and also because it is a tack that none of the other characters has tried. The doctor appeals to her intelligence, where the others have appealed only to her sense of propriety or self-love.

Arabella's delusions are interesting, also, as part of the continuing novelistic discussion of the status and rights of women. To her contemporaries, her fears of being made love to, or raped and kidnapped, make no sense. Charlotte and the other female characters like being made love to, and don't fear being "carried away"; their greater concern is to appear more innocent than they are. This is certainly because they live in a safer world than the world of *The Heptameron*. The underground river of the French romance has carried medieval conflicts between love and virtue, honor and power into the mundane modern world of eighteenth-century England, where they still have enough ambiguity to compel a great deal of interest. Arabella's dilemma (will she marry as the dictates of her father and property demand, or will she pursue her own course?) is the same old dilemma, though benignly rendered in this case. What to do with the girls is the perennial dilemma of the novel, sometimes given first place, sometimes given second place, but clearly a preoccupation of European life in every country and in every era. Where do Lennox's own sympathies lie? The ending to *The Female Quixote* is not well developed (evidence is that she had too much material for two volumes but not enough for three and decided to wind things up as quickly as she could), but it does give a clue that the enterprising Lennox, who had sufficient talent and wit to interest the greatest literary men of her day, thought that including women in the discussion of their own lives and fates was at the very least an excellent place to start.

14 · Laurence Sterne · The Life and Opinions of Tristram Shandy, Gentleman

ED. MELVYN NEW AND JOAN NEW

(1759–67; REPR., NEW YORK: PENGUIN BOOKS, 1997), 543 PP.

Tristram Shandy may be the most masculine novel ever written. Sterne was a middle-aged, long unhappily married clergyman when he began his novel, and he seems to have had no interest in the marriage dilemmas of young people. His novel is comic, or at least funny, but dispenses entirely with comic structure as borrowed from plays—there is no happy ending, symbolized by a series of weddings, and what is really of interest is not marriage and money but the interplay of the individual mind with its circumstances. The novel's sources are in sermons, scientific and philosophical treatises, military histories, anecdotes, and conversation. It was conceived and carried out as a serial work, rather like a set of sermons, and was, from first publication, a sensation that Sterne strove hard for the rest of his life to keep alive. It was highly esteemed by twentieth-century critics and writers, who much appreciated the novel's complexity and self-consciousness.

Explanatory notes in the Penguin edition run to 130 pages of small type, and even so are not enough. The reader may be forgiven for not fully understanding the novel, because it is not only replete with obscure references and written in a highly and even aggressively non-linear style, it also takes shame as its theme, and explores it by means of blank pages, unclear allusions, and information implied but stated only through series of asterisks.

The novel opens with the conception of Tristram, and the joke/tragedy is that just as Tristram's father, Walter, is climaxing, Tristram's mother asks him if he has remembered to wind the clock, thus distracting him and scattering "the animal spirits, whose business it was to have escorted and gone hand-in-hand with the HOMUNCULUS, and conducted him safe to the place destined for his reception." Walter, his brother Toby, and Toby's man, Trim, are the main characters of the novel. Walter is a philosopher and autodidact with many cherished and eccentric notions. Toby is a veteran of campaigns of the early eighteenth century on the European continent and has suffered a mysterious and debilitating wound in his groin. Trim, too, is a wounded veteran. The two brothers live near one another, and Toby and Trim occupy themselves by reproducing in miniature, on the bowling green of Toby's estate, the battles and sieges they read about in the newspapers. Although all three men and the other male characters (Dr. Slop and Yorick the curate) consider themselves worldly and up to date, all are, in fact, figures of radical and irredeemable innocence, especially in contrast to the female characters, Mrs. Shandy, Susannah, the midwife, and the widow Wadman, who ignore ideas in favor of practicalities and represent the workings of ignorant, or perhaps natural, chance in the formation of Tristram.

Tristram is undone by four events: his mother's inopportune question, the crushing of his nose at birth, Susannah's failure to remember the proper name ("Trismegistus") at the christening, and Susannah's suggestion that instead of peeing in the chamber pot, the young boy simply pee out the window. Unfortunately, the window sash falls just at that moment, causing an unexpected circumcision. But it may also be that Tristram is undone, not by the events themselves, but by Walter's convictions that such details are formative for the character and the fate of the child, and so the novel repeatedly poses this dilemma: is it the events themselves or the interpretation of them that dictates their outcome?

As the novel progresses, Uncle Toby becomes more and more the central character, and the last volume depicts his wooing by a neighbor, widow Wadman. Widow Wadman loves Toby and is not herself unattractive, but before she accepts his proposal, she very much wants to know the nature and effects of the wound in his groin. Toby has had so little to do with women that he seems not to understand the facts of life. When Trim reveals to him what the widow wants to know and why, he is overwhelmed, though delicately so, by a sense of shame that is fatal to his continued affections, and that is that for the widow Wadman.

Sterne's theme of shame is strongly linked to the overt display of masculinity. Toby and Trim are hobbyists of war, embracing the very activity that injured them. At a gathering where clergymen are debating a point of doctrine, another entirely masculine activity, a hot roast chestnut drops into the open fly of one of them, who attributes his injury to Yorick's malice. Later, when Trim is disporting himself with widow Wadman's cook on one of Toby's model bridges, the bridge collapses and reinjures Trim's knee. In other words, all of Sterne's men live in a world where male activities present a constant and immediate danger of injury or embarrassment to masculinity itself. Women either do not notice or haven't the intellect to appreciate this. The efforts of Walter, in particular, to forestall these dangers are unavailing: he suffers the death of his elder son, Bobby, and the strange fate (not entirely disclosed) of his younger son, Tristram, in spite of his carefully thought-out system, which includes the composition of "Tristra-paedia," his work on educating his son, which so distracts him from Tristram himself that the boy is left too long in the hands of the women.

Bawdiness is the inevitable accompaniment of Sterne's theme of manly shame, but it is the bawdiness of privacy and innuendo rather than the openly tawdry, realistic, cultural bawdiness of Fielding, Defoe, and Richardson. Each of these great eighteenth-century writers takes up the overt sexuality of the period and addresses it in a different way—for Defoe the issue is guilt; for Fielding, social decay; for Richardson, individual worth as against social power; and for Sterne, the unavoidable and unrelieved experience of shame, thus his appeal to the twentieth century, which also was interested in and sensitive to the workings of shame.

Tristram Shandy also reminds us that the novel was not invented as a page-turner—in some sense this novel was not even invented as a novel, since Sterne wrote later volumes that were outside the original plan as a way of prolonging his success—plot is minimal here, and style is the organizing principle. But suspense is only a contingent virtue of the novel, not a necessary one; *Tristram Shandy* is often charming and even profound, and while reading it, if she is in the mood, the reader may not care at all that it is not compellingly told as a story. Reading *Tristram Shandy* feels like eavesdropping on a truly unique sensibility in a truly intimate way.

15 · Voltaire · Candide

(1759; REPR., NEW YORK: W. W. NORTON, 1991, 1966), 60 PP.

Every novel is a social document in prose with something wrong with it, but not every social document in prose with something wrong with it is a novel. *Candide,* in some ways a profound and influential piece of philosophical fiction, is not a novel, but illustrates by contrast some characteristic features of the real novel. Maybe the closest relative to *Candide* that we have already discussed is *Lazarillo de Tormes.* The one we haven't discussed is Rabelais's *Gargantua and Pantagruel* (1542), a piece of work so masculine and French that I find it unreadable. Like Lazarillo and Pantagruel, Candide is forced to go out into the world. Like the previous two, the requirement suits him because he is interested to discover the nature of the world. In this he differs from Don Quixote, who thinks that he already knows the nature of the world and plans to redeem it by doing knightly deeds. The world Candide finds is Uncle Toby's world, strangely darkened, a world of endless wars and battles, less the scene of military pattern and strategy than the scene of pointless destruction and torment. In this world, though, there is no Shandy Hall, a safe haven where theories are spun out of predilections and affections. There is only chaos and accident. The goal of the characters is to make sense of the world; the goal of the author is to show that sense cannot be made of it.

In this regard, it is interesting to contrast Voltaire with English novelists writing at the same time. Voltaire was a wealthy and influential man who created and lived upon a great estate just inside France, near the Swiss border (when he got into political trouble with the king of France, he could cross into Switzerland). He lived to a great age, surrounded by friends and relatives, apparently in good health (owing to an abstemious diet). Yet his view of life is far darker than that of Fielding, Sterne, and Smollett (see below), who were plagued by financial troubles and ill health, who died young, and yet give us worlds of great beauty that are shadowed by darker events but not dominated by them.

A novel starts with an action or an event; *Candide* begins with a premise—that all things are for the best in this best of all possible worlds. It is the raison d'être of the characters Candide, Pangloss (Candide's tutor), Cunégonde (Candide's beloved), and their friends to test this premise, and it is immediately found wanting—in the first few pages of the book, Candide is kicked out of his home, the castle is invaded by enemies, Cunégonde is raped and killed, and Dr. Pangloss contracts a venereal disease that maims and disfigures him. No effort is made to render these events with any texture; the reader is not asked to empathize with the characters (that is, imagine their experience of things), only to observe and marvel. The characters themselves hardly suffer. Even though they lose parts of themselves, are bereft of loved ones, watch the sufferings of others, are injured, robbed, endangered, betrayed, enslaved, and isolated from all they know, they are always resilient enough to survive, to tell their stories, and to speculate about how their stories fit into the larger scheme of things. The world Candide travels through is a world of godless chaos and suffering. It is, in many ways, suddenly the modern secular world of huge energies wasted in pointless conflict. Voltaire's essential point is that the world is not the result of intelligent design, and certainly not the object of care and scrutiny by a higher power (Voltaire was famous for his atheism and anticlerical views). His quick pace and broad scope depersonalize every incident, and the narrative achieves a vertiginous effect—the point of view is so distant from the characters that every feeling they have, from hope to despair, from love to vengefulness, is simply evidence of folly. In sixty pages Voltaire does not take the time to develop scenes, characters, or even conversations; he is far more interested in giving the illusion of great distances traveled and great events witnessed. But in the end, the very resilience of the characters goes to support Pangloss's contention rather than contradict it—even though things have not turned out as Candide expected them to when he still lived in the castle of Thunder-ten-Tronckh, he is married to Cunégonde and he lives in comfort with his friends at his estate near Constantinople, where he tends his own garden. The necessities of a story (that we end with the same characters we begin with) undermine the philosophical assertion that the torrent of incidents seems to illustrate.

In fact, prose narratives of a certain length with something wrong with them do not lend themselves to being used as philosophical proofs. They are too transparent; it is too easy for the reader to see that the writer is setting up the story to demonstrate what he already supposes rather than to investigate some significant unknown question. Because it is a narrative, the novel is inescapably subjective. Every word that the writer chooses, every manner in which he constructs a sentence bears witness to the subjectivity of his argument. The power a novelist brings to his argument is never objective information or the power of reason (though intelligence illuminates lots of novels), it is always the power of emotion—the reader feels what the characters are feeling, so she accepts their point of view as true. Every fictive argument must be circular, because all its attempts at objectivity are false.

Candide is an eloquent social document testifying to the spiritual and humanitarian failures of European colonial exploration and settlement. It is as harsh in its representation of Europe's export of its own troubled culture as any twentieth-century revolutionary tract could be. It represents the world as polluted and destroyed by greed, cruelty, social inequity, and blindness. Everywhere Candide goes, Europeans have already been there and wrecked it, or else the natives (as in El Dorado) have taken precautions to protect themselves. Much of *Candide* has the ring of truth. In addition, of course, it is representative of its period—the eighteenth-century French Enlightenment—in its anticlerical and in many ways humanistic ideas, as well as in its cynicism. I read it first as an assignment in ninth grade and didn't understand a word of it, though many of the images of suffering and disfigurement shocked me and stuck in my mind. Perhaps schools assign it because it is short and full of action, but it is not a novel because the "agon" is missing from the "protagonist"—Candide acts but he has no inner life that invites us to empathize or sympathize with him. *Candide* exists alongside the novel as a separate form of discourse, succeeding in making its philosophical arguments only to the degree that it gives up being a novel.

16 · Tobias Smollett · The Expedition of Humphry Clinker

(1771; REPR., NEW YORK: W. W. NORTON, 1983), 336 PP.

Now mostly unread, Tobias Smollett was a famous writer in his day, the author of five well-received novels and many volumes of historical and political commentary. Like Defoe and Fielding, he was first a polemicist and only later a novelist. Unlike Defoe and Fielding, Smollett was born in Scotland and trained at the University of Edinburgh to be a doctor. He was regularly referred to by his contemporaries as "Dr. Smollett." In the eighteenth century, Scotland and the University of Glasgow were the home of what was known as "Scottish Empiricism"—a philosophical and scientific school of thought that has been highly influential in shaping the modern world around objectivity, pragmatism, and systematic observation. Its most famous product, of course, was Adam Smith, author of *The Wealth of Nations*. Dr. Smollett was well known for being crusty and Scottish and skeptical, and one thing that differentiates *Humphry Clinker* from most comic English novels is that it doesn't make the resolution of the gentle young lovers' romance the sole end of the plot, but accords it a rather small proportion of the narrative, setting it into the context of the differing concerns of other characters, who all have their own intentions, plans, and learning tasks. It therefore has considerable crusty and skeptical mature appeal.

A family sets out upon a long journey. The principals are Matthew Bramble, a country squire in Wales; his sister Tabitha, a spinster of about forty-five; their nephew, Jery, who has just left Oxford and is considering his career; their niece, Lydia, who has left her school and is in love with an unsuitable young man; and Tabitha's maid, Win, somewhat older than Lydia, along to take care of Tabitha. The ostensible purpose of the journey is to take the waters of various spas in an effort to relieve Matthew's ills, which seem to be digestive. Their longest sojourns are in Bath, London, Yorkshire, and Edinburgh, but there are plenty of stops in between. Each of the five writes letters to someone at home, and these letters constitute the text of the novel. Humphry is a character they encounter on the way, who links up with their family in a surprising plot twist.

The greatness of Smollett's novel is in the simplicity of his formal idea. Each writer has his or her own concerns, his or her own style, and his or her own observations. The five sets of letters work together to progress the strands of the plot and to comment upon the various scenes the travelers encounter. Most of the adventures are told from more than a single point of view, and the effect is to reduce the dominance of the narrator and create the illusion of a more inclusive and various world through which all travel together, no one's opinions taking precedence over those of the others. This, of course, is in striking contrast to both Fielding and Sterne. Smollett is no less than they a man of strong opinions and partisan feelings, but his polemical purpose is forwarded indirectly, by his molding of the plot and his depiction of what his narrators see and do, rather than by assertions of a strong narrator. The result is wonderfully sophisticated and almost modern—and as an exponent of a school of thought that has come to dominate the way we see the world, Smollett seems less dated to us than his contemporaries.

Humphry Clinker's complexity works by seeming simple; its profundity works by seeming mundane. The characters tell their stories and express their opinions, while the author constructs the relationships between the themes and the motifs in the background, there to be understood by the astute reader but not forced upon her. The novel seems to be an entertaining story or a typical eighteenth-century travel narrative, but really it is, among other things, a story of spiritual redemption and reconciliation, a story of the re-creation of the pastoral order and of the right order of society. It takes up the same question as *Candide*—how can we understand the world and how can we live in it?—and it gives a similar but better worked-out answer: cultivate the estates we are given, avoid ambition and luxury, and enter into relationships with those who are given us to love, even if they are not very appealing. Smollett successfully solves the paradox of the novel form—how can the specific lives of ordinary characters represent the commonality of human life, both as it's lived in society and as it's lived subjectively? The adventures the characters have on their expedition add up to maps of the inner world and of the outer world—every episode is both plausible and meaningful. But by contrast to *Candide,* many of the episodes are routine—at one point, Matthew's rest is disturbed by some men who are playing musical instruments on the staircase of his boardinghouse. At another, he is mistakenly saved from drowning by Humphry, who interprets Matthew's gasp at the frigidity of the sea as a cry for help. At another point, Humphry catches sight of Win's bare buttocks as she is climbing down a ladder, escaping a fire, and falls in love with her. Every incident is plausible and funny and realistic, which is no doubt why some readers thought Smollett was the funniest writer of his day. But his jokes are subtle, inviting laughter rather than demanding it.

Humphry Clinker was Smollett's last novel, and like all mature work, it was written with the instinctive knowledge that the author no longer had to force it—that his style naturally expressed his views, and that it could do so with artless subtlety. It is not so much that the writer now trusts the reader to be alert to every word and intention, more that he now truly knows what he wants to say and how to say it—he no longer has to say it twice for it to be clear to himself. Additionally, Smollett's novel is forgiving and open-hearted. The ridiculous figures have their say and their achievement of self-knowledge just as the attractive figures do. Baser human motivations are forgiven—when Matthew's sister, Tabby, finds a man to marry her, the fact that both are marrying for practical as well as romantic reasons is acknowledged. After the triple wedding, in a moment possibly unique in English fiction, Smollett remarks (in the voice of Jery) upon the physical evidence that each character has enjoyed the sexual connection with his or her new spouse—the gentle lovers with their eyes, the middle-aged couple through attentive and exuberant behavior, and Humphry (illegitimate) and Win (a maid), through words (Humphry says, "For what we have received, Lord make us thankful"). Such an acknowledgment of the joys—and godliness—of sexuality combines with the usual English sentiment at the end of a comic novel that at last the money and the love are brought together to add an unusually humane strand to the history of English narrative.

Another feature of *Humphry Clinker* worth remarking upon is that it really does work as a reliable social document. Because Bramble and Jery (and, of course, the author) are interested in the world they travel through and are observant (at the University of Edinburgh, Dr. Smollett would have been trained to be particular and systematic in his observations), there is a great deal in the novel about how people lived in eighteenth-century Britain. Matthew discourses on architecture, medicine, politics, society, customs, modes of travel, and much else. To an American it is particularly interesting to note that while you could read Fielding, Richardson, and Sterne and never know that the North American colonies existed, Smollett makes one of his most interesting characters a man who has been to America, has been captured and scalped by the Indians, and is planning to return there.

17 · Choderlos de Laclos · Les Liaisons dangereuses

TRANS. P. W. K. STONE (1781; REPR., NEW YORK: PENGUIN, 1961), 393 PP.

When Laclos conceived *Les Liaisons dangereuses,* he wanted to create a sensation, and when he published it, he succeeded. It was a great *succès du scandale* and sold many copies. Some twenty years after Laclos himself died in the Napoleonic Wars (1802), the novel was tried in a criminal court, condemned, and burned. Laclos, by the way, married at forty-six and later became known for his life of conventional family happiness.

The premise of the novel is that two experienced libertines, the vicomte de Valmont and the marquise de Merteuil, set out to manipulate the relationships of several of their associates, both for fun and for revenge. The marquise wishes to get back at a former lover by compromising his intended bride, and Valmont wishes to seduce a legendarily virtuous woman merely to exercise his powers. The tangle of intrigue and deception that ensues leaves two dead, one in a convent, one disgraced, and one in exile. That Valmont and Merteuil will succeed in their seductions is never really in doubt, so one problem of the novel is lack of suspense, but the compensation is the intricacy of the arguments each character puts forth to support his or her position and the complex psychology of each of the intersecting relationships.

Like *Humphry Clinker, Les Liaisons dangereuses* is composed of letters written during several months by different characters, though the recipients of these letters are also these characters (the recipients of the Smollett letters do not figure in the plot of that novel). The letters therefore not only report events and comment on them, they also precipitate events. The characters' secret intentions and the forms of polite discourse of the era dictate that much of what the letters communicate is insincere or exaggerated, but Laclos is superb at juxtaposing letters to reveal layers of deception and imply the deeper story (or not—the true feelings, especially, of Valmont are enticingly myste-rious; perhaps he is the heartless libertine that he purports to be in his letters to the marquise, perhaps he truly loves the présidente de Tourvel beyond his expectations and is ashamed of how he has treated her and is glad to die in the end). The reader has only clues to any interpretation. The mysteries surrounding the marquise are fewer and less interesting, but the main ones are: Does she really love the vicomte from the beginning? Is the whole plot simply a way to win him back? Is her cool manner simply a coquettish cover?

Both Valmont and the marquise seem to be respected members of society, and they live in accordance with the self-contradictory prin-ciples laid down in *The Heptameron*. Indeed, Valmont might be quot-ing the assembled party of the earlier work when he writes, "I know a hundred, a thousand ways of robbing a woman of her reputation; but whenever I have tried to think how she might save herself, I have never been able to think of a single possibility." Then he adds, "You yourself . . . whose strategy is masterly, have triumphed a hundred times . . . more through good luck than good judgment." The mar-quise sets out her ideas and strategies in another long letter that also may be considered a response to the untenable position of women in a society where men feel obliged to prey upon their bodies and feelings in every way they can and then to humiliate them. Her method is to set up scenarios where any sort of subsequent gossip by the man is so implausible in the context of the woman's reputation for virtue that he dare not say anything. She has trained herself to hide every feeling and manipulate every circumstance—she demonstrates her methods with a man Valmont meets in society and dislikes. As a result of her plot, he is thrown in prison and socially destroyed.

Valmont and the marquise are certainly unsympathetic characters, but through the reader's continuous exposure to how they think, they achieve a certain appeal. They are not, perhaps, the most intelligent people in their circle, but they are the most rational in that they dis-count all emotions even as they are feeling them, and they recognize that the society they live in is merciless but also the only one they value. The portrait their letters paint is convincing (especially in light of what else we have read of the pre-Revolutionary French aristocracy). Ad-ditionally, the world they live in is not unrecognizable. French lit-erature from *The Heptameron* through Zola is continuous—nasty people motivated by greed, selfishness, lust, and schadenfreude doing nasty things with wit but no good nature, corrosively honest except in personal relationships, where secrecy and deceit rule. It is hard to know whether Laclos's avowed intention to create a stir is the intention of all French novelists, but while English novels, especially eighteenth- and nineteenth-century ones, depict an England that is perhaps more appealing than England truly was, French novels depict a nation of vipers. One can only hope that for all that French novelists present themselves as social documentarians, they were actually just trying to make money.

18 · The Marquis de Sade · Justine

(1791; REPR., NEW YORK: GROVE PRESS, 1965), 290 PP.

In the context of *Pamela, Tom Jones,* and *Candide, Justine* is eminently recognizable. A young girl is left without protectors in the world. She embarks upon a forced journey, seeking asylum and some means to support herself. Like Pamela, Cunegonde, and Sophia Western, she is betrayed by those she trusts and whose job is to protect her. She is raped or threatened with rape. Many of those she meets are happy to sell her to the rich and powerful. Her task is to preserve her virtue and her life, or, if she can't, to develop some sort of worldview that accounts for her choice to accept what has happened to her or not to accept it and die. To the question of whether a woman is to be allowed to be an agent and live freely, de Sade answers, "Only if she is willing to abide by the chaotic system of exploit or be exploited that is the rule of modern life." His answer is not different from the answers of the other authors, only more extreme. Several women characters do manage to prosper, at least temporarily, but to do so, they not only give up their sexual virtue, they also commit arson, infanticide, and murder; they steal, betray, and destroy out of necessity and gratuitously. The men characters generally not only survive but get wealthier and more powerful—the young count who murders his aunt for the inheritance becomes wealthy beyond his dreams; the doctor who dissects his living daughter after raping her repeatedly becomes a respected government official; the monk who is the torturer and murderer of uncounted abducted girls is made head of the entire Benedictine order. Justine, whose only desires are to keep her virtue and find something useful to do, is condemned to go from one enslavement to another, until, at last having disburdened herself of her story, she is killed by a bolt of lightning.

De Sade relates all of Justine's torments in a tone of excited, sentimental relish, as, for example, when Justine witnesses the torture of a younger girl at the monastery: "Rodin contemplates . . . his inflamed eye roves, his hands dare profane the flowers his cruelties are about to wither; it all takes place directly before us, not a detail can escape us: now the libertine opens and peers into, now he closes up again those dainty features which enchant him" (p. 537). Such incidents alternate with cool discussions about her fate that Justine has with almost all of her tormentors—for example, the count of a remote château. His particular fetish is bloodletting. Justine's job becomes taking care of his fourth young wife as he prepares to murder her. He remarks to Justine (who is traveling under the name Thérèse), "How are you justified, pray tell me, Thérèse, in asserting that a husband lies under the obligation to make his wife happy? and what titles dares this woman cite in order to extort this happiness from her husband?" (p. 645).

Nevertheless, *Justine* (Rousseau declared that any girl who read a single page of the novel would be lost) is not nihilistic. The key to the novel is that since Justine's world is entirely without fellow feeling, what happens to her is impersonal. People do not betray her and torture her out of personal enmity or malignity, they do so because they feel no connection to her or to anyone else. Justine becomes a little ridiculous because she is always throwing herself upon the mercy of men who have tortured her in the past, but she does so because her psychology is the virtuous mirror of their vice—she cannot unlearn the sense of common humanity that they cannot learn. It can hardly be said that virtue triumphs at the end of *Justine,* or even that Justine attains a Voltairean truce with the world. But one character does point out that given the world they both inhabit, the fact that she is still alive, vigorous, and virtuous (as opposed to virginal) is something to be grateful for, almost a sign of having been among the elect. Justine and some of the other destroyed women characters retain their sense of who they are and what they believe to the end of their lives—examples of the inability of Sadist culture to annihilate all humanity in spite of its enormous power. Justine never betrays herself; her mind is never changed; the sympathy of the reader is never lost.

It is indeed true that Justine's adventures are told very graphically, but what is more shocking about them than the acts committed is that they offer repeated and insistent evidence of the absence of any feeling of shared humanity in the world of pre-Revolutionary France. Justine's torturers (a gang of thieves, a young count, a group of monks, a counterfeiter, a doctor, a financier, and others) constitute a catalog of the French ruling class and of masculine power. Everyone Justine meets is more than without pity—is, rather, actively cruel, vicious, deceitful, selfish, and cold. When they exercise their intelligence and imagination, they do so only to invent more perfect methods of torture, that either cause more pain or cause pain to more women. Men are not shown as being capable of feeling pain or of empathizing with the pain of women. Had *Justine* been written by a woman, it could well have functioned as a revolutionary political document, a real man-hating polemic, but the context of de Sade's other writings casts ambiguity over his intentions for what seems to have been his favorite novel.

As a social document, *Justine* perhaps helps explain the chaotic violence of the French Revolution and is thus an important book for students of European history. It portrays as a given the absolute selfish corruption of an entire society and foretells certain attitudes that have become features of modern life—the idea that destructive acts are part of the natural order, the idea that the winnowing out of the weak is positive (the free market, anyone?), the idea that certain populations are expendable because they produce nothing the society wants, the idea that because customs differ from country to country, all virtues and vices are relative. *Justine* is as full of argument as graphic violence. In fact, one of the charms Justine has for her tormentors is her persistent desire to convince them of the error of their ways. There is an odd psychological truth to this—they not only want to exercise power, they also want to view themselves as right. Justine's many debates with her captors give the novel much of its formal sophistication, because through their voices and arguments, Justine's tormentors become characters rather than figures.

The marquis de Sade was a contradictory man, as most authors are. He was not as isolated or powerful or wealthy as the male characters of *Justine*. Nor does he seem to have been as impervious to the claims of virtue, since the woman to whom he dedicated *Justine* seems to have been a long-term companion with a reputation for virtue that de Sade acknowledged in several letters as well as in his dedication. Authors often fail to live up to their narrative personae—de Sade seems to have aspired to a purity of viciousness as others have aspired to wit or charm or benevolence.

19 · Sir Walter Scott · The Tale of Old Mortality

(1816; REPR., NEW YORK: OXFORD UNIVERSITY PRESS, 1999), 353 PP.

The night before he fights the climactic duel in *A Hero of Our Time* (see below), Pechorin, Lermontov's protagonist, picks up a novel to while away the time. He writes, "It was Walter Scott's *Old Mortality.* At first it was an effort to read, but I was soon carried away by the magic of the tale. The Scottish bard must surely be rewarded in heaven for every moment of pleasure given by his book." This excellent review is the least ironic and most wholehearted remark the embittered Romantic Pechorin makes.

The Tale of Old Mortality is part of Scott's tetralogy of novels about the history of Scotland in the seventeenth century, one for each of the four regions of the country—the Borders, the Highlands, the West, and Fife. *The Tale of Old Mortality,* the second of the four, concerns the 1679 insurrection of the Presbyterian Scottish Calvinists against King Charles II of England and Scotland. The first three-quarters of the book follows the fates of several characters caught up in the conflict— Henry Morton, a young moderate Protestant; the woman he loves (Edith), who is the daughter of royalist aristocrats; Henry's rival Lord Evandale, also a royalist; a career soldier, Claverhouse, who commands the regular troops; and a career rebel, Balfour, who initiates the action by murdering the archbishop of St. Andrews. Although the historical event is of minor importance, and the love story a bit perfunctory, *Old Mortality* is insistently compelling for the depth and complexity of Scott's understanding of the personal and political implications of the rebellion and for the psychological astuteness with which he draws the characters. It also resonates with events at the beginning of the twenty-first century in a way that at first seems almost uncanny.

Scott was born in 1771 and was thoroughly a member of the revolutionary generation. The great news of his youth and early adulthood, when he was writing his famous poems and beginning his novels, was the French Revolution and the career of Napoleon, who was finally defeated by the British just before Scott began writing his tetralogy on factional strife in seventeenth-century Scotland. "What is a revolution for?" and "How far is it permissible to go?" are the questions that Scott addresses in *The Tale of Old Mortality*.

Scott's literary style is both limpid and nimble. He effortlessly moves among all the required dialects—the thick Scottish of the peasant characters, which almost requires formal translation (there are extensive notes), the elevated formal English of the royalist characters, and the various colorful mixes of the two. He is especially remarkable at reproducing the biblically influenced testifying and preaching of the more extreme members of the rebel party. The narrative style that binds it all together is witty, intelligent, and fast-paced. All in all, there is nothing at all tiresome or even old-fashioned in *Old Mortality*. Scott has caught just the right tone of organized conversational intimacy— not unlike the tone of his contemporary Jane Austen.

For the modern reader, the history known to Scott and his contemporaries is largely unknown, so the plot has an added dimension of suspense, but there is a kind of gloomy familiarity to it—a band of "criminals" or "revolutionaries" (depending upon your point of view) happen upon a "rightful" or "miscreant" religious leader late one night and kill him. The government sends in troops, who go house to house looking for the killers and sweeping into their nets all sorts and shades of dissenting citizens. Soon two camps have formed—the progovernment camp and the pro-insurrectionary camp—and they are required to do battle, but in fact most of the people involved do not believe wholeheartedly in one side or the other, in particular Henry Morton, a young gentleman of modest education and modest ambition whose father had been a leader in an earlier antiroyalist rebellion. Henry finally sides with the rebels because he believes in freedom of religion and opposes the cruel methods of the government, but he continues to argue for forbearance and moderation as the war progresses. One of Scott's signal achievements is that he depicts the more fanatical evangelical elements of the rebel party with insight—they lose partly because they do not understand how the world works, and they don't understand partly because they don't care. When they are finally beaten and executed, they go to their deaths with bravery because they truly do expect a glorious reward—Scott understands both the strangeness and the strength of mystical religious conviction without ridiculing it or sharing in it.

Scott is equally clear and evenhanded about the military aspects of conflict. He depicts the battles in a natural and organized way, so the most neophyte modern female reader can see how and why they turn out as they do and what that means. He also understands how soldiers' minds work. The cool, elegant, ruthless Claverhouse is fascinating, and so is the ruthless, crude, and fanatical Balfour. The telling sign of a great novelist of rich imaginative gifts is the ability to draw beautiful minor characters and to allow them to remain minor. Scott is such a novelist.

What Scott is awkward at is changing the scene. He must follow the battle, the propaganda campaign, and the love story, and this requires more than a few "meantime, back at the ranch" sorts of transitions. The modern novel has discovered some techniques that weave disparate sections together more seamlessly and naturally than Scott was able to do, but his own voice is the compensation for this awkwardness—it is a frank but artful voice, reasonable but evocative, and both reassuring and enlightening. Modern readers generally avoid Scott as outdated and potentially tedious, but issues and dilemmas that interested him are still with us, and his desire, as a novelist, to imagine an enlightened and humane outcome deserves revival.

Sir Walter Scott · The Bride of Lammermoor

(1819; REPR., NEW YORK: OXFORD UNIVERSITY PRESS, 1998), 349 PP.

The Bride of Lammermoor is the fourth of Scott's tetralogy of Scottish novels of the seventeenth century but is utterly unlike *Old Mortality* and, according to most critics, utterly unlike anything else Scott wrote. He was suffering from extremely painful gallstones while composing the novel (which he dictated), and according to one of his secretaries, when he read the published version "he did not recollect one single incident, character, or conversation it contained!" Perhaps this is evidence that the id, or the limbic brain, or the muse can compose without the faculty of reason, because *The Bride of Lammermoor* is never confused or disorganized. It is especially rich in themes and motifs that remain consistent throughout the novel and that give it a pleasing sense of completeness.

The plot is simple: an ancient aristocratic family, the Ravenswoods, lose their estate through bad management, political upheaval, and legal wrangling to another family, the Ashtons. Sir William Ashton is a talented and wealthy but base-born lawyer; his wife, Lady Ashton, is a member of a very powerful family. Edgar Ravenswood is bent upon revenge, but an accident intervenes through which he is introduced to

Lucy Ashton while her mother is away in England for some months. Sir William allows the acquaintance, partly through oversight and partly as a political maneuver, and Lucy and Edgar fall in love and betroth themselves. When Lady Ashton returns, she is unalterably opposed to the marriage, and forces Lucy instead to marry another suitor, who is wealthy and has similar political and religious loyalties to those of the Ashtons. Even though Lucy shows obvious signs of mental stress, the marriage goes forward. On the wedding night, Lucy attempts to kill her new husband with a dagger she has stolen. She then succumbs to madness and dies. The novel became a famous opera by Donizetti, *Lucia di Lammermoor,* and obviously has many romantic and operatic elements. But it is also a technically interesting novel because even though its elements don't seem as though they are going to mesh in an affecting and illuminating way, Scott manages to make it work.

One striking characteristic of the novel is that Scott uses the forms and tones of realism to depict his romantic and folkloric elements. He explores the psychology of the Ashtons' family life very carefully, delineating the ways in which Lady Ashton dominates her husband, the ways in which the cleverness that has made him successful also makes him vulnerable to manipulation, and the ways in which the dysfunctional family romance among husband, wife, and daughter make everyone vulnerable to destruction. Edgar Ravenswood is no less carefully analyzed. His nurture as the son of an irascible, traditional, and probably not very intelligent aristocrat is contrasted nicely with his gentler nature as a man who understands that the world is changing and would like to live on the new terms, and also as a strong man who feels tenderness for a weak and apparently vulnerable woman in spite of his intuition that someone with more vitality and enterprise would suit him better.

Scott is clear that all the power relationships in this world are out of whack and in flux, from political ones (as represented by the marquis of Atholl) to familial ones (as represented by the parents' relationships to their offspring) to master/servant ones (as represented by Balderstone and Ravenswood, but also those of minor characters) to gender ones (Lady Ashton has openly usurped her husband's power, but the relationship between Ravenswood and Lucy is equally unbalanced). The polity is out of joint, and there is nothing romantic love can do to redeem it.

The novel is full of supernatural elements, such as three old hags who are reminiscent of the three witches in *Macbeth,* and omens, signs, legends, and prophecies. Many of these are accounted for or debunked by the narrator. For example, the sudden exchange of one portrait for another at the marriage feast is traced to the agency of one of the malevolent old women. Her malevolence is not of mysterious origin— she is envious, full of class resentment, and angry at the way Lady Ashton has treated her in the past. Nevertheless, the exchange of paintings serves to forward the prophecy that disaster will ensue if the master of Ravenswood returns to his old castle to seek a wife. Scott, in fact, has a quite sophisticated view of the way stories and gossip sometimes dictate events, not because prophecies have innate power, but because they gain social power through agreement.

Scott was a natural novelist because he understood and portrayed ambiguities and complexities with seeming effortlessness, in prose that even in the twenty-first century seems accessible and clear. His narrators always tell the story with an automatic tone of reasonableness that keeps the narrative anchored in the world, yet they do not discount any potential source of motivation or action. He is a natural psychologist, too, who can convincingly motivate characters of all social classes and temperaments, both minor and major. He hasn't fared as well in the modern world as Jane Austen, but he is somewhat like her—one of a long line of liberal British writers for whom human individuality is a source of inspiration as well as psychological, social, political, spiritual, and philosophical speculation.

20 · Mary Shelley · Frankenstein

(1818; REPR., NEW YORK: PENGUIN PUTNAM, SIGNET, 2000), 198 PP.

Mary Shelley was the wife of Percy Bysshe Shelley, the great Romantic poet, and the daughter of Mary Wollstonecraft (author of *A Vindication of the Rights of Women,* who died a few days after Mary's birth) and William Godwin (a radical polemicist and author). *Frankenstein* was conceived and written when Mary was nineteen years old and much under the influence of her husband and Lord Byron, when they were all living on the shores of Lake Geneva. The two poets and Mary, along with Byron's companion, Dr. Polidori, had been reading ghost stories, and decided to try writing some. The poets quickly got bored with their humdrum and, you might say, prosaic task, but Polidori and Mary each produced pieces. Mary's novel was published anonymously, and most readers assumed that Percy had written it. It was not until 1831, after Percy's death and Mary's return to England, that she published an edition under her own name with her own explanation of the circumstances of authorship.

Frankenstein poses a challenge to the modern reader's willingness to suspend disbelief because Mary does not detail how Frankenstein actually creates the monster. She is far more interested in feelings and reactions than she is in processes and events, but by eliding over the mechanics, she tempts the modern reader to dismiss the actuality of the monster—we all know how long it takes a multitude of inventors to do something as relatively simple as creating a robot that can walk up stairs. That it takes Victor two years of solitary work (imagine a graduate student robbing graves) to make a thinking and growing creature is simply ridiculous. But the implausibility of the science isn't the only difficulty; Victor's own reactions are also implausible—or, perhaps, not rendered carefully enough so the reader is drawn into empathizing with them. The author has not found a prosaic style that gives objective context to the feelings of the characters—their sentiments are high, low, exalted, tender, grand, unmixed. In other words, they are poetic sentiments spoken by poetically conceived characters—the wise father, the perfect friend, the beautiful and virtuous young woman. Much of the narrative is dialogue, but it is ideal rather than vernacular dialogue.

For the modern reader, the novel fails in its intention to depict and evoke horror. In part this is a failure of style, and in part it is a failure of technique—the author dwells too little on grisly details. We have to take the horror too much secondhand. Though objectively the events of the novel are horrifying—three murders, a wrongful execution, another death—the author, for whatever reasons of sensibility or youth, chooses not to make a spectacle of them. Since the novel was a popular sensation at publication, it is possible that we are simply inured to the ideas, and require visuals to elicit a reaction—most horror stories from the period don't seem horrible to us (this is not true of plays—Shakespeare's *Titus Andronicus,* John Webster's *The White Devil,* and Percy Bysshe Shelley's *The Cenci* can produce revulsion). Nevertheless, *Frankenstein* is an advance on *Justine* in the sense that Shelley (and other Romantics) were looking for a way to successfully depict horror that the reader would feel as well as observe. Nineteenth-century realist novelists subsequently built on Mary Shelley and the writings of other Romantics to render these states of mind in greater detail and set them into a more mundane context that would make them more believable and produce a bigger thrill.

Where *Frankenstein* succeeds is as a novel about an idea—once again, as with many great novels, the idea is simple. A man creates a humanlike creature, a train of events is set into motion, and the narrative follows them. *Frankenstein* was the first "high concept" idea of the modern era; the idea was actually new, and Mary and her friends did receive it as a revelation. That didn't mean that it had no sources. Mary and her whole group were moved and impressed by Coleridge's long poem "The Rime of the Ancient Mariner," about the terrors of an outcast, and they were also much influenced by the portrayal of the relations among God, Adam, and Satan in Milton's *Paradise Lost.* Byron and Shelley both professed sympathy for the Devil in their writings, and explored the Promethean ideas that Milton had, possibly inadvertently, hinted at. Mary, though, stays firmly on the side of Frankenstein and his family—although she allows the monster to state his point of view, his desires never prevail, and he, unlike Frankenstein, remains unredeemed in the end. Though Frankenstein looks forward to reunion with his loved ones beyond the grave, the monster's only future is nonbeing. Because he is an unnatural creation, his outcast state cannot be relieved; both of his creators, Frankenstein and Mary Shelley, are merciless toward him.

The novel does not easily take up the subject of horror, and most ghost stories and narratives of horror date fairly quickly. *Frankenstein* worked in its day. Though it has since become a model of what not to do if you really want to frighten the reader, it is an excellent social document that combines the drama of Mary Shelley's life with several of the ideas and modes of expression current when she was writing. In addition, *Frankenstein* shows the capacity of the popular novel to change the way society looks at things. One of the truisms of human existence that the monster comments upon, and that seems also to dictate the plot of the novel, is the idea that "the human senses are insurmountable barriers to our union"—in other words, that the monster's ugly strangeness cannot be overcome in his relations to humans, and he can live only in isolation. *Frankenstein* is possibly the first novel to have explored this assumption, and in doing so, undermines it without challenging it. The reader cannot help empathizing with the monster's isolated state and feeling at least some sympathy for him. One is tempted to ally herself with him against his creator. By portraying the inner life, the novel as a form contradicts the importance of appearance in a way that drama and film do not. *Frankenstein* set in motion the processes that created the world we live in, where ugliness and strangeness do not dictate a person's isolation and where intolerance of an unorthodox appearance is viewed as a primitive attitude that education can remove. The 1931 movie *Frankenstein* demonstrates a related effect—when it first came out, Boris Karloff as the monster was frightening, but familiarity bred affection. Now audiences hardly see his threatening qualities at all; it has been a long time since Hollywood tried to use human deformity as intrinsically scary. Scary humans in movies these days are often quite beautiful; what is scary about them is that appearances are deceiving, not revealing. In part, it is the empathy that is essential to the success of a good novel that has changed the way we respond to appearances.

21 · Jane Austen · Persuasion

(1818; REPR., NEW YORK: DOVER, 1997), 188 PP.

I have read *Persuasion* many times. When I first read it, I was younger than any of the characters, and now I am older than any of the characters, and also older than the author, who died at forty-two. I have read *Pride and Prejudice* as many times, and I have read *Emma* several times as well. The clarity of Jane Austen's literary style and the fineness of her sensibility are worth revisiting over and over. I could have indulged myself by including all of her novels on our list, because though the pleasures to be taken from her novels differ as one ages, they never lessen. I chose *Persuasion* because Austen gives her heroine not only the poignant Cinderella bonus of being chosen over all the more apparently appealing girls, but also because in her last novel, her insights into her social milieu are especially brisk and broad.

Anne Elliot is twenty-seven years old. She has lost her looks and is very much on the verge of becoming a spinster. In addition, her father and sister, vain of their own looks and social position, have been extravagant, and the family must now retrench. Rather than simply economizing, they decide to rent out the family estate and move to Bath. The couple who take the estate turn out to be the sister and brother-in-law of Anne's former suitor, a career naval officer, whom she hasn't seen in the eight years since his proposal was turned down by her family as not sufficiently prestigious. Captain Wentworth, however, has changed his circumstances, and, now both rich and respected, is looking for a wife.

Austen was a revolutionary novelist in several particulars that are somewhat hidden by her clever and charming writing style. First among these is that she focused on the emotional lives of women at a time when virtuous women were not allowed to have emotional lives. In *Tom Jones,* for example, Fielding allows Sophia to decline to marry Blifil, whom she abhors, but she is not allowed to express, or even feel, a preference for Tom. Female virtue in the eighteenth century (and into the Victorian period, as in the novels of Anthony Trollope) required that young women be entirely ignorant of love and choice until they were solicited. But all of Austen's novels pay close attention to the desires of female characters—in *Pride and Prejudice,* the fact that Jane Bennet cares for Mr. Bingley and wishes for a proposal from him without knowing whether he cares for her is fully explored. With utter naturalness, Austen gives her female protagonists both ambition and the intelligence to realize it without impugning their virtue. Austen was also alive to the position of women who had no alternative to marriage or continued submission to parents. Anne Elliot, who is constantly at the beck and call of her married sister and yet is repeatedly demeaned by her relatives, can claim nothing for herself in the way of privileges, independence, or money.

By the time Austen wrote *Persuasion,* she had become something of an egalitarian. The powerless Anne is surrounded by vanity, selfishness, and social climbing. Those who follow standard social norms, such as Anne's father and sister, are portrayed as silly and venal. The naval officers Anne meets who have risen through merit are portrayed as worthy of respect and affection because they have traveled and learned interesting things. And they have the perspicacity to appreciate her. The core of the novel is Austen's record of Anne's private thoughts about Frederick Wentworth. After many readings, the satisfaction of her wishes is pleasurable but hardly suspenseful. What remains interesting and new about them, however, is the intimacy of Austen's relationship to her heroine. Anne is attentive to every nuance of the social intercourse around her; she is almost, in some sense, a spy among her relations, calculating the meanings of their actions and moods and gauging how they will affect her.

The larger aspect of Anne's quietly observing habit is Austen's depiction of the social codes of the English gentry early in the nineteenth century. No doubt it is impossible for a modern reader to understand all of the refinements of gesture and implication that Austen catalogs, but the gist remains—almost every social signal is codified. Knowing the code is a sign of proper breeding and education, and is the key to social acceptance, and yet following only the code without true feeling is equally a sign of moral emptiness. Anne (and Austen) recognizes that the code is as much a device of oppression as a set of manners, and the novel's good characters are those who have inner lives—cultivated through private systems of belief—that reveal themselves not only in proper behavior, but also in proper motives. In all her novels, Austen satirizes individual selfishness, irresponsibility, foolishness, and egotism. In *Persuasion* she enlarges her critique and shows that personal failings grow out of social distortions. She is neither as lighthearted as in *Pride and Prejudice,* nor as forgiving as in *Emma.* But the passion at the heart of Anne's unchanging love for Captain Wentworth softens the novel. It is a haunting, appealing, and yet disquieting example of Jane Austen's almost perfect sense of character, style, and pace, an example of the way a true master novelist (and lover of novels—Austen often defended novel-reading and in this novel gently pokes fun at too much poetry-reading) employs all of her tools to their best advantage.

22 · James Hogg · The Private Memoirs and Confessions of a Justified Sinner

(1824; REPR., NEW YORK: PENGUIN, 1987), 242 PP.

James Hogg was a self-taught literary man, a shepherd by birth who wrote and farmed for much of his life. He knew Scott and wrote a book about him. Depending upon your point of view, *The Private Memoirs and Confessions of a Justified Sinner* is either a political novel about faith and doctrine, or a religious tale with political overtones, but it is very much about how controversies over religion express themselves both psychologically and sociologically. It begins, appropriately to our study, with a forced marriage. A wealthy young woman is married for property considerations to an older man whose religious beliefs she does not share. She avoids consummating the alliance on the wedding night, but her husband then locks her up and rapes her repeatedly until she flees to her father, who beats her and sends her back to her husband. This episode, very much in the spirit of *The Heptameron,* only stiffens her resistance. She and her husband live in separate parts of the castle for some years thereafter, and she produces two sons. The elder shares his father's beliefs, which are Church of Scotland, and the younger his mother's, which are Calvinist.

These unfortunate preliminaries pave the way for a sibling rivalry from hell. The elder son, raised by the liberal father, is inexplicably harassed by his brother, who appears to be a sanctimonious prig and mischief-maker, egged on by the resentful mother and her religious mentor. After he is imprisoned for murder, however, the younger son leaves a memoir explaining his actions in terms of what the reader readily identifies as satanic possession (though the Devil does not enter into him, rather becomes his unshakable companion). Like *The Tale of Old Mortality,* Hogg's novel is set in the late seventeenth century, when religious controversies raged in Scotland, partly defining and partly defined by class conflicts and regional antagonisms, and also when, as in *The Bride of Lammermoor,* visions, ghosts, supernatural figures, and superstitions were typical beliefs among members of all classes.

The two brothers, George and Robert, contrast in temperament, religion, and politics. George is a hale fellow, a lover of games and society, openhearted and well meaning. He is also the heir to the family lands and wealth. Robert's legitimacy is questionable, though he is acknowledged by the father as his son. Robert is annoying from the beginning—he first introduces himself to George, and to the reader, by interfering in a tennis match, standing in the middle of the play until he is knocked down and injured. He acts churlish and resentful toward George and the other boys and soon is hounding George unmercifully, but with a condescending, sanctimonious air. According to the narrator, he has been convinced by his foster father, his mother's spiritual adviser, that he is a particular type of privileged believer, a "justified sinner"—that is, a member of God's elect, a person already awarded "grace," so that no act he might perform on Earth could endanger his election (salvation). This notion is a logical extension of the Calvinist idea of grace—if no human act of goodness, generosity, or penance could influence or limit the power of God and His capacity to anoint His privileged few, then no evil act could influence Him, either, so there exists a class of believers who can do no wrong—whatever they do is right, no matter how harmful it might be.

Satan, of course, is drawn to Robert's pride, and befriends him almost immediately after his parents declare that they have seen a valid sign that he is among the elect. Robert wonders about his new companion but finally decides that he must be a prince, and possibly he is Peter the Great of Russia, who was rumored to be traveling about at the end of the seventeenth century, educating himself. Robert is not happy with his new companion, though. Even while he is listening to the prince's flattery and using his powers to pay back old scores, he realizes that much about their relationship is inexplicable, especially the fact that he himself feels no pleasure and considerable uneasiness in the prince's company. Soon, it seems, there is evidence that Robert has committed crimes he has no memory of—either the prince is committing them disguised as Robert, or Robert is committing them himself in some sort of oblivious state.

The suspense of the novel is not in who Robert's mysterious companion is, but in whether Robert will ever understand and acknowledge his mistaken view of himself as a "justified sinner." *The Private Memoirs and Confessions of a Justified Sinner* is very much a tale—the third-person narrator never commits himself as to the verifiability of the strange events he relates, and the novel is supposed to raise a thrill of gothic dread in the reader. Even so, Hogg places every incident and character within the realistic confines of known Scottish history, including a destructive riot that ensues in Edinburgh after the first contretemps between George and Robert, which Hogg analyzes sociologically as a function of party loyalties in a period of heightened partisanship. Hogg, though himself the son of Calvinists, sees how extreme religious beliefs are apt to destroy all sense of common humanity and infuse political life with inflexible passion—this, he is saying, is where Satan finds an entry, and mayhem ensues.

Hogg's novel may have seemed eerie or unearthly at the time it was written. These aspects of the narrative have faded and the horror is no longer so horrible. But the psychological and sociological observations he makes have not faded. Robert's feelings about his devilish mentor sound very much like addiction; rigid religious self-righteousness still has the same effect on civil society as it did hundreds of years ago; unhappy, violent marriages produce unhappy, violent children. Ideological passions in novels do not enter American literature from the

English novel, but perhaps from the Scottish tradition, along with Scots-Irish Calvinist religious traditions that have shaped much of our culture.

23 · Stendhal · The Red and the Black

TRANS. MARGARET R. B. SHAW (1830; REPR., NEW YORK: PENGUIN, 2002), 509 PP.

Stendhal (né Henri Beyle) was forty-five when he began to write his first novel, and it was published at about the time of the Revolution of 1830, in France, which ratified and regularized the changes in French life and politics begun by the French Revolution. It is thus a social document of a high order as well as a wonderful novel. Stendhal did what many novelists have done—he took a story he found in a newspaper and fashioned it into a work of the imagination by inferring the feelings and thoughts of the principal characters. The novel was meant to be current and socially engaged—Stendhal was a liberal and a freethinker, and he intended to portray French politics, French provincial life, and Parisian life. He had specific political views—that the royalists and the Catholic Church were in collusion against the interests of the rest of the population and that they planned to aid Charles X in reinstituting absolute monarchy. But the novel doesn't only display these views; it also stands on its own as a psychological portrait and as a depiction of the causes and effects of sexual passion.

Julien Sorel is a good-looking peasant boy with ambitions and aptitudes above his station in life. Looks are important, because they allow him to gain access to places and groups that would otherwise be closed to him, and they encourage others to attribute noble qualities, such as pride and fineness of feeling, to him even before he has learned enough to actually possess such qualities. In part, *The Red and the Black* is a study of the social effects of manner—Julien ends as he does because others have expected great things of him, and he has come to expect them, too. It is not clear whether he has great talents or only certain facilities—part of Stendhal's point is that Julien's development is public rather than private, and that he acts out the expectations of others. But perhaps as an effect of the resentful pride he has developed as a result of the antipathy of his father and brothers, he is always willing to take a dare. From beginning to end, whenever there is a choice between caution and boldness, Julien cannot allow himself to choose caution. He thus has the predispositions of a Romantic hero, if not the talent, passion, or singularity.

Missing by a generation the occasion for great military prowess, Julien enters the church, thinking that he can realize his ambitions there, but the church is split along partisan lines and he casts his lot with the wrong side (the Jansenists as opposed to the Jesuits). It is women who save him.

His first love affair is with the wife of the mayor of his small town, who hires him to tutor her three sons. Madame de Rênal is as interesting as Julien—a retiring, innocent product of a strict upbringing, with no real friends or position in society, she has never even read a novel. She is entirely unprepared for the surge of passion she feels for Julien. At first Julien doesn't respond to her feelings, but the excitement of the liaison eventually arouses him, too, until the gossip of the town and the suspicions of M. de Rênal force the two of them to part.

Church politics bring Julien to Paris, to a position as secretary to a wealthy aristocrat and government minister, M. de La Mole, who has a son and a daughter about Julien's age. Julien quickly realizes that he has more on the ball than the son or the other young aristocrats who hang around. In the meantime, his employer begins to treat him with kindness and familiarity, and the daughter, Mathilde, a great beauty, begins to involve him in her self-created drama of grand, doomed passion. Julien is not precisely reluctant to go along, but his motives grow more out of pride and daring than out of actual love for Mathilde. The climax is precipitated by her discovery that she is pregnant.

Stendhal is matter-of-fact about the passions of his female characters, neither prudish nor sentimental. For Madame de Rênal, love only just overwhelms her religious scruples, but it does overwhelm them. For Mathilde, virtue is a social necessity, but neither a moral nor a religious imperative. Almost to the end, her goal is to be married to Julien on any terms, even the most compromising. It is Julien who repeatedly attempts to figure out how to reinsert her into society with as little damage to her reputation and her fate as possible. At the same time, Stendhal pays minute attention to the progress of each character's feelings—they are not defined as being "in love," but rather the interplay of desire, pride, resentment, fear, second thoughts, prudence, and gamesmanship is carefully depicted, making Julien's love affairs seem rather cold by contrast to, say, the love of Tom Jones and Sophia Western, but infinitely more interesting. For Julien and his mistresses, the growth of love is political rather than natural, and, indeed, love has no goal except moment-by-moment sensation. Julien is not courting either woman, so a happy ending is not to be expected. Rather, the means justify the end: the passions of the characters set them so completely outside the normal run of mercenary, mean, and empty French society that they must die or go insane—Julien is executed, Madame de Rênal dies of a broken heart, and Mathilde acts out her mad ideal of a medieval queen (by coincidence, Marguerite de Navarre), burying her lover's head with her own hands, then building a shrine to it. The ending is neither comic nor tragic but ironic, made so by the carefully detailed social portrait of contemporary provincial and Parisian France that Stendhal never loses sight of.

Julien, Mathilde, and Madame de Rênal are complex and fascinating characters, but the character of the narrator is at least as fascinating, and acts as a countervailing realistic consciousness in which their Romanticism is always submerged. He never fails to have a wide perspective, never fails to set their actions and feelings into social context, never fails to analyze the steps by which they arrive at decisions and actions. His France is never a transcendent or sentimentalized place—it is a place where greed, ambition, envy, and hatred are always at work, appearances are deceiving, and prudence is an essential virtue but no guarantee of safety. His voice is entirely ironic—he neither respects nor denigrates Julien's aspirations; he merely observes them with a degree of sympathy. He seems to like Madame de Rênal for the innocent profundity of her love and to respect the intensity of Mathilde's determination, but he recognizes that the three characters lose as well as gain by their actions. He doesn't offer them as models; there is an absurd quality to their choices that surely comes from the fact that Stendhal found the story and made himself its primary observer, but did not generate the story out of his own experience.

The Red and the Black is not formally perfect. It seems to ramble, and the parts don't quite fit together. The shooting and the trial and the execution at the end go too quickly, and the novel has to cover more territory than it can handle with the degree of leisurely detail it employs in the first half. Julien is not entirely sympathetic. At times he is too scheming and at other times too proud. The case is made that he is extraordinary, but maybe he is really only something of a misfit. His psychology seems complete but not appealing. All the same, this is an incredibly rich novel, much more straightforwardly bold than the nineteenth-century novel is conventionally credited with being.

24 · Nikolai Gogol · Taras Bulba

TRANS. BERNARD FARBAR (1835; REPR., PRESTIGE BOOKS, 1962), 125 PP.

On the back of this out-of-print edition is a blurb from Ernest Hemingway, "One of the ten greatest books of all time!" Well, maybe yes. If not one of the ten greatest, certainly one of the greatest, if by great we mean that much of the time a reader is reading *Taras Bulba,* she experiences a conscious and pressing feeling of pleasure and admiration, or if by great we mean that some of the feelings one experiences are simultaneously strange and profound, as if the author's take on things is not merely original, but uprecedented.

Taras Bulba is brisk and refreshing and constantly communicates a sense that is more than authenticity and more than intelligence and more, even, than love. It is as if by thinking so continuously and with such concentration about his subject, Gogol (who was in his twenties when he wrote *Taras Bulba*) arrived at truth. This, of course, is the illusion of supreme art. The time is the sixteenth century. The place is the Ukrainian steppe, which is nominally controlled by Poland but subject to the depredations of the Tatars and the Turks. Taras and his family and friends are Cossacks, Slavic warrior bands who follow the Russian Orthodox religion and have been constantly at war for about two hundred years. Taras is a vigorous man of middle age with two sons just returning from school in Kiev. He takes them to the "Setch," which is a townlike permanent encampment of Cossacks. Because treaties prevent the sort of raiding Taras would like for the training of his sons, he begins to instigate mischief by appealing to the pride of the warriors. Soon, though, a band shows up reporting that Jews have taken over churches and are charging Russians money to hold services and that Roman priests have harnessed Orthodox Christians to carriages. The Cossacks set out to avenge these insults and eventually lay siege to a walled Polish town.

It is impossible to read this novella without looking through the lens of the 175 years that have intervened between Gogol's time and ours. Russians, Poles, Jews, and Muslims lived in proximity, all on fire with orthodoxy, all tempted and enraged by rumors and prejudices, and all armed. Gogol felt great admiration and kinship for the Cossacks (he was from Ukraine), and his admiration encompassed both the cruelty and the stoicism that were the terms of sixteenth-century existence.

Out of this admiration, he forged a literary style that is intensely modern in the way it depicts paradoxes of feeling and sensation. At one point early in the novel, Gogol evokes a peace that truly passeth understanding:

> Meanwhile the beauty of the July night had acquired a magnificent and awesome quality. It was the glare of the neighboring districts that had not yet burned to the ground. In one place the flame spread slowly and majestically over the heaven. In another, meeting with something inflammable and bursting into a whirlwind, it hissed and flew upwards to the very stars, and its severed tongues died in the highest regions of the sky. Here stood the charred, black monastery, like a stern Carthusian monk, displaying its gloomy grandeur at every new outburst of flame; there blazed the monastery garden. One could almost hear the trees hissing as they were wrapped up in smoke; and as the fire broke through, it suddenly lighted up clusters of ripe plums with a hot, phosphorescent, violet gleam or turned the yellow pears here and there to pure gold; and in the midst of this, hanging against the wall of the building or from a bough, would be seen the black figure of some poor Jew or monk whom the fire was devouring together with the building.

Taras's intentions for his sons, which amount to some enjoyable raiding and plunder, do not work out as planned. Taras, like most Cossacks, is disdainful of the softer attractions of women—the boys are meant to be warriors. But during the siege of the walled Polish town, his younger son, Andrei, betrays the Cossacks and his father, for the sake of the love of a seductive Polish beauty. Taras must kill him, which he does without remorse. The older boy, Ostap, less romantic, is brave and tough, but when the Cossacks are defeated, Ostap is captured and taken to Warsaw. Taras himself is wounded, but when he recovers, he persuades a Jewish merchant to sneak him into the Polish city, where he witnesses Ostap's dramatic torture and execution. The Cossacks' subsequent revenge is violent and unmerciful, and Taras's last words call for war, not peace. Gogol's Cossacks are as unremitting and matter-of-fact as the Vikings of *Egilssaga* (and probably related to them, since Scandinavians under Rurik settled the north–south-flowing rivers of Russia in the Middle Ages).

But the medieval Icelandic writers did not display a refined sense of the beauty of the landscape or a complex sense of the characteristic psychology of the Norsemen as Gogol does of the Cossacks. Taras and his sons are always shown in the context of Cossack culture, on the broad and beautiful stage of the central Asian grasslands. Like many Russian writers, Gogol employed his gifts in trying to discern the nature of Russianness and in forging a literary identity for Russia that would somehow help to engender a road to the future. Gogol's ideas were deeply conservative—true Russianness is defined, in *Taras Bulba,* as bold, muscular, nationalistic, and backward-looking. Each life is dictated by Fate and must be endured and challenged rather than thought through or arranged. National characteristics persist: Poles are Catholic, gaudy, effete, and treacherous; Tatars are unknowable; Jews are well connected (the novella's anti-Semitism is one of its more uncomfortable features); Cossacks are real men. But these national characteristics do not necessarily lead to salvation or redemption—in the context of sixteenth-century Ukraine, they only lead to more and more complex dilemmas and more grueling challenges that must be endured.

Gogol's most famous novel is *Dead Souls,* which he partially destroyed before he died, and his most famous stories are "The Overcoat" and "The Nose." He wrote several plays; the production of his satiric play *The Inspector General* resulted in his departure from Russia for Western Europe when it seemed to offend the czar, who left the theater during the first act. Gogol was and continues to be an immortal but controversial Russian writer whose works are difficult to categorize. Later, more ideological Russian authors often tried to enlist his works as evidence for his belief in one program or another, but Gogol's forms are so various and his tone so idiosyncratic that it is impossible to come up with a consistent set of beliefs that can be attributed to him. When he burned the final manuscipt of *Dead Souls,* it may have been because of a conversion to fanatical Russian Orthodox belief, or it may not have been for that reason at all—scholars don't agree. But individual completed works make perfect sense and are wonderfully enjoyable because Gogol is so inventive that the reader cannot resist suspending disbelief. He is the perfect example of a writer who cannot help but express the idea of artistic freedom even if, perhaps, it isn't in his best interest (as when he offended the czar and felt he had to exile himself) or something he wants to do (as when he completed *Dead Souls* in a way he himself rejected).

25 · Mikhail Lermontov · A Hero of Our Time

TRANS. PAUL FOOTE (1840; REPR., NEW YORK: PENGUIN, 1966), 185 PP.

Lermontov wrote one novel, many poems, and some dramas and critical essays. He was born in 1814, and became an acclaimed literary figure, the heir to Pushkin, before he turned twenty-four. He was exiled twice to the Caucasus, first for an inflammatory essay about Pushkin's death, and later for dueling. He fought three duels, and died in the third one at age twenty-eight. *A Hero of Our Time,* though it is short and in some sense fragmentary, and though all of its themes are outdated and it depicts an era that passed quickly and had few ramifications for the modern world, is truly a fascinating novel—for me, perhaps one of the most fascinating ever written.

Lermontov's protagonist, Pechorin, was modeled on the eponymous hero of Pushkin's famous narrative poem *Evgeny Onegin* (1831). Part of the fascination of *A Hero of Our Time* is in the efficient and evocative way in which Lermontov constructs his narrative. Pechorin appears in five self-contained stories, the first two written by an unnamed narrator who is traveling in the Caucasus, meets up with an old soldier named Maxim Maximych, and elicits from him a tale of horse-stealing and abduction as an example of local color. He is intrigued by Pechorin, who has figured in that story, and becomes more intrigued when the two of them happen to run into Pechorin sometime later. When, in the second story, Pechorin refuses to take possession of his own journals, which Maxim Maximych has saved for him, the narrator asks to have them, and then "publishes" them. The last three stories are in Pechorin's voice. Of these, the longest, and the centerpiece of the novel, is "Princess Mary," in which Pechorin coolly seduces and then disdains a girl he does not care for in full view of her cousin, Vera, a married woman who is the love of Pechorin's life, and also in full view of an old associate of his, Grushnitsky, who is himself in love with Mary. The intrigue leads to the death in a duel of Grushnitsky, a nervous breakdown for the girl, and ruin for Vera when her husband realizes he has been cuckolded. The last story is a meditation upon Fate, and ends just before Pechorin meets Maxim Maximych for the first time. The sequence of stories makes a narrative circle—"Bela" comes after "Princess Mary" chronologically, but before it in the novel; enigmas of Pechorin's character as it appears in "Bela" are explained in "Princess Mary" and "The Fatalist." All five of the stories resonate with one another, as does the third-person narrative by "Lermontov" juxtaposed with the first-person narrative by Pechorin. At the end, the reader feels she has become remarkably intimate with Pechorin and, given his pleasure in manipulating people and wrecking lives, such intimacy carries a measure of discomfort. But only a measure. Pechorin's voice is so simultaneously confiding, honest, clear, and reasonable that he does seem remarkable in the end—the reader is seduced as the women had been. Is he exceptional? Is he one of a kind or just a glib example of a type? What are the wellsprings of his character? Is his life an example of social and political waste, an example of the workings of Fate, the inevitable result of poor upbringing and education? Do we like him? Does his honesty make up for his selfishness? Is he cold or despairing?

The key to Pechorin's success as a narrator of his own adventures is his impeccable manners. He details the action clearly and reports on his own feelings and doubts about what he is doing calmly, without any sort of undue emotion. He even reports on his emotions (such as his fear and despair after the fatal duel) without undue emotion. Nothing is so seductive in a narrator as self-knowledge, and Pechorin seems to have some. He doesn't know why he is as he is, and he doesn't know how or why he might change, but he does seem to know who he is, and in the end, that is enough.

The narrator's ostensible reason for writing is that he is keeping travel notes, and in the first two stories in particular the mountain scenes of the Caucasus region of central Asia—high, snow-covered peaks, rough roads, native families in huts and tents, Cossacks in forts—are beautifully evoked. To the modern reader, the references to the Chechen rebels and the Muslim villagers are eerie and striking. We understand the plight Bela is in once she has been kidnapped and seduced by Pechorin because we have seen Afghan women in veils in the news. At the beginning of the twenty-first century, *A Hero of Our Time* turns out to be a compelling historical document in a way that it might not have been in 1975, and this is a testament to Lermontov's powers of observation and his sense that descriptions of the exotic regions he passed through were appropriate to the form of the novel.

Pushkin was the younger Lermontov's friend and model, but for our purposes, a key difference between each author's work is that one is poetry and the other is prose. Pushkin's lovers and their story typify certain Russian qualities that are lovingly described in his poetry—this is how lyricism in poetry works. Images are coordinated by poetic forms so they will coalesce into a larger meaning that makes something general of their particular qualities. Prose makes no such promises. The mountains in the distance may mean something, but they may not—they may only be a majestic backdrop, their exotic appearance sufficient reason for them to be described, especially when the novel explicitly presents itself as a travel narrative. The very ambiguity that defines Pechorin comes from the contingent elements of the narrative about him. The structure of the novel shows that certain events took place; materials narrating those events were gathered together by means of a separate sequence of events; the book we have in our hands represents still another sequence of events—an interpretive sequence. The conceit is that all of these sequences came about by chance. Do they add up to something? This is the novel as casual and natural, as almost not a novel, as having only a fortuitous existence, not an intentional one. It is conceit that might not have worked except that the idle confiding coolness of Pechorin's tone makes it work.

A Hero of Our Time demonstrates that flawless judgment and technical genius of an author can go a long way to overcome being passed over by history. A novel need not fall entirely into the historical document category, as so many, once thought great, have done. If a narrator, either third-person or first-person, strikes up a comfortable and interesting relationship with the reader, the reader is happy to read about almost anything.

26 · Honoré de Balzac
Cousin Pons

TRANS. HERBERT J. HUNT

(1846-47; REPR., NEW YORK: PENGUIN, 1965, 1968), 334 PP.

Cousin Bette

TRANS. MARION AYTON CRAWFORD

(1846-47; REPR., NEW YORK: PENGUIN, 1965, 1968), 448 PP.

Balzac's greatest work is a cycle of novels called *La Comédie humaine,* in which he attempts to capture the vastness and variety of life in Paris in the middle of the nineteenth century. Each novel and story is different, and meant to stand alone, but many characters recur in different capacities. The result is a dense fictional kaleidoscope of materialism, envy, spite, worldliness, and occasional virtue—characters of all ages and types and social positions encounter one another, act in one another's dramas, and then go on, in many cases, to something completely different. Two important novels in the larger project are *Cousin Bette* and *Cousin Pons,* which were written as a pair on the theme of "poor relations."

Balzac was a great materialist. His novels always discuss money, and most of his characters are motivated largely by greed, though occasionally by lust. How much income each has, the expenses of each, what each wants to earn by gaining some sort of position, how much it costs to live in Paris or to marry a daughter to a desirable husband are all central concerns in Balzac's world. In this sense he is the quintessential realistic novelist, since nothing drives sentimentality out of a novel like exact sums of money, and monetary anxiety is a common feature of novel plots, both because the opposing temptations of greed and true feeling offer efficient moral choices for characters and because authors themselves are often writing for a living and pressed for money, and so monetary questions are interesting to them.

For Cousin Bette and Cousin Pons, considerations of poverty and dependence on wealthy relatives are central to their characters. Bette is the plain cousin; her pretty benefactor has been married long ago to a dedicated libertine whom she loves very much. This woman, Baroness Hulot, who is exceptionally religious, has tried to help Bette, but Bette has secretly cultivated her resentments. She attempts to harm the family in every way possible while all the time pretending to be grateful and affectionate. Cousin Pons is a small-time musician and big-time collector of objets d'art. Because he is devoted to and jealous of his collection, he lives in poverty—his only pleasure is gastronomy. He is in the habit of dining with his wealthy friends and benefactors, but over the years he gets less and less welcome at their tables, and eventually he is insulted and dismissed by his cousins, who have no idea he owns an enviable treasure. He has one friend, Schmücke, who is, indeed, a schmuck—an utter innocent who loves Pons but can hardly help him against the vultures who gather once the news of his wealth emerges. Most of the novel describes Pons's decline toward death as everyone but Schmücke and a couple of people from the theater where he works scheme to steal, defraud, and murder.

Both novels have several gruesome fascinations. In *Cousin Bette,* Bette's protégée, a young woman she sponsors as a seductress, contracts a fatal and disfiguring venereal disease, which Balzac describes in some detail. In *Cousin Pons,* Pons is tormented by his concierge, whose attempts to bully him to death by haranguing and contradicting him are portrayed at length. In both novels the sordid habitations of the poor or low characters are described with relish. It is also true, though, that Pons's cherished collection is carefully depicted—Balzac himself was a knowledgeable and ambitious collector who perhaps awarded to Pons pieces he himself might have wished to own.

Many novelists of the mid-nineteenth century had social theories, and Balzac's narratives are regularly interspersed with expository asides on such things as the course of Pons's illness or the reasons certain dying people have visions and others don't. Balzac was not as careful of his authorial voice and narrative position as certain more artful authors such as George Eliot and Henry James were later, but he was writing very quickly—the cycle of novels (projected to be 115 volumes, with 85 completed) was organized and written in about ten years (some of the volumes were already written when Balzac decided how he was going to shape his larger project). The author had to devise a natural and eloquent storytelling method that enabled him to deliver both information and drama easily and quickly. His stories are suspenseful and his intrusions seem automatic, as if the conversational voice is right there beside the composing voice, ready to offer additional insights at any time. Balzac seems almost uniquely unself-conscious as an author, as if, in the rush of events and analysis, he simply doesn't have time to ponder and cultivate his narrative presentation.

Nor does Balzac seem to have a larger political theory. Many of his characters are vile—inhumanly greedy, callous, cruel, and almost too cold even to be called sadistic. Bette is one of these—on her deathbed "quite wretched at the good fortune that was shining on her family," her only comfort is that they have no idea how she hates them and are, therefore, "mourning her as the good angel of the family" (p. 458). Her cousin-in-law, Baron Hulot, who seems in the last chapters to have been redeemed by the suffering of his wife and family, ends up in the bed of the kitchen maid; his saintly and devoted wife overhears him say to the girl, "My wife hasn't long to live, and if you like you can be a baroness" (p. 461). Balzac accounts for their natures by depicting Paris,

France, and Frenchness in ever more detail, leaving the reader to con-
clude that the characters are horrible because they are French, and perhaps even more horrible because they live in Paris (although the
narrow-minded greed of some of the provincial characters, like Bette
and like the father in the opening chapters of *Lost Illusions,* is perhaps
more brutishly automatic than that of socially calculating Parisians). In
Cousin Pons, innocence is reserved for Schmücke, who is German, and
kindliness is reserved for some of the hardworking theater people,
who seem to actually have fun from time to time, but at any rate to be
relatively free of the status anxiety that motivates the others. In *Cousin
Bette* Madame Hulot plays the same role, though her innocence is a
result of faith rather than nationality. These characters do not figure in
the plots as models to be emulated, though. Rather they end up as con-
senting dupes for the others, simply because they do not have the
energy or the perspicacity to counteract the endless plots against them.

Balzac, therefore, expresses a version of novelistic conservatism—
humans are unredeemed and apparently unredeemable; France is a
Boschian landscape of iniquity, Paris its sewer. Even so, Balzac's novels
have a comic liveliness, as if the author's fascination with the social
scene were unbounded and its very energy compensated for its repellent inhabitants.

27 · Charlotte Brontë · Jane Eyre

(1847; REPR., NEW YORK: W. W. NORTON, 2000), 397 PP.

If many, or most, European novels take up the question of what is to be
done about, or with, girls, *Jane Eyre* is one of the first to most steadily
and resolutely address the question of "What do girls (or women)
want?" Jane's great characteristic, from the moment we meet her, is to
be immovably certain about what she wants. She is not influenced by
the opinions of those in authority about what she should want or must
not want, and punishment only reinforces her sense of self. She is
never deluded, like the heroine of *The Female Quixote,* for example,
and never unsure of her feelings, like Pamela. She recognizes that she
might not fit into the world as it is constituted, that she might have to
settle for less than she knows is available, but, romantic as she is, she is

an intransigent realist about herself. Her journey of self-knowledge is never about discovering true feeling; it is always about making connections between appearances and realities, about separating truths from lies.

Jane's is the archetypal orphan tale. A plain girl, reviled by her relatives, sets out on her lonely life journey. She must use the tools she has. In her case, these are intelligence and a passion to minutely observe everyone around her. Given the chance, she can love and respect those worthy of her love and respect—the nurse Bessie, her friend Helen Burns, her teacher Miss Temple—but she offers neither love nor respect to those who treat her badly or are in themselves unworthy. In a hierarchical society she refuses categorically to be servile or even to show the normal forms of respect. As a result, she is profoundly lonely, but she has no idea, except through work, of how to assuage her loneliness. She encounters the Beast—in this case Mr. Rochester, the unhappy and intimidating lord of the manor—and she readily understands that he is more bluff than bite. He, for his part, recognizes something in her—honesty in every sense—that he finds intriguing and then seductive. He decides that he must have her, and engineers that very thing that Pamela was so afraid of, a false marriage (full of true feeling, but illegal). Jane escapes, becomes destitute, and is rescued by kind strangers who turn out to be long-lost relatives. She gains a fortune through the death of a distant uncle, shares it with her relatives, and escapes, at the last moment, another false marriage—this one legal but without feeling. She returns to Rochester, discovers that he has been maimed, blinded, and widowed all in one unlucky (lucky) accident, and, Reader, she marries him.

Jane Eyre is as satisfying as it is unsatisfying. The material is as powerful as the strongest wish—that the fascinating man is yielding and loving within, that the plain girl appeals, that a connection can be so powerful as to express itself telepathically across a hundred miles, that the chastened groom and the vindicated bride can live happily (and in good conscience) forever after, that good can grow out of evil. However, realism keeps inserting itself. At the highest moments of the drama—particularly when Jane hears Rochester calling her and when she discovers his newly reduced condition—the reader is tempted to back away, sensing that this is not how life works, and Jane's unique journey is atypical and therefore unlikely and implausible.

Now we are at the heart of the dilemma of the novel. Are the stories

the novel relates typical or unique? Do we expect the novel to recon-
firm our beliefs about the world or to challenge them? Is the point of
the novel the revelation of the ideal or the depiction of the real? In fact,
no individual novelist can decide which side of this dilemma to adopt.
Realism or idealism is native to his or her temperament and intrinsic
to his or her vision of the world. But *Jane Eyre* reveals something
about the dilemma—compelling idealistic novels, novels that grow
from wishes—are beloved. Compelling realistic novels, novels that
grow from astute observation of likely outcomes, are respected. A diet
of too many idealistic novels comes to seem shallow. A diet of too many
realistic novels comes to seem sordid.

For some readers, the idea that Jane and Rochester communicate
telepathically at the moment when both are experiencing their greatest
distress is perfectly plausible. The two of them have demonstrated in
several ways before this point that even though their intentions and
social positions are different, their spirits are joined. Jane, especially,
believes in the tangible expression of spiritual qualities. Brontë has
prepared the ground rather carefully, with her depiction of Jane's
school friend Helen Burns and Jane's discovery of her cousins. In fact,
the whole novel demonstrates the power of projection. The orphan
girl of unique mental strength summons up both her trials and their
rewards. All the scenes she passes through are vivid, dramatic, and
essentially solitary, as if displayed for the education of herself alone.
The novel seems to be, and only works as, a document of subjectivity.
For some readers this subjectivity coincides with their own experience
of the world and is right. For others it is ridiculous.

Nevertheless, it takes a novel of unique subjectivity and stubbornness to even ask the question "What do women themselves want?" as
opposed to the question "What should be done with women?" Jane's
answer is, women want independent, equal, and loving connection at
whatever social cost. The vitality of *Jane Eyre* in the 158 years since
publication and its niche in the lives of adolescent girls have given it
political as well as artistic power. Many girls have come to know,
through *Jane Eyre,* what it is possible to want, even if, as they grow up,
they back away from the cost.

28 · Emily Brontë · Wuthering Heights

(1847; REPR., NEW YORK: OXFORD UNIVERSITY PRESS, 1995), 338 PP.

Whereas Jane Eyre is a recognizable young woman, uncompromising but not terrifically unusual, who makes the case that governesses, though quiet and plain, have full inner lives and deserve consideration, the characters of *Wuthering Heights* are hardly recognizable at all, and most readers encounter them with fascinated amazement. I would suggest that they come to seem stranger and more inhumane as the reader gets older—their absolutism and passion seem more normal to a girl in her early teens, caught in the tangle of junior high school, than they do to someone who has married, had children, and gotten in the habit of conforming to social expectations.

Emily Brontë was only thirty when she died, and although Charlotte lived with her and had known her all her life, she did not profess to understand her, or even to understand her novel, which was published in the same year as *Jane Eyre*. Charlotte seemed wild and intransigent to her biographer Elizabeth Gaskell, but Emily seemed "stronger than a man, simpler than a child" to Charlotte. She likened Emily's novel to a mountain crag become human. It had not so much been written by Emily as come through her, fully formed. Additionally, Emily didn't have much to say—she left no letters and few diary entries. There are no reported conversations. Heathcliff, Catherine, Linton, and their children seem real: it is Emily who seems ghostly.

Reviewers at the time didn't know quite what to make of *Wuthering Heights*—it was almost as if it arrived from another country, where the customs and the national character were much different, and not even really English; and indeed, it did. The Yorkshire moors were settled in the tenth and eleventh centuries by Vikings, who brought both language and culture with them. Even in the nineteenth century, the Yorkshire dialect owed a lot to Norse, and by the evidence of the novel, Yorkshire character owed a lot to the bitter passions, hatreds, and feuds of the sort frequently detailed in the Icelandic sagas.

The outline of the story is simple. Two families live near one another, one on the mountain, a rougher, harsher family, the Earnshaws, the other in the valley, a better-educated, more sociable family, the Lintons. Mr. Earnshaw walks to Liverpool one day to do some trading and brings home Heathcliff, a wild child, whom he comes to favor over his own two offspring, Catherine and Hindley. The three children grow up in relative isolation until two of them, Heathcliff and Catherine, try spying on the children in the valley, Edgar and Isabella. Catherine is bitten by a dog and ends up staying with the Lintons. When she returns home, her horizons have widened to include the books and dresses and social attainments that the Lintons care about. Catherine, a passionate girl, then attempts to balance and reconcile the wilder and the more domesticated forms of existence, but various bits of bad luck foil her attempts, and Heathcliff runs away, only to return several years later, a wealthy man, even stronger and also more sinister than before. He intrudes upon Catherine's marriage to Edgar. After she dies, he ensnares Catherine's older brother through drink and gambling, then systematically wreaks revenge upon the Lintons until eventually he is the only member of the older generation still alive. All of the offspring are in his power—Cathy (daughter of Catherine and Linton, beautiful, affectionate, and plucky), Hareton (son of Hindley and his wife, rude and uneducated but good at heart), and Linton (son of Heathcliff and Isabella, sickly and mean). The children, now in their late teens, are living with Heathcliff at the estate on the moor when the novel opens. The story is related by two narrators: Lockwood, a visitor from London who is the tenant of the valley estate, and Nelly, housekeeper and childhood companion of the older generation.

While the story is startling and even shocking, the narrative frame is brilliant. Lockwood is a conventionally educated, pompous, and rather stupid man. His flat-footed sensibility lends authenticity to his part in the narrative, since he is clearly too dull to make this sort of thing up. Nelly Dean, while more intelligent than Lockwood, is as conventional in a moral sense. She is observant, orderly, and enduring without being passionate or imaginative. Many critics dislike her, and blame her for balking the passions of her employers, as if the plot of *Wuthering Heights* could possibly go some other way than it does, but the novel resides in the Norse tradition of fated action. Once Heathcliff is introduced, his alien nature and heritage must cause conflict until it is removed (through his death and that of Linton, his son). Nelly does her best to ensure the survival of the body of the family until it is cured of the infection. Nelly serves the important function of forgiving Heathcliff all his sins, even as she witnesses them. It is her commentary that renders him human, because it is to her, a lifelong and not judgmental companion, that Heathcliff can reveal the workings of his own mind. Without this dimension, he would simply be a villain or a devil, since his actions are relentlessly calculated to destroy others (also see the discussion of Nelly in chapter 9, "The Circle of the Novel").

Lockwood tells the story in three parts: part one is his own story of being trapped at the Heights by a storm and seeing what may be Cathy's ghost; part two is the background related to him by Nelly while he is recovering from the illness he contracted escaping from the Heights to the Grange; and part three is what Nelly relates some six months later, when he returns to give up his lease and retrieve his possessions. His story echoes Heathcliff's in part—his intrusion unbalances the isolation of Heathcliff's power over the three children, and he unwittingly sets in motion the release from bondage of young Catherine and Hareton.

The greatness of *Wuthering Heights* arises from the fact that it unfolds with absolute conviction. Not only does each scene follow the previous one with superb narrative economy, the author also offers very little interpretation of the events or the characters. *Wuthering Heights* is possibly the only English novel that ignores the reader so thoroughly, in such a European, and even Kafkaesque, way. The characters do what they do, events take place, enough said. Such novels have an undeniability about them that renders them vivid and concrete, as if they were mere artifacts of existence than of minds. The reader may, and in fact must, make of them what she will. Intransigence is the root charm of *Wuthering Heights*—characters in other novels live by passion, as Cathy and Heathcliff do, but these characters are unapologetic about it—they don't seem to understand that there is any other way to live. Their intransigence is a significant factor in the reader's willingness to suspend disbelief—every character in the novel, major and minor, might in some way be off-putting (selfish or feckless or petty or unkind), but they persist in being who they are, as the wild moors persist in being wild. And when the reader is in the mood, most other novels seem all too civilized by comparison.

29 · William Makepeace Thackeray · Vanity Fair

(1848; REPR., NEW YORK: PENGUIN, 2003), 809 PP.

At the beginning of *Vanity Fair,* two girls leave school. One is the sweet-natured daughter of a prosperous commercial family, Amelia Sedley. The other is her friend Becky Sharp, whose background is far more suspect (her mother was French, for one thing). Becky is smart and pretty, but never for a moment sweet-natured; she knows that she will have to use her wits to survive, and she intends to do so. The period is the Napoleonic Wars. Amelia is soon engaged and then married to an officer in the British army, and in one of the great set pieces of the novel, she accompanies him to Belgium, where he is killed in the Battle of Waterloo, leaving her with a son and a sentimental attachment to his memory. In the meantime, Becky flirts with Amelia's foolish brother, home from India, and then marries the rakish younger son of a wealthy country family, Rawdon Crawley. Rawdon lives in hopes of a large inheritance from his aunt, whom Becky attends to and flatters unceasingly. One by one, the plans and dreams of each character (and there are many besides these) come to nothing, wrecked by history but also by greed, selfishness, shortsightedness, and sentimentality.

I don't think it is possible to understand *Vanity Fair* without acknowledging Thackeray's extensive familiarity with French literature, because this huge novel takes up a Balzacian purpose—to depict English life over a period of twenty years, with an array of characters of all classes (at least all classes middling and above), and to depict it with the cool detachment implied equally by the title *Vanity Fair* as by Balzac's title *La Comédie humaine*. At the beginning and the end of the novel Thackeray explicitly likens his characters to puppets on a stage whose actions reveal general truths about human nature. Thackeray's purpose is essaylike (to demonstrate and argue) rather than poemlike (to evoke) or dramalike (to move). Becky is skilled in ways similar to characters in French novels—she dresses beautifully, she is smoothly hypocritical and coquettish, she has almost professional-level talents in music, she is unmotherly (she sends her child to a wet nurse, for one thing), and she is without any apparent profound emotions. She is greedy and always aware of where her self-interest lies. The plot of the novel can be understood in accordance with this French/English contrast—the typical English plot brings the love and the money together at the altar, and the typical French plot explores the ramifications of passion after the marriage has taken place. In *Vanity Fair* the characters marry for love and suffer the consequences—the novel explores what happens when those who have the money cannot be reconciled to the romantic aspirations of their children, and in fact never forgive the children for their acts of independence.

Unlike most of the other great Victorian novelists, Thackeray was born a gentleman and educated at a public school and at Cambridge. His allegiances were not with energetic upstarts, such as Dickens, or Nonconformists and women, such as Eliot, or sui generis provincials, such as the Brontës. His vision was conservative; it was colored by the fact that he lost his property as a young man through speculation and high living. The darkness he saw in human nature was thus a general sinfulness and vanity. He was not a liberal, like Dickens, who felt that social and economic circumstances accounted for most if not all of mankind's propensity to transgress. For Thackeray it is in human nature itself, even in the nature of virtuous characters, to be selfish and dissatisfied. As he says, "Which of us is happy in this world? Which of us has his desire? or, having it, is satisfied?" This is much more a French view than an English one, since many great English characters *are* happy in the possession of their desires—Tom Jones in the possession of Sophia, Darcy and Elizabeth in the possession of one another, as are even Cathy and Hareton, even Jane and Rochester, while many French characters, such as Julien Sorel, not to mention the more extreme characters in *Justine* and *Les Liaisons dangereuses,* are never happy in possession of anything they act to achieve.

The liberal satiric vision promotes specific reforms to get rid of specific evils and thereby enable people to gain their desires, but the conservative satiric vision is a wholesale one, asserting that nothing works and life must only be endured. Is either one truer or more profound? The answer for most readers is a matter of temperament as much as reason.

Thackeray's exploration of Becky's nature and her circumstances is detailed and profound, and says much about women that continues to be convincing. For one thing, Becky is smart. She understands her situation and knows that she must act to better it or sink into some sort of degradation. She gambles, using her charm and her wits to gain access to the money belonging to others, and she occasionally wins, but at several junctures her reading of the characters of those around her is mistaken—they turn out to be more selfish and more irrational than she had expected. Aunt Crawley, for example, cannot be reconciled to Rawdon's marriage to Becky in spite of the fact that she rather likes Becky, who attends to her and flatters her. Pitt Crawley, who benefits from Aunt Crawley's peevishness, can never be brought to make reparations for what he knows are his ill-gotten gains. Becky expects each of them to put sentiment or right ahead of greed, and her errors of judgment mean that she never has a respite from her plotting and scheming. Her husband, Rawdon, has no useful skills other than gambling and card playing, and Thackeray leaves it unclear whether Becky actually markets her attractiveness the way French women characters on the make tend to do. Becky's plotting finally destroys her when she and the powerful Lord Steyne have Rawdon arrested for debt and thrown in the sponging house so they can perhaps manage a tryst. The result is that Rawdon leaves her, Steyne is humiliated and does likewise, and Becky must shift for herself. Since her reputation is famously and fatally tainted by this incident, her situation deteriorates until she manages at the very end to hook the hapless Jos Sedley and inherit his insurance.

Although her decline is not edifying, Becky, of all the characters in the novel, is the only one capable of giving unalloyed pleasure to others. She is selfish and self-interested but observant. Every other character is blinded by his or her own desires. Becky alone sees what others want and occasionally acts to give it to them. She is remorseless but sometimes compassionate. My favorite moment in the novel comes when Becky at last gets to dine at the home of Lord Steyne. While the men are present, the women are marginally polite to her, but once the ladies leave the dining room and go to the drawing room, they ignore Becky completely. Finally Lady Steyne speaks to her out of pity, and, grateful, Becky plays and sings Mozart for her. Thackeray writes of Lady Steyne, whose life is one of almost Sicilian submission to the power of her husband, "She was a girl once more, and the brief period of her happiness bloomed out again for an hour" (p. 573). Toward the end of the novel it is Becky who understands that Amelia's illusions about her dead husband are dangerous for her, and it is Becky who acts to disabuse her of them.

My guess is that Thackeray was fonder of Becky than he let on, and that the narrator's steady abuse of her was a way of distancing himself from her. If the narrator judges her for her failures of virtue before the reader has a chance to, and the author succeeds in thoroughly punishing her, then her story is not shocking and disreputable but

just, and the author can delineate her virtues and vices in their fascinating combination without suffering harm to his own reputation for
respectability.

Vanity Fair is ruthlessly satiric. Some readers consider it the greatest
English novel because of its sweep and sophistication. Other readers
find it heavy going—interesting but not innovative enough (like *David
Copperfield* and *Madame Bovary*) to make the effort worthwhile. The
good stuff, I would say, is at the end rather than the beginning. In the
latter half, the style, the characters, and the plot mesh more smoothly,
and the author's wisdom grows somewhat less angry and more
resigned. And in the end, the love and the money do come together,
thanks to Becky.

30 · Harriet Beecher Stowe · Uncle Tom's Cabin

(1851; REPR., NEW YORK: MODERN LIBRARY, 2001), 662 PP.

Uncle Tom's Cabin was the most famous American novel of the nineteenth century, and Stowe the most famous American author. In the
twentieth century, as critical standards and social norms shifted, the
novel lost stature, especially in comparison to *Moby-Dick* and *The Scarlet Letter,* two contemporary novels that were not as popular in their
day. Nevertheless, *Uncle Tom's Cabin* is essential reading both as a
novel and as a social document. It is compelling and dramatic, full of
vividly wrought characters, wonderful and intelligent dialogue, and
ideas that were sophisticated in their time and remain so today.

Stowe's story begins simply—a Kentucky plantation owner gets
into financial difficulties, and to save the farm, he decides to sell two
slaves—his farm manager, Tom, and the child of his wife's favorite
house slave, Eliza. The scenes that ensue were as familiar to Americans of the nineteenth century as, let's say, scenes from the movie *Star
Wars* are to modern Americans. Eliza escapes with her son by leaping
from ice floe to ice floe across the frozen Ohio River. Tom is taken on a
riverboat down the Mississippi; he is sold to a benevolent but indecisive
owner and goes to live in New Orleans. After the famous death of his
owner's daughter, the saintly Eva, and the death of his owner in a bar
fight, he is then sold to Simon Legree, whose plantation is a sort of
agricultural concentration camp lost in the bayous of Louisiana. At

Legree's plantation, Tom meets Legree's bitterly angry slave concubine Cassy, and advises her to escape. When she does so, using a clever ruse, Legree beats Tom to death for not betraying her plans. Cassy, Eliza, her son, and Eliza's husband, George, are reunited in Canada at the end of the novel.

Stowe's plot is inherently suspenseful, full of heroic action, dangerous encounters, and threatening situations; it is made more so by the fact that she is an astute psychologist, capable of drawing a variety of interesting characters who play off against one another while also serving Stowe's larger purpose of exploring how the institution of slavery fit into and corrupted American life in the antebellum era. Stowe took up the two most controversial subjects in America, black-white relations and religion, and addressed them directly, and it is impossible, even at the beginning of the twenty-first century, to read *Uncle Tom's Cabin* without being impressed, moved, or offended. I attribute the continued currency of her novel to the continued unresolved dilemmas surrounding her subjects, but also to the author's own unshrinking and passionate convictions.

In style and tone, *Uncle Tom's Cabin* owes something to Dickens novels such as *The Old Curiosity Shop* and to nineteenth-century conventions of melodrama—the author intends to arouse pity, horror, and anger in the reader in order to move her to action. At the same time, some of the best parts of *Uncle Tom's Cabin* are discussions between such characters as Ophelia and Augustine and Cassy and Tom, or between the Shelbys, discussions that develop Stowe's argument against slavery while also developing complexity in her characters. Stowe has a sophisticated sense of humor, too. Early in the novel, two of Shelby's slaves are sent to help the slave trader catch Eliza. They foil the capture partly by knowingly playing the typical musical-hall roles of stupid "niggers" that the slave trader expects. They defeat him, laugh at him, and avoid punishment all at the same time. Toward the end of the novel, when Cassy and her charge escape Legree, they perform a similar jujitsu—Cassy plays upon Legree's superstitions, and Stowe makes knowing use of the conventions of gothic horror. The reader is tempted to laugh at the fool Legree until he avenges himself by beating Tom to death.

The modern reader has been warned away from *Uncle Tom's Cabin* by several generations of scholars who prefer the nineteenth-century male sensibility (*Moby-Dick, The Scarlet Letter*) and by several generations of black writers who prefer to tell their own history. Stowe's reputation has also suffered from the fact that Christian belief has become a taboo point of view in any modern novel worthy of critical consideration. But no one interested in American history, or in the history of the novel, or in the work of women writers should miss *Uncle Tom's Cabin*. This novel is one of the most important, and one of the most intriguing and readable, too.

31 · Herman Melville · Moby-Dick; or, The Whale

(1851; REPR., NEW YORK: PENGUIN, 1992), 625 PP.

The Hungarian critic György Lukács maintained that the difference between the novel and the drama is that while the drama works by precipitating and then accelerating the action, the novel works by retarding the action. The requirement that the author put off the climax is both his boon and his bane. On the one hand, while he is digressing, the author can expand his focus, deepen his psychological and sociological analysis, and engage in speculation. On the other hand, he must do all of this subtly, without either losing track of the plot (and therefore the suspense that carries the reader forward) or by telegraphing too quickly what is going to happen, which shuts down the plot entirely. *Moby-Dick* demonstrates the pleasures and profundities of digression and is an excellent example of how a novelist can excel at what he perhaps should not have tried in the first place.

In spite of the fact that the first line of the novel is "Call me Ishmael," Ishmael's own personality and fate are very little explored in *Moby-Dick;* the novel is not about character transformation. Ishmael takes up with Queequeg and goes to sea with him, but their relationship is not developed, nor are any other relationships on the *Pequod*. It is Ahab, in his obsession (he intends to find and kill the white whale), who becomes the main focus of the narrative, but his character is no more transformed than Ishmael's, though some of the ship captain's doubts and complexities are revealed from time to time. The *Pequod* looks for the white whale for hundreds of pages; the encounter itself takes thirty pages, or less than 5 percent of the novel. There is never any doubt about whether the whale will be found or pursued. At no juncture in the novel is there even the illusion of choice by Ahab, nor are there intervening circumstances. And so the novel is not about whether or even why the climactic event is to take place. The reader is simply asked to wait until it takes place and to contemplate it.

Moby-Dick relies on two things to maintain the reader's interest: the inherent strangeness of whaling, and the author's quest (expressed in his varieties of style) to exhaust the spiritual meanings of obsession (or "monomania," as it was called then). Melville excels at picturing what the reader may not have ever previously imagined—"the peeled white body of the beheaded whale flashes like a marble sepulchre; though changed in hue, it has not perceptibly lost anything in bulk" (p. 336), or the sensation of losing oneself in staring over the calm sea, or the appearance of the ship on a dark night, with all the furnaces stoked, rendering the blubber into oil. Some readers skip some of Melville's more essayistic, informative passages about types of whales and so forth, but the true lover of this novel—its ideal reader—savors even those passages that are outdated, as more examples of the variety of thoughts Melville brings to his theme; maybe a good analogy for this novel in another artistic medium is Bach's "Goldberg Variations." Much of the pleasure for the reader has to be witnessing the endless but systematic variety of the author's technique. *Moby-Dick* must be long because it takes a while for the author to impart to the reader enough information to enable the reader to make sense of everything the author wishes to communicate, just as it takes Bach a while to accustom the listener's ear and the listener's mind to his musical ideas. Part of every artist's job is to train his audience, though the artist may fail in his training and the audience may decline to be trained. But the reader willing to be trained to read and appreciate *Moby-Dick* gains a rare and steady pleasure—a prolonged experience of rightness and felicity of style and a vision of something entirely unknown suddenly made known. Othello is said by Shakespeare to woo Desdemona by telling her strange tales. So Melville, and all novelists who deal in the exotic, woo their readers. Those who love *Moby-Dick,* those who think it the best novel ever written in English, are those who relish the double strangeness of Melville's vision—the exotic locale and the visionary ideas—above every other joy that novels can afford.

Note added later:

I read *Moby-Dick* in the winter of 2003, and wrote this entry within a couple of days. When I came back to rethink and rewrite the entry in the winter of 2005, I found that I could hardly remember the novel, and certainly could not remember enough of it to expand my entry to include themes that other readers find compelling in Melville's vision. In some ways I consider this failure on my part odd. I have strong memories of most of the other works, including those I read before *Moby-Dick,* such as *The Princess of Clèves* and Scott's *The Tale of Old Mortality,* not to mention *The Red and the Black,* where, after two and a half years, I can remember how certain words looked on certain pages and where those pages were in the text. The interesting thing to me is that while *Moby-Dick* is possibly the greatest American novel and is beloved by many readers and scholars, it clearly didn't make much of an impression on me even though I was reading it attentively and not idly. The question, I think, is, can a reader read a book intentionally— that is, can she decide to be impressed by it, decide to take it in, decide to have a relationship with it? Some of the books on this list were difficult for me to relate to—I had internal arguments with the author all the way through; Ian McEwan's *Atonement* is a good example. These arguments helped fix those books in my mind even when I was not conscious of enjoying them. Other novels, of course, I liked very much and I remember them fondly every day or two in the ongoing flow of mental images that constitutes my inner life. But even though I had no argument with *Moby-Dick* and felt as though I was enjoying it and appreciating it without truly loving it, very little lingers, and I rarely think about it. Is this only because the concerns of the novel are extremely masculine and I don't really care about them? Is it because the style seemed heavy and ornate to me and didn't really communicate much about the psychology of the characters even though I wanted it to? Is it because the characters don't relate to one another in a way that I intuitively comprehend? More important, do I need to read it again and try to get more out of it? That strikes me as possible but not likely, rather like going out on another date with someone who was okay but not compelling the first time. On the other hand, even though the world is full of tempting new novels one can always go on to (I would like to go on to Michael Chabon's *The Amazing Adventures of Kavalier & Clay* and Marguerite Yourcenar's *Memoirs of Hadrian,* for example), the novel that one didn't connect with is always there on the shelf, waiting to be reexperienced by the different person you are going to be when you notice it again and are moved to pick it up.

32 · Nathaniel Hawthorne · The House of the Seven Gables

(1851; REPR., NEW YORK: RANDOM HOUSE, MODERN LIBRARY, 2001), 227 PP.

The House of the Seven Gables begins with what amounts to a prologue tracing the history of the house and the Pyncheon family, who own it. The first Colonel Pyncheon, in the time of the Salem witch trials, had coveted a property owned by another man, named Maule. He engineered an accusation of witchcraft against Maule, then confiscated Maule's land and built a house on it. Subsequently Colonel Pyncheon died, fulfilling the curse Maule had laid upon him prior to being executed. At the time of the narrative, the Pyncheon family is represented by two branches—the branch that lives frugally in the house, consisting of the middle-aged spinster Hepzibah and her brother Clifford, recently released from jail, and the branch that still has wealth and influence around the town, consisting of Judge Pyncheon. The way the novel is structured foreshadows that the two-hundred-year-old curse upon the family and the property will be realized and that justice will finally be done. The agent of this retribution/redemption is a distant cousin, Phoebe ("light"), who comes from the country to help Hepzibah in the tiny shop she establishes to support herself and Clifford. Eventually a boarder moves in, Holgrave, who seems to be the perfect new American man—enterprising, energetic, and interested in new technology (he is a daguerreotypist)—and he turns out to be a descendant of the Maule family. He and Phoebe come together at the end.

The House of the Seven Gables is not especially appealing. It bears comparison with *The Bride of Lammermoor* because it makes use of similar materials—old curses, fated outcomes, and family histories. But whereas Scott is careful to make the psychology of the characters and their interactions mesh with the omens and predictions, so that by acting within character the characters seem to work out their destinies as predicted, Hawthorne is less of a psychologist and more of a moralist. His few characters are not so much agents of the plot as objects of the narrator's observations and victims of circumstances. It is, in particular, the manner in which Hawthorne toys with ideas of spirits and ghosts that robs the novel of both supernatural operations *and* realistic motivation. Rather, each character seems to be a manifestation of a certain type of atmosphere. What prevails instead of logic and action is

aesthetic. Phoebe and Holgrave are attractive—she represents forgiveness and innocence, he represents reason. Judge Pyncheon is unattractive—he represents hypocrisy and is motivated principally by
greed. Each character rather mechanically acts out what he or she represents, and eventually, through the agency of the ancient curse (and
the author), Judge Pyncheon dies suddenly and then is held up by the
narrator as an example of the suddenness of death in the midst of life
(and egomania). At the same time, the family curse is revealed as not a
curse but a natural process—Holgrave theorizes that the judge has
died of natural causes (perhaps a heart attack or a stroke, the reader
thinks) and that predisposition to such a death is inherited and also
accounts for the earlier sudden death of Colonel Pyncheon. At the climax, the author does not take the opportunity to intensify his drama
but rather to ratchet up his eloquence—*The House of the Seven Gables*
turns out to be a sermon. The contrast with *The Bride of Lammermoor*
is apparent in terms of style, too. Whereas Scott uses a clear, more or
less objective style that naturally weighs the curses and superstitions
against the more mundane forces shaping the lives of his characters,
Hawthorne uses a highly charged and floridly ironic style that continuously reminds the reader what to think of the characters and the
events.

All of Hawthorne's characters have psychological possibilities, but
the plot hardly develops them. Hepzibah, a loving but unattractive
old maid, gains neither grace nor self-knowledge. The narrator repeats over and over that her brother Clifford's losses can never be redeemed and are without a larger purpose. Holgrave and Phoebe's love
is barely developed, and the judge is simply an emblem. Since the characters cannot, by the author's definition, change, the pages of the novel
have to be used for something other than character development, so
they are used for description (my favorite is of the chickens in the
yard) that is often quite lyrical and that gives the novel its romantic air.
But the reader has to wonder—well, *this* reader has to wonder—what
Hawthorne was getting at to begin with. Is there some political purpose here? If so, is the original sin that has cursed the Pyncheon family
really so simple as the fact that the first Pyncheon stole a small lot from
a neighbor? Or is there a larger uneasiness?

The House of the Seven Gables was written in 1850, when Americans
were broadly conscious of both the moral compromises of slavery and
of the eradication of Native Americans but had not decided how to act
upon their misgivings. It is possible, I think, to read the static and

heavily moralistic qualities of Hawthorne's novel as a resistance to considering larger questions of injustice and guilt in favor of contemplating minor ones. The novel is attempting to interpret history as entirely personal, through the lens of a family curse, but the characters cannot as yet imagine how to solve even their minor dilemmas—they are stuck in a state of unhappiness and moral unease until something happens that is outside their control, and miraculously, that thing brings prosperity. Hawthorne pays very little attention to the social context of the family—the history of the town, for example, or what the town is like at the time of the novel; as a result, the family can be redeemed solely through the original terms of the curse, which makes the plot (for example, that Holgrave turns out to be a Maule) too predictable. This sort of talelike wishful thinking works in some novels, but Hawthorne doesn't deliver on the promise of the tale—that the story will be entertaining. The novel turns out to be sober but not realistic, mysterious but not entertaining, and so doesn't succeed as either a romance or a realistic novel. *The Bride of Lammermoor,* by contrast, does face up to history and acknowledge its moral complexities; characters act and react to the consequences of their actions, but Scott also makes canny use of folkloric elements, so the novel gives the pleasures of both realism and romance. Scott has a political philosophy that encompasses injustice, hatred, revenge, and the passage of time that leads to reconciliation. Hawthorne (in my opinion as a reaction to the charged issues of his time) is unsure of the meaning of the history he wants to depict. The result is strange and flat—if the reader cannot respond to his style, there is little else to respond to.

33 · Gustave Flaubert · Madame Bovary

ED. PAUL DE MAN (1857; REPR., NEW YORK: W. W. NORTON, 1965), 255 PP.

Everything about *Madame Bovary* has been passionately discussed since publication: is it good, is it great, is it a novel, is it a "realist" novel, is it true, is it worthy, who is Emma, how did the author feel about her, about the rest of the characters and the setting, about himself, about literature, about the form of the novel? It is Flaubert's single greatest achievement that he systematically excluded the answers to these questions from the text itself by focusing intently on his subjects, only once, at the very beginning, allowing the narrator to speak in his own voice, to introduce Charles Bovary in school. Thereafter, Flaubert insistently presents his story as an objective reality, giving clues to its meaning only through tone. When Charles dies, the story ends. No overt lessons are drawn from it. If Flaubert's letters are to be believed, this was an exceptionally difficult technique—it takes the novelist's inherent and necessary subjectivity and pretends it doesn't exist. The result is to introduce the author's subjectivity into the reader's mind, unapologetically and successfully taking over her mind.

Flaubert famously remarked, "Emma Bovary, c'est moi" (several versions of the remark survive). The context of the remark is sometimes reported as Flaubert's exasperated answer to repeated questions about whether the portrait of Emma was based upon a real person. We can interpret Flaubert's identification with Emma in different ways— as a simple rejection of questions that he felt impugned his imagination, as a recognition that every character depicted in the work of every author is a product of that author's inner life, or as a closer, conscious identification between Flaubert and Emma, pointing up his "feminine qualities," or his "romantic nature," or whatever. My own inclination is to see his remark as the answer to what I would call "the French paradox." What is striking about *Madame Bovary*? It is not the plot. A hasty marriage to a boring husband, followed by several love affairs and ending in the destruction of everyone is the staple plot of French fiction. That the protagonist alone, or the lovers together, are surrounded by stupid, boring, unimaginative associates is the further ingredient of most such plots (in *The Princess of Clèves,* even the highest, most elegant court is by definition cruder than the princess and the duc de Nemours). These auxiliary characters are routinely portrayed as greedy, selfish, libertine, and nasty—Cousin Bette is the paradigm, and not a very extreme one at that. The French paradox is, how can a world as beautiful and delightful as France produce a literature universally peopled by vipers and fools?

It is *Madame Bovary* that resolves the paradox in a new and profound way—and like all paradoxes, it is easier to apprehend than to analyze. Emma's singular characteristic, which the style of the novel asks us to identify also as Flaubert's singular characteristic, is that she is repeatedly and perennially seduced by appearances. She is not merely sensuous. Rather, in how things look and feel, how patterns are created into images and scenes, Emma finds meaning that she then feels compelled to act upon. New drapes are as important to her as a new lover;

having champagne at a hotel in Rouen tells her who she is, and who she is is entirely different from who she had thought she was not long before. She has a strong sense of taste—a striking image of this occurs early in the novel, when she is looking at a keepsake (a book of sentimental poems and pictures), and she is moved by the way the paper film that covers the pictures folds over itself. But such images abound—all of Emma's existence is permeated by such moments. It is as if she can never detach herself long enough to get her thoughts together (and, indeed, she has no method of objectification, being poorly educated, having no friends, and lacking any feeling of kinship with her husband). If Emma is Flaubert, then she is Flaubert without his resources of companionship, money, and purpose, but her stylistic aspirations are the same as his—to have things right and suitable. She thus is strangely similar to Balzac's and Laclos's, and even de Sade's selfish characters, but she is more sympathetic, because we see the world as she sees it, everything heightened by her passionate intensity.

The fact that Flaubert reserves his judgment of Emma guarantees that she will be a revolutionary figure in French literature. She can be contemptible, and what she does to Charles can be reprehensible and frightening, but Flaubert never gives the reader permission to feel contempt for her (contrast this to Balzac's repeated condemnations of his characters—first he judges, only then does he offer mitigations of his judgments). Perhaps this very thing was the temptation of Gustave Flaubert that he found so arduous—the temptation to let himself judge rather than to suspend judgment. But as with *Pamela,* a personal, apparently artistic choice had a political effect once the novel was published. Flaubert's acceptance of Emma's kinship with him guaranteed that others would be able to feel a kinship with her in spite of her lack of virtue, kindness, intelligence, compassion, or true faith. As her inner life becomes the reader's, the reader can empathize with her, and perhaps even sympathize with her, without needing a traditional excuse (in *The Red and the Black,* for example, Madame de Rênal is not unlike Emma, but Stendhal gives us permission to sympathize with her by making her a well-meaning woman and a good mother).

The other important thing about *Madame Bovary* is that there is something wrong with Emma. She does not fit into the world she was born into. Flaubert himself offers no theory of what the problem is— either with regard to origins or to any possible solution. One critic suggests it is simple bad luck, another that her education is wanting. There are plenty of characters in the history of prose fiction who have something wrong with them, but Flaubert's relentless depiction of Emma's life and death makes her seem comprehensible, like a case history. Because he depicts her in such detail, she ceases to be merely a person among others; in spite of her mediocrity, her life has been found dramatic, she has been found worthy of analysis. Her "case" predates Freud and the other literary theorists of psychology, but it sets them up—it prefigures that facet of the modern world, the minute analysis of the average man or woman.

34 · Charles Dickens · A Tale of Two Cities

(1859; REPR., NEW YORK: BANTAM, 1989), 352 PP.

In the 1840s and '50s, Dickens wrote a series of deeply serious political novels that explored the inequities and the suffering that grew out of the rise of urban capitalism in England. The last of these, *Little Dorrit,* contains some of Dickens's most insightful writing and harshest criticism of the world he lived in, but the plot became so tangled over the course of eighteen lengthy installments that Dickens had to include a note at the end explaining what happened. He then turned to what surely must have seemed like an even vaster and more confusing theme—the French Revolution. But the novel he came up with has an elegant and simple plot, while at the same time it is perhaps the most astute portrayal of the psychology and sociology of violent social change ever written.

Dickens's guide and mentor for *A Tale of Two Cities* was the historian Thomas Carlyle, whose work on the French Revolution Dickens had read more than once and much admired. His plan was to dramatize Carlyle's ideas, not to improve upon them. Nevertheless, Dickens's novel remains current while his friend's history does not. The reason is surely that Dickens is able to vividly embody the ambiguities of the Revolutionary period as well as to cogently characterize the social forces at work. Carlyle may have supplied the analysis, but Dickens understood the human truths at the source.

The characters of Dr. Manette, Lucie, Charles Darnay, Miss Pross, the Defarges, and even Sydney Carton are less complex, psychologically, than is usual for Dickens, signaling that his novel is, indeed, a "tale"—Lucie and Charles, in particular, are a simple and virtuous couple with almost no characteristics apart from their virtues. Dr. Manette *is* his imprisonment. Madame Defarge is relentlessness personified. The only characters with the usual Dickensian flourishes and idiosyncrasies are Jerry Cruncher, Miss Pross, and Mr. Lorry, but they hardly ever get out of hand, as quirky characters such as Mr. Micawber do in other Dickens novels. The plot is all, and it is a cinematic plot. Dickens was passionately interested in theater, and was an accomplished amateur actor. He wrote or collaborated on several plays over the years, and *A Tale of Two Cities* has the tightness of a play—it is full of coincidences, twins, doubles, and repetitions. But because of the spaciousness and grandness of Dickens's themes—the differences between France and England, the nature of mass movements, and social violence—it does as a novel what a play can't quite do—it moves through time and space, panning over crowds, capturing the surge of large groups in flux. The narrator's voice, which is particularly rich and insightful in this novel, works like a camera, pointing out what is important and focusing the reader's attention on particulars that make sense of the chaos.

As a rule, the novel and the cinema don't work in similar ways, and as a rule the novel has not been good at depicting wars and revolutions, but in the sections where Dickens wants to give a sense of what groups are doing, he uses powerful and archaic images of fire, flood, and wild dancing. When he wants to depict the significance of a murder, he uses metaphors of stone gargoyles. He is communicating figuratively that the forces at work are elemental and morally natural—there is, after all, nothing so logical or implacable as the consequences of tyranny.

But revenge, the basic motive of the republican characters, works like a machine, inhumanly mirroring and reproducing the tyranny that gave rise to it. As the Revolution progresses, Dickens's insights into the republican mind are no less unsentimental than his earlier insights into the aristocratic mind. Through Sydney Carton and Mr. Lorry, Dickens depicts what it is to remain human in the midst of fear and rage—it is to keep order, to maintain attachments and affections, to make plans with a cool head, to sustain a sense of compassion, to endure, and to accept defeat knowing that the body is not the only manifestation of life. *A Tale of Two Cities* is Dickens's most openly faithful novel, but his faith is simple—merely a faith in redemption through sacrifice and kindness.

Dickens always strove to depict the web of connections he saw between all individuals, no matter how far apart they appeared to be.

The connections in *A Tale of Two Cities* are very tight—defying plausibility for some readers. But I see the novel as a discourse on that very theme—the responsibilities and the pleasures of the connections to all around us that we barely see or feel and sometimes are reluctant to acknowledge, but exist anyway, whether we can sense them or not.

35 · Wilkie Collins · The Woman in White

(1860; REPR., NEW YORK: BANTAM, 1985), 564 PP.

The Woman in White was one of the first, if not the first, great novels of detection, though the "detective" is not a private eye or a police official, but merely an interested party, Walter Hartright, an artist and drawing master. The crime is fraud rather than murder, and Collins depicts nothing grisly or violent, but nevertheless *The Woman in White* is a page-turner, showing that a good riddle, an intelligent style, and compelling characters are plenty sufficient for a thriller, and that questions of good and evil do not require large effusions of gore.

Like many English novels, the story begins with a rich young woman and a poor young man, who fall in love but are separated by difficulties of class and wealth. Laura Fairlie has already been betrothed for two years at the novel's outset, to a man of large property from a distant part of England, in accordance with her father's last wishes. Walter and Laura fall in love, but are properly circumspect, and renounce one another within the first hundred pages. The stage is thus set for the typical English outcome, but Collins chooses a new way to get there.

There is nothing apparently wrong with the prospective bridegroom, Sir Percival Glyde (except his sinister name), but Laura's beloved half-sister, Marian, and her dog are both suspicious of him. Nevertheless, the marriage goes forward even as symptoms of a coming disaster begin to accumulate. The pleasure of *The Woman in White* is not that it avoids damsel-in-distress clichés, but that it embraces them and converts them into actual complexities. Collins owes a lot to the tradition of *Pamela* and other virtue-beset novels, as well as gothic novels such as Mrs. Radcliffe's *The Mysteries of Udolpho* (1794), but he locates every scene and event in a specific, modern, and prosaic landscape. The characters meet on Hampstead Heath, in Cumberland, Hampshire, and in St. John's Wood in London. They ride in trains and cabs and speak in typical dialects. Most importantly, Collins's style is solid, objective, and reassuring (though he adopts several different points of view and styles of composition). He seems to be asking, can the old bogey of false marriage, of kidnapping and even rape happen right here, in England, in the sunshine of every day? And he seems to be answering yes.

And yet the end is never really in doubt, because Laura and Walter's love is true. The compelling quality of the narrative comes from the ambiguity of Collins's characters—in several situations, certain characters could make dangerous or harmful choices; other, more sympathetic characters are at their mercy. The momentum of the plot argues for the happier choice, but the complexity of the characters seduces the reader into imagining things going differently. Thus Collins fully exploits the paradox of the thriller. The thriller is essentially a tragicomic form. Maybe a paradigmatic model is Shakespeare's *Measure for Measure,* in which a false marriage is threatened; one character appears to die but revives; and a powerful, high-ranking character must sort out the difficulties and bring about the happy ending. "The danger but not the death" is simultaneously suspenseful and reassuring—the perfect entertainment for a reading public that lives in basically secure circumstances, as the literate middle class was beginning to do in the high Victorian period, when Collins's novels were published with great success.

A necessary requirement of Collins's sort of ungruesome thriller was that he create complex characters who could or might do anything, rather than mechanical types who were certain to act predictably. In *The Woman in White,* Count Fosco, his wife, Sir Percival, and Laura's half-sister Marian have a suspenseful richness. Following the workings of their minds and the ramifications of their relations with one another is enough—no need for bloodier shocks. And yet, in the end, the novel is less satisfying because of its suspenseful form—the wonderful prose, the fabulous characters, the astutely depicted settings have failed to reveal anything larger than the plot. The plot has taken over the author's point of view, and the critique or vision he might have offered has been sacrificed. This is the further paradox of the thriller, which subsequent authors have continued to wrestle with. The thriller posits various forms of evil and goodness that come into conflict. The next step, of course, is some sort of philosophical program that reflects upon the nature and sources of good and evil, but plot complexity prohibits discussion that is productive, and anyway, the demands of the plot beg the question—evil exists in the last analysis so that the author can write a thriller. While the thriller form addresses the classic concern of literature—the nature of and the interplay of good and evil—it addresses it tautologically, and proposes the discussion of good and evil as essentially an entertainment. Thriller writers after Collins tried to solve this ontological problem by depicting more gore and destruction (more danger and more death for less important characters), but still they cannot escape its paradoxes.

One of the interesting features of cultural history since Collins's time is that the entertaining, tautological, and tragicomic form of the thriller has almost entirely taken over cultural considerations of good and evil, through best sellers and movies, and these have accustomed us to the evils in our world, reassured us that escape is possible for a few main characters (and we are all the main characters of our own stories), and so inured us to the existence of evil that it causes no outrage or even disquiet.

Wilkie Collins · The Moonstone

(1868; REPR., NEW YORK: OXFORD UNIVERSITY PRESS, 1999), 466 PP.

In narrative form, *The Moonstone* uses the same device of multiple tellers as *The Woman in White*. It also has a similar charming liveliness of style and similar typical English characters—the beautiful young heiress, the attractive scapegrace lover, the kindly faithful servants, and the villain who is virtuous on the surface and corrupt underneath. It is a novel designed to be reassuring, in which the temporarily cursed characters (cursed by the Moonstone, a jewel) are exiled from the beautiful country estate, and then restored to it by truth, love, and money.

What *The Moonstone* has to offer is delightful ingenuity of plot. The premise is simple—a jewel is bequeathed to a young girl coming of age, and then stolen. A detective is called in. Some danger and some death (which I won't reveal the nature of) intervene before the fate of the jewel is discovered. The author uses a fairly elementary deduction strategy (which the modern reader may be a little too astute for) to mislead the characters and to tempt the reader to skip forward to discover the solution (the novel was originally published in thirty weekly parts, so skipping forward wasn't possible for its first readers). What the novel also has is something modern scholars like very much—the beginnings of a critique (or at least a consideration) of British colonial activities in India. The novel begins with British soldiers plundering an Indian town and stealing a holy jewel. It does not overtly analyze who has the right to possess the jewel, but it does, in the end, return the jewel to its original location. There are several Indian characters, a character of mixed race, and some discussion of opium-eating (Collins took laudanum, a form of opium, for a painful illness that modern scholars have not diagnosed). The morality of the opium trade was a topic of public debate while Collins was writing the novel, and to modern thinkers is a prime example of the callousness and corruption of British imperialist capitalism.

Collins is a perfect candidate for literary rehabilitation, because it is tempting to see a great deal that is subversive encoded in his novels, and so they are novels that seem to argue against their own affirmation of rational and traditional English life. Collins himself was a complex man, not nearly as respectable, or eager to appear respectable, as most English novelists, and he was a great protégé of Dickens's, who upheld respectability in his writings but not in the last thirteen or fourteen years of his life. But is *The Moonstone* really subversive? As I pointed out in the entry on *The Woman in White,* the detective novel is a conservative form—the purpose of detection is to ferret out evil and dispose of it, temporarily righting the imbalance in the world created by criminal activity. In neither of these novels does Collins show any propensity to argue that the imbalance in the world can be righted in the sense that the pervasiveness of evil can be mitigated in general—the lesson the characters learn is to be more careful and perhaps take refuge behind large gates.

Collins's style is attractive, objective, and accessible. It is felicitous, like Scott's style. It does not open out into an irrational, visionary world as Dickens's style does. Collins the writer seems like a versatile but basically sanguine fellow for whom happiness is made up of normal forms of human love, comfort, stability, and companionship. Collins's emotional state never seems to drive his works—Dickens was often sentimental, or outraged, or awed, or overjoyed, or transported, and his characters and plots existed as embodiments of these intense states. Collins, by contrast, writes like a member of a society into which he fits fairly well and whose norms he feels comfortable with.

Collins's works give pleasure rather than pity, terror, or transcendence, like those of Dickens, the Brontës, or Shakespeare. Whether it was Collins's temperament, or the form of the detective novel itself, or Collins's ambitions for popular success that made these novels "encoded" or self-contradictory is not, I think, susceptible to critical understanding. Best to just enjoy.

36 · Ivan Turgenev · Fathers and Sons

TRANS. RICHARD FREEBORN

(1862; REPR., NEW YORK: OXFORD UNIVERSITY PRESS, 1998), 201 PP.

Fathers and Sons is the transitional work between Russian novels of the Romantic period and the great Russian novels of the realist period. It even has an aged and attenuated Romantic character, Pavel Petrovich, who has sacrificed his life to unavailing passion and in the course of the novel fights a duel of his own instigation, even though duels are sadly out of date. Mostly, though, it has the ineffable charm and brevity of the Russian fiction that grew out of "Eugene Onegin," Pushkin's great and much-beloved narrative poem of the 1830s. The style of Turgenev's language and the way in which the narrative develops are suggestive and lyrical rather than dense. Detail seems to accumulate almost incidentally (though, of course, that sense of casualness is carefully contrived by the author).

Turgenev's central character is Bazarov, a "new man," whose intellectual inspirations are German and scientific rather than French and Romantic. He is openly contemptuous of every received idea, including ideas of love or morality. The paradox of Bazarov's character and his social position is that he seems, both to himself and to those around him, to be Russia's only chance to save herself, but he has no belief in Russia's saving herself. Bazarov's friend Arkady is made of kinder, more conventional stuff. When the two men meet two sisters and fall in love, the reader can't help desiring a happy ending for Arkady, and that happy ending is achieved. But there is no happy ending for Bazarov, and in fact he rejects all ideas that would lead to a happy ending. A conventional happy ending would so betray Bazarov's principles that it would be more horrifying than the ending he achieves.

Turgenev addresses Bazarov's nihilism, but because of the lightness of his technique he does not judge it. He is a realist in the sense that he holds up five characters for the reader's consideration—Bazarov, his father, Arkady, his father, and Arkady's uncle—and he follows their progress over the course of about a year, almost without comment. He doesn't weigh their fates morally; rather he observes them with a muted but natural generosity of spirit and then parts from them once their fates are decided. It may come as a surprise to the reader that the other characters seem to have such respect for Bazarov, since he is brusque and churlish and has none of their charm and feels none of the attachments they revel in. But he looks forward to Dostoevsky and is, in some sense, a true Russian type, a man who is resolutely searching for a way into a new and different era, a way to solve social, economic, and political problems that didn't exist in England or France. In this sense he is a modern, ideological man and thoroughly recognizable to modern readers, who have seen youthful nihilists with no manners come and go again and again.

Like *A Hero of Our Time, Fathers and Sons* is a bit enigmatic—beautifully even in tone, suggesting more than it states, modest, never didactic, and yet true and important because of rather than in spite of its brevity. It is the sort of book a reader returns to, not because there is so much material there that she has to read it over and over to excavate it all, but because what is there is ephemeral, easily lost, and yet seductive.

37 · Émile Zola · Thérèse Raquin

TRANS. AND ED. LEONARD TANCOCK (1867; REPR., NEW YORK: PENGUIN, 1981), 255 PP.

Thérèse Raquin was Zola's first success, but initially it was a *succès du scandale,* since Zola was accused of writing pornography—there was such a critical outcry that he felt he had to defend himself in his preface to the second edition of the novel. Zola also wrote a stage version of the novel, which was popular at the time and more lasting than any other of his plays.

The plot is focused and dramatic: two children are reared together, a boy and his cousin, by the boy's mother, a woman of some means who lives in a small French town. When the cousins reach marriageable age, they do what the mother wishes, which is to marry one another, because they have lived such a circumscribed life that they don't have any idea what else to do. Thérèse, the girl, is quiet and submissive, but secretly passionate. Camille, the boy, is sickly and spoiled. Though the three members of the small family live and work together, they have no intimacy with one another, and the inner life of each develops entirely in isolation from the inner life of the others. The mother eventually decides to take the money she has saved and open a small shop in Paris. Camille finds himself an office job, and the family gains a circle of friends, one of whom, Laurent, is about Camille's age and is strongly drawn to Thérèse, who reciprocates his lust.

Laurent and Thérèse plot to kill Camille and successfully make his death look like an accident, but while the scheme works and they end up marrying, their relationship is entirely contaminated by their secret, and their once-passionate attachment becomes a daily exercise in repulsion and panic. They live with Camille's mother, who eventually has a stroke, and they care for her with all apparent tenderness (her friends marvel at how considerately they treat her), but once again, each one puts his or her faith in arduously maintained secrecy, and each lives a hellish existence right beside the others, never comforted but always tormented by their presence (and by the growing presence of Camille, who obsesses each of them differently).

Thérèse Raquin demonstrates that a carefully worked-out psychological theory can be dramatic and compelling, even when the characters are not appealing or sympathetic. Zola himself, as both author and narrator, embraced the idea that characters without charm, education, or even notably human qualities were entirely worthy of literary depiction as examples of behavior patterns. In fact, the fewer special qualities his characters (you might call them, not protagonists or antagonists, but simply "agonists"—beings with feelings but requiring no partisanship by the reader) had, the more valuable they were as objective examples. Zola wanted to write fiction in the scientific mold—he called his style "naturalism."

The melodrama of the story of Thérèse and Laurent is suspenseful, but it barely hides the theory supporting the action of the plot, which can be outlined as follows: the failure of Madame Raquin to reckon with Thérèse's nascent sexual feelings when she reared Thérèse and Camille together through childhood and adolescence made the young woman immune to Camille but susceptible to Laurent. The feelings these two had for one another were solely physical and depended heavily on the exciting secrecy of their initial relations. After the murder, the simultaneous presence of guilt and lust eventually destroyed the lust, and neither Laurent nor Thérèse were capable of any other form of connection to another human being. Guilt is all-consuming and works by a process of association, overwhelming, bit by bit, every aspect of the lives of the guilty. It cannot be expiated or relieved, but in the last scene, when Laurent and Thérèse drink poison with Madame Raquin as their silent and immobile witness (she has suffered a stroke), they achieve a single ambiguous moment of oneness.

This is both a psychological and a spiritual theory—it asserts the inescapable solitude of the individual and the irredeemable natural selfishness of human nature. Zola's theory is a train of logic backed up by shrewdly chosen details of setting, action, and revealed thought. The premises, however, require the same leap of faith that any theory requires—his story demonstrates his theory because it was designed to do so.

This self-referential quality does not disqualify *Thérèse Raquin* from being a good novel—I happen to like it—only from being a good scientific experiment. In fact, every novel requires the author to have a psychological theory—every train of logic (which in a novel is made up of actions, dialogue, and expressed thoughts) requires theory to progress from one step (one plot point) to the next. Some theories are more conventional than others, some are more profound than others, some date more quickly than others, but an author with a theory, even a theory that dates very quickly, is in general more humane and large-spirited than an author with no theory or no interest in theory. The very attempt to come up with a theory expresses a broader humanity and a wider perspective. In Zola's case it was as though he were saying, "Even these sorts of persons are interesting to me, and I can make them interesting to you."

38 · Anthony Trollope · The Last Chronicle of Barset

(1867; REPR., NEW YORK: ALFRED A. KNOPF, EVERYMAN'S LIBRARY, 1993), 768 PP.

Marcel Proust was only the most famous novelist to try out the virtues of what might be called the meganovel. In the 1830s and 1840s Balzac wrote his eighty-five novels that were loosely linked as *La Comédie humaine,* and Trollope wrote six novels of the fictional cathedral town of Barchester in the 1850s and 1860s, as well as a series of linked novels about English political life known as the Palliser novels. Many of these novels worked somewhat like Balzac's *Comédie,* with characters who appear as major in one and reappear as minor in others. The mega-novel allows the author to explore a milieu in depth and to follow his characters as they age and develop. *The Last Chronicle of Barset* is Trollope's last novel about Barchester, but the reader need not have read any of the others to enjoy it thoroughly.

The premise of the novel is that an impoverished country curate, Mr. Crawley, passes a check for twenty pounds (maybe the equivalent of seven hundred dollars in modern money) in payment of a past due bill. When the check goes to the bank, it turns out that it is a check that had been lost by the estate agent of the signer of the check, Lord Lufton. Mr. Crawley gives two stories about where he got the check, but in fact he can't remember the origin of the check because of his perennially confused mental state. He is thus in danger of either being proved a thief or proved a madman. Neither will be to his benefit in demonstrating his competence to retain his curacy and continue to support his family.

The depiction of Crawley is a marvelously detailed and insightful portrait of a very antisocial, proud, and meticulous man, a domestic tyrant, a brilliant scholar, a flawed but compassionate human being. The analysis of his marriage and family life is no less compelling: his wife loves him but fears him, and never knows from one day to the next how to deal with him—she is always in danger of offending his pride with her concern, and yet she doubts whether he is competent to act on his own behalf (he isn't—for example, when he must go to court to be indicted on the charge of theft, he is too proud to get a lawyer, and he is indicted even though the justices are looking for some way, any way, to let him off).

Crawley's difficulty works as an instrument to expose a cross section of the entire town. His guilt or innocence is a matter of wide discussion, and his impending trial serves to put a kink in the marital plans of a local squire, Major Grantly, who loves Crawley's nineteen-year-old daughter, but whose family is appalled at the thought of being allied through marriage with the daughter of a thief. And when Crawley's daughter, Grace, goes to stay with a friend, because he and his wife can no longer afford to keep her, she meets another young woman to whose hand her cousin aspires. Trollope is the master who orchestrates this social symphony, who engages the reader's sentiments and loyalties over these less than life-and-death issues, and who then very neatly and yet plausibly brings them to a graceful conclusion.

Trollope has many virtues as a novelist. He is organized and efficient; he has a good sense of pace and of proportion, too. His characters are more than believable—they seem perfectly familiar, both as types and as individuals. Trollope's wisdom about the workings of marriage seems almost modern, and contrasts strongly with that of almost every other Victorian writer—he seems actually familiar with intimacy as most people know it, especially the way marriages have two manifestations—the one presented to the outside world, and the one the spouses themselves know. But the best thing about Trollope is that he is always one step ahead of the reader, who comes to feel that there is nothing in the world that the author doesn't know everything about. And Trollope's style, which is objective, understated, detailed, and eloquent, is perfectly suited for his sort of sociological and psychological expertise.

Trollope was a worldly man—his mother was a popular novelist and travel writer who supported the family while he was growing up. He made his way in the British civil service and traveled extensively. Dickens, for example, went to America, France, and Italy. Trollope lived in Ireland, traveled to the United States and Europe more than once, and also to Australia, New Zealand, and South Africa. For purposes of his writings, he was perfectly familiar with how the English ruling class worked, both socially and politically. Judging by his composing style, he went about all things with care and deliberation—in fact, the sympathetic young men in his novels are often beset by indecisiveness about romantic versus monetary concerns; young men in other Victorian novels usually disdain such practical considerations.

Trollope is a master at entering the minds of a variety of characters and showing how their thoughts progress, and also at showing how they are often deluding themselves or how their views of themselves contrast with the way others see them. Each vivid character is fully enmeshed in a social network, and this enmeshment has consequences—Major Grantly and his father, for example, get into a very entertaining tug-of-war about his prospective engagement that involves anger, resentment, stubbornness, and empty threats on both sides that could easily result in the disinheritance of a beloved son by a beloved father, and which is almost entirely carried out through a discussion about foxes on the family estate. Truly odd characters, such as Crawley, are explored as astutely as more normal ones, but Trollope is

unusual in that he can individualize normality and make it compelling—he can give the reader a picture of lives not so unlike her
own, and concerns not so different from those she herself has. Trollope
is not a sensualist like Flaubert, or a visionary like Dickens, or even a
strict moralist like George Eliot. In the Barchester novels Trollope's
view is essentially benign, and his endings comic in the red-blooded-
Englishman tradition of Fielding and Scott. Trollope writes as if his
reason is in charge, but also as if his reason is entirely cognizant of the
irrational, the romantic, and the unscrupulous. In fact, he makes all
those other Victorians seem a little overheated and melodramatic. This
is a lovely and delicious novel.

Anthony Trollope · The Eustace Diamonds

(1873; REPR., NEW YORK: PENGUIN BOOKS, 1986), 770 PP.

The Eustace Diamonds was one of Trollope's later novels—he wrote it
at fifty-eight, long after he had completed the Barchester novels, which
gained him his reputation and his status, and at about the same time as
The Way We Live Now, which was his darkest satire of contemporary
English life. He acknowledged that his ideas for the novel were influenced both by *The Moonstone,* with its jewel theft, and by the character
of Becky, in *Vanity Fair.*

The possession of the necklace in question is subject to dispute—
Lizzie Eustace, the twenty-year-old widow of Sir Florian Eustace and
the mother of the heir to the Eustace fortune, claims that her husband
gave it to her free and clear before his death. The Eustace family solicitor, Mr. Camperdown, claims that she cannot possess it because it is an
heirloom belonging to the estate and tries to insist upon its return, but
Lizzie is not a young woman with whom insistence is possible. She is
akin, in a way, to Melville's Bartleby the Scrivener—she carries stubbornness to a level previously unknown to her friends (a level quite
irritating and even frustrating to the reader, whom Trollope does not
allow to feel sympathy for Lizzie). Lizzie is selfish, stubborn, beautiful,
manipulative, and almost successful, a girl no one likes but few can
resist. Eventually her success is thoroughly compromised by her flaws
of character, and those she had hoped to ensnare escape her, but it is

not without cost to them. If most novels depict some positive or negative transformation of character by the protagonist, *The Eustace Diamonds* does not. The fact that Lizzie cannot learn from her experience, or even comprehend the differences between herself and others with more integrity, is the essence of her nature and is, actually, the great genius of Trollope's portrayal. What he is interested in is only secondarily Lizzie herself. Her place in society and her effect upon others are his real subjects, which he anatomizes minutely and in a cool, eloquent style. The result is that the reader nods and nods in agreement—Lizzie leaps from the page, unfamiliar in literature but utterly familiar in life, a portrait of a sister or a cousin or a friend whose behavior one is always trying to account for and failing.

Lizzie isn't the only one—Frank, her cousin; Lucy, Frank's beloved; Lord George—almost every major character of the novel is alive, true, not clichéd. Trollope is as insightful about the minor characters as he is about the major ones, and in that sense totally throws off what the English novel owes to the theater—no plot elements and no characters are coasting on theatrical conventions. All are depicted with the attention to detail and to the inner life that only the novel can accomplish.

Trollope is often criticized for being habitually digressive, and in fact *The Eustace Diamonds* could have been shortened by about 15 percent if an authoritative editor had controlled Trollope's tendency to repeat himself. Nevertheless, Trollope's method is one of incremental accumulation of detail. He reminds us of what we know, then adds to it, always bringing in the new material in the context of the familiar. The result is an unparalleled sense that the reader understands everything about the situation and the characters (and, over the course of Trollope's entire oeuvre, the class society of Victorian England). He does not have Proust's sensibility—Trollope is cerebral and ironic rather than lyrical and evocative—but his works add up to a similar compendious exploration of a certain place and a certain time. Trollope is not overtly comic or satiric, like Dickens or Thackeray, but is generously ironic. His typical view of his characters is honest and astute but forgiving. The virtuous ones are not so very virtuous as to be unbelievable, and the villainous ones are not so much evil as ignorant and small. Trollope gives them plenty of opportunity to grow wise, and some of them take it while others do not.

A few years after *The Eustace Diamonds* Trollope wrote an autobiography in which he portrayed his novelistic enterprise not as a quest for high art but as a daily task not unlike other professional work. He also outlived his own popularity by a few years. Trollope didn't advertise his gifts very well, and his reputation suffered in consequence, but the entertainment value of his works, and their value as social documents, has grown. His characters have a familiarity and an immediacy that those of writers with a more distinct style do not, and the friendly density of his style has worn well, too. He is not as weird as Dickens, nor as jaded as Thackeray. Trollope doesn't mind a little sin, and he knows that lives go on after the plot ends (Lizzie Eustace turns up again in *The Prime Minister,* unimproved morally but believably older and more knowledgeable). He is a novelist for adults.

39 · Fyodor Dostoevsky · The Idiot

TRANS. ALAN MYERS (1868; REPR., NEW YORK: OXFORD UNIVERSITY PRESS, 1998), 652 PP.

The "idiot" is Prince Myshkin, a young man who returns to Russia from years at a Swiss clinic, where he has been treated for epilepsy. In addition to his illness, and perhaps because of it, Myshkin is (and was intended to be by Dostoevsky) a representation of pure goodness. "Pure goodness," as embodied by the prince, is made up of a cluster of characteristics—he is solitary, poor (at first), innocent and naive, honest, intuitive, generous, easily imposed upon, forgiving, "democratic" (in the sense that he cares little about social status), socially awkward, passive, afflicted by a magical disease, and susceptible to visions of love and brotherhood. He is also both strangely attractive and strangely repellent to those he meets. At least some of these characteristics Myshkin shared with his creator—epilepsy is the most obvious. It is fair to say, I think, that Dostoevsky built his protagonist around some image he had of himself. But the "idiot" is an idea trying to be a character. At times in the novel he almost achieves fullness, but he never throws off his origins in the author's ideas rather than in the author's world—he contrasts strongly, for example, to Raskolnikov, the main character of *Crime and Punishment,* who was based on a real murderer Dostoevsky read about in the newspaper (rather as Stendhal read about the man upon whom he based Julien Sorel). The problem with Prince Myshkin is that Dostoevsky has to give him a story, and the story Dostoevsky gives him is jumbled and overly dramatic.

Almost as soon as the prince arrives in St. Petersburg, he encounters two beautiful women. One is the former mistress of a wealthy old man, a young woman who had been taken up as an orphan by the owner of the estate her family lived upon, and both educated and raped by him for several years. Her attempts to free herself of this man are the talk of the city. She arouses both pity and desire on the part of those who know her, and she seems to court the dangers of her position. The other woman is the spoiled youngest daughter of the prince's only living relative. The prince is drawn to both of these women, but he is too naive to understand, or perhaps feel, the difference between eros and agape. And perhaps Dostoevsky is pointing out that in a truly good man, especially one who is a virgin, as Myshkin certainly is, there is no difference. At any rate, he is the passive recipient of the passions of both women. But while both are strongly drawn to him, neither is capable of feeling or acting in a consistent manner, or even a kind manner. The prince is unable to choose between them, and unable to really understand the intentions of either of them. The reader may be forgiven for having the same problem.

Dostoevsky may be exploring the age-old European problem of, on the one hand, whether a virtuous woman can truly love a man and retain her virtue and, on the other hand, how young women are to be disposed of in opposition to their own wishes. Toward the end of the novel, the father of the second young woman attributes the whole fiasco to the fact that the prince had been interested in "the woman question."* His real focus, though, seems to be the array of Russian characters the prince encounters after his sojourn in Switzerland, and whether he can handle them. He cannot. It's possible that the average reader can't handle them either, since they seem to be a bunch of drunks, hysterics, liars, madmen, and manic-depressives.

The novel, as I suggested with regard to Flaubert, was one of the immediate sources of psychoanalytic theory, and Dostoevsky, like Dickens (whose work he loved), had a strong interest in mental illnesses—addictions, mood disorders, character disorders, personality disorders. All of the characters of *The Idiot* show symptoms of these. They do almost everything on impulse—marry, betray, attempt extortion, go into the country, forgive, commit murder, make assignations. Their reactions to these impulses, in themselves and in others, are distorted, and everyone's distorted reactions reinforce the distorted reactions of the others. For example, when an elderly and rather crazy

*The nineteenth-century precursor to feminism.

man dies, even those characters who hadn't liked him grieve vocifer-ously, but when a character is murdered, the two characters most involved hardly show any reaction at all. One thing that almost every character does at one point or another is discourse at length in a man-ner that is totally inappropriate to his or her social situation at the moment, about himself or herself. Histrionic display and disorder are the norms of their lives; giving vent to momentary feelings, their most natural form of expression. In such a society, mere perfect goodness must inevitably fail, simply because the success of passivity, honesty, and generosity depend on at least a degree of self-knowledge and con-sistency by those who are being benefited, or upon the acceptance of social norms about what is good. Fielding is able to depict Squire All-worthy as perfectly good because Squire Allworthy has a social func-tion that gives his goodness a responsible and powerful outlet. His aims correspond to the creation and maintenance of social order in a cultivated and fertile landscape. The characters of *The Idiot* are con-stantly at loggerheads about every aspect of their inner lives and their outer lives, and this conflict is only just veiled by manners. Myshkin is conceived as a character without any power at all—with even less power than those around him. Powerlessness is an essential part of his goodness, so he is doomed.

Would both the female characters be ruined, each in her separate way, if Myshkin had not entered the scene? Dostoevsky seems to me to be saying that they would not, but to me, each of the women is so dedi-cated to contrary and perverse actions that each would have eventually enlisted someone or other in her self-destructive psychodrama. And yet if Myshkin doesn't precipitate the tragedies, the plot of the novel falls apart and Myshkin himself remains a man without a story. This, in fact, is the source of the failure that Dostoevsky felt in the finished novel. There is no inevitability to it—Myshkin has qualities but no intentions. It is not only that this makes him not tragic, it also makes him not a believable character. While Dostoevsky readily portrays characters who manifest extreme psychological states, he is not very good, at least in this translation, at finding a language that mimics their thought processes, except when they are spouting off to one an-other. He often has astute things to say about the characters—he can analyze, for example, what effect they have on others, or their motives for acting—but he cannot demonstrate how their trains of thought progress, as Trollope does, or how things seem to them, as Dickens does. Thus he cannot enable the reader to empathize with them. Such a language would be essential to making Myshkin's perfect goodness convincing, on the one hand, and to organizing the novel, on the other.

Of Dostoevsky's major works, *The Idiot* is the only one that takes up the typical English and French subject of marital alliance. There are moments when the novel seems to be moving toward a French or English comedy of manners—the ideas and especially the speeches of some of the characters are full of absurdities that could easily show up in Thackeray, Dickens, or Balzac as idiosyncrasies of the human condition. The marital alliance project itself is plenty absurd in this novel, but the prince is too good to have a sense of humor, and none of the other characters has the detachment required of wit.

It is perfectly all right to read Dostoevsky and wish you were reading Trollope. The extremity of the Dostoevskian world is a good reminder that the prolonged exposure to a novelist's sensibility required by a lengthy novel is akin to a long train ride with a stranger, sometimes more demanding and uncongenial than the reader is prepared for. In that sense, every novel is, in the end, a social experience as well as an experience of solitude. Even so, a dip into Dostoevsky's world is stimulating; Dostoevsky's boldness as a thinker and an artist set many of the terms for art, philosophy, and psychology that shaped the twentieth century and that are still influential in the twenty-first.

40 · Louisa May Alcott · Little Women

(1868-69; REPR., NEW YORK: SCHOLASTIC, APPLE, 1995), 562 PP.

Little Women is a hugely famous perennial best seller that is in some ways less interesting than Louisa May Alcott herself, who based the novel on her adolescence in Concord, Massachusetts, as the daughter of Bronson Alcott, a crony of Emerson, Thoreau, and Hawthorne. It was written in two volumes. The first ends with Meg's betrothal. The second begins three years later, with Meg's wedding, and follows the differing ways in which the four daughters and their ambitions are disposed of.

Alcott wrote the novel for young women at the behest of a publisher she knew. It was instantly successful, and it has an openly didactic purpose—to teach moral lessons about proper values and attitudes. In the first chapter, for example, the sisters give their meager Christmas breakfast to a poor family who has no breakfast at all. As a result, they are given a treat by a wealthy neighbor, Mr. Laurence, at suppertime. Somewhat later in the novel, Amy vengefully burns some of Jo's writings. Jo is unforgiving, in spite of her mother's admonishments, and then suffers terrible remorse when Amy nearly drowns as a result of a skating accident. Adults reading the novel for the first time since childhood may be put off by such obvious lessons, but young readers are so accustomed to taking a dose of moralizing with their stories that to them Alcott's style seems perfectly natural. In fact, most girls, if they like *Little Women,* tend to prefer the first volume, when all the sisters are living cozily at home together, making do with what they have and relating mostly to one another.

It is in the second volume, though, that Alcott puts her mind to solving the long-standing question of how girls are to be dealt with, of whether and how money and love are to come together, and what is to be the goal and purpose of women's lives. Her answers are both bolder and more naive than those of some of her more respected contemporaries, such as George Eliot and Henry James. Four girls, four temperaments, four sets of desires mean four plausible outcomes, all linked together by the example of Marmee, whose principal ambition for her daughters is that they "be well and wisely married, and . . . lead useful, pleasant lives, with as little care and sorrow to try them as God sees fit to send." She expressly disapproves of seeking high-status marriages, and aims to equip the girls mentally and spiritually for future challenges.

No activity is proscribed—in fact, from rather early in the novel, Jo earns money by selling sensational stories to tabloid newspapers (as Alcott herself did). The family cautions her, but welcomes the money and lets her find her own way to her real voice and subject. Alcott rather neatly avoids the trap Eliot falls into in her autobiographical novel *The Mill on the Floss,* of endowing her heroine with many of her own characteristics and dilemmas but none of her options. When Amy marries Laurie, the wealthy boy next door, after he has proposed to and been rejected by Jo, Alcott is careful to bring the two together slowly. In fact, her portrait of Amy, a rather unpleasant little girl in the first volume, is one of the most satisfying aspects of the second volume. Jo manages to find both publication and romance with Professor Bhaer; there could be no Prince Charming less appealing in the eyes of an eleven-year-old reader. To an older reader, he is far more attractive—intelligent, kind, comfortable, and well educated, in every way more suitable for the volatile Jo than Laurie.

Little Women may have lost its appeal for young adults simply because Jo and her three sisters aren't recognizable teenagers anymore, so the novel's concerns are no longer current enough to fit into our culture as timely lessons. Freed of its former purpose, though, the novel can take its place among other nineteenth-century novels whose preoccupying subject was the problematic status of women. Because Alcott wants to supply four happy endings, she works through and weighs not only what is to be achieved but also how to get there, while the necessity of having a moral lesson to teach forces her to be explicit about issues that many other novelists discuss but cannot solve. Having posed the question of what an intelligent mother might want for her daughters, she can then systematically demonstrate different ways by which the laudable goal might be achieved. She reminds us in doing so that all novels (not only novels for young people) are stories but also models—they demonstrate how a small thing might be done, such as stealing a valuable jewel, and also how a large thing might be done, such as pursuing a white whale or escaping from slavery.

41 · George Eliot · Middlemarch

(1872; REPR., NEW YORK: NEW AMERICAN LIBRARY, SIGNET, 1992), 811 PP.

In *Middlemarch,* George Eliot's conception is so intricate and yet spacious, so detailed and yet broad, that it seems impossible to summarize. The subject is the town—Middlemarch—and its immediate environs in the 1830s, at the time of the Parliamentary Reform Bill in Britain, and yet the subject is several families of that town, the Brookes and their neighbors, who are wealthy gentry, the Garths and their relatives the Vincys, who are prominent tradespeople, and the Farebrothers, who live at the vicarage (Mr. Farebrother holds the living). And then there is Lydgate, the new doctor who comes to town. The subject of *Middlemarch* is all the relations among all these friends and relatives, young and old, and yet the subject is really how Dorothea Brooke, Mary Garth, Fred and Rosamond Vincy, and Tertius Lydgate pair up and marry. But that is not the real subject either, since every character

has far more on his or her mind, and much more to learn, than traditional questions of romance. But we begin with Miss Brooke, who
marries Mr. Casaubon, who is far too old for her. Mr. Casaubon calls in
Dr. Lydgate, who is falling for Rosamond Vincy in spite of his better
judgment. The plot, like all plots, develops from there, but because of
the richness of Eliot's conception it seems to develop in all directions,
less a story than a network of stories.

I always think of *Middlemarch,* which I love and have read many
times, as an example of the principle that a novel may not be perfect,
may, in fact, be too grand to be perfect. Surely George Eliot (the pen
name of Mary Ann Evans) brought as much intelligence, insight, wit,
learning, evenhandedness, and native talent to the writing of her
greatest novel as any novelist ever. She peopled it with an extraordinary range of characters whose actions and words seem to arise out of
wholeness and complexity, even though some of them appear only
briefly. Each character seems to live within a fully realized network of
relationships that are simultaneously social, economic, personal, and
intimate. Every scene is fully realized; the structure of the novel is spacious and satisfying, the pace deliberate but not slow—very much the
pace of a rational mind contemplating one thing and then another, but
dwelling unduly on none. Most important, perhaps, every sentence is
so smart that the reader cannot help but feel little jolts of pleasure, one
right after another, on every page. Eliot is often considered to be a Victorian moralist who could have lightened up a bit and lost nothing by
it, but in fact her style is higly ironic and often dryly funny. For example, early in the novel, the doctor, Lydgate, follows an actress for
whom he has a passion, to her new town. In the midst of shocking revelations about how her husband had come to be killed, Eliot has the
woman speak: "'You have come all the way from Paris to find me?'
she said to him the next day, sitting before him with folded arms
and looking at him with eyes that seemed to wonder as an untamed
ruminating animal wonders. 'Are all Englishmen like that?'" Lydgate
subsequently swears off romance and considers himself safe from
Rosamond Vincy, since she contrasts so strongly with Laure, "the
divine cow." Elsewhere Mr. Brooke, Dorothea's shallow uncle, is
suggesting to Casaubon, Dorothea's pedantic husband, that she divert
herself with some eighteenth-century novels:

'Smollett—Roderick Random, Humphry Clinker. They are a
little broad, but she may read anything now that she's married,

you know. I remember they made me laugh uncommonly—
there's a droll bit about a postilion's breeches. We have no such
humor now. I have gone through all these things, but they might
be rather new to you.'

'As new as eating thistles,' would have been an answer to represent Mr. Casaubon's feelings. [p. 280]

Virginia Woolf famously said that *Middlemarch* was "one of the only
English novels written for grown-up people," and other critics have
declared it the greatest English novel, or even the greatest novel. And
it certainly follows the natural inclination of the novel to expand and
grow more various. The other candidates for greatest novel ever—
Anna Karenina, Our Mutual Friend, Moby-Dick, Don Quixote, even the
seven volumes of *The Past Recaptured*—hardly contain more. And
everything that *Middlemarch* does contain is exquisitely considered
and beautifully rendered.

But a novel is less and less likely to be perfect as it grows because as it
fills out and expands, the connections between the exquisitely rendered smaller parts grow more and more attenuated—they grow
beyond the capacity of both the writer and the reader to keep track of
them and thus remain compelled by them. Some novelists are able,
sometimes, to overcome this tendency by using the reader's emotional
investment in the characters to bolster suspense. An example of a novel
that succeeds in hanging together, though very long, is *Anna Karenina.*
Another is *Our Mutual Friend,* into which Dickens slips a chase sequence of almost unbearable suspense right at the moment when
he might be beginning to exhaust the reader's powers of attention.
Middlemarch doesn't have much suspense. The tales of three couples at
the core of the novel (Dorothea and Will Ladislaw, Lydgate and Rosamond, Fred Vincy and Mary Garth) are told with such wisdom and
measure that it is easy to imagine what will happen. What Eliot is after
is analysis of their relationships rather than emotional investment
in them. Characters whose fates might be suspenseful—Bulstrode and
his wife—are unsympathetic. Suspense is not dependent on the reader's not knowing what is about to happen—a reader can read *Pride and
Prejudice* half a dozen times and still feel a quickening of delight when
Elizabeth and Darcy get together. But the pleasures of *Middlemarch*
are more in the intellect and less in the emotions—the narrator stands
at a greater distance from her characters, moving into their consciousnesses and then out again, making them the objects of her marvelous

phrases rather than the originators of them, looking at how their senses of themselves fit into the sense other people have of them. As a result, it is not only that in the end, the reader feels more edified than gratified by the outcome of the novel, it is also that the dynamic energy of the novel is somewhat dissipated by the requirement of detailed understanding.

Nevertheless, the three central relationships, which are surrounded by several smaller ones, are uniquely penetrating analyses of marriage unmatched in the work of any other author. The depiction of Lydgate and Rosamond, his limited but resolute wife, could serve as a whole course in the nature of marriage based on presuppositions and appearances (and with no possibility of divorce). Eliot's portrait of Dorothea and her dried-up scholar, Casaubon, is no less insightful, only less generally applicable. These marriages do not seem any more true of their place and time than they seem generally true—there are always well-meaning but ignorant men who marry beautiful but shallow women, always idealistic women who completely misapprehend male psychology. Of special note in this regard is the richness of what Eliot adds to literature about the natures and powers of women. By contrast, the writings of her male contemporaries about women (except possibly Anthony Trollope) seem deluded and sentimental or simply vague.

Middlemarch is also a wonderful social document, because Eliot was much interested in the intellectual and scientific issues of her time and embraced the power of her novel to depict such issues. Her characters have aspirations beyond money and happiness—Lydgate wants to add to the stock of scientific knowledge, Casaubon wants to discover the ancient roots of myth, Dorothea wants to benefit others. Among the three of them, they mark specific moments in the history of ideas. In fact, nineteenth-century philologists and folklorists did succeed in linking modern languages and modern literature with each other and with earlier roots, as Casaubon aspires to do. Philosophers of religion and ethics did take up the question of how an individual is to live a virtuous life, which Dorothea thinks about. Biologists, chemists, and others eventually found the key to the nesting layers of matter and energy that make up the world as we understand it. The specific hypotheses of the *Middlemarch* characters may be outmoded (and were in Eliot's day—she was writing in 1870 about the 1830s), but Eliot has a good deal to say about the psychology of intellectual endeavor. She gracefully incorporates into her novel aspects of human life that had never found novelistic expression before she brought to bear her unique combination of gifts—wit, sensitivity to language, intelligence and learning, psychological insight, ambition, reasonableness, and courage, too, since much of what Mary Ann Evans learned, she taught herself.

Perhaps Virginia Woolf considered *Middlemarch* the only English novel written for adults because Eliot keeps her characters working and striving past the denouement of the novel. Lydgate eventually earns money with his medical practice, but only at the cost of all his aspirations. More interestingly, and perhaps echoing Eliot's own life with writer George Lewes in a distant way, Fred Vincy and Mary Garth both write books and both contribute to the family income as tenants upon an estate that Fred had once hoped to inherit. Eliot's romantic ideal is not landed companionate marriage, but common work, equal contribution to the household, and vital intellectual development for both spouses.

42 · Leo Tolstoy · Anna Karenina

TRANS. CONSTANCE GARNETT, REV. LEONARD J. KENT, AND NINA BERBEROVA

(1877; REPR., NEW YORK: MODERN LIBRARY, 2000), 923 PP.

The premise of *Anna Karenina* is simple and even basic—a wealthy Moscow family, the Oblonskys, are hoping to marry their younger daughter, Kitty, to a desirable aristocrat, Vronsky, even though another young man, Levin, a rather somber and countrified landowner, is in love with her. When Vronsky accompanies Oblonsky to the train station—Vronsky to pick up his mother, and Oblonsky to pick up his sister, Anna, who is married to an important government official—Vronsky meets the woman who really moves him. He begins to court Anna almost immediately, abandoning his suit of Kitty and his future in respectable Russian society. While Anna's marriage is breaking apart under the weight of this passion, Levin begins to find his purpose, first in the improvement of his estate and the condition of his workers, and later in his renewed and ultimately successful pursuit of Kitty.

The great nineteenth-century novelists all aimed at comprehensiveness. George Eliot's portraits of Casaubon, who is writing a key to all mythologies, and Lydgate, who is trying to find the unifying principle in disparate forms of living tissue in *Middlemarch,* are portraits of herself, and Dickens and Trollope and Balzac, as much as they are of scholars and scientists. Tolstoy, in *Anna Karenina,* seems to have felt that he could portray two marriages (the novel was originally called *Two Marriages*) in sufficient detail that they could stand as models for how marriage works in general, with Anna's marriage and adultery standing for one form (based on property, social status, lust, and a failure to grasp the spiritual life, what you might call the French form) and Levin's marriage to Kitty (based on love, common goals, usefulness, and spiritual redemption, a Russian version of what you might call the English form) standing for the other. There is a third marriage, too—the one that begins the novel, between Kitty's sister, Dolly, and Anna's brother, Stepan, which is based on the principle of getting along as best they can and having lots of children, but no real relationship between the spouses.

Tolstoy's method of comprehensiveness is the key to the novel's greatness—a close, realistically rendered attention to sensory details and details of emotional states. Each of his main characters—Karenin, Anna, Vronsky, Levin, and, to a lesser extent, Kitty—has chapters in which the narrator depicts in vivid detail the progress of a certain mood. For example, Anna falls ill with childbed fever when her illegitimate child is born. She writes Karenin, who has resolved to hate her and to ruin her by divorcing her, and asks him to forgive her on her deathbed. Karenin arrives in a state of deep rage and antipathy, but the scene at her bedside brings him to such a state of exalted forgiveness that he can never return again to precisely how he felt before he forgave her. His inner journey must and does progress, in his case to a weird form of fraudulent spiritualism. The reader is made to see Karenin's point of view in every detail and then to understand his transformation and to sympathize with it—the sympathy grows out of the empathy. The same method works with Levin, who is an irritable and irritating character. By the end of the novel, the reader is more or less in sympathy with Levin's ideas because she has experienced the events and emotions that gave rise to them along with Levin. As the novel progresses, it takes more and more mental effort to resist Levin (Tolstoy's stand-in) and disagree with him. It becomes almost overwhelmingly tempting, given Tolstoy's method, to yield to both the experiental details and the ideas and declare, with nineteenth-century critic Matthew Arnold, "We are not to take *Anna Karenina* as a work of art; we are to take it as a piece of life." But it is not a piece of life—that it could be a piece of life is an illusion imparted by the passion, intensity, and technique that Tolstoy brings to his story. Tolstoy's method of composition was arduous—he wrote and threw out hundreds of pages—but as a result, he thought through all of his ideas until he had exhausted all of their possibilities, thereby staying one step ahead of the reader at every turn. It is this willingness to work everything out that gives Tolstoy's work its characteristic sense of authority.

But Tolstoy's desire for comprehensiveness presents him with the essential novelist's paradox and difficulty. Because mental states that are felt and understood in an instant take much longer than an instant to describe, he must pick and choose the ones he wishes to focus upon—that is, he has to make the time pass in some consistent way. The way he chooses inevitably imposes meaning on the text; although his choice is "technical," it limits the universality of the story and it opens the author to "mistakes." In the case of *Anna Karenina,* Tolstoy chooses to show how each relationship develops over the course of several years. Therefore he must pick the most dramatic moments in the plot and show how the characters are changed by them (a novel with a briefer time span or a tighter plot can unfold through both high drama and routine activity, thereby depicting the interplay of the two in creating character). The incidents that Tolstoy does pick are beautifully and truthfully portrayed (not in the sense that Tolstoy is telling the truth, but in the sense that the reader recognizes the action to be true to her experience), but, especially early in the novel, they are grand and therefore distancing.

For me, the central difficulty of *Anna Karenina* is whether the reader believes in Vronsky and Anna's love or merely accepts it on faith. How they act and what they say demonstrate that something dramatic is going on between them, but the author offers no quiet and apparently routine scenes that show why him, why her (in this, of course, Tolstoy is also hampered by nineteenth-century reticence about intimate matters). In part two, chapters 9 and 10, Karenin confronts Anna and attempts to get her to admit to and recant her feelings for Vronsky. At this point she and Vronsky have not had sexual relations. Chapter 11 begins with a postcoital confrontation between Anna and Vronsky—she is humiliated and ashamed at giving herself to him, and he is desperate. According to the narrator, it has been almost a year since they first met each other. The author has chosen not to depict the private aspects of their courtship—the moments, for example, that Stendhal depicts in *The Red and the Black* between Julien and Madame de Rênal, moments that would show the stages by which Anna has been brought to shame and Vronsky to satisfaction of his desires. So dramatic is her reaction to their union, in fact, that the reader has to ask how she let this happen—by what process has she been lulled and persuaded to give up her virtue? When Tolstoy skips over this process, he chooses not to give the reader essential access to Anna's psychology, but to let some sort of typical female psychology stand for her individual female psychology. The author begins to make up for this omission only after Anna's mental state begins to disintegrate. Still, she is less interesting and less true than she could have been if she had been more sharply individuated. This specific flaw is echoed over the course of the entire novel by the fact that while the reader may be observing the characters in some detail, she doesn't often feel especially intimate with them. The primary reason for this choice—the choice of dramatic moments over routine moments or over a mixture of dramatic moments and routine moments—is Tolstoy's technical need to have time pass as efficiently as possible, to show the process of development that constitutes his rhetorical point.

There is no satisfactory solution to the requirement that time in the novel must pass in some way. If it passes in a routine, intimate way, the reader may wonder why she is bothering to read such a dull novel, and if it passes in a consistently dramatic way, the reader may wonder what relevance this has to her own rather routine life. (Some feminists might say, also, that Tolstoy did not imagine a female audience for his novel; for example, Kitty, Tolstoy's primary virtuous woman, feels terrific unease, which her husband supports, in having anything to do with Anna. It's hard to imagine that Tolstoy considered the depiction of Anna's sin and disintegration an appropriate subject for Kitty-like young girls reading in their bedrooms.)

Many novelists solve the time difficulty with a vivid and idiosyncratic literary style, which serves as an incentive to the reader to keep reading in spite of the dullness or the irrelevance of the events, and also makes the events seem more or less subjective, which has the effect of begging the question of how the time passes. But realistic novelists such as Tolstoy have also chosen not to do that—they don't want to suffer the fate of Dickens or the Brontës, the fate of having their ideas dismissed as too out of the mainstream to be accepted as universally true.

The realist novel does offer the reader the illusion of a certain sort of freedom, though. The style, felicitous but not intrusive, seems to ask the reader to make up her own mind as to the themes and intentions of the work as a whole, seems to allow her to divorce herself from the narrator's direction and look at the scenes as if they were real. On that score we can wonder if Tolstoy himself realized that one of the persistent themes of his novel is how females in general and women in particular pay for the pleasures of men, or if such observations came together in the work without his conscious intention. Vronsky's English mare is killed when Vronsky wants to ride her in a race himself and makes a mistake. Anna, of course, never recovers from Vronsky's successful seduction of her. Stepan sells off pieces of his wife's estate to pay for his pleasures. Levin is assailed by self-doubt when he sees Kitty in the pain of childbirth. Even so small a detail as the sex of Levin's hunting dog, Laska, implies foolish male appetite contrasted with submissive but knowing female effort. Tolstoy doesn't offer a solution for this unfairness, but it is so evident that the reader herself may begin contemplating political solutions.

Is *Anna Karenina* the greatest novel by the greatest novelist? Let us compare apples and grapefruits and peas and dogs, not to mention oranges and dreams. *Anna Karenina* has nothing in common with *Tristram Shandy,* so how can they be on a scale together? Indeed, *Anna Karenina* has nothing in common with *Taras Bulba.* I might feel, as I do, that *Taras Bulba* offers a unique stylistic experience—words brought together in a manner unmatched before or since, simultaneously original and right, operating instantly—let's call that "revelation." *Anna Karenina* works upon me rhetorically, convincing me with insight after insight to share or at least accept the author's contentions. Let's call that "wisdom." But the pleasures of each are not comparable with the other. Tolstoy had read Gogol and knew his work quite well. He had even learned from Gogol, but still he could not possibly be like Gogol because the novel itself promotes difference rather than similarity. For that reason the quest for "the greatest" is particularly futile with novels and novelists.

43 · Henry James · The Portrait of a Lady

(1881; REPR., NEW YORK: PENGUIN, 1986), 641 PP.

Although *The Portrait of a Lady* was James's fifth novel, it was the first in which he developed all of his talents as well as all of his interests. He was thirty-seven when he began it, and he had high hopes. James had met and dined with George Eliot, and he admired her version of the realistic novel; Isabel Archer directly inherits the earlier dilemmas of Maggie Tulliver and Dorothea Brooke. But even though James was writing only a few years after Eliot wrote *Middlemarch,* he was a generation younger than she, and the novel has a much more modern feel. Still, what is to be done with the young woman? James disposes of the traditional English answer within the first hundred pages. Isabel appears on the scene, an attractive and moneyed aristocrat presents himself and proposes to her, and she instinctively turns him down, to the amazement of everyone around her. Then an old suitor appears, an American named Caspar Goodwood, and she very explicitly turns him down, also, though he is more importunate than the English lord. The problem of what to do with the young woman is not to be solved in the traditional way. James gives her money of her own, and the rest of the novel asks a new question: what is a young woman to do with herself?

European society, and the Old World in general, do not have an answer. The course Isabel chooses, to marry Gilbert Osmond, an expatriate aesthete, is famously wrong. All of the characters in the novel and the author himself hint that Gilbert is meant to be diabolical. The couple have a child who dies, and by the time of that death there is such a breach between husband and wife that the option of motherhood has been foreclosed for Isabel. Several other models are supplied—Mrs. Touchett, who, though married, lives as if she were single; Madame Merle, who is entirely charming but without her own establishment and who whiles away her life congenially living off others; Countess Gemini, who is trapped in a loveless marriage of a coarser sort than the Osmonds; and Henrietta Stackpole, an employed journalist, distinctly new and American, a little attractive and a little silly. But after a brief separation, Isabel returns to her marriage, almost for lack of anything better to do. In 1881 James could not answer the old question except by supplying Isabel with the conviction that she has to adhere to the old form, empty as it has become.

The Portrait of a Lady, paragraph by paragraph, page by page, is exceptionally satisfying. James writes in a highly metaphorical style that continuously invites the reader to impute refined and yet dramatic meanings to the actions and feelings of his characters. If Dickens's characters move in a landscape of inner visions projected outward as monsters and innocents, James's characters live in an apparently real world, but only by analogy. James is always pausing to brilliantly characterize, not their feelings, but the feel of their situation. For example, discussing the character Edward Rosier, a childhood acquaintance of Isabel's, James writes, "His father was dead and his *bonne* was dismissed, but the young man still conformed to the spirit of their teaching—he never went to the edge of the lake." This is typically Jamesian in tone and is very much extremely elevated and advanced gossip. His great analogies and intelligent analyses are attempts to characterize small psychological states and shifts rather than endeavors to depict the world (which for James is made up of estates and ruins and buildings as backdrops). James builds on the Victorian novelists by developing a theory of human psychology that deepens and complicates their insights, but much of what he says about his characters is not and cannot be known to themselves—they do not have the larger perspective that he, the master analyst, has. His purpose is to find commonalities in human nature and the inner life that his characters represent, and his tool for doing this is his style.

The Portrait of a Lady, as a whole, therefore, can be irritating, especially, perhaps, to a female reader, because there is no satisfaction in Isabel's fate; though the question is asked, the answer is wanting, and the author seems not to know this. He seems to think that by supplying Isabel and her fellows with vast amounts of detailed motivation he can give their actions a tragic dimension, but in fact their paralysis seems self-imposed and very youthful, as if they simply aren't experienced enough to think of an alternative. The greatest insight of the novel occurs near the end, when it is suggested to Isabel that she will get over what has happened to her and become young again, but James doesn't linger over the idea—no doubt because to do so is to diminish the drama of the previous six hundred pages.

For me, Isabel's dilemma is not in her character but in her world. She has three suitors plus a cousin who loves her without hope. All four are seriously flawed marital prospects—Lord Warburton is attractive and well-meaning, but like Darcy in his first proposal (in *Pride and Prejudice*), he doesn't bother to court her, only to present himself.

Caspar Goodwood, Isabel's last hope at the end of the novel, is so aggressive as to strike the modern reader as akin to a stalker or a rapist, and in fact he does force a kiss on Isabel that she responds to, but then she does the most sensible thing, which is to flee—Goodwood's love expresses itself no less hatefully than Osmond's hate. Osmond is sly, weak, and insidious, but finally less dangerous than Goodwood. Cousin Ralph is well-meaning but fatally ill. There are no matches; the marriage market offers no attractive prospects. And then, as if to reiterate his point, James introduces Pansy, Osmond's daughter, who has been raised, unlike Isabel, to be perfectly submissive. She cannot be satisfied in the marriage market either, because Rosier, whom she loves, is too weak to claim her, and Warburton finally doesn't want her. She ends up immured in a convent, being further trained to submit, as if Osmond's will to efface her simply cannot be satisfied. Only Henrietta comes up with a companion, and her ability to do so comes from her willingness to live unconventionally with her friend Mr. Bantling, until she knows him well enough to marry him. Hers is an unorthodox and singular solution not generally applicable in James's world (though pretty workable from the perspective of the twenty-first century).

What motivates Isabel is not, in the end, as interesting as what motivates Gilbert Osmond to hate her once she has become his wife. James makes it clear that her independence of mind combined with her independent means arouse his resentment, but given his attitude toward Madame Merle, whom he also hates in spite of their long intimacy, what really seems to be the case is that he has an abiding resentment of women that he attempts to assuage by insisting upon their submission. There is the sense at the end of the novel that he is immuring Pansy because he is coming to hate her, too. Isabel's provisional tragedy is that she has wedded herself to his misogynism, but the relationships between the women are still in flux at the close of the novel. Osmond is a paper tiger—his power derives from the concessions of his sister, wife, and daughter. The potential for alliance among them remains at the end, when Isabel returns to Rome rather than save herself.

It is tempting for the modern reader to make up her mind that changes in divorce laws have solved Isabel's problem. She has made a false marriage—the thing that preoccupied European authors from Boccaccio to Charlotte Brontë. Fifty or a hundred years later, she would have divorced and started over. Tragedy would have been transformed into error, and Isabel's life would not have been wasted.

Isabel's dilemma traces straight back to *The Heptameron*—is it allowed for women to live freely? In the 1550s, the answer was no—women without protectors were in danger of rape and murder. In the 1880s the answer was still no, but in spite of Caspar Goodwood, the strictures are more self-imposed than they had been.

James was a sly and comic novelist. He pretended to treat his characters and their fates seriously and in great detail, but in fact every character, including Isabel and Osmond, verges on the absurd because the author is so interested in observing them that he detaches himself from them. They are all amusing—that is implicit in the gossipy style, though some, such as the countess and Henrietta, are more openly amusing than others. He can wring from the reader a sense of disquiet as the characters realize and lament their fates, but in the end they are limited by the very thing James offers in such abundance—the knowledge he has of them that is vaster than the knowledge they have of themselves. James liked to be known as "the Master," as Dickens liked to be known as "the Inimitable," but the epithet contains James's limitation as well as his genius—he couldn't cede a larger unexpected humanity to his creations and thereby touch his readers' deepest feelings.

Henry James · The Awkward Age

(1899; REPR., NEW YORK: OXFORD WORLD'S CLASSICS, 1999), 321 PP.

In addition to writing many novels, Henry James wrote plays that were not, on the whole, popular or successful. When he finally gave up the drama and turned his attention back to the novel, he wrote a succession of mature, complex, and profoundly "Jamesian" novels in which his style was exactly as he wished it—particular, calculated, and highly modulated (as he got older, he stopped writing and dictated his work; Ford Madox Ford once remarked that if the reader were to read late James aloud, with much expression, the prose would make a lot more sense). His first novel after giving up the drama was *The Awkward Age,* which concerns marital arrangements of a group of upper-class Londoners at the end of the nineteenth century. The thematic premise is the contrast between two eighteen-year-old girls who are just becoming marriageable. One, Aggie, has been raised in a sequestered Italian fashion by her aunt; the other, Nanda, has been allowed more freedom by her mother and father (in part because the parents, who have aristocratic obligations but no money, want to farm their older children out at least some of the time so they can save money on their upkeep while possibly finding them wealthy mates). If there was ever a novel about marriage as a system of covert but acknowledged dealmaking, this is it.

As mentioned above, *The Awkward Age* was an experiment for James, who attempted to use some of the techniques he used in his plays. He communicates all the narrative information through scenes in which two or more of the characters are gathered together for a social occasion, and all the action of the novel is reported through the conversation of the characters, conversation that is complex, allusive, sometimes witty or playful, and always discreet. Part of the pleasure (or difficulty) of the novel, for the reader, is inferring what is going on through what amounts to eavesdropping. James uses several dramatic devices to maintain order. The characters are clearly distinguished from one another and identified, most of them in contrasting pairs. Nanda and Aggie are contrasted through their innocence (or naïveté); Aggie's aunt, the duchess, and Nanda's mother, Mrs. Brookenham, through their opinions and social positions. Of the two primary young men, Vanderbank is handsome, charming, and poor, while Mitchett is ugly, charming, and rich. The character who precipitates the action is Mr. Longdon, an old admirer of Nanda's grandmother who suddenly reappears from deepest Suffolk, after, it appears, pining for forty years. Mr. Longdon has also been the unsuccessful suitor of Vanderbank's mother.

The characters consider their own London society generally dangerous, because it is full of sexual intrigue among the married. The reader can easily see that it is also dangerous because the inequitable distribution of money, social power, and approval makes everyone sneaky and manipulative. One sign of the general danger of this social group (and by extension, the rest of London society) is that they are careful to praise and show affection to one another at all times, rather like denizens of Hollywood or the members of a large group of chimps who perform submissive behaviors so as not to alienate one another. The unwary reader might think they actually like one another, but their relations are based much more upon intrigue and having nice places to congregate than a sense of real connection. Nanda, whose "contamination" by her mother's free and easy ways comes up for a lot of discussion, is a natural innocent, so it is no surprise that she and Mr. Longdon, another innocent, end up together, even though Nanda is very much in love with Vanderbank, who likes her, but can't bring himself to propose, in spite of the fact that Longdon (without Nanda's knowledge) has promised to settle a large property on her. Vanderbank himself is having a serious flirtation with Nanda's mother (though several of the characters testify that the two haven't actually become lovers by the time the question of proposing to Nanda comes up).

James was proud of the way he structured the novel—entirely through dramatic scenes using for each the point of view of a different character. These points of view work as vantage points from which to both convey and interpret the progress of the plot. James was pleased with the subtlety of using arrangement and inference as substitutes for a strong narrative voice. He willingly gave up one of narrative's best devices, which is access to the inner life, no doubt to emphasize human nature as a social construct. Nonetheless, having given that up, he forces his conversations to carry a great deal of weight and ends up forbidding the reader the sense of intimacy that many readers look for in a novel first and foremost—it is hard to feel genuine intimacy with characters on whom you seem to be eavesdropping. The convention of the stage—that a play is going on and people are watching—turns into a kind of voyeurism in *The Awkward Age.* And it is hard to relax with this novel, or to feel oneself carried forward, because it is so easy to lose the thread of the narrative. Nevertheless, suspense does build as the reader grows more familiar with the characters.

James's style always poses a problem that Ford Madox Ford's suggestion somewhat alleviates. James is as highly metaphorical a writer as Dickens, and rather like him in some respects. Both use metaphor not as ornamentation but as the primary method of communicating mental states, and both are interested in the interplay of fictional characters as a group of subjectivities communicating with one another and at the same time contrasting to one another. But whereas Dickens's metaphorical language is fully expressed and easy to understand, James's is partially submerged. The reader is repeatedly asked to infer the larger metaphor from a few words. Early in the novel, for example, Longdon is described: "He had at all events, conclusively, doubled the Cape of the years—he would never again see fifty-five: to the warning light of that bleak headland he presented a back sufficiently conscious. Yet, though, to Vanderbank, he could not look young, he came near—strikingly and amusingly—looking new . . ." (p. 20). The overt metaphorical language of the sentence is separated by modifiers and adverbs that imply the consciousness of the perceiver almost as tone of voice would—the perceiver (Vanderbank, but really James) wants to go beyond the precision of nouns and verbs into a quality of intensification or deintensification that can be supplied only through other parts of grammar or the rhythm of the sentences. If you take a paragraph of James and strip it of all adverbs, nothing is lost but the fussiness; and yet the fussiness is James's consciousness at work, which is why his style is unique.

James was an insightful observer of English society—Harold, Nanda's brother, is given the task of speaking unpleasant truths. A profligate young man always borrowing five-pound notes from anyone he can, he understands the marital bazaar and is willing to talk about it. About two-thirds of the way through the novel he says, "London, upon my honor, is quite too awful for girls, and any big house in the country is as much worse—with the promiscuities and opportunities and all that—as you know for yourselves. *I* know some places . . . where, if I had any girls, I'd see 'em shot before I'd take 'em." He goes on to discuss the interest of Mr. Longdon in Nanda: "Oh yes, dear man, but what do you *give* us for her. . . . I'll be hanged . . . if he shall have her for nothing!" Nanda agrees to marry Mr. Longdon (who has perhaps successfully, in his own mind, scared Vanderbank off by offering to pay him to take her). *The Awkward Age* is officially, then, comic. But once again, the outcome is a little disconcerting. After all, Longdon is more than forty years older than Nanda, and though kindly and innocent, not much of a man that the reader can tell. But then neither is Vanderbank, who is indecisive, or Mitchett, who is unattractive (and whom Nanda doesn't like). James does some characteristic special pleading to match up the couples morally, but their relations seem reserved and too much manipulated. The pattern of their relationship is formal, almost ritualistic, like a minuet—they come into contiguity with one another, they act with some kindness and tenderness, but there is no sense of passion springing from the inner life of one character into the consciousness of another and galvanizing the two of them. James was a great parser of social connections, but the energy comes from the parsing rather than the connections.

44 · Oscar Wilde · The Picture of Dorian Gray

(1891; REPR., NEW YORK: OXFORD UNIVERSITY PRESS, 1998), 184 PP.

The Picture of Dorian Gray was reviled as scandalous and wicked when it was published, which seems to have pleased its author. From the distance of more than a hundred years, though, it is possible to see that the outline of the plot is hardly scandalous—a young man makes a thoughtless pact with the Devil and suffers for it almost unremittingly until he finally kills himself. Perhaps the only new twist that Wilde brings to this ancient idea is that both the young man and the Devil exist entirely in the world. There is no implication that Lord Henry (Lord Harry, a common nickname for Satan) retains Dorian's soul into eternity or that there is an eternity.

What may have been more scandalous was Wilde's scathing critique of English hypocrisy combined with his overt depiction of homosexual and bisexual affections carried out within the social structures of marriage and conventional property alliances. The standard resolution of English plots is shown thereby to be impossible because no true affection exists and the real purpose of money is to purchase ever more exotic sensual pleasures.

The reader may or may not care for Wilde's epigrammatic style. Many of his paradoxes seem both arresting and true—"Nowadays people know the price of everything and the value of nothing," for example—but epigram piled upon epigram seems more like a thoughtless habit or a form of neurosis than art. What is more appealing is Wilde's catalog of sensual pleasures. Dorian, who has plenty of money and has prayed for eternal youth and the appearance of innocence so he might experience as wide an array of pleasures as possible, goes far beyond mere sexual passion. He collects perfumes and jewels and embroideries and enjoys them as much as romantic affairs. He collects all sharp sensations—including the experience of having someone die for love of him, the experience of murder, and the experience of escape from being murdered. He takes opium and lures others to addiction. What he can't do—and his inability is the source of his torment—is to detach himself from his feelings and become a spectator of his own torments and those of others. In this, his highest aspiration, he can but intermittently emulate his mentor, Lord Henry.

Lord Henry, the Satan figure, cannot remain young, as Dorian seems to, but has perfected his artistic distance. All developments in the social life around him arouse his interest, but none arouses his sympathy. He is no less cold toward Dorian, his protégé, than he is toward his wife or his other associates. He is entirely solitary and untroubled by his condition. Epigrams about hypocrisy are his greatest pleasure. Since Lord Henry shares his author's verbal style, he was widely considered to be speaking for Wilde, which was part of the scandal. But as with de Sade, the fictional creation is colder and more inhuman than the creator was. Like de Sade, Wilde could, and in fact was required to, inhabit the victim, Dorian, as fully as he inhabited the torturer. There is a third character, Basil Hallward, an artist, the man who discovers Dorian and paints the magic portrait. Through him, the novel reflects on some aspects of art. Both Basil and Lord Henry understand that Dorian and Basil have transgressed a boundary through the making of the painting—Basil has been more than ordinarily inspired and has in turn inspired Dorian with love of himself as an object (in some sense, Basil has allowed Dorian to fetishize his own beauty), but Basil remains secure in the knowledge of what is art and what is life. He, too, represents Wilde, of course. When Dorian reveals to Basil that the portrait has magical powers, the artist urges the younger man to pray for salvation. Dorian, inspired indirectly by Lord Henry, has lost his sense of the difference between art and life and promptly tries out the sensation of murder. But he is ambivalent. It is only Lord Henry who can sustain the artist's technically inspired remoteness from life, always appreciating and critiquing but never feeling.

The Picture of Dorian Gray was written almost exactly a hundred years after the far more brutal and cruel *Justine* and there are some similarities, especially in the argument that morality is "against nature," or that moralists are essentially exercising caution rather than manifesting a real allegiance to goodness. And the narrator of *Justine* inveighs against religion, while the narrator of *Dorian Gray* mostly ignores it. Perhaps the outrage that greeted the later novel was more than anything an index of how much less jaded Victorian sensibilities were than those of the ancien régime in France. *Justine* still can shock; *Dorian Gray* does not. In some ways the later novel seems more dated than the earlier one—a testament to psychological theories then current that Wilde was using to motivate the plot and the characters. For example, the premise of Dorian's ability to escape the results of his iniquities is that he looks youthful and unmarked in spite of them. Conventional wisdom in our day is that illness, poor nutrition, and sun damage change one's looks more than sin does.

What remains after more than a hundred years is not the novel of ideas that Wilde once wrote, but a novel of sensuous surfaces that still beguile and give the pleasure that Wilde so clearly found ambiguous.

45 · Bram Stoker · Dracula

(1897; REPR., NEW YORK: RANDOM HOUSE, MODERN LIBRARY, 2001), 365 PP.

The idea for *Dracula* came to Bram Stoker in a dream. The novel was a great sensation at the time of its publication and, like *Frankenstein* (also the fruit of a dream), quickly became part of popular culture. Because it was one of the first novels to be sold to the movies, and the movie was an even greater success than the novel, it is probably impossible for a twenty-first-century reader to come to the material fresh and capable of being horrified by the count. It is easy, instead, to feel knowing and Freudian about what must have really been going on in the minds of the characters and the mind of the author (all about repressed sexual feelings) as well as jaded about what constitutes true horror.

Stoker's novel remains in print as a horror classic, though, because he plotted the rise and fall of Count Dracula with great care. He then adopted the strategy of multiple narrators, as Wilkie Collins had done with much success thirty years previously, making good use of the variety of effect such a strategy offers. And such a strategy enhances the suspense, because what each character, including the count himself, has at stake comes into play as the plot progresses.

The novel begins when an English solicitor goes to Transylvania, in the Carpathian Mountains, to transact a bit of business, and finds himself trapped in a mysterious castle with a courtly but sinister aristocratic host, Count Dracula. Count Dracula, it turns out, is much feared by his own people as the principal representative of the undead, a soulless folk who achieve a form of immortality by drinking the blood of others. The count's country has become rather depopulated (possibly as a result of his depredations), and he is planning to move to the much more busy and accessible city of London. His existence is entirely circumscribed by rituals and rules, but when the count has surprise and ignorance on his side, he can find victims and drink their blood.

The characters in *Dracula* are drawn from the same categories as

James's and Wharton's characters—two marriageable young women, an American fellow, an English lord, and a young lawyer, plus a sinister European and a benign European. And *Dracula* in part asks the same questions as James and Wharton do: What is the role of the women? Can they be agents of their own salvation or destruction? What constitutes virtue, and what are the social implications of the definition? Especially interesting is the new notion Stoker brings to the idea of feminine purity. *Dracula* has two women characters, Lucy and Mina. Both are engaged to be married, but Lucy is restless and likes to walk in her sleep. One night, Mina follows her, and she finds her friend sitting on a bench by the sea, her head thrown back and two tiny wounds in her neck. The reader knows by this time that the count has claimed her as his source of sustenance. Lucy is eventually transformed into one of the undead. To save her soul, one of her friends must cut off her head and drive a stake through her heart, grisly work that is eased by the knowledge that she is damned otherwise (and not all that different from the fate of an unvirtuous woman in earlier centuries—it may not have been her fault, but she's tainted and must be destroyed).

Mina marries her fiancé and helps the men look for the count, but through the unwitting agency of an inhabitant of the house where she is staying, Mina, too, falls victim to the count in a scene that can only be interpreted as sexual—he holds her by the neck and forces her to drink blood spurting from a vein he has opened in his chest. The author is clear that Mina, like Lucy, has been polluted, and her virtue has been stained. But she insists upon coming to her own aid, going with the men to Castle Dracula, guiding them by means of hypnotic visions of the count. She transcribes notes, keeps a journal, and helps to plan the attack upon the vampire. In fact, it is when the men treat Mina in the Victorian style, keeping things from her and trying to protect her for her own good, that she is most vulnerable and falls victim to her destroyer. Mina is one of the first female characters in Western literature who redeems herself. In a tradition that holds women suspect even if they are raped, Mina thoroughly "cleanses" her honor by acting against her defiler.

Stoker gains this enlightened vision as a side benefit of thinking through his plot. We can think of his novel as requiring two things above all—putting something precious and vulnerable in jeopardy, and bringing the love and the money together in the end. Clearly, a woman had to be the victim, but a woman, the same woman, had to be redeemed. The count had to have some sort of uncanny power over his victim (and hypnosis and mind reading were popular ideas at the end of the nineteenth century). The clever part was making the mind-reading a two-way street—giving Mina her power over the count. Another of Mina's powers grows out of the multinarrator format for the novel. It is Mina, from time to time, who types and collates all the parts, thus affording herself an overview of the whole adventure. The structural and mechanical requirements of the novel pave the way for a new mode of looking at the characters.

Stoker did not have a string of solid, respectable successes, like some of his contemporaries. He was a smart popular novelist rather than a great literary novelist, and some of his horror material seems laughable today, but *Dracula* is well worth both reading and emulating, if only as a lesson in the thoroughness and seriousness Bram Stoker brought to his potentially silly material.

46 · Kate Chopin · The Awakening

(1899; REPR., NEW YORK: AVON BOOKS, 1972), 190 PP.

Possibly Kate Chopin read Henry James. Probably Henry James did not read Kate Chopin, though *The Awakening* was considered so scandalous when it was published that it was banned in the author's hometown library, and she herself was barred from the Fine Arts Club in the same city, so maybe he did. If he had, he might have enjoyed her boldness and been scandalized by her choice not to judge her protagonist, Edna Pontellier. What *The Awakening* has to offer, among other things, is honesty. To the eternal question of how women are to be disposed of as both objects and agents, Chopin offers an antecedent question: why is there a problem? And she also asks: what if society cannot provide the answer?

As the novel opens, Edna, age twenty-eight, and her husband and two children are ensconced for the summer at a lake retreat north of New Orleans, where they are a prosperous, socially prominent family. Edna is just beginning to realize that she is different from the other women around her—not so consumed by husband and family, more susceptible to outside influences. As the summer progresses, Edna finds herself periodically ravished by sensual experiences—she learns to swim, she responds with a kind of swoon to an evening performance of piano pieces by Frédéric Chopin (no relation). Eventually she falls in love with the son of the woman who runs the guesthouse and finds evidence that her affections are returned. When the family moves back to New Orleans for the winter, Edna must resume her bourgeois life, which includes much entertaining and formal visiting. Edna refuses, and begins to wander about the city, discovering places and ways of life she had never before been aware of. She takes instruction in painting and begins to sell her pictures through a dealer. Her actions only feed her dissatisfaction. She decides to utterly change the terms of her existence by moving out of the large mansion she shares with her family into a smaller house nearby.

Toward the end of the novel, Edna suffers a couple of disappointments that lead her to realize that even the terms of her new life cannot be borne. Her newly awakened sensuality must have a worthy object, but it does not—there is to be no outlet for her passions. In addition, she can't, in the end, betray the honor of her children. Instinctively making a kind of death-before-dishonor decision, she swims out into the ocean and drowns, but not with a sense of fear, more with a sense of discovery and liberation.

It is very interesting to read *The Awakening* along with James, Wharton, and the other novelists of the turn of the twentieth century, because they all had the same thing on their minds, but James and Wharton weren't straightforward about the sexuality implicit in their protagonists' dilemmas. Chopin, on the other hand, makes wonderful use of her exotic setting, evoking the heat, beauty, and physicality of not only her southern Louisiana landscape, but also of the Creole society she lives in, where men and women are much more open about all matters of sexuality and reproduction, even though virtue and the appearance of virtue are as important to them as to those in James's and Wharton's milieu. Chopin is no less definite than the others about the effects of such an awakening, though Edna does not die in defeat, as Lily Bart (Edith Wharton, *The House of Mirth*) seems to. Rather Edna recognizes that once she has awakened, it is better to sacrifice her life than to sacrifice her new sense of herself. When she swims out, her suicide is far from despairing, and quite unlike Lily's overdose of sleeping pills in a dingy room in New York City.

The Awakening was Chopin's only novel—she died about five years after its publication—but it is well worth reading, not as much for the plot (though I think she makes a pretty good argument for Edna) as for the depiction of the gradual change of Edna's way of seeing the world and for the sympathy she shows her. Flaubert may have stated "Madame Bovary, c'est moi," but his empathy was not quite sympathy. Not so Kate Chopin. Edna is a woman throughout *The Awakening,* and her quest for a sense of authenticity is never demeaned.

47 · Sir Arthur Conan Doyle · The Hound of the Baskervilles

(1901; REPR., NEW YORK: NEW AMERICAN LIBRARY, SIGNET, 2001), 240 PP.*

Compared with Bram Stoker and the thriller writers who have come after him, Conan Doyle seems unusually, even boringly, squeamish. While purporting to delve into evil and danger, he keeps away from anything distasteful. Dickens was more graphic and horrible in parts of his sunniest works than Conan Doyle ever is. If *The Hound of the Baskervilles* is meant to impart a shudder, then the British reading public was more susceptible to shuddering at the turn of the twentieth century than they had ever been before. Many eighteenth- and nineteenth-century novels are more gruesome and uncanny than this one. But even so, we have to reckon with Sherlock Holmes, and in him, Conan Doyle created a unique figure who has served modern culture as an intriguing and reassuring model of civilized man. Holmes is a man of his time, but with a difference—what appeared in contemporary characters as anomie and isolation appear in Holmes as savoir faire. What appeared in others as coldness and suspect scientific rationality appear in Holmes as coolness and practical intelligence. What appeared in others as sensuality appears in Holmes as taste (in music and art). And what appeared in others as misogynism appears in Holmes as a mysterious and perhaps romantic choice. Holmes is the quintessential man of the British Empire—self-confident and self-reliant, athletic and active, intelligent and moral, a Tory in values but

*I learn from Michael Chabon's piece in *The New York Review of Books* that Conan Doyle and Oscar Wilde were once invited to lunch by the editor of *Lippincott's Magazine,* and asked to write long stories for the publication. The resulting works were *The Sign of Four* and *The Picture of Dorian Gray.* (Michael Chabon, "Inventing Sherlock Holmes," *The New York Review of Books,* vol. 52, no. 2, Feb. 10, 2005.)

free of snobbery and political cant. And he likes to solve puzzles. And he is discreet, important, and famous. He ought to get tedious and even ridiculous, but he doesn't.

The premise of *The Hound of the Baskervilles* is that a certain wealthy family from a rather wild part of Devonshire is subject to a family curse involving a large infernal hound. One heir has died of mysterious causes before the novel opens, and another has just come to England to take up his inheritance. Can Holmes save the new heir and solve the mystery surrounding the death of the former one? Of course he can. The pleasure is in how Conan Doyle sets up the mechanics of the plot so that the reader, and Watson, don't figure it out before Holmes reveals what he knows. The trick is that Conan Doyle withholds no information from the reader, but turns it into misinformation through Watson's interpretation of it. The reader, used to Watson, knows he's wrong, but follows him pleasantly on various wild goose chases without reinterpreting the information until Holmes makes his revelations.

Conan Doyle tried to get rid of Holmes at least once, and apparently detested writing about him, but Holmes is as popular at the beginning of the twenty-first century as he was at the beginning of the twentieth (maybe more so). My view is that the reason for this is that somehow he truly predates the First World War, and that reading Holmes stories is endlessly reassuring—when Conan Doyle was writing most of the Holmes stories, the horrors of the war and the twentieth century could not be imagined, and while she is reading them, the reader can hardly imagine them, either. Many readers read them over and over, perhaps as escape, but perhaps as a way of imagining the world we live in as a manageable place, where all we need to orient ourselves is a little systematic brainpower. Holmes and Watson, with some help from Hollywood, have endured while other, more graphic thriller writers have not. But the intriguing thing about the Holmes stories is that the Hollywood versions have dated, while the originals have remained perennial. Holmes is the model all other detectives wrestle with because he is the coolest puzzle solver. Perhaps the lesson is that it is not the brutality or shock of the crime that invites willing suspension of disbelief, but the intrigue of the puzzle.

48 · Joseph Conrad · Heart of Darkness

(1902; REPR., NEW YORK: W. W. NORTON, 1971), 89 PP.

Heart of Darkness is a good example of how even the best-intentioned, most respected piece of fiction can devolve into a social document when attitudes change and history overtakes the thematic material of a given work of art. A hundred years after publication, Conrad's repeated images of the Africans Marlow meets in his journey up the Congo River seem racist and inhumane. Even when they are dying from the cruel treatment they receive at the hands of the Belgians (treatment that Conrad protested), they die as a group of pitiful creatures, not as individuals who have been exploited and handled unjustly and unmercifully. Conrad's habit of individualizing whites and generalizing blacks, arrogating consciousness and intellect solely to Europeans, no longer rates the respect it once received—for many years *Heart of Darkness* was considered a great novella, one of the half dozen great short novels in the European tradition.

But the problem of *Heart of Darkness* is not merely a historical one—that attitudes changed—or a psychological one—that Conrad himself overlooked or avoided seeing evidence of vital African cultures when he visited the Congo in 1890 (as some scholars assert). The problem with *Heart of Darkness* is artistic, too, and it is a good lesson in how technical choices shape artistic vision. The symptom is that from beginning to end, the author and the narrator are victims of a thoroughgoing imperialist sentimentality that persistently substitutes false feeling for true observation. The first hint of this is when Marlow says of his aunt, "It's queer how out of touch with truth women are. They live in a world of their own, and there had never been anything like it, and never can be." Such a remark could be made only by a man who had never actually listened to a woman or observed any of the women around him on any street in any city of Europe. Or, perhaps, read a novel by a woman. Or, perhaps, cared about women's lives. At any rate, Conrad's tendency to generalize from these sorts of feelings rather than to actually observe what is around him is clear from this point forward. Sentimentality is often defined as fake or exaggerated feeling, but it also may be seen as feeling that has no basis in the sentimentalist's actual experience—he does not truly observe or perceive the object, but rather projects fears or wishes onto the object and then reacts to them as if they were real.

Marlow's reaction to the coast of Africa is similar to Crusoe's two centuries earlier—the jungle seems impenetrable and fierce. When he enters at the mouth of the Congo River, however, his perception doesn't change—the vegetation along the river continues to hide something or someone whom Marlow hardly dares to look at or imagine. He is the opposite of an explorer, if an explorer is someone who actually looks for what is present in the new landscape, as Crusoe does. And then there is Kurtz. The reverse side of his fear-induced sentimentality is his impulse to worship Kurtz. Even before meeting him, after no more than hearing his name and a bit of his reputation, Marlow is ready to attribute all sorts of greatness to Kurtz. He is thus enthralled. After he picks up Kurtz and returns him downriver, he spends lots of time listening to Kurtz and pondering his meaning, but he doesn't actually hear anything Kurtz says clearly enough to remember it or communicate it to his listeners. He is far more interested in his own feelings about Kurtz—what Kurtz symbolizes in his emotional life. When he subsequently visits Kurtz's fiancée at the end of the novella, the two of them collude in memorializing Kurtz by sentimentalizing him. It is clear from how they converse that each wants to claim Kurtz's "greatness," but neither one actually remembers any specifics about it.

The real problem with *Heart of Darkness* is that Conrad substitutes eloquence for details and incidents. Marlow makes a long journey—from Belgium to Africa, then months in Africa waiting to go upriver, then downriver and back to Belgium and England. Clearly there is a story here, full of adventures and particulars, but the particulars are not related—they are summarized and interpreted for a rhetorical purpose. The author is less interested in telling a story than in making a point, but the point he makes is unconvincing because there is no evidence in the form of a well-constructed narrative with believable characters to back it up. Marlow's fear (and Kurtz's and Conrad's) approaches terror. What they fear is so overwhelming that it is unspeakable. At the root of such fear is guilt, perhaps. The Africans in the novella work not like human characters but like ghosts, or like the undead in *Dracula*—they are meant to infuse the reader with a sense of uncontrollable forces at work in the world, of dread that the reader is supposed to accept and partake of.

Heart of Darkness asks us to consider the idea of greatness in the novel, because it was considered great until dissenting voices, such as that of the Nigerian writer Chinua Achebe (in his 1975 lecture "An

Image of Africa: Racism in Conrad's *Heart of Darkness*"), invited the literary establishment to reconsider it. The important thing to remember is that thematic material in any novel—that is, the author's ideas about the world he lives in—goes in and out of style. A novel always documents the period of its composition; sometimes the story it tells transcends the period and transcends the themes the author thought he was using it to express. Sometimes, indeed, the period of a novel's composition becomes so distant that the thematic material ceases to mean anything, while the story remains compelling, as with Boccaccio's stories of feuding Florentine parties. It's hard to see how Conrad's novella will come back into the general canon, given his penchant for talking about Africans and women in casually demeaning terms. Perhaps if it did come back, that would be a sign that such talk and such views had returned to respectability. Resurrection is always possible as long as a book remains in print and someone is around to champion it. My own view, however, is that because the novella is artistically flawed—because the balance between thematic material and narrative material is off—*Heart of Darkness* will remain an interesting historical document but a bad work of art. _I AGREE!_

49 · Edith Wharton · The House of Mirth

ED. CYNTHIA GRIFFIN WOLF (1905; REPR., NEW YORK: PENGUIN, 1985), 329 PP.

The House of Mirth begins with a minor indiscretion. An unmarried New York society woman, Lily Bart, who is twenty-nine years old, gives in to the temptation to visit the apartment of a man she knows, Lawrence Selden, and her departure is witnessed by an unsavory social-climbing character named Rosedale. Lily is awkward during the encounter with Rosedale and manages to alienate him, but since she is to all appearances firmly planted in the highest society, the very society that Rosedale would like to frequent, she shrugs off her sense of unease and pursues her already formed plan, which is to secure herself a wealthy and socially prominent husband, an unappealing mama's boy named Percy Gryce.

But Lily does not succeed. Though she brings Gryce to the point of a proposal, she ends up offending him and he goes off without making an offer. Lily is now in considerable financial and some social danger.

Though beautiful and possessed of perfect manners and only the best connections, she has come to an age where she has to play her cards right to gain an establishment. For the rest of the novel, Lily plays her cards wrong every time. Finally, socially and financially ruined, in part by the malice of others and in part by her own circumspection, she dies of an overdose of a sleeping draft in a shabby room, her life a beautiful, dignified, and in some sense perplexing wreck.

Wharton's characters consistently act out of what may seem to the reader to be a self-destructive reserve. It is clear to everyone around Lily, including the reader, that to survive she must marry for money, but throughout the novel she toys with making a more companionable connection with Lawrence Selden, who appreciates her but does not have enough money to marry. He also lives a kind of aesthetically perfected life that he doesn't care (except briefly) to disrupt. He comes closest of all the characters to feeling love for Lily, but his real role in the narrative is to observe her fall with a finer sensibility than the others around her are capable of. However much the reader may deplore Lily's downward spiral (which Wharton depicts in graphic detail), and however much the reader may wish for Selden to rescue her, it is clear from the first time she enters his apartment that he is incapable of really connecting with Lily or with anyone else. Her circumspection finds its echo in his core selfishness.

It says something about Wharton's milieu—the wealthiest and oldest New York families—that by contrast to everyone they know, Lily and Selden are the hero and heroine of *The House of Mirth*.

Wharton writes with judicious self-assurance and detailed, deliberate observation. Like James, Wharton was intent upon raising the artistic claims of the novel to the heights of great poetry, drama, or painting, and like James, she considered a finished or perfected quality to be the sign of a truly artistic novel. Her models were French rather than English—Flaubert rather than Dickens—and she admired the French novelists for their psychological probing and for the care with which they shaped their material. Herself possessed of wealth, she had the leisure to perfect her work rather than rush it into print at so many cents per word, and *The House of Mirth* does have a polished and deliberate style that is frequently mesmerizing. Wharton lived and wrote with an equanimity that is unusual in a productive novelist—she had one passionate affair in the course of an otherwise unsatisfactory marriage, she seems to have been sensible and charitable in all of her relationships, to have been in general drawn to doing the right thing, both morally and socially, all her life. These characteristics certainly were reinforced by the fact that the great success of her work did not change her circumstances. She lived the life she had been destined by birth to live, but with the added advantage of intelligence and moral sensibility. She is an excellent role model not often emulated.

The modern reader may find Lily Bart just on the verge of being a case study in a science, psychology, that was just on the verge of being invented. She is interesting in psychological terms as well as in social terms (the terms Wharton chooses). She can't commit herself to the life she seems to prefer to lead. At every critical juncture, she torpedoes the very plans she has worked assiduously to bring about, and yet she also can't accept the working world—when she gets a job she needs very much, making hats, she is too clumsy and inexperienced to do the work and gets fired. She has been raised and trained to make a rich, loveless marriage, but she can't bring herself to do it.

Wharton does not condemn or satirize Lily's world, but neither does she glamorize it. She does not question Lily's preference for this world, but she does present the world coolly, inviting the reader to observe that while it is a world full of beautiful things and places, delightful treats and privileges, it is also cold and destructive, a world where it is easier to do damage than to do good, easier to exclude than to connect. Therefore the reader is left to question whether there was ever any hope for Lily, since her preferred environment is one in which her sensibility cannot be satisfied.

Lily's problem is not being disposed of against her wishes, but disposing of herself against her wishes. Wharton indicates that the problem is not solved by female freedom of choice, only complicated by it. Without parents to push her, Lily can't act. Having passed the age of ignorance and become an astute observer of those around her, she is too far gone—paradoxically, it is not she who is past being desirable, but her surroundings, mansions and privileges and all, that are past being desirable enough to compel the fatal choice among the various less than ideal mates.

The House of Mirth also raises an interesting formal question. Although Lily's fall is dramatic and compelling, it is not especially representative and therefore not especially meaningful. Her unique qualities of beauty and circumspection combined with the special nature of her milieu—great wealth and impeccable breeding—mean that her story is not susceptible to being generalized. Lily's interest for Wharton, and for Lawrence Selden, is that she is unique on the surface and unique underneath. It is only in her psychological profile—her nascent identity as a case study—that she becomes like others, like people who may be reading about her, for example. But a novel is different from a case study in that it looks past surface distinctions to the similarities underneath. Therefore, though Lily is interesting to witness, she is hard to learn from. Every novel of fatal decline has intrinsic dramatic excitement (à la *Thérèse Raquin*), but Lily's decline is so specialized that *The House of Mirth* falls just short of greatness.

50 · Max Beerbohm · The Illustrated Zuleika Dobson, or an Oxford Love Story

(NEW HAVEN, CONN.: YALE UNIVERSITY PRESS, 1911), 350 PP.

Max Beerbohm was an artist, a reviewer, an essayist, a caricaturist, and a generally beloved fellow about town, and upon publication, *Zuleika Dobson* was greeted with a chorus of delight that perhaps no one alive in the twenty-first century quite understands. The author of the introduction to the Yale University Press edition wonders, if the novel is a satire, what is it satirizing?, and that is perhaps a fair question. My guess is that it is not satirizing as much as it is making fun out of irresistible women, manly men, and undergraduate callowness. For our purposes, *Zuleika Dobson* also pushes to its ridiculous extreme the old question of what women are for. Zuleika, who is by profession a magician but by avocation a siren, is clearly for nothing. She has no money and no life goals other than to captivate the hearts of undergraduate men. When she first arrives at Oxford during "Eights Week," she meets the duke of Dorset and, certain of his indifference, falls in love with him. The next day at breakfast, however, he reveals that he has fallen in love with her. She is stung and betrayed. She has no use for a man who actually loves her, and at once recoils. The duke now vows to commit suicide for her, and tries to do so at once, but circumstances intervene, and he has to put off his plan for twenty-four hours. In the course of the next day, he, too, falls out of love, but nonetheless he is bound by honor and tradition to go through with his vow. He is more than a little disconcerted to discover that every other undergraduate in Oxford has made the same vow, thereby diluting the drama of his plan. Witty complications ensue.

Zuleika Dobson is lighthearted to the core, exuberant to the end (when Zuleika looks up the train schedule to Cambridge). Like the works of P. G. Wodehouse, it is undarkened by the least hint of social commentary. But unlike the novels of Wodehouse, it uses romantic conventions only to turn them upside down, not to reaffirm them. It is a model comic novel in that it exploits the comedy inherent in logic. Everything Zuleika, the duke, and all the other characters do is logically perfect, given their assumptions about virtue, honor, and social class, but everything they do is also ridiculous. If Beerbohm had a satirical agenda, no one seems to have discovered it. He twitted or killed off all his characters, to the delight of all his readers. *Zuleika Dobson* was a success when it came out, in 1911. Whether it had any larger purpose at the time is impossible to know now, because it quickly took on a different meaning. Bertrand Russell noted much later in the century, "I read *Zuleika Dobson* with pleasure. It represents the Oxford that the two World Wars have destroyed with a charm that is not likely to be reproduced anywhere in the world for the next thousand years."

The Yale University Press edition is illustrated with Beerbohm's original drawings.

51 · Ford Madox Ford · The Good Soldier

(1915; REPR., NEW YORK: RANDOM HOUSE, VINTAGE, 1989), 256 PP.

The Good Soldier is an odd and maybe even unique book in that the fact that it is a masterpiece, almost a perfect novel, comes as a repeated surprise even to readers who have read it before. In a dedicatory letter to the second edition written some ten years after the publication of the novel, Ford depicts himself "taking down one of [his] ten-year-old books [and exclaiming] 'Great Heavens, did I write as well as that then?' . . . And I will permit myself to say that I was astounded at the work I must have put into the construction of the book, at the intricate tangle of references and cross-references" (p. xx). Ford wrote other very good novels—his tetralogy *Parade's End* is moving and innovative—but he called *The Good Soldier* his "auk's egg" ("having reached the allotted, I had laid my one egg and might as well die"); it does have the quality of saying absolutely everything about both his story and his theme—not just everything he has to say, but everything there is to say.

The story seems simple. Two wealthy couples, one American and one English, meet at a spa in Germany and spend several years in comfortable friendship until it is revealed that the American wife and the English husband are carrying on an affair that the English wife knows about but the American husband does not. After the deaths of the adulterers, more and more is uncovered about both the conduct and the emotional meaning of the affair. The story is narrated by the American husband and is in some sense a detective story, but he is no investigator. The facts come to him unwillingly, since he would have preferred from the beginning not to know; the suspense depends not on what has happened, as dramatic as it turns out to be, but on the narrator's unfolding interpretation of the passionate emotions manifested in very small gestures or brief remarks.

Ford's greatest gamble is in the naïveté of the narrator (Dowell), supposedly an idle but well-meaning wealthy man from an old Philadelphia family who readily accepts a sexless marriage with a woman (Florence) whose emotional life is a secret and a deception. Florence persuades Dowell at the commencement of their honeymoon that marital relations might so tax her weak heart that they are out of the question—she turns him into a servant who takes care of her every need while also leaving her lots of free time to carry on with at least two lovers of her choosing. Dowell's idiom and mode of thinking are not perfectly American, and Ford's insights into American ways are slightly off, but America is not his subject, England is, and Dowell is convincing enough. His real virtue is that he is disarming, and he does not pretend to reliability. He freely offers his own self-doubts about his competence, both as an actor in the drama and as an interpreter, and he manages not to seem either untruthful or self-serving. He paints four portraits—Edward Ashburnham, the owner of a large estate in England; his wife, Leonora, daughter of impoverished Irish gentry; Florence, heiress to a New England fortune; and Nancy Rufford, Leonora's ward, who has lived with Edward and Leonora from age thirteen.

Edward and Leonora have every appearance of grace, character, and respectability. Edward, too, is suffering from a bad heart, but he has been in the army in India, and has also been an excellent landlord and magistrate back in England. His failures are failures of self-knowledge and intelligence more than morality—he is upright, generous, and responsible. But, fatally, he is "a sentimentalist," which makes him susceptible to the appearance of suffering or weakness, and also makes him immune to his wife (theirs is an arranged marriage), whose virtues are those of strength and reserve. She is repeatedly termed "cold" by Dowell, but her coldness seems more in the nature of untapped warmth (for example, she wants children, which she and Edward can't seem to produce). The first startling fact about them that the reader learns is that they haven't spoken in private for thirteen years, though they are gracious to one another in public (surely this is possible only in an especially grand setting, with perfectly trained servants). Everything about Edward is plausible for, even typical of, a man of his position, but Ford takes a different approach from every previous English author to have contemplated the landed gentry, because he takes Edward's inner life, as empty as it is, seriously, anatomizing and sympathizing with its very emptiness.

It is clear as the novel proceeds that not only do Edward and Leonora have no idea what intimacy is, they also have no way of having found out: for one thing, they don't read novels, and for another, Leonora consults priests and nuns for marital advice, and what they have to offer are thirdhand clichés such as "men are like that." Edward consults no one, and there seems to be no structure in his life that would permit such consultation. Other men of his social class tell dirty stories, perhaps as a form of sharing information, but these make Edward uncomfortable. Thus, when Edward begins to feel out of sympathy with Leonora some three or four years into their marriage, he is ripe for exploitation, and he ends up making a costly liaison and losing about 40 percent of the principal value of his estate. Over the next ten years Leonora takes over management of the estate and brings it back to its original value, but the balance of their relationship is fatally undermined by her control and his untrustworthiness.

Both the American marriage and the English marriage suffer from the emasculation of the husbands, and Dowell criticizes Leonora and Florence, but Ford depicts the husbands more complexly. They have fully colluded in their emasculation by not knowing how to be men—the reason for Dowell's failure (symbolized by the fact that unlike other Americans, he has no interest in earning money) is unclear, but the reason for Edward's failure is that he has received no instruction in anything but duties and forms. He is also slightly stupid. Dowell is content in his emasculation, but Edward has unfulfilled yearnings for companionship and support that he finds in a series of women, with Leonora's tacit acceptance. Leonora holds out the hope that once their financial imbalance is righted, he will get interested in her again, and things seem to be moving in that direction when Florence entangles Edward in her much colder and less sentimental designs—Dowell says that she "annexes him."

Dowell maintains that Florence is a woman of the most shallow possible motivations—she wants to look good, dress well, display herself to intellectual advantage, and be catered to. She is purely and discreetly a social climber. Until Florence comes along, Leonora has accepted Edward's liaisons as well-meaning and necessary, worthy of her respect and even her care, but when he links himself with Florence, whom Leonora despises, she loses all respect for and sympathy with him, though she still loves and desires him.

While I don't want to retell the entire novel—especially since it interprets itself quite well—I do want to comment on Ford's style, which makes great use of paradox. At one point, for example, while giving the history of Edward's military career, he says, "It would have done him a great deal of good to get killed." There is something quite reckless about that sentence, and yet it is perfectly understandable in context—it comes late in the novel, when we know that not only is Edward's end to be tragic, but also that the downward path to it is painful and pathetic. How much better for the dumb animal to have died heroically, in accordance with the system by which he lived. There are those who believe that *The Good Soldier* is one of the few stylistically perfect novels in any language, and perhaps what Ford was alluding to in his remarks about references and cross-references is this sense that the contradictory and complementary meanings in every paradoxical sentence are entirely understandable because he has made such a clear explication of his fictional situation—the psychologies of his characters, the interweaving of character and event, intention and chance.

Ford originally titled his novel *The Saddest Story*. After the outbreak of the First World War and his departure for the front, his editor changed the title to *The Good Soldier,* which Ford did not care for. But the editor was right—Ford's title is empty and meaningless. *The Good Soldier* subtly cues the reader to the larger social dimension of Ford's subject. Leonora and Edward, and to a lesser degree Dowell and Florence, are struggling with ignorance as much as moral failure. They are representatives of a system that fails them and fails in their failure. It is the subtler side of Dickens's Circumlocution Office, of Thackeray's *Vanity Fair*. In Dickens and Thackeray's day, the landed gentry could still be attacked. By Ford's time, all of the social and cultural arrangements of feudal Europe were imploding in the First World War. Ford was astute enough to depict both the inevitability of the implosion and its sadness—the world of Jane Austen a hundred years on, depopulated, lonely, and dark.

52 · Sinclair Lewis · Main Street

(1920; REPR., NEW YORK: NEW AMERICAN LIBRARY, SIGNET, 1998), 474 PP.

Sinclair Lewis may be ripe for a revival; his books bring up several interesting issues of art and fashion. *Main Street* is his most famous book, though certain critics prefer *Babbitt* as a better novel. *Main Street* was a tremendous best seller, published when Lewis was thirty-five, and cited by the Nobel Prize committee as a major reason he was given the Nobel in 1930. *Main Street* is the story of Carol Kennicott, who graduates from a small women's college in the first chapter of the novel with rather vague aspirations to achieve something or reform something. After a reasonably long (but not very enlightening) courtship she marries small-town doctor Will Kennicott and moves with him to Gopher Prairie, Minnesota (based on Lewis's hometown of Sauk Centre). She is immediately dissatisfied with the town and her life there, and the rather episodic novel traces the simultaneous evolution of her marriage, her life in Gopher Prairie, and the passing of her youth. The novel is rather like a bildungsroman in that it describes the education of a young person through a series of trials, but Carol's is a domestic education, and it is hard to decide whether she grows or is simply overcome. In the end, under some protest, she manages to agree to life in Gopher Prairie, but not quite to accept it.

Lewis is careful to present Carol as immature but well-meaning, an unreliable spokesperson for the valid idea that there is something more to life than bridge, something more to politics than voting the straight Republican ticket, and something more to human relationships than empty forms and eager gossip. He sets up her husband, Will, as her foil—he is steady and, on the surface, unimaginative. He defends the town and his friends there against her denigrating comments, though as the novel progresses, he softens in his insistence on having their marriage conform to a traditional model. Carol is ambivalent. She is moved by all forms of beauty, including that of the Minnesota landscape and that of a young man who comes to town as a tailor late in the novel and who courts her (she entertains his crush but doesn't concede her virtue). In fact, she has no consistent allies and no rational program, only feelings that sometimes offend her fellow citizens and sometimes are offended by them. She not only criticizes their aesthetic but also crosses social boundaries by maintaining a friendship with her housemaid and her housemaid's husband, a jack-of-all-trades who is a Communist sympathizer. Carol's fecklessness is believable and sometimes irritating, but the townspeople's general resistance to every form of nonconformity is also believable. Lewis perfectly renders the frequently nice and friendly narrow-minded prejudice of small-town America that is all the more difficult to combat because it is well-meaning and patriotic.

Lewis was a satirist, but his plots were realistic plots rather than fabulist ones, so an element of exuberance is missing in the novel, and the tone sometimes seems unclear. Satirists such as Swift often signal the reader that it is time to laugh at the characters by making them or their situations fantastic. Other satirists, such as Fielding, use a certain elevated language or comic tone to do the same thing, but Lewis was satiric without being overtly funny or comic, which means that the signals the reader is supposed to pick up are easily missed. He called himself a "scold," and that was an appropriate characterization—his criticisms of American life are far from lighthearted. He manages to be intelligent and interesting and even hopeful; his characters are well drawn and lively. But his plots meander and his tone is unclear. His novels aren't well-made wholes, but nor are they shambling stylistic charmers. In their time they dealt with issues that Americans wanted to read about—small-town life, the mind of the businessman, revivalist religion—but when those issues seemed to fade in importance, so did Lewis's reputation.

Lewis adhered to a strongly felt social theory that was basically leftist, and he wrote at a time when almost all writers were required to declare their allegiance to the right or the left, at least in America. In *Main Street,* Lewis's loyalties sometimes come across as simply a democratic sensibility, and therefore aesthetically acceptable, and sometimes as an outmoded and false-seeming program for building the utopia of the future. No novelist can quite escape the social theories of his time, and in fact must be drawn to them, because the novel is a social investigation. So to some extent the reputation of every novelist will rise and fall according to how his social theory holds up. For example, in the 1960s and '70s, the era of the new left, Dickens was considered well-meaning but naive; his "program" was thought to be poorly worked out and inconsistent—not Marxist enough (though Marx was a great fan of Dickens). After Marxism went out of fashion, Dickens's amorphous social critique came to seem more universally true because it was not programmatic but based on feelings of generosity and brotherhood combined with specific criticisms of practices common in England during his lifetime.

Novelists of a conservative or more purely aesthetic bent hold up better on the surface, but their novels go in and out of fashion according to relevance or irrelevance. Trollope, for example, in some eras seems interesting and in others trivial but not, like Dickens, right or wrong. Some novelists are luckier than others in the eras of their formative intellectual years, but all weltanschauungs return, which means that most novelists have at least a chance of a revival.

53 · Sigrid Undset · Kristin Lavransdatter, vol. 1, The Wreath

TRANS. TIINA NUNNALLY (1920; REPR., NEW YORK: PENGUIN, 1997), 336 PP.

Sigrid Undset, who won the Nobel Prize in literature in 1928, went one way and modernism went another, but *Kristin Lavransdatter* holds up quite well in any number of ways, even compared with the more experimental works of Undset's contemporaries. Her portrait, in three volumes, of the whole life of a Norwegian woman of the fourteenth century could not have been written with such frankness before Undset's day, and probably would not have been written at all outside of Scandinavia. Undset's success in creating the illusion that we are reading about the Middle Ages as they actually were lived is striking. Her details are not only rich, they are also subtly presented rather than paraded ostentatiously before the reader; every bit of local color is worked into the plot or the character development or the thematic material. The Nunnally translation, too, is excellent—straightforward but also evocative, lyrical enough in places, but not, like earlier translations, overtly romantic or archaic.

Kristin is the beautiful daughter of an unlucky marriage between Lavrans Bjorgulfsson and his wife, Ragnfrid. For a long time she is their only surviving child. Three sons die in infancy, and Ragnfrid is a reserved and melancholy mother. The family lives on a prosperous estate in northern Norway, but there is some sense that Lavrans could have done more with his life, and that Ragnfrid is viewed with suspicion by the neighbors.

Two more daughters are born, but no sons. It appears that Kristin is destined to be married off in the usual fashion to a dull but good man of her own social class. But one evening she goes out to say farewell to a young man who has been her childhood friend, and on the way home, another local fellow attempts to rape her. The shame and disquiet that grow out of this episode (like every other episode, the subject of much gossip) lead Lavrans to send Kristin to a convent in Oslo as a student for a year, and there she falls passionately for a very well-born but unsuitable man. He seduces her, transforming her character and her social position and setting her at odds with everything she believes and everyone she loves.

So far, *Kristin Lavransdatter* is not unlike *The House of Mirth* or George Eliot's *The Mill on the Floss* except that Undset is more explicit about the workings of sexual passion than either Wharton or Eliot. Nor is Undset intimidated by the failure of Kristin's virtue, since she doesn't kill her off, as Wharton and Eliot kill off their protagonists. The shame is great, as Kristin herself knows, but to Undset, the hard work of redemption is more interesting than sacrifice, and she allows Kristin and her seducer, Erlend, to get married. Their marriage (they produce seven sons) is explored in volume 2, *The Wife,* and Kristin's experiences as a widow during the Black Death are explored in volume 3, *The Cross.*

Perhaps the biggest difference between Undset's protagonist and most other female protagonists is that she is never without work to do. Even though she is a member of the gentry and her father owns an estate, she spins and weaves and makes beer and sews and helps with the planting and the harvesting. In Norway, all hands work, so Kristin never wonders, as Lily Bart does, why she exists. The choices are two—marriage or the convent—and the obligations are many. Life is arduous in a way that is never true in novels about women of the middle and upper classes in France and England. Undset writes about work and weather and famine and accidents, illnesses, pregnancy, animals, and the natural world with immediacy and ease. Though Undset, too, explores the classic conflict between female virtue and female desire, she sets it into the context of female usefulness. It is clear by the end of *The Wreath* that Erlend and his friends think Kristin is not only worth possessing as an object of beauty and property, they also think she is going to get things organized on his estate, and she thinks so, too, though she is barely seventeen years old. No heroine out of Trollope or James would ever aspire to such a life.

Undset was a great lover of the Icelandic sagas, and she learned more from them than just the details of the fourteenth-century lifestyle. An important convention of the Icelandic sagas is that small events have large ramifications. In *Hrafnkels Saga,* a servant's disobedience results, eventually, in a serious feud and the deaths of many men. *Kristin Lavransdatter* works in the same way. Lives are changed and fates are decided. The chain of cause and effect may go back to something as incidental as, in this novel, the escape of an imported panther from its cage and the subsequent panic that results in Kristin and her friend getting separated from their escort. This very tracing of cause and effect, this sense that one knowable thing leads to another, is where Undset parts from modernism (as exemplified by *The Trial*). Every detail of *Kristin Lavransdatter* is significant, because the author knows what every detail means and how they all fit together. This makes the novel a rich and satisfying read. What happens to Kristin is not happy, but it does have meaning that she is able to understand (and that reflects Undset's own belief system after her conversion to Catholicism). The world Undset creates for Kristin is full of senseless suffering, but those who suffer are given full instructions for how to endure their suffering and make something of it. Undset's world is frightening but coherent.

Undset was a patient and painstaking novelist. In addition to the literary pleasures of her work, the reader finds as well an underlying sense of honor and a willingness to wrestle with moral questions as moral questions rather than as political questions or questions of perception. Her works are well worth reading and reviving.

54 · James Joyce · Ulysses

(1921; REPR., NEW YORK: RANDOM HOUSE, VINTAGE, 1990), 783 PP.

Whether a reader enjoys or appreciates *Ulysses* or not, it is absolutely true that it is interesting because it demonstrates several things that happen when an author exploits to a logical extreme the possibilities inherent in every novel. Its story is fairly simple—two men, a young man of twenty-one named Stephen Dedalus (based on Joyce himself), and an older man of thirty-eight, named Leopold Bloom, pass a single day and night, June 16, 1904, in parallel, at first missing each other and later meeting up before Bloom returns to his home and the bed of his wife, Molly. Joyce bases his story loosely on *The Odyssey,* making Bloom an Odysseus (or Ulysses) figure, and Stephen a figure of Telemachus, Odysseus' son. A complicating factor in Bloom's day is that he knows that Molly is to be visited by a sexual rival, Blazes Boylan, while Bloom is away. A complicating factor in Stephen's day is that he is to be paid his monthly wages, and he will be tempted in a number of ways to dissipate his money, waste his time, and betray his talents.

The most obvious characteristic of *Ulysses* is its complex and, to some people (including me), forbidding variety of styles. Even the most straightforward chapters, such as chapters one and two, are not easy to follow the first time through, and several of the chapters require repeated rereadings and true dedication (as well as some sort of companion learning aid, such as a key or a set of taped lectures, which is what I chose). It is impossible to read *Ulysses* without paying attention to every word (some readers advocate not really paying attention at all, just sort of letting the prose wash over, but to me, at least, this method results quickly in boredom). Most devotees of *Ulysses* maintain that every word rewards attention and that the system thus created is uniquely rich ("life itself" is the common claim). Since every novel is, in fact, a system of words in which each could, in theory, relate to every other, a novel that forces the reader to pay attention word by word and to reread it until many or most of the possible connections emerge and stick in the memory, then the difficulty of *Ulysses* serves as gatekeeper, luring those with the capacity for full enjoyment, deterring those without it. *Ulysses* also requires the reader to judge for herself whether the tendency of prose to elaborate itself into an ever more complex linguistic system serves or detracts from other elements of the novel. For some readers, the difficulty of *Ulysses'* style mitigates its emotional impacts; for others, the style enriches the emotional basis of the story. Because the style is so extreme, though, the novel can seem abstract and arid, or uniquely rich.

Joyce's main protagonist, Leopold Bloom, is not traditional. He does not do much in the course of the day except observe, and in fact one of the unusual things about him, in addition to the fact that he is a Jewish outsider in Dublin, is that he is an avowed voyeur. Joyce gives him lots of venial faults and also lots of excuses. On the one hand, he is portrayed as an ordinary man, with some talents but not many (not like Stephen, who is a literary genius in the making and a wonderful singer to boot), but then again, Bloom is not typical. He's kinder, more vulnerable, more knowledgeable, more long-suffering, more fastidious, and more self-doubting than the Dubliners around him. He is, in spite of his possibly unsavory sexual proclivities, a better person than those he meets, and he thereby raises the moral tone of those sexual proclivities.

Young Stephen is prickly, sensitive, and arrogant. He acts the part of a prodigal roysterer, and Bloom is moved, toward the end of the novel, to save him from himself, but in fact, Stephen seems too self-conscious to ever actually let himself go to the degree that Joyce seems to want the reader to accept. At least when he is sober, Stephen seems chary of being taken advantage of, or even of being denigrated in any way; it is not plausible that he would suffer a wastrel's fate. His view of himself is grandiose. He is convinced that his failure to kneel and pray at his mother's dying bedside is what killed her (even though she was dying of cancer). He recognizes the same lack of generosity in himself that the reader does, but he gives it a bigger name. The story seems to suggest that Bloom needs a son to care for and Stephen needs a father to care for him, at least on this one night in June 1904, but the reader may have her own opinion about whether this emotional armature for this story is compelling. There is some sense that stylistic pyrotechnics hide what is essentially a sentimental yearning by Bloom that results in a sentimental gesture (he even suggests that Stephen marry his daughter Milly; Stephen declines).

Molly Bloom, is, of course, famous as the woman with the very beautiful large breasts (according to Bloom's testimony) who says "yes." We see her from a distance at the beginning of the novel, when Bloom prepares her breakfast for her, and then again at the end, when the novel winds up with her long, interior monologue. Bloom thinks about Molly all day. He buys her a few things, he recalls their first few

times together, he meditates upon her with desire, fondness, and forgiveness. But there is no evidence that they actually relate in the sense
that they share their thoughts, have ongoing discussions about anything, or are truly intimate. He remembers one time when she had
expressed physical desire, and it was after looking out the window at a
passing man. She is a figment of Bloom's imagination, a representative
of many feelings he has, but she seems to be a stranger to him. She is
thus an object of sentimentality as much as Stephen is, and the novel
seems to have at its core Bloom's deep loneliness, a sadness so normal
to him that Bloom himself doesn't recognize it, and, what's worse, it
doesn't seem as though Joyce recognizes it, either. The stylistic fireworks come to seem like an elaborate surface distraction from what is
missing at the core of the plot, that substitutes for the exploration of the
dilemmas and crises of a real relationship (or two). When Molly engages in her own monologue, her view of their life together contradicts
Bloom's in material ways. It is also significant that they are in the habit
of lying to one another and suspecting one another. None of these
issues is resolved by the end of the novel, no doubt because to resolve
them in the course of a day when the members of the couple do not see
one another would be implausible, so the novel ends up as a lengthy
demonstration of the uncrossable (except by the author) abyss between
men and women.

Molly's monologue is supposedly an interior one, but it demonstrates, I think, the limits of Joyce's conception of her. She uses many,
many verbal expressions, such as "of course shes right," "who did I get
the last letter from," and "its all very fine for them but as for being a
woman." If this is indeed meant to render her inner life, then she has
completely internalized talking as a way of thinking. She reminds me
of Flora Finching, a character in Dickens's *Little Dorrit,* who is well-
meaning but pathologically garrulous, and whose inner life is continuously paraded in front of, and contrasted to, that of the more discreet
and less comic characters. Supposedly Joyce's wife said that he did
not understand women, and Molly's style is, I think, a rendition of a
woman observed rather than seen into.

Joyce befriended and helped Italo Svevo, who wrote *Zeno's Conscience*. *Ulysses* and *Zeno's Conscience* form an interesting contrast,
because Zeno is nearly as self-involved as Stephen and nearly as neurotic as Bloom, but one of the satisfying aspects of Svevo's novel is the
solid sense of the presence of Zeno's wife as an intelligence that meets
and matches his own rather than as a symbolic location in his mind.

Since every novel is also a social and historical document, Joyce exploits this possibility to the full, too. Bloom and Stephen perambulate around Dublin, filming the life of the city, both close-up and wide-angle, for some twenty hours. June 16, 1904, is an ordinary day, a representative day in the life of the Irish, more or less peaceful, more or less prosperous, perfectly contemporary, and one of Joyce's points is that an epic portrayal of life in Ireland must capture the ordinary with the seriousness and detail that are possible only through the deployment of many styles and forms (one lengthy section is written as a play). The reader has to find the depiction of Dublin life appealing, I think, to find it worth the effort.

Is *Ulysses* the ultimate novel? Yes, in two or three ways mentioned above. It is also the ultimate novel in another way—it cannot be judged at all except by the individual reader. It is either to one's taste or not, and no amount of lobbying by readers with other tastes can change one's mind.

55 · Italo Svevo · Zeno's Conscience

TRANS. WILLIAM WEAVER

(1923; REPR., NEW YORK: VINTAGE INTERNATIONAL, 2001), 437 PP.

"Italo Svevo" was the pen name of Ettore Schmitz, a well-to-do businessman who was educated as an Austrian and a German but who lived in Trieste and wrote in Italian (even though he says that the dialect of Trieste was his native tongue and that "with our every Tuscan word, we lie . . . by predilection, we recount all the things for which we have the words at hand, and . . . avoid those things that would oblige us to turn to the dictionary!" (p. 404). *Zeno's Conscience* was published when Svevo was sixty-two years old, and to his delight, it became much celebrated. He remarked to a friend, "Until last year, I was the . . . least ambitious old man in the world. Now I am overcome by ambition. I have become eager for praise. I now live only to manage my own glory."*

The novel purports to be the journal of a man undergoing psychoanalysis, written at the behest of the analyst, and then published by

*Quoted in the introduction of the Weaver translation, p. xxi.

the analyst to embarrass his patient and avenge his termination of the analysis. Zeno tells five interrelated stories: the story of his last attempt to quit smoking cigarettes, the story of the death of his father, the story of his marriage, the story of his mistress, and the story of his doomed business partnership with the husband of his wife's sister. Zeno's narrative style is plain and even ingenuous. He tells each story straightforwardly. But as the novel progresses, its themes, along with Zeno's feelings, get complicated. Zeno acts—the complications do not paralyze him—but he becomes more and more unsure of the meaning and the rightness of his actions until the last chapter, where he contemplates his psychoanalysis and decides that his doctor's very attempt to cure him is wrongheaded and that the images and memories the doctor wants to do away with are the ones Zeno himself cherishes the most. At one point he remarks, "I believe that he is the only one in this world who, hearing I wanted to go to bed with two beautiful women, would ask himself: Now let's see why this man wants to go to bed with them" (p. 413).

Confessions are difficult to pull off, because, as Zeno himself says, "A confession in writing is always a lie" (p. 404), but a novel that takes the form of a confession doesn't have to be true, it only has to be alluring or intriguing, and Zeno's voice is both. His avowed motives are simple: to tell what happened and why. His actions don't speak well of Zeno. He is deceitful, lustful, envious, impulsive, lazy, and easily distracted. But in fact, major sins like these are often acceptable to readers because they make for an interesting narrative. Zeno is honest and generous. He seems to be telling the truth, at least to himself and the reader, even if not to his wife and his friends. And even though he deceives his friends, he almost always speaks well of them. Such generosity in a narrator (who is simultaneously speaking ill of himself) is appealing.

The five stories have some surprising twists. The story of his marriage is the best one—he begins visiting the house of a businessman he is fond of and discovers four daughters, all of whose names begin with "A" and all of whom have reputations for beauty. He promises himself that he will marry one of the beautiful daughters, but one turns out to be too young; one has "a squint" (which I take to mean strabismus); one wants a career instead of a husband; and the fourth one, the eligible one with whom he falls in love, can't stand him. He ends up with the exact sister he had vowed never to take, and as soon as they are engaged, he is filled with unexpected happiness. They have a very satisfying marriage, at least in part because he tells her about every-thing (except the mistress) and she trusts him. Admittedly, by modern American standards this is an odd marriage, but in comparison with the other marriages in the novel, it is companionable and mutually lov-ing, and the reader has the feeling that if Augusta, Zeno's wife, with-holds judgment, then the reader might as well do so, too.

Another aspect of Zeno's charm is that while he is more than a little feckless, he is also quite observant. Above all, he observes the para-doxes of human behavior, both his own and that of others. At one point he is asked to help someone he knows cannot be helped because the man won't take responsibility for his own affairs. Zeno says, "If I had been calmer, I would have spoken to her of my inadequacy for the task she was assigning me, but I would have destroyed all the unfor-gettable emotion of that moment. In my case, I was so moved that I had no sense of my inadequacy. At that moment, I thought no inade-quacies existed for anyone" (p. 345). Zeno is always doing something unreasonable, quixotic, even self-destructive just because he enjoys the largeness of the feelings involved.

Zeno's retrospection brings him to 1915, in the First World War. He sends his family to Tuscany and waits out the dangers of the war by himself in Trieste. By this time he has told his story in detail and also has pondered the requirements of psychoanalysis. He considers intro-spection, war, memory, health, and sickness and comes up with a remarkable peroration that casts a lyrical and reflective light backward over the whole novel and makes something profound of its apparently simple materials. I think it is justly celebrated, and forms, with *The Trial* and *Ulysses,* a trio of orthodox modernism wherein the conscious-ness of the passage of time and the parsing of consciousness itself are more important than the story or the plot elements. *Zeno's Conscience* is the Italian version, with recognizably Boccaccio-like elements of wives, mistresses, business, speculation, trickery, and sex that *Ulysses* and *The Trial* have less of, or have in a less shameless way. Perhaps it was inevitable that Boccaccio would meet Freud and that Boccaccio would win.

56 · E. M. Forster · A Passage to India

(1924; REPR., SAN DIEGO, CALIF.: HARCOURT BRACE JOVANOVICH, 1965), 322 PP.

A Passage to India is a good example of a novel that, as a result of history, lost and then regained the potency of its ideas. In 2005 it is far less outmoded than it may have seemed in 1955, only a few years after Indian independence and partition. The keys to the novel's persistent currency are partly to be found in it—Forster's consistently personal (as opposed to institutional) focus and his exceptionally graceful style—and partly to be found outside it. Can Westerners, Muslims, and Hindus communicate across religious, cultural, and political boundaries? With American and English soldiers and officials once again trying to shape Eastern cultures to their own specifications, Forster's insights into how members of each society misread and read into each other's statements and actions are both timely and depressing.

Forster tells the story of Dr. Aziz, about forty, who works in a hospital in a part of India governed directly by the English. One evening, he is visiting his local mosque when he happens upon an elderly Englishwoman, Mrs. Moore, who has recently come out to India to visit her son, a low-level government official, and to bring his propective fiancée, Miss Quested. Aziz is at first offended to find an Englishwoman in the mosque, but when he realizes that she has behaved respectfully, and when she is effortlessly friendly toward him, he warms up, and after some negotiations, he offers to take Mrs. Moore, Miss Quested, and some others to visit local caves. Something unaccountable happens at the Marabar caves, and Miss Quested flees, later to accuse Aziz of molesting her. The English colony is outraged, and the accusation and subsequent trial turn into a political scandal. Forster's sympathies lie with Aziz and with Fielding, a teacher who dislikes his fellow countrymen and tries to live a more cosmopolitan life than the other officials. Miss Quested, who is confused but well intentioned, goes along with the legal machinery of the trial, but she has her doubts about what actually happened. At the trial she recants her accusation, throwing both sides into confusion and incurring the enmity of everyone. Individual doubts and second thoughts result in further conflicts and bitterness, and by the end of the novel each of the characters has been thwarted in his or her attempts to connect genuinely with the others.

From the beginning of the novel Forster limits his portrait of India to personal relationships and subjective experiences. The narrator's voice draws back from the characters mostly to depict the natural world—the stars or the caves or the rains. Each character is both an individual and a self-conscious representative of his or her group, but only insofar as he or she experiences it. For all of the characters, this self-consciousness causes a greater or lesser degree of defensiveness, irritability, and shame, but no one can imagine a different set of circumstances—the English seem to be in India to stay, and whatever any one person does or feels is rendered false by that evident and apparently permanent fact. The "realists" at the officials' compound are crude and philistine in their opinions, but the idealists, such as Miss Quested and Mrs. Moore, come to grief as well.

A Passage to India is simultaneously profound and narrow because Forster eschews as a narrator what might be called the authoritative voice. The voice he does use recognizes that for the time being, it is enough to pose the problem without even implying or hoping that the problem can be resolved. Instead of guiding the reader toward a solution—that is, subtly or not so subtly advocating one policy or another—both the plot and the narrator guide the reader away from a solution. Each time a solution, even a sense of relief, seems imminent, the possibility explodes. For example, when Mrs. Moore, now despairing and ill, persuades her son to send her back to England, and a cabin and an escort are miraculously produced at the last minute, she dies in transit and has to be buried at sea. When Fielding persuades Aziz not to accept the penalty Miss Quested is supposed to pay, Aziz becomes convinced that Fielding means to marry Miss Quested and keep the money for himself. Only at the end, at a Hindu festival that none of the characters really understands, do the principals begin to be reconciled, but even when they do begin, the moment is followed by the recognition that full reconciliation is impossible. Forster demonstrates that the imposition of tyranny, even for the best motives by decent people, unfailingly distorts true feelings and relationships and requires ambivalence and double-dealing.

Nevertheless, Forster's style is so elegant and smooth and his tone so apparently light that the novel is far from tragic, but rather infused with the sensibility of Professor Godbole, an enigmatic Hindu Brahman to whom both Aziz and Fielding are drawn but can't make sense of. The final section of the novel takes place at a yearly festival of the rebirth of Krishna. This is the most extended scene in the novel, and

Forster carefully describes the town, the temple, and the rituals. But he also makes sure that the Western reader knows that none of these add up in the way Christians and Muslims would expect them to, and indeed that their meaning contradicts all ideas of "adding up." Just as Hindu folk religion has, earlier in the novel, taken up the name of Mrs. Moore as "Esmiss Esmoor" and made of her a minor deity, now the larger moral implications of friendship and subjection, good and evil, are muddied and lost in the variegated complexity of the whole picture. Most novels, of course, express the idea that nothing is as it seems, but this one offers the idea that "is" and "seems" are interchangeable terms.

And yet, because Forster's voice is so specific, clear, and conversational, the reader is never confused about the action or the characters. One of the main assertions of the novel as a form is that the personal is political (as with *Pamela*), but few authors have quite the ability that Forster has of making every character's most idle action represent both his psychology and his sociology. My guess is that he focused on the psychology and let the sociology write itself out of the fraught political atmosphere he found when he went to India in the early 1920s. The result is that even though many of the larger political issues of Anglo India were "solved" after the Second World War, *A Passage to India* remains profound because the deeper issues surrounding Western power and colonialism and its aftermath simply shifted to other areas of conflict. The novel, as a form, is about connection. By focusing on that very thing, Forster in some sense defies history itself.

But any novel written by a white man about colonialized people is suspect to some readers, because the author can only more or less successfully infer thoughts, motives, ideas, and values from characters who are unlike him. The novelist's only tools in his portrayals are observation, ideas, and a reader's willing suspension of disbelief. Ideas, of course, are often suspect, since most historical periods generate ideas that later seem wrong. If those ideas are egregiously self-aggrandizing, as many English ideas about Indians were, they become highly unsympathetic as times change. Most ideas later seem silly, but some of them seem harmless, such as Balzac's ideas about physiology, and some of them seem harmful, such as Victorian ideas about the nature of women and Conrad's ideas about Africa as expressed in *Heart of Darkness*.

It isn't enough to point out that "for his time" an author was enlightened (that is, like us); relative enlightenment is good enough for a social document but not for an enduring work of art. Forster, I think, comes pretty close to being actually enlightened, even though here and there the voice of the narrator makes some generalization about Indians that probably would not bear scrutiny. What Forster does quite skillfully is deploy the special qualities of the novel to bolster his depictions. The first of these is giving each character good and bad moral traits as well as attractive and unattractive personality traits. This makes the characters seem rounded, and readers instinctively believe that mixed characters are more true than vicious or virtuous ones. The second of these is giving each character a degree of agency so that he or she seems realistically responsible for what he or she does. Aziz is the victim of British injustice and prejudice, but his own vanities and insecurities feed into the events that lead to his arrest, and these events are evident to the reader. Forster's focus on small moments and social occasions serves him, too, because his objection to the British is not that they rule India, or are bad rulers, but that they are rude and unkind— the reader is hardly allowed to reflect to what degree these are characteristics of culture, personality, or political structure; it is enough that she is offended, and therefore agrees with Forster's basic premise of shared humanity, as expressed by Mrs. Moore. Since the novel is always a social occasion, a reader is always offended by social transgressions even though she might not be by other antisocial plot occasions, such as murder. Forster's fourth claim to immortality is the precision of his observations. A long sequence of small, precise, and convincing observations gracefully and clearly expressed gives the reader a habit of complicity with the author that is hard to break if some small observation offends—the next small and perfect observation might make up for it.

This is not to say that every reader willingly suspends disbelief in *A Passage to India,* only that Forster makes excellent use of the peculiarities of the novel to prolong the life of its apparent historical truth. Other novels of the period, such as *The Great Gatsby* or *Main Street,* do not seem to illuminate our own time nearly as cogently.

57 · F. Scott Fitzgerald · The Great Gatsby

(NEW YORK: CHARLES SCRIBNER'S SONS, 1925), 194 PP.

It is hard to read *The Great Gatsby* with a fresh eye, not only because it is a famous novel by a famous author, but also because, along with his characters, Fitzgerald's observations and phrases have become so much a part of the way Americans think of themselves. The novel is also a principal American entrant into the pantheon of world greatness, so it bears the burden of universal critical acclaim.

Most Americans are familiar with the story. Jay Gatsby, a man of vast wealth, mysteriously appears in a fashionable town on Long Island and begins throwing fabulous parties to which everyone comes, not because they have been invited or know the host, but just because everyone else is there. As our narrator, Nick Carraway, comes to know Gatsby, however, he learns that Gatsby has two secrets—that he is in love with Nick's cousin, Daisy, who is married to an unpleasant man named Tom, and that Gatsby's apparent wealth comes from questionable investments and gangster connections. When Gatsby reveals himself to Daisy, she at first resumes their five-year-old romance, but Tom quickly reasserts his power over her. Then, during a drive from New York to Long Island, Gatsby's car is involved in a hit-and-run accident in which Tom's mistress, Myrtle, is coincidentally killed. Myrtle's husband then finds Gatsby and kills him, afterward shooting himself. Gatsby has told Nick that Daisy had been driving the car, but this crime is covered up and Tom and Daisy famously "retreat . . . back into their money or their vast carelessness, or whatever it was that kept them together, and let other people clean up the mess they had made . . ." (p. 188). In the meantime, Nick arranges Gatsby's funeral, to which no one comes. Sound implausible?

I have to admit that I don't care as much for *The Great Gatsby* as many people do. I think it should have been a hundred pages longer and that Fitzgerald should have developed the characters and their relationships more meticulously and in more detail. As it is, each character has only a few scenes, and those are mostly short. Once the author elaborately introduces each character, they do not develop or change as a result of the action, they only reveal their true natures, and their true natures are shallow. This is especially true of Daisy. Even Gatsby is disappointed in her; when he finds her again, it takes him only an hour or two to realize she is not what he thought she was. Nick admits that he

THIRTEEN WAYS OF LOOKING AT THE NOVEL

can't describe her particular charm—it is in her voice or her face, but he doesn't actually describe either one, he merely tries to capture in a couple of phrases the impression her face and her voice give. Tom's signal quality is that he is threatening; Gatsby's, that he is romantic; Nick's, that he is honest; Daisy's, that she is strangely desirable. But Fitzgerald doesn't build these personalities so that they are truly convincing, by showing them to us action by incremental action. For scenes and dialogue he substitutes his own aphoristic style (rendered by Nick Carraway). Some of it is apt and smart, but much of it is sentimental and even nonsensical. The problem is that the tone of the novel is bittersweet before the action has earned the right to be bittersweet. Nick is already elegiac before anything is lost. A good comparison can be made to Zeno. Zeno is straightforward and occasionally ironic until the reader comes to know what has been lost and what Zeno feels about it; only then does Svevo allow his narrator to wax lyrical. A good example of Fitzgerald's sort of mistake takes place in the first two pages. The novel opens with the line, "In my younger and more vulnerable years, my father gave me some advice that I've been turning over in my mind ever since.

"'Whenever you feel like criticizing anyone,' he told me, 'just remember that all the people in this world haven't had the advantages that you've had.'" On the next page Nick rephrases the advice: "I am still a little afraid of missing something if I forget that, as my father snobbishly suggested, and I snobbishly repeat, a sense of the fundamental decencies is parcelled out unequally at birth." Whether these two ideas are related is unclear. They seem not to be. Fitzgerald should have been aware that they are not the same, and he should have developed his argument beyond these flashy phrases to make it clear. The same is true of his last observation: "So we beat on, boats against the current, borne back ceaselessly into the past" (p. 197). The image is lyrical and paradoxical but it doesn't really make sense.

What is Fitzgerald arguing for? The only way in which Gatsby is great is that he has devoted himself to an illusion and given up every virtue except the virtue of style to attain it. The illusion is not precisely Daisy, but rather the class that Daisy seemed to embody, with its comfort and elegance. We know that he doesn't actually honor Daisy from a dropped remark about their earlier interlude—that he seduced her or, as Nick says, "took her" before they were married or even engaged, and then didn't contact her because he wasn't wealthy yet, and he didn't want her without the wealth. Nick is skeptical of the sort of illusion Gatsby is susceptible to from the beginning (because he went to college and also has known Tom for a while), but for some reason he respects Gatsby for not being as skeptical as he is. This is a vividly written novel of a very young man (Fitzgerald was twenty-nine when it was published). It is not the wisdom of the ages. All the qualities of youth are present in the novel—snap judgments about others, overblown emotions, sharp observations about surfaces, self-doubt, self-hatred, and a lack of insight into women—plus considerable promise, of course—but I don't think it is careful enough, wise enough, or well enough thought through to be a masterpiece.

58 · Franz Kafka · The Trial

TRANS. BREON MITCHELL (NEW YORK: SCHOCKEN BOOKS, 1925), 231 PP.

The Trial was published after Kafka's death by his friend Max Brod, who defied Kafka's own expressed wish that all of his papers and manuscripts be burned. Although Brod was right to save and publish his friend's work, thereby furnishing the twentieth century with its most uncannily truthful voice, it is also easy to understand why Kafka might have wanted to keep his work private. What is new in Kafka's work is an astonishing degree of intimacy and honesty—what is utterly original in fiction is always more private than what is original in other forms, because it is uncircumscribed by conventions (like poetry) or the presence of other people (like drama and movies). What makes novels public are traditional themes and stories: Will the boy and the girl get together at last? Will the husband be cuckolded? Will the individuals be reconciled to their communities? But Kafka's works have no traditional stories and so possess a much smaller public dimension. Reading Kafka's work can seem like no less an intrusion upon him than reading his diaries. His protagonists, often full of shame, also seem shameless in their readiness to confess their shames.

In the opening chapter of *The Trial,* Josef K., a bank manager in his twenties in some central European city, is arrested for an unknown crime by authorities whose jurisdiction he doesn't recognize. In the course of the novel, he solicits help and advice from all sorts of associates, but their advice is contradictory and untrustworthy, and everything he learns about the court and the law system he is attempting to deal with indicates to him that the court is strict, arbitrary, senseless, and merciless. Finally (and Kafka himself did not finish the manuscript—it was found after his death and published in a somewhat patched-together form) Josef K. is killed by the side of the road, anonymously and, to all appearances, meaninglessly. Most Kafka protagonists suffer a similar fate—Gregor Samsa, who is turned into a bug, dies and gets thrown on a dust heap. The hunger artist loses his commercial value, dies of starvation, and is replaced by a much more crowd-pleasing panther. For Josef K., and all the others, though, the "process" (*Der Prozess* is *The Trial*'s German title) of affliction, judgment, and guilt takes place as much within the mind as it does between the protagonist and the authorities. Its primary effect is to make him painfully self-conscious, so that he second-guesses his every action and intention, trying to decide what will work and whether he can justify his life, trying to decide, in fact, what is true or real and what is guilty projection.

With his characteristic brilliance, Kafka, who was from Prague, focuses completely on Josef K.'s experience of his ordeal, and, most important, he tells a lively tale. Every Kafka story is dynamic and entertaining—in fact, Kafka himself is said to have found his stories to be tremendous fun when he read them aloud. His ability to keep the action moving forward not only encourages the reader to suspend disbelief but also seduces the reader into taking the narrative on the author's terms. While telling his story, Kafka makes no allusion to whatever analogous situations the reader may perceive—to arbitrary governments, to the judgment of God or religion (Kafka was Jewish), to the operation of guilt itself, to neurosis. The tight narrative focus quickly begins to accumulate symbolic power that more casual narratives cannot achieve. Most novelists give both sides of an analogy, for example. George Eliot does it best—on the one hand we have a character or a feeling or an event—let's say Mr. Casaubon. On the other we have the groping animal that Mr. Casaubon is like, and thus Mr. Casaubon's character is illuminated. With Kafka we have only the groping animal. We may link it to whatever or whomever we like. The groping animal does not illuminate merely a single character; we are not invited to relate it to a single character's individual quirks. The animal illuminates life itself, the nature of groping itself, which, after we think about it, turns out to be universal.

It is common for readers to wonder if a particularly original novelist is sane or insane, and to look into his life for evidence one way or the other. Evidence of some sort of mental condition (for example, Dostoevsky's epilepsy or Fitzgerald's alcoholism) can come to color a reader's attitude toward whether the work is genuninely profound or visionary. Sometimes this comes up with Kafka, but his perfect logic, the evenness of his tone, his exquisite German style, and his knack for keeping the action moving forward make him seem transcendentally sane, so the question is thereby cast back into the world—if Kafka's protagonist makes so much sense in the way he tells his story, then it must be the court, or the family, or the town that is insane, and in fact the twentieth century itself seemed to prove this to be true. At the beginning of the twenty-first century it's hard to remember that while Kafka may have intuited much of what was latent in the world he lived in (he died in 1924), he didn't actually foresee what was to come.

Nevertheless, Kafka is a good example of the astute way in which some novelists seem to see patterns and movements in the world that others do not see. Such insight contributes, of course, to the lasting fascination their work arouses in generations of readers. *The Trial* must be read not only through the lens of the Holocaust, but also that of all the show trials and oppressive, arbitrary legal systems that the nations of the world imposed upon their citizens throughout the twentieth century. The details were different but the experience is the same: What do I do? Do I laugh or cry? Do I remove myself or engage? Is the legal system ridiculous or cruel, inhumane or only too evidently human? Am I a fool to think there is any possible outcome other than execution? Can this really be the world I live in? Part of Kafka's genius was that in his willingness to throw off conventional subjects and narrative modes, he concentrated more clearly on his intuitions. As a result, his "private" experience of his world turned out to be not only uniquely intimate but also uniquely subtle, insightful, and fascinating.

59 · Hermann Broch · The Sleepwalkers

TRANS. WILLA AND EDWIN MUIR

(1926; REPR., NEW YORK: RANDOM HOUSE, VINTAGE, 1996), 648 PP.

The Sleepwalkers is another monument of modernism, which in some ways can be defined as the reaction of ambitious novelists to the breakdown of European culture that seemed to result from the First World War. Broch, like Sholokhov, attempted to address the subject of the war directly (showing individuals taking sides, trying to figure things out, suffering, being destroyed, and surviving) rather than indirectly (depicting individuals outside of the war through the shared but unexplored lens of the war, such as Joyce and Svevo). Like the other modernists, Broch found that he had to break up and remake the traditional form of the realist novel to begin to communicate what he wanted to say about his world, and, as with other modernist novels, this very disintegration of form has become a historical artifact. The First World War and even the Second World War no longer mean what they once did. The much-heralded end of rationality, or end of civilization, or even of consciousness, of course did not arrive with the transmutation of Europe from several warlike, armed mini-empires into the postcolonial European Union.

The Sleepwalkers concerns the convergence of three men of different generations and classes. Von Pasenow is the first, a hereditary Prussian aristocrat and career soldier whose marital and social fates are set by the end of the first novel, when his father, who both frightens and repels him, marries him off to the daughter of wealthy neighbors, and the two estates are united (the old happy ending translated into an unsavory and calculating piece of business that in spite of Pasenow's sexual queasiness does result in offspring). The second is Esch, twenty years younger, who is an up-and-coming urban bookkeeper at the beginning of the twentieth century. Esch is impetuous and volatile. Like Pasenow, he suffers from sexual uneasiness, which in his case is a combination of attraction and repulsion to the older maternal proprietress of the cafeteria he frequents. He can't stay away from her, but he beats her and repeatedly rapes her (which she allows, or seems to expect, as if the properest form of intercourse requires the woman to become as passive as possible).

In fact, *The Sleepwalkers* is a perfect Freudian gallery of various

sublimated erotic dysfunctions that seem to be imposed upon the protagonists by the rigidity of the society they live in. Broch is exceptional
at characterizing how each of his protagonists and several minor characters experience themselves and project those sensations onto the
world around them. Both Pasenow and Esch suffer from a streak of
hysterical overreaction to small things, which grow disproportionately
large and distorted. For example, during Pasenow's interview with his
prospective bride, her face stops looking like a face and starts looking
like a landscape, which frightens and repels him. Later, Esch becomes
convinced that his old boss has committed a crime and should be
reported to the authorities. This conviction continues to weigh upon
him through most of his section of the novel, even though it is apparent to the reader that the root of Esch's conviction is simply resentment
at being fired.

As with Kafka and Robert Musil, the protagonists' most essential
relationships seem to be with the state rather than with other people. If
we contrast the German novelists with, say, Anthony Trollope, who
was the English novelist who wrote most directly about government
(in the Palliser novels, whose characters actually do govern England),
it is striking to note that the average German citizen (or rather, citizen
of the Austro-Hungarian Empire) feels the impersonal state as a
palpable personal presence he must think about and relate to as much
as or more than he relates to wives or children (though mothers and
particularly fathers are often overwhelming and oppressive when they
occur in the narrative). In the German novel, government is a sense of
inescapable authority present in every mind; in the English novel, even
the prime minister hardly has a relationship to the state at all—his
relationships are to particular allies or functionaries or social arbiters.
Government, in Trollope, is reduced to a network of friendship and
influence much like any other English social network.

The third volume of *The Sleepwalkers* brings Esch and Pasenow
together and subjects them to Huguenau, who is twenty years younger
than Esch (about thirty when the volume begins, in 1918). Huguenau
is Alsatian and Catholic; he speaks French. He is represented by contrast to his elders as having few sexual feelings at all, and as being of a
purely commercial and mercenary bent. Huguenau doesn't mind
hurting others if he has the chance, whereas Pasenow is afraid to hurt
others and Esch hurts others only for the sake of a higher good.
Huguenau is the most competent of the three—he successfully deserts

the army (breaking off his relationship to the government and to all moral authority) by watching for an opportunity and having a sharp sense of timing. After he arrives in Esch's town, he uses the same instincts to take over Esch's newspaper and make himself a prominent citizen. But even though he has severed his relationship with authority, he cannot resist soliciting the attention of the town commandant (Pasenow) and attempting to achieve some sort of father/son relationship with him. Pasenow, now representing the remnants of decency, is much put off and tries to avoid the younger man. After Huguenau rapes Frau Esch and murders Esch, he engineers his escape and goes back to his home city, where he becomes a prosperous entrepreneur, husband, father, and solid citizen who never gives another thought to his crimes or betrayals. He epitomizes the amoral modern man who buys low and sells high no matter what else is going on.

Broch was not a happy novelist. He preferred philosophy to fiction, and he interpolates a philosophical essay supposedly written by one of the minor characters into the novel. In the essay he makes explicit and universalizes the arguments that his characters are meant to demonstrate. At one point he also writes the narrative of the three men as a drama, and he sometimes uses poetry to communicate certain ideas that prose is not intense enough for. The philosophical sections of the novel now seem dated, but are made relevant in the novel by the narrative sections, which, because of Broch's skills in character drawing, psychology, dialogue, and even plotting, hardly seem dated at all. Broch is an incisive stylist, similar to Robert Musil but without his dry wit, though bolder in his willingness to grapple with the events of the war itself rather than to imply them.

Pasenow and Esch have what we would probably call mental illnesses—Pasenow seems to be obsessive-compulsive, and Esch seems to suffer from hyperactivity and attention deficit disorder accompanied by oppositional-defiant disorder. Huguenau is recognizable, too— antisocial personality disorder—though even today, people are divided about whether this is a mental illness, a spiritual fault, or simply a form of evil. Does the end of European civilization produce or result from the widespread occurrence of such mental conditions? In his philosophical sections, Broch traces the sources of his characters' mental dysfunctions to the Reformation and the rise of Protestant individualism—Huguenau represents a Max Weber sort of figure, who is good at business because he feels no human connections. But the reader is, of course, free to disagree with the philosopher, and to make other cause-and-effect connections, because Pasenow, Esch, Huguenau, and the minor figures live more vividly as characters than as representatives of a philosophical system.

60 · **Marcel Proust** · In Search of Lost Time
vol. 1, Swann's Way;
vol. 2, Within a Budding Grove;
vol. 3, The Guermantes Way;
vol. 4, Sodom and Gomorrah;
vol. 5, The Captive;
vol. 6, The Fugitive;
vol. 7, Time Regained

TRANS. C. K. SCOTT MONCRIEFF, TERENCE KILMARTIN, ANDREAS MAYOR, AND D. J. ENRIGHT

(NEW YORK: RANDOM HOUSE, MODERN LIBRARY, 1913-27), 4,200 PP.

In many ways, *In Search of Lost Time* is the most extreme example of what can be done with the novel form. It is almost six times the length of *Ulysses,* five times the length of *Our Mutual Friend.* It is as ambitious as *The Man without Qualities* and was essentially complete at the time of the author's death. It is truly a lengthy written prose narrative with a protagonist. In terms of theme, plot, characters, style, and time scheme, it is both cohesive and coherent; easy to read in the course of a summer or a winter; and, for some aficionados, worth rereading over and over.

The most interesting thing about it is that while it is indeed a novel, it employs the conceit of a memoir. The narrator's subject, as with any memoir, is what he has done in the course of his life and what he has made of it; and, indeed, the plot of the novel concerns what he has made of his life, not what he has done. The climax of Proust's thousands of pages occurs in volume 7, when he goes to one last party and realizes as he arrives both what is important about his life and how it may be represented as a work of literature. In this, of course, he sets his novel in contrast to most other novels, in which events coalesce to form the plot and the climax takes place in an action or series of actions between the protagonist and an antagonist. But Proust chooses a more private sort of plot in which the reader, like the reader of a memoir, is asked to ponder at length and in detail the relationship between the protagonist's activities on the one hand and his feelings, sensations, thoughts, and observations on the other. As with Kafka, when Proust throws out standard plot conventions, he gives the reader a sense of unprecedented intimacy with the narrator, who may be the author, and who once or twice refers to himself as "M." or "Marcel" but is not the author. *In Search of Lost Time* is a novel that uses the conceit of the memoir, is in no way a memoir, and assumes simultaneously the authority of the novel and the authority of the memoir. It is perfectly convincing.

Proust's protagonist, "M.," is slightly younger than Proust himself and seems to have been born in 1878 (Proust was born in 1871). He is an only child (Proust had a younger brother), and grows up in Paris and the small town of Combray, southwest of Paris (the town, originally called Illiers, is now called Illiers-Combray). He is a sensuous, observant, sickly, and emotional child who is deeply attached to his mother and grandmother, for whom he is a somewhat perplexing darling. The central incident of the first section of the novel is little M.'s success in gaining his mother's company for a single night—she stays with him because he is upset, and during the night reads to him aloud from George Sand's novel *François le Champi,* thus setting in motion both his ultimate downfall (his connoisseurship of emotional suffering) and his ultimate triumph (his mastery of literature).

As M. grows up, he cultivates numerous relationships, some with men and some with women, that recapitulate and expand his early attachments. As he remembers the earlier ones in light of the later ones and is reminded by the later ones of the earlier ones, he constructs a theoretical and sensual network of connections that comes to constitute a portrait of his inner life, which he presents as both uniquely his and as representative of the typical workings of the inner lives of men in general. Almost every idea Proust offers is both particular and general, which is the paradox of the novel as a form working in the most absolute possible way. It is the construction of this network rather than the idiosyncrasies or dramas of the people he knows that actually interests him; he goes out of his way to remind the reader over and over that his characters aren't especially worthy of his affections or his analysis. Those who appear most often in the narrative—Madame de Guermantes, Robert Saint-Loup, the baron de Charlus, Gilberte Swann, Françoise, M.'s servant, and even his great love, Albertine—are routinely found to be conventional, uninspiring, and shallow. Personal qualities that the reader might think M. would respond to positively—

Saint-Loup's kindness to and affection for M., for example, or Gilberte's long-standing loyalty to him, or Madame de Guermantes's friendliness—are systematically demeaned. Nevertheless, these characters do form the world that he lives inside of and obsessively contemplates. Only the baron de Charlus, who is almost always arrogant and rude, gains M.'s steady respect.

Of course, the most difficult aspect of a first-person narrative, especially a lengthy one, is the adoption of a voice that allows the narrator to talk endlessly about himself without offending the reader, and Proust is careful to create a voice that is both appealing and worth paying attention to. Some of his devices are obvious ones—whenever he talks about himself in the act of relating to the others, he is self-effacing and makes jokes at his own expense. According to his story, he is generally cherished and loved, but at the same time he is modest and tries as much as possible to stay in the background. He implies that when others distinguish or value him, they might well be making a mistake—but he is careful to repeat the affectionate or respectful things they say to him. He is surrounded by social climbers, but he isn't one— his social rise is mysterious, rather like a natural phenomenon, and happens in spite of his expressed desires. He himself would rather focus on other desires, especially the desire to get to know girls of a certain age, particularly attractive girls of obscure background. Proust's second device is to analyze himself as coolly as he analyzes others. He is a master at observing himself from a distance—never swayed so much by his own emotions that he can't delve deeply into them (sometimes in more detail than the reader cares for). This painstaking objectivity serves not only to give him something to talk about, but also to reassure the reader that he is telling the truth, or at least being more honest than any memoirist ever.

But of course he is not—he is writing a novel, and not a word of it is honest.

French literature offered Proust plenty of examples of prestigious and successful memoirs—the novel has not dominated French literature as it has English and American literature, and in fact to be a critic, a man of letters, a memoirist, or a theoretician of some sort is possibly more respectable for an ambitious Frenchman than to be a novelist. But like many novelists, Proust preferred the freedom of the novel form for several reasons. One of these was overt—the actual details of his life and loves were more complicated and less interesting than details that would illustrate his theme. In addition, the love of his life was not a woman but a man, not Albertine but Alfred Agostinelli, upon whom Albertine was based. And many of the other acquaintances he would transmute into characters were still living (possibly to take offense) when the novel began to be published.

Proust's real purpose, though, is one that he advertises in his title, *À la recherche du temps perdu*—he doesn't want to simply recall and perhaps justify the past, as memoirists do, he wants to give it palpable existence, which is what novelists do. That this is his intention he makes clear repeatedly in the course of the novel. He is in search of emotions that are as strong as those he once felt, and the route to those emotions is through sensation—most famously the taste of the madeleine dipped in lime-flower tisane—but also through other sensations that he delineates in the final volume of the novel, *Le Temps retrouvé,* or *Time Regained.* His power to make something of his life comes to him one evening as he is entering a party given by old friends. In the course of a few moments he has three madeleinelike sensations that fill him with feelings he thought lost forever. These in turn persuade him that other formerly cherished but forgotten (in a visceral way, though not unremembered) emotions are available to him if he uses certain techniques to evoke them. The implication is that on the day after the party, he intends to sequester himself from society and dedicate himself to recapturing what he can (though in fact, a few days of illness intervene between his plan and its execution). This party is reported to take place during the First World War. The first volume of *In Search of Lost Time* had already been published, in 1913, and volume 2 had been ready for the printer at the outbreak of the war, so M.'s revelation of his powers is a fictional incident as it is written, but it forms a beautiful simultaneous prologue and recapitulation in volume 7 of everything that has gone before in volumes 1 through 6. The seven volumes of the novel become a cycle—volume 7 predates the other six in composition, but they lead ineluctably to it in M.'s "life."

It is just about impossible to read Proust's novel without wondering how close the incidents and characters are to Proust's life, but in fact in writing the novel, Proust owed as much to literature as he did to his life, and for all that he asserts that his inspiration is the moment-by-moment passage of inner and outer time, the novel conforms very closely to conventions of French literature, especially in the depiction of M.'s relationship with Albertine.

Even though the original of the relationship in Proust's life was a homosexual one, Proust is careful to portray Albertine convincingly as a woman and M.'s relationship with her convincingly as heterosexual (though he implies that sexual relations were not common between them). M.'s love for Albertine is developed over the course of five volumes. At first, when he is visiting a seaside resort in Normandy, M. sees Albertine laughing with a group of girlfriends. All of the girls are sporty and jovial, and M. enjoys being with them without especially distinguishing any one as the object of his affections. That he is a lusty young man, eager to fall in love and occasionally resorting to prostitutes, he leaves no doubt. Albertine wins him by being ambiguously available—she seems to have experience, which arouses him, but she is incensed when he assumes that she will give him what he wants, at least when he first approaches her. Her behavior and thought processes always to some extent mystify him, and this mystery intensifies his desire. He discovers that when he is satisfied that she loves him, he is bored, but when she is acting as if she has something to hide, he is intensely jealous and avid for her.

At the beginning of volume 5, *The Captive,* Proust invites Albertine to return to Paris and live with him (his mother is going to the country to take care of a relative). Their living arrangement quickly turns into an imprisonment of the woman by the man. Albertine lives in accordance with myriad rules established by M., from the time when she can enter his room in the morning to where she is allowed to go and whom she is allowed to see. He is endlessly suspicious of her activities, both in the present and in the past, and he is repeatedly devastated by some thought that she might be acting in a certain way, or might have acted in a certain way. He questions her and assumes that her responses are lies; he questions others about her, and persuades her best friend to accompany her everywhere and report her activities to him, but in the end he doubts the testimony of the friend, too. In particular, he cannot tolerate the thought that she is a lesbian, or had been a lesbian before he came along. Nevertheless, he obsessively cultivates his suspicions as a way of keeping his emotional attachment to her in turmoil because he actually doesn't like her much and there is nothing she can do to satisfy him. In one striking, and you might even say necrophiliac passage, he admits that really he only loves her when she is sound asleep, quiet and still, on his bed. Otherwise she drives him crazy. Even when she is living with him, what he really enjoys is his own sensation of things such as the morning light through the curtains. In another telling passage, he invites a young girl he meets to come into the house and sit on his lap; he then gives the girl five hundred francs. He is later taken to the police station and investigated after this incident is interpreted by the girl's parents as suspicious. He is released but told to be careful. In fact, whether or not Proust ever read de Sade (he does refer to Choderlos de Laclos), volumes 5 and 6 explore many of the same themes as *Justine*. By turning the love of his life into a woman in his novel, Proust ends up addressing the most traditional and central question of the French novel, and, indeed, of the European novel: what's to be done with women?

Even so, M. is a new sort of man. He does not feel himself to be powerful in relation to Albertine—even though she is imprisoned in his house and surrounded by his spies, her secretiveness and his conviction that she doesn't love him cause him to feel powerless, so he redoubles his efforts to control her, on the one hand, and bribe her, on the other. He thus probes the impossibility of actually treating a woman as a possession. In the end, he ruins himself financially (at one point he offers to buy her both a Rolls-Royce and a yacht) and she manages to escape. Because throughout volumes 4, 5, and 6, he is narrating his feelings in ever finer detail, the reader has what she may consider to be an excessive and tedious exposure to them. Just behind M.'s feelings, though, are Albertine's reported actions and responses. From these it is easy to infer Albertine's point of view, if not her motives—she is attempting to please and placate M., she is restive in her captivity, and she is ambivalent. M. is clear that he will never marry her, so what is in it for her? M. doesn't know, the reader doesn't know, and Albertine doesn't know. Albertine eventually escapes and returns to her hometown, where she is killed in an equestrian accident (Proust's real lover was killed in an aviation accident—he also, unlike Albertine, had a wife and children, whom Proust attempted to aid after his death). M. expresses minimal regret at the end of the relationship—he grieves for a while and then it is over, convincing him that since his passionate feelings did not last, Albertine was not worthy of them and that passionate feelings themselves are dependent upon circumstances and upon keeping the relationship in a turmoil—true love is actually intense jealousy. A woman's job is to promote jealousy and a man's job is to feel it. When the jealousy dissipates, the love does, too, since no other form of companionship with a woman is satisfying. Proust cites numerous examples of this idea throughout the novel—it is his guiding theme, first expressed in *Swann in Love*. M. never loves again, even though subsequently he does imprison nameless and faceless girls in the family house in Paris so he can make idle use of their companionship. The implication of Proust's entire discussion of Albertine and the other girls he is drawn to is that while his nature as a weak, unhealthy, kindly, and generous man prevents him from true sexual predation à la de Sade, in principle there is nothing wrong with it, and in fact it is the way of the world.

And Proust does take up the subject of homosexuality, as de Sade does, through the characters of the baron de Charlus and Robert de Saint-Loup. These two characters are complementary—they belong to the same aristocratic family. The baron is effeminate, outrageously rude, cruel when he can be, and intelligent, while Saint-Loup is a sort of Adonis—manly, athletic, thoughtful, and kind, but not especially smart or insightful. The baron, whom M. witnesses, at the beginning of volume 4, having sex with a tailor who lives in the same compound as Proust, is always homosexual, and becomes, in the novel, a model for how homosexuals exist in French society. Robert begins with a mistress, marries for love, and ends as a homosexual. Between them they suggest that the point de Sade makes in *Justine,* that women exist to facilitate the transfer of property but real Frenchmen prefer to be buggered by their servants, is still as valid in 1890 as in 1790. The climax of the baron's juxtaposition to Saint-Loup takes place in the seventh volume, when, during the war, M. happens upon a strange hotel that turns out to be a male brothel, where he witnesses Saint-Loup leaving and the baron, tied to a chair, being whipped by a young man he thinks has committed several murders (when M. subsequently talks to the male prostitutes, it turns out that they have committed no murders and are actually using the brothel money to support their aged parents). This, of course, is the terror de Sade attempted to evoke turning up as farce, but the point is the same—this is how the world really works, behind the facade of bourgeois marriage and notions of heterosexual "love."

It is not common for the average reader to make it all the way through the seven volumes; the reason for this, most people suppose, is that the seven volumes are tedious or difficult. In fact, they are neither. Once the reader has gotten familiar with Proust's voice and the rhythms of his style, his way of thinking about and discussing things is fascinating and full of substance. He is the number one do-it-yourself psychoanalyst. He believes that an individual can plumb the depths of his own mental life and experience and learn true, valuable things about himself and the world he lives in by doing so. No "subconscious" exists beyond his ken that can be explored only with the help of an analyst. In this sense, *In Search of Lost Time* is, in spite of itself, a hopeful novel, because the author's sense that his endeavors are rewarding and productive is apparent on every page, whether the reader actually likes M. or not. At the same time, Proust's morality doesn't conform to what most people, and, more particularly, most women might consider to be comfortable. His views are ultimately narcissistic; he not only doesn't understand Albertine's point of view very well, he also doesn't care about it and finds no potential satisfaction in making an effort to do so. Any sort of real connection with another person, based on actual interest in that person, is beyond him, so he gives no thought to whether his desires and actions hurt others. He is a kindly narcissist, but a narcissist all the same, and at great, almost persuasive length.

61 · D. H. **Lawrence** · Lady Chatterley's Lover

(1928; REPR., NEW YORK: BANTAM, 1983), 328 PP.

Lady Chatterley's Lover is really the story of Lady Chatterley, Connie, with whom Lawrence is sympathetic and in whose consciousness Lawrence convincingly places his narrative center while employing the flexibility of third-person omniscient point of view to occasionally gain access to the inner lives of some of the other characters. Connie's dilemma is that she is not only trapped in a loveless, childless marriage to Chatterley, who has been paralyzed and emasculated in the First World War, she is also lonely, isolated by class and geography on an ugly estate in the English Midlands. Chatterley is dependent, physically, but he is also exacting and jealous of his authority. Lawrence thoroughly anatomizes all of his unattractive qualities and traces the downward progress of Connie's attempts to be a good if not loving wife, even after she meets and begins to be interested in the estate gamekeeper, Mellors, who has also, in a more subtle way, been changed by his experiences in the war. Like Chatterley, Mellors now knows with more certainty what he wants from life. It is not, to begin with, an affair with Connie, but rather independence from English class society. Mellors represents a new sort of working-class Englishman, worldly and self-possessed and no longer content to know his place; he is, therefore, a worthy title character for Lawrence's novel,

but it is only with Connie that the reader is allowed to feel at all intimate or comfortable.

This, Lawrence's last novel, was his most scandalous. After the
author oversaw its printing in an Italian print shop, a friend suggested
that if the printer had been able to read what he was printing, he
would not have been able to concentrate well enough to arrange the
type. In the twenty-first century, perhaps because we are less easily
shocked by mere sex, we can more readily appreciate all of the ways in
which Lawrence challenged his readers.

Of course there are the sex scenes. They are explicit but not graphic
in a cruel way, and certainly not pornographic. The manner in which
Connie and Mellors make love is revealing of their characters rather
than simply titillating. Both characters have sexual histories that dictate how they approach each other and intercourse itself; their images
of themselves and their sense of the world around them change as a
result of their sexual relations.

Lawrence possessed subversive views of all kinds, though, and in
this novel he is utterly frank about them—that is its boldest element.
Just because Chatterley, for example, has been paralyzed in the war
doesn't mean Lawrence is going to give him any leeway—he is
depicted as cold, selfish, hypersensitive, snobbish, and weak—and it is
these very qualities that enable him to transform himself into an English captain of industry. Lawrence lavishes plenty of analysis on what
he considers to be the essential faults of England, the English class system, and the essential English character. At one point, when Chatterley wants to be a writer and is successful, Lawrence portrays his work
as empty and worthless—its very success in England is a sign of its
emptiness and worthlessness.

For the modern reader, perhaps especially for the modern female
reader, Connie presents something of a dilemma. Lawrence is far
more sympathetic toward her and also toward the other women characters, Mrs. Bolton and Connie's sister, than toward the men. For one
thing, he doesn't require them to betray one another, a requirement
many male authors impose on their female characters. Connie's sister
strongly disapproves of Connie's love for Mellors, but she remains
loyal and sympathetic in a believable way. But Lawrence also makes
Mellors's first lovemaking with Connie into more or less a rape, since
she doesn't quite seem to know what is going on and gives no consent.
There are two ways of looking at this. On the one hand, Mellors takes
Connie, which makes her seem a bit foolish and him a bit brutal. On

the other hand, though, Connie, like many English heroines before her, does not risk possibly losing the reader's sympathy by acting wanton. As a result, Lawrence gets to have it both ways: Connie enjoys sex with Mellors, but she doesn't foresee it.

Mellors is hardly kind, cordial, and spiritually enlightened. He has particular sexual requirements, and he has given up looking for a woman who can fulfill them until he discovers Connie. Part of his manly appeal is that he does acknowledge his appetites, but he's opinionated and not easy to like. If he weren't so outspoken about his opinions, he would be a kind of green-man-of-the-forest figure; in some ways, he is more reminiscent of an American cowboy type than he is of any English type (and Lawrence lived for a while in the American West). Mellors is not a dreamboat to begin with, however, and there is no sense at the end of the novel, as there is with, say, Mr. Darcy in *Pride and Prejudice,* that he is willing to give up either his pride or his prejudice, or that Connie and Mellors will necessarily live happily ever after. It seems as though they will, like most couples, love and adjust. The basis of their marriage will be a strong sexual bond, and given that, they will make concessions and find a way of getting along. The last few pages of the novel peter out into practicalities—Connie and Mellors are living apart so he can get his divorce, and they are hoping to find a farm somewhere, with Connie's inheritance to provide the capital (love and money coming together once again). Lawrence's disaffection with England is so strong that he can't imagine a happy ending taking place there, only plenty of hard work.

What I like about *Lady Chatterley's Lover* is that in the midst of all these innovative and, for their time, astounding scenes, Lawrence managed to put together a traditionally well-made novel. The characters are compelling and complex, the scene is rendered vividly, the themes of sexuality and class antagonism and the motifs of nature versus industry are carefully developed and understandable. Lawrence uses the classic tools of realism in a way that does not subvert the form, but rather extends the discussion of ideas that already underlie the form: What is to be done with women? How do women negotiate their simultaneous identities as agents and as possessions? What is authentic love? How do pastoral scenes and industrial scenes, money and work fit together? Lawrence doesn't quite have the answers, as the ending shows, but he is especially daring in how he asks the questions.

62 · Virginia Woolf · Orlando

(1928; REPR., SAN DIEGO, CALIF.: HARCOURT BRACE JOVANOVICH, HARVEST, 1956), 329 PP.

Orlando is a confection, light and airy in tone, undercutting even its most serious insights with a certain coyness that probably came from Woolf's desire to flatter Vita Sackville-West, the object of her affections and the inspiration for her protagonist, Orlando, who is born during the reign of Queen Elizabeth yet is only just over thirty years old in 1928.

Orlando has several adventures in four hundred years and meets many noteworthy personages. As a boy, he is introduced to Queen Elizabeth, who is so pleased with his "innocence, simplicity" that she gives his family a large property (evidently based on the estate where Vita Sackville-West resided). Later Orlando spends a century or so in Constantinople, only to return to England as a woman in time for the London literary era of Pope, Dryden, and Swift. She lives through the high domesticity of the Victorian era, marries, produces a child, and emerges in the twenties shopping at a department store and driving a motorcar out of London on the old Kent Road. Throughout, Orlando has been composing a poem called "The Oak Tree," which survives numerous literary fashions and is finally published and wins an award. Her enduring qualities are a habit of independence, a love of the English countryside, and a certain reserve about marriage.

Orlando is full of famous and delightful passages and set pieces. In perhaps the most famous, the Thames freezes all the way to the bottom, and King James puts on a great winter festival, with feasts, skating, and fireworks. When Orlando returns to England as a woman, after the sojourn in Constantinople, she is struck by the differences in how she is treated, and also how she feels: "Which is the greater ecstasy? The man's or the woman's? And are they not perhaps the same? No, she thought, this is the most delicious (thanking the Captain but refusing) to refuse, and see him frown. Well, she would, if he wished it, have the very thinnest, smallest sliver in the world. This was the most delicious, to yield and see him smile" (p. 155). But it is the whole last section, where Orlando finds herself in the present, that is the heart of the novel:

And so for some seconds the light went on becoming brighter and brighter, and the clock ticked louder and louder until there was a terrific explosion right in her ear. Orlando leaped as if she had been violently struck on the head. Ten times she was struck. In fact it was ten o'clock in the morning. It was the eleventh of October. It was 1928. It was the present moment. [p. 298]

This is a remarkable example of Woolf's talent for folding perception into consciousness—moving quickly back and forth between what the character is perceiving and how she feels about it. Such passages even now have a kind of utter freshness that makes other forms of narrative, even those with more exciting plots, seem a little thick. Nonetheless, *Orlando* does not have the weight and perfection of *To the Lighthouse* and *Mrs. Dalloway*.

Orlando lives through everything without really living through anything. What Woolf is best at in her other works is breaking down the passage of time so the reader experiences a single day or two days that are divided by several years as utterly significant, moment by moment. When Woolf focuses on the events of a single day and the interactions of several characters who don't consciously have much to do with one another, she shows that traditional narrative significance, made manifest by large events, is not real—reality is in tiny threads of connection, tiny shifts in perception. Woolf is after meaning rather than events, showing that events and their meaning do not necessarily coincide, and important actors in events do not necessarily understand them as well as peripheral witnesses do. *Orlando,* because it takes place over some four hundred years, has only a few representative moments from each era. Woolf can't afford to linger. And Orlando has no society to interact with. Every relationship, every activity is doomed to be transient and therefore not especially vivid, so Orlando him/herself is not very vivid. What is vivid are Woolf's reflections on the idea of Orlando.

In fact, *Orlando,* which was made into a movie in 1993, is an ideal vehicle for film. Costumes, sets, new and intriguing ideas, lots of scene changes, and an androgynous actress are exactly what *Orlando* needs to fill in the narrative blanks that Woolf leaves where Vita and her house would be if the reader knew them as well as Woolf does. As a rule, a good novel can't be made into a movie—it is too rich in the reader's consciousness to be reduced to film. But many almost good novels can be enhanced by the color, movement, and actors that film has to offer. *Orlando* is one of these.

However, it is also true that a novel doesn't have to be a good example of the form to be important and influential. All women writers after Woolf owe her an unprecedented debt. I think it is safe to say that women writers of my generation could not have conceived of themselves as they did—conceived of themselves as writers with a right to compose their works—without two things that Woolf offered: in her fiction, a serious depiction of female and male consciousnesses as they exist in themselves and interact with one another, equal and equally detailed, and, in her criticism, a consideration of literature (in the *Common Reader*s and *A Room of One's Own*) in which Woolf's rights as a critic and reader are quietly and authoritatively asserted. *Orlando* is more a part of this second body of work than it is part of her fictional oeuvre. What Orlando has that few women in fiction had before her is power—power *not* to have to consider, as Lily Bart and Isabel Archer do, whom to marry and whom to yield to. Her power is so thorough that the questions of marriage and childbirth come up only as choices, never necessities. Perhaps the operative fact is that she has no father, only a house—and money.

Orlando does not have the poignant undertone that Woolf's other works do. It was composed out of exuberance and love, not out of fear and loss. But even though beautiful style gets you only so far in a novel, the style of *Orlando* is indeed beautiful.

63 · William Faulkner · As I Lay Dying

(1930; REPR., NEW YORK: RANDOM HOUSE, VINTAGE, 1987), 242 PP.

William Faulkner was working as a night watchman at a power plant in Mississippi when he wrote *As I Lay Dying* in about eight weeks in the autumn of 1929 (oddly enough, commencement of work on the novel almost exactly coincided with the great crash of Wall Street on October 29). The novel was one of the first he set in Yoknapatawpha County, Mississippi, a region based upon Faulkner's own home county. It made him famous and brought him to the attention of Hollywood, where he later spent some twenty years writing screenplays and doctoring scripts.

The simple plot of *As I Lay Dying* is easy to understand and therefore allows for considerable southern gothic embroidery. A woman, Addie Bundren, dies, mother of Cash, Darl, Jewel, Dewey Dell, and

Vardaman, wife of Anse. In accordance with Addie's wishes, Anse resolves to take her remains, in a coffin built by Cash, back to her original home, some forty miles away, where she wishes to be buried with her own family. The journey is impractical and costly, ill-fated from the beginning. Like most fictional journeys, it is full of adventures (the first set of mules drowns trying to cross the river, a barn burns down, buzzards follow the coffin, etc.), but given the purpose of the journey, the adventures are macabre and horrifying, not at all exciting or enlivening. Anse is never deterred, even though each of his children is injured in one way or another. Addie is buried. Anse buys himself a set of false teeth and finds a new wife.

As I Lay Dying is a powerful and moving novel, widely considered one of the greatest novels by a great American novelist, but it is not an easy novel to agree on. Some readers think the Bundren family's misadventures are meant to be humorous, or at least absurd; others see biblical echoes, Homeric echoes, or tragedy. Some critics focus on Faulkner's modernist innovations in point of view and variety of language and on his attempts to characterize the inner life of madness (Darl), youthful innocence (Vardaman), and death itself (Addie). The fact is, Faulkner's technique is similar to Kafka's—to present, without comment, the putative experience of a character in an extreme situation and to let the reader follow the logic of both the situation and the experience as best she can. For Kafka's single typical Central European citizen and clarity of style, though, Faulkner substitutes American eccentrics and a multitude of voices, some conversational and familiar, others unique and difficult to make out. The result is oddly similar to Kafka in effect, since the reader begins in a state of confusion and ends in a state of acceptance (or not—such a technique is relatively high risk in that a certain irreducible percentage of readers simply do not care for the challenge and stop reading).

Faulkner was not the first novelist to use the technique of multiple points of view—Virginia Woolf explored the idea only a few years earlier in *To the Lighthouse* and *Mrs. Dalloway*—but Faulkner was more interested than Woolf in extremity of setting and situation. Anse Bundren perhaps qualifies as one of the voiceless ignorant masses that middle-class literature overlooks—he is poor and feckless. His sons and daughter seem to have no recourse against him—they, too, are uneducated country people who seem odd even to their neighbors, and their neighbors are by no means part of the American mainstream. The Bundren children are more than unlettered—they have had no moral education in how to understand themselves and make choices. The precise diagnosis of Darl's mental illness is hard to figure out, and Vardaman seems to be about ten but to have the consciousness of a three- or four-year-old. Dewey Dell at least knows she is pregnant and that she needs to purchase an abortifacient—she has been instructed that far by her seducer—but she doesn't know enough to protect herself when her instructions don't work out as hoped. When the mules drown, the Bundrens are unmoved—they are so used to such acts of God (or carelessness) that they are numb to suffering. When Vardaman drills holes into the coffin, damaging Addie's face, the holes are patched, but an appropriate reaction is beyond everyone in the family. Each has a single emotion that he or she can express—Anse, self-pity; Jewel, anger; Darl, a sort of wonder; Vardaman, dogged curiosity; Dewey Dell, patience; and Cash, stoic acceptance.

As Virginia Woolf does, William Faulkner radically democratizes the novel by rendering the voices of those whom earlier literature had ignored, but there are several facets to his technique. Everything depends, for one thing, on the reader's willingness to believe that the characters are authentically presented—that the boy is a boy and the girl is a girl and the setting and circumstances are plausible. Initial confusion and ignorance on the part of the reader can only afford the author a certain degree of leeway. Once she becomes familiar with the characters, they have to embody the same logic as characters in any other novel. Individual stories have to be surprising as they happen but perfectly understandable in retrospect, so Darl has to be capable of setting the barn afire before he does it, even if the reader doesn't realize before he does it that he is going to do it. Dewey Dell has to be capable of keeping the secret of her plan even while the reader doesn't know she has a secret. It is such capacities that bring the characters close to the reader even as their looks, behavior, and diction move them further away. Of crucial importance to this feel of authenticity are Faulkner's theories of psychology and sociology. His view of the characters and how they coordinate the plot and the themes can't undermine how they allegedly think of and present themselves, or else certain actions and expressions will pop awkwardly out of the text, destroying its effect of seamlessness. It is in just such a circumstance, when the themes and the theories are supposed to be artfully disappearing because the author's voice has been subsumed by the characters' narrating voices, that the author runs the greatest risk of seeming overbearing or manipulative. A straightforward narrator, who tells the story in his own voice, runs less of a risk, because he isn't trying to hide his presence. Faulkner has gotten in some trouble for his presentations of women, which even male critics haven't found especially sympathetic or convincing, and also into a bit of what you might call political-correctness trouble: Are the Bundrens garish types or true portraits? Would they see themselves as Faulkner sees them? Is their story tragic with ridiculous overtones, or ridiculous with tragic overtones? Is he honoring their humanity, or poking fun at their strangeness? Of course these questions can't be answered objectively—much depends on a reader's intuitive apprehension of the novel. I find that in spite of Addie's and Dewey Dell's too-predictable lapses from female virtue, the pathos of how Dewey Dell is doubly cheated in the end is the real heart of the novel.

As I Lay Dying is both original and odd, and it points up the way in which American literature has decentralized respectability. The aim is not to bring outliers into the mainstream, but to broaden the mainstream so it includes the outliers without destroying their uniqueness. It is the countervailing force against the homogenization of American life, states' rights versus federal power—the part undissolved in the whole, representing it and reproducing it.

64 · Robert Musil · The Man without Qualities

VOL. 1, TRANS. EITHNE WILKINS AND ERNEST KAISER

(1931; REPR., NEW YORK: PENGUIN PUTNAM, PERIGEE, 1980), 365 PP.

The Man without Qualities is one of the most prestigious novels of the twentieth century, the sort of book that no one has read but everyone has heard of. It is well worth reading, even though it is very long, very slow, and was unfinished at the time of Musil's death. This first volume runs 365 pages, and the dilemma of the protagonist, Ulrich, is presented only on about page 300. Nevertheless, the writing is so precise and the argument Musil makes about Ulrich and his situation so intricate that it is intellectually and aesthetically involving even before it becomes emotionally involving.

Ulrich is an unmarried man in his early thirties who has recently returned to Vienna from several years abroad. He is ostensibly a mathematician, but although his mind still works like that of a scientist, he has ceased to be inspired by his vocation, and finds himself in the midst of an existential crisis. He is a habitual thinker whose most characteristic activity is to continually refine his analysis of himself and the people around him. He is not meditative or contemplative—that is, he seeks neither peace nor enlightenment. Earlier, once through love and the natural world, and later through mathematics, he had sought truth, but not long before the novel begins, he slacks off, no longer passionate enough about it to be disappointed. He finds and redecorates a house and then takes up the typical activities of Viennese gentlemen—he procures himself a mistress and falls in with bureaucratic projects. As an idle pastime, he gets to know the leading lights of the Austro-Hungarian Empire, who, somewhat like their counterparts in the American South of the 1850s, have no idea that they are passing into history.

The novel has eight principal characters: Ulrich; his cousin Diotima, a tall, robust, beautiful middle-class woman who epitomizes a certain type of self-satisfied German-speaking Austrian; Diotima's lover, Arnheim, a Prussian mogul and man of letters whom Ulrich detests; Bonadea, Ulrich's own mistress, whose promiscuity and spiritual corruption sometimes intrigue him; and Leinsdorf, a highly placed government official who is in charge of the celebrations for the jubilee of Emperor Franz Josef. A sixth character, Moosbrugger, is a murderer whose trial interests Ulrich and a friend of his, Clarisse, who is married to Ulrich's estranged childhood companion. All of these characters have plenty of leisure, including Moosbrugger, who is in prison for the murder of a young prostitute.

Like most modernist novels, *The Man without Qualities* is not tragic, but it is not comic, either, if we take comic to mean that at least some of the characters achieve authentic connections with one another by the end of the novel (of course, there is no ending, since the novel was unfinished). It is, however, quite funny, or at least witty, as a result of Musil's amazingly specific and complex figurative language. The reader is quite often struck by epigrams and remarks that gracefully offer images and insights that are utterly original and right. At one point, for example, he writes, "this non-plussed feeling refers to something that many people nowadays call intuition, whereas formerly it used to be called inspiration, and they think that they must see something suprapersonal in it; but it is only something nonpersonal, namely the affinity and kinship of the things themselves that meet inside one's head" (p. 129). And in a remark that must surely apply to many of the

unacccountable things that rogue governments and rogue corpora-
tions still do, he writes, "for it is only criminals who presume to damage other people nowadays without the aid of philosophy" (p. 227).
The chapters on Moosbrugger and Count Leinsdorf are contrasting
masterpieces of empathy—on the one hand, with a murderer whose
grasp of reality is utterly logical but scarily tenuous, and on the other,
with an aristocrat who has no idea what is going on in the nation he is
responsible for.

Some novelists excel at giving the reader the emotional feel of a
character's mind (Dickens), others at the sensuous feel of a character's
mind (Flaubert). Musil is wonderful at both of these—even though
Ulrich isn't very emotional, a couple of the other characters are, and
Musil enters into them quite smoothly. He is astonishing at characterizing the logical way in which the thoughts and perceptions of a thinking man progress, climax, and begin again with another subject. Musil
uses the third-person omniscient point of view, and is perfectly at ease
entering the minds of all his characters; he seems to get especially close
to them, as if what he were saying about them is so concise that it must
be absolutely true. Ulrich is both attracted to and disdainful of Diotima; for example, Musil writes, "What it really came to always was
that Diotima began talking as though God had on the seventh day put
man, like a pearl, into the shell of the world, and Ulrich then reminded
her that mankind was a little heap of dots on the outermost crust of a
midget globe" (p. 333). But as foolish as Diotima is, it grows apparent
that Ulrich is even more foolish, because, just as his friends and relatives keep telling him, he is going nowhere. He is always right, but
never productive, never happy, and never, except momentarily,
engaged. The reader may enjoy his talents and his state of mind, but
Ulrich himself is building to something that may not be pleasant.

The Man without Qualities requires and rewards patience. Like most
modernist novels, it forgoes plot in favor of ideas, character, and, in
this case, many very funny insights into modern life. Most novels come
to seem, while one is reading Musil, rather coarse; most characters, too
easily satisfied. The older editions and translations show that Musil is
due for a revival in English. It can't come too soon.

65 · Mikhail Sholokhov · And Quiet Flows the Don

TRANS. STEPHEN GARRY

(1934; REPR., NEW YORK: RANDOM HOUSE, VINTAGE, 1989), 554 PP.

Although there was, of course, a radical breach in Russian culture and politics between the czarist era and the Soviet era, Sholokhov wrote his epic of war and revolution among the Cossacks in the most traditional epic and realistic style, and this remained the preferred style of Soviet literature until the demise of communism in Russia in 1991. For that reason alone, it is interesting to analyze the differences between Sholokhov's novel and those of his Western contemporaries, but in fact *And Quiet Flows the Don* is a compelling novel in its own right, full of historical incident and human interest.

Sholokhov's progenitors were Gogol, who wrote about the steppe and the Cossacks in many stories and in *Taras Bulba,* and Tolstoy, who wrote about the Cossacks and also the Napoleonic Wars, in *War and Peace.* Like Gogol, Sholokhov wanted to portray a Cossack nation within the Russian nation, and like Tolstoy, he wanted to show the sweep of Russian history through a, or perhaps the most, pivotal period. He begins in about 1910, several years before the start of the First World War, and ends this volume during the civil war, after a defeat of the Red Army in Cossack territory, before the final resolution in favor of the Communists.

The novel begins with the family of Melekhov. The patriarch, Pantaleimon, is the half-Turkish son of Prokoffey and a woman he has brought back from the Turkish war, whom the women in the village consider to be a witch. She is attacked toward the end of her pregnancy and dies while giving birth to Pantaleimon. He grows into a prosperous member of the village, but he is hotheaded and has a difficult time getting along with his own sons, especially Gregor. Gregor is in his early twenties when the main action of the novel begins, and his first act is to commence a scandalous affair with the wife of a neighbor who is away training in the army.

Gregor, his mistress, and his wife form an odd triangle. For many years Gregor spurns the wife, and at one point she attempts to kill herself, but after the death of his daughter with his mistress, he returns to his wife and impregnates her with twins. In the meantime, war, revolution, and civil war disrupt the life of the village and bring everyone abruptly into the modern age, where they discover that all of their presuppositions about how things work are outmoded and suspect. This is epitomized in the relationship between two subsidiary characters, Bunchuk and Anna. Bunchuk is a modern man—a specialist in Marxist theory and the machine gun. Anna is a Jew and a female comrade. They meet and fall in love without parental permission or oversight, thrown together by events. They try to resist their passion because it is inconvenient to the revolution, but they succumb. She becomes pregnant, but is then shot in a street battle.

Sholokhov is careful to show the Marxists' analysis of the Russian Revolution, blaming the agonies and the discontent resulting from the senseless cruelty of the First World War for the outbreak of class warfare. The Cossacks are fighters, but according to Sholokhov, they do not really understand why they are fighting the Hungarians and the Germans. As in Gogol's depiction of the sixteenth century, they are cavalrymen—Sholokhov is especially good on their feelings for their horses—but in a world of machine guns, bombs, poison gas, and trench warfare, cavalrymen are more vulnerable, not less, because of their skills. Once the Cossacks have become inured to fighting, injury, and death, though, and once they have lost their sense of connection to the czar, then it is only a matter of time before they bring their expertise as killers home (one character comments that the short Russo-Japanese War resulted in the Revolution of 1905, and so the much longer and more brutal world war will certainly result in a much longer and more brutal revolution). Sholokhov organizes his narrative by vignettes, many of which are moving and surprising.

But Sholokhov was not as disciplined as either Gogol or Tolstoy in organizing his material and understanding how to use a few protagonists to illuminate all parts of the plot. No doubt he wanted to avoid "heroic" clichés. But the effect is that in the second half of the novel, forward motion dissipates into a catalog of events that don't have much more than historical meaning. The novel becomes an occasionally vivid history movie where many actors have cameos but none carries the action. At the same time, Sholokhov does avoid the abstractions of modernism, where the protagonist's state of mind and experience of consciousness are given more weight than events. The First World War seems to have challenged every European writer's ability to portray reality—some opted for narrow focus (Svevo), others for altered consciousness (Ford Madox Ford in his *Parade's End*), some for lyricism (the "Time Passes" section of Virginia Woolf's *To the Light-house*). Others ignored the war altogether and began with a fresh consciousness in the twenties (*The Man without Qualities, The Great Gatsby, Lady Chatterley's Lover*). Inspired by the great nineteenth-century Russians, though, Sholokhov attempted to trace the path from one form of consciousness and one era of history to the next, doing so chronologically, never forgetting that the events happened to men and women and that men and women lived and died in the events, and also that they were mass events in a way that almost no European events had ever been before. Like Lawrence, Sholokhov attempted the realist solution to dilemmas that had rarely or never been portrayed before, and as with Lawrence, some of the outcomes now seem weak because there was no way to truly imagine the future when Sholokhov was writing.

Nevertheless, the novel is not a good medium for portraying mass events—words and sentences are too sequential and linear to evoke the overwhelming without making it abstract by using figurative language (as Dickens did in *A Tale of Two Cities*). What movies can show in a couple of minutes the novel lumbers through in many pages. The novel can detail the inner experience of mass horror by slicing small events finer and finer, evoking their cruelty more and more exquisitely (often through the memories of the protagonist rather than his or her immediate experience). For various reasons, Sholokhov opted not to do this by not giving any of his Cossacks the capacity for introspection. It is only through Bunchuk and Anna, who appear late in the novel, that the reader even begins to see the personal gains and costs of modern life.

This novel's sometimes pedestrian and sometimes lyrical and sometimes horrific realism give it the feel of authenticity even as it slips out of the mainstream of the twentieth-century novel. In particular, what was once set decoration—Sholokhov's evocation of the timeless beauty of the steppe—has become another entry in the catalog of the lost world. *And Quiet Flows the Don* has become a historical document—not a bad fate, I think, for a Marxist novel.

66 · Zora Neale Hurston · Their Eyes Were Watching God

(NEW YORK: HARPER, 1937), 193 PP.

Zora Neale Hurston was a trained anthropologist who produced two novels, several field studies, and an autobiography. At about the time of *Their Eyes Were Watching God,* she was celebrated and successful, but for ten years before her death in 1960, she fell into deep obscurity—working as a maid, falling victim to illness, and finally dying in a welfare home, only to be buried in an unmarked grave. Her work and her reputation were resurrected in the late 1960s in black studies courses. In 1973, novelist Alice Walker searched for and marked her grave in Eatonville, Florida. By the late 1970s, Hurston's novel had become a classic of American literature, and it has remained continuously in print since then.

Hurston's protagonist is Janie, who is married off by her grandmother at sixteen to a prosperous but authoritarian farmer who has land and a house but who intends that Janie will work, breed, and do what he says. Janie and her grandmother have different opinions about what constitutes a good life for a woman—the grandmother knows that a beautiful woman on her own is in considerable danger and is likely to fall into not only a state of unvirtue, but also a dangerous life of vice. Janie, though, is both sensitive and sensuous—she wants love and pleasure, and she is seduced away from her first husband by the ambitious Joe Starks, a city man passing through on his way to a new and entirely black town. Within days of their arrival in the new town, Joe makes himself the mayor, builds himself a store, and soon becomes the wealthiest and most influential citizen. Janie is married to him for some twenty years, but he, too, proves unsympathetic and tyrannical. She is not sorry to see him die, but she is more or less indifferent to the fact that he leaves her a wealthy woman—wealth and safety had never been her goals in the first place. Some months after Joe's death, she meets Tea Cake, who is much younger, but very lively and affectionate. Defying her cautious friends, Janie marries Tea Cake and goes with him to the Everglades, where they work on the farms during the winter planting and harvesting season. Tea Cake is no parent's idea of a good catch—he's a musician and a gambler who is nearly killed in several fights and is not above flirting with other women from time to time, but his love for Janie is sincere and he is manly, fun, and smart. His end is unusual and horrifying, making full use of the setting and milieu that Hurston has chosen for her novel.

But while *Their Eyes Were Watching God* is illuminating and exciting, it does not fit into any political program. The point of Janie and Tea Cake is that they do not conform. They are not good or even wise, they are free, and the essence of their appeal to one another is this freedom. Their idea of a good time is laughing, talking, and teasing one another (and, of course, by implication, having terrific sex). How their good times are to be earned or paid for is another question. Two or three times, Tea Cake goes off unexpectedly and without saying a word. The first time is when he finds Janie's money and goes on a bender. He returns, though not in shame, exactly, having lost most of it. He then proposes to win it back playing dice and poker, and he does, though he gets cut in a fight while doing so. He is not a middle-class striver by any means. But the implication is that his pleasure- and freedom-oriented personality is valuable because he hasn't given up a sense of wider possibilities in favor of property and authority. Janie goes with him and lives the exciting but insecure life that he prefers because she loves him and also because that life is more fun than the alternatives.

One aspect of Hurston's novel is her rendition of Florida black vernacular. While she narrates in standard English, the characters always speak in dialect, which simultaneously sets the scene, broadens both the subject and the audience of the novel, and gives Janie's and Tea Cake's choices a context. White people are peripheral in this novel, and generally to be avoided. The reader has the sense that she is being invited to witness a place and a life that are hidden, and, in the twenty-first century, largely lost. The same device is at work in Halldór Laxness's novel of rural Iceland *Independent People*—men sit around and gossip, producing an ad hoc cosmology that is simultaneously local and universal. Janie and Tea Cake overtly agree or disagree with the prevailing wisdom only once in a while, but it reveals them to the reader and to themselves. As an anthropologist who returned to her home territory to observe the local customs, Hurston put herself in an interesting intermediate position between writing from the place and writing of the place. A lesser novelist might have found the balance difficult, but Hurston is well aware that her allegiance must be to the integrity of her characters and that the other aspects of a novel will sort themselves out if the drama of the plot and the logic of the character development seem authentic.

67 · Elizabeth Bowen · The Death of the Heart

(GARDEN CITY, N.Y.: DOUBLEDAY, ANCHOR, 1938), 418 PP.

Americans, I think, may be forgiven if they don't quite understand what is going on in this novel, because almost all of its emotional dynamic takes place beneath the surface, and the characters, wealthy Londoners not long after the First World War, speak almost entirely in language codes that refer to behavior codes that are either now lost or were always understood by only a select few. On the surface, there are two stories that intersect: that of Anna Quayne, in her thirties, who, as a result of a failed early love affair, has married a rather boring but respectable man; and that of Portia Quayne, Anna's sixteen-year-old half sister-in-law, who comes to live with the Quaynes for a year when her mother dies, leaving her an orphan. Portia is not only young; she is also diffident and alienated, fully aware that her position in the family is compromised by the fact that the father she shares with Thomas Quayne had been kicked out of the family home by Thomas's mother when he confessed that he was having an affair with Portia's mother, who had become pregnant. Anna, though more aggressive and self-assured than Portia on the surface, also feels compromised. Unable to produce children, she lives an idle, superficial life of social contacts, fashion, and gossip. The action begins when Anna confesses to her friend St. Quentin that she has read Portia's diary, and that the diary is not terribly complimentary about Anna herself or about anyone Portia has come to know in her new life.

The principal action of the novel is that Portia falls in love with Eddie, an irresponsible young man who hangs around Anna and to whom Thomas has recently given a job. Eddie acts out a kind of romantic hysteria that Portia takes seriously as love and thinks will lead to marriage. Eddie at least understands that he is utterly incapable of commitment or even generosity. He is akin to the Oscar Wilde young men of a previous generation whose object is to parasitize as many people as possible for as long as possible before coming to a bad end.

But none of Bowen's characters is appealing. Anna is heartless; Thomas is ineffectual; St. Quentin, a novelist, is a social troublemaker; and family friends of Anna's whom Portia visits are simply not respectable, whatever other insights or talents or vitality they might have. Only Major Brutt, an old friend of Anna's who turns up, is in the least bit kindly, but he cannot find a job and appears to be heading toward some sort of netherworld that Bowen leaves nameless. In other words, once again, what is to be done with the girl? Bowen's answer seems to be that first her heart is to be killed, as Anna's has been before the outset of the novel and as Portia's is by Eddie, and then she might be found some sort of husband who would not be worthy of her respect or her affections, and then they will live out their lives in a formal marital sham.

This is not to say that *The Death of the Heart* isn't a fine novel. Bowen's style makes it work. She writes with precision and pungency. At one point she observes, "On that early March evening, Anna and Portia both, though not together, happened to be walking in Regent's Park. This was Portia's first spring in England: very young people are true but not resounding instruments. Their senses are tuned to the earth, like the senses of animals; they feel, but without conflict or pain. Portia was not like Anna, already halfway through a woman's checked, puzzled life, a life to which the intelligence only gives a further distorted pattern. With Anna, feeling was now unwilling, but she had more resonance" (p. 158). Elsewhere, she writes of Portia's friend Lilian, "She walked around with the rather fated expression you see in photographs of girls who have subsequently been murdered, but nothing had so far happened to her" (p. 61). Every page has some sharp, arresting observation. Bowen's voice is cool, specific, rarely asking larger emotional questions, but always alluding to them indirectly. Anna, for example, may be unsympathetic—all of her feelings have become selfish—but Bowen indicates that it is life itself, or at least respectable life as it is constructed around Regent's Park, that has formed her.

Portia is not to be saved because there is no one to save her. Major Brutt would like to save her, but when she comes to him from Eddie at the end of the novel, the mere sight of her in his hotel goads him to recognize that he has nothing to offer her. Only Matchett, Anna's housekeeper, cares about Portia, but Matchett herself is hard and judgmental, fond but not welcoming. Bowen's London is a cold place, far from Austen's Hampshire, where the people may be hard to take, but at least there are plenty of them. Bowen's characters find some solace only in going to the movies; conversations (such as Anna's with St. Quentin) can easily lead to betrayal and intrusion, and parties, such as those Eddie goes to or the one Portia is taken to when she is away on her visit, lead only to embarrassment or sometimes debauchery. All the characters act toward all the other characters as if attempts at intimacy or even warmth are at the least embarrassing, certainly impossible, and always in very poor taste.

Bowen was a generation younger than Virginia Woolf and about the same age as Nancy Mitford. Bowen wrote at a time when women's lives were beginning to change under the pressure of modern urban life, which offered more freedom of every sort, but Anna and Portia, still suspicious of education and work, don't know what to do with their freedom. Only Matchett, the housekeeper, has a vocation, know-how, dedication. But even she has been exiled from her true home, the Quayne family estate in the country (Bowen grew up on family property in Ireland). There is some sense that all of the characters would be better off there than in the house next to Regent's Park, but as with *The Good Soldier* twenty years earlier, that traditional English paradise has shut down and there is nowhere else available.

68 · P. G. **Wodehouse** · The Return of Jeeves, Bertie Wooster Sees It Through, Spring Fever, The Butler Did It

(1953, 1955, 1948, 1956; REPR., NEW YORK: GRAMERCY BOOKS, 1983), 682 PP.

To all appearances, P. G. Wodehouse is that rarest of comic novelists, a writer with no ax to grind. His novels are similar in feel but diverse in plot and point of view. They are like stock theatrical comedies or Hollywood romantic comedies of the 1930s—they seem simply to exist, more alike than different, and with no visible social analysis or intent. They are above all else well disposed. For some readers, this may seem naive or suspect. For others, it is a relief and a delight.

In some ways, Wodehouse's plots are strictly traditional. More often than not, they involve bringing a charming and well-meaning but impecunious young person together with another charming and well-meaning and very pecunious young person. But the emphasis in Wodehouse is not on the young lovers—it is enough that she is beautiful and has a couple of other desirable traits (for example, the young woman in *The Butler Did It* has a melodious speaking voice and is an excellent cook). And it is enough that the young man is well spoken and honorable. In a Wodehouse novel, the emphasis shifts to the older, more knowing, and more idiosyncratic characters—Jeeves and other butlers, members of the House of Lords who have fallen on hard times, bachelor friends of the loving couple (Wodehouse wrote many books in the narrative voice of Bertie Wooster, who remarks, "Florence gave him the swift heave-ho and—much against my will, but she seemed to wish it—became betrothed to me"), or knaves of various ilks. He is more interested in the efforts of men of a certain age (earls, barons, retired butlers) to find some comfort and the opportunity to live out their quirks and crotchets in peace.

Wodehouse's great genius is in his comic style, which works in part by paradox, like that of Oscar Wilde. Of Lord Shortlands's daughter and antagonist in *Spring Fever* he writes, "She was a girl who had an annoying habit of paying no attention to questions, being brisk and masterful and concentrated on her own affairs; the sort of girl, so familiar a feature of the English countryside, who goes about in brogue shoes and tweeds and meddles vigorously in the lives of the villagers, sprucing up their manners and morals until you wonder that something in the nature of a popular uprising does not take place" (p. 297). In *Bertie Wooster Sees It Through,* Bertie muses, "When you are trying to raise a thousand quid, the first essential, of course, is to go to someone who has got a thousand quid, and no doubt he had learned from Florence that I was stagnant with the stuff" (p. 152), illustrating another aspect of Wodehouse's charm—his way of inventing phrases that sound like slang but that are original to him. Bertie, in particular, has a distinct narrative rhythm that carries his novels and makes them seem especially jaunty. His style always contrasts with that of his butler, Jeeves, who is far more knowledgeable and cultured than Bertie. When Bertie asks him his opinion of a play Bertie is considering investing in, Jeeves remarks, "it seemed to me a somewhat immature production, lacking in significant form. My personal tastes lie more in the direction of Dostoevsky and the great Russians." Jeeves's savoir faire combined with his loyalty to Bertie is very reassuring, implying that the English upper classes, while feckless, are also harmless, and easily used for a higher purpose by their much more enterprising servants.

In his characters and plots, Wodehouse takes the tragic material of such earlier novels as *The Good Soldier* and reimagines it with grace and joy. Wodehouse, born in 1881, was a near contemporary of Ford Madox Ford, but Wodehouse immigrated to America in 1909 and got to Hollywood soon thereafter. He quickly saw the absurdities of

English-American relations—that the Americans had the money but the English had the class, and that much fun could be made of the exchange of money for class. The real repositories of tradition, for Wodehouse, are not the aristocrats themselves, but their servants, especially their butlers, whose job is to run the household and also to uphold forms of respect. Wodehouse's English society is not like Austen's or Ford's—it is far more permeable and various. Butlers turn out to have been safecrackers, lords turn out to be bookmakers. Everyone is in search of the same thing—a good meal, a comfortable establishment, and some time to pursue one's hobbies. The breakdown of the class system is not the occasion for regret, but the occasion for ingenuity (an ingenuity that mirrors Wodehouse's own).

Wodehouse wrote film scripts and plays, and his novels are all plotted in the same way, which eventually becomes tedious—the outcome of the action is never in suspense, and the compensatory motive for turning the pages is intended to be humorous or farcical plot twists, but these don't have anough substance to actually work. Enough Wodehouse is enough after a while, but some Wodehouse is essential to a happy literary life.*

69 · T. H. White · The Once and Future King

(1939; REPR., NEW YORK: PENGUIN PUTNAM, ACE, 1958), 639 PP.

The Once and Future King is steeped in learning and literature, and yet it is not quite literarily respectable in the way that the works of, say, Kingsley Amis or Virginia Woolf are. Maybe it has been contaminated in the minds of critics by popularity and Walt Disney animation. Nevertheless, it is a serious work, delightful and witty in many ways and yet very somber overall. The volume published as *The Once and Future King* is actually four works separately composed during about twenty years. The first, *The Sword in the Stone,* concerns the lost childhood of Arthur, future king of England, and his education by Merlyn. The second, *The Queen of Air and Darkness,* tells the story of adolescent sons of

---

*For a balanced and detailed look at Wodehouse's controversial career during World War II please see Anthony Lane, "Beyond a Joke," *The New Yorker,* vol. 80, no. 9, Apr. 19, 26, 2004, pp. 19–26.

Orkney (Gawaine, Agravaine, Gaheris, and Gareth) and their mother, Morgause, who, unbeknownst to him, is Arthur's half sister. The third, *The Ill-Made Knight,* takes up the story of Sir Lancelot and his uneasy relationship with Queen Guenever and with Arthur. The fourth, briefest book, *The Candle in the Wind,* concerns the end of the Round Table and Arthur's death.

White, born in India in 1906, was a brilliant student at Cambridge in the twenties, when he was already reading Malory's *Morte d'Arthur.* He clearly saw in Malory's cycle the British version of the Oresteia— an epic creation myth in which the violation, even the unintentional violation, of a cluster of taboos eventually leads to the disintegration of the nation created, even though, in White's work, almost everyone involved is reasonable, compassionate, and well intentioned. The out- lines of the story are well known: the young Arthur, rushing to find a weapon for his foster brother, Kay, pulls a magic sword from a magic stone, revealing himself as the rightful king of England. He then engages in several wars, and during one of these he finds himself in Orkney, where he is seduced by means of a charm into sleeping with his half sister Morgause. The child of this union is Mordred. He then duly marries Guenever, but she subsequently falls in love with the greatest knight of the Round Table, Lancelot, who has come from France. The Orkney brothers, including Mordred, repeatedly use Guenever and Lancelot's adultery as an excuse for forwarding their own resentments, until finally all loves and all friendships have been sacrificed. Morgause is beheaded by her own sons. Lancelot mistak- enly kills Gareth and Gaheris, Guenever is nearly burned at the stake. Lancelot kills Agravaine during a raid and Gawaine in a battle. Arthur is left bereft, only to die at the end, wondering if it is possible to govern at all.

The Once and Future King is full of insights, scenes, and flourishes that are really quite astonishing. No doubt because of the material, for one thing, it is one of the few English novels that are utterly frank about the power of love and sex. Morgause is portrayed as a beautiful but trivial and silly woman, a witch like her sister Morgan le Fay, but not serious enough to do real spells. The harm she does is in the seduc- tive and yet neglectful way she rears her sons, deforming their emo- tional lives so they are always subject to violent jealousies, outbursts, and hatreds. At one point they hear that she has gone with a couple of visiting knights to search for a unicorn but hasn't found it (not being a virgin, of course—and there is the implication that Agravaine has witnessed her seduction of one of the visiting knights that was the real purpose of the hunt). So the brothers persuade the kitchen maid, who is a virgin, to accompany them on a unicorn hunt of their own—they are intent upon winning their mother's attention by presenting her with a unicorn's head. The unicorn does indeed come to the kitchen maid and lay his head in her lap. Both moved and frenzied by the beauty of the unicorn, the four boys kill it and attempt to take the head as a trophy, creating only pain, grief, and mess with their efforts, and then getting in trouble when they return home.

White seems to know all there is to know about boys. Arthur and the knights of the Round Table are so many boys grown into man-hood, seething with ambitions, conflicting desires, strong emotions, and barely recognized motives. At one point he writes of the Orkney brothers, "The idea which the children had was to hurt the donkeys. Nobody had told them it was cruel to hurt them, but then, nobody had told the donkeys, either. . . . So the small circus was a unity—the beast reluctant to move and the children vigorous to move them, the two parties bound together by a link of pain to which they both agreed without question. The pain itself was so much a matter of course that it had vanished out of the picture, as if by a process of cancellation" (p. 242). This is prose at its prosy finest, an observation made in a con-versational tone with profoundly moving implications, that grows out of a simple scene, preceded and followed by many other equally apro-pos and yet simple observations.

White's novel is intense and rich. The first volume, which tells the story of Arthur's education (he is transformed into several animals and birds), is a treasury of English natural history and increasingly obscure forms of sport, such as falconry and boar hunting. The same is true in the third volume, which tells how Lancelot became the greatest knight. White writes, "Uncle Dap was the only one in the family who took Lancelot seriously, and Lancelot was the only one who was seri-ous about Uncle Dap. It was easy not to be serious about the old fellow, for he was that peculiar creation which ignorant people laugh at—a genuine maestro. His branch of learning was chivalry." And then White shows convincingly what a maestro of chivalry would know and how he would think (p. 324). White uses the inherent flexibility of prose to deliver a lot of information, not only background in-formation that makes it easy for the modern reader to picture twelfth- and thirteenth-century England, but also good analogues to modern society—jousting as a form of cricket, for example—that work not only to clarify what might be confusing, but also to show the continuity of English life from the Middle Ages to the twentieth century.

The Once and Future King is about male society, but White is not a misogynist. His portrait of Guenever is sympathetic and rich. Of particular note is the moment when Lancelot and Guenever first fall in love. They are out hawking, and Guenever makes a mistake in her task of helping Lancelot with his hawk. He rebukes her, and then, when her feelings are hurt, he suddenly recognizes that "she had been giving kindness, and he had returned it with unkindness. But the main thing was that she was a real person." This recognition of common humanity is the source of their inconvenient and passionate love.

The Once and Future King is full of comic scenes. One of the ways White deals with some of Malory's absurdities is to make them funny, as with King Pellinore and the Questing Beast or the visit of King Pellinore and Sir Palomides to Orkney. But he never forgets that underlying the good fellowship and prosperity that Arthur brings to "Gramarye," or medieval England, are violence, rape, and incest. And there is human nature, too. In his efforts to substitute "right" for "might," Arthur discovers that the human urge to win, to prevail, to gain status and revenge offers a constant challenge to any system of governing that hopes to promote cooperation rather than conflict.

In the final volume, White does explicitly what is always tempting to the novelist—he analyzes the circles of relationships that begin with the most intimate and move toward the most impersonal and political. He is intent upon discovering the links between the personal and the political, between love and power, between the family and the nation. The promise of such an analysis is that the proper arrangement and resolution of personal relationships, with all their betrayals and disappointments and pleasures and satisfactions, will result in social peace and, conversely, proper laws and governance will result in healthy intimacies. The underlying premise of the novel as a form is that such rationalization and reconciliation is possible, because the novel always tries to set the individual into the social context. Merely making the links implies that a good fit is possible—if not for this protagonist, then for some other, less recalcitrant one. It is not that liberal social institutions have created the novel, it is that the novel is in its very organization liberal, because the individual always continues to exist and be compelling and the social group always continues to exist, also, containing in its very existence the idea that the individual can be reconciled to it. King Arthur recognizes before he dies that he has not succeeded in creating the kingdom he hoped for, owing, of course, to the effects of his own sins. But he is the once and future king. The novel ends with the implication that upon his return, he will try again, with better results.

70 · Christina Stead · The Man Who Loved Children

(1940; REPR., NEW YORK: PICADOR, 2001), 576 PP.

The Man Who Loved Children is one of the few novels that come close to attaining the grandeur of tragedy, and the tragedy it most recalls, perhaps, is *Medea.* It is also a thoroughly modern novel and a fascinating social document. Stead's father was a Fabian socialist, and Stead was born in Australia. She lived for many years in the United States, was married to a prominent Marxist writer, and was up to date in her understanding of all the myriad subjects and ideas that come up in the course of this long and dense work of fiction. Most important, though, is that she actually does give her ordinary government bureaucrat and his unhappy wife that sense of unstoppable and fated intensity that literature usually reserves for kings and queens.

Sam and Henny Pollit, husband and wife and parents of six and then seven children (the eldest, Louisa, Sam's child by his former wife, is the novel's protagonist), live in a large house in Washington, D.C. Henny is a former southern belle, one of twelve offspring of a wealthy and influential man, David Collyer. Sam is self-made, also from a big family, but a big family without money or status (one of his sisters is a schoolteacher). Sam is smart but impolitic, and Stead is masterful at communicating the maddening excesses of his demeanor. He is drunk on his own words, on his own elevated ideas, on his grandiose sense of himself and his mission. In a normal novel he would be a comic blowhard waiting for a comeuppance, something of a clown, but with the dark addition of unmitigated narcissism. Henny is dissatisfied and angry, disappointed in her marriage, and unsuited to her role (though more capable of performing it than Sam gives her credit for). She is maternal but not kind; toward Louisa she is often cruel and openly unloving. Toward the other children she is irascible and unpredictable. Sometimes she seems fond and indulges them, but at other times she is rejecting and impatient. At the outset of the novel she hasn't spoken to

Sam in some years (they communicate by notes or through the children), and she has a lover named Bert, a large career bachelor she goes
out with from time to time (Sam also has his flirtations). In the course
of the novel, Sam and Henny enlarge. At first eccentric, they grow
beyond dysfunctional, neurotic, and even psychotic, until they eventually become simply, irreducibly, hugely themselves, as beyond help or
even diagnosis as King Lear or Prometheus.

Not every novel that wants to be a tragedy gets to be one. Usually
novelists and readers have to be content with melodrama or somber
realism, but Stead avoids both, and her techniques are very specific.
Most commentators, including the poet Randall Jarrell (who resurrected *The Man Who Loved Children* twenty-five years after its first
failed publication), complain of Sam's and Henny's excess—they have
no sense of decorum, and they parade their disagreements openly in
front of the children, their families, and the neighbors while all the
time protesting that they prize discretion. For another thing, both are
more than eloquent—Henny specializes in arias of invective, while
Sam never shuts up about anything, but especially about his ideas and
projects. He pries constantly into the private lives of his children and
also, when he feels like it, holds children who don't please him up to
the ridicule of the other children. He is a smiling tyrant, all-seeing, all-
questioning, an atheist god in his own mind and in the minds of the
younger children, who have no defense against either his crimes or his
charms. Henny is the anarchist, or the nihilist, since no system, no government, no order, and, eventually, no life at all are preferable in her
mind to the interminable presence of Sam. Sam and Henny are as dramatic as any stage characters, always demonstrating the progress of
their inner lives to an audience. The excess is what saves their story
from sober realism or Zolaesque naturalism. The only character who
has an inner life is Louisa, the witness, and in many ways the consciousness through which the action is distilled.

What saves the Pollits' story from melodrama is the presence of the
chorus, the five younger children, who respond with exquisite sensitivity and evenhanded affection to each parent. Ernie, the oldest boy, is
especially fond of Henny, even though she betrays him repeatedly.
Evie, who looks like Henny, is always being enlisted by Sam to do such
things as come into his bed in the morning and scratch his head. He
baby-talks her and woos her or criticizes and abuses her by turns, en-
suring her future, according to both Louisa and Henny, as a wifely
doormat or worse. Little Sam and Saul, twins, are no less transgressed

upon and invaded, but they have solidarity with one another and serve mostly as an audience for the ridicule of the older children. Stead is wonderfully adept at individualizing the children and showing how each reacts to and is molded by each parent. The reader's constant sense of this chorus, of the damage the parents are doing both individually and together, is finally overwhelmed but never suppressed by excess and relentlessness. There is no sense by the end of the novel of cause and effect, no understanding of the specific costs the children will have to pay as adults for the storm of their childhoods. Stead wisely doesn't even address this question. It is enough to present the storm. The reader coexists with the children in the inescapable and enormous world that Sam and Henny have made, a family as horrible, irredeemable, and incurable as the family of Agamemnon or Atreus.

Nevertheless, Stead has a lively and informed political consciousness. What is at stake in the Pollit household is power, and even given all of Henny's failures as a parent, it is she who understands this. Sam Pollit is an absolutist who desires not only to invade his children's every thought, but also to have all their love and devotion. Big Brother in Orwell's *1984* is no more totalitarian than Sam Pollit. One of his more unsavory habits is to call himself "poor little Sam," to make the children pity him as a victim, usually when he has just finished ordering them around or has just been challenged by Henny or Louisa. He is a constant fount of propaganda about himself, about the neighbors, about unnamed hostile strangers, about history, culture, science, geography, religion, and the proper way to live. At the end of the novel it appears as though he is going to have a radio show and become a media celebrity, thus unstoppably expanding his audience far beyond the family circle (Stead hardly seems to be a satirist in *The Man Who Loved Children,* but this is surely a quietly satirical moment). Stead clearly understands that the family is not sentimentally walled off from politics, but is the source of all political feeling and understanding. When Louisa runs away at the end of the novel, Stead explicitly shows that her sense of who she is, what the world is, and what her "home nation" is shifts as soon as she crosses the bridge that separates the house from the other side of the creek. For Stead the good news is that freedom of thought is possible—at least it is if Big Brother has had to live with an opposition, even an opposition that has been wrong-headed and unwise. The presence of the opposition allows at least some of the chorus (or audience) space for constructing notions of reality that are independent. At the same time, only Louisa escapes. She has to leave the other children to their fates, which is not a collective solution and reaffirms the underlying premise of tragedy that when kings and queens do battle, the general outcome for most of mankind is not a happy one.

The Man Who Loved Children was a critical and commercial failure when it was first published, and it is easy to see why. In the first place, it was unprecedented in its seamless integration of politics, psychology, and tragedy. Stead was a true heir to Charles Dickens in her understanding of how personalities project themselves outward and create symbolic worlds that are limned by eloquence. Most of Dickens's heirs intuitively grasped the truth of his depictions of the power of mental universes, but only Stead was able to do what Dickens did routinely, which was to have two or more of these universes abut and challenge one another. But Stead the sociologist was colder and more honest than Dickens, whose sentimental attachment to a Victorian ideal of family comity was sometimes shaken but never destroyed. Stead seems never to have had such a thing. At the opening of her novel, Sam and Henny are way beyond the point where most people (including Dickens himself) would have sought separation or divorce.

This novel is not for everyone, nor for every mood. I have read it twice with great admiration. When I tried to read it a third time (when I had a young family myself), I couldn't stand it. If *Hamlet* runs four hours and *Lear* almost five, well, *The Man Who Loved Children* runs fourteen or fifteen hours, and though the plot is actually quite neat and progresses steadily, novel-readers are not used to fifteen-hour storms. The catharsis here, compared with any other tragedy, is a long time coming. Nevertheless, Stead's novel is like Ford Madox Ford's *The Good Soldier* in its power to astonish and compel with each reading. It is sui generis among novels, and Stead, too, never wrote anything else like it.

Some commentators have wondered why this novel has not entered women's studies curricula or even twentieth-century literature curricula. I think it is because the novel is so anomalous that it can't easily be accommodated on a list with other novels. I would teach it along with some Greek tragedies or maybe a Russian novel or two written about Josef Stalin.

71 · Junichiro Tanizaki · The Makioka Sisters

(NEW YORK: RANDOM HOUSE, VINTAGE, 1948), 529 PP.

All novels eventually become historical documents, because they either chronicle everyday life taking place all around the author as he writes, or they chronicle his ideas of what is true or important, which are always strongly determined by his circumstances. But some novels are conceived as historical documents, and one of these is *The Makioka Sisters*. Tanizaki wrote many novels in a long career—he was born in 1886, and continued publishing until he died in 1965. *The Makioka Sisters* was written during the Second World War, largely, it would seem, to depict a traditional Japanese way of life that was fast disappearing. Even so, Tanizaki's treatment of the four Makioka sisters— Tsuruko, Sachiko, Yukiko, and Taeko—and the husbands of the older two—Tatsuo and Teinosuke—is evenhanded and has, on the surface, an idle tone. The family dilemma is a rather simple one: Yukiko, the third sister, is approaching age thirty unmarried. Taeko, several years younger, has a liaison, but can't marry until Yukiko does.

The fault, for Yukiko, may be in her stars and it may be in herself. She is small, retiring, and old-fashioned, but stubborn. Many proposals have come and gone over the years; always something has happened to obstruct each one—either the man has been found deficient at last, or Yukiko has been unable to commit herself. Though the Makiokas are no longer a wealthy and powerful family, they do have prestige— Sachiko, the protagonist, often wonders if family pride has forestalled marriages that would have been perfectly acceptable. Over the five years of the action of the novel, the breakdown of each marriage negotiation is an index to how the Makiokas think of themselves, how others think of them, and how the Makiokas attempt to divine how others think of them and what this means for how they are to estimate their own value and status. In the meantime, Taeko, in her twenties, acts like a Westernized, liberated woman—she wears Western clothes, smokes cigarettes, and supports herself, at first by making elaborate dolls and then by setting up as a dressmaker. She gets into more and more trouble, and with each incident there is the ever-increasing danger that Yukiko's prospective suitors will be put off by scandal.

Though Tanizaki's plotting seems casual, the novel builds considerable suspense with each change in the fortunes of the characters. It is similar in technique to a novel by Anthony Trollope, or perhaps to an

Icelandic saga. Events move along at a steady pace. The author writes of dramatic moments in much the same way as he writes of insignificant moments, and pretty soon the reader understands that in the chain of cause and effect, what seems insignificant might be more important than what is dramatic—in fact, there is no way to know, so the characters are always going over incidents in their minds, trying to find the thread that will make the action work out.

The Makioka Sisters has plenty of action: Taeko is nearly drowned in a huge flood; Sachiko finds herself in a typhoon; the Second World War begins, first in China and then in Europe; Taeko's boyfriend is disinherited for stealing from the family jewelry store; Sachiko's daughter contracts scarlet fever; Taeko's other boyfriend gets gangrene from an operation and must suffer an amputation before he dies; Taeko herself contracts dysentery. Even so, the style of the novel, which is to portray the dialectical progress of Sachiko's and to some extent Teinosuke's thoughts as they deal with the difficulties and problems of five years, never varies—whatever the event, and whatever the characters' emotions, consideration is all, calculation is all. Each marriage negotiation is a microcosm of the characters' lives in general— what information is going to get out and to whom? Can leaks (for example, through the maids) be controlled? Is confession the best strategy, and if so, how is it to be expressed? What must be put up with and what can be manipulated? For an American reader, who perhaps sees impulsiveness as more passionate and true than endless calculation, the Makiokas are saved, I think, by their evident fondness for one another and the desire to preserve one another from as much pain as possible—these characters are hardly ever selfish, and even Taeko, some of whose actions come to seem selfish to Sachiko, is given the benefit of the doubt—perhaps she is simply more like the sisters' father in temperament, perhaps she has been poorly trained or poorly guided by the sisters themselves.

As the reader gets more comfortable with the novel and its milieu, Sachiko's perennial second thoughts and cautions come to have their attractions. As they ponder and discuss the ramifications of every step, Sachiko and Teinosuke are actually creating the continuity that is otherwise vanishing around them—part of Tanizaki's theme of the disappearance of the old ways. Sachiko's and Teinosuke's worries serve to link this year's cherry blossom viewing with last year's and that of many previous years. They make of the parade of Yukiko's suitors a train of logic—this is who we were then, this is who we are now, and this is how we have become what we are now. When Tatsuo declines to spend much money on the sixteenth anniversary of the father's death, it says something about everything having to do with the family—who the father was, what Tatsuo's estimation of himself is, what has changed in Japanese society. Impulsiveness, as represented by Taeko, comes to seem not pure and innocent as much as a way of dispensing with the past that must have the effect of turning the continuity of individual lives into a series of unrelated explosions. As a result of her contemplations, Sachiko is often anxious, but as a result of cultivating her awareness of her history and putting all new events into context, she is also often reassured.

The Makioka Sisters is a good example of the notion that a novel does not so much need a plot as an organizing principle. Though Tanizaki was quite familiar with Western novels, the sense of an Aristotelian sort of plot, based on conflict and aiming toward a large climax, meant to be cathartic, was not second nature to him, as it is to most literate Westerners. The marriage finally contracted for Yukiko is not self-evidently the best marriage or the worst—it is the one everyone finally manages in the end, and the reader understands that it does not promise to be extra happy or extra unhappy—it promises to fit in with the marriages around it. The same goes, in large part, for Taeko's marriage—a bartender with entrepreneurial aspirations who will let her do her dressmaking is the best she can hope for, but he is a kindly, presentable fellow, and maybe it will all work out. Tanizaki's intent is neither to damn nor to redeem his characters. For the most part, they are distinct within their group, but not inherently in conflict with it. It is neither a defeat to be subsumed within it nor a victory against nature to find integration. It is simply a detailed example of how something happens, how things work.

Tanizaki's novels are not all so based in ordinary life. He was strongly influenced by The Tale of Genji and other highly dramatic Japanese cultural traditions, and he disagreed with the increasing Westernization of Japanese culture, but in The Makioka Sisters he resisted both anger and polemic, relying instead upon what seems almost like mere gossip to create a novel of the highest art.

72 · Vladimir Nabokov · Lolita

(NEW YORK: RANDOM HOUSE, VINTAGE, 1955), 317 PP.

Most people know the basic plot of *Lolita*—for one thing, two movies have been made from it, one with James Mason and one with Jeremy Irons. Humbert Humbert, an educated European middle-aged man with a fetishistic attraction for twelve- to fourteen-year-old girls, inserts himself into the domestic arrangements of a woman with a twelve-year-old daughter. When the woman is fortuitously killed, HH, as he calls himself, takes the daughter on a prolonged cross-country car trip, repeatedly raping, molesting, bribing, and imprisoning her as they travel from motel to motel. After she escapes, he pursues her and her "rescuer," first discovering Lolita, now eighteen, married, and pregnant, but still not interested in HH, then shooting the rescuer (a playwright named Quilty). The novel purports to be HH's jailhouse confession.

Lolita is a controversial novel, of course. It has made it into the critical pantheon of great twentieth-century novels, but it is also notorious, and it does not seem possible that it will be dislodged from either category. Even more than *Ulysses* it stands as a kind of index of literary taste. If you don't like it, then you don't truly understand great art. On the other hand, if you do like it, then what kind of person are you? Nabokov himself was opinionated about the nature of art—working as hard as James or Tolstoy to promote a theory of art and of the novel that led straight to him and his sort of greatness. As a teacher and an essayist, he was a tireless self-promoter who relentlessly demeaned as philistine those who didn't share his perceptions and ideas. His particular whipping boy was Dostoevsky, whose reputation he attempted to puncture at every opportunity, possibly because he had read Dostoevsky's books in his youth and didn't remember them very well (as recent translators of Dostoevsky have suggested), possibly because Dostoevsky was very popular in the United States (Nabokov promoted Gogol, for example, who was less well known to a general American audience), or possibly because the two were so philosophically at odds. At any rate, whereas Dostoevsky was always engaged with political and moral questions, Nabokov maintained that he disdained such things as being outside the realm of true art, and at first glimpse *Lolita* seems to bear out Nabokov's view.

Philosophically, *Lolita* is in the tradition of conservative novels by novelists who accept the innate evil of human nature, such as Thackeray. In conservative novels such as *Vanity Fair, The Picture of Dorian Gray,* and *Lolita,* redemption is as impossible to achieve as true connection, and the protagonist either remains isolated at the end or achieves a new degree of isolation as a result of the action of the novel. Conservative novelists are much more likely to reserve a special place for art (or at least aesthetics) as a (or the) pure moral category in a world where all other moral categories have failed. They are also more likely to disdain the social programs of more liberal and socially active novelists who see human nature as either inherently good, or at least neutral, and capable of positive moral change. Nabokov made a vigorous case against the novel as a social or biographical document. In particular, he ridiculed psychological ideas current in the midcentury, especially Freudian ideas, that attempted to make causal connections in the emotional and mental lives of both characters and authors. He does not explore *how* HH and Lolita became, respectively, a pedophile and a slut; he simply accepts that they are, and that most of the other characters in the novel have secret sins as well. The pleasure and the redemption in the face of human nature is to use the artistic materials at hand to create a beautiful and interesting pattern, preferably one that is as intricate and convoluted as possible, full of internal and external references, wordplay, and complexities that enhance the game aspect of the work of art (and thereby make it more exclusive).

Lolita is an American novel, but Nabokov was a Russian and a European novelist. He was, in some sense, the major heir to the nineteenth-century Russian novelists, and in spite of his own distaste for biographical connection, I think it is fair to observe how the pattern of Russian history produced his ideas. Nabokov's father was an enlightened liberal jurist in Russia who went into exile in 1919 and was assassinated in 1922, when Nabokov was twenty-three. The assassins were czarists. The great Russian novels of the nineteenth century were energized by a single quest—to find a way for Russia to enter the modern world without losing its Russian identity. Nabokov's father's assassination represented the path that Russia did not take, the constitutional Western secular path, and the author never stopped disdaining the path Russia did take. He readily saw that the fervor of the nineteenth-century novelists had resulted in a cruel and irrational upending of Russian society. As far as Nabokov was concerned, that closed off the two traditional forms of redemption—social change and spiritual change. The only alternative was to make the best of the physical world, flawed though it is.

Lolita has to be seen as the story of a man who is making the best of the world as he knows it—his only higher faculty is a particular aesthetic response to a certain sort of girl. He wants to manipulate her as if she were a set of artistic materials. Early on, in fact, before the death of Lolita's mother, Charlotte, when Lolita happens to sit on his lap and he happens to climax without her realizing it, HH says, "Lolita had been safely solipsized," and then, "What I had madly possessed was not she, but my own creation, another, fanciful Lolita—perhaps more real than Lolita; overlapping, encasing her; floating between me and her, and having no will, no consciousness—indeed, no life of her own" (p. 62). Except that fate intervenes to tempt him with custody of the real Lolita, and his instincts are the worst possible guide to either fostering her or finding satisfaction himself. The result is that she escapes, he never stops loving her or regretting his treatment of her, he fails to expiate his sins in his own mind, and he discovers that their relationship has always been unpleasant and meaningless to Lolita.

Nabokov was thoroughly familiar with French literature and certainly recognized that the physical trap that the imprisoned girl finds herself in is mirrored by the mental trap the libertine himself resides in—the more HH seeks satisfaction from Lolita, the less he can find it and the more obsessed with her he becomes. Her outer hell is his inner hell, and his inner hell drives him to reinforce her outer hell at every possible point. The difference between HH and other tormentors, even Proust's M., is that HH believes in love and they don't, but the practical methods they all use to imprison their victims are the same. More than that, *Lolita* is a classic European novel in its preoccupation with the classic European theme of the irreducibly ambiguous nature of women and girls. Nabokov's answer to the traditional question is muted but distinct—when HH finds Lolita married, pregnant, eighteen years old, and living in a shack with her husband, he respects her autonomy—not only her right to choose her life but also her right to judge her history for herself. He gives her money he owes her from her mother's estate and leaves, more or less getting his papers in order so he can finish his tasks. But this recognition doesn't resolve his frustration. He can't possess her, but he also can't leave the mental hell he has made for himself. Unfortunately for this autonomy theory, Lolita soon dies in childbirth, killed by the author, thereby rendering all of the action of the novel more or less meaningless except as an expression of HH's aesthetic.

Is *Lolita* a great novel? How does it compare to *Anna Karenina,* a novel that Nabokov himself respected, or to *Middlemarch* or to *Madame Bovary*? How does it compare to the monuments of modernism such as *Ulysses* or *The Trial*? For one thing, in 315 pages, *Lolita* is much more limited and less capacious than the socially descriptive and expansive nineteenth-century novels; it is less stylistically ambitious than *Ulysses,* less profound and original than *The Trial*. It doesn't quite sustain each third of the narrative (before Charlotte's death, between Charlotte's death and Lolita's escape, the pursuit of Quilty)—the last third is sketchy and not very interesting, as if the author can't realize HH without Lolita, or as if the stalking and the murder aren't that important to him as a theme, but he has to follow out the plot anyway. The last third shows that his observation of the American landscape is pictorial rather than analytical, not very insightful and similar in this to his observation of Lolita herself (as HH points out toward the end of his narrative). It might be assumed that since both novels ran into censorship difficulties, *Lolita* is similar to *Ulysses* in the way *Lolita* challenges sexual taboos, but Joyce's hero, Leopold Bloom, is a social outcast, not a moral outcast—Joyce makes the case for him that he is kinder and more truly connected than the people around him. Nabokov makes no such case for HH, and in fact HH never defends his abuse of Lolita; rather he never stops expressing his remorse. *Lolita* is more similar to *Madame Bovary,* in which the reader is asked to experience the subjective life of a character conventionally considered immoral. But the precedent of Flaubert's technique was a hundred years old by Nabokov's time, so technically *Lolita* is an advance upon *Justine* but not upon *Madame Bovary*. *Lolita* is a compelling, complex, and intriguing novel, but the only value it expresses is the value of freedom, and freedom, as Nabokov explores it, is highly ambiguous. When HH and Lolita are driving around the country, doing whatever they wish, their freedom is a prison of idleness and fear. When Nabokov is asserting his artistic freedom from the political and moral traditions of the novel (and the Russian novel in particular), he finally has nowhere to take his plot—the action leads to no revelations that aren't already present in earlier sections of the book. He must fall back on reiteration of his original ideas to wind everything up. So no, I don't think *Lolita* is a great novel, but I also don't think, as an example of artistic experimentation, that it can be avoided by anyone truly interested in the history and nature of the novel.

73 · Rebecca West · The Fountain Overflows

(NEW YORK: VIKING, 1956), 313 PP.

Rebecca West is better known as a journalist than as a novelist—she wrote a monumental history and analysis of the Balkans, *Black Lamb and Grey Falcon,* in the 1940s, and had a long and illustrious career (she died in 1982, at age ninety, and her output of books of all types numbers many volumes). She was especially famous for her clear and pointed writing style, and *The Fountain Overflows,* written when she was in her midsixties, is emphatically the work of someone for whom writing is as natural as breathing. Everything about the prose of the novel is subtle but lucid—diction and pacing, the voice that moves effortlessly between past and present, evocation and comment. By turns, the narrator writes as an opinionated and willful adolescent observer and with the cooler judgment of a mature woman. While the action of the novel is often painful, the style is never lugubrious, yet there is an undercurrent of muted sadness in the contrast between past and present that is very affecting. This novel has many emotional layers, but is so readable that its technical sophistication (not to mention its wisdom about family life, women, men, girls, and history) has been too much overlooked.

The Fountain Overflows opens when Rose, the narrator, is about eight or nine. She is one of four children. The oldest sister, Cordelia, is twelve or thirteen, and Rose has a twin sister, Mary. The boy, Richard Quin, is not yet of school age. They are the offspring of a famous Anglo-Irish conservative theorist and journalist, who is under some sort of a cloud that the children don't understand, and a Scottish pianist, who has given up her concert career in favor of domestic life. Socially they occupy a particular niche—educated and influential but not prosperous, and not English, gentry. It is clear from the first page of the novel that Papa is a bounder—brilliant, untrustworthy, and profligate, though charming and idealistic—while Mamma is volatile and long-suffering, with a true artistic temperament (that is, focused, as she says, on the fact that "there is a great deal in life that is not affected by what happens to you" (p. 307). Mamma's attitude both ensures the survival of the family and makes for a good deal of eccentricity—the girls, for example, often shudder at the spectacle of their mother's appearance when she goes out, but they are passionately devoted to her and to their father. They are forgiving and understanding and strong in a way that would make any modern child psychologist shudder.

The novel opens just after Papa has taken an editorial job with a small suburban London newspaper—his first job in London—and the family moves into a house he had lived in as a boy. It ends when the three girls depart in some sense into their adult lives—Rose and Mary take musical scholarships, and Cordelia discovers a talent for clothing design. West chooses and develops her themes and weds them to her plot very slyly and smoothly. By using the form of the memoir, she seems merely to be retailing incidents and adventures, with many colorful characters along the way, but really she is exploring the nature of family life, emotional inheritance, and love between parents and children, siblings and friends.

Papa is a womanizer and a gambler. The children notice that their smooth, happy times are punctuated by troubled times, in which not only is there no money, but also people keep coming to the house angrily seeking payments on past due bills, and that these times are followed by sudden removal to new lodgings. Mamma is sensitive and impractical, not at all equipped to be the wife of such an unreliable man. One early crisis in the novel results from Papa's refusal to communicate with his family—on the date when Mamma is to take the children from one house to another, he hasn't bothered to tell her the address or to send her a key. Embarrassment is Mamma's frequent lot. But just as she doesn't allow the children to resent and demean their father, West doesn't allow the reader to judge him for his sins. She quite skillfully portrays him from Rose's point of view as a complex human being who is not exactly doing the best he can but is subject to many conflicting impulses. Not the least of these is that he is Irish by birth but conservative by temperament, not unlike Joyce's Buck Mulligan, a natural traitor to everyone, including himself.

West's subtlety is beautifully displayed in an incident late in the novel: Mamma's cousin Jock, Scottish by birth, is considered by Rose to be a cruel, selfish, and crude man who plays at being a stock comic Scotsman while refusing to provide for his wife and daughter, who live much of the time with Rose and her sisters. He has the family gift for music, and Rose is both puzzled at and disdainful of what he has done with his gift. One night he comes by after playing his flute in a rehearsal of Handel's *Messiah*. After behaving obnoxiously, he takes out his instrument and plays a solo from Gluck's *Orpheus*. When afterward the women confront him with his earlier behavior, he says, sincerely for the first time in the novel, "Life is so terrible. There is nothing to do with it but break it down into nonsense." This is clearly how Papa feels, also—West's sense is that somehow the men they know are less resilient and more despairing than the women.

Papa finally leaves the family. His motive is not quite clear, but the catalyst is a pamphlet that he had been writing for a fee about the future (this is set in about 1906). Papa is not sanguine, and the picture he paints is both horrifying and unbelievable to the man who has commissioned the pamphlet. Papa is a man whose despair is both personal and political, and when Mamma discusses his departure with the children, she tries to get them to understand how his complexity, her complexity, the complexity of family life, and the complexity of the rapidly changing world around them fit together. In retrospect, of course, from the point of view of 1956, Papa is not wrong in his predictions, but West makes her point tactfully and then leaves it alone. It is a mark of her skill as a novelist and the richness with which she paints her world that when she makes comments in her narrator's voice they flow in along with the rest and do not disturb the artful illusion of her narrative.

West is much interested in the nature of art, especially as represented by music, and one part of her plot has to do with Cordelia, the oldest sister, who does not play the piano and, according to the mother, Rose, and Mary, has no musical talent of any kind. She takes up the violin and then is befriended by a woman teacher of a certain age who also plays the violin and thinks Cordelia has talent. The give and take between Cordelia and Miss Beevor, as seen through the eyes of a judgmental (and talented) younger sister, is quite entertaining, and serves as an occasion for West to develop her argument about truth, talent, and the requirements of art. This thread of the novel is quite unusual and original as a way of laying out the protagonist's inner struggle to become the artist who has written the novel, and the climax of *The Fountain Overflows* proves to be both surprising and stimulating.

Of course, it is always difficult to end a memoir, because life goes on and the protagonist is still alive, so why stop now? West does so in a smart way, giving Mamma and Papa both their due, serving up a realistic but upbeat denouement, and working out the thematic material, too. It is quite an accomplishment, and all the greater for being written with such verve and smoothness that the novel was serialized in *Ladies' Home Journal* before publication.

The Fountain Overflows is a perfect example of a certain kind of woman's writing that is so smart it seems as though it must have been as easy to compose as it is to read, so smart that it doesn't seem important compared to more difficult and experimental novels. Lots of modernists of West's generation had so much trouble integrating theme and story that they let the story aspect (narrative, plot, the smooth buildup of incident to climax and denouement) break down, asserting that the realistic novel didn't have the capacity to communicate what had to be said. A novel such as West's shows that a flexible, subtle, and intelligent style can communicate almost anything if the novelist is willing to accord the reader respect. The breakdown of narrative happens when the author wishes to emphasize thematic points rather than integrate them and risk that the reader will remain unconvinced (or unaware) of the author's opinions. It is the didactic novelist who doesn't have patience for narrative structure. Modernism might be seen as an attempt to coerce the reader, or at least convince her, rather than let her make up her own mind. But West is so in control of the emotional dynamic of her narrative that no opinion she offers in her voice as Rose, the child, or as the mature narrator, or in the voice of Mamma ever goes unnoticed. The story *is* convincing because it is wise, graceful, and thoroughly thought through.

74 · Nancy Mitford · The Pursuit of Love, Love in a Cold Climate

(1945, 1949; REPR., NEW YORK: RANDOM HOUSE, VINTAGE, 2001)

Don't Tell Alfred

(1960; REPRINT, NEW YORK: CARROLL & GRAF, 1990), 698 PP.

While it's not necessary to read Nancy Mitford's three linked novels about the Radlett clan all at once, it is almost irresistible to do so, they are so humane, worldly, and hilarious. Mitford, of course, was the eldest daughter of the famous Mitford family, the subject of numerous biographies and memoirs (the most informative of which is sister Jessica's *Hons and Rebels*). From a purely theoretical point of view, reading Nancy's novels in conjunction with Jessica's memoir is enlightening as an example of how a novelist selects, changes, and enhances given material to make it appealing and to make it fit a given form. Nancy Mitford was a great comic novelist, and her novels necessarily ignore some of the darker threads of the Mitford story, and of midcentury history, in which she and all the rest of them were deeply involved. The astute reader becomes aware of shadows and echoes that give the novels depth, even though the novelist does not linger over them but fits them into the comic form and tone of her work.

The Pursuit of Love takes place in the 1930s and concerns the ultimately successful quest of Linda Radlett, the family beauty and the daughter of extremely eccentric parents, to find a satisfying romantic attachment. She is two generations younger than Isabel Archer or Lily Bart and fully ready to dispose of herself. And she does what Isabel and Lily do: she makes a mistake the first time. But two generations after Isabel and Lily, she is able to happily rectify her mistake by running off with another man, who also proves unsatisfactory, and then to rectify it again.

Love in a Cold Climate is a "paraquel" to the first novel. Fanny, the narrator of *The Pursuit of Love,* returns to narrate another story of the thirties, this one about neighbors of the Radletts, Lord and Lady Montdore and their daughter, who are the last manifestation of a supremely ancient and wealthy aristocratic family. Once again the story turns on the daughter's search for love, and once again her first try is unsuccessful, but Mitford adds several wonderfully clever twists to the plot—the real protagonist is not the daughter but her imposing, selfish, middle-aged mother, who also seeks and finds love.

By the time of *Don't Tell Alfred* it is the late 1950s, and Fanny and Alfred are parents and foster parents to the children who were born as a result of the unions in the first novel. Those children are now falling in love and beginning their own adult lives, but Fanny's (and the author's) attention has shifted slightly to Fanny's mishaps and adventures as the wife of the British ambassador to France; the children's pairings are secondary.

Of the three novels, *Love in a Cold Climate* is the most playful and makes the most unconventional use of the comic form. It is delightful from beginning to end, perfectly sustained in tone and style, always recognizing disappointment and even tragedy from a distance, but ever willing and able to make the most of whatever circumstances present themselves. The key is expressed by the Radlett "chorus," Jassy and Victoria. At one point they come into Fanny's house after Lady Montdore has left. Whereas she had complained offensively about the tea, they exclaim, "Not digestives! Vict—look! Digestives! Isn't Fanny wonderful? You can always count on something heavenly—weeks since I've tasted digestives, my favorite food, too!" (p. 397).

The central figures in the "love plot," Lady Montdore's only daughter, Polly, and Boy Dougdale, rumored to be a former admirer of Lady Montdore herself, could be the couple in a realistic novel, a tragedy, or a melodrama, since he has a habit of abusing little girls (established at the beginning), and their marriage (which Polly insists on) is a huge disappointment to everyone in the family and a scandal in the neighborhood. Likewise, the fact that upon the death of Lord Montdore the estate is to pass into the hands of a Canadian cousin who turns out to be homosexual could also function much differently in a different sort of novel, but Mitford works all of these connections exuberantly into the mix. In fact, the cousin turns out to be a fabulous deus ex machina who comes from his own rather compromised circumstances in France and exerts his charms and his skills to sort everyone out and make everyone happy.

The bracing answer, for Mitford, to the dilemmas of passion, selfishness, and loneliness is generous worldliness, especially of the French sort. She doesn't hesitate to laugh at the contrasting foibles of the French and the English (at one point Lady Montdore hosts a French noblewoman for dinner, and is for the first time in her life brought to speechlessness by the marquise's unceasing and detailed questions about the estate's every practical and financial arrangement), but in the end the French have the answers—good clothes, good food, settled methods of dealing with love and passion, and in general a reasonable approach to life that protects from the emotional ups and downs that bedevil the English characters. At the same time, the English characters have a liveliness and energy that literally populates Fanny's world. Mitford would have been growing up with her parents on the family estate when Ford Madox Ford was writing *The Good Soldier,* but there is quite an opposite feel in her novels—the English aristocracy is not stupid and attenuated and on its last legs, good riddance, it is passionately making its way into the modern world, full of ideas, political disagreements, and jokes.

The best thing about Nancy Mitford is that she's funny. The humor, like much of the humor of the English novel in general, grows out of appreciation of human idiosyncrasy. Lady Montdore and Cedric, the Canadian, in particular, are beautifully observed. Powerful and rich, Lady Montdore is also opinionated and selfish, but Mitford insightfully depicts the unhappiness that gives her narcissism poignancy. Cedric's former life in Paris is very lightly sketched in, but the details indicate that Cedric, too, has been saved by those he is saving, and knows it. The second best thing about Nancy Mitford is that she has been everywhere that the reader may not have been, and has kept her eyes open and her wits about her. Though her canvas is personal, like Jane Austen's, she is not at all blind to either political events or social movements; she just happens to filter her insights through characters that preexist them. For a politically astute and experienced midcentury novelist, that is an unusual choice. It may have made her seem frivolous at the time, but it makes her seem perspicacious now. Ideology changes, she might have said, but gossip lasts forever.

Research on the Web indicates that while the Mitford family is of continuing popular interest, Nancy's virtues as a novelist are somewhat overlooked. It should be the other way around. She is a wonderful novelist who added a distinct vision to the tradition of the English comic novel. There is much more to her work, technically and substantively, than meets the eye, but only if the reader can stop wallowing in pleasure long enough to notice it. Reading Nancy Mitford makes me believe that writing comic novels is one of the most purely humanitarian endeavors civilization has ever come up with.

75 · Harper Lee · To Kill a Mockingbird

(1960; REPR., NEW YORK: WARNER, 1982), 281 PP.

To Kill a Mockingbird is perhaps the *Uncle Tom's Cabin* of the twentieth century (and no doubt it is no coincidence that the man Atticus Finch defends from a charge of rape is named "Tom"). The instant and enduring popularity of *To Kill a Mockingbird* as a Pulitzer Prize–winning novel and, very shortly thereafter, an Academy Award–winning film (for adapted screen play) shows that liberal ideas about the sources, problems, and solutions to American racism have wide appeal and that Americans would like the challenge of racism over-come, but only as an extension of other liberal values of fairness and individualism. *To Kill a Mockingbird* is now frequently taught in high schools in the United States. It is in many ways a perfect high school text—the plot is understandable, the characters are appealing, the light tone masks a serious purpose, and the motivations of the children, Scout and Jem, are considered typical (at least by many adults) of real American children (children born before the era of pop culture at least). In addition, the lessons of the novel are clear and can hardly be contradicted in a moral society—every man deserves a fair trial, no matter what his skin color, and educated people, people with sense and honor, prefer the rule of law to the rule of prejudice and revenge.

Most Americans know the plot—Scout and Jem are growing up in Alabama in the 1930s. Their childhood is made up of the traditional amusements—staying out of trouble as much as possible, running around the neighborhood, tormenting the neighbors, engaging in make-believe and other imaginative games. They have a friend, Dill, who visits in the summer. The widowed father, Atticus, is assigned by a local judge to defend a black man who lives in the town against a charge of rape pressed by a girl and her father who are the town dere-licts—dirty, drunken, and violent. Although Atticus defends Tom elo-quently and everyone in the court knows that he has proved that Tom cannot have committed the rape, Tom is convicted anyway and sent away to prison, where in spite of the hope for a successful appeal, he tries to escape and is shot. The derelict father, humiliated by Atticus, attempts revenge and is killed in the act.

One of the chief appeals of the novel is Scout's voice. Only six but literal-minded, outspoken, and tomboyish, Scout offers a rough, inno-cent perspective on the pretensions and compromises of the adults around her. She is quick to judge and hot-tempered. The author relies for irony throughout the novel on the disparity between what the reader knows is happening and what Scout thinks is happening. Both Scout and her brother, Jem, are educated by the events of the years cov-ered by the narrative (three or four), but they are educated in different ways because their temperaments are distinct. Scout learns to control her emotions and understand, at least to some degree, that adult soci-ety is complex and nuanced. Jem learns what bravery is—not taking dares as much as taking responsibility. There is some sense early in the novel that Jem is disappointed in Atticus's manliness, but by the end he has learned to respect him.

The lessons Atticus teaches all have to do with respect—he considers even the Ewells, father and daughter, worthy of courtesy. When provoked by interfering relatives or childish misbehavior, he chooses to exhibit respect rather than to correct or offend. Is he a rounded, vivid character? At this point it is hard to know, because it is impossible to imagine him outside of his portrayal by Gregory Peck in the film of the novel.

There is no sense as the novel progresses that structural change is possible in the world Scout lives in. Maycomb County is small—there have apparently been no immigrants since the first settlers took their land and their places in society. Just as the Ewells have always been bums, the Finches have always been eccentrics. Just as the whites inhabit the main part of town and occupy all the important economic and social positions, the blacks live south of town and keep to themselves. The death of Tom and the death of Ewell cancel each other out, and Scout observes that talk of the trial quickly subsides. She accepts, in some sense, that she and Jem may have been the only people in town to have learned something from the event—when the sheriff insists on keeping the circumstances surrounding the death of Ewell quiet, he, like everyone else, is accepting that trying to change the town is more trouble than it is worth.

When we look back to *To Kill a Mockingbird* through the lens of the intervening years, we can see why the civil rights movement in the United States had to be instigated and led by black people themselves—even the most well-meaning white people (Atticus Finch is the model) didn't have the understanding and the will to break up the status quo and reimagine American life as socially, culturally, and politically as well as legally egalitarian. The virtue that Atticus represents—respect, and especially respect for privacy and eccentricity—is a virtue that makes change more difficult because it fails to question social forms that, Lee shows, are a significant part of racism. Atticus and the children, for example, make no headway at all against racist gossip. The best they can do—and Scout is always admonished to do this—is not to pay any attention. Maintaining the surface appearance of propriety is too important for her to declare her allegiances.

Thus *To Kill a Mockingbird* is doubly a social document—it documents small-town southern life and attitudes in the 1930s (rigid and antediluvian) but also liberal attitudes in the 1950s (stuck in legalism and individualism, unable to actually effect change). At the same time, it is an essential American text because it is so readable and straightforward. Teachers enthusiastically teach it along with novels written by black writers about similar subjects, and it serves as a safe introduction to more challenging material.

It is interesting to speculate what Harper Lee might have written if she had kept writing novels, but she has been exceptionally reclusive. When asked why she didn't write another novel, she replied that the Pulitzer and the Hollywood success spoiled her. Perhaps they did. But perhaps she simply had only one story to tell, and her telling of it carried her to the limits of mainstream white liberal possibilities for imagining the great American subject—relations between black and white. After *To Kill a Mockingbird,* the right to tell the story went to black writers, where it still resides at the start of the third millennium.

76 · Jetta Carleton · The Moonflower Vine
(NEW YORK: SIMON & SCHUSTER, 1962), 318 PP.

This novel may be the most obscure contemporary novel on our list, but those who have read it, if the customer reviews at Earth's Biggest Bookstore are any guide, are very loyal to it. Jetta Carleton wrote only this novel, which appears to be autobiographical, at least in part, but Carleton's style is so dense and precise and her method of imagining the inner lives of each character so daring that she seems to have been unconstrained by fears either of remembering things wrongly or of offending her relatives. Her subject is the romantic passions of five members of the Soames family—Matthew and Callie, the husband and wife, and Jessica, Leonie, and Mathy, the older three of the four daughters (Mary Jo, the youngest, is understood to be the narrator). These adventures are narrated out of sequence—the first to be told is how Jessica falls in love at eighteen with the hired hand and runs off with him to his family in the Ozarks, where she subsequently makes her home even after her husband dies of what appears to be tuberculosis. The novel then flashes back to the youth of the patriarch, Matthew, who is the somewhat remote but controlling and dominant presence in the family. Far from being the cold and sometimes frightening figure he appears to be to the women, he is inordinately susceptible to female charms, and over his years of employment as a teacher and superintendent of schools in his small Missouri town, he succumbs to the

attractions of numerous young girls, some of whom he flirts with and
even dallies with in spite of conscientious resolves not to. Carleton's
attitude toward Matthew's peccadilloes is forgiving—in the context of
twenty-first-century strictures on sexual harassment, maybe surprisingly forgiving; the girls are portrayed as not actually seductive, but in
some sense responsive, using Matthew for their own romantic designs
as much as he uses them. The result of one of these flirtations is Callie's
assertion, late one night in the woods, of her marital rights, and the
conception of Mathy, the third daughter, whom Matthew is a little
afraid of, since she represents to him the wages of sin (he had been
thinking of the girl he was infatuated with while making love to Callie). The next section is about Mathy, who grows up wayward, independent, and self-willed, and ends up running off with an attractive
young man, Ed, whom Matthew knows from his school and doesn't
like. The reader can see that Ed and Mathy are certain to come to a bad
end—the question is what the family will make of it. After Mathy dies,
Matthew uses the adoption of Mathy's son, Peter, who is much like his
mother, as a way to make more of his second chance with her than he
had of the first. Callie's reaction is more mysterious—to the girls she
seems to go crazy with mourning but they decide that that is a mother's
right, and anyway, she eventually comes out of it. After the other two
girls run off, Leonie stays home with her parents, subjecting them to
her various virtues until she realizes that they would prefer that she
left them alone. She then goes to Kansas City, intending to throw off
all restraint and have some fun. She ends up connecting with Ed himself, and eventually marrying him.

Carleton mostly avoids the perils of this material, which, baldly
summarized, sounds scandalous and best-sellerish, a *Peyton Place* of
the Midwest, by depicting the southern Missouri landscape of the family farm in exceptional detail. The farm is small but much beloved, full
of fields and grasses, trees and shrubs, rocks and flowers that present a
seasonal drama to the members of the family. All admire and appreciate their natural surroundings, sometimes in spite of themselves. Since
most of the novel takes place in the summer, when the family is settled
on the farm, the characters frequently suffer from the heat, which has
the effect of making the scenery palpable and especially sensual.

The five characters are a convincing family in several ways. They
resemble one another but are ill-assorted, as members of families often
are. Their contrasts to one another are exaggerated by proximity.
Matthew loves Callie and she is essential to his sense of his identity and

self-confidence, but her lack of interest in intellectual things (she can't read, though she pretends sometimes she can) means that he can't share things with her that are important and satisfying to him. Callie is sexy but submissive, and hardly ever dares to challenge Matthew, or even ask anything of him. She recognizes, though, that he had been the best bet of all the young men she might have chosen, and in the end he is a good husband even though he hasn't shown her the tenderness she might have liked. Carleton excels at depicting the personalities of the girls, who often don't understand one another at all, and would never, they think, make the choices that the others have made, or even have similar relationships to their parents. And yet there is familial loyalty and attachment, mostly arising out of a shared sense of the enjoyment of the farm and each other.

To my mind, this is a novel characteristic of its time, the 1950s, because it completely avoids all political themes. To read it you would never know that black people existed in southern Missouri, that the area was still a hotbed of post–Civil War resentments, that the Cold War was raging, and that World War II had taken place. The novel exists in a timeless world of seasons and of girls coming of age, love their greatest concern, with earning a living teaching school or giving music lessons a distant second. The Soames family thinks only of religion, love, nature, and sometimes music. They are American innocents in spite of their lustiness, quite untainted by the compromises of American history. The novel is neither liberal nor conservative— more, perhaps, tribal, in the sense that while the characters do make authentic connections, these connections are only within their own family rather than with anyone outside (except for Jessica, who moves away). In addition, the world is repeatedly redeemed, not by human action but by natural renewal, as symbolized by the nightly flowering of the moonflower vine (a relative of the morning glory). In the end, none of the characters comes to an understanding of Christianity or Christian precepts—doctrines of fundamentalist Protestant religion don't seem to fit what they have learned—nor do they embrace their sexuality (though they seem to learn that they can't get rid of it), but they do come to an understanding of the nature and purpose of forgiveness, and each character achieves a feeling that happiness, even fleeting happiness, is to be recognized and cherished.

Several American novels on our list—*The House of the Seven Gables, The Awakening, To Kill a Mockingbird,* and *The Moonflower Vine*— gain considerable dramatic tension from secrets that the characters are

required to keep to maintain respectability in the towns where they
live. The conflict between who a character feels herself or himself to be
and what is acceptable to friends and colleagues is as constant a theme
in American novels as, say, a character's relationship to the state is in
German novels. In exploring the romantic secrets of each member of a
single family, Carleton offers something of a catalog of ideas on the
subject of secret desires—*The Moonflower Vine* could have been a scandalous novel. But by presenting each character's desire as a moral
dilemma for that character, and especially by consistently depicting the
bonds of love that eventually hold the family together, she succeeds in
arousing both empathy and sympathy in the reader. At the same time
that she portrays the "normality" of her family, she demonstrates that
"normality" is always more complex than it appears on the surface.

77 · Yukio Mishima · The Sailor Who Fell from Grace with the Sea

TRANS. JOHN NATHAN

(1965; REPR., NEW YORK: RANDOM HOUSE, VINTAGE, 1994), 181 PP.

Mishima is a good example of a novelist whose novels are more ambiguous and nuanced than his press releases. Philosophically, Mishima
was very conservative in a specifically Japanese way—he adhered to
traditional samurai ideals of warrior-based masculinity and felt that
the modernization and Westernization of Japan following the Second
World War was a catastrophe. He committed ritual suicide in 1970, at
age forty, after attempting to rouse the Japanese army with a small
paramilitary band called The Shield Society, which he had founded.

Mishima was almost unbelievably prolific. Between his years at the
university and his death, he published 150 novels, plays, and short stories, many of which were made into movies. *The Sailor Who Fell from
Grace with the Sea* was made into a movie set in England six years after
Mishima's death.

The novel is a tale with realistic trappings and, in our era of single
parents, a familiarity that it did not have upon first publication.
Noboru, thirteen, lives with his mother, Fusako, a widow who owns
and manages a luxury shop specializing in Western clothing and gifts.
Through Noboru's fascination with ships (they live in the port city of

Yokohama), they meet Ryuji, a second mate on a large cargo ship, who falls for Fusako. Unbeknownst to the adults, Noboru has discovered a peephole between his room and his mother's room, which he is making frequent use of, and he is also involved with a group of boys who spend their time cultivating perfect dispassion—no attachments, no pity, etc. The unnamed head of the group uses humiliation, arrogance, logic, and the grievances the boys feel against their parents to establish power over the others and "train" them. Early in the book they eviscerate a kitten.

Noboru is ambivalent about Ryuji—he is attracted to the romance of being a sailor and enjoys Ryuji's stories of his adventures, but he has an idea of pure heartless manliness that he feels Ryuji should adhere to; when Ryuji is kind or shows any sense of connection to either Noboru himself or Fusako, the boy is offended. The other boys, especially the Chief, nurture Noboru's feelings and encourage him to believe that Ryuji is transgressing some objective ideal of masculine purity. In the meantime, when he looks through the peephole, Noboru's own view of his world becomes estranged and fetishized. He watches his mother dress and undress, he watches the adults make love, he sometimes just watches the empty room, but each time he sees a dramatically artful scene that seems to him to have more meaning than what he sees without the peephole.

As the romance between the adults progresses, the boys decide to exert their power before they turn fourteen (the Chief tells them there are no consequences if they commit violent acts before turning fourteen), so they lure Ryuji to a secluded spot and drug him. The implication at the end of the novel is that they eviscerate him as they had the kitten.

Apart from plot suspense, the interest of the novel arises from the fact that Ryuji holds pretty much the same ideas that the boys do, he just happens to be twenty years older. An austere, solitary man, he had gone to sea in the first place because he sensed that he was destined for some perfect and unique transcendent moment that would give his life special meaning. But even though he has seen much of the world, been in danger, and lived his life according to his own rules, life on the ocean has turned out to be as mundane as life on land (for which he has habitual contempt). His relationship with Fusako appears at first to offer the sort of gratification he is looking for, too—he is very drawn to her—but when he gives up sailing and begins to prepare for married life and life in the shop, his ideals are disappointed. His murder

at the hands of the boys may not be grand, but at least it is unique
and strange. It preserves him from what he might discover to be a
worse fate.

Mishima builds his novel by juxtaposing the perceptions of each of
the three main characters and showing that none of them, but especially Ryuji, can communicate what he or she really feels. When
Fusako comes to love Ryuji, she loves not what he means to say, but
what he manages to say, which, according to the narrator, is always a
misrepresentation of his true feelings, though not exactly a lie.
Noboru's feelings, too, are more complex and various than the adults
can understand, partly because he is secretive, partly because he is
under the influence of the Chief, and partly because he doesn't know
himself what he is feeling and thinking. There is the strong implication that without the Chief, stepfamily life would have proceeded in
the standard manner—fine enough on the surface, dissatisfaction and
resentment below the surface.

Even though *The Sailor Who Fell from Grace with the Sea* fits well
enough into the Western tradition of "wild child" novels such as *Lord
of the Flies,* which was published at about the same time, it's important
to remember that Mishima was a Japanese writer, and a conservative
one at that, whose ideas were inspired by non-Western traditions of
Zen Buddhism and warrior discipline. Structurally and stylistically he
sets the novel up to explore questions of transience, aesthetic opposition, purity, and the workings of impersonal Fate. In some sense it
doesn't matter what the boys' motives are, or whether they are "evil"—
their actions form part of a pattern. The origins of the pattern are
within the other characters as well as within the boys. The reader is encouraged to focus on the pattern rather than on moral questions (perhaps this is why the tale ends before the consequences begin). All of the
characters are more strongly motivated by "rightness" in an aesthetic
sense than they are by "rightness" in a moral sense. Ryuji, for example,
interprets his passion for Fusako as the perfect fleeting love for the
perfect-looking woman (she is very slight and beautiful) he has been
waiting for. As he relates to Noboru, he is self-consciously attempting
to follow a picture he has in his mind of how fathers act and people on
land relate to one another. Fusako is an arranger, too—when she sees
Ryuji off a few days after they meet, she wears a particular type of
kimono so he will remember a particular view of her as his ship
departs. The Chief's ideals are especially ruthless, but they are no different in their sources than the ideals of the others—purity is all.

But the novel is a tale, not a polemic. The Chief is hardly a re-spectable spokesman for nihilism—it is clear that he is being badly raised by his own parents, who are wealthy, shallow, and abusive. There is no sense that Ryuji's youthful view of his unique destiny was warranted by unique abilities—he is just a guy. Whatever Mishima's political views, he perfectly understands the resistance of the novel as a form to use as bald propaganda, and he opts instead for evocative, ambiguous subtlety, which is what gives this novel its staying power.

78 · Jean Rhys · Wide Sargasso Sea

(NEW YORK: W. W. NORTON, 1966), 190 PP.

In *Jane Eyre,* Charlotte Brontë's version of *Beauty and the Beast,* the beast turns out not to be the man, Mr. Rochester, but his first wife, Bertha Mason, the Creole madwoman he had been tricked into marry-ing for the sake of money as a young man. Ugly (her eyes are described as "red balls"), brutish, dangerous, and sexually dissolute, she is reviled by Jane as well as by Rochester, and everyone, including the reader, is expected to breathe a sigh of relief when she dies, because she doesn't deserve to live and to come between the soulmates Jane and Rochester. However it was that she struck the reader of 1847, though, she strikes the modern reader as a failed depiction—our understanding of mental illness and its care has changed so completely that the way in which Bertha is treated seems cruel and her response to it natural—she is more sinned against than sinning. Added to that, a modern under-standing of the cruelties of European colonialism makes Bertha an interesting figure in her own right, rather than just a figure in the lives of Jane and Rochester.

Jean Rhys, who was born in Dominica, in the West Indies, exca-vated Bertha, renamed her, and gave her her own novel. In the pro-cess, she gives *Jane Eyre* a political and historical context that only enriches the ambiguities of that novel and of all English and European fiction. Bertha Rochester begins life as Antoinette Cosway (a much more appealing name), a Creole girl whose father has died and whose beautiful mother cannot handle either the plantation she owns or the servants who people it. She is saved by an English planter named Mason, who takes over a plantation nearby. He is well-meaning but

completely misunderstands the colonial cultural mix, according to Antoinette and her mother, who live in considerable fear. As a result of
a slave revolt, Antoinette's mysteriously afflicted brother is severely
burned and her mother goes out of her mind. Antoinette herself goes
to school, where she is happy for a while. Rochester enters the picture
as a young man. His marriage with Antoinette and his removal to the
plantation take place while he is ill and disoriented, and though he is at
first well disposed toward her, he soon backs away as a result of the
insinuations of a disgruntled local man, whose motives are suspect.
Rochester then sleeps with one of the house servants, thereby offending and rejecting Antoinette. She grows increasingly jealous, fearful,
and unstable, until at last he forces her to leave Jamaica and move to
England, where her incarceration exacerbates her mental instability.
The novel ends just as she is leaving her attic to set fire to the house.

A novel is a piece of logic, and Rhys's logical analysis of how Antoinette Cosway is transformed into Bertha Rochester is utterly convincing. The premises are cultural instability, pervasive mistrust, and
childhood trauma. The logical steps are progressive misunderstanding
and isolation, which eventually evolve into outright cruelty. The conclusion is Bertha's inner nightmare, which results in an objective
inferno.

Since the novel thrives on subjectivity, any consciousness is sufficiently interesting to be made into one. *Wide Sargasso Sea* uses Brontë's
own insight against her—she had asserted that even the inner life of a
poor, plain, and overlooked governess could be compelling, but made a
repulsive object of a madwoman. Rhys shows that the line between
sanity and madness can't be drawn either, and that Bertha has a back
story as worthy of sympathy as Jane's. What Rhys seems to be saying is
that *every* female consciousness presents a problem that marriage as a
property arrangement cannot solve and can only complicate.

79 · John Gardner · Grendel

(NEW YORK: ALFRED A. KNOPF, 1971), 174 PP.

Five years after Jean Rhys rewrote *Jane Eyre* and three years after Tom
Stoppard rewrote *Hamlet* (in *Rosencrantz and Guildenstern Are Dead*),
John Gardner rewrote *Beowulf*. In general, I like the idea of recasting

earlier works, but every recasting is an interpretation and therefore thematically based, and the resulting works are as much or more the products of their own times as the works that inspire them. Those of us who risk the extra measure of ephemerality that comes from rooting a novel overtly in another work take comfort in a couple of things. One is that reworking old material is a tradition as old as literature. Certainly *Beowulf* was the written culmination of an oral tradition that was at least several centuries old in Anglo-Saxon and that was itself based on narrative patterns that go back to the earliest Indo-European epics. Beowulf's and Hrothgar's concerns have a dark, cold, northern flavor, but they are not terribly different from Arjuna's concerns in the *Bhagavad Gita* and Agamemnon's concerns in *The Iliad*—glory and heroism versus death and mass murder. Likewise, *Hamlet* and *King Lear* (the source of my novel *A Thousand Acres*) are Elizabethan reworkings of earlier stories. Old stories have more than staying power; they force the reader and the writer to contemplate the most basic human concerns once again—the nature of love, death, art, and existence, of family, fear, injury, and hope. They also give the author a rare and precious treat, the chance to follow an earlier mind step by step into a knotty artistic dilemma, to test with each word and idea what has changed and what has remained the same about the story. In addition, every work of literature exhausts the inventiveness of its author and could use another rewrite. A work that evokes in a reader enough fascination so he or she will put in the hours to try to solve those last little problems of logic, continuity, or thematic contradiction is a work that speaks especially clearly out of the past.

John Gardner was a motorcyle-riding medievalist in a black leather jacket, a true representative of his era. He was daring, he was dedicated to writing and teaching writing, and he believed in the tour de force, a novel so glittering and unusual that it would take the literary world by storm, and if it more or less bypassed the larger world of readers, that would be okay, too. He wrote eleven books before his death in 1982 at age forty-nine. *Grendel* was the one that made his reputation. *Grendel* is the memoir or meditation of Beowulf's monster enemy, who turns out, like Jean Rhys's rendition of the monstrous Mrs. Rochester, to have a logical, and even an appealing, point of view. Like Bertha, Grendel is a complete outsider, marked by isolation and loneliness and doomed to act out the fascination he feels for those who fear and reject him. He lives in a sordid cave with his mother, who has devolved in old age into a grumbling, suffocating, lumpish beast unable to offer Grendel, who is quite garrulous and inquisitive by contrast, any companionship. Grendel suspects that he is related in some way to humans, because he understands their speech, though they only intermittently understand his. His relationship to them is complex. He has a natural desire to eat them, which he often does, but he is moved by their poetry and by the beauty of the queen to a frustrated, lovelike state. Mostly, since they can't hurt him but are always boastful and fearful simultaneously, he feels contempt for them. He seeks wisdom from those he can talk to—the dragon in particular—but he is the only one of his kind, and no general theory applies to him. He is doomed to live out his avid alienation until the arrival in a longship of Beowulf and the Geats, a tribe of humans that seems, even to Grendel, to possess actual power.

Grendel, of course, is not Beowulf's only victim, and because he dies, the novel cannot follow the poem to the end, but anyone familiar with the poem can infer what happens after Beowulf, by means of a trick as well as his superhuman strength, manages to destroy the monster.

Gardner's novel has the merit of extreme cleverness, which is the hallmark of a tour de force—with one simple idea it presents the reader with a whole new way of looking at something she thought she already knew all about. In *Beowulf* Grendel is all physical—a huge, hairy, dark beast who kills and eats Hrothgar's thanes in a senseless and erratic manner. In *Grendel* the monster is all talk—he says of himself, "Talking, talking. Spinning a web of words, pale walls of dreams, between myself and all I see." He kills and eats the thanes, but that is mostly because they are such fools. Otherwise he is their witness. He watches their settlements, their tribal battles and wars, their attempts to gain themselves peace by waging war, and he can't understand how their minds work—their actions are too illogical and futile and their lives are too short. What they consider to be a long time is only a brief span in his much longer and more tedious existence. In addition, he has the wisdom of the dragon to go on, and the dragon is for all intents and purposes eternal—he can see the future and the past. To him, sitting on his hoard of jewels, all relationships are meaningless, and Grendel's longing for some sort of understanding or connection is as silly as the same sort of longings in the humans.

Since there is no point in writing a tour de force without making a case for something, Gardner makes a case for the necessity of the dark side. Grendel comes to justify his existence, which he otherwise cannot understand, as the required antagonist who drives the humans to a height of bravery and philosophy they would not otherwise reach without his presence. In this he subtly shifts the balance of literature, especially plotted literature, away from the protagonist and toward the antagonist—it's all too easy to say that without Claudius, for example, Hamlet would have lived a decent and peaceful life—Grendel would say that without Claudius, Hamlet would be a nobody. But Grendel is not only interesting for the case he makes, he is also entertaining because, though the humans speak translated Anglo-Saxon, Grendel speaks like we do (as does the dragon, though he speaks more like a philosophy professor than an English professor). This is a technique that serves Gardner well, because it simultaneously diminishes the epic size of the humans, adds wit, makes the story a novel, and brings the novel into the modern era. The other good effect of this technique is that through his narration, as through a small lens, we can see medieval Denmark in the primitive period of the early Germanic tribes. Gardner does not paint these scenes grandly and in detail, as T. H. White paints his medieval world, but he evokes it, especially with descriptions of animals, such as mountain goats, that have since vanished from Europe. His dark ages are dark, indeed, but the reader has to wonder after reading this novel of foolish, vainglorious, aggressive human folly how much has changed.

But is *Grendel* profound as well as smart? The critical faculty, the faculty that takes such pleasure in analyzing literature that it wants to fix it, is sometimes impatient with the details and texture that give a novel staying power, and in the end the problem with *Grendel* is that it is long enough to explore its ideas but not dense enough to be a really good story. Gardner's idea itself limits his execution, because since Grendel must live in a solipsistic universe, his plot doesn't have much action. What he learns he must learn in the abstract because he is conceived to be without any other interests except his interest in those who can't interact with him. Gardner sticks close to the plot of *Beowulf,* and we admire his erudition and imagination in doing so, but his fidelity to his source prevents him from really fleshing out a world of his own.

80 · Alice Munro · Lives of Girls and Women

(NEW YORK: PENGUIN, 1971), 278 PP.

Munro has a special genius for understanding the profound implications of incidents that most people, even most writers, notice and forget, or perhaps turn into anecdotes. She is truly, in Henry James's phrase, someone "upon whom nothing is lost." The short-story form has showcased her talents because she has been able to transform it. Avoiding the tricks and surprises of earlier exponents, and writing with an unprecedented complexity of insight and precision of style, she has given her stories the weight of novels.

But Munro did write one novel, *Lives of Girls and Women.* It is both a fine novel and a wonderful introduction to Munro's subsequent work. Like many first novels, *Lives of Girls and Women* is semiautobiographical—it takes place in rural Ontario; the protagonist is Del, who seems to be about the same age as the author would have been in the 1940s; and it is told in the first person. But Munro's semiautobiographical first novel already fully displays her characteristic gifts, in particular her ability to judiciously consider every aspect of a situation or a scene, to subtly highlight the details that make her argument, and to suggest more than she states.

Del's family is unorthodox, which Del understands from the beginning of the novel (which opens when Del is about ten). For one thing, her father is trying to earn a living raising silver foxes for fur coats, so they live in the country, on a road where her mother feels out of place and bored, and where Del, too, is mildly alienated. Already, at ten, Del is an observant and inquisitive child. She does what she is told, and passes no judgments upon the adults and their choices, but her inner life, both imaginative and moral, is full and convincing. Del's nuclear family is a small cell of both a larger community—the town where Del and her mother eventually move—and the extended family that Del visits and observes on her father's side. Both town and countryside are depressed—what had not been a very promising agricultural region to begin with has declined because of the Depression and has not revived because of the war. When Del's mother takes up selling encyclopedias to earn more money, Del goes along. The farms and families she visits are eccentric in the way that subspecies become eccentric when they lose contact with the rest of their fellows—they pursue old habits and make the best of things and accept that life is the way it is and there is no escape. As Del gets older and her horizons extend beyond her family, she makes a little tour of her region and samples what it has to offer.

Her maiden aunts and her history-buff uncle give way to ladies of the town that her mother tries to befriend, then her uncle and his American wife. After that, she begins going to church, not the family church, the one they know, but a smaller, poorer, and more ritual-filled Episcopal church on the other side of town. After that, her circle widens to include boys and other, more conventional girls. With each expansion, though, Munro never fails to keep track of the characters and scenes she has previously introduced. The maiden aunts not only grow older and more feeble, they also change in some ways but stay the same in other ways. Her mother tries one thing after another to lift the boredom of life in Wawanash County; nothing works, and she, too, subtly grows older and less hopeful. The parents' marriage changes while at the same time Del comes to understand more about it. As she grows up, so does her brother. As she evolves to be more like her mother, so Owen evolves to be more like her father, who is also changing. The delicacy with which Munro portrays these characters is smoothly kaleidoscopic—one manifestation shades into another as Del herself matures and solidifies.

All of Munro's themes are subtle; the reader is hardly aware that she deploys them. A second time through the novel, though, shows her purpose. She is writing a bildungsroman, a story of how the writer became herself. It begins immediately: when Del can hardly read, she notices and is fascinated by tabloid newspapers that collect in the shack of the tenant:

I read faster and faster, all I could hold, then reeled into the sun, onto the path that led to our place, across the fields. I was bloated and giddy with revelations of evil, or its versatility and grand invention and horrific playfulness. But the nearer I got to our house, the more this vision faded. Why was it that the plain back wall of home, the pale, chipped brick, the cement platform outside the kitchen door, washtubs hanging on nails, the pump, the lilac bush with brown-spotted leaves, should make it seem so doubtful that a woman would really send her husband's torso, wrapped in Christmas paper, by mail to his girlfriend in South Carolina? [p. 6]

This juxtaposition between the dramatic and the mundane, which sheds light on both, will be the essence of Munro's vision from then on. Equally, she writes as soon as she knows how. She is employed by the tenant to answer an ad in the newspaper seeking a position for a "Lady with one child." Del, only in fourth grade, isn't content to serve as amanuensis—she has stylistic objections to his dictation: "'You start with *Dear* and then the person's name,' I said, 'unless it's a business letter and then you start with *Dear Sir* or *Dear Madam* if it's a lady. Is it a business letter?'" (p. 13).

Each subsequent chapter offers her other models for how to think of writing—her uncle's life work, much cherished by her aunts, is a local history in which every small incident gets equal, even, thorough treatment:

> "Nearly a thousand pages."
> "More pages than *Gone with the Wind*."
> "He typed it so beautifully, no mistakes." [p. 67]

At school, Del encounters art in the form of the yearly operetta, which the third-grade teacher, Miss Farris, and the organist from the church, Mr. Boyce, seem to mold the children into by sheer force of showbiz will. Del is alert to how children who had seemed to have no special qualities at all somehow blossom during the rehearsals and performances of *The Pied Piper*. When Miss Farris subsequently drowns (accident? suicide?), Del takes it in—it conforms to her sense of how the dramatic and the mundane mesh, and also reaffirms her sense that many things occur beneath the rather drab surface of the town that the adults won't, or don't know how to, talk about.

As Del gets older, her rather conveniently chosen and not very congenial best friend, Naomi, begins experimenting with clothes, makeup, men, and sex. Naomi seems sure of herself; Del is less so, on the surface, but more truly inquisitive, as she always has been, underneath. Naomi wants to find for herself what amounts to a good position in life, and she marshals all of her resources to do so. Del, whose position in life has always been anomalous, cares only about novel experiences—what they feel like and what they mean. Naomi wants to catch a husband. Del wants to feel passion, and she succeeds with the mysterious Jerry, whom she meets at a revival meeting and instantly recognizes in some visceral, sexual way. Jerry, far from Del's educational or social equal, works in the local lumberyard. Del can't get enough of him, and they engage in a frenzied relationship that distracts her from the university exams she has been preparing for all her life. But Munro is careful not to account for Del's choice in any clichéd, Freudian way. Jerry speaks to her, he changes the course of her life; he is, though she doesn't quite realize it, the pivot between conventional success, as represented by examinations, university, professional life, and the alternative Del achieves, which is artistic vision. It is through Jerry that the odd layers of her childhood and youth, the foxes and her parents' marriage and the bookishness and her aspirations to faith as well as passion, meld into a whole.

81 · Naguib Mahfouz · The Harafish

TRANS. CATHERINE COBHAM (GARDEN CITY, N.Y.: DOUBLEDAY, ANCHOR, 1977), 406 PP.

Naguib Mahfouz was born in Egypt in 1911, wrote dozens of books and novels, and won the Nobel Prize in 1988. He was the great twentieth-century chronicler of the Arab world, and his most famous work is *The Cairo Trilogy,* written in the realist tradition about a neighborhood, called an alley, in Cairo, and following the lives of the inhabitants as they encounter the modern world. *The Harafish* dispenses with realism and tells a cycle of tales about a single family, also in a particular alley, over the course of ten generations, or hundreds of years. Of particular interest to Mahfouz are only a few concepts as they work in the lives of each successive generation—virtue (defined as both personal propriety and the correct uses of power and wealth), ambition, love, and the self-consciousness that comes from inheriting power and influence.

The founder of the family is an abandoned infant, Ashur al-Nagi, discovered by a blind reciter of the Koran as he is making his way toward the mosque one evening. He takes the child home and raises him to be virtuous and strong, an able protector of the "harafish," or working poor of the alley he lives in. Ashur's great adventure and piece of luck is that he has a dream that tells him to leave the alley during a bout of the plague. When he returns, all the wealthy families have died, and he assumes both their wealth and their power, but he devotes himself to the benefit of the neighborhood. His descendants are well aware of his example as the generations pass, but they dishonor it more than they honor it—most often the most powerful and ambitious man of each generation is either seduced by love into some sort of unwise marriage or sexual adventure, or is seduced by wealth into selfishness and dissipation. In each generation the great temptation is to become the clan chief, but when each man realizes his ambition, he discovers that the chieftaincy is also a test of courage, fighting skill, and character. In one case, the ambition falls to a woman—Zahira—who decides to use her beauty to gain wealth and power rather than love. She marries and divorces several times and causes quite a scandal. Eventually she is beaten to death by one of her betrayed husbands, and the sight of her bloodied face then haunts her child, Galal, who becomes possessed by either nihilistic despair, or madness, or the Devil, depending on who is interpreting his behavior.

For the Western reader, *The Harafish* is appealingly alien. Mahfouz strips the narrative of the usual indicators of the passage of time—there is no sense of progress, or even of how daily life takes shape. The characters have jobs and ideas and plans, names and looks, but the details are left out, as if they are too common and unchanging to be worth describing. They pass between the bar and the café. They wander into the vicinity of the mosque, where they hear singing, but the door of the mosque never opens, and no one ever enters or emerges. The mosque shows no recognition of the people—even when they are starving, the mosque passes out no alms, and the people, no matter how virtuous or interested in the doings of the mosque, never participate in the joys of the mosque—God is present, but it is the job of the people to be attentive to Him, not His to be attentive to them.

The Harafish is a string of tales. Tales are often overt or covert parables, and if *The Harafish* eventually suggests causes and effects, they are not sociological but psychological, since the sociology of the alley never changes. The psychology of the characters is rooted in their temperaments and their social positions. Some protagonists are hot-blooded and pugnacious. Others are greedy, others selfish, others beneficent and self-effacing. The appearance of these characteristics is random to a certain degree—for example, the luck of a father's marriage choice may dictate whether the son is graceful and strong or self-indulgent and shortsighted. Or circumstances may intervene to cut off a promising career. There is a persistent sense of danger—in every generation, both men and women must be wary of crossing powerful enemies, or even relatives, who are full of hatred or resentment. The clan chief is the only person capable of giving the harafish protection, but he himself is always beset and insecure. By the last pages of the novel, the triumphs and defeats of all the characters, major and minor, come to seem futile (though Mahfouz is too skillful to make them repetitive). The long history of the al-Nagis doesn't add up to what they think it does—in fact, it doesn't add up at all. The return of Ashur in the tenth tale ends up being a respite rather than a climax.

It is possible to utterly enjoy the stately drama of the history of the al-Nagis without being at all drawn to the violent and dangerous world they live in. Betrayal is commonplace and can occur between the closest relatives. Enmity is expected from most associates outside the family if they haven't been bought off or made into allies. Women are as unpredictable as men, and even the most helpful and faithful wife is likely to be displaced by a younger one. Family relationships depend entirely upon the character and circumstances of the patriarch, and he can devolve into a hashish-smoking drunk at any time. Mahfouz's tone is even throughout. Though he is skillful at engendering suspense, in the end even the most suspenseful adventure ends as gossip and then turns into a story or a legend. Whether the reader finds this reassuring or disheartening is in some sense beside the point—this is one of those novels that subordinates individual dramas to a larger pattern than comedy or tragedy. It is a good example, like *The Makioka Sisters,* of the adaptation of a European form to a non-European culture. The result shares some characteristics of all novels (in this case, readability and accessibility) but arrives at different meanings and makes a subtly different impression on the reader.

82 · Iris Murdoch · The Sea, the Sea

(NEW YORK: PENGUIN, 1978), 495 PP.

The Sea, the Sea is a disquieting novel, substantial and serious but puzzling in many ways. It is the self-told story of Charles Arrowby, a successful London theater director who decides to retire to the seaside and write something rather like a memoir. It turns out to be a confession and an account of how a man comes to terms with his own egoism, but it is also a demonstration of how difficult the confessional mode is, especially if the narrator is supposed to be morally transformed by his experiences. In *The Sea, the Sea,* Murdoch has given Charles Arrowby a rich sensual appreciation of nature and sharp observations of his friends, but she also has taken on the added challenge of writing from within his consciousness while portraying him as not merely foolish and heedless, as Flaubert, for example, portrays Emma Bovary, but boorish, contemptuous, and selfish—less forgivable traits in the social world of writer, reader, and protagonist. She then piles plot twist upon plot twist, taxing the reader in several ways. She achieves a high degree of suspense but also of implausibility, and resolves it all through the deus ex machina of Charles's cousin James, who acts as Charles's savior for unexplained reasons of his own and then passes on to a higher plane of existence, or so Charles is led to believe.

At first Charles seems quite attractive. He is worldly, articulate, gossipy, witty in some ways, and full of information and stories. He seems forthcoming about his likes and dislikes, as if, by sixty-three, he has earned the right to live as he pleases. His most unattractive quality is that he gives in to the temptation to fiddle with the lives of others, especially the affections of an old girlfriend, Lizzie, who is at this point happy enough living in an unorthodox relationship with another old friend, Gilbert, who is homosexual. Charles is in the midst of breaking this relationship up when he realizes that his real first love, a girl he had known in youth, is living in his new town with her husband, who seems to be something of a bully. Charles immediately becomes romantically obsessed with this woman, Hartley, and attempts to rescue her from her marriage by kidnapping her and holding her hostage in his house while other houseguests party around them. A long section in the middle of the novel consists of Charles's obsessive self-justifications and hysterical fantasies about Hartley, who, it is clear to the reader, is both frightened of Charles and not worthy of his interest, even on the score of renewing first love. As if to compound his errors in judgment, Charles also conceives an infatuation with Hartley's adopted son, Titus. Charles is a heavy burden to his author because his best quality, his eloquence, is also his worst, since his habit of applying the full force of his eloquence to every idea, no matter how foolish or misguided, inures the reader to believing him, or even paying much attention to him.

Murdoch's Flaubertian gambit is to give Charles a profound and appealing talent for describing the natural landscape around him, especially the look of the sea as it changes moment by moment. This facet of his eloquence gives his voice the substance and attractiveness it has and in some sense works to make him seem more reliable as a narrator through most of the novel. No doubt this fineness of perception is a trait Charles shares with his author, and perhaps it is meant to stand at the beginning of the novel for disregarded and unexploited moral qualities that the action of the novel is meant to develop. However, the steady alternation of the narrative between precise description of the scene and precise description of Charles's unbelievable wishes, scenarios, and inferences works to give all of his thoughts a sameness—his finer thoughts and potentialities come to seem equally tainted by self-delusion, so it is hard for the reader to see the moral growth the author seems to have intended.

But what did she intend? The standard novel depicts moral transformation through the operation of the plot, which is made up of actions, reactions, and interactions among the characters. The pact between author and reader is that a particular sequence of events is being described because these events above all others are pivotal in the protagonist's life. Such a pact is easy to make with classic novels—in the English novel that ends in a marriage or two, the importance of the events as life-shaping is obvious, especially since marriages in classic times were lifelong. In the classic French novel of romance and adultery, too, events are pivotal, because usually death is the result of the action. In *The Sea, the Sea,* the only person to experience both the action of the novel and the moral transformation of Charles Arrowby is Charles himself. After the fatal weeks, the other characters either die or go about their business. At the most, they are relieved that Charles is less of an egomaniac. The drama throughout the novel takes place in Charles's own mind, without much reference at all to other people. The reader can thus see these five hundred pages as fairly trivial— Charles is an emotional loner who should never have solicited the attentions of the other characters in the first place, and by the end of the novel he is back where he started, only with a few more sentimental feelings about himself than he had at the beginning. The one aspect of the novel that gives it more seriousness than this is its eloquence— we want Charles's sensibility to be more worthy than it seems. Murdoch does her best to endow him with her own worthiness, but in my opinion it doesn't quite come off. She tries to objectify and subjectify his moral life at the same time, but her tool—his writing style— muddles her effort. Her ideas about how moral transformation works do not come across believably, either through the plot or through the telling of the story.

The Sea, the Sea is a good example of the principle that no novel can transcend its conception. Iris Murdoch was certainly an important and ambitious novelist, with rich measures of intelligence, style, knowledge, and experience. In this novel she brought all of these gifts to bear upon her subject, but the more Charles partakes of Murdoch's talents, the less credible he becomes, so that at the emotional climax of the novel, when he is living in his cousin James's house and finally understanding the true emotional sources of his life, the reader feels no answering sympathy. The idea of redemption applies, but the reality of it does not.

83 · David Lodge · How Far Can You Go?
(NEW YORK: PENGUIN, 1980), 244 PP.

One of the results of the competing fashions in academic criticism that seized English departments on college campuses in the 1970s and 1980s was that novelists came to understand and in many cases to embrace the political aspect of the novel. Art, especially art that advertised itself as universal or timeless, came to be seen as another area in which the dominant social, cultural, and economic groups could press their views and close off discussion of subversive or challenging subjects. One result of this critical ferment was the remaking of literary history, which meant the inclusion in the canon of authors previously excluded as well as the redefinition of standards of value. Another result was a sharper understanding of contradictory impulses in individual novels. David Lodge, who taught English literature at the University of Birmingham, has written both novels and critical works, usually alternating between the two. He was (and is) both quite astute and up to date in literary theory and quite entertaining and smart as a novelist. *How Far Can You Go?* shows pretty much how far you can go in turning a story into a historical inquiry if you have a lively intelligence; a clear, comic, and detailed style; and a humane sensibility.

There is possibly no more straightforward novel than *How Far Can You Go?* It opens in a cold, damp Catholic church in 1952, during weekday Mass. Eight or nine characters are introduced, all English Catholic university students, along with the priest, who is a few years older. The five men and four women are set very particularly in time, given not only a specific historical moment but also a list of doctrines they have been taught and believe in. The novel then follows them as they study, fall in love, graduate, marry, have children, grow older, and find their faith tested in any number of ways. Lodge is always clear that they are based on people he knows; that they are representative of their time, place, and situation; and that he is ruthlessly summarizing their inner lives for the sake of his argument. Drama is subordinated to pattern, the characters' experience of emotion to the narrator's ideas about what their pleasure and torments signify. And yet the novel is rigorous but not cold, objective in tone but compelling to read, no doubt thanks to Lodge's very crisp and insightful and funny style.

Lodge's characters have only first names, as befits examples. Dennis and Angela, already a couple at the beginning of the novel, become the most prosperous but encounter the greatest challenges—not only is their fourth child born with Down syndrome, their third child is killed in traffic. Michael is obsessed with sex. He and Miriam, who had converted to Catholicism to marry him, have the most companionable marriage, but he is most troubled by the pleasures of the flesh he thinks he has missed by adhering to doctrinal strictures. Edward is a doctor whose practice of medicine is troubled and distorted by the church's insistence on limiting birth control to the rhythm method, or "Vatican roulette," as Michael calls it. Miles is a supercilious homosexual who finally accepts his sexual orientation, and Adrian is a revolutionary always agitating for liberal changes with pamphlets and meetings. Ruth, the plainest of the girls, becomes a nun. Her whole way of life is repeatedly modified by changes of doctrine. Polly, always the most experimental, marries a television producer and winds up wealthy, successful, divorced, and liberated. The novel ends arbitrarily, before the stories of the characters end, right about the time John Paul II is elected pope. The characters are now in their forties. Lodge gives each a small send-off, but there is no overall plot structure, meaning no climax and no denouement.

It is the author himself, as narrator (and his narrative voice seems to be identical with his personal voice), who makes *How Far Can You Go?* work. When he introduces his characters in the first chapter, he also introduces himself contemplating them. One lengthy early paragraph introduces all the outmoded beliefs they have been taught and still hold at eighteen but will soon abandon. At the end, he reintroduces himself in the first person, saying, "While I was writing this last chapter . . ." Thus Lodge signals his satirical but generous attitude—he doesn't blame them for anything they do, whether it is proscribed as sin by the church or is simply foolish or egotistical. They are, after all, his friends, and he worries about the same things they do. The novelist is not concerned with punishments and rewards (that is, with how they experience their lives) but with how what they do fits in with what they have been taught and what they learn once they are faced with the adventures and choices of adulthood.

Like Lodge's other novels, *How Far Can You Go?* is preoccupied with sexuality, and much of the poignancy of the characters' stories comes from their ambivalence about sex and love. When they most want it—as young men and women—it is forbidden. Once they are married, there is the constant danger of pregnancy. The rhythm method of birth control introduces further disincentives, especially, as Edward comes to believe, because the failure of the rhythm method is more likely to lead to genetic anomalies. By the time all of the characters finally overcome their doubts and begin to take the Pill, marital sex has become routine. Each of the characters, but especially Michael, is beset by the feeling that he or she has missed something, a feeling that dogs their marriages and careers even as liberalism sets in and takes hold. They don't want to adhere to strict doctrines as earlier generations did, but once they give them up, a residual anxiety is accompanied by the feeling that adhering to them thus far has been a waste of time.

I have read *How Far Can You Go?* several times, and I am always impressed by how satisfying it is. Its subject is not one I have any special interest in, and probably I wouldn't read a novel about English Catholicism that had a more internal sensibility. Lodge's influences—Joyce, Graham Greene, and Evelyn Waugh—are ones I am fairly indifferent to. Nevertheless, I admire Lodge's willingness to bring his entire mind to every novel he writes, and this means his good nature as well as his intellectual curiosity, his perplexity as well as his hopefulness, his sadness as well as his sharp narrative skills, and his pleasure in experiment as well as his vast knowledge of literary tradition. And he is very funny, too.

84 · Muriel Spark · Loitering with Intent

(NEW YORK: NEW DIRECTIONS, 1981), 214 PP.

Muriel Spark is a true woman of letters who has written many novels and many volumes of poetry, as well as short stories, biographies, criticism, and other essays. She has been at work for fifty years or more, and her output has been consistently of high quality as well as consistently unlike the work of any other author. *Loitering with Intent* purports to be a memoir by an older woman of letters about the fate of her first novel, written exactly at the middle of the twentieth century, when the novelist was lingering on the fringes of London intellectual life and waiting for the onset of success. It is not actually autobiographical in the strictest sense, in that it does not relate events that appear in Spark's biography; it is rather a reflection on the strange condition of being a novelist and finding events of one's life beginning to echo and reflect the incidents in one's work. Spark has a thesis, but it may be that she is also enjoying a joke—pressing the plausibility of her thesis to extremes and daring her voice, her style, and the apparatus of the realistic novel to carry it off.

Fleur, Spark's protagonist, takes a job with Sir Quentin, who appears to be a wealthy, disinterested, though snobbish, man of letters. Sir Quentin runs a club of people whom he is encouraging to write, called the "Autobiographical Association." His motives are unclear, but Fleur begins to suspect him of something unsavory, largely because he is such a snob and because he treats his mother as if she were senile when she does not appear to be so to Fleur. In the meantime, Fleur is working on and completing her novel. It is taken by a publisher, but then, after the proof stage, returned to her. The manuscript is stolen from Fleur's room and, to all appearances, destroyed.

Loitering with Intent is set at a particular moment in English history, five years after the end of the Second World War, but it is strangely vague as a social document. Fleur is hardly interested in the world around her, or is interested in it only as it begins to behave like her novel. There is rationing, there are bombed-out craters, jobs are hard to find, characters have been demobilized from the armed forces, but these are so incidental to what is important to Fleur that they do not gel into any kind of depiction of a passing cultural or political moment. Fleur's world is as eternal to her as the conventional plots of novels or the insights of the authors of the books she likes. She has no theories, almost no interests other than her books and friends she likes because they are fun and kindly (including Quentin's mother, who is far less senile than she lets on).

As in other Spark novels, the plot is elaborate, but at the same time Spark doesn't seem to particularly care about it, nor does she develop her characters in the conventional way, by giving them important tasks that simultaneously develop and reveal them. Rather, they have certain taglines (Quentin always querulously addresses his mother as "Mummy!," for example, and Dottie, Fleur's friend, is repeatedly referred to as "an English Rose"), and their activities form a sort of background pattern or armature for Fleur's observations about herself, her world, and her work. The most important thing about Fleur is that she is happily and intently writing a novel. She enjoys everything about it and has great faith in it while she is writing it. As she discusses it in her "memoir," it sounds juvenile and highly plotted, a run-of-the-mill English potboiler about strange goings-on among the upper crust, or at least among upper-crust wannabes. What stands out about it (even for Fleur, once she has gone on to her next novel) is her pleasure in writing it and her love of it as her production. She is never oppressed by self-doubts or doubts about the novel—even after she finishes it and falls out of love with it, she still honors it for what it is, the prologue to the rest; *her* novel, but just a novel.

Loitering with Intent is an oddity, a bildungsroman that is a farce rather than an epic. Idiosyncratic charm is the hallmark of Spark's work; *Loitering with Intent* is a good introduction to her sensibility as well as her oeuvre.

85 · Anne Tyler · Dinner at the Homesick Restaurant

(NEW YORK: ALFRED A. KNOPF, 1982), 303 PP.

Dinner at the Homesick Restaurant is interesting in part because it doesn't seem to have a reason to exist. It does not seem to be autobiographical; it sets forth no political or social analysis—no ideas about anything except how the Tull children, Cody, Jenny, and Ezra, were shaped by their family life, especially by the sudden departure of their father, Beck, and the erratic, prickly behavior of their mother, Pearl. It is a serious though not overly sober narrative of the life of a particular family whose members consider themselves ordinary, and whom the author, too, seems to consider ordinary in a sociological sense—none of them has any claims to outstanding accomplishments or talents—but each is full of idiosyncrasies, though no more so than any other family. On the surface, Tyler seems to be engaging in a form of comic natural-ism—like Zola, she details the ordinary and never proposes that a change in social conditions would change her characters' lives. But unlike Zola's characters, hers do not come to grief, they come to under-standing and accommodation. Things go on as they begin, and how they go on is satisfactory enough in the end.

The novel begins with Pearl on her deathbed, then moves quickly backward to her meeting, as a young girl turning into an old maid, with Beck Tull, who is good-looking and travels for a living and is not quite the mate Pearl had originally imagined for herself. Nor does she plan to have more than one child, but when Cody, the eldest, suffers a frightening childhood illness, Pearl persuades Beck to give her two more. Beck leaves the family when Cody is fourteen. Tyler's character-izations are especially sharp—the reader can see in the way Beck combs his hair and the style of his dialogue that he is a certain type of mid-twentieth-century man, flashy but unreliable, an employed drifter in a suit, not a bum but not quite committed to the middle class. Pearl is filled with resentment at her situation. She, too, is a mid-century type, a woman with social pretensions fallen on hard times, who is fanatical about keeping up appearances and incapable of friendships outside the family, fearful that someone might get the op-portunity to look down on her as she looks down on most others. She is devoted to her three children but resentful of them, prone to hysterical rages in which she demeans and denounces them for not considering her desires in some way. She is a bad mother, something of a witch, but Tyler doesn't allow the children or the reader to come to a final judg-ment of her; rather she asks the reader to patiently consider Pearl and, at the very end, to empathize with her, as Ezra does.

Ezra is Pearl's favorite child and Cody's hated rival, an easygoing, almost oblivious caretaking sort whose only ambition in life is to cook good meals and see families (including his own) enjoy dining together. Ezra owns the Homesick Restaurant, which is a quirky establishment without a menu or a particular style of cooking. He has a knack for getting along with others that Cody, more observant and selfish, lacks and resents. The only girl, Jenny, is smart and pretty. She does well in college and becomes a doctor, but she is Pearl's opposite in her chaotic family life and her indifference to appearances.

Tyler's novel covers some forty-five or fifty years, progressing by means of certain family incidents that are told through the different memories of each of the characters. There is no controlling consciousness, but Cody's seems the most observant, and he opens and closes the narrative. He is, in some sense, the villain of the family, full of grievances and meanness, unhappy and unforgiving, always replaying his old contempt for, fear of, and resentment of Ezra. A turning point in family history is when Cody, who is, like Beck, successful with women, steals the only girlfriend Ezra ever has and marries her, though they have nothing in common. Pearl, who realizes what is going on, can't stop it. But eventually this betrayal is incorporated into the family history along with every other misadventure and mistake.

Tyler is subtle and retiring as an author. Her style is precise and insightful, her incidents are full of interest and psychological weight, and her structure works to lay bare the workings of the family. But what is her point? *Dinner at the Homesick Restaurant* is Jamesian in the sense that it reads like very advanced gossip: all of the ideas it explores are about personal relationships—what they feel like, what they mean, how they work—but nothing about their larger political context. In the background I sense all sorts of psychological theories that exist in the culture but are outside the purview of Pearl and her children (even Jenny). In some sense, *Dinner at the Homesick Restaurant* stands as Tyler's answer to Freud, Jung, the behaviorists, the attachment theorists, and the ranks of therapists and clinicians. She is saying, here is a family; here is a bad mother; here is dysfunction. But the meaning of their family life is not in any theory about it, but in the details of what happened, how they experienced it, and what wisdom they took from their experience. She also excludes other forms of self-improvement, such as religion. The Tulls are entirely secular and not intellectual. They don't seek to know themselves through God or through ideas. Tyler seems to be saying that a good memory is enough for some measure of redemption as long as someone, in this case Ezra, has the right attitude.

But, of course, Tyler does have theories, like any other author. She does not overtly display them, but she constructs her story so they are demonstrated. Ezra, for example, is not typical of a successful adult. His restaurant is not a great success, and he lives at home with his mother. He has no artistic aspirations, though he enjoys music. He is not physically prepossessing, nor is he universally appreciated by anyone but the author. Nevertheless, his kindness and patience supply the Tull saga with its redeeming moment, which takes place after Pearl becomes blind, during a period when she asks Ezra to read her youthful diary aloud to her. Other than that, I am not going to give the moment away, but it constitutes Tyler's idea about what is moral and of value in ordinary human existence. In other ways, too, she orchestrates the action of the novel to demonstrate a certain theory about how to live a good enough life even with flaws and vulnerabilities. While Tyler is remarkably self-effacing for an author—always writing in the third-person limited point of view and never digressing from the story or taking any opportunity to comment on the historical or social context of the story—the reader comes away from the novel with a strong sense of her presence and her take on life—clear-eyed but benign, principled but full of good humor and insight.

86 · Milan Kundera · The Unbearable Lightness of Being

TRANS. MICHAEL HENRY HEIM (NEW YORK: HARPERPERENNIAL, 1984), 314 PP.

Kundera is a philosophical novelist in the tradition of Hermann Broch, and like Broch, he likes to break up the narrative in several ways to give the themes primacy over the story and characters. Whether this works is, I think, more a matter of taste with Kundera than with other novelists of the same turn of mind, because Kundera's tone is not charming, like that of, say, Italo Svevo, but cool and even condescending.

The protagonists of *The Unbearable Lightness of Being* are Tomas and Tereza, a couple living in Prague who begin their relationship not long before the Prague Spring and Soviet invasion of 1968. Tomas is a doctor who has left his wife and young son because he doesn't like them and prefers the life of a libertine. Tereza is an unhappy and vulnerable young woman who more or less gives herself into Tomas's hands after one or two meetings. She has some talents and a love of books, but it is not what they have in common that appeals to Tomas, rather Tereza's capacity for grief and suffering (most of it self-imposed by means of terrifying nightmares). Tereza is jealous and insecure, but Tomas does not give up his persistent womanizing—he justifies his

"epic" pursuit of sex with many women as a separate category of connections and emotions from his feelings for Tereza. The two other
characters in the novel are Sabina, an artist who has been Tomas's mistress, and Franz, a lover she meets in Geneva after she emigrates from
Prague following the occupation. Franz and Sabina are not capable of
understanding anything they experience together in the same way
because of the wide differences in their previous lives, nor do they
seem to be able to communicate these differences, but after Sabina
leaves him, Franz remains attached and loyal to her as a kind of larger
conscience or perspective that reminds him that his life is trivial and
unheroic. When he does make a small attempt to do something heroic,
he is accidentally killed, and his whole life disappears as those around
him interpret it for their own benefit. Sabina, too, eventually dies in
alien territory (California). Her vocation, painting, is portrayed more
as a way to make a living than as an expression of her inner life.

The one thing Tomas and Tereza share is a dog, Karenin, who is a
female, but has a male name and is always referred to as "he." The
action of the novel more or less spans Karenin's life, and after he dies of
cancer, Tomas and Tereza are killed in a truck accident.

The gist of Kundera's theme is that the continuous falsehood of life
under Soviet communism renders every action, emotion, and aesthetic
response empty and meaningless. The great drama of Tomas's professional life occurs when he loses his career as a surgeon because of a letter to the editor of a newspaper written during the Prague Spring. The
entire experience of the letter, printed in a truncated version that distorts Tomas's point, makes no sense because there is no action Tomas
can take sincerely—everyone involved wants to use him and his prestige for purposes that do not originate with Tomas himself. Even
though he loves surgery and knows he saves lives, he soon realizes that
his only choice is to give up every form of success and privilege in order
to remove himself as a tool for others. When he then becomes a window washer, it turns out to be a wonderful vacation, because he now
has access to many more women than ever before, and he is shielded
from Tereza's unhappiness by the mismatch of their daily schedules,
since he is out all day and she works all evening. After two years,
though, this life, too, becomes untenable, and Tereza persuades him to
move to the countryside, to a collective farm. In the end she decides
that he really does love her because he has given up everything for her,
and he pretty much decides the same thing, though they differ in their
estimations of what he has given up.

The salient characteristic of all four of these figures is that they never share their inner lives and that in fact it is impossible for them to do so. Tereza's grief is private, lived out mostly in dreams and in her relationship to the dog. Tomas can't communicate to anyone either the nature of his feeling for Tereza or what he thinks of his own epic womanizing. Franz and Sabina don't take the time or make the effort to connect—she seems to forget about him, and he internalizes an image of her that may or may not have anything to do with her. It is only by coexisting in Kundera's novel that they become available to anyone other than themselves, but while that may be enlightening for the reader and a good occasion for Kundera to make some points, it does the four of them no good.

Kundera's method is to remove the veil of verisimilitude from his characters—to treat them as characters and talk about them as characters rather than pretending that they are real people. He then defies his own assertions about who they are or are not by evoking their inner lives and external circumstances as if they were real, but as soon as those begin to solidify, he speaks up again (his intrusions don't seem intrusive because his tone is conversational and because he prepares the reader early on for his method) and reminds the reader that these are just characters. There is a certain degree of playfulness in this, but Kundera's style is so humorless that the playfulness doesn't come across very well.

The Unbearable Lightness of Being is openly a novel of ideas, but ideas, or themes, are the most time-sensitive element of any novel. Kundera's ideas about communism became outmoded and of current relevance to groups of people growing smaller by the year within five years of the novel's publication, when Eastern Europe threw out the Russians, and then the Russians threw out the Communists. As themes lose currency, the narrator's authoritative tone comes to seem egotistical rather than insightful, and seems to prevail at the expense of his characters rather than in support of them. It is possible that *The Unbearable Lightness of Being* will emerge from history like *The Sleepwalkers,* which has a large thematic investment in changes wrought in the human psyche by the First World War, but Kundera is much less interested in ideas of good and evil than Broch is, and it is the evils that the characters do, still shocking after more than eighty years, that furnish *The Sleepwalkers* with its engine. Kundera also, in this novel, contrasts with Arnošt Lustig, another Czech writer, who focuses on the Holocaust rather than the Communist period. For Lustig, the Holocaust is an example of the nature of humanity, and therefore worthy of interest both as circumstance and as theme. For Kundera, the nature of humanity is influenced or even altered by communism. One of the problems with this idea is that when communism vanishes, Kundera's insights into humans under communism lose immediacy, too.

87 · Jamaica Kincaid · Annie John

(NEW YORK: NEW AMERICAN LIBRARY, 1985), 148 PP.

Annie John is a narrowly focused and intense portrayal of the inner life of an adolescent girl growing up in Antigua in the 1950s and 1960s. It begins in paradise. Annie is ten years old. She lives an orderly and affection-filled existence with her mother and father in a small house he has built and that her mother keeps perfectly in order. Annie adores her mother and loves being in her presence, helping her with her daily tasks, dressing like her, being made to feel cherished and protected by her mother's knowledge and special rigor. The next nine chapters detail Annie's simultaneous disillusionment and quest for independence as she becomes "a young lady" (a very suspect category), a star student in a rigidly British educational system, and her mother's loved and hated antagonist. The last chapter details Annie's vivid ambivalence about her departure from the island and from her parents. She is now taller and stronger than her father, disdainful of her mother, and in a fever to leave the island, but the reader knows through the very richness of the novel she has just read that Annie can never quite leave behind the sharp combination of pleasure and pain that has been the strongest feature of her passionate childhood.

The spread of general education after the Second World War swept all sorts of potential novelists, male and female, into the net, and one of the special features of the generation of novelists born in the forties and fifties (Kincaid was born in 1949) is its range of national and ethnic diversity. Kincaid has said that she became a novelist almost by accident—after leaving Antigua to work as an au pair in New York City, she went to college for a few years and began meeting up with writers and writing herself. But her education in Antigua, based on English classic literature, was both a perfect education in literary taste and a perfect education in political ambiguity.

Kincaid's only apparent subject is the evolution of Annie's emotional state as she is growing up. Her style is precise, ironic, and evocative—Annie's world is full of people and places that intrigue her, draw her, or alienate her. She is full of appetites and hates to be crossed. The reader quickly has the sense that her mother's standards of doing everything according to plan and order have created in Annie a felt but not quite articulated aesthetic—different from her mother's but equally powerful—and that this difference in taste is added to the other, more common rivalries of mothers and adolescent daughters. Annie's maturation is objectively the most routine of processes, but it is so strongly felt by the child herself, and as narrator she brings such a wealth of inference to it, that it seems to be the paradigm of tragedy and epic. It does not overtly remind the reader of other deeply felt tragedies and epics as much as it resonates with similar vibrations while purporting to be nothing more than a very particular record of a very particular childhood.

In later works Kincaid expresses more specifically political ideas and emotions about Antigua, class, race, illegitimacy, colonialism, AIDS, and other topics that some readers may find informative in the context of *Annie John* or of Kincaid as a writer who is also a representative figure of her time and place, but the genius of this particular novel is that whatever those ideas are, the author doesn't use them as any kind of explanatory reference in accounting for Annie's successive states of mind. Like most children, she exists outside of time. Her life is all of life and her world is the whole world. Her view of things recapitulates the way the world works and the way human psychology works, and subtly comments upon political and social ideas if the reader wants it to. Like *The Trial, Annie John* expands into larger meaning or doesn't, depending upon the reader's frame of reference. It is more likely to expand than not, but it also works on its apparent terms—a simple story of a particular girl in an out-of-the-way place.

Annie is a figure of both sympathy and empathy—even when her emotions seem inappropriate, she is so honest about them and she evokes them in such detail that the reader stays right with her. In some sense the flowering of the novel around the world in the seventies, eighties, and nineties stands as the fulfillment of the potential of the novel as a social document, if not as an artistic document (the potential of the novel as an artistic document is always equally fulfilled and unfulfilled). Of this flowering, *Annie John* is an especially excellent example. The superb precision of Kincaid's style makes it a paradigm of how to avoid lots of novelistic pitfalls. By staying very close to her protagonist, always moving the argument and the narrative forward, choosing concrete incidents and examples to portray, having a goal but not anticipating it, and knowing her subject in such depth that every episode seems to distill many other episodes that have to go undepicted, Kincaid never allows the reader to either wish for something more or to wish for something less.

88 · J. M. Coetzee · Foe

(NEW YORK: PENGUIN, 1986), 157 PP.

J. M. Coetzee is a winner of the Nobel Prize, and best known for his novel *Disgrace,* which was published in 1999 and won the Booker Prize. A novel of his that I especially like is *Waiting for the Barbarians,* which evocatively explores the question of how a man of good will can negotiate daily life in a tyrannical world, portrayed in the novel as hypothetical, but clearly based on anticolonialist ideas growing out of Coetzee's life in his native South Africa. Even though *Foe* is not one of his more famous novels, I was drawn to it through my admiration for Defoe, and my fascination with his life, which Coetzee seems to share.

Like *Wide Sargasso Sea, Foe* is the meditation of a modern author upon the power of a classic author, in this case Daniel Defoe, and upon the history and tragedy of British colonialism. The premise is that a woman, Susan Barton, has come to London with a story of being cast away on a tropical island. She hopes to persuade the famous Daniel Defoe to write her tale and make her fortune, but "Mr. Foe," as she calls him, has his own troubles—he has fled from his house in an effort to escape his creditors. Much of the novel details her attempts to communicate with him by letter, explaining her situation and making suggestions about the writing she hopes he is doing. She is accompanied by a wordless Friday, whose exact relationship to Cruso (the original of Robinson Crusoe) she doesn't have any means to understand, because Friday has either lost or never had the power of speech—Cruso has told Susan that slavers cut his tongue out, but in fact Susan doesn't know whether this is the case.

Foe refers nearly as much to *Roxana* and several of Defoe's other works as to *Robinson Crusoe*—for example, Susan is pursued by a mysterious girl who claims to be her lost daughter, just as Roxana is pursued by the daughter she abandoned after the departure of her profligate husband. What Coetzee seems to be getting at is the disorder of a writer's themes and subjects before he orders them into separate books. Whereas life is a mishmash of events, books are ordered and sequenced; whereas life is rather dull, books are exciting—one of Susan's observations is that Cruso's real life on the island contained neither cannibals nor introspection. Mr. Foe will have to make up something in order to give the island any interest for a reader.

Foe has several gamelike features—Defoe's disappearance, Susan's pursuit of him, the basic proposition that among the three characters, they are producing a work that is to be entertaining as well as enlightening—but the tone of the novel is oppressive. Instead of discovering something or achieving something or, at least, coming to a degree of self-knowledge, Susan grows more confused as she becomes less and less able to clearly remember her own history (part of Coetzee's theme about the costs of novel-writing). As she writes about herself and Friday to Mr. Foe, she becomes more and more uncertain, especially about who Friday is and what his capacities are: Does he have language and feelings? Does he understand what she is saying to him? What should she do with him? (At one point she is about to send him away on an English ship when she realizes that the captain is actually planning to sell him into slavery.) Friday's wordless suffering also serves to root the novel (and, by extension, all novels) in pain.

Coetzee's points are all thematic—Susan's adventures are not fleshed out; very little action and process are supplied to go along with the dissipation of certainty and meaning. Coetzee is South African, and what he really wants to emphasize is the central mystery of Friday, who could be anything and could mean anything. The novel is short because Coetzee wants to make a certain point—that the usual novelistic tricks of the trade, such as detailing the setting (London in the early eighteenth century), fleshing out the characters, and filling in the gaps of the story are exactly the parts of novel-writing that, according to *Foe,* are dishonest and suspect. Since Coetzee does not have a playful sensibility and has written other novels about the moral compromises of writing novels, such as *The Master of Petersburg* and *Elizabeth Costello,* he is not the sort of novelist to simultaneously perform the tricks and send them up.

In the latter third of the twentieth century, European literature itself came to seem coercive to some readers, especially for promoting the white male Christian supremacy that even when not its subject has been its assumption. The women's movement proposed the principle that the personal is political—that is, all personal choices have their source in power relationships (a principle that was gleaned from the nature of the novel as well as 250 years of novels about choices made by and about women). This principle became a useful lens for looking at how all power relationships work—always a subject that the novel is interested in—but it doesn't always make for readable and compelling novels, especially if the novelist is preoccupied with the problem of subjectivity. Susan Barton, for example, spends very little time depicting her activities around London and a lot of time depicting her doubts and fears. Her thoughts go round and round about the same moral concerns without resolving them, at least in part because the author hasn't constructed a plot that organizes and carries forward their resolution. The lesson is that characters in a novel must keep on doing and interacting or the novel will sink under the double weight of its inherent subjectivity combined with the theme of subjectivity. Infinitely nesting thoughts eventually get tedious, even in only 157 pages. If we look at *Roxana* or Defoe's other novels that play with subjectivity, we see that in them survival comes first and is of intense interest. Moral considerations follow, and when they sometimes conflict with the means of survival, that is fascinating, too. Coetzee can't reproduce Defoe's characteristic practical, clear, and generous tone or his illusion of real concrete life, so his accusation against Defoe—that he exploited and misrepresented the "real" subjects of his work—falls flat. Defoe was a novelist; he exercised a rich imagination and wrote novels that were compelling to read. That's all, in the end, that the reader holds him responsible for.

89 · Toni Morrison · Beloved

(NEW YORK: NEW AMERICAN LIBRARY, PLUME, 1987), 275 PP.

It is clear from Morrison's dedication ("Sixty Million and more") that she intends to embrace the social-document potential of the novel, as, indeed, any novel that treats injustice and its effects must do. This acceptance of the novel's power to shape opinion actually frees her to do anything she wants artistically—novelists who are careful to avoid social questions tend to limit their subjects to personal relationships or aesthetic questions that seem, on the surface, to be perennial, though in fact the novelist is usually simply avoiding the social and economic implications of what he or she is saying. For Morrison and most other writers of the 1980s, though, everything about the novel, from plot to style to characterization, that had once seemed fairly neutral was seen to be fraught with political implications. Like Tolstoy, who also embraced the novel as a social document and openly used the novel to express his opinions, Morrison had a theory—a vision of slavery and black/white relations in America—that was in some ways old hat, but still inflammatory and unresolved. The task was to remake the old story in a compelling way, and also to separate her own telling from that of earlier writers, especially Harriet Beecher Stowe and possibly Harper Lee as well as several male writers.

Beloved is not as easy to read as, say, *To Kill a Mockingbird,* but it is easy to get used to, and once the reader begins to distinguish among the elements, they fall into place quite clearly. As it opens, Sethe, in her late thirties, is living with her eighteen-year-old daughter, Denver, in a house that the neighbors avoid because it is haunted. The time is the early 1870s, right after the first wrenching dislocations of the Civil War and its aftermath. Sethe and Denver live in an uneasy truce with the ghost until the arrival of Paul D, one of Sethe's fellow slaves on her former plantation in Kentucky. Paul exorcises the ghost, but then a mysterious female stranger shows up. She is twenty years old and strangely unmarked—she has no lines in her palms, for example, and her feet and clothing show no signs of hard traveling. She calls herself "Beloved," and Sethe and Denver are happy to take her in.

Sethe, Denver, Paul D, and every other character in the novel live simultaneously in their present and in their history—the chapters of the novel alternate between the two stories—that of the growing contest between Sethe and Beloved and that of Sethe's life on the plantation, her escape, and the traumatic events that followed her crossing of the Ohio River and her appearance at the home of her mother-in-law, Baby Suggs. A crucial, revealing, and in some ways impossible to assimilate event takes place about halfway through the text—Sethe's former owner shows up with some officers to recapture the escapees, and Sethe attempts to kill her children. The two boys and the newborn survive, but she succeeds in slitting the throat of the two-year-old.

Everyone is astonished and appalled by this turn of events (which Morrison discovered in an old newspaper account of the period). Baby Suggs is never the same again; Sethe is shunned by her fellow citizens; Denver grows up isolated and suspicious. Morrison is careful, though, to indicate that while this is a pivotal event in the lives of everyone, it is not, in spite of its shock value, either the climax, or the worst thing to have happened to Sethe and her loved ones. The climax of the historical narrative is, in fact, the night of the escape, when several of the escapees were hanged and mutilated, while the present-time narrative builds to Denver's decision to separate herself from what is apparently a life-and-death struggle between Sethe and Beloved, and to go out and find work and friends that will help her save herself.

One of the reasons *Beloved* is a great novel is that it is equally full of sensations and of meaning. Morrison knows exactly what she wants to do and how to do it, and she exploits every aspect of her subject. The characters are complex. Both stories are dramatic but in contrasting ways, and the past and the present constantly modify each other. Neither half of the novel suffers by contrast to the other. Especially worth noting is Morrison's style, which is graphic, evocative, and unwhite without veering toward dialect (which can strike the reader as unintentionally humorous if the writer isn't careful). Even though Morrison rejects realism, using a heightened diction and a lyrical narrative method returning again and again to particular images and events and adding to them so they are more and more fully described, the reader never doubts the reality of what Morrison reports. Just as Sethe recognizes Beloved toward the end of the novel and knows at once that she has known all along who she is, the reader is shocked at the sufferings of the black characters and the brutality of the whites, but knows at once that every torture and cruelty is not merely plausible but also representative of many other horrors that go unmentioned in the novel and have gone unmentioned in American history. Harriet Beecher Stowe was accused in her time of exaggerating the cruelties in *Uncle Tom's Cabin,* and she replied that in fact she whitewashed events to render them publishable. Morrison is her heir, in the sense that she dares to discuss and publish more (though certainly not all) of the truth.

Beloved has held up quite well over the years in spite of the fact that Morrison was as much a product of her time as any other novelist. The novel seems, for example, more current and compelling than *The Unbearable Lightness of Being.* One reason for this is, of course, that racist attitudes in the United States change very slowly, but another is that Morrison is far more subtle in her exploration of her ideas than Kundera is. Morrison depicts every incident with such concrete expressiveness that the reader takes it in willingly as truth. She is also entirely matter-of-fact in her assertions—equally so about the presence and identity of the ghost as about the character flaws of whites. No aspect of the novel is presented as speculation, and so to read on, the reader suspends disbelief. In this, *Beloved* works something like *The Trial* or "The Metamorphosis." With a tale, the reader is asked to suspend disbelief completely and at once. If she can't do it, she won't read on; if she does do it, she is in the mood to accept everything the author asserts as true. The bonus of the tale form, for Morrison, is that she is also tapping into a vital store of black folklore that feeds her style as well as her story.

Beloved is one of the few American novels that take every natural element of the novel form and exploit it thoroughly, but in balance with all the other elements. The result is that it is dense but not long, dramatic but not melodramatic, particular and universal, shocking but reassuring, new but at the same time closely connected to the tradition of the novel, and likely to mold or change a reader's sense of the world.

90 · A. S. Byatt · Possession

(NEW YORK: RANDOM HOUSE, VINTAGE, 1990), 545 PP.

Possession begins with the theft of a document from the London Library. A young researcher in the 1980s happens across the draft of a letter written in the 1850s by a Victorian poet whose relationships and activities had been thought to be perfectly understood and accounted for. Investigation reveals the poet's great secret—a love affair with a rather obscure poetess. Through straight narration, poems, and fictional documents such as diaries and letters, Byatt develops the parallel stories of the secret affair, the scholarly detective story, and the growing attachment between the researcher who found the document and a famous scholar who is a specialist in the life and works of the poetess.

Possession is a remarkably rich novel, so painstakingly constructed and so multivoiced that it is hard to believe it is the work of a single novelist. It is a true example of astonishing inventiveness but also astonishing insight, thought, and research. George Eliot appears early on—evoked as a shade in the stacks of the London Library—and surely she is Byatt's model and muse. Byatt's prose has a deliberate pace and imaginative density that is reminiscent of *Middlemarch.*

The nonscholarly reader, though, may wonder at first whether she cares about this subject. Victorian poetry, the works of Tennyson and Arnold, don't have much appeal for the modern audience, at least in comparison with the Romantics and the moderns. *Possession* may seem so erudite as to be inaccessible, but Byatt is deft with her modern and her Victorian characters. Although Roland and Maud (the modern scholars) are fairly standard, virtuous, and well disposed, their supporting characters are eccentric and appealing—Roland's testy girlfriend; Maud's overbearing American lover; and Roland's employer, who is named "Blackadder." And the Victorian characters seem authentically Victorian—Ash, the poet; Christabel LaMotte, the poetess; and Blanche Glover, Christabel's artist-lover. One theme that interests Byatt is the differences in the ways the modern era and the Victorian era experience passion. Although the novel implies that there is something deeper and bolder in the Victorian manner, it is the modern characters who achieve the happy ending, with satisfying connections all around and the ever-pleasant infusion of plenty of money.

I mention Byatt's use of names because she is openly cluing the reader in to her use of the tradition of the romance and the epic. Ash is a poet in the epic tradition—his major work (of which Byatt supplies a lengthy selection) is titled "Ragnarök." He also writes about science and history, all male subjects. The ash tree, of course, is an ancient representation of male potency and strength. "Christabel" is a reference to Coleridge's famous poem of the same name, and "LaMotte" refers to medieval fortifications (Christabel is not easily won). Roland, of course, is the subject of the French chanson de geste *The Song of Roland.* "Maud" refers to a Tennyson poem. Through her poets and scholars, Byatt manages to introduce a great deal of European literary history. *Possession* is not weighted down by it—it is more like music in the air. As the interlocking stories proceed, the reader begins to sense a grander, more intriguing, and livelier atmosphere than she has sensed in other novels. With its wealth of references, *Possession* successfully throws off the customary novel-burden of linearity and succeeds in expanding in a new way. The names, the references to other authors, the layered narratives, the poems, diaries, and letters begin to reside together in the reader's mind—not, in the traditional way, creating a self-contained world, but in a new way setting up the resonances of many imaginative worlds coexisting together.

Possession is a novel of ideas, and illustrates some of the joys and the pitfalls of using the novel to put ideas across. Byatt tries to construct the novel as an example of her ideas, while for the most part avoiding overt comment upon them. She wants the reader to feel the ideas as they shape the characters' lives and to accept the rightness of how they feel. *Possession* has held up fairly well because Byatt's ideas are expressed through traditional forms and styles—her choice is not to create new forms and styles but to add layer upon layer of readily understandable forms and styles (and if a reader chooses not to stick with the lengthy poems, she can still enjoy the prose). If and when Byatt's ideas lose their currency, the novel can survive as a story without them. Even though the central modern relationship seems a bit thin and tentative, and the villains are a bit too villainous, the whole is so various and full that everything works well enough as a story and marvelously as a display of literary virtuosity.

91 · Nicholson Baker · Vox

(NEW YORK: RANDOM HOUSE, 1992), 165 PP.

Vox seemed like a shocker when it came out—the premise of the novel is that a man and a woman are having a transcontinental bout of anonymous phone sex, through a calling service. Although their purpose is to arouse each other, their conversation repeatedly digresses, and although they do arouse each other periodically, the more conversational sections are meant to be compelling as well, luring the reader into empathizing and sympathizing with them as characters, and into possibly even having a few vicarious wishes that two people as compatible as these (it is a costly phone call, after all) might overcome distance and anonymity and get together happily ever after.

Baker is trickier than that, though, and far more austere. Whatever the reader takes away from *Vox* is the reader's responsibility. There is no reassuring frame saying what happened before or after the events of the novel, and absolutely no indication of who these two people are outside of their phone call, or of whether they are as they present themselves. The phone call itself may well be a work of collaborative fiction in which both assume personae and false presentations of self. *Vox* is a tour de force of a kind—a genuinely intriguing and unique premise that, in my opinion, had to be executed exactly as Baker executes it in order to be interesting at all.

The originality of Baker's work lies in its meditative nature. My favorite of his novels is *A Box of Matches,* in which a man comes down every morning and lights a fire. The novel records his thoughts as he lights the fires and day by day uses up his box of matches. He ruminates on all sorts of things, but there is a cozy quality to the situation— the family is asleep, he is inside the house, it is winter, and so forth. But Baker brings his meditative nature to all kinds of subjects, and it transforms them. When *Vox* was published, it was considered especially bold, but the story, such as it is, progresses too idly and too routinely to be pornographic and thereby comments on the artificially lurid quality of pornography. No matter what is happening in *Vox,* the reader has the underlying sense that the author is a decent, normal person, just the sort of person who could ponder a box of matches or a punctuation mark (*The Fermata*) at length and in an intriguing way.

In 2004, Baker published a much more controversial novel even than *Vox,* titled *Checkpoint: A Novel,* in which two men discuss the assassination of George W. Bush. One of the men talks through various schemes and the other tries (apparently successfully) to dissuade him from acting out his fantasy. *Checkpoint* was denounced in the *New York Times Book Review* as a betrayal of liberalism, and it was seen in other publications as a joke—after all, there is no indication that the would-be assassin in the novel can even begin to carry out his notion. Both *Vox* and *Checkpoint,* I think, are daring moves in the novel-as-a-game genre of experimental fiction. What differentiates them from racy popular bodice-rippers and political thrillers that have similar themes is Baker's refusal to situate them in a recognizable genre and give them the trappings of commerce, such as suspenseful plots. The reader is asked not to go along for an exciting ride but to meditate along with Baker upon ideas of phone sex, politics, and assassination. He also refuses to add flourishes of obfuscatory literary style (à la Joyce) that serve to deflect all but a select audience. Baker's style is always plain and clear. It is also sometimes tedious and even dreary— intentionally so, since fidelity to the conversation of average people sometimes requires that they seem tedious and dreary in order to seem average. Baker also never communicates his own feelings about phone sex and assassination to the reader, as political thrillers and bodice-rippers do—he presents the conversations and the ideas. The reader meditates upon them. The author seems to be absent, or, if not absent, then morally neutral.

Baker's strong suit as a novelist is that he is intriguing. No one else's mind works quite like his, and he never seems in any way to make apologies for it or to try to be a different kind of writer. When we read his books, we are only in part reading them for themselves—that is, as individual narratives. What we are also reading for is just to find out what Nicholson Baker has been thinking about lately.

92 · Garrison Keillor · WLT: A Radio Romance
(NEW YORK: VIKING, 1992), 401 PP.

If Garrison Keillor were not a radio personality famous for his smooth, good-natured delivery and generally good-humored skits and anec-dotes on *A Prairie Home Companion, WLT* might not have been such a surprise when it came out in 1992. *WLT* is both dark and funny—it is as dark as it is funny—and lots of Keillor fans, used to the lighter, more rueful tone of his earlier collections of pieces, were put off by the novel. Nevertheless, it holds up very well thirteen years later. Keillor's vision is all of a piece, and his style is supple and provocative.

The novel begins in the 1920s with Ray and Roy, two brothers from Minneapolis who start a radio station in a small lunchroom and quickly discover that the eagerness of listeners to devote themselves to the radio is matched only by the eagerness of "personalities" and musi-cians to get on the air. WLT becomes popular and powerful—the sig-nal can be heard throughout the American heartland, and Ray, Roy, and their sister Lottie (who sings old standards on a show of her own) get rich enough to indulge their eccentricities. Ray happens to be a ladies' man, who samples the pleasures of most of his staff over the years but has a jaded view of both humanity and radio. Roy is a frus-trated inventor who retires to the country and invents things such as "the radio chair"—an overstuffed prototype of "surround sound." Lottie, who is wheelchair-bound, lives near the station and sings as "Lily Dale" for fifteen minutes a day, spending the rest of her time speaking well of others and trying to maintain a cheerful attitude. The other writers, singers, engineers, and actors who work for the station come and go over the years, putting out an always wholesome product (except for mistakes) but otherwise living by principles of self-interest, self-deception, and lust. Ray, who benefits the most from the hypocrisy of broadcasting (especially broadcasting to middle America) has the sourest view of it.

About a third of the way into the novel, Keillor introduces Francis With, who turns out to be Keillor's real protagonist. Francis is a young boy living in a small town in North Dakota, whose father is killed in a railroad accident and whose mother thereupon falls into unredeemable despair. Francis changes his name to Frank White and finds occupation, love, and eventually success at WLT and then, as radio goes into decline, in television.

Keillor's style is fast-paced and lively, full of jokes, set pieces, and anecdotes quickly and vividly sketched in. It takes a while for the main characters to come alive because the author's first task is to give a sense of the sociology of the radio station, which he does in an informal and colloquial style, very evocative of both the way midwesterners use language (full of colorful expressions) and the way they confide in one another and gossip about each other. The reader must infer the author's point of view and themes entirely from what the characters do and say.

Most of the characters' lives are marked by foolishness, mistaken choices, and tragedy. WLT is a collection of knaves and dupes who happen to be able to sing or act and who, in addition, often hate or envy one another. Original sin abounds, as with the child stars Little Marjery and Little Buddy, and the Shepherd Boys' gospel quartet, and where sin doesn't obtain, sheer wretched luck does. The afflicted get more afflicted, and the unafflicted get pretty afflicted, too. Fans of the shows, who are full of admiration and affection for the characters, are shown to be gullible and easily manipulated, always ready to send in a dollar or a letter, unable to tell the difference between fiction and reality.

Keillor's style is the backbone of the novel. He constructs his story and his characters out of a mix of colorful expressions and conventional wisdom, often contrasting the cynical with the wholesome and thereby skewering the native hypocrisy of American conformism, midwestern variety. He doesn't always avoid mean-spiritedness by any stretch of the imagination. In some sections, as in those about Lottie and some of the other women, it is hard to tell what it is about them that is being satirized—that they are ugly or that they are silly.

Satire, of course, is often a sour dish. Jokes depend on the teller of the joke and the listener sharing enough values and references so the double and triple implications of the words can be understood. The theory of life evident in *WLT* is that nature is bad and nurture is worse, and efforts to avoid this truth are at best forms of delusion and more likely forms of calculated corruption. Beyond that, the broadcast media, in particular, can't help but exaggerate and consolidate the inherent evils of human nature, disseminating them into every corner of modern life. The reader has to wonder: Is this what Keillor really meant? Did he mean it in general, or was he just going through a bad period?

Dark satire is always problematic in the novel because the novel is so long and often the reader can't tolerate, or doesn't care to tolerate, such a sustained cynical tone. One of the difficulties with *WLT,* as with other satiric works, is that the author's integrity, as he presents his vision, doesn't allow for much variety, but the reader, who finds herself in the presence of the author for hours on end, yearns for variety and even relief. Wit works to a certain degree to carry the reader through the novel, and *WLT* is indeed exceptionally witty. It helps that Keillor's insights into hype, self-aggrandizement, and pomposity, not to mention capitalism, are uncomfortably astute. But an entertainment this is not—it is a polemic with an entertaining demeanor.

93 · Kate Atkinson · Behind the Scenes at the Museum

(NEW YORK: PICADOR USA, 1995), 333 PP.

On the second page of her novel, Kate Atkinson acknowledges her source of inspiration in the line "and the scratch-scratch of the Reverend Sterne's quill." Indeed, the narrator begins the novel as Sterne begins his, with her conception, which coincides with the chiming of the hall clock (in *Tristram Shandy,* the source of all Tristram's troubles is his father's distraction when the clock chimes just at the moment when the "homunculus" is setting forth). Ruby's locale, like Tristram's and Sterne's, is Yorkshire and the city of York. One of Atkinson's

themes is that York is not the same England, even in the twentieth century, as London and the South. And just as Sterne focuses on the male
members of Tristram's family—Father and Uncle Toby—Atkinson
focuses on the female members of her family: her mother, Bunty; her
grandmother Nell; her great-grandmother Alice; and her sisters Gillian and Patricia.

Theirs is not a happy family and has never been a happy family.
Atkinson alternates Ruby's narrative of her childhood with chapters
that jump around in time and show the larger background to the small
incidents she remembers and that account for the inability of the family members to enjoy and value one another. Bunty is a cold and unaf-
fectionate mother, much put upon but also unaccountably nervous
about every little thing. Father George, it turns out, is habitually
unfaithful, but in fact no one's affections work as they ought to, beginning with Alice, whose fate is a mystery to her children (they think she
died in the night, but actually she ran off with an itinerant French pho-
tographer) and a family curse—Alice is quickly replaced by a wicked
stepmother who actively abuses the children.

But Atkinson's exploration of the family's history and circumstances
is not confined to domestic particulars. The history of the family is
profoundly intertwined with twentieth-century British history. Each
generation's youth coincides exactly with the onset of a world war, and
the decisions each character makes about whom to love, whom to
marry, what to do, and where to go are shaped and distorted by who
lives, who dies, and who is injured in the wars. Atkinson has none of
the sentimentality about the wars that other English writers show. She
counts costs very carefully—dead soldiers, dead suitors, maimed bodies, and maimed hopes. She seems to be saying that the same English
intransigence that won the war makes intimacy and simple familial attachment impossible, either because affections are repeatedly betrayed
or because no one has the occasion to practice any form of relating
besides resentment.

For Ruby, the first and strongest object of resentment is her sister
Gillian, four years older. Ruby's resentment is a reciprocation of
Gillian's intense sibling rivalry, which at first seems to have no larger
implications. Ruby comes to be fond of the oldest sister, Patricia, who
returns her affection, but Patricia is unnaturally self-contained, as if
planning her escape from the family from her earliest moment of consciousness. And, indeed, one by one the sisters disappear, leaving only

Ruby and Bunty and Ruby's increasingly avid excavation of the family history.

Behind the Scenes at the Museum sounds depressing, but Atkinson's lively and idiosyncratic style and irreverent tone make the novel work brilliantly. Her take on family life and English history is deeply and consistently ironic. She banishes sentimentality from the novel—no being sentimental about absconding mothers or dying children or war heroes or a fire in a pet shop, no being sentimental about an uncongenial childhood, about not achieving one's heart's desire, or about the blows of history. Better to make a joke out of it all—to detach and observe—than to lament. In the end this is as much a characteristic of the English, and the English novel, as Atkinson's portrayal of coldness, intransigence, and resentment. But in her use of language, Atkinson plays exuberantly over her subject and illuminates it with profound wit and pleasure.

94 · Rohinton Mistry · A Fine Balance

(NEW YORK: RANDOM HOUSE, VINTAGE, 1996), 603 PP.

A Fine Balance is a novel that won many awards and is also much loved by readers. It seems to have effortlessly spanned the cultural divide between high literary culture and mass literary culture. It seems to appeal to Western readers as well as to Indian readers (though this is somewhat hard to discern), and many readers consider reading it to be a life-changing experience. It is frequently compared to works by Charles Dickens, but I think that comparison is not quite apt—maybe Balzac is better (and, indeed, Mistry invokes Balzac in his epigraph, which is from the beginning of *Père Goriot*)—Dickens's most characteristic feature is his unique, highly subjective prose style. Mistry's style is far more objective and detached; his straightforward precision is the source of the novel's power, since it never occurs to the reader (or, at least, the Western reader) to doubt Mistry's depiction of Bombay life.

Edith Wharton counseled thoroughness in novel-writing, and in constructing his story, Mistry is both organized and thorough. He begins with Ishvar and Om, two low-caste Hindu tailors riding a train in a large Indian city. They happen to meet a Parsi student, Maneck, who is from the foothills of the Himalayas. Both the tailors and the student are going to the same residence, an apartment rented by a woman named Dina, who intends to hire the tailors to do piecework and to take in Maneck as a lodger. The first half of the novel details, in part, what brought each of the four to the apartment, and also follows the tailors as they attempt to make a home for themselves somewhere in the city, even though overpopulation and government corruption make their quest just about impossible. Each of the four has a wish. Dina is an educated woman who would like to live independently of her well-off brother, who has been trying to marry her to one of his friends for twenty-five years. She has suffered a good deal of bad luck, especially the accidental death of her self-chosen husband on the third anniversary of their marriage. As the novel opens, she has been supporting herself for twenty years by simple sewing, but now her eyes are failing and she can't see to thread the needle or make the stitches. She decides to turn her apartment into a small factory even though such a thing is forbidden in the lease.

Ishvar and Om, the tailors, have a complicated history. Traditionally of the untouchable leatherworkers caste, they have benefited from a career switch engineered by Ishvar's father (and Om's grandfather). But religious strife and envy have destroyed the family—before the novel opens, all of their relatives have been burned to death as a result of an election dispute. Their ambition is to earn some money in the city and return to the village. Ishvar, in particular, wants Om to have a wife, though Om seems indifferent to the idea. Maneck, who is about Om's age, has had a happy, prosperous childhood as the only son of shopkeepers, but his father is worried that the family business will not survive, and is determined for Maneck to have an education. At the opening of the novel Maneck has gotten peripherally embroiled in political conflicts at the university and is looking for another place to live so he can continue his studies. By this point in the novel the reader may think she is inured to cruel events—each of the characters has had to endure and survive something shocking by Western standards (though portrayed with the same flat precision as all the other events in the narrative). And the characters themselves are appealing and neatly delineated—Mistry relies heavily on dialogue to progress the narrative and to depict social conditions as well as to reveal the characters. That Dina, Ishvar, Om, and Maneck endure constant daily indignities as well as brutal injuries and keep on in quite a lively way in some sense keeps the tone of the narrative hopeful and forward-moving rather than lugubrious—Mistry's empathy is such that his characters' lives may be cruel, but they are not sordid.

In the classic historical-novel tradition, the four protagonists find themselves embroiled in large political events—in this case the governmental emergency of 1975, when Prime Minister Indira Gandhi maintained her administration by force and cracked down on indigent and homeless people as well as on the political opposition. The main action of the novel begins when Ishvar and Om are forced to board a bus one morning instead of going to work. They are taken, along with thousands of others, to a staged rally and paid to clap and cheer when the prime minister makes a speech. Soon thereafter, the shantytown where they are living is destroyed and they find themselves on the streets.

Mistry's pacing remains even, his tone remains quiet, and the story continues to develop in exactly the same manner as it has so far, but the situations of the four characters get more and more dangerous, and eventually each loses the very thing he or she wanted and more. It is not that they have sinned or that their losses are deserved. There is not that moment, as there is in, say, Icelandic sagas and other Scandinavian fiction, where the character did some small (or large) proscribed thing that set the train of disaster in motion. It's clear from the lives of the incidental characters in Mistry's novel that violence and disaster are the norm (at least during the emergency) and that in fact the difficulties of life in India, or at least in Bombay (though there is plenty of violence elsewhere, too), are beyond cause and effect, more like impersonal natural disasters. What is remarkable is that the characters wrest some connections, however brief, and some pleasures, however transient, from the vast Hobbesian world that is their home. In fact, the characters (and the author) offer no de Sade–like arguments about whys and wherefores. Events simply transpire, and sometimes characters make a comment or two upon them, but everyone is more or less resigned to pain, disfigurement, death, and brutality having no meaning except as facts of life. The novel is Balzacian in the sense that the way people treat each other seems to come from their national identity—as Balzac's nasty Parisians are simply acting French, so Mistry's indifferently brutal citizens of Bombay are simply acting Indian. Nor does he blame colonialism or history. As in Kafka, this happens and then this happens and then this other thing happens. The reader can make what she wants to out of it—what Maneck makes out of it is different from what Dina, Ishvar, and Om make out of it.

Religion, which most Western readers associate with India, hardly appears in the novel, and when it does, it is not as a solace but as a source of conflict, class inequities, and physical identity (at one point Ishvar and Om have to take down their pants to prove to some marauding Hindus that they shouldn't be killed). The only "holy man" turns out to be a murderer whose powers are tricks and cons.

A Fine Balance is a remarkably restrained and powerful novel, but it is hard to know how to react to it. The reader ends up not unlike the protagonists of Francine Prose's two novellas (below), morally uncertain, stunned by too much casual cruelty. The author seems to assert that there actually is nothing to be done about it; it is only to be witnessed and understood.

95 · Francine Prose · Guided Tours of Hell
(NEW YORK: HENRY HOLT, 1997), 241 PP.

In both of the novellas that make up *Guided Tours of Hell,* Americans with some aspirations to culture and education go to Europe and are confronted with the task of assimilating, or comprehending, or at least responding to the horrors of European history. The first of these is Landau, a playwright who has been invited to a conference in Prague to give a reading of his play *To Kafka from Felice,* which is based on Kafka's letters. He quickly discovers that not only is he not the star of the conference, he also is unpleasantly overshadowed by a quite famous diarist of the Holocaust named Jiri Krakauer, who has written a book about his relationship with Kafka's sister, Ottla. Jiri is some twenty years older than Landau, a true witness to the death camps, and Landau can't stop resenting Jiri, envying him and trying to impress him, but Jiri is no saint, either. He is demanding and selfish, and has shamelessly exploited his suffering in the camps for personal gain. Landau is petty—whether or not he is normally this way, the conditions of the conference (not only is he overlooked, but also accommodations are bad) spur him to take a jaded view of all the other participants as well as everything he sees and does in Prague. And then they take a tour to a death camp.

In the second novella, some three times the length of Landau's story, Nina, an American travel writer, is sent to Paris by the owner/editor of the travel newsletter she works for, who is also her lover, Leo. From the first it is clear that Leo has Nina completely off balance. She does not know when she goes, for example, whether he is planning to join her or not, and then when she goes to the hotel he reserved for her, she discovers that not only is it a dump, it is also owned by one of his former lovers (he is much older than she is), who takes her aside and gives her all sorts of details about the old love affair.

Like Landau in *Guided Tours of Hell,* Nina is forced by the circumstances of her trip to take history personally. Jiri and Leo are both quick to claim special status—Jiri by virtue of his experience in Auschwitz and Leo because he is a Jew and Nina is not. But simple moral judgments can't be made—Jiri does behave in a sleazy manner, and Leo is cruel and manipulative toward Nina—sometimes openly and sometimes subtly. For Nina in particular, the very health and integrity of her personality seem to be at stake as she endures and tries to assimilate Leo's treatment of her. She believes in love, and she and Leo have a passionate sex life they are proud of, but as the novella progresses, Nina knows less and less how to define love. If she defines it as passion and excitement, then she is all the more subject to Leo's unkindnesses. If she doesn't accept the definition that she and Leo have agreed upon, then she is not only isolated and lost, she also must accept the existential crisis of profound ignorance (and the certainty that she has also wasted her life). At the same time, Landau and Nina accept Jiri's and Leo's claims—Nina in particular is struck by the anti-Semitism she sees in France. She is supposed to be having a good time, but she feels more and more oppressed by the relics everywhere in Paris of past crimes, revolutions, terrors, and wars. The title of this novella, *Three Pigs in Five Days,* comes from something Nina keeps seeing on French television—shows in which the French countryside and French heritage are celebrated through the slaughter of pigs and the making of sausage (which Leo interprets as coded images of the rise of French fascism). Love is the only antidote to history, but in the city of love, there is no evidence of love.

Prose's special talent, particularly evident in the second novella, is in the texture and density of telling details. Nina's ambiguous situation is palpable and suffocating, just indeterminate enough to be authentically confusing (obviously Prose has learned a lot from Kafka, though the feared authorities in her novellas are not functionaries of the state or fathers, but boyfriends and literary rivals). Her intent is satiric, but her satire is dry and ambivalent, not angry and overt. Leo is cruel and Jewish. Is he being satirized as a male chauvinist pig, or is Nina being satirized as a shallow fool? Landau is a small-time egomaniac. Does that make him better or worse than Jiri, who is a big-time egomaniac? Certainly, Prose seems to be saying, European history leaves no one either redeemed or unscathed—not Americans, whose innocence is really egotistical naïveté, and not Europeans, who are still in thrall to the same old horrors as they begin to surge up again in the form of right-wing xenophobia and general anti-Semitism (not to mention the brutal romance of pig slaughter).

Prose's satirical sensibility is conservative—she locates the foolishness and knavery that are her satiric targets in human nature rather than in social arrangements. For that reason she is stuck with the sort of unsatisfying endings that other conservative satirists are stuck with—the characters make some last meaningless gesture that simply ratifies what has been learned in the course of the novel, and the narrative stops. For that reason she has not, perhaps, had the sort of general success she has deserved—American readers like their characters' revelations to be, if not life-affirming, then at least hopeful, or, barring that, at least energetic and lively. At the end of these two novellas, Landau and Nina are left with nothing even though, objectively, they have actually lost nothing. But Prose is one of the few American women writers who engage seriously with the Eastern European tradition, especially with more difficult figures such as Isaac Babel. In these novellas in particular, her voice is precise, original, and continuously intelligent.

96 · Chang-rae Lee · A Gesture Life

(NEW YORK: PENGUIN PUTNAM, RIVERHEAD, 1999), 356 PP.

Chang-rae Lee's protagonist, Doc Hata, in *A Gesture Life,* has had to fit into two alien cultures—he was born into the Korean community in Japan; then adopted into a Japanese family; and then, after serving in Burma as a medical officer in the Second World War, he has immigrated to the United States and lives in a small town outside of New York City, where he owns a medical supply store. When the novel begins, he is about to retire from his business.

From the opening pages of the novel it is apparent that Hata's main goal is to follow all the rules and social codes he can understand in an effort to maintain an orderly and unsullied existence. Although he is a Japanese man in an American small town, he prides himself on how well he has fit in, and feels that his friendly and neat demeanor, in particular, has endeared him to his neighbors. It soon becomes apparent, though, that Hata's idea of belonging is actually a form of isolation. The remotest social gestures and the most routine friendliness are enough for him. When acquaintances seem to want more intimacy, he quietly but firmly turns them down. The question of Hata's motives is somewhat open. Any lover of Japanese literature will certainly attribute much of Hata's punctiliousness to a strongly felt and eagerly developed aesthetic of the sort expressed in all types of Japanese literature, and at first Hata and Lee seem to invite this interpretation (but of course that isn't enough motivation for a whole long novel). Hata is not without dilemmas—he has missed out on a relationship with a nice woman in his neighborhood, he is selling his shop to a family with a very ill child, and he would like to be reconciled with his estranged adopted daughter. These dilemmas would be plenty for a standard-issue American novel.

But Lee's subject is how Hata's psychology manifests more than temperament and circumstances. His predilections seem like choices to him, but as the novel unfolds, it becomes clear that his desires and what appears to be his inborn psychology are really the natural results of caution borne of long experience. As a Korean boy in prewar Japan, he was forced to develop habits of extreme self-effacement, since Koreans were targets of ethnic hatred, and his self-deprecating correctness as an old man at first seems to come from the same source. As the story of Hata's present-time relationships develops, though, his wartime experiences are narrated, and it becomes evident that he is a man whose every desire, no matter how normal, has been punished, sometimes horrifically.

Lee develops Hata's story as two unfolding narratives that alternate and reflect upon one another. It is unclear whether this unfolding is meant to mimic what is happening in Hata's mind (that there are experiences he hasn't assimilated yet and has to come to terms with in order to purge them or to achieve some sort of reconciliation with his past) or whether Hata is perfectly aware of his experiences, and the unfolding is taking place entirely in the structure of the novel, to reveal the sources of Hata's psychology to the reader. While the effect of the two narratives is suspenseful, this small technical confusion means that it is impossible for the reader to really know what Hata's existential task is—to know himself or to act in accordance with his conscience. On the one hand, the evidence of the first sections of the novel is that Hata doesn't miss a trick—he is like a prey animal in his constant awareness of where he is, who is around him, and what the meaning of every gesture he makes and others make might be. This hyperalertness makes it hard to believe that he would not be perfectly aware at all times of what has happened to him. So then the question arises, does his tremendous carefulness come out of an attempt to hide his terrible experiences or to escape them?

The author is to all appearances sympathetic to Hata, but the novel is told in Hata's voice, so it is hard to figure out whether his narrative and his story are supposed to undercut one another or support one another, and whether Hata ever understands himself in the way the author understands him. The events Hata remembers from his time in Burma are stunningly dramatic, and in some sense they drive out subtler considerations. The ending of the novel seems to fall apart— Hata's motivations for resolving everything as he does are unclear. The reader is left to wonder whether anyone could assimilate such experiences and go on to a life of normal intimacies and relationships. In addition, the American reader is not quite able to gauge the importance of Hata's adoption as a child and his removal from his family into Japanese society. I think one thing that is missing is more information about Hata's first experiences in the United States, the transitional period, after the war, perhaps, between Japan and the United States (even if not between horror and normalcy). Who he is at seventy-five is so far away from who he was at twenty-five that without some sort of information that is still missing in this novel, the reader cannot quite make connections.

Even so, *A Gesture Life* is a serious and beautifully written contemplation of the intersection of personal history, cultural ideals, and history. It is ambitious and extremely complex as well as readable and suspenseful.

97 · Arnošt Lustig · Lovely Green Eyes

TRANS. EWALD OSERS (NEW YORK: ARCADE, 2000), 248 PP.

Arnošt Lustig is a Czech writer living in the United States who writes in Czech. Most Americans are not as familiar with his work as with that of Elie Wiesel and Primo Levi, but Lustig has made a literary life of exploring the Holocaust through fiction rather than nonfiction. Lustig was eighteen at the end of World War II, the only survivor in his family, the rest of whom were lost in concentration camps. He lived in Czechoslovakia until the Soviet invasion of 1968, and has also written about and discussed Eastern European communism in films and interviews.

The protagonist of *Lovely Green Eyes* is Skinny, a fifteen-year-old Czech girl whose family is sent to Auschwitz toward the end of the war. She sees her parents and brother killed, and goes to work in the office of a doctor who is experimenting on camp inmates before killing them. To escape this situation she accepts a spot in the soldiers' brothel being established not far from the camp. She must pretend to be eighteen and Aryan to work there with the other girls. When the Eastern Front crumbles as Germany is defeated, she manages to return to Prague, where she tells part of her story, regains her health, and finds ways to survive both physically and emotionally.

Wisely, Lustig, who has eight works of fiction in print and has written at least twelve books since the early seventies, does not try to encompass the vast subject of the Holocaust in only one or two books. Instead, he has used various stories that take place during the Holocaust as a lens for investigating his larger subject, which is the mysteries of human interaction. This allows him to focus on individual characters without feeling pressure to depict collective experience. In this case, Skinny has several lengthy "relationships" (though, of course, they are coercive ones). One is with a German officer who is almost kind to her, another is with an officer who must be the son of Broch's Huguenau—his sense of himself is brutally narcissistic—he kills with enjoyment and admires killing as a way of life. He also likes bondage, and teaches Skinny how to tie him up. Skinny has slight relationships with the madam of the brothel and some of the other girls (most of whom do not survive), and from time to time the novel skips forward into the period after the war, when Skinny and her fellow survivors are trying to assimilate their experiences and also to find jobs and lives.

The narrator presents himself as Skinny's eventual husband, to whom she has told most if not all of her experiences.

Lovely Green Eyes is hard to read, and not because it isn't readable—it has appealing characters and plenty of suspense. The style is lively and the narrator's voice is reassuring. In some sense Lustig's narrator stands at the end of the road, the goal that Kafka, Musil, and Broch were moving toward without realizing, and his voice is an answer to theirs. His is more horrifying because more explicit about the actual tortures and torments that their narrators only suspected could happen, but it is also less dreadful, because the murders, tortures, and modes of survival are concrete rather than inchoate and unknown. It is more than that the narrator and Skinny herself are survivors, it is also that they have wrestled with what survivors need to learn and ponder in order to not only survive but also to live another fifty years. Lustig writes, of course, in the Kafka-Musil-Broch-Kundera tradition, but he also writes in the Boccaccio tradition—he demonstrates with the very existence of his work and the complexity of its structure that unimaginable mass death doesn't reduce human civilization to nothing—complexities of thought, emotion, desire, and taste continue to exist and constantly reassert themselves even as those who think they have been reduced to nothing are grappling with their experiences.

One notable feature of *Lovely Green Eyes* is Lustig's empathy (not sympathy, of course) toward Skinny's captors. He never for a moment allows the reader to lose sight of the inherent cruelty and injustice of the Nazi system, but he does force the reader to experience the point of view of Hentschel, the kinder officer, and Sarazin, the crueler officer. The reader experiences it because Skinny herself can't avoid it—they want and have paid for more than the usual quick intercourse, so they talk and expound and try to relate to her, or, at least, to fit her into some preconceived expectations they have about women. These prolonged episodes are more difficult for Skinny than twelve regular soldiers in one day because she is in greater danger of mistakenly revealing her Jewishness or her age, or of doing the wrong thing (especially with Sarazin, who has previously had a girl whipped to death for not precisely fulfilling his fantasy), or of showing her true feelings about these men. The men themselves are entirely deluded, but the novel shows that their delusions have a compelling context—the general delusions of the Germans about who they are and how the world works.

A novelist who takes up and explores a single subject, no matter how large it is, is always in danger of repeating himself and testing the patience of his audience, but Lustig has avoided these problems by understanding and exploiting the techniques of the novel. He has chosen to look at individuals rather than groups, thus avoiding the technical problems of portraying collective action as well as the philosophical difficulties inherent in ideas of collective guilt or innocence. He has focused on the inner lives of his characters, but he doesn't give an inner life to only one character—the juxtaposition of mutually exclusive inner lives is a constant source of suspense in *Lovely Green Eyes.* He also understands that Skinny's experiences have to be told in real time and also in retrospect, because her understanding of them will be different as she experiences them, remembers them, and retells them— the "truth" about them can't be arrived at through one rendition only. The effect upon the reader of Lustig's supple and varied technique is to lead her through what might otherwise be an unbearable learning experience—to show her something essential in a way that she can "enjoy" as well as understand.

98 · Zadie Smith · White Teeth

(NEW YORK: RANDOM HOUSE, VINTAGE, 2000), 448 PP.

From time to time, *White Teeth* made me think of Wilkie Collins's *The Moonstone.* Possibly of all the novelists of his day, it was Collins, who began his tale with the theft of a holy jewel from the forehead of a holy statue in India, who had an inkling of the English world that would grow out of the British Empire, a world that Zadie Smith depicts with richness and intelligence, and with a stylistic exuberance that would be worthy of some of her Victorian predecessors. In Smith's North London there is hardly a white Englishman to be seen other than Archie Jones, whose wife, Clara, is Jamaican and whose best friend is a Bengali, Samad. The people they know who act most English are a Jewish geneticist whose grandfather came from Central Europe and his protégé, Samad's son, who has returned from Bengal, where he had been sent to an Islamic religious school at age ten. The rule of the new British culture is mixing—blood, religion, DNA, ideas, names, foods, languages, accents. But as the cultures mix more and more thoroughly,

the characters find themselves striving with ever-increasing frustration (and angry conflict) for purity and tradition. Or, rather, the men
do. With good and bad motives and good and bad results, the women
characters in the novel all strive to connect to someone or other across
some boundary or other.

The story of *White Teeth* is loose, more of a progress than a plot. The
first generation consists of Archie and Samad, both soldiers in World
War II, and their much younger wives, Clara and Alsana. Irie, Archie
and Clara's daughter, grows up with Millat and Magid, Samad and
Alsana's twin sons. Although the novel is told from the omniscient
point of view, Irie comes to be the central consciousness of the narrative, and it is through her that all of the warring factions are finally reconciled. "Plot" elements are really thematic elements—events and
motifs that recur in the lives of the characters, informing actions that
seem random, or at least free, to the characters themselves with a certain fated, or at least inherited, pattern evident to the reader. The richness of Smith's depiction of her characters and their milieu allows the
reader to entirely give up all allegiance to plot. The novel does not
move quickly or suspensefully; rather it moves majestically, first considering one thing and then another, tying thread after thread into a
compelling and vivid fabric that comes to seem a true picture of
English life at the turn of the millennium.

Smith was in her early twenties when she wrote *White Teeth*. That
plus the broad liveliness of her canvas resulted in comparisons to
Charles Dickens, who wrote his first book in his early twenties and
was also remarkable for the abundance of characters and scenes he
seemed to portray with utter natural genius. Without denigrating
either author's wonderful skills, I think that what *White Teeth* and *The
Pickwick Papers* both show is the remarkable effect the English language itself has on the nascent novelistic mind. Like Smith, Dickens
was exposed, and consciously exposed himself, to a garden or even a
jungle of English dialects—speakers of all classes and from everywhere, gathered together in London, entertaining themselves and
doing business day and night. Dickens's characters, especially his
minor characters, are never reticent. They are always spouting off,
announcing their opinions, narrating their lives, trying to put something over on someone else. For whatever reason, English people prize
verbal fluency and use it. The result has been logorrhea given form
and purpose, the novel. A hundred fifty years after Dickens, and in a

new way and a new world, *White Teeth,* too, demonstrates the pure capaciousness of the English language—the characters may seek purity, and even purgation by violent means, but the language, as written by Zadie Smith, incorporates and grows, promoting its own all-inclusive form of cultural intelligence.

I waited all the way to the end of the novel to see if Smith would, perhaps unconsciously, yield to the English habit of bringing the love and the money together at the last minute, and I have to say that she did, though I won't say how. I will say that after exploring several realms of ideology, including Islamic and Christian fundamentalism, and giving a good deal of insight into religiously based critiques of Western empirical, racist, and imperialist ways of looking at the world, Smith proves herself a novelist to the core, because she saves the humane in her characters and lets them connect in the time-honored manner, not because they are pure or right or just or true or powerful or holy, but because they are good enough individuals who have affection for one another and for whom the reader, too, has developed an affection.

99 · John Updike · The Complete Henry Bech

(NEW YORK: ALFRED A. KNOPF, EVERYMAN'S LIBRARY, 2001), 509 PP.

This volume began in 1964 as a short story about the novelist's somewhat older Jewish alter ego, living a literary life rather different from Updike's but on the same turf. Over the years, stories were added, and the result, published in 2001, is a single, somewhat episodic, but unified contemplation of the artistic life as lived in the latter third of the twentieth century in the United States. The Bech stories, both in conception and in execution, are irresistibly clever and good-natured, even though Bech himself is often sour, mean-minded, lecherous, and lazy. For the reader, contemplating Updike contemplating Bech, and doing so with unparalleled eloquence and insight is a fabulous joke in itself that only twists and expands with each additional tale. It is not Updike's masterpiece, because a novelistic masterpiece cannot be about the writing life—such a subject is too narrow and self-involved—but it is an exquisite addendum to Updike's more straightforward novels, an assertion that John Updike can be John Updike, but he can be Philip Roth, too, if he wants to be, and he can do it in his spare time.

The first Bech story, "The Bulgarian Poetess," is the most famous. The young Bech, unmarried and in the midst of a prolonged writer's block, finds himself a U.S. emissary in Bulgaria, possibly the most distant country in the world from the New York City Bech knows and inhabits. He has no reason to be there except that he has nothing else to do with his time, nor is he eager to remain. It is only that he meets a woman there, the Bulgarian poetess, who is possibly the only woman he ever has met or will meet with whom he might form a truly loving and mature connection. They are doomed to part—that is that. It is a poignant and evocative tale. My favorite, though, is "Bech Panics" (1969), in which Bech travels to a southern women's college in the spring, purely for the money he is to get by giving a reading and a couple of classes. The easy money turns out to be hard-earned. The beautiful spring and the well-behaved young ladies induce in him a serious existential crisis that includes self-loathing, intimations of the vastness of the universe, and sexual vertigo. Updike depicts each of the stages of Bech's panic attack with virtuosity and allows the reader to sympathize but also to smile—the novelist is safe, after all, from death, if not from the cultural trivialization he should fear (and sometimes does, as the years pass and he finds himself on the best-seller list). Another one I like and can easily empathize with is "Three Illuminations in the Life of an American Author," in which Bech agrees, in exchange for a free vacation to a Caribbean island, to sign autographs, which he thinks will be an easy job. He signs until signing becomes difficult, and then he keeps signing until he can't even remember his own name—a beautiful and funny evocation of the paradox of the novel, where the individuality of an author and its vast commercial duplication exist side by side. Bech is temporarily destroyed by his own books—but it is only temporary. He soon finds himself not only touring the Third World but also writing his "big book." Almost every story maintains the same high quality, and all work together beautifully. Since Updike wrote the Bech stories off and on during almost thirty years, he was free to exploit the possibilities of topicality. As a result, of course, there are quite a few witty cultural references to such fads as adults trying marijuana for the first time (it "looked like a residue of pencil shavings in a dirty tobacco pouch" [p. 67]) and "an actor in the White House" (p. 320) that add to the sense that Bech's life

is passing before the reader as it is lived, and that Updike's inventiveness is more and more stimulated by his protagonist.

John Updike, of course, has written dozens of books of all kinds—
not only novels and short stories, but also books of poetry, essays, and
criticism. The Bech stories are not his major work, but they are a flour-
ish upon it, similar to an ornamental trill in a piece of eighteenth-
century music—I like to think of them as the bonus that demonstrates
the inspiration, virtuosity, and exuberance left over when all the other
work of this amazingly prolific writer is finished, and that shows the
pleasure he has received from his vocation.

The depiction of making art, or writing novels, is not a very important story in the end. It is a drama more exciting to the dramatist than
the audience, and writing about the ups and downs of being a novelist
is not what the culture has hired its novelists to do. Imaginative insight
into other lives, and into the life of the larger culture, is what novelists
have to offer. Updike understands this, which is why his Bech stories
are serious fun rather than serious work. But it is the very game-
playing aspect of these stories that frees the author to be honest and
eloquent and to write about how painful the artistic life can be as well
as how silly. Bech is not a character most readers would sympathize
with (he even commits several murders late in his career), but Updike
has given him large capacities—larger capacities as a person and as a
consciousness than as a writer.

100 · Ian McEwan · Atonement

(NEW YORK: DOUBLEDAY, ANCHOR, 2001), 351 PP.

The four layers of *Atonement* fit inside one another like nesting dolls.
McEwan, born in 1949, is writing about an elderly novelist, Briony
Tallis, born in 1922, who is writing about herself as a novelist, who is
writing about herself as a child of thirteen, her older sister, Cecilia, and
her sister's lover, Robbie Turner. The premise of the plot is that Briony,
imaginative and precocious, witnesses several events that lead to
Robbie's arrest and conviction for the rape of Briony and Cecilia's
fourteen-year-old cousin. As a result of the conflict, Cecilia breaks off
relations with her family. Five years later, the Second World War
begins, and Robbie is freed from prison to join the army just before it is

driven back to Dunkirk by the overwhelming German advance.
Briony, now eighteen and a student nurse, has come to realize that she
fatally misinterpreted what she had seen, and attempts to atone in several ways, one of which is by writing a true account of what she saw
and how it fit into what really happened. The reader is given to understand that this account is the novel *Atonement*.

Atonement was universally acclaimed—nominated for the Booker
Prize in England and declared the best book of the year by ten American newspapers—and also a huge best seller, so it is worth analyzing
what it has to offer. For one thing, the outline of the story is simple, as
is the structure of the novel. Rather like Virginia Woolf in *To the
Lighthouse,* McEwan picks three pivotal days and records each almost
moment by moment. The first, a summer day in 1935, ought to be
quiet and straightforward. Briony plans to enlist her three cousins in
putting on a play she has written as a welcome home gift for her
beloved older brother. But the cousins are uncooperative, her mother
comes down with a migraine, and everyone acts at cross-purposes to
everyone else, resulting in confusion and, ultimately, catastrophe. The
second day, told from Robbie's point of view, bodes ill from the first
sentence. The English forces in Belgium have been routed and are on
the run. Robbie, a private, is carrying a piece of shrapnel in his
abdomen. He manages to get to the beach, but is feverish by the time
he settles down for the night. The third day is another summer day.
After some months working as a student nurse (an arduous and
thankless task), Briony receives word that her cousin, the one who had
been raped, is getting married in a quiet ceremony, even though the
parents of both bride and groom are wealthy and socially prominent
enough for a large, ostentatious wedding. Briony attends the wedding
uninvited and realizes that it was the groom, not Robbie, who committed the rape. She then finds Cecilia and Robbie.

The passage of each of these days is related in detail through intense,
almost Woolfian depiction of the consciousness of each character. The
nature of consciousness is not McEwan's focus, though—he is more
interested in the building blocks of belief. It is assumptions, mistakes,
moods, chance, and misapprehensions that doom Robbie—the workings of tragic irony. It is further tragic irony, the irony of history and
war, that possibly prevent his rehabilitation and redemption. Briony
the novelist never quite comes clean about the success of her effort at
atonement, but she implies that the modestly happy ending of part
three is a fiction and that her long and successful artistic career has

been fatally compromised from the beginning by her first foray into narrative.

As its title implies, *Atonement* is not fun. In spite of the mix of social classes, it contains little overt social analysis, and strives to be about as apolitical as a novel can be. The characters do their best, but destiny thwarts them—even Briony's destiny as an acclaimed novelist thwarts her need to be punished for ruining the lives of her sister and Robbie. Nor does the novel contain any lighter moments. There is not even any repartee. Briony's mistake (and she never admits that it was anything but a mistake) seems to be interpreted by herself as narrator as an honest outgrowth of the inherently treacherous novelistic mind. If it reflects on anything, it reflects on the idea that novel-writing (like art-making) is a suspect activity that takes perfectly innocent acts and turns them into sins and crimes just for the sake of a thrill. But McEwan never explores what really did happen—the cousin was raped by the man who eventually married her. This is a significant moral issue that should be explored. In particular, it is never made clear to the reader whether the cousin knows that her future husband raped her, and if so, how it came about that she was reconciled to life with him, and what she thought about it. In the end the reader (this reader, anyway) can't help feel that by choosing to have Briony tell her half of the precipitating incident and its consequences, and by not finding a way to tell the other half in a plausible manner, McEwan has undermined the very realistic, objective tone and tools he uses, because the realistic novel always promises that the reader will understand the difference between what the characters think is happening and what is really happening. As a result of this significant lapse in the plot, Briony's self-blame comes to seem easy rather than difficult, trivial rather than truly dramatic.

Atonement is ambitious, serious, and clever. The detailed and seemingly random workings of tragic irony are suspenseful and in some sense profound if the reader is willing to be moved by tragic irony. Possibly what critics liked about it, in addition to the skill with which McEwan builds the scenes and depicts the characters, is the sense of guilt that pervades the narrative. The pieces add up in a way that seems to indicate that atonement, and therefore redemption, are not achieved in life and that art as consoling fantasy offers very little. As a final punishment, Briony discovers that she is to suffer "vascular dementia," a process of mental deterioration not unlike Alzheimer's. My own feeling is that the novel-within-a-novel bits demean the other parts of the narrative, and by making an overt game out of them, ask us to care less about all three of the characters. And they also preempt any criticism of sentimentality that might be lodged against the Second World War sections, where the tone is uniformly sober and respectful.

What I like about *Atonement* is that it is a good lesson in what the novel can and can't do—what it can do is portray complex and serious scenes in a complex and serious way. When we revisit the 1930s and 1940s by means of McEwan's prose, we are compelled by his narrative technique to care about and contemplate people who never existed doing things they never did, and to reconsider in detail issues that may not seem all that important anymore. We are asked to hold many ideas in our minds at the same time and to make a piece of logic out of them. Suspense, empathy, and sympathy help us do so. The gravity of *Atonement*'s themes make it a worthy effort. What I also like about it is that, for me, it fails as a work of art—a made thing. I like that McEwan thought it through and put it together, and that I can see through it. I feel cheated by the fact that I never learn whether the cousin understands who her rapist is and whether Robbie dies at Dunkirk. This means that McEwan is trying something out, taking a risk. I like the fact that it is a risk worth taking. When any reader, reading any hundred novels, loves some, likes some, doesn't care about a few, and hates one or two, she is asserting her freedom and casting her vote. I like that best of all.

And one more:

Jennifer Egan · Look at Me

(NEW YORK: RANDOM HOUSE, NAN A. TALESE, 2001), 432 PP.

After I finished rewriting *Thirteen Ways of Looking at the Novel,* I went to Mexico with my daughter, who had four or five specimens of "chick-lit" in her suitcase. I got bored with the book I was reading, and she tossed me this one, which I had never heard of (I think when it came out, I was busy reading about the decline and fall of the savings and loans for *Good Faith*). While the paperback edition of *Look at Me* was not pink—a sure sign of chick-lit—it was pastel. Still, the premise was intriguing—a New York model, Charlotte, visiting her family in Rockford, Illinois, has a terrible car wreck in which her face is so damaged that when she goes back to New York after a series of reconstructive surgeries, she is unrecognizable and, she soon realizes, no longer employable as a model. In a parallel plot, Charlotte's teenage namesake, the daughter of her best friend from high school, who still lives in Rockford, gets more and more involved with a mysterious new teacher at her high school. The teacher proves to be a chameleonlike prototerrorist from a nameless Middle Eastern country who is part of a fairly unformed conspiracy to commit some sort of ambitious terrorist act, but in the end—thanks, I think to the younger Charlotte—makes up his mind not to, though he does disappear without telling her who he is or where he is going. Young Charlotte's eccentric uncle also figures prominently in the plot, which shifts between New York and Rockford and deftly explores issues of identity on several levels and in all of the characters. The young Charlotte, for example, has typical teenage identity problems, but they are exacerbated not only by the fact that she is the plain-looking and quiet daughter of a beautiful mother, but also by the lengthy health crisis of her charming and handsome younger brother. Charlotte's uncle, who teaches at the local college, has identity problems, too—at one time a star scholar and athlete who seemed to be heading for fame and fortune, he has suffered a prolonged existential crisis that may be craziness or may be a larger and more astute apprehension of the reality of American life. The prototerrorist, of course, lives by hiding his identity.

But the most interesting of all these dilemmas is that of the model Charlotte, when she returns to New York, and is approached by an Internet entrepreneur whose scheme is to purvey life stories over the Internet in what appears to be a cross between blogging and novel-writing. Charlotte, who was once famous, will be paid a high price for the simultaneous drama and celebrity of her story, which will be written up with pictures and posted on the Web (the ghostwriter has several lives, too). The entrepreneur, though, is also alive to the potential of everyday drama, so he also purchases the drama and noncelebrity of a homeless man Charlotte knows, who lives near her apartment building.

Egan's special talents in this novel are organization and empathy. She uses both to keep the many characters and their many identity confusions distinct in the reader's mind, while at the same time unfolding the mystery plot of how the older Charlotte got to Rockford in the first place and why she was in the car wreck. Charlotte is required to move forward, resolving her employment situation and her identity crisis, and to work backward, figuring out her accident, simultaneously. She is not a sympathetic character—aggressive, resentful, and shallow—but she is brave, which keeps the reader reading. The younger Charlotte is more sympathetic, but her life is also more painful and in some ways less promising.

Look at Me is not explicitly about novel-writing—no one becomes a novelist in the course of the story—but it does offer an uncanny and believable solution to the question of the death of the novel. When Charlotte's ghostwriter writes about her life and her accident, she inevitably fictionalizes her; when the Internet entrepreneur contracts to put her on his Web site, he buys her identity from her, knowing full well that it is her story—the plot of her life—that is his salable commodity. He is commissioning a new type of novel, one based on gossip and letters (blogging) but that gains energy and importance from his conception that the people he puts on his Web site are representative characters in the epic he is putting together of life in America and life on Earth. It is the lengthiest written prose narrative of all, with many protagonists. Egan turns the idea of the novel as we've explored it in this book upside down. If *Little Women* and *The Harafish,* to take two examples, are compact missiles shot from the inner life of the author into the public life of the literary world, then Egan's vast Internet novel is a kind of public explosion that invades the privacy of people all over the world and transforms them into creatures of the media with no private life at all, only the seductive appearance of one (necessary to arouse the voyeuristic impulse of viewers, who then pay a subscription fee to read all about it). Part of Egan's genius is that her entrepreneur is idealistically convinced that his idea is going to not only make him rich, but also bring about the brotherhood of man.

Look at Me is full of ideas that sometimes go unreconciled in the narrative, but they are truly innovative and fascinating ideas. Her terrorist, for one thing, is a triumph of empathy. I may have never met a terrorist, and Egan may never have met one either, but it is easy to suspend disbelief in this one, because she so skillfully evokes his resentment, deracination, and intelligence. At the same time, she tosses off a portrait of the American Midwest that is as true to the spirit of that region in the year 2000 as any in American literature. Her observations on celebrity culture are convincing, too.

Novels of ideas, of course, come and go—that's their job—and it is impossible to tell at this point whether *Look at Me*'s more basic components of character, plot, and setting will hold up after the ideas have been outmoded. For one thing, though the novel is highly ironic, it is never funny, so it is not very entertaining—the reader has take these issues as seriously as the author does in order to keep reading. But it is also only a second novel. Most of the novels on our list are mature efforts, written after their authors had learned to employ their basic narrative tools almost automatically. *Look at Me* is a snapshot of a passing moment, not only in history, but also in the life of a young author. In our list we have looked backward over and over. Paradoxically, even though Egan gives us a frightening image of the novel subsumed and radically transformed by technology, she also gives us a chance to appreciate once again the power and vitality of that simple and complex object, a long story bound enticingly between the closed covers of a book.

INDEX

A NOTE ABOUT THE AUTHOR

Jane Smiley is the author of eleven novels, including
A Thousand Acres, for which she won the Pulitzer Prize;
Horse Heaven; and, most recently, *Good Faith.* She has also
written three works of nonfiction, including a critically
acclaimed biography of Charles Dickens and *A Year at the
Races.* She was inducted into the American Academy
of Arts and Letters in 2001. Smiley lives in
Northern California.